Educational Psychology

Educational Psychology

Principles in Practice

Rosemary A. Rosser

Glen I. Nicholson

University of Arizona

LITTLE, BROWN and COMPANY

Boston   **Toronto**

Library of Congress Cataloging in Publication Data

Rosser, Rosemary A., 1946–
    Educational psychology.

    1. Educational psychology. I. Nicholson, Glen I.
II. Title.
LB1051.R66 1983   370.15   83–11265
ISBN 0–316–60633–2

Library of Congress Catalog Card No. 83–11265

ISBN 0-31b-b0b33-2

9 8 7 6 5 4 3 2 1

HAL

Published simultaneously in Canada
by Little, Brown & Company (Canada) Limited

Printed in the United States of America

Credits and Acknowledgments

COVER ART

ARTIST — Stanton Macdonald-Wright, American (1890–1973). **TITLE** — *Abstraction on Spectrum (Organization, 5).* **DATE** — 1914. Used by permission of the Des Moines Art Center, Coffin Fine Arts Trust Fund, 1962.

PHOTOGRAPH CREDITS

p. 4: Paul Conklin

PART I — p. 10: Ralph Granger; p. 16 (top): Union Pacific Railroad/Wide World Photos; p. 16 (bottom): Wide World Photos; p. 22 (top): © Susan Lapides 1981; p. 22 (bottom): David M. Grossman; p. 39: © Elizabeth Hamlin 1976; p. 44: © Elizabeth Crews 1978.

Credits and Acknowledgments continue on page 608.

Preface

As the words imply, educational psychology is a bridge between two subject areas—education and psychology. It follows that an educational psychologist not only must possess a thorough knowledge of psychological principles and theories, but also must be able to apply salient principles in an educational setting.

Our overriding goal in writing this book has been to provide teachers, future teachers, and anyone else interested in the teaching-learning process with a background of psychological principles and with a knowledge of how these principles may be used by those who teach in any educational or instructional setting. To help accomplish this major goal, we employ a format of paired chapters. The lead chapter, the *a* chapter, contains relevant principles derived from psychological research. Because psychology is an ever-changing field of study, we have included in these chapters some discussion of the historical precedents of current theories. Further, we have selected for each of these chapters an illustrative research project that exemplifies the methodologies used by psychologists to derive principles and theories. The changing nature of psychology is also reflected in a feature we call "New Directions in Research." These essays suggest the direction of current research efforts and provide ideas for further exploration of topics.

The second member of each pair, the *b* chapter, is designed to provide examples of how a teacher might use or apply the principles and theories presented in the *a* chapter. Although these chapters are not meant to exhaust all potential applications, sufficient examples are provided to make the subject matter relevant to those who plan to teach. Each *b* chapter begins with a teaching scenario. By focusing attention on a problem that a teacher is likely to encounter, the scenario helps set the stage for realistic applications. At the end of the chapter, we present a possible solution to the problem. To further exemplify and promote the application of principles, we have suggested practice activities. The activities provide an opportunity either to apply what was learned in a teaching-learning situation or to discover the relevancy of the principles through observation.

The content of the book is based on our conviction that behavior is a function of the interaction between environmental and person variables. The organization of the body of material that makes up the book was also determined by our position. Part I introduces the basic theme and serves as a framework for the ensuing chapters. The spotlight shifts from one variable to another as the content unfolds.

In Part II, emphasis on environmental and person variables is reflected in our presentation of learning theories. Chapters 3a and 3b are devoted to the behavioral theories. The interactionist viewpoint, that of Albert Bandura, is considered in Chapters 4a and 4b. In the final chapters of this section, Chapters 5a and 5b, the processes within the individual are examined and cognitive and information-processing theories are featured.

Although person factors are the major focus of Parts III and IV, we refer frequently to the environmental context that impinges on the person. Part III explores the role of developmental processes in cognition and language. Jean Piaget's theory of cognitive development is the topic of Chapters 6a and 6b, while theories of language development and the challenges of facilitating language development are presented in Chapters 7a and 7b.

Individual and group differences are studied in Part IV. Chapter 8a is an innovative explication of the construct of intelligence. Instead of considering intelligence as an exclusively person variable, which is characteristic of conventional trait theory, we maintain that intelligence is a complex process involving both environment and person influences. We also show how current controversies concerning intelligence testing have evolved from trait theory, and we suggest alternatives to traditional perspectives on intelligence. In Chapter 8b, approaches commonly used in measuring intelligence and achievement are presented. Differences among groups are the topic of Chapter 9a. We suggest that variability within a group is often a more important consideration than variability among groups. Again, we emphasize the role of environment in creating and maintaining these differences. Motivation, as a construct, is treated in the content of Chapters 10a and 10b. Again, as with intelligence, we illustrate the movement away from considering motivation as purely a trait to that of motivation resulting from an interaction of environment and person.

In the concluding section of this book, we look at the significant behaviors that are the outcomes of education. Concept learning and its corollaries of rule/principle learning and problem-solving are the content of Chapters 11a and 11b. Since much of the learning in schools involves learning from prose, we have devoted Chapters 12a and 12b to this timely topic. And finally, we examine prosocial behavior and positive classroom management in Chapters 13a and 13b. Throughout these chapters, we have continued our emphasis on the environmental context and the person variables, which interact to produce these behaviors.

The last two chapters of this section, Chapters 14 and 15, present methods for measuring and evaluating student progress. Tools used to gather such evaluation data as teacher-made tests, rating scales, and checklists are examined. We examine how the data serves as a base for grading and reporting to parents.

Three supplements were developed to accompany this text. For students, the Study Guide, written by Carolyn S. Anderson, contains many study aids useful in mastering material in the textbook. Each chapter has a list of the key ideas presented in the corresponding book chapter, questions that focus on important concepts, practice test questions, and suggested activities. For instructors using our text we have created an Instructor's Manual and a Test Bank. Included in the manual are alternative strategies for using the text in courses with differing formats, extended outlines and explanatory summaries of content, and suggested sources for supplementary information and related available films. The Test Bank consists of an extensive set of test items for each chapter.

We gratefully acknowledge the contributions of our colleagues and students who provided significant input in the preparation of this book: Darrell Sabers, Carolyn Anderson, and Patricia Horan. We also wish to express our gratitude to the reviewers of our manuscript in its various stages of development: Lewis Bossing, Murray State University; Steven L. Christopherson, The University of Texas at San Antonio; Peter A. Cohen, The University of Texas at San Antonio; Donald Cunningham, Indiana University; John P. Gaa, University of Houston; Shawn M. Glynn, University of Georgia; Robert Gross, formerly of Swarthmore College; John Hampton, Oklahoma State University; Wayne Moellenberg, University of New Mexico; Thomas J. Shuell, State University of New York at Buffalo; Albert Solomon, formerly of Tufts University; Myron Trang, Texas Tech University; and Joan R. Yanuzzi, Indiana University of Pennsylvania. Their thoughtful and incisive comments helped us to sharpen our thinking and writing and provided us with many suggestions that we have incorporated in this book.

A special thanks to Little, Brown and Company, specifically Mylan Jaixen and Victoria Keirnan, for their support in the development of this text from a germinal idea, through many revisions, to this final product. Also, we wish to express our appreciation to Dan Otis for his fine efforts in helping us convey our ideas in a smooth and consistent writing style. We must also thank our typists, Alice Schoenberger and Jessie Fryer. Without their invaluable assistance this book could not have come to fruition. Lastly, we could not have accomplished this task without support, encouragement, and understanding from our spouses, Marty Floerchinger and Phyllis Nicholson, and our families. Thank you.

R. A. Rosser
G. I. Nicholson

This book is dedicated to:

My parents—Willis and Ivy Rosser
—RAR

My wife and children—Phyllis,
Marc, Jon, and Beth
—GIN

Brief Contents

Contents

Educational Psychology

Chapter 1

The Challenge of Education and the Resources of Psychology

Introduction

Every spring hundreds of colleges and universities award thousands of education degrees to graduating students. Many of these students soon join the work force as teachers. They enter new classrooms in the fall and begin the process of educating others—a process that they themselves only recently completed. Will they all succeed? Some will persevere and evolve into effective, competent, resourceful educators; others will not. What makes the difference? To even begin to answer this question, we must examine the challenges teachers face, what they must do to meet these challenges, and what they must know to act effectively.

A teacher's primary task is to help students acquire the information, facts, and skills needed for academic success. Another task is to ensure that each student achieve his or her potential. Think about the context in which these two tasks must be accomplished. A teacher operates within the physical boundaries of a classroom, the philosophical boundaries of an educational structure, and the political boundaries of school board policy. A teacher faces a varied class of individuals, not a homogeneous group of learners. Some are cooperative, motivated, and eager to learn; others are not. Some are very capable; others are not. Some have all the economic, social, and physical advantages on their side; others do not. The tasks of teaching must be accomplished in the context of these physical, philosophical, political, and individual constraints. As a society, we charge teachers with a major role in the socialization of youth. The teacher occupies a front-line position, attempting to meet the challenges of the charge. How can they be met?

To get some perspective on the charge, consider the following scenarios. In each, a teacher faces a challenge; the challenge raises questions; the questions require answers.

The Scenarios

1. Dr. Marshal regularly teaches a required freshman algebra course. Although the class is large at the beginning of the semester, many students drop out before the first test. Over the years, Dr. Marshal has observed that the drop-out rate is highest among female students, many of whom report that they expect to fail. He would like to do something to lower the drop-out rate. Dr. Marshal wonders, "Why are these women afraid of mathematics? What can I do to convince them that they can succeed if they stay in the class? How can I give them a sense of efficacy for mastering the content of the course?"

2. As a result of budget cuts, the school in which Ms. Turner teaches has eliminated teacher aides in elementary school classrooms. Consequently, Ms. Turner must manage a classroom of forty students alone. She still wants to individualize instruction as much as possible. She asks, "How can I organize the classroom for maximum individuality? Can I still manage small-group activities with this many children? What can I plan for the rest of the children while working with a few?"

3. Mr. Galvez teaches kindergarten in an urban school system. At the beginning of the school year he notes how different his students are, how much they vary. Some have well-developed language and number skills and seem comfortable during classroom activities. Others lack these skills and are frightened and bewildered by what is, to them, a novel environment. He wonders, "How can I prepare them all for first grade starting with this kind of variability?"

4. Ms. Jefferson is a new teacher in an eighth grade general science class. One of her students is performing very poorly, despite an above-average intellect. In an attempt to improve the student's performance, Ms. Jefferson has a conference with him to discuss his work. The youth claims he is not interested in science and does not see why he should put in the effort needed to pull up his marks. Ms. Jefferson's dilemma: "What can I do to increase the boy's motivation?"

5. A sixth grade teacher has recently resigned, and Mr. Swanson takes the teacher's place. The pupils appear to lack self-discipline. Children fight, shout, move around the classroom at will, interfere with each other, and generally create havoc. Mr. Swanson knows that under these circumstances his chances of teaching are nil. His question: "How can I gain control over the students in the classroom so that they can learn?"

6. A girl in Ms. Bolla's fourth grade classroom is very well behaved and quiet, seems motivated and pleasant, but academically is achieving

little. Ms. Bolla is concerned about the girl's lack of progress and wonders why she is not doing better. In an attempt to understand the situation, she examines the girl's cumulative files. She finds records of past achievement and standardized test scores, but what do they mean? Ms. Bolla is curious: "What do these measures tell me about what to expect in the classroom? What do they mean for the design of instruction?"

The Answers

Obviously, none of these questions can be answered quickly and easily. They typify the kinds of challenges most teachers face at some point in their careers. Helping teachers address these challenges is what this textbook is all about.

The Purpose of Schooling

Schools are unique institutions. Their primary aim is to help young people acquire the skill, competence, knowledge, and behavior needed to function effectively in society. Many other groups, organizations, and individuals share these goals, but schools are unique because they must serve large segments of the population at one time, and they must reflect communal needs and goals rather than the goals of any one group, family, or individual. Like parents, psychologists, counselors, and others, teachers are agents of socialization who supervise the growth, development, and evolution of children into effective adults. Unlike the others, teachers must accomplish their task in classrooms, with many individuals at the same time.

When communities establish and support schools, either public or private, they provide guidelines for educating the young. These guidelines are typically broad, reflecting the values of the community as a whole. The professional educator's task is to translate these guidelines into workable terms. This involves translating general goals into achievable ends, devising methods for reaching these ends, determining whether the ends have been reached, and overcoming the obstacles encountered along the way. Teachers are involved in all four parts of the process.

A teacher, then, is much more than a dispenser of knowledge. To be effective, teachers acquire a body of knowledge and a set of skills that help them accomplish these tasks and meet these challenges. Where does this knowledge come from? One source is the discipline of psychology. Teachers and psychologists are interested in the same things: behavior and changes in behavior. Psychologists study behavior and the processes involved in changing it. Teachers must deal with

Teachers must supervise the growth, development, and evolution
of children into effective adults. Each class consists of individuals differing from each other in abilities, needs, motivation,
and skills.

behavior in the classroom, attempting to bring about changes in behavior in accord with educational goals.

Processes of Behavior Change

Every human being contains a complex network of abilities, potential-
ities, competencies, propensities, attitudes, feelings, thoughts, and past
experiences. In addition, we all inhabit a world that makes demands,
offers opportunities, provides stimulation, erects barriers, fulfills our
hopes, and blocks our wishes. Each of us is a complex system, a person,
existing in another complex system, the environment. Through our
behavior, we do our best to adapt to that environment, make the best

of it, and profit from it. Sometimes we are successful and sometimes we are not. When we are not, we must adjust, produce new behavior, and attempt to adapt more successfully. We change.

Successful adaptation is more likely if we have many options and skills—alternative behaviors to use when faced with different environmental demands. These options, skills, and alternatives are acquired with experience; the greater our experience, the more tools we have. Education supplies one kind of experience that helps people acquire those tools and learn more adaptive behavior. How does change occur? Why does experience affect behavior? What are the mechanisms, the causes of adaptive change? In order to be effective agents of change, teachers, who direct the educational process, must know the answers to these questions, at least in part. The job of the psychologist is to supply answers to these and similar questions.

The Purpose of Psychology

Psychologists try to understand what people can do, how they learn, how they change, and why they behave as they do. They attempt to identify the causes of behavior and behavioral change. This is a very large task, and psychologists have been pursuing it systematically for only a little over a hundred years. They have not yet developed definitive explanations of human behavior. They do, however, have some approximate explanations, some alternative solutions, and some evidence that at least bears on the phenomena.

Most psychologists contend that people's actions are determined by both their personal characteristics and the demands placed on them by their surroundings. There is, therefore, no single cause of human behavior; there are, rather, a number of causes acting together. Some of these causes are personal, originating in the individual, and some are environmental. Psychologists attempt to understand and explain this process of interaction; teachers attempt to direct it.

The Relationship Between Psychology and Schooling

To teach effectively and facilitate productive learning, one must understand human behavior. Psychology can provide some of this understanding, this required insight. Since educators and psychologists deal with the same phenomena, the two professions are closely related. In fact, there is a field known as educational psychology that is devoted to the psychological study of educational issues.

A number of educational psychologists work directly in the classroom and study the teaching process itself. Most psychologists, however, do not work in classrooms and do not study teaching. Their work thus may appear to have no immediate and obvious bearing on education, but our contention is that it has. The purpose of this book is to demonstrate the relevance of psychology to education and to apply psychological principles and knowledge to educational concerns. We wish to provide a knowledge base that can help answer questions such as those raised in the scenarios.

Knowledge alone, of course, is not sufficient to make a competent teacher, but it is surely an important prerequisite. Successful teachers know how the environment influences student behavior and how student characteristics affect this influence. They have a broad familiarity with the content of psychology.

Bringing Psychology to Bear on Education

If you examine the remainder of this text, you will discover a number of organizational features. You will note, for example, that there are five major sections in this book, and that most of the chapters have an *a* and a *b* section. The *a* chapters present current theory and research in psychology, and each includes a section called *New Directions for Research* and a *Research Report*. The *b* chapters cover school-related activities, and each includes a section called a *Teaching Scenario* and a *Scenario Suggestion*. These organizational features reflect our view of the relationship between education and psychology. The text's organization in many ways reveals our perspective on human behavior and on the two disciplines.

The Five-Part Organization

To explain human behavior and give us insights into its causes, psychologists must do several things. First, they must know what they wish to study; they must define the content of the discipline. Second, they must identify the factors that influence this content. Third, they must have a method for figuring out how the factors influence the content. The content is behavior, what people do. We will call that B. The relevant factors are the environment (E) around the person, and the characteristics of the person himself or herself (P). The method is the means of identifying how these three elements fit together, the relationship between the person, the environment, and behavior.

We have, then, three components, E, P, and B. Most psychologists agree that behavior is caused by environmental forces acting in conjunction with individual characteristics; in other words, $B = E \times P$. Behavior changes as the environment changes, as the person changes, as experience is accumulated. Learning is one kind of change, development is another, the ways in which we express our individuality a third. All of these changes are studied by psychologists, and all occur in the classroom.

In Parts II, III, and IV of this textbook we examine one particular kind of change. In Part II, for example, we focus on changes associated with learning, and in Part III on changes associated with development. In Part IV we examine the expression of individual differences. All result from the combined effect of E and P.

Psychologists differ, however, in their views of the relative importance of E and P in changing behavior. The emphasis depends upon the behavior in question and the perspective of the psychologist. In changes associated with learning, for example, some psychologists emphasize the role of the person, others the role of the environment. The same applies to development and to individual differences. Accordingly, rather than there being one explanation of learning or one explanation of development, there are several.

Psychology is a young discipline, too young to have determined which of the several explanations is best. The discipline is still emerging, growing, and changing. When we present explanations of learning, therefore, we give more than one. In each of the major sections we present multiple perspectives on the phenomenon.

You might ask why we do not begin with Part II. The reason is that how psychologists study human behavior is almost as important as what they find. The *hows* are the methods of psychology, the techniques of gathering information, building explanations, and developing theories of human behavior. We begin the text, then, with Part I, *Method*— how the information you will read about was acquired in the first place.

Our final section, Part V, focuses on the aspects of behavior particularly relevant to education. This last section focuses on the outcomes teachers are most eager to achieve—for example, comprehension, the acquisition of concepts and information, and the acquisition of social skills.

The Chapter Pairs

Although psychologists study change in human behavior and teachers direct change in some aspects of human behavior, the link between the two disciplines is not always readily apparent. Often, the relevance of psychological methods, findings, and explanations is not immediately self-evident to teachers. Conclusions from laboratory studies or research in settings other than classrooms do not automatically suggest applications to teaching. Moreover, the results of psychological studies are usually disseminated in sources not readily accessible to teachers, often in highly technical language. There is therefore often a gap between what psychologists discover and what their discoveries suggest to teachers.

We contend that teachers can benefit from knowing what happens in psychological laboratories and research settings. The psychological literature is an important source of information for teachers; but a link to practice is needed. These necessary links are provided in the *b* chapters.

In the sections that follow, we have presented two chapters on each major topic. In the *a* chapters we summarize the psychological methods, theories, and research findings relevant to the topic. In the *b* chapters we apply those findings and perspectives to certain aspects of education. Of course, the psychological knowledge base is relevant in many more ways than we can demonstrate; but, through our discussions of practice, the teaching scenarios included in each chapter, and the activities designed to help you observe psychological principles in action, we hope to show how research can be linked to teaching. That link and the scope of the content is stressed in the overview preceding each chapter pair.

New Directions in Research

Psychology is a rapidly expanding and changing field. As the discipline matures and new information is added to what we already know, dramatic changes will continue in the future. As new findings, new methods, and new theories emerge, some current information will become obsolete. We wish to give you a glimpse into the future as well as to summarize the current state of the art.

Our *New Directions in Research* is a preview of the changes occurring at the cutting edge of psychology. We know you will want to become an intelligent consumer of psychological research. By considering current developments, you may learn what developments you want to follow. These future trends will be discussed more fully in the epilogue.

Summary

We opened this chapter, as we will subsequent chapters, with teaching scenarios from the classroom. These scenarios raise questions; the content of this book will suggest answers. Because there are a number of perspectives on human behavior, there are several answers to any query. We will present some probable answers and suggest some alternatives. In doing so, we will emphasize the relationship between psychology and education. Our purpose and hope is that you will derive from this text an understanding of psychology's pervasive influence and will learn to appreciate how it may be useful to you as a prospective teacher.

PART I

A Scientific Approach

PSYCHOLOGY did not emerge as a science until the latter part of the nineteenth century. Prior to that time, psychological questions were considered the province of philosophy. Philosophy and psychology still retain close ties, and both focus on the same general issue—the nature of man. Today, however, the two disciplines have come to use different methods. Philosophy depends on a purely logical method, psychology on a scientific one.

In the next section, we outline briefly the major characteristics of the scientific method and discuss its applicability to psychological investigation. This method is an approach to the answering of questions, to the gathering of information, and to the drawing of conclusions. Borrowed from the older sciences, it has proven itself a useful technique, one based on *demonstration*. Implicit in the method are certain assumptions about the way we should view human behavior, analyze complex events, and make decisions. Since teachers, like psychologists, must also examine human behavior, analyze complicated situations, and make intelligent decisions, the scientific method has implications for the educational process as well.

In future chapters we will examine a variety of human performances and a set of possible explanations for those performances. This is the content of psychology, which has broad ramifications for educational practice. Before we proceed, however, we must examine the tools of psychology. Tools as well as content have implications for the classroom.

Chapter 2a contains an outline of the research psychologist's tools derived from the scientific method. We describe that method for science in general and for psychology in particular. In Chapter 2b we demonstrate how the same methods, or variations of them, apply to educators as well as to scientists. There are useful techniques, for example, that teachers can adapt for use in classrooms from the working plans of psychologists.

Chapters 2a and 2b are meant to establish a framework, a perspective, applicable to all subsequent chapters.

Chapter 2a

The Methods
of Scientific Investigation
in Psychology

Introduction

Suppose you have been given the assignment of visiting a first grade classroom. Your tasks are to *observe* the events that take place there, to *describe* them, and to *explain* them. With notebook in hand you go to the school, find the classroom, locate a clear vantage point, and begin to observe. Where do you start? It is soon evident that it is impossible to observe and describe all the activity in the classroom, so you begin your assignment by making some choices. You decide to attend to and record some events at the expense of others. On what basis could you make your decision?

The choices of classroom observers noticing and recording different events in the same environment depend on their individual perspectives and background. The architecture student will probably notice features of physical space and the way people utilize it. The sociology student might consider the formation of small groups within the larger group structure. The education student preparing for the teaching profession might pay close attention to the activities of the teacher. The psychologist—what might a psychologist watch? Faced with a complex event, each individual makes choices about what to observe and describe. The choices vary depending on individual perspectives, and therefore the methods of attending, describing, and recording differ, too. If descriptions of what took place are made from different perspectives, the explanations based on these descriptions are bound to vary.

Psychologists bring a particular perspective and method to the problem of analyzing human events in complex settings. The approach and techniques are borrowed from other scientific disciplines and applied to the examination of human phenomena, including the teaching-learning process. The scientific method is not the only possible analytic tool, but it is a very useful one. In this chapter we examine the roots and essence of psychological methodology, considering its origins, the logic behind it, and the way we can use it to understand human behavior.

Psychology and Science

The application of scientific methods to the study of human behavior is a relatively recent development. Before the late 1800s the nature of man was approached and explained from the perspectives of philosophy and theology. Philosophical discourse on human events occurred during the Classical Greek period and the Renaissance, and it continues today. With the rise of science, however, human nature also became a subject open to scientific inquiry. Psychology officially separated from philosophy in 1878 when Wilhelm Wundt founded in Germany the first scientific psychological laboratory. At that time psychology began using the tools of scientific investigation and established an identity of its own. The assumption that human events can be approached scientifically remains an integral part of modern psychology.

When psychology shifted away from philosophy, the kinds of questions asked about human events changed very little, but the means employed to answer them changed dramatically. No longer were purely logical approaches considered acceptable. Scientific proof demands data, empirical evidence.

Psychology and philosophy employ different methods, but they have common roots, which they also share with education. Such eighteenth century philosophers as England's John Locke (1632–1704) and France's Jean-Jacques Rousseau (1712–1778) wrote philosophically about the nature of children and made recommendations for educating them. Since they were primarily philosophers, they did not base their position on empirical evidence, and they expressed very different views. Their writings exemplify the historical connection between philosophical discourse, psychological issues, and educational concerns.

Psychology and education share more than common philosophical roots, however. As noted in the last chapter, there is a special discipline, educational psychology, in which educational matters are directly addressed with psychological methods. In addition, such modern psychologists as B. F. Skinner and Jean Piaget have made recommendations on educational practices, although they are educators only tangentially.

Psychology differs from philosophy and education in its reliance on the scientific method. This approach, which is based on careful and objective observation, description, experimentation, and demonstration, is common to all disciplines that consider themselves sciences, regardless of their subject matter.

The Logic of Science

We must understand the basic logic of scientific inquiry before we can learn how to apply it to human behavior. All scientists base their approaches on a particular sequence of steps and manner of proceeding. These procedures, which were developed over many years, are based on certain assumptions about the nature of proof and how it can be established.

The Focus of Science

The scientist's task, irrespective of discipline, is to examine *happenings* (Harre, 1965). A happening occurs when one state of affairs is transformed into another state of affairs. The change from a seed to a plant is a happening, as is a house catching fire or a child solving a problem. We can ask the same questions about each of these happenings: (1) "*What* happened?" (2) "*How* did it happen?" and (3) "*Why* did it happen?" Other questions might also be asked (Harre, 1965), but these are the kinds of queries for which science is best suited.

If a happening is a change in a state of affairs, then a happening is essentially a relationship between two different states of nature. The change in the two states did not occur spontaneously, however. It was caused by an event of some kind. Events take place in a temporal sequence; that is, at Time 1 a state of affairs exists, at Time 2 an event occurs, and at Time 3 a different state of affairs exists. The elements of a temporal sequence are depicted in Figure 2a–1. We look to this sequence to explain how a change in states of nature takes place.

When we examine a temporal sequence for the purpose of understanding a happening, we are trying to identify the event that caused the change. The altered state of affairs would not exist unless something caused it. According to Western logic, the cause of the transformation must occur between the first state of affairs and the second. Logically, the cause of a change could not occur after the change itself has taken place. To uncover the causes of happenings, therefore, one begins by looking at a temporal sequence associated with change, and only events that precede the end state can logically be identified as *causes* of it.

FIGURE 2a–1.   The Temporal Elements in a Happening

Time 1	Time 2	Time 3
Stable state of affairs	→ An event →	An altered state of affairs
A happening		

Scientists attempt to explain the causes of happenings—changes in the state of affairs. The change of Mount St. Helens from a majestic mountain (above) to a holocaustic scene (below) exemplifies a kind of happening of interest to the physical scientist.

We can propose, for example, one possible temporal arrangement of the events associated with a house catching fire. At Time 1, the house exists in an intact state; it is not burning. At Time 2, an event occurs; lightning strikes the house. At Time 3, the house exists in a transformed state; it is burning. Once we know that sequence, we are inclined to make a causative statement: "Lightning striking the house caused the house to burn." We explain a happening by examining a temporal sequence and looking for the event that preceded the altered state of affairs.

A great many phenomena can be described in terms of a temporal sequence. There are physical happenings: An object is at rest (Time 1), force is applied to it (Time 2), and the object moves (Time 3). There are biological happenings: An organism exists in a hungry state (Time 1), the organism eats (Time 2), and hunger dissipates (Time 3). There are chemical happenings: A base and an acid are contained in two beakers (Time 1), they are mixed (Time 2), and water and heat are produced (Time 3). There are psychological happenings as well: A child is frustrated with an arithmetic problem (Time 1), the teacher demonstrates the problem's solution (Time 2), and the child arrives at the answer (Time 3). All the outcomes that exist at Time 3 can be attributed to events at Time 2, prior to the transformed state of affairs. The problem for the scientist is deciphering cause-and-effect sequences or links, discovering whether the links are reliable, and eliminating other events that might also explain an outcome. These examples and their temporal sequences are summarized in Table 2a–1.

So far we have discussed the causal relationship between events (Time 2) and outcomes (Time 3) in a happening. Other circumstances also influence happenings, however. *Existing conditions*, the initial state of nature (Time 1), also play a role. If the house struck by lightning had had a lightning rod, for example, would the same outcome have occurred? Would a house with a wooden shingle roof and a house with a nonflammable roof have been equally likely to burn if each experi-

TABLE 2a–1. **Examples of the Temporal Elements in a Happening**

Time 1	Time 2	Time 3
State of Affairs	*An Event*	*Altered State of Affairs*
1. An intact house	Lightning strikes house	A burning house
2. An object at rest	The application of force	A moving object
3. A hungry organism	Ingestion of food	A satisfied organism
4. A frustrated problem-solver	Demonstration of problem solution	A happy problem-solver

enced the same event at Time 2? The presence of a lightning rod or the material in the roof, existing conditions, can also influence the effect of an event.

Existing conditions must also be taken into account when we attempt to explain happenings involving human behavior. Individual characteristics (existing conditions) influence the final outcome. The frustrated problem-solver in the previous example would not solve the arithmetic problem even after the teacher's demonstration if his anger kept him from attending to the demonstration.

Whether the scientist attempts to explain the burning of a house, the movement of an object, or the arithmetic accomplishments of the child, the task is very much the same: (1) identify existing conditions, (2) identify outcomes or results, (3) identify possible causal events, (4) identify the temporal relationships among the elements in the happening.

The Goals of Science

Scientists focus on happenings, and their general goal is to understand the causes associated with a happening. This is a large task, however, and some intermediate steps are necessary before the job can be completed. First, scientists must be able to *describe* the happenings they wish to understand. Second, they must *explain* the happening, the events and causative sequences that made it occur. Third, scientists try to *predict* the circumstances in which a happening can be expected to recur. Description, explanation, and prediction are the particular components that comprise general understanding. When these tasks have been completed and a base of understanding has been developed, scientists can make recommendations that will be useful in decision-making. We can demonstrate this process with physical, sociological, and psychological examples.

The 1980 eruption of Mt. St. Helens in Washington state was a rather dramatic happening. A serene mountain was transformed into an active volcano and then a devastated crater. Scientists and the general public certainly wish to understand the nature of this volcanic eruption, but understanding requires a few preliminary steps. First, the eruption and the events associated with it must be *described*. Second, scientists must try to understand events associated with the eruption, such as earth tremors, to help them *explain* the eruption. Once they have explained it, they may be able to *predict* when future eruptions will occur. *Decisions* to warn and evacuate people in the area will probably be based on those predictions. As you can see, a scientific endeavor does not proceed in one big step toward one final goal. The process takes a while, and a few intermediate steps are necessary.

Scientists interested in understanding human happenings proceed in the same manner. An environmental psychologist studying the effects of crowding on human behavior also begins with description. How do people act when they must live in high-density environments? Once descriptive information has been gathered, the relationship between density changes and behavioral changes can be studied and, it is hoped, explained. Then predictions about density changes and behavioral outcomes can be made. Finally, recommendations for future housing patterns may be offered.

In psychology, investigators have tried to show how young children acquire mathematical concepts, including concepts in geometry (Lesh, 1976). Once again, description of geometric and spatial abilities comes first (Piaget & Inhelder, 1956; Martin, 1976), followed by explanations of how geometry learning takes place (Montangero & Smock, 1976). In the future, to ensure the growth of geometric knowledge, scientists will try to learn how to predict the outcome of learning experiences. The information they acquire will help them make recommendations to mathematics educators and decisions about appropriate teaching methods.

Scientists try to follow this sequence from description to explanation, prediction, and application, but in practice science seldom follows its models perfectly. Answering the questions at any stage of the process takes time. Although it is slow, it is precise, and scientists have a collection of proven tools for which no suitable alternative has yet been proposed.

The Tools of Science

It is important to recognize that science is a procedure, not a particular subject or outcome. In a sense, the means by which a scientist reaches an outcome are more important than the outcome itself.

During high school or college you probably enrolled in a laboratory science course in biology, physics, or chemistry. The laboratory assignments you were given were designed to demonstrate some relationship between phenomena. You were given a set of instructions; you recorded in a lab notebook precisely what you did; and you described the outcome. The grade you received on your lab assignment was probably based not so much on the final outcome but on how well you followed the instructions and recorded what you did. It was *method*, not outcome, that really mattered.

Method is the essence of science. Regardless of who is conducting the experiment, the procedures and results must be accurately recorded. In the previous example, another student should have been able to pick up your lab book, follow your description of procedure, and replicate the experiment. This is another aspect of the scientific method: It is public and repeatable. Conclusions based on information known only to a single person are unacceptable evidence in science. Conclusions should be accessible to anyone who can follow the procedures.

How are conclusions made accessible to others? Scientists work very hard to be objective and complete. During observation and the recording of events, personal interpretations are either minimized or kept separate from the data. Examine an article in a psychological journal and you will note that it is divided into sections, the last three of which are (a) method, (b) results, and (c) discussion. The method and results sections are straightforward accounts of what was done and what was found. The discussion section allows the author to express an individual interpretation of the meaning and importance of those findings. The two parts, however, procedure and interpretation, the objective and subjective, are usually kept separate.

Two scientists reading the same account should reach the same conclusion about what happened, even though they might disagree about the meaning of the outcome. In the same way, the observations of two individuals watching the same event should be very similar. Objective observation, public information and scrutiny, and repeatability of a sequence of events are essential to scientific examination. Private experience, idiosyncratic knowledge, and individualistic conclusions fail to yield an acceptable data base.

Scientists interested in analyzing a happening begin by formulating a *hypothesis*. A hypothesis is a provisional statement that relates two events in a possible cause-and-effect sequence. An investigator might, for example, contend that the application of heat will cause water to boil. If you refer to Figure 2a–1, you will see that this hypothesis relates Time 2 and Time 3 occurrences in a possible causal relationship. Until the sequence is actually demonstrated, however, it remains a possible, or hypothetical, connection. Hypotheses are expressed in the form of "if . . . then" sentences: If heat is applied to water, then the water will boil.

After developing a hypothesis, the scientist designs a situation to test it, to see if the proposed relationship actually holds. The designed test situation is an *experiment*, a demonstration of the empirical relationship between the two elements in the hypothesis. Then the scientist conducts the experiment and observes, records, and describes the results. The conclusions drawn indicate whether the proposed hypothetical cause-and-effect sequence occurred as predicted. If the outcome occurs as expected and if it can be replicated, then the hypothesis becomes a scientific principle.

Hypotheses are not generated out of thin air; scientists develop them, often basing them on past work or on the observations of others. By keeping abreast of research in their area, scientists can generate more interesting and relevant hypotheses.

A second source for hypotheses is scientific theory. In any area of research, experiments are run and data are collected. The meaning of the results, however, is not always clear. Often, scientists must interpret data, weaving many results together so that they make sense and relating outcomes to a larger context. Interpretations of research outcomes that bring together many results in a meaningful way are *theories.*

By bringing diverse information together in new ways, theories can suggest previously unsuspected relationships between events, relationships that enable scientists to predict causal sequences. These predictions serve as the bases for future hypotheses and experiments, the results of which reflect on the adequacy of the theory.

These, then, are the tools of the scientist: theories, hypotheses, experiments, and data. How a scientist uses these tools will depend on the content under scrutiny. The tools, however, are the same for everyone, as are the criteria for their use—objectivity, repeatability, public scrutiny, and replication.

Science and the Psychologist

Psychologists conducting research studies use the same tools and the same criteria as other scientists. The happenings to be explained, however, are changes in human behavior. Like other scientists, psychological researchers first describe human happenings, then explain them, and ultimately hope to predict them.

Explaining human happenings is a complex task, for several reasons. The happenings themselves are often complicated or subtle changes in behavior that are sometimes difficult to observe. In many cases, it is difficult to distinguish the time sequence of related events and states. Another problem is that a great many events can occur in the sequence. Finally, there are so many unknowns associated with changes in human behavior that the task sometimes seems monumental. Since specifying cause-and-effect relationships for human events is extremely difficult, the knowledge base developed so far from scientific inquiry is limited. Much remains to be discovered and explained.

Happenings and Variables

The first difficulty one encounters in a science of human behavior is the variability of the content itself. Human behavior varies from person to person and situation to situation. Even individuals in identical circumstances are almost certain to behave differently. This is true because people's behavior is influenced by their make-up and experiences, which vary remarkably. To deal with individuality, the psychologist frames descriptions of happenings in terms of relationships between

Psychologists, as scientists, attempt to explain the causes of happenings. For educational psychologists, the happenings involve children in learning situations. Children changing from cooperative behavior to aggressive behavior would be a happening of interest to the psychologist.

variables rather than between specific states and events. Even so, predictions about human outcomes must always be stated in terms of probability rather than certainty.

The term *variable*, which comes from mathematics, indicates a measure that can assume more than one value. In the physical world, temperature is a variable, since temperature can have different numerical values. In human events, age, intelligence, and height are variables. Even experience is a variable, since individuals differ in the amount and nature of their past experience. Actual behaviors can also be expressed as variables. Scores on a measure of reading skill, for example, will vary across individuals: some will score very high, others will perform poorly. In attempting to explain human happenings, psychologists describe content in terms of variables.

A number of relationships can exist between two variables. In some cases, variables are not directly connected. Human noses, for example, come in different sizes; nose size is a variable. Intelligence is a variable also, but the size of one's nose is unrelated to one's intelligence. On the other hand, some variables change together in a similar manner. During childhood, for example, height increases as age increases. These variables are said to covary, to change together. Other variables are causally related; changes in one variable are followed by changes in another. A change in diet, for example, may be followed by a change in weight. The latter two types of relationships, covariance and cause and effect, are the specific focus of psychological study.

Identifying relationships between variables is a reasonable way to approach the study of human behavior, but it is important to recognize that scientists' statements about relationships hold most of the time, not all of the time. Most children get taller as they increase in age, for example, but certain physical defects can prevent physical growth with increased age. In these cases, the specified relationship between age and size would not hold. Similarly, most children who receive instruction in a specific skill will learn it, but some will not. Most of the conclusions we draw about relations between human variables hold most of the time, not all of the time. Psychologists' findings must therefore be expressed as probabilities.

Earlier in the chapter we listed the questions addressed by science: (1) What happened? (2) How does it happen? and (3) Why did it happen? We can reexamine these questions in terms of variables. *What* questions are concerned with individual differences on a specific variable. If nose size is of interest, we can measure the noses on a group of people and describe the differences. Using different measurement devices, we can examine how children of a given age differ in mathematics proficiency, in the use of problem-solving strategies, in reading speed, and in innumerable other characteristics. In short, answering *what* questions involves describing differences on a given variable. *How* and *why* questions go beyond the description of a single variable to address the relationships between variables.

Investigative Procedures

To find answers to questions about relationships between variables, psychologists must conduct research. Several different kinds of studies are possible, including (1) experimental studies, (2) correlational studies, (3) field studies, and (4) case or clinical studies. The studies vary in their settings, the types of information they yield, and their suitability to specific questions, but the goal of all of them is to discover something about causation.

The Experimental Paradigm.   The approach closest to that used in nonsocial science research is the experimental paradigm. Experiments are conducted in laboratories or laboratory-like environments. The hallmark of the experiment is the experimenter's control over events. Precision and the careful use of procedures are also characteristic. Earlier in the chapter we suggested that a happening can be analyzed as a temporal sequence that suggests cause-and-effect relationships among events. In the experimental paradigm the experimenter decides in advance what the temporal sequence will be and controls the timing. To do this the experimenter creates a particular event and then carefully records its effects or results.

The investigator begins with a hypothesis about the relationship between two events, the "if *A*, then *B*" proposition discussed earlier. The "if *A*" part of the statement refers to an event the experimenter can create and control; this event is manipulable. The "then *B*" part is the outcome, which follows the manipulation and occurs because of it. The goal is to be able to conclude that *A* causes (or does not cause) *B* to occur.

Consider, for example, a hypothesis about human behavior: If children view violent television content, then their aggressive behavior will subsequently increase. A hypothesis similar to this one guided a number of laboratory studies in the 1960s (Bandura, 1969, 1977a). Another hypothesis behind an actual research effort (Pressley, 1976) was this: If children are provided with pictures when they read prose, then they will recall more prose content. These hypotheses are both statements about a possible causal link between two events, and the experimenter can create and control the first event when examining the plausibility of the statement. An investigator who has set up a study, created the prior event, and recorded the subsequent occurrence of another event has completed an experiment.

In psychological research, a hypothesis is a causal proposition about the relationship between two variables. It states essentially that changes in one variable (the "if" part) will be followed by changes in a second variable (the "then" part). Returning to the previous examples we see that viewing violent television is a variable because different values are possible. The programming could contain many violent acts, few violent acts, or none at all. The number of pictures accompanying a prose passage can also vary. These, then, are examples of variables.

The second half of the hypothetical statement also concerns a variable. The number of aggressive acts a child produces after watching violent television could vary from a great many to few or none. In the prose-learning example, recall proficiency could also vary from near perfect to near zero. Resulting performances thus also involve variables.

Variables are given different labels depending on their role in the hypothesis. The prior event (the "if" part), is called the *independent variable*. The independent variable is the possible cause of the change in the second variable; it is thus the proposed causal variable. The outcome is the *dependent variable*. The dependent variable results from changes in the first variable and is thus dependent on those changes. The independent variable, then, is the cause, and the dependent variable is the effect. This relationship is depicted in Figure 2a–2.

When we study human behavior in this manner, the independent variable is any event or situation that experimenters control so that the effects of the manipulation can be observed. The independent variable could involve providing individuals with a particular experience, a learning program, a strategy for problem-solving, or a set of instructions. The dependent variable is some aspect of human behavior, some action that the subject performs after receiving the experience provided by the experimenter. The experience is a possible cause of the performance.

If, after conducting a study like this, the experimenter gets positive results, the hypothesis is reformulated as a causal statement. The causal statement is a statement of a *functional relationship*. The TV-

FIGURE 2a–2.   The Temporal Arrangement of Elements in a Hypothesis

The "if" part	Time →	The "then" part
Independent variable	→	Dependent variable
Cause	Causal link	Effect

aggression hypothesis, for example, could be reformulated as: "Aggression is a function of watching violent television programs," or "Viewing violent television leads to increased aggression." The prose recall hypothesis could be restated as "Prose recall is a function of reading with pictures," or "Providing pictures with prose leads to better recall performance."

It is sometimes difficult to clearly demonstrate a functional relationship. Results tend to be equivocal, and many experiments do not permit us to make precise statements of this nature. This is true primarily because variables other than the independent one may influence the outcome. Suppose, for example, that Vern Victim views an aggressive television show, after which he goes to a room where his imitative aggressive behavior can be observed. On the way to the room, however, Bernie Bully appears and slugs Vern. Once he is in the observation room, Vern behaves very aggressively, destroying and throwing toys. Is Vern's violent behavior a result of watching the aggressive show, or is it caused by Bernie's behavior? One cannot be sure, because two events rather than one occurred during the time span of the happening.

To draw cause-and-effect conclusions, the experimenter must control not just the independent variable, but all other events as well. The researcher may not be interested in manipulating some of these extraneous variables, but they, too, can affect the dependent variables. Research psychologists use many procedures to control extraneous variables. A laboratory setting is often preferred because control is easier to attain there. Less structured situations can present control problems.

Psychologists must also be concerned with the variability of individual subjects in an experiment. Characteristics of experimental subjects that may influence the study's outcome are called *attribute variables*. Different people may not react the same way when exposed to the same independent variable. Among the many attribute variables are such characteristics as age, sex, abilities, past learning, and past experience. The scientist examining human behavior must take such characteristics into account when identifying a functional relationship.

Unlike the independent and extraneous variables, attribute variables are not subject to the experimenter's complete control. These variables can be controlled to some extent through the selection of participants; the investigator may choose to study only girls or only high-ability individuals. However, people's characteristics cannot arbitrarily be changed. These characteristics are part of the existing conditions, the qualities that a participant brings to the experiment.

Consider once again, for example, the laboratory studies of the effect of violent television on children's subsequent behavior. Many studies show that aggression does increase following exposure to violent programming (Lesser, 1977). Some studies, however, yield more varied results: aggression increases in some children but actually decreases in others. Moreover, a child's reaction is influenced by past socialization experiences as well as by what is watched. Children who have been punished for aggression or taught that aggression is inappropriate may react differently. Violent programming may cause them to feel anxious; they may aggress less rather than more. Past socialization about aggression is something the child brings to the laboratory. Since it is out of the experimenter's direct control, it is an attribute variable, a condition existing before the experiment begins. Expanding our earlier diagrams to include attribute variables produces Figure 2a–3.

The experimental paradigm, or *laboratory analogue,* as it is sometimes called, is a precise scientific approach to the study of human behavior. It has proved extremely useful in helping psychologists become more scientific and less philosophical. It has limitations, however.

First, many questions that might be asked about human events cannot be examined experimentally. Some variables are not subject to manipulation, and the experimental paradigm requires manipulation and control of an independent variable to demonstrate cause and effect. The effects of malnutrition in babies may be a legitimate scientific question, for example, but it would obviously be highly unethical to starve a group of babies for the purpose of collecting data. We might also want to study the relationship between an attribute variable, such as age, and an aspect of behavior, such as language skill, but attribute variables cannot be manipulated, so the experimental paradigm would be inappropriate in this study, too. There are many questions about human behavior that need asking; some cannot be answered in the laboratory.

Furthermore, some scientists (McCall, 1977) contend that the experimental paradigm is not always appropriate because it is artificial. The precise, controlled environment of the laboratory is very unlike the natural environment in which people actually behave. In noncontrived settings many variables act together to influence behavior, but this situation is hard to replicate in laboratories. Other techniques are needed for the study of human behavior occurring naturally in complex settings. The techniques used are correlational procedures, field studies or ecological methods, and case studies.

FIGURE 2a–3. The Expanded Temporal Sequence

	Time	
Independent variable	→ Attribute variable →	Dependent variable
Cause	Person	Effect

Other Paradigms.   In correlational studies, researchers examine a relationship between attribute variables or between attribute variables and behavior. After measurements are collected, the data are examined to determine if and how strongly the variables are related. This approach is well-suited to the study of some questions. A psychologist interested in the relationship between age and language skill, between gender and behavior, or between intelligence and achievement could use a correlational approach. Independent variables are not manipulated. Correlational studies can only suggest, not prove, cause-and-effect relationships, but the information obtained is still very valuable.

Field studies, of which there are many varieties, are done in the natural environment rather than a laboratory. In some cases, independent variables are manipulated and cause-and-effect statements drawn. In others, the experimenter examines the effects of an event that occurs naturally. These studies lack the control found in laboratory investigations, but they have the advantage of realism.

Another technique, the individual case study, is conducted with one person or several persons. Sometimes this method involves merely describing an individual's behavior, but in other instances the procedure can be as precise and controlled as the laboratory experiment. It is sometimes possible to make cause-and-effect statements with this technique, but conclusions based on the behavior of a single individual may not hold for others, so generalizations must often be limited. On the other hand, the value of information about the behavior of a few subjects should not be minimized. Jean Piaget originally developed his highly influential theory of intellectual development by observing only three persons—his own children (Gruber and Voneche, 1977).

Essential Features of Research Paradigms

Regardless of the form of research paradigms, they have several features in common. All methods yield information about human behavior and help to explain it. Explanations permit us to help people with difficulties, predict what people will do, and teach effectively. A second shared feature is that all forms are based on scientific methods. Empirical science is public, so procedures must be described objectively. Replication is possible only if scientists do their job well and describe their studies fully.

The psychologist is no exception. Regardless of the type, psychological studies must also be public and thus objectively described. Objective description involves *operationalization*. In a research report the investigator must describe the operations performed in (1) creating the independent variable, (2) assessing attribute variables, (3) controlling extraneous variables, and (4) measuring the dependent variable.

Operationalizing the independent variable entails describing the

Research Report

In most of the chapters that follow, we will include research samples drawn from the empirical literature, as we do here. There are several reasons for these additions. The first is, quite obviously, to provide illustrations of exemplary research. The second is to demonstrate a psychological principle or fact. The third, however, relates to the thrust of the current chapter. We have stressed the fact that science is essentially a method that can be used to study a wide range of content. A psychological study, then, is a concrete demonstration of the way these methods of science are applied to the content of human behavior. There are special problems involved in trying to do this. In fact, the psychological literature is replete with examples of both the problems encountered and their ingenious solutions. Our first selection illustrates this last point quite nicely.

T. G. R. Bower, one of the authors of our selection, is a master of psychological methodology. He has to be; he studies one of the most difficult topics in contemporary psychology—what we perceive and know of physical reality, and he examines this topic in a truly difficult population—infants. In short, he tries to empirically determine what babies know. The pursuit raises many problems with respect to operationalization, control, and the precision demanded by science.

The Swiss psychologist, Jean Piaget (about whom you will learn much more in Chapter 6a), proposed that babies do not know that objects exist when not in view. For a baby, he said, an object that is out of sight is out of mind; when it disappears from view, it ceases to exist. Piaget came to this conclusion by noting that babies fail to search for hidden objects. Bower has taken issue with this conclusion, contending that babies know that out-of-sight objects exist but lack the motor skills to search for them. A systematic investigator, Bower has undertaken a research program comprised of many individual studies of this issue (for example, T. G. R. Bower, 1971). Our selection is only one of many.

Just think of the problems involved in determining whether a baby knows something. Knowing *per se* is unobservable; scientific data must be based on observation. The scientist must therefore develop an operational definition of an externalized act that will indicate what babies know about the continued existence of objects they cannot see. To judge whether adults know something, the scientist could ask them; the verbal response is an external act. But one cannot, of course, ask babies for a meaningful verbal response. The scientist might also watch how adults act, observe what they do on the basis of their knowledge. But again, young babies cannot do much; they are capable of few acts.

Bower reasoned that one act of which babies are physically capable is reaching for an object; reaching is an observable performance. He further reasoned that babies will reach for an interesting object if they know it is there, but they probably will not if they doubt its existence. If knowledge of the existence of objects is dependent on actually seeing an object, then one would not expect babies to reach for objects they cannot see.

To test this hypothesis, Bower devised an ingenious task. One at a time, he placed twelve twenty-week-old babies in a light-tight room. He then dangled an interesting manikin from a string directly in front of each baby. Before the baby could reach for the manikin, he turned out the lights, plunging the baby into total darkness. Bower wanted to know whether the babies would reach for the toy even though they could no longer see it. How did he manage to reliably record the responses? He used a special infrared television system to film the babies' actions without light visible to the human eye and produced an observable, public record of their responses.

Interestingly enough, all of Bower's babies not only reached out for the manikin, they actually grabbed it. With careful design, ingenious equipment, and the control typical of a laboratory study, this psychologist empirically demonstrated something about what babies know.

Bower, T. G. R., & J. F. Wishart. The effects of motor skill on object permanence. *Cognition*, 1972, *1*, 165–171 (second experiment).

experiences that the participants in the study were subjected to. The instructions used by the experimenter, the study's setting, the materials employed, and similar information should be included in this description. If the experiment is done properly, a knowledgeable reader will understand exactly what took place and be able to replicate the study. The psychologist also describes the control procedures and attribute variables taken into account.

Equally important is the process of operationalizing the dependent variable. The investigator needs to develop a procedure to accurately describe not just what was done in the study, but what the subjects did as a result. The behavior of the subjects is stated in the form of an *operational definition.*

Creating a good operational definition for outcome performances is more difficult than you might suppose. It involves designing procedures to measure human performances, and the measurement must meet certain requirements. First, the measurement of performance must be logically related to the research hypothesis. A researcher concerned with learning outcomes will measure some aspect of learning. If the hypothesis pertains to memory, then performances involving memory processes must be assessed. This may seem like an obvious point, but it is often difficult to accomplish. Outcomes involving aspects of human behavior are often difficult to measure precisely. Human performances associated with such characteristics as cognitive skills, thinking processes, comprehension, learning, and understanding sometimes seem impossible to tap, but it is precisely these aspects of human behavior that are most important to those concerned with instruction and educational processes.

Suppose, for example, that a researcher hypothesizes that experience in role-playing activities (an independent variable) will enhance children's abilities to be empathetic about the experiences of other people (a dependent variable). What does the researcher mean by *empathetic*? How will empathy in a child's behavior be recognized and measured? The researcher's operational definition of empathy is determined by the operations or procedures used to measure empathy. Various investigators have used different measures of empathy in past research (Rosser, 1981). We may personally disagree with a particular investigator's operational definition, but it is important to know precisely what aspects of behavior were being measured and labeled.

A second requirement of operational definitions concerns reliability. Reliability, which you will learn much more about in later chapters, is an assessment of the consistency with which we measure behavior. In research, it often means that two individuals examining an incident of human behavior will classify it the same way. Suppose, for example, we observe two youngsters engaged in physical activity on a playground. They are in close physical contact, rolling on the ground, physically touching each other. Are they fighting? Engaging in healthy horseplay? Is it part of a sports activity? You would need clear guidelines for classifying a specific act in order to decide. Establishing those guidelines is part of devising a good operational definition. Armed with well constructed guidelines, two observers watching the youngsters should reach the same conclusion most of the time.

An important issue closely related to reliability involves externalization. Human behavior must be defined in terms of an external performance or action. Such internal performances as thinking, imagining, and self-verbalizing are not directly observable, nor are they always accompanied by observable signs. In the absence of clear outward signs of an internal event, we must make inferences about what we think is going on, but inferences are less likely to be reliable than direct observations. Suppose we give a child a three-dimensional puzzle, and the child sits quietly for several seconds without responding. Is the child thinking? Daydreaming? Is the child evolving a mental strategy? We cannot know for sure. We must guess: Inference involves guessing.

To reliably measure human phenomena, we need outward signs. These signs are external performances, observable actions. Operationalizing the dependent variable is the process of obtaining those signs, collecting measurements of them, and reaching agreement about their meanings.

Conclusion: Science, Methodology, and Theory

Explaining human happenings is an undertaking that requires skill, ingenuity, and the mastery of a set of tools. Even behavioral scientists who use their tools skillfully face additional problems. What happenings most deserve study? In a particular happening, what key variables can be stated as hypotheses that will direct the investigations? Once data have been collected, how should they be interpreted? Choices made before the investigation will influence what is studied. How does the scientist make those choices? Selections are made primarily on the basis of theory.

Like any other event, scientific investigation is also a happening, and it does not occur in a vacuum. It is itself part of a temporal sequence: Every study has been preceded by some investigations and will be followed by others. Previous studies influence the choices and

New Directions in Research

One facet of science fascinating to many is that it continually changes. Scientists make new discoveries, describe new phenomena, and explain old phenomena in more sophisticated ways. As the science changes, so too must the tools and methods of the science change to keep up with the cutting edge. Methodological innovations both reflect the state of the art and permit the art to evolve. In fact, one could propose that a science can progress only within the limits of the available tools. Psychology is no exception.

What we see happening in psychology right now is a shift in both theory and methodology toward greater complexity. Contemporary theories of behavior have a systems flavor—that is, the person is viewed as a complex network of interrelated components responding to multiple simultaneous influences. You will read more about these newer approaches in subsequent chapters. The relevant point for now is that this theoretical shift is accompanied by a methodology shift.

The laboratory analogue is a good fit for breaking down complex phenomena into parts and testing, one at a time, the hypotheses associated with the parts. One might not, however, discover the nature of a system by studying the parts if breaking it into parts destroys the system. Instead, it may be wiser to test the system as a whole. In this way, single hypothesis testing is re-placed by its extension, multiple hypothesis testing, or *model testing.*

Hypothesis testing and model testing are both based on the same basic tenets of science and are related. They differ in the size of the chunks studied. Traditionally, we examined the influence of one or two variables on one or two others while controlling for other factors—that is, a relatively small chunk. In model testing, we have multiple variables affecting another set of multiple variables. We want to specify all the relationships among the variables and test them as a unit—a large chunk. The question is whether the full model, rather than the individual relations, is a good fit with human behavior. You thus test the model; in fact, the model becomes the hypothesis.

This level of analysis is not possible without a computer. What we see in contemporary psychology is a growth of sophisticated computer methodologies like those associated with causal modeling (Heise, 1975), confirmatory factor analysis (Joreskog & Sorbon, 1979), and computer simulation (Newell & Simon, 1972; Simon, 1979). These are the tools for testing systems.

The methods are new, and they are not without controversy. They may signal, however, a coming of age in psychology. In the near future, testing theory rather than hypotheses that comprise the theory may become commonplace.

investigative procedures selected for a current study. In short, what will be done is related to what has been done. Research data from a number of investigations are compressed into systems that summarize previous findings. These systems also assess the implications and meanings of previous findings and suggest hypotheses that may lead to new discoveries. These systems are the various psychological theories.

Theories are units of explanation about human behavior that cover more than a single experiment or set of experiments. Moreover, theories go beyond data, judging the relative importance of research findings and directing future examinations. Theory, then, influences what is studied and how it is studied.

For every human happening there is more than one theoretical explanation. We have several theories of learning, theories of personality, and theories of development. Each has its own system of explanation and its own body of empirical evidence. In the course of this book you will encounter many of them. Perhaps as psychology matures as a scientific discipline some of these theories of human behavior will emerge as clearly superior to others. At present, however, the discipline is in its infancy, or at best in early childhood. For this reason we must consider a number of perspectives and a varied body of evidence concerning how and why people act as they do. Despite their differences regarding human behavior, however, all of the theories have one feature in common. Theory may act as a guide, but empirical data are the evidence, evidence gathered on the assumption that people are an appropriate subject for scientific investigation.

Summary

The science of psychology, like other sciences, employs methods and logic based on the objective analysis of happenings. The *tools—theories, hypotheses, experiments,* and *data*—and the *criteria—objectivity, repeatability, public scrutiny,* and *replication*—are common to all scientific disciplines, including psychology.

Psychologists seek to *describe, explain,* and *predict* happenings in human behavior. These goals comprise an understanding of human behavior, so the decisions and applications that understanding yields are empirically based. A number of techniques are used to meet these goals, including *experimental methods, correlational procedures, field studies,* and *case studies.* All help to reveal the causes of human behavior, the essence of human nature.

In the process of building explanations, the psychologist looks at happenings as relationships between variables. Some of those variables are causal in nature; when manipulated by the experimenter these are called *independent variables. Dependent variables* are effects, the human performances that result from the causal events. The scientist must also be concerned with *extraneous variables,* other events occurring during the happening, and *attribute variables*—individual characteristics. All must be accounted for in explanations of the causes of human behavior.

To meet the criteria of science, investigators *operationalize* their procedures and measures so that others can objectively judge the work conducted. Operationalization involves describing how data are collected and makes psychology public, like the other sciences.

TEACHING SCENARIO

One task facing virtually all teachers is communicating information about student progress. The information must be transmitted to a variety of individuals including parents, other educational personnel, and, of course, the students themselves. What is communicated and how the communication process proceeds is vitally important. Educational decision-making is based in part upon this process. It may affect how parents perceive their children and can even influence how the children perceive themselves. How best to proceed is not easily outlined. Our teaching scenario involves one aspect of the communication process, one part of the challenge.

Mr. Baker teaches a third grade class in an urban school. The children in his class come from a wide variety of backgrounds, economical, educational, social, and ethnic. Late in the fall and again in the spring Mr. Baker will hold parent-teacher conferences with the parents of his pupils. He wants to do a good job of communicating to all the parents the progress of their children. He needs a good method for doing that, anticipating that the parents will differ in their familiarity with the school and with the curriculum. Some parents will find standard reporting measures—that is, grades and test scores—more meaningful than will other parents. Yet all parents need and deserve relevant information about their children's progress.

Mr. Baker's challenge is to develop a method of collecting and reporting student progress that is meaningful, that accurately depicts what the child is doing in school, and that reflects changes between fall and spring performance. What is a viable procedure for meeting that challenge?

Chapter 2b

Psychological Approaches and Classroom Happenings

Introduction

In the last chapter we discussed the methods psychologists use to analyze, study, and explain human behavior. To the student of psychology, the relevance of Chapter 2a is probably self-evident; this is the methodology in which psychologists are trained. The methodology's relevance to teaching may be less apparent, however. The purpose of this chapter is to highlight the applicability of psychological methodology to educational settings.

An important point made earlier is that education is a process of changing human behavior. Teachers, as directors of the learning process and managers of the educational environment, are major agents of change. They devise procedures to increase the chances that desired changes will occur. When teachers encounter students who fail to improve in spite of instruction, they may pose several questions similar to those asked by scientists. What happened or failed to happen that caused the lack of progress? How did it happen that the specified outcome was not obtained?—and, of course, Why? These questions are the ones best suited to the application of scientific methodology.

Teachers need to ask themselves the same questions when they design instruction. What do I want to happen as a result of the instruction? How can I achieve that outcome? If successful, why was the end achieved? Answering the *why* question permits the teacher to achieve the same outcome again in the future.

Both teachers and psychologists are change agents. In laboratory experimentation, psychologists design changes to demonstrate the causes behind them. In a field setting, psychologists try to outline past sequences of change for the same purpose—to identify independent variables that produce desired outcomes. Psychological clinicians use established change procedures to achieve a positive outcome for their clients. When designing instruction, the teacher is planning something like an experiment to bring about a specific outcome. When examining an existing classroom, the teacher analyzes past happenings just as the psychologist does in the field. Teachers assisting children with a problem fill a role similar to that of the clinician. Since teachers and psychologists fill similar roles, it seems logical that the tools of one may be helpful to the other.

Three essential features discussed in the previous chapter apply to classroom happenings as well. The first is the manner in which the psychologist analyzes events on the basis of variables. The second involves identifying cause-and-effect relationships, and the third concerns operationalizing variables in terms of observables.

Variables in the Classroom

Happenings are comprised of essentially four types of variables: (1) independent variables, (2) dependent variables, (3) attribute variables, and (4) extraneous variables. Similar variables operate in the classroom.

The independent variables in an experiment are the events that are manipulated and controlled by the change agent. These variables are seen as causal, since manipulation of the independent variables leads to a result. Independent variables occur in the classroom, too; they are the events over which the teacher has control. Instructions, learning experiences, materials, assignments, tasks, and lectures are all events the teacher plans, designs, and creates. Why do teachers spend time on these activities? Implicitly, and perhaps explicitly, we assume that these experiences promote learning, that they function to cause the desired results. Instructional activities, then, are like independent variables, which we manipulate to achieve results.

Teachers use hypotheses about learning outcomes to design instruction in much the same way that scientists use them. The independent variable is an activity the teacher designs and implements; the dependent variable is the outcome that results from the activity. The following statements are examples of hypotheses pertaining to classroom learning outcomes. These statements reflect how a teacher might employ hypothetical thinking:

If	practice is provided with addition problems	*then*	the students will increase their scores on tests of addition operations.
If	time is devoted to the presentation of words	*then*	the students will increase their sight word vocabulary.

If	the teacher designs interest centers for measuring and cutting wood	*then*	the students will become more proficient at measuring.
If	children are given opportunities to write about their own experiences	*then*	they will become more fluent in the use of their developing language skills.
If	the teacher asks high-level questions when discussing social studies	*then*	the students will increase their verbal reasoning skills.
If	the teacher provides frogs and dissection materials and demonstrates procedures	*then*	the students will learn about the internal structure of animals.
If	the teacher responds nonjudgmentally to all student inquiries during a discussion	*then*	student verbal interaction will increase in frequency.

Independent Variables in the Classroom

Look at the *if* statements in the list of examples. They all concern the design of an activity directly under the teacher's control: providing practice, developing an interest center, asking certain kinds of questions. In addition, these events would all occur before any change in student behavior. These classroom events thus correspond to the independent variables of psychological experiments. In fact, events very similar to some of these have been studied by educational psychologists. You will be reading about many of them in subsequent chapters. The important point for now is that teaching activities function just like independent variables, as procedures that promote change.

Dependent Variables in the Classroom

You will recall that dependent variables are outcomes, the result of implementing an independent variable. Outcomes occur in both the psychological laboratory and the classroom.

Look again at the list of exemplar hypotheses above, but this time examine the *then* statements. They all concern aspects of student behavior, something the learner will be able to do as a result of the designed experience. The dependent variables in the classroom are aspects of student behavior or learning outcomes; they take place after the provided experience and as a result of it. They are hence influenced by exposure to that experience, that independent variable. The correspondence between experimental analysis and learning events is depicted in Figure 2b–1.

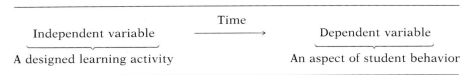

FIGURE 2b–1.   **The Temporal Sequence in the Classroom**

Cause and Effect in the Classroom

A major tenet of the previous chapter was that the events comprising a happening occur in a temporal sequence, a sequence that reveals the cause-and-effect relationship. The same can be said for sequence in a classroom. Causes are prior events that occur before outcomes. Prior events, learning activities—independent variables—are the same thing, causes of change. Learning outcomes—dependent variables—are also one and the same, the effects. In teaching, we try to link the causes and effects to understand the process of educational change. Until those links are established, we are without a sound basis for choosing among different learning activities or instructional methods. Delineating cause-and-effect sequences is thus as important to the teacher as it is to the scientist.

To determine cause-and-effect sequences, the scientist must take into account not just independent and dependent variables but existing conditions as well. Among the important existing conditions are attribute variables, the characteristics of the experimental subjects. Attribute variables also have a parallel in the classroom: the characteristics of the learners.

As a teacher, the groups of students you encounter will vary in a number of ways. If you teach more than one grade, the students will vary in age—an attribute variable. Most classes include both male and female students; sex is another attribute variable. Numerous other attribute variables also show up in most classrooms. Differences in ability level, intelligence, past learning, language fluency, and experience are but a few of the possible attribute variables. Virtually every one of them influences how well teaching promotes learning.

Let us take an example from the list on pages 36–37 to clarify the importance of attribute variables in establishing cause-and-effect sequences, in linking the proposed causal event (teaching) with the outcome event (learning).

The Hypothesis.   If practice is provided with addition problems, then students will improve their scores on tests of addition problems.

For the group as a whole, scores will probably improve following sufficient practice, but this is not necessarily true for every student. One obvious limitation is children's past learning of addition operations. Some children may have had very limited experience in addition

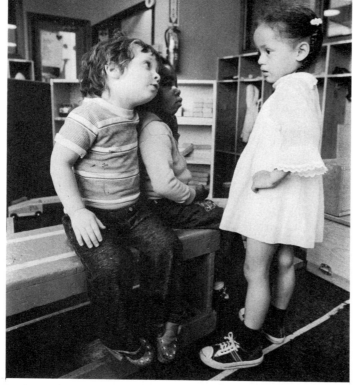

Such attribute variables as sex, age, ability, intelligence, language fluency, and experience must be considered by the teacher. The teacher's understanding of the effects of these variables on learning will determine the effectiveness of instruction.

and need much more than practice and drill. Even when provided with opportunities to practice, their lack of knowledge may interfere and their scores may not improve appreciably. Others may have had so much experience that they find practice boring and redundant; in their case, boredom could conceivably result in scores that decrease rather than increase. Students in the middle who understand the basic operations but need opportunities for application and rehearsal may improve their test scores. We thus see that attribute variables can influence outcomes, too, and can depict this effect, as in Figure 2b–2.

What does this sort of variability in outcome mean? It means that

FIGURE 2b–2.   The Relevance of Attribute Variables

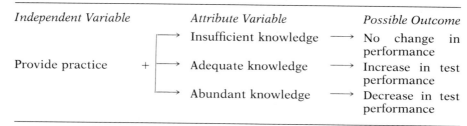

Independent Variable		Attribute Variable		Possible Outcome
Provide practice	+	Insufficient knowledge	→	No change in performance
		Adequate knowledge	→	Increase in test performance
		Abundant knowledge	→	Decrease in test performance

depending on student characteristics, in order to alter the learning experiences provided to students we must take into account not only teacher activity (independent variable) but learner background (attribute variable). Psychologists who conduct experimental learning studies often examine the role of attribute variables in their experiments. Whether functioning as teachers or researchers, we cannot delineate cause-and-effect sequences without taking personal characteristics into account.

A Second Hypothesis.   If the teacher responds nonjudgmentally to all student inquiries during a discussion, then student verbal interaction with the teacher will increase in frequency.

What attribute variables could interfere with outcome in this case? See if you can determine which learner characteristics might be influential.

From these examples you can see that attribute variables as well as independent variables affect achievable outcomes. Teachers can rarely, if ever, directly change attribute variables. Instead, they must modify their own actions to achieve the same end. This is essentially what individualizing instruction is about—matching the type and degree of the independent variable to the characteristics of the learner.

We can now rediagram the sequence of cause-and-effect relationships taking attribute variables into account. This relationship is depicted in Figure 2b–3.

The Classroom and Extraneous Variables

Psychologists cannot outline cause-and-effect sequences clearly in the laboratory unless they can control other events that might interfere. As you will remember, these undesired events that confound causative conclusions are called extraneous variables. Extraneous variables are found in classrooms, too. Distractions, excessive noise, interruptions, and chaos are just a few of the possible sources of extraneous variation. If a teaching approach fails to increase learning, is it the fault of the approach itself, or could it be due to the fact that the noise level was so high during instruction that few students paid attention? Control over interfering events, then, is also necessary.

FIGURE 2b–3.   A Comparison Between the Classroom and the Experiment

The Experiment			
Independent variable	+ Attribute variable	$\longrightarrow$	Dependent variable
The Classroom			
Created teaching activity	+ Characteristics of the learners	$\longrightarrow$	Learning outcomes

The means by which psychologists analyze human behavior are not restricted to the laboratory. Human happenings of many types can be examined with similar procedures. Identifying cause-and-effect relationships, testing causal hypotheses, assessing the contributions of attribute variables, and maintaining sufficient control to draw meaningful conclusions are processes as relevant to the educator as they are to the researcher. Breaking happenings into their components, looking for relationships between these components, and identifying possible causes of change are procedures that can be applied to human happenings anywhere.

▶ *ACTIVITY 1.*   Most teachers construct formal lesson plans. Sometimes these plans are quite sketchy, designed simply to serve as reminders about planned activities. Other times they are so extensive that a substitute teacher could use them to continue the regular teacher's activities. Regardless of their completeness, lesson plans reflect teachers' analyses of instructional activity, expected learning outcomes, and the relationship between them.

Select a teacher who is involved with a grade level and with subject matter that interests you. Arrange to interview the teacher about a unit of instruction for which lesson plans have been designed. Formulate a series of questions that will help you obtain information about the following: (1) specific instructional activities (independent variables) that will be used to teach the unit, (2) the general goals (dependent variables) that are desired as a result of instruction, and (3) specific goals (operationalized dependent variables), statements about what the students will be expected to do following instruction. See, too, if any adaptations are planned with regard to individual characteristics (attribute variables). Examine the lesson plans to see if and where these elements are included. Diagram the information obtained in a manner consistent with the system depicted in Figure 2b–3.

When you have identified the general goals for the unit, replan it yourself. Create some possible instructional activities (independent variables) that might help achieve the goals. Identify individual student characteristics (attribute variables) that could bear on your plans. State as specifically as you can what you would want the students to be able to do following instruction. Make a list of these student outcomes and keep it; you will need it for another activity.

Operationalizing Outcomes: The Use of Performance Objectives

Applying a cause-and-effect analysis to classroom learning helps educators make informed decisions about instruction. Knowing that one teaching activity yields a desired outcome more efficiently than another allows you to select instruction on the basis of sound reasoning. To make such informed decisions, you must be able to determine if and when the desired outcome has in fact been attained. How will you determine when learners have learned the skill or material desired? How will you know when understanding has occurred? You must specify your outcome.

Psychologists, when planning an experiment, define their dependent variable operationally; that is, they describe how they intend to *measure* outcome. You will recall that operationalization is based on objectivity; one must be able to clearly assess outcomes with as little subjective inference as possible. Again, what holds for the experiment holds for the classroom. We must operationalize the learning outcomes of the teaching process. Without such a procedure, it is virtually impossible to make sound decisions.

In the classroom, we operationalize desired outcomes by preparing instructional objectives (Mager, 1975). An instructional or *performance objective* is an objective statement about outcome, one that ideally requires a minimum of inference. In fact, a well-stated performance objective includes a statement of the performance desired and the method of assessing it.

Objectifying Performance

Performance objectives specify the dependent variable in the cause-and-effect relationship. They are stated so that we will recognize the performance when we see it. Poorly-stated objectives lead to ambiguous assessments of the validity of the relationship. Three essential elements are required: (1) a clear statement of the desired *performance*, (2) a statement of the *conditions* under which the performance is expected, and (3) a statement of the *level of performance* considered acceptable.

Performance Statements. Dependent variables are aspects of learner behavior, what the learner will do or perform. Human beings can do a number of things, some of which are external and involve observable action, and some of which are internal, like thinking, and are not directly observable. Psychologists studying human behavior must externalize what people do, since assessing internal performances requires subjective inference, which is not public.

As a teacher, how would you determine if learners understand the operation of addition? If they know the concept of measurement? If they appreciate the complexities of national economic policy? You could make a personal judgment about these internal events, or you could require them to *demonstrate* understanding, knowing, and appreciating. Demonstration is an externalized performance.

The most important part of a performance objective is a statement of the way the outcome will be demonstrated. Rather than assessing whether a learner understands the operation of addition, we ask him to compute the sums of addition problems. Computation is demonstration. Knowing the concept of measurement is tapped by writing the correct lengths of objects. Computing and writing are external performances; each requires the learner to perform an explicit act.

Demonstration may be evident from the verb used in the objective, but verbs can involve either internal or external actions. We try to use external actions because they are less subjective. Table 2b–1 includes lists of performances that are possible learner outcomes. Some are stated externally and some internally. The external ones would be easy to recognize; the internal ones would not be, since they require too much subjective judgment on the observer's part. Which would you rather assess?

Statements about external performances use *action* verbs that specify an observable performance. Only learner outcomes stated in this way are amenable to objective verification. Creating performance objectives that indicate externalized performances can be a difficult task, particularly for outcomes related to affect, such as feelings, attitudes, or likes and dislikes. Both educational psychologists and educators attempt to make clear statements of this nature as they assess cognitive, psychomotor, and affective performances.

TABLE 2b–1. Examples of Internal and External Performances

Internal performance	*External performance*
The learner will:	The learner will:
1. ... *understand* the difference between rectangles and circles	1. ... *sort* a set of rectangles and circles into two sets
2. ... *comprehend* the meaning of a passage	2. ... *verbally paraphrase* the essential meaning of a passage
3. ... *recognize* the importance of good nutrition	3. ... *list the reasons* for maintaining a sound diet
4. ... *know* the square footage in a given house plan	4. ... *compute* the square footage in a given house plan
5. ... *grasp* the significance of scientific methodology for the classroom	5. ... *describe* in writing how scientific methodology applies to the classroom
6. ... *empathize* with an unfortunate peer	6. ... *provide a verbal description* of a peer's feelings

To determine a student's understanding or knowledge, some behavior must be performed. Observation of a student computing an arithmetic problem provides the teacher with information regarding the child's understanding of the multiplication process.

Statement of Conditions.   Describing the actual performance is the first important element in constructing performance objectives, but it is not the only one. We must also indicate the circumstances under which the performance will take place. When and under what conditions a learner performs are as important as the performance itself.

By this time in your educational experience you have taken innumerable tests. Some were multiple-choice tests in which you had to select the correct answer from among a number of foils. Others required you to supply the answer yourself by listing, describing, or preparing an essay. Both types of examination assessed your skills and knowledge, but the circumstances of assessment differed. Perhaps you favor one kind of test over another because you are more comfortable or perform more competently with that type. If so, then how and under what circumstances you perform are also important considerations, in addition to your performance itself.

For another example, think of how many ways a child could apply addition operations. A sum can be computed in a number of circumstances. The following are examples of different circumstances:

(1) $\begin{array}{r} 7 \\ + 4 \\ \hline ? \end{array}$ (2) $7 + 4 = ?$ (3) If Johnny has 7 pennies and finds 4 more in the street, how many pennies does Johnny have?

Are these precisely equivalent tasks? Probably not. Many children would find one or two of these problems more difficult, depending on their past experience and practice.

In a third example, five-year-old Nancy is given a picture containing a number of black dots. Then she is presented with a set of new pictures that contain more, the same, or fewer dots than the original. Nancy must make judgments about the equivalence or nonequivalence of the new cards and the original. It will make a difference whether the number of dots depicted varies from one to five or from twenty to twenty-five. Whether she must produce her judgments with the pictures in front of her or from memory will also make a difference.

These differences are variations in the *conditions* under which a response is expected. When writing performance objectives, we must include the conditions of performance as well as the performance itself. Table 2b–2 contains examples of ways we might assess one performance under a number of circumstances.

TABLE 2b–2. **Examples of the Importance of Conditions**

General	*Performance*	*Particular circumstances*
1. Knowing types of geometric shapes	1. The learner will be able to differentiate geometric shapes	a. Given a set of 4-sided figures, the student can sort them into squares and rectangles b. Given a series of line drawings, the learner can circle all the triangles c. Given a plain sheet of paper, the learner can draw a square, a triangle, and a rhombus
2. Comprehension of a paragraph in a foreign language	2. The learner will translate a short paragraph from a foreign language into English	a. Given an hour and a dictionary, the student can translate in writing the short paragraph b. Given a short class quiz, the student can translate the short paragraph in writing without the aid of a dictionary c. In a given class period, the student can orally translate a passage in front of other students

Table 2b–2 (continued)

General	Performance	Particular circumstances
3. Understanding the scientific method	3. The student can describe the variables in the paradigm	a. Given a description of a psychological experiment, the student can describe the important variables b. Presented with an educational problem, the student can describe the relevant variables c. Given a list of hypothetical statements, the student can describe the dependent variable in each
4. Physical stamina	4. The athlete can swim the distance of a mile	a. Given a warm day and a heated pool, the athlete can swim the distance of one mile b. In a turbulent ocean, the athlete can swim one mile c. Following a night of partying and no sleep, the athlete can swim one mile

The difficulty and nature of a specific performance depend at least in part on the conditions under which the performance is expected. The statement of the performance specifies what the learner is expected to do—the action, and the statement of conditions, when and under what circumstances the learner will do it. There is one final component: how well the performance is to be done.

Statement of Criteria. The proficiency level of a performance is also important and is often included in the statement of performance objectives. Is perfection expected, or is something short of perfection acceptable? Must the swimmer complete the mile in five minutes or thirty minutes? These are statements of criteria—how well the learner must perform. Examine the pairs of objectives presented in Table 2b–3. In each pair, the conditions and performance required are the

TABLE 2b–3. Examples of Different Criteria

Condition	Performance	Criteria
1. Following a semester in a typing class	the student can type	a. 45 words per minute without errors b. 80 words per minute without errors
2. When presented with addition problems orally	the learner can compute the correct sum	a. fifty percent of the time b. without error
3. Given a five-minute oral presentation in a foreign language	the student can translate the passage in written form	a. with 100 percent accuracy b. with no more than five grammatical errors
4. After listening to ten short musical selections	the student can identify the composers correctly	a. for nine out of ten passages b. for at least five of the passages

same but the criteria differ. Are they equivalent or different? A criterion, or expected level of proficiency, is necessary to establish the acceptability of a performance. How well the learner should perform, like what and when the student should perform, plays a role in assessment.

> ▶ *ACTIVITY 2.* In Table 2b–4, a series of behavioral objectives are listed. See if you can determine whether or not the objectives are well stated. For those that are poorly stated, tell which of the three elements is missing and design a well-stated objective that contains all three important components.
>
> ▶ *ACTIVITY 3.* Resurrect your list of student outcomes from the lesson plan activity referred to earlier in the chapter (p. 41). Select from your list any outcomes that contain no performance verb, an externalized performance, and rewrite them with the performances specified. Then redo all your outcomes, adding first conditions and then criteria. At the end of the activity, you should have a list of performance objectives for a unit of study. Reorganize the list in terms of the importance of the outcomes. Does the list offer any hints about planning instruction so that important outcomes will be more likely to be achieved?

TABLE 2b–4. **Well-Stated and Poorly-Stated Behavioral Objectives***

1. Given a series of colored blocks, the learner can pick out all of the red ones.
2. Following a unit on the Civil War, the student will know three major causes of that conflict.
3. Presented with a written test of ten addition problems, the learner will compute the correct sums for at least nine of the ten.
4. The learner can identify three classes of psychological variables without error.
5. After six weeks of regular exercise, the adult runner can cover four miles.
6. At the end of a course in art history, the student will appreciate the contributions of five major Renaissance painters.

*In this list of examples, 1 and 3 are completely stated, 4 lacks the specification of condition, 5 lacks a criterion, and 2 and 6 use nonperformance verbs.

Pros and Cons of Performance Objectives

It is important to remember that a performance objective is a tool, one borrowed from operationalizing variables in psychology. The value of a tool, whether it is a psychological technique, a hammer, an automobile, or a computer, rests in its usefulness. Tools should not determine what the goal is; their value is in helping us reach the goal more efficiently and straightforwardly. Tools help us get there; they do not tell us where to go. When the tool determines the goal, then the tail is wagging the dog.

One of the authors is reminded of the time she obtained a fancy food processor capable of performing the marvelous function of pulverizing food. This elaborate tool was accompanied by a cookbook of recipes that made use of the tool. Fascinated with the new device, the author concocted a variety of dishes, all of which involved using one of the various complicated facets of the tool. More often than not, the results had a couple of features in common: a messy kitchen and unpalatable food. Can one blame the tool itself? The tool did what it was supposed to do, and it did it efficiently. The tool-user, however, chose poor goals or outcomes; the tool dictated the end. Later, the tool-user learned to use the food processor to reach previously determined goals, to prepare foods that she wanted to eat, not just to exercise the tool. When used in this way, the tool proved productive, efficient, and useful.

This rather pedestrian example makes an important point. Tools should not dictate ends; rather, they should facilitate desired outcomes. Many of the criticisms leveled at the use of performance objectives reflect confusion between ends and means. Some critics of performance objectives, for example, have warned that their use focuses on low-level outcomes of the learning process. Low-level objectives, such as

Scenario Suggestion

The effective transmission of information about student progress requires a variety of communication tools as well as sensitivity about the impact of the information on recipients. The precision and meaningfulness of the information reported is an important consideration. Class rankings, for example, indicate the way a student compares with his or her classmates. Grades imply a judgment about how total performance is valued. More is needed, however. Parents, students, and others may wish to know precisely the kinds of skills a student has demonstrated.

One reporting tool that can help Mr. Baker meet his challenge is the use of performance objectives. Working within the boundaries of the school philosophy and the curriculum of the grade level, Mr. Baker can develop a set of performance objectives at the beginning of the school year. The objectives should reflect the kinds of accomplishments the school deems important achievements for third grade learners.

During the course of each semester, Mr. Baker could keep records of the number and kinds of objectives each child is mastering. When he meets with the parents he will be able to tell them in fairly precise terms what the child can do, under what circumstances, and at what level of proficiency. Moreover, at the spring conference, Mr. Baker will be able to describe precisely where progress has been made. Grades alone do not directly communicate either performances mastered or specific progress. By discussing objectives as well as grades and test scores, Mr. Baker will be giving his pupils' parents a very precise and straightforward accounting.

Of course, although there is much more to a parent-teacher conference than reporting performance, the use of objectives is one tool that Mr. Baker may find useful and parents may find informative.

---

spelling, computing, and *recalling,* are easier to write than objectives that tap higher intellectual processes like comprehending, drawing inferences, and solving problems. Is that the fault of the tool itself, or of the tool-user? If higher intellectual functioning is a desired outcome, then care must be taken in creating objectives that tap those outcomes. It is not the tool itself, but the tool's usage, that deserves the criticism.

Higher-level performances are difficult to specify, but this may be because we do not understand them very well. This difficulty is reflected in the problems we experience when we try to state them explicitly. Psychologists study this type of performance, and they must operationalize them in order to investigate them. Psychological operationalizations are often unsatisfactory, but better operational definitions are continually being developed. Performance objectives have the same feature; they are sometimes unsatisfactory for tapping sophisticated functioning. We can, however, keep trying.

A second criticism involves the time necessary to devise good performance objectives, especially since teachers are busy people. It is a time-consuming job. As a result, it is obviously not possible to prepare objectives for every teaching activity. Teachers have some goals that are more important than others, however, and for those goals surely the extra effort is worthwhile. If a teacher takes the time to develop well-designed activities, preparing accompanying objectives will take additional time; it may also make the activities more efficient and directed.

There are also advantages to using performance objectives. They provide a contract between teacher and learners; they specify what teachers must teach and inform learners of what they must achieve. The contract can save time, energy, and needless guessing. In addition, well-prepared objectives specify the assessment procedure, so they have built-in accountability. No doubt the arguments about the usefulness of this tool will continue (for example, Ebel, 1970), but we do have evidence that it works (McNeil, 1967).

Summary

Happenings in a classroom, like happenings in a psychological experiment, can be analyzed as relationships among variables. *Independent variables* in the classroom are features of instruction under teacher control. *Dependent variables* are the aspects of student behavior the teacher seeks to change. *Attribute variables* are the characteristics of the learners themselves, and *extraneous variables* are all the other events that might inadvertently affect learning outcomes.

A causal relationship exists between what the teacher does in instruction and what the learner does in performance, but to determine the effectiveness of the causal variable the outcome must be *operationalized*. We operationalize learner performance in the form of *performance objectives*, which contain a statement of (1) *action,* (2) *condition,* and (3) *criteria.* By using performance objectives as a tool, we know when the results are attained.

The classroom and the psychological laboratory differ in many ways. Human happenings occur in both, however, so the tools and methods of the psychologist are relevant to those who would teach. Educators are in charge of a crucial human happening—learning.

PART II

Focus on Environmental Impact

IN THE PREVIOUS CHAPTERS WE described a framework for examining human happenings. Analyzing changes in behavior on the basis of variables, cause-and-effect relationships, and operationalized outcomes is part of this approach. At this point we turn to one kind of happening that can be examined in this way—*learning*.

We generally regard learning as a process that alters human behavior so that the person can do things that were impossible before the process occurred. Performance changes, then, are the outcomes of learning. They can also occur as a result of other factors. These changes, rather than being the results of learning, are biologically based. Learning is one kind of performance change process.

Learning occurs when events in the environment influence a person and a behavior change results. The environment is in the role of the *independent variable*, which creates alterations in performance—the *dependent variables*. The alterations are *experiential*. Virtually all psychologists include these two elements, the environment and the person, in their explanations of learning, but they may interpret them differently. Various learning theorists, for example, differ in the importance they assign to specific independent variables (environmental events). They also differ in the emphasis they place on the *person* in the learning process. We thus have not one explanation of learning but many.

Any behavior results from the interaction of environmental forces (E) and person characteristics (P), or, as psychologists express it, Behavior = $E \times P$. E and P need not carry equal weight. Some learning theorists place more importance on P. However, the environment is perceived by most as playing the major role. Thus, Behavior = $E \times p$.

In the next section we present three approaches to learning, ones that place different emphases on the person. The first, *radical behaviorism*, looks primarily to environmental events to explain learning; in this approach the person is deemphasized. The second, *social learning theory*, considers some person variables but still focuses on environmental ones. The third, *cognitive learning theories*, gives person characteristics the most weight. We include summaries of all three approaches, explaining the rationales behind the explanations and the research findings that serve as the impetus for theory building.

In this section we will examine a number of learning theories—psychological attempts to explain how individuals learn to accomplish new performances. The first learning theory we present is that of behaviorism, a controversial explanatory system that places major emphasis on the way the environment affects behavior.

Chapter 3a contains a description of the behavioral approach and the historical events that led to its primacy in American psychology. Behavioral principles and the methods used to validate them are explored. Our purpose is to present the flavor of the behavioral perspective and its basis. Alternatives to the behavioral approach are detailed in subsequent chapters.

Behavioral psychology is the foundation of an important and influential behavioral technology—behavior modification. This technology, and its application to classroom phenomenan, are the subject matter of Chapter 3b.

Chapter 3a

*Behavioral Approaches
to Learning*

Introduction: Historical Background

In the early 1900s changes were taking place in psychology that were to dramatically affect the discipline. Before that time psychologists had focused on the study of consciousness: the sensations, thoughts, images, and perceptions that occur in the human mind. Known collectively as *mental events*, these occurrences presented some methodological problems. They are private happenings, and science, you will recall, must be public. A person can describe these private experiences—and description makes them public to some extent—but independent verification of a description's accuracy is not really possible. How, then, could these private happenings be studied scientifically? A number of psychologists questioned the prevalent methodology of psychology because of this problem (for a summary, see Boring, 1950). The logic and rules of science seemed to be in conflict with what psychologists were doing, and therefore presented a threat to the discipline.

A second threat to the state of the art in psychology came from a different source. Psychology encountered Sigmund Freud. Freud proposed that much of human behavior is motivated not by conscious mental events but by unconscious events of which the individual is unaware. If one accepts the idea that human behavior stems from an unconscious mental realm rather than a conscious one, how can an understanding of human behavior be achieved by studying consciousness, which is what psychologists were examining? People can hardly be expected to describe private events they are unaware of.

Freudian theory encompassed a very different view of human nature, one that could not really be incorporated into the mainstream of contemporary psychology. Freud's perspective was provocative enough that it could not be ignored, either. While the methodology of studying consciousness was thus being attacked on the basis of scientific methodology, Freud challenged the very importance of consciousness itself.

Even before Freud, another monumental scientific event had shaken the intellectual world: Charles Darwin published *The Origin of Species*. We are all familiar with Darwin's propositions, but some people are unaware of the controversy surrounding their initial publication. One reason Darwin's theories had such an impact was his notion that human beings could be placed on a continuum with other animal species; perhaps humans were more complex, but they were not basically different from other organisms. If one accepts that idea, it follows that human behavior and animal behavior have important characteristics in common. The scientific study of animals, then, could provide at least some information about human nature.

The implications of Darwinian and Freudian theories challenged the intellectual world. Add to that the questioning of psychology's methodology, and the stage was set for a revolution in psychology, a change of direction, or a *paradigm shift*. The final impetus for that shift came in 1913 when John Watson published his work, *Psychology as the Behaviorist Views It*.

In retrospect, Watson's treatise appears overly simplified, somewhat naive, and overstated; but he made two influential points. First, he proclaimed that behavior, not consciousness, is the appropriate subject for psychological study. Behavior is public and observable, whereas mental events are not. Second, he argued that humans can be extremely malleable beings, subject to being strongly influenced by their environment. Moreover, he proposed that the cause of an individual's produced behavior is the environment. Most psychologists of the time did not heartily embrace Watson's point of view, but his proclamations did receive widespread attention.

At about the same time as Watson's revelations, the work of the Russian psychologist, Pavlov, was also attracting attention. Pavlov, too, investigated behavior, examining the role of environmental events in his studies of dogs. The challenges facing psychology were crystallized with the work of Watson and Pavlov, and dramatic changes began to occur in psychology, particularly in the American branch. Animals as well as human beings were the subjects of psychological investigations. The focus changed from private mental life to produced behavior, and the causative role of the environment became a primary interest.

The Rise of Behaviorism

American psychology has never been ideologically unified, since several theoretical perspectives can flourish simultaneously. Behaviorism has, however, been an extremely important force in psychology and remains highly influential today.

In the decades following the proclamations of Watson and his contemporary, E. L. Thorndike (1913), behaviorism in psychology grew and much research was produced. Its impact was widely felt. Guthrie (1952), Hull (1952), and others produced numerous studies, refining, elaborating upon, and sometimes confirming Watson's prophecy. These people provided the basis for what is known as *methodological behaviorism* (Achenbach, 1978). Methodological behaviorists are those who adopt behavioral ideas in their investigative procedures: they study behavior, they adhere to the rules of science, and their experiments rely on public evidence. In short, it is their methodology that is behavioral; they may or may not agree with Watson's view of human nature. Today, however, a second branch of behaviorism is more prevalent and influential. This controversial branch, *radical behaviorism*, is associated with B. F. Skinner.

B. F. Skinner is clearly one of the most important psychologists of our time. His work has had a unique influence on all facets of psychology and education. He was born in Pennsylvania in 1904 and educated at Hamilton College in New York and Harvard University. He has had and continues to have a prolific and productive career (Skinner, 1976). Continually a center of controversy, Skinner has conducted voluminous research, writing treatises not only on psychology in general (Skinner, 1953, 1974), but on language (Skinner, 1957) and on education (Skinner, 1968). He has also written books for the lay public, such as *Beyond Freedom and Dignity* (Skinner, 1971), a book that may be familiar to you. You may also be aware of such instructional devices as programmed instruction and teaching machines, which were popularized by Skinner. In short, Skinner is a psychological giant both to those who agree with him and to those who question his explanations of human behavior.

Skinner's approach to human behavior interests psychologists for several reasons. First, perhaps more than any other psychological theory, radical behaviorism has adhered closely to the classical tenets of scientific logic in building a science of human behavior (Skinner, 1953). Second, the system is parsimonious and consistent: it explains most aspects of human behavior with a limited number of psychological laws. Finally, its psychological laws have been derived from the voluminous data of a great many empirical studies. The behavioral system developed not from conjecture or inference, but from actual experimentation with animals and humans.

Radical behaviorism is important to educators because its principles translate directly to classroom applications. These principles provide teachers with a methodology for fostering learning, with techniques for evaluating whether learning has indeed occurred and with procedures for making objective observations. You have probably already heard such terms as *behavior modification, reinforcement, token systems,* and *time out.* These terms refer to psychologically based teaching technologies with roots in behaviorism. We turn now to an explanation of this psychological system.

The Logical Underpinnings of Behaviorism

Every psychological theory is based on a set of assumptions about reality, about causation, and about human nature. These assumptions come from philosophy, a fact that again demonstrates the relationship between psychology and philosophy. Because there is more than one philosophical approach to human nature, there is more than one set of philosophical assumptions and more than one psychological theory. Behaviorism derives its assumptions from British empiricism (Boring, 1950) and thus represents only one philosophical approach to reality, to causation, and to explanation.

Where Does Cause Reside?

As we stressed in earlier chapters, every psychological system attempts to explain human behavior, to identify its causes. The approaches people use to determine causes can differ, however. The following example shows the problems associated with locating causes and demonstrates how a behaviorist approaches them.

Suppose the year is 1965. At a large university, a young man has been diligently studying in the library—eight hours without a break. We wish to determine why this student has undertaken this task, to find the *cause* of his studying. We choose three unrelated observers who do not personally know the persevering young man, and each of them watches the student's behavior. We then ask each to explain the behavior's causes.

The first observer declares that the student must indeed be highly motivated to spend so many hours studying. Long studying (the result) is caused by high motivation (the cause). This may seem like a satisfactory explanation, but it presents a problem. How did the observer determine that the student was motivated? Knowing nothing else about the rabid studier, the observer had to *infer* motivation from the behavior. Then the cause, which was inferred from the behavior, was used to explain the same behavior. This explanation involves circular reasoning: *B* is used to infer *A*, which in turn is used to explain *B*. This circular explanation, as illustrated by Figure 3a–1, is in fact a tautology that explains nothing.

Our second observer offers a different explanation: The student is studying because he must do well in school or he will lose his student deferment and be subject to the draft. Recall that our scenario takes place in 1965, during the Viet Nam war and before the beginning of

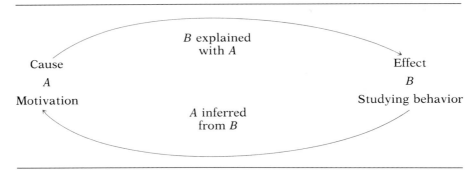

FIGURE 3a–1.   Circular Reasoning Diagram

the draft lottery. The second observer explains studying (result) as fear of the draft (cause). This cause, however, is also inferred from behavior and has the same problem of circularity as the first explanation. It also points up a second problem. Observers 1 and 2 made different inferences from the same data—and that reveals a problem of reliability. How can you be certain about an inferred explanation when disagreements arise from the same data?

The third observer offers another explanation: The student must have a test the next day. This explanation is a likely one, too, but it points up another logical problem. The suspected cause, a forthcoming test, is a *future* event in relation to the studying. How can a future event explain a current one? To an empiricist, and therefore to a behaviorist, it is logically impossible for a cause to follow its effect (Boring, 1950; Heise, 1975).

Thoroughly frustrated with our attempts to explain this young man's behavior, we approach him and ask him why he is studying with such ardor. His reply: "I have a test tomorrow. Before the last test I studied for ten hours because I didn't have anything else to do. I got an A, so I'm doing it this time, too." This explanation is acceptable to a behaviorist. There is no inference, no circularity, and no need to find a cause in the future. A past event, receiving A's after studying, caused the result, studying again.

Two important points about behavioral explanations are illustrated here: (1) causes must be past events, and (2) inference must be avoided.

The Chain of Events

To determine causation, the behaviorist begins by looking at phenomena in a temporal sequence. The phenomenon of interest, according to the legacy of Watson, is observable behavior. In our example, the observable behavior is studying, which in behavioral terminology is called a *response*. Events that precede the response are called *antecedent stimuli*. The announcement that a test will be given is an antecedent stimulus preceding the response of studying. Events following the response are called *consequent stimuli*. The *A* received after studying for a test is a consequent stimulus. Stimuli (*S*) and responses (*R*) can thus be placed in a temporal sequence or chain. Any behavior can be analyzed in this way, and a long chain of sequential behaviors can be divided into these units, as in Figure 3a–2.

To explain behavior, however, we must identify past events that are causative, ones regularly associated with a particular outcome. The regular association between two events is a *functional relationship*. A functional relationship between a stimulus and a response is called a *contingency*. When a particular stimulus and a particular response are regularly associated, a contingency exists between them. If the occurrence of the stimulus is regularly followed by the occurrence of the response, the contingency has functional properties.

Most stimuli are environmental events, whereas responses are events produced by the organism. The functional analysis of behavior is the process of determining the connections between the two. The importance of environmental stimuli is their relationship with behavior. What the stimulus is remains irrelevant; the behaviorist is concerned with what it does.

Behavioral Perspectives on Learning

Behaviorists consider learning in terms of response changes. Some responses grow more frequent, others become less frequent. Simple responses may be combined into more complex ones. A response may come to be produced in many situations or be restricted to very few settings. Learning includes all these kinds of changes in the frequency, complexity, and generality of particular aspects of behavior. Whether or not a person produces a specific response in a given situation depends on the individual's learning history—what has happened in the past regarding that response. Changes in responding occur through a learning process called *conditioning*.

Most behaviorists recognize two types of *conditioning* in learning: *classical* or *respondent* conditioning and *instrumental* or *operant* conditioning. Both processes involve response changes, but these are associated with different types of stimuli.

FIGURE 3a–2.   The Temporal Sequence Chain

Time →

S	*R*	*A* . . . .
Antecedent stimuli ——→	Observable response ——→	Consequent stimuli

Classical Conditioning

The Russian psychologist, Pavlov, was one of the people associated with the radical changes in psychology discussed at the beginning of this chapter. Pavlov, through his research efforts with dogs, developed the classical conditioning paradigm. Watson conducted research in the same area. Both men observed a particular type of association that can exist between a stimulus and a behavioral response.

Respondent Behavior

When certain kinds of stimuli are presented to an organism, a response follows virtually automatically. If a bright light is directed into a human eye, for example, the pupil will automatically constrict. The bright light is a stimulus; pupil constriction is a response. If a loud noise occurs in the presence of an infant, the infant will probably cry. Again, the noise is a stimulus, the cry is a response. If an electric shock is applied to an animal's limb, the animal will withdraw the limb. If a puff of air is projected at your face, you will blink.

These examples have something in common: each involves what we call *respondent behavior*. The first common characteristic of respondent behavior is the temporal sequence associated with occurrence. A stimulus is presented, and the response follows. The stimulus is an *antecedent* event. The sequence is presented diagrammatically in Figure 3a–3. A second feature common to these examples is the regularity of the relationship between the stimulus and the response. Virtually every time the stimulus occurs, the response will follow. This kind of regularity between two events is called a *contingency*. The occurrence of the second event, in this case the response, is contingent on, or depends on, the occurrence of the first event, presentation of the stimuli.

The time sequence and the regularity of the reaction enables us to make statements about cause. Presentation of the stimulus causes the behavior to occur; it elicits, triggers, or brings on the response. The causative nature and the regularity of the relationship between the two events can be demonstrated with experiments. The experimenter manipulates the presentation of the stimulus and records the occurrence of the response. The stimulus acts as an independent variable and the response is the dependent variable.

FIGURE 3a–3.   The Temporal Sequence Associated with
Respondent Behaviors

Time

(1) Presentation of a stimulus ⟶ (2) Occurrence of a response

Antecedent event   Observable behavior

Through a great deal of experimentation, psychologists have identified much animal and human behavior that has this kind of relationship with environmental stimuli. The eye blink response, pupil constriction, crying and withdrawal in response to pain are a few of these behaviors. Individuals apparently need not learn to perform these acts; the process seems automatic. We respond innately in reaction to these stimuli. The number of these innate reactions is limited, but those that exist appear to be species characteristics that the organism can perform at birth.

In psychological terminology, behaviors that occur automatically like this, in the absence of prior learning, are referred to as *unconditioned*. An automatic, unlearned response is an *unconditioned response (UCR)*; the antecedent stimulus that evokes the response is an *unconditioned stimulus (UCS)*. Relabeling the events in the sequence with the appropriate terminology produces Figure 3a–4.

We all know, however, that many thousands of stimuli in the environment evoke regular responses. Certain odors, such as those of perfumes (stimuli), may cause us to feel pleasure (response). The sight of a spider (stimulus) may cause us to withdraw (response). There are innumerable associations of this type, and all individuals have their own set. Associations such as these, however, are not automatic—they involve learning. This learning can be explained by the process of *classical conditioning*.

The Classical Conditioning Paradigm

The research of Watson and Pavlov demonstrated how certain responses, rather than being innate, become associated with antecedent stimuli through learning. Pavlov observed this learning process in experiments with dogs. When food is given to a dog, the dog will salivate; food is an unconditioned stimulus and salivation in the presence of food is an unconditioned response. Pavlov, however, paired the presentation of food with the sound of a bell. After a number of these pairings, the sound of the bell caused dogs to salivate even in the absence of food. The dogs had learned to salivate to a new stimulus. This learning process is one type of conditioning.

Prior to the conditioning, the bell was a *neutral* stimulus—it was

FIGURE 3a–4.   **The Elements in an Unconditioned Sequence**

	Time	
(1) Antecedent stimulus	⟶	(2) Subsequent response
UCS		UCR

not associated with any particular behavior on the dog's part. We might say the bell had no meaning for the dog. After conditioning, however, the bell was associated with a particular behavior, salivation. When a formerly neutral stimulus comes to have a regular relationship with a particular behavior, we call it a *conditioned stimulus (CS)*. The word *conditioned* is chosen because the association is learned through experience rather than being innate.

After sufficient pairings of the bell and the food, Pavlov's dogs would salivate with the sound of the bell alone. The salivation response is then a *conditioned response (CR)*, since its association with the bell was learned. The mechanism of learning is *pairing*. The bell and the food were paired; that is, the bell, too, could elicit a regular response.

> *Step 1:* The automatic sequence
> (1) presentation of food (*UCS*) ⟶ (2) salivation (*UCR*)
> *Step 2:* The conditioning process
> (1) food (*UCS*) ⟶ (2) salivation (*UCR*)
> \+ ↗
> bell (*neutral stimulus*)
> *Step 3:* The conditioned sequence
> (1) bell alone (*CS*) ⟶ (2) salivation (*CR*)

Watson demonstrated the same sort of learning process in humans by classically conditioning a fear response in an infant, Little Albert. In this experiment, the *UCS* was a loud noise, a stimulus that usually evokes a fear response without prior learning. The neutral stimulus was a white rat, a stimulus not innately associated with fear. The presentation of the noise did cause Little Albert to cry:

> *Step 1:* The automatic sequence
> (1) loud noise (*UCS*) ⟶ (2) crying (*UCR*)

Then the loud noise and the white rat were paired; as Albert reached toward the rat, the loud noise was presented, and Albert cried.

> *Step 2:* The conditioning process
> (1) loud noise (*UCS*) ⟶ (2) crying (*UCR*)
> \+ ↗
> white rat (*neutral stimulus*)

After this process, poor Albert would cry when the white rat was presented alone; the noise was not required anymore.

> *Step 3:* The conditioned sequence
> (1) rat alone (*CS*) ⟶ (2) crying (*CR*)

Fortunately for Little Albert, a *CS* eventually loses its power to elicit the *CR* unless the *CS* is occasionally paired with the *UCS*. Albert did not have to go through life crying every time he encountered a white rat. What is learned can be unlearned; Albert unlearned his rat fear through a process of *desensitization.* By encountering the *CS* a number of times in different circumstances when it was not occasionally paired with a fear-producing *UCS*, the damage was undone.

The effects of classical conditioning can generalize in a number of ways. A conditioned stimulus, for example, that acquired its power to elicit a response through being paired with a *UCS*, can later serve the same kind of role as a *UCS* and become paired with other neutral stimuli. This is called *higher-order conditioning.* The process operates the same way except that the *UCS* is replaced by an already-acquired *CS*.

Since the time of Watson and Pavlov, many researchers have used the classical conditioning paradigm and established that it is a valid explanation for some learned behaviors (Reese & Lipsett, 1970). Classical conditioning is associated primarily with the learning of emotional behaviors, such as fears, phobias, and attractions. Techniques have also been developed to break the associations learned through this process, particularly such maladaptive associations as severe phobias. Systematic desensitization and other clinical procedures have their roots in the classical conditioning paradigm.

Relevance of Classical Conditioning

Little Phreddie Phobia is having trouble attending school. Every time he gets close to the school grounds, he cries, shakes, and is generally miserable. It seems that on the first day of school, Bernie Bully slugged little Phreddie. Bernie is the stimulus for Phreddie's fear. The school grounds, which were originally a neutral stimulus for Phreddie, were paired with Bernie, so now they produce fear, too. A classical conditioning process may be behind Phreddie's school phobia.

Knowledge of classical conditioning helps us understand emotional reactions better, but classical conditioning is rarely used deliberately as a learning procedure. One reason the principles are not very useful for teaching is that no new responses are learned. The subject learns to respond to more varied stimuli in the environment but not to make new and different responses. The *UCR* and the *CR* are virtually the same behavior, differing only in strength or intensity. The difference between the responses is not the responses themselves but the stimuli that elicit them. This sort of learning may inadvertently occur in a classroom, however, so we must be aware of its operations. Few teachers, for example, would wish to become a conditioned stimulus for fear, but that could happen in some circumstances. Perhaps Ms. Chalkboard

A child's fear of a dog may result from classical
conditioning. Pairing a dog's loud barking with the sight
of the dog may instill fear which could generalize to
other dogs encountered later.

was also present when Bernie terrorized Phreddie; Bernie's fear-producing power could generalize to her. Then Phreddie's fear might be
elicited not only by Bernie and the school but by Ms. Chalkboard, too—
an unfortunate state of affairs.

Classical conditioning is discussed in this chapter to illustrate the
general principles of behaviorism. It has several important features: its
emphasis on observables, its conception of the relationship that can
exist between stimuli and responses, and its idea that learning can
occur through pairing. Examining the functional relationship between
features of the environment and behavior is the characteristic most
relevant to teaching.

We do not define, describe, or catalogue stimuli on the basis of
their physical characteristics—what they are. Bernie, the school
grounds, and Ms. Chalkboard are physically different stimuli; their
physical features were not important in figuring out the causes of

Phreddie's phobia. Rather, we examine and define stimuli in terms of their *function*, their effect on behavior. A particular *CS* can be any aspect of the environment; what makes it a *CS* is what it does, how it affects behavior. The functional properties of the environment are important to all aspects of the behavioral approach.

Operant Conditioning

In addition to respondents, behaviorists examine another class of responses. Many of the behaviors we produce have an effect on the environment. Turn the ignition key in a car (response) and the car will start (effect). Ask for the salt (response) and the salt will be passed (effect). A child who follows an instruction (response) is likely to get a hug or pat of affection (effect). In these examples, the response produces some kind of effect on the environment. Behaviorists describe this class of behaviors as *operants*, since we use them to operate on the environment, to have an effect on our surroundings.

Relationships between operant behaviors and their produced effects can also be analyzed in terms of function. Certain responses cause specific kinds of effects; hence, a functional relationship exists between the behavior (R) and some aspect of the environment (S). Now, however, the time sequence begins with the behavior rather than with the presentation of the stimulus. This sequence is depicted in Figure 3a–5. Compare this diagram with Figure 3a–4. It differs from the scheme for classical conditioning; the stimulus events follow rather than precede the behavior. These stimulus events are called *consequent* stimuli; they follow a behavior and provide a consequence to it. It is the relationships between behaviors and their consequences that are of interest in this second type of learning, which is called *operant conditioning*.

Behaviorists using an operant paradigm have conducted a great deal of research to determine if and how future behavior changes as a result of the consequences associated with the behavior in the past. Is a produced behavior more or less likely to occur again if pleasant or unpleasant consequences follow it? If a gambler places a nickel in a slot machine and wins a hundred dollars, will the gambler repeat the behavior and try another nickel? If a child asks a question in the

FIGURE 3a–5. The Temporal Sequence Associated with Operant Behaviors

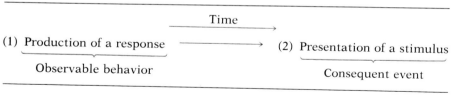

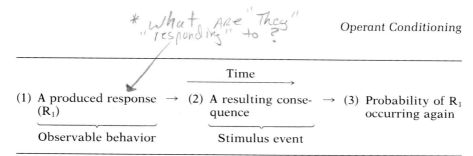

*"What ARE "They"
"responding" to?*

Time

(1) A produced response → (2) A resulting conse- → (3) Probability of R_1
    (R_1)   quence   occurring again

Observable behavior   Stimulus event

FIGURE 3a–6.   The Issue in Operant Conditioning

classroom and is yelled at for being stupid, will the child ask questions
in the future? If a soft drink machine keeps eating your quarters but
fails to give you a drink, will you keep putting money in? These are all
questions about principles of operant conditioning. The fact that you
can answer them indicates that, at least informally, you know about
these principles and have observed their effect in your own experience.

Essentially, the psychological issue concerns the effect of consequences on subsequent behavior. Stated more formally, what is the
probability that a response will occur again after it has met with
specific consequences in the past? This question is depicted in Figure
3a–6.

The probability that a given response will occur following a specific
consequence can do one of three things: increase, decrease, or remain
the same. Determining the sorts of consequences associated with these
three outcomes is the task of operant psychology. The principles of
operant conditioning have been developed by examining probability
changes and determining how to predict them.

Increasing Response Probabilities Through Reinforcement

Consequences that lead to increases in the probability of a response
involve a process called reinforcement. It is the whole process that is
referred to as reinforcement, however, not just the specific consequences. You will recall that behaviorism examines relationships or
contingencies between things, not just the specific things. For reinforcement to occur, three things must happen in sequence: (1) a response
must occur, (2) a consequence must occur, and (3) the likelihood of the
response occurring again must increase. It is the relationships among
the three events, not the events themselves, that define reinforcement.
This is outlined in Figure 3a–7.

FIGURE 3a–7.   The Sequence of Events in Reinforcement

Time

(1) R_1 →   (2) S   →   (3) Increased p of R_1

Positive Reinforcement.   The examples in Table 3a–1 depict the kinds of events that can follow a response. Certain features common to these examples exemplify reinforcement. In Column *A* a behavior is performed by an individual. These behaviors are the *operants*. In Column *C*, each operant is performed again; its probability has increased. To explain why the behavior has increased, we must examine Column *B*. In each case, the responder received something as a result of his or her response: a paycheck, an allowance, a hug, or praise. An event or element was added to the situation as a result of the response, and the response subsequently increased. To emphasize the importance of the

Reinforcement of appropriate behavior will increase the probability of that behavior occurring again. Parents often reinforce appropriate behavior with affection.

TABLE 3a–1. **Examples of Positive Reinforcement**

Column A	Column B	Column C
Response	*Consequence*	*Outcome*
1. A man works for two weeks	He receives a paycheck	The man continues to work
2. A student answers a question correctly	The teacher tells her the answer was a good one	The student answers the teacher's questions more frequently
3. A toddler plays quietly with her blocks for ten minutes	Her mother gives her a hug "for being good"	She continues playing with her blocks for fifteen minutes more
4. A teenager keeps his room clean for three days	He receives his allowance for keeping his room clean	The fellow continues to keep his room clean for five days at a stretch
5. A second grader writes a short paragraph	The teacher pins up the paragraph as "a good example"	The child's next story is two paragraphs long

consequent event, look over Column *B*. If these events had not occurred, would the outcome described in Column *C* be the same? Would the man continue to work if he did not receive a paycheck? Would the student answer questions if her answers were ignored? Probably not. The consequence served a function for the behavior: it increased or maintained it.

These scenarios are examples of *positive reinforcement*. Positive reinforcement occurs whenever a thing or event (*consequence*) follows a behavior (*R*) and as a result increases or maintains that behavior. There are three key elements to this definition: a positive reinforcer, a contingency, and an outcome. First, an event or thing is added to the situation. This is the consequence, which is called a *positive reinforcer*. The added event follows the behavior; this is the contingency. The response then increases; this is the outcome. We all behave in ways that earn positive reinforcement in the form of praise, rewards, recognition, or money. We even persist in difficult and perhaps unpleasant tasks because persistence has been rewarded in the past. Different people prefer different sorts of positive outcomes or rewards. Some people find money highly reinforcing; others place less importance on it. Some strive for public attention; others try to avoid it. In short, the actual positive reinforcer may vary from person to person. The critical element is not what the reinforcer is but what it does. If behavior increases, reinforcement has occurred regardless of the form of the reinforcer.

To emphasize the functional rather than the physical aspects of this procedure, let us examine the term itself. There are two words in this descriptive term, *positive* and *reinforcement*. The second term refers to the fact that the behavior will increase: reinforcement equals response increase. To what does the *positive* refer? Since anything can be a reinforcer, the *positive* cannot refer to any quality of the stimulus. Instead, *positive* is used here to indicate the operation of addition (+); something is added after the behavior. It may help to think of it as + *reinforcement*.

Negative Reinforcement. Looking at the term this way may help you understand the second form of reinforcement, *negative reinforcement*. Again, look at the words. We still have the term *reinforcement*, so we are still talking about consequences that increase behavior. Now, however, the term *negative* is included. Here, *negative* denotes the operation of subtraction (−); some thing or event is taken away as a result of the behavior, and the behavior increases. The relationship between these two types of reinforcement is depicted in Figure 3a–8.

Suppose a child has a mother who constantly nags when the child is in the house. The child probably finds the nagging unpleasant. If the child discovers that he can escape the unpleasant situation by going to his bedroom and shutting the door, we may find that he learns to spend a great deal of time in his room. The behavior (R) in this case is going to the bedroom. The reinforcer is the removal of the aversive agent, nagging. Reinforcement has occurred because going to the bedroom is increased as shown diagrammatically in Figure 3a–9.

For negative of reinforcement to occur, an aversive stimulus must be present. How else could it be removed? Table 3a–2 presents a number of examples.

Reinforcement Principles in Psychology. The principles of reinforcement have been investigated extensively in both the laboratory and in naturalistic conditions. The research evidence for this phenomenon is voluminous and varied, covering a wide scope of both animal and human behaviors. An example is included in the Research Report on page 72.

FIGURE 3a–8. Positive and Negative Reinforcement Compared

R ⟨ S is added ⟶ R increases { Positive reinforcement; S is subtracted ⟶ R increases { Negative reinforcement

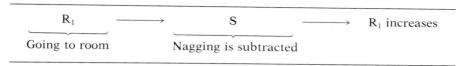

FIGURE 3a–9. **Effects of Negative Reinforcement**

Critical Features of Reinforcement Principles

Scientific investigations of the principles of reinforcement shed further light on important characteristics of the process. The results of studies tell us, for example, about different types of reinforcers and how individual stimuli become reinforcing in the first place. Moreover, operant researchers have developed objective procedures for demonstrating the functional power of stimulus events. These procedures are also important to an understanding of behaviorism.

Types of Reinforcers.   Almost any event or stimulus can serve to reinforce behavior in particular circumstances. In research with animals, the reinforcers are usually food. With humans, the reinforcers are frequently *social reinforcers,* such as praise, recognition, a reward, or permission to take part in a desired activity. Such reinforcers as food, water, and warmth are called *primary reinforcers,* because they are associated with physiological processes and because they function as reinforcers virtually automatically, without prior learning. Primary

TABLE 3a–2. Examples of Negative Reinforcement

Stimulus (S) Present	*Response (R)*	*Consequence: The stimulus (S) is subtracted*	*Outcome*
1. The TV is on very loud while a student is trying to study	The student turns off the TV	The loud noise is removed	Turning off the TV in similar circumstances is increased
2. A young child is ridiculed by his peers	He punches one in the mouth	The ridicule ceases	The child fights more in the future
3. A baby is crying at high volume and has been for ten minutes	The father picks up the baby	The baby stops crying	The next time the baby cries, the father picks up the baby as soon as it cries

Research Report

The study we have chosen to present in this chapter captures some of the essential features of both operant principles and operant methodology. A number of these features are fairly typical of research in the Skinnerian tradition. First, for example, this is a *single-subject design* in which only one person participates. The single-subject format is used in most operant studies. Second, the investigators examine the functional power of *positive reinforcement,* a main focus of radical behaviorism. Third, they use a *reversal design* to demonstrate the cause-and-effect relationship between reinforcement and behavior. Moreover, the research involves a real problem in a real environment: the maladaptive behavior of one preschool child. The origin of this research problem thus differs from that of many laboratory studies. For these reasons, this example should suffice as a concrete illustration of how operant psychologists pursue their science. The methodology is clearly described by the investigators themselves, who exemplified the behaviorist's passion for clear, observable phenomena, and a clear, observable science.

METHOD

Subject

Mark was one of the twelve children enrolled in the three-year-old group at the laboratory preschool. He was three years and eight months old when the study began. It became apparent during the first six months of school that Mark spent little time in physical activity. He possessed few skills for using materials or equipment or playing with other children. During his first half-year he spent much of his time wandering randomly from one activity to another. When he occasionally tried to join other children in play, he disrupted their activities. He avoided most of the climbing equipment—boards, ladders, and boxes—and he almost never used a piece of outdoor equipment referred to as the large climbing frame.

Procedures

The procedure for getting Mark to play on the climbing frame consisted of making adult social reinforcement contingent solely upon his use of this piece of equipment. Use of the climbing frame, hereafter called climbing-frame behavior, was defined as follows: physical contact with the frame or with the auxiliary boards, blocks, ladders, or ropes temporarily attached to it. Social reinforcement was defined as follows: a teacher standing within ten feet (the length of the climber) of the subject and watching, speaking to, smiling at, or touching the child, or bringing him supplementary equipment to amplify his play on the climber. To withdraw or withhold social reinforcement, the teacher turned away and did not look at, smile at, or speak to the child, focusing her attention and activity elsewhere. One of the two teachers who were regularly in charge of the group was assigned the task of reinforcing the child to make sure that the above procedures were carried out consistently and promptly. This teacher also supervised other children who came to the climber. The other teacher, who assumed major responsibility for guiding the rest of the group, followed identical procedures in reinforcing Mark whenever his proximity to her made it appropriate. No other adults interacted with the children. The study was carried out in five phases.

BASELINE. The subject's behavior during the outdoor play period, before reinforcement procedures were systematically applied, was recorded to determine the operant level of his climbing-frame behavior. Recording was carried on for nine days.

FIRST REINFORCEMENT. Continuous social reinforcement was given whenever the subject was using the climbing frame; reinforcement was withheld whenever he engaged in other activities. Since Mark initially had no climbing-frame behavior for teachers to reinforce, it was necessary at first to reinforce successive approximations to his behavior. The reinforcing teacher, stationed near the climbing frame, smiled and spoke to him when he approached or walked by, withdrawing her attention when he moved away. When he began to come closer and stay longer, she narrowed her criteria for reinforcement; that is, at first she paid attention to him when he came within about six feet of the climber, then not until he came within five feet, and so on. Eventually, he touched the frame and was soon climbing on it. From this point on, the teacher gave him attention only for climbing-frame behavior, as previously defined. Only the amount of time he actually engaged in climbing-frame behavior was recorded, over a period of nine days.

REVERSAL. Contingencies for delivering reinforcement were reversed; that is, the teachers withheld attention from Mark's climbing-frame behavior but gave him continuous attention during all of his other activities. Although the reinforcement teacher assumed the major responsibility for giving this attention, the other teacher also reinforced Mark for activities away from the climbing frame. This procedure was followed for five days to determine whether the contingency employed (adult attention) was a significant variable in the change in climbing-frame behavior observed during the first reinforcement period.

SECOND REINFORCEMENT. Continuous social reinforcement for climbing-frame behavior was again instituted for five days. No reinforcement was given for other behaviors.

GENERALIZATION. The reinforcement schedule for climbing-frame behavior was gradually shifted from continuous to intermittent, and all other physical activity was likewise intermittently reinforced. This procedure was carried on for four days. During this change in reinforcement procedures,

FIGURE 1. Percentages of each morning spent by a nursery school boy in using a climbing-frame apparatus.

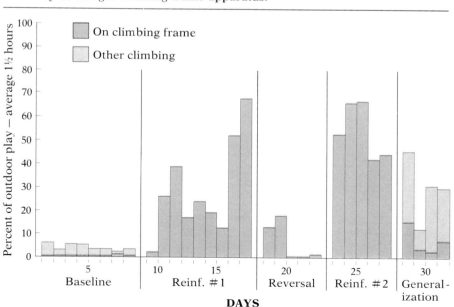

teachers began to give reinforcement less frequently and for shorter periods of time. On the schedule of continuous reinforcement, the teacher gave Mark attention every time and for as long as he played on the climbing frame. When he left it, the teacher immediately turned to other children or duties. When an intermittent schedule was instituted, the teacher first attempted to reinforce approximately every second incidence of this behavior for as long as it continued. Next, she gradually reduced the duration of the reinforcement until she stayed only a few minutes. Slowly, then, the teacher increased the number of responses required for reinforcement and shortened the duration of reinforcement, flexibly adjusting her schedule to maintain the child's climbing-frame behavior. In the final stages of this phase, teachers reinforced Mark on an intermittent schedule consistent with that given to any child in the group.

Changes in the above procedures were to be instituted whenever the behavior reached a consistently stable rate, showing no extreme variation for three days. No changes were to be made on a Monday or a Friday, however, to minimize possible effects of the weekend holidays.

The results, depicted in Figure 1, are dramatic. They demonstrate both the format for presenting data in a single-subject study and the remarkable power of applying reinforcement contingencies. The author's conclusion provides an interesting personal note on Mark:

> It appeared that, along with the planned manipulation of Mark's climbing-frame behavior, desirable modifications had occurred in two other classes of behavior over which no control had been attempted and no data recorded. These behaviors were: (1) improved skill with all the active play equipment and (2) an increase in social and verbal behaviors that enabled him to interact more effectively with his peers.

Johnston, M. K., C. S. Kelley, F. R. Harris, & M. M. Wolf. An application of reinforcement principles to the development of motor skills of a young child. *Child Development*, 1966, *37*, 379–387.

---

reinforcers promote life directly. They function to increase behavior in all organisms under most circumstances.

The effects of social reinforcers can vary greatly. Different people react differently to the same reward, for example. Social reinforcers are a type of *secondary reinforcer;* that is, their reinforcing value must be acquired. We must learn the reinforcing value of grades, money, and praise. Unlike primary reinforcers, social reinforcers have no intrinsic value biologically.

One way that social stimuli gain reinforcing value is through being paired with primary reinforcing stimuli. If you have ever trained a puppy you have seen this pairing process in action, even though you may not have known the name of the process. To train a puppy to sit, for example, you start by giving him a dog biscuit, a primary reinforcer, every time he sits on command. As you give him the biscuit, you also give him a pat and a "Good boy." The latter is a social reinforcer which you are pairing with food. Eventually, the puppy will sit on command,

and only the social reinforcer will be needed to sustain the behavior. When maintained with pats and praise, the behavior is under secondary rather than primary reinforcer control. Since the social reinforcer becomes effective only after it is paired with a primary reinforcer, its reinforcing value is learned.

Human beings learn to respond to social reinforcers as infants. Such social events as smiles, physical attention, and the sound of a human voice acquire reinforcement value early in a baby's life. These

Teachers display students' work so that the students may receive public attention. The attention may serve as reinforcement for the behavior that led to the production of that work.

events acquire reinforcing power, however, on the basis of past experience. Since people's experiences vary, the effectiveness of a particular reinforcer will, too. Therein lies the individuality of reinforcement.

When children begin to attend school, social reinforcers can usually be used effectively to increase or maintain their behaviors. Their effectiveness will vary, however. Some children will be under strong social control; others will not. Some may perform for intangibles, such as praise, attention, and individual recognition; others will not find those intangibles particularly reinforcing.

In naturalistic settings, we rarely expect each of our responses to receive attention or praise. Sometimes this happens, but more often it does not. Yet we often persist in activities even in the absence of obvious reinforcement. How can this be explained? One explanation involves extending the notion of secondary reinforcement.

When children produce responses valued by others—cleaning their rooms, for example—some sort of social reinforcer, such as praise, often follows. If on the basis of past experience praise functions as a secondary reinforcer, receiving praise leads children to feel good about themselves. The response, room cleaning, is paired with the delivery of the secondary reinforcer, praise, but it is also associated with that good feeling. For clarity, this can be diagrammed as shown in Figure 3a–10. If this pairing occurs often enough, simply producing the behavior will cause the consequence of the good feeling. A girl who is often praised for cleaning her room may associate room cleaning with good feelings and do it without being told. Producing the response alone functions as a reinforcer, and hence behavior is maintained. Obviously, this is a desirable state of affairs, since delivery of a reinforcer no longer requires another person's presence.

Similarly, simply discovering that a response is appropriate sometimes serves as a reinforcer. In this case, the effective reinforcer is knowledge of results (Skinner, 1968). If learners are externally reinforced for correct responses, discovery of correctness and an external reinforcer are again paired. If the pairing occurs often enough, the discovery of correctness alone will function as a reinforcer. Again, this situation is desirable, since the presence of another person is unnec-

FIGURE 3a–10.   **Effects of a Secondary Reinforcer**

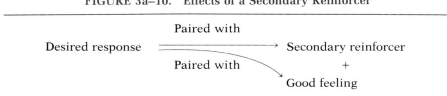

essary. Only confirmation of correctness is required. This can be supplied by someone else, but often children can determine correctness themselves.

Reinforcing events like good feelings and knowledge of results share two important features. First, both are secondary reinforcers— that is, their reinforcing function was acquired through being paired with another reinforcer. Second, pairing is a learning process that depends on past experience. Since people differ in their experiences, they also differ in whether or not these nebulous events function as reinforcers for them. Reinforcing value must be learned, and because every person has a different learning history, the same stimuli do not work identically for everyone.

Recording Behavior. Since reinforcement is defined in terms of its effect on behavior, the only way to determine whether a specific stimulus is reinforcing is to observe its effect. To begin this process, operant psychologists observe the frequency of a particular defined behavior, recording how often it occurs under existing circumstances. This record of behavioral frequency, called the *baseline,* is the observed frequency of a response before the experimenter has applied any contingencies. Without a baseline record, it would be impossible to evaluate changes in behavior after reinforcement is applied.

After a baseline data record is established, a particular reinforcement plan is devised, and the reinforcer is provided for the behavior being examined. Data collection continues during this phase. If the frequency of the behavior increases during intervention, then reinforcement probably is occurring. If it does not increase, then by definition reinforcement has not occurred, regardless of the researcher's intention.

When behavior frequencies do increase, the researcher double-checks to find out if the increase was simply a chance occurrence. One way to do this is to repeat the process a second time. This involves returning the situation to the initial conditions and discontinuing the experimental reinforcement plan. During this phase, which is called a *reversal,* data are also collected. Then the reinforcement plan is reinstituted. If the target behavior increases again, the researcher can be reasonably certain that the reinforcement plan is actually responsible for the behavior change.

There are other procedures for checking the effects of reinforcement, but they share emphasis on data. If the data show that the behavior increases, then reinforcement is occurring. If the behavior fails to increase, reinforcement has not occurred. This emphasizes again the point that reinforcement is defined in terms of *function,* regardless of the particular behavior or stimulus.

Decrease Procedures: Extinction

So far we have discussed how environmental consequences increase behaviors, but consequences can also decrease behaviors. If people working at a difficult job are no longer paid, chances are they will quit. If students study diligently but fail to receive passing grades, their studying will probably decrease. If a child is ignored in the classroom even though he or she is working hard and completing assignments, the child may stop working. These are examples of another operant process—*extinction*.

Like reinforcement, extinction describes a relationship among three events: (1) a behavior, (2) a consequence, and (3) a performance effect. Examine the list of examples in Table 3a–3. The examples have several things in common. First, in each example a behavior decreases, as we see in Column *C*. Second, the performer had been reinforced for the behavior in the past, as indicated in Column *A*. Third, in each case reinforcement is not received; examine Column *B*. These three elements give us our definition of extinction: the process of decreasing a previously reinforced behavior by stopping its reinforcement.

Extinction demonstrates how non-reinforcement functions to decrease responses, a phenomenon which is reliably observed across organisms (Reese & Lipsett, 1970). The decrease, however, is often very gradual. The rate of decrease is related to two conditions: (1) the past reinforcement history of the response, and (2) the availability of alternative responses that facilitate reinforcement.

The first condition relates to *schedules of reinforcement*, the timing and frequency with which reinforcement has been received in the past. Basically, reinforcement can be delivered in two fashions, on either a *continuous* or an *intermittent* schedule. A continuously reinforced response results in reinforcement every time it is performed. The rate of responding with continuous reinforcement increases rapidly. With an intermittent schedule, reinforcement occurs not for every response, but only after certain ones. With intermittent reinforcement, the rate of response increases less quickly than it does with a continuous schedule.

There are four types of intermittent schedules: (1) *fixed interval*, (2) *fixed ratio*, (3) *variable interval*, and (4) *variable ratio*. Each type is associated with a different rate and pattern of response increase. With fixed schedules, reinforcement is delivered on a specified basis—after a certain period of time in the interval variety, or after a certain number of responses in the ratio variety. The time period or the number of responses required does not change but is held constant. A worker who is paid every two weeks, for example, is on a fixed-interval schedule of reinforcement. It is a *fixed* schedule because the time period, two weeks, does not change. It is an *interval* schedule because time, not some other criteria, serves as the basis for reinforcement. On the other hand, a

TABLE 3a–3. Examples of Extinction

Column A	Column B	Column C
Response	*Consequence*	*Outcome*
1. A rat in an experiment presses a bar that in the past always produced food	No food is forthcoming	The rat eventually stops pressing the bar
2. A gambler places many nickels in a slot machine that in the past has paid off	The machine returns nothing	The gambler leaves
3. A father politely asks his son several times to clean his room	The son ignores the father's request	The father ceases to ask politely
4. In a grocery store, a toddler asks his mother for candy	The mother quietly continues shopping	The toddler stops making the request
5. A child raises his hand frequently in class to get the teacher's help	The teacher fails to notice the child's hand-raising	The child stops raising his hand
6. A student spends hours preparing a special project	The busy teacher neglects to examine and evaluate the project	The student does not undertake other projects that semester

factory worker who is paid on a piecework basis is reinforced on a fixed ratio schedule. A specified constant number of pieces, that is, responses, earns reinforcement.

In variable schedules, the time period or the number of responses required before reinforcement varies around some average amount. If you were paid on a variable interval schedule you might sometimes receive your paycheck once a week, sometimes once a month, sometimes twice a month. The time period would vary, and it would be hard to predict when payment was coming. The factory worker on a variable ratio schedule based on piecework would earn reinforcement for *X* number of pieces sometimes, *2X* other times, and perhaps *3X* other times. Again, predicting when reinforcement was forthcoming would be difficult. Few unions would accept such conditions.

In the natural environment, it is usually difficult to determine the precise schedule of reinforcement for any particular response. Intermittent schedules of some sort are more common. In the laboratory, the specific schedule can be determined by the researcher, so patterns of responding associated with different schedules have been extensively studied. One feature of these patterns is rate decreases under extinction conditions, that is, when reinforcement is terminated. In general, these findings can be summarized as follows:

1. Rate decreases are fastest with responses previously reinforced on a continuous rather than on an intermittent schedule.
2. Previously fixed schedules produce intermediate rate decreases under extinction conditions.
3. Previously variable schedules produce the slowest rate of decrease under extinction conditions.
4. Under extremely thin variable schedules, the rate decrease under extinction conditions can be very gradual indeed. A thin schedule is one in which a high rate of responding is required for a unit of reinforcement.

Although an operant psychologist would not use these words, we can interpret these research findings in terms of expectations of reinforcement. With continuous or fixed reinforcement schedules, the performer knows when to expect reinforcement. If reinforcement ceases, the expectation is violated, and the performer stops responding, since reinforcement is obviously not forthcoming. If you normally received your paycheck weekly but suddenly stopped getting it, you would not continue to work for very long. Your expectation of reinforcement would be violated, and the violation would be easy to detect. With a variable reinforcement schedule, however, the expectation is not as clear. Since reinforcement is unpredictable, it is not easy to tell when it has stopped. Under those circumstances, responding might continue for a longer time, since the next response might in fact result in reinforcement. The gambler at a slot machine is a case in point. Slot machines deliver on a thin variable ratio schedule, so the gambler cannot predict when he might win and get reinforcement. It is therefore not unusual for gamblers to persist for a long time, even after considerable losses.

The second condition that affects the rate of decrease during extinction is the availability of alternative responses that might lead to reinforcement. If an alternative behavior is available, extinction will proceed more quickly, since the performer will try something else. The rat described in Table 3a–3, who has received food only by pressing the bar in his cage, has a problem when reinforcement ceases. What else can he do? In desperation, he may keep pressing the bar, despite lack of reinforcement. The poor thing has no alternative. On the other hand, the youngster who fails to obtain the teacher's help by raising his hand does have an alternative. If calling aloud to the teacher gets attention, handraising will be rapidly abandoned for this new strategy.

Extinction is an effective and reliable behavioral principle. It works. How quickly it works depends on past reinforcement history and the availability of alternative responses.

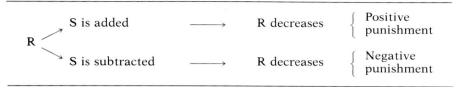

FIGURE 3a–11. **Positive and Negative Punishment Compared**

Decrease Procedures: Punishment

We defined reinforcement in terms of its function on behavior: responses increase. Extinction was also described in terms of function: responses decrease. The same holds true of punishment. Punishment is an operant conditioning technique that results in the decrease or reduction of a behavior.

Types of Punishment. Like reinforcement, punishment comes in two varieties, positive and negative. You will recall that positives are associated with addition (+) and negatives with subtraction (−); these terms do not describe the goodness or badness of the procedures. In *positive punishment,* some event or thing is added following a behavior and decreases the incidence of the behavior. With *negative punishment,* a stimulus is subtracted after the behavior and again results in a rate decrease. This is depicted in Figure 3a–11.

We are all familiar with positive punishment. Some examples are given in Table 3a–4. In each of these examples, the response in Column C is decreased; this is essential to the definition of punishment. In addition, a consequence is added following the behavior; this is what makes the punishment positive. With negative punishment, removing something leads to the decrease. Examples of that process are depicted in Table 3a–5.

TABLE 3a–4. **Examples of Positive Punishment**

Column A	Column B	Column C
Behavior	*Consequence*	*Outcome*
1. A toddler touches a hot stove	The child's hand is burned	The child does not touch the stove again
2. A child mistreats a younger sibling	The parent delivers a spanking	The child does not bully the young child again
3. A student talks out in class without raising his hand	The teacher scolds him for doing so	The student is quiet for the remainder of class

TABLE 3a–5. Examples of Negative Punishment

Column A	Column B	Column C
Behavior	*Consequence*	*Outcome*
1. A child is misbehaving with his friends	The mother sends the friends home	Misbehaving decreases
2. A child is playing too roughly with a new puppy	The puppy is given away	Rough playing with animals is decreased
3. A child steals money from his mother's purse and is discovered	Mother states she "cannot love such a bad boy" and withdraws love	Stealing does not occur again
4. A girl is physically aggressive with her mother	Father refuses to take the girl with him on an outing because of her "bad behavior"	Physical aggressiveness toward the mother is reduced
5. A student misbehaves during class with his peers	He is denied recess period	Misbehaving in class decreases

Conditions Affecting Punishment.   Like reinforcement, the effectiveness of punishment in decreasing behavior has a great deal of empirical support. Certain conditions must be present and punishment must be delivered in a precise manner, however, or it might suppress behavior only minimally or temporarily.

In laboratory investigations, researchers find that punishment is most effective in decreasing a response when it is delivered with maximum intensity. This finding is based on animal research in which the subjects were given electric shocks of various strengths following a produced behavior. Higher intensities suppressed behavior more effectively and for longer periods of time than milder intensities (Walters & Grusec, 1977). Even under these conditions, however, the response is very likely to reappear when punishment ceases. Studying the influence of punishment intensity with children is much more difficult. One cannot, of course, ethically apply high-intensity electric shock to youngsters. As a result, investigative laboratory studies with children differ from those used with animals, and the findings are less clearcut (Walters & Grusec, 1977). In these studies, punishing stimuli sometimes decrease responding and sometimes do not.

Punishment is also more effective when delivered on a continuous rather than an intermittent schedule (Left, 1969; Walters & Grusec, 1977). This finding suggests that consistency of punishment is important if we wish to suppress a behavior. The effect is also greater when punishment is delivered immediately after the response rather than after a time delay (Aronfreed, 1968; Cheyne & Walters, 1969; Parke, 1969). Again, the findings for children are less clear than those for animals.

Ensuring that the conditions improving the effectiveness of punishment—maximal intensity, consistency, and immediacy—are all present can be very difficult, especially in the natural environment. Even under ideal conditions the rate and degree of behavioral suppression is unpredictable. This fact alone may cause one to question the efficacy of punishment for changing behavior, and punishment often presents other even more serious problems.

Side Effects of Punishment.   Besides being unpredictable, the use of punishment can lead to side effects, some of which are quite serious for the recipient, the punisher, or both. One side effect, for example, is that it may encourage aggression on the part of the recipient, particularly if the punishment is physical (Bandura & Walters, 1963; Mitchell, Arling, & Moller, 1967; Sears, Maccoby, & Levin, 1957). Positive physical punishment is especially likely to cause problems. Aggression disrupts social relationships, and once it is exhibited it may be reinforced. Creating circumstances that make aggression more likely is a questionable procedure. Negative punishment, which involves withdrawing approval or privileges, is less likely to cause aggression (Walters and Grusec, 1977).

Punishment also increases the probability of escape behavior. Who voluntarily remains in a situation when he or she expects to be punished? The problem is more serious when the situation is associated with punishment exclusively and reinforcement is not provided. A person who consistently delivers aversive stimuli, however, is very likely to be avoided by recipients.

A number of other side effects have been associated with punishment. One is that punishment can overextend its effect and suppress behavior in general, not just the specific punished response. A second is that the deliverer of the aversive contingency can actually become a fear-producing stimulus through classical conditioning. Again, however, results are equivocal with regard to human subjects (Walters & Grusec, 1977). Moreover, most findings relate to physical punishment. We know less about the side effects of softer forms of positive punishment, such as verbal reprimands, and the side effects of negative punishment, such as withdrawal of love or privileges.

Although punishment is difficult to use successfully, it can be effective. We possess little certain knowledge of its short- and long-term effects on children, particularly in naturalistic settings. Punishment

New Directions in Research

Radical behaviorism is an internally consistent theoretical system comprised of a limited set of empirically validated principles of behavior. New research, then, focuses not on the development of new principles but on increasing the precision of these principles under laboratory conditions, and on the *validation* of the principles in non-laboratory settings. Many contemporary researchers seek to demonstrate that the same general principles hold across settings, individuals, and behaviors. This latter issue reflects a concern with the *ecological validity* of reinforcement principles.

Since behaviorists take many of their research questions from the real environment, they work with real problems in natural settings. In the course of doing so, they are conducting research on behavioral phenomena like phobic disorders (Morris & Kratochwill, in press; Mauissakalien & Barlow, 1980), hyperactivity and learning problems (Lahey, 1978; Bijou & Ruiz, 1981), language disorders (Kratochwill, 1981; Ross, 1981), and affective disorders (Eastman, 1976; Carson & Adams, 1981). These kinds of problematic behaviors have traditionally been addressed by personality theorists using non-behavioral treatment methods. By working with these complex problems in complex settings, behaviorists

face some new challenges Skinner did not have to contend with.

The behaviorist is first and foremost operating from a scientific value system: Objectivity, therefore, is always a high priority. To obtain that objectivity with complex behaviors, behavioral researchers must develop accurate methods of collecting and examining data tapping those behaviors. We thus see many new efforts in sophisticated techniques of behavioral assessment (Ciminero, Calhoun, & Adams, 1977) and data analysis within single-subject designs (McCleary & Hay, 1980; Kazdin, 1976; Kratochwill, 1978).

There is another relatively recent development not quite as true to the original system—the reintroduction of cognitive factors, unobservable mental events, into the analysis and treatment of behavioral problems. Known as *cognitive behaviorism* (Kendall & Hollon, 1979; 1981) or when used in treatment *cognitive behavior modification*, this approach is more eclectic than radical behaviorism. Perhaps it mirrors a general shift of interest in psychology as a whole—increasing concern with the nature of thought.

In the next theory chapter we examine in some depth one of the more cognitive behavioral perspectives, social learning theory.

may be accompanied by unpleasant side effects, so it should be used with caution. If used, it should be applied judiciously. Physical punishment may be the most questionable procedure of all.

Evaluation

Behavioral principles are among the most thoroughly researched and validated principles of human behavior. The phenomena of classical and operant conditioning are well substantiated in both laboratory and field research. With its emphasis on observables, its establishment of clear cause-and-effect relationships between environmental stimuli and behavior, and the demonstrated reliability of those contingencies, behaviorism is a very useful body of psychological principles. These principles have been accumulated from scientific study.

There are, of course, many people who question whether all human behavior can be reduced to behavioral contingencies. Behaviorists study observable behaviors, which means they do not address such private mental events as thinking (Skinner, 1974), but look instead at the outcome of the mental event, performance. Behaviorism contends not that mental events do not exist, only that they cannot be objectively studied.

There is a logical reason for this position. Conceivably, a mental event could also be placed in a temporal sequence. Let us symbolize a mental event as M' and place it in a temporal sequence:

$$(1)\ S \rightarrow M' \rightarrow R$$

We can observe (S) and (R) directly, so the temporal relationship between them can be determined. However, we cannot observe M'; we can only infer it. We thus cannot rule out other possible temporal relationships.

$$(2)\ M' \longrightarrow S \longrightarrow R \quad (3)\ S \begin{array}{c} \nearrow M' \\ \searrow R \end{array} \quad (4)\ S \longrightarrow R \longrightarrow M'$$

Unless we know the temporal relationship between the three elements (S, R, M'), how can we know which is the cause and which the result? If mental events could be directly observed and therefore located in the sequence, behaviorists might study them also; but at present the technology to observe mental events does not exist, so behaviorists do not study them. Psychologists from other perspectives who wish to study nonobservable mental events have to use inference and make other assumptions that radical behaviorists are unwilling to make.

Summary

To summarize the content of this chapter, a few contrasts may be helpful. We have described two forms of behavioral conditioning, classical and operant. Classical conditioning relates to the control of *respondent behaviors* by *antecedent stimuli*. A specific respondent behavior becomes associated with numerous stimuli through an association or pairing process. Classical conditioning explains how a single behavior comes under the control of many environmental events. Operant conditioning is concerned with response changes that result from *conse-*

| | | Stimulus Condition | |
		S added	S subtracted
Behavioral Result	R increases	Positive reinforcement	Negative reinforcement
	R decreases	Positive punishment	Negative punishment

FIGURE 3a–12.   A Summary of Operant Procedures

quent stimuli. Experiences with specific consequences influence the rate, type, and regularity of *operant behaviors* produced by an organism.

In operant conditioning, we examined two types of consequences: those that increase behavior rates and those that decrease behavior rates. The definition of each conditioning principle is based on its function on behavior rate rather than some other quality of the procedure.

Reinforcement, an increase procedure, and punishment, a decrease procedure, can each be either positive or negative. In the positive forms, a stimulus is added following a behavior. In the negative form, the stimulus is subtracted after a behavior. These relationships are represented in Figure 3a–12. Another procedure, *extinction*, involves decreasing a behavior by terminating reinforcement. The speed of a behavior's extinction depends on its prior reinforcement schedule and on the availability of alternative responses.

These three behavioral principles, in elaborated form, have served as the basis for a wide variety of techniques useful in managing behavior in many different settings. The resulting technology, its effectiveness, and its application to the classroom will be examined in the next chapter.

TEACHING SCENARIO

Of primary concern to most teachers, and certainly to teachers-in-training, is the issue of classroom control and management. The teacher is the individual responsible for maintaining a sense of order, for creating a setting where learning can occur and where individual learners will flourish. That is no small feat when a single teacher is faced with more than thirty individuals, some of whom are not always committed to the same end. Chaos limits learning; disruption interferes with learning. The maintenance of order is an important classroom goal.

Classroom management is a multifaceted skill. Teachers-in-training learn a variety of methods for achieving a smoothly-running classroom. Behavioral techniques are one of the many tools useful for reaching that overall outcome.

In Mr. Bench's third grade classroom, there are some periodic interruptions leading to disruptive behavior by a number of students; the situation needs to be brought under control. Apparently, two boys who sit near each other in the back of the room start clowning, attracting the attention of others, and before long a group of students are both off task themselves and interfering with the work of others as well. The flow of classroom activities is thus affected. Mr. Bench has tried scolding, ignoring, and sending students out of the classroom, all to no avail. Is there a way Mr. Bench might employ behavioral principles to gain control over this situation?

Chapter 3b

The Use of Behavioral Principles for Classroom Management

Introduction

A knowledge of behavioral principles and their use is an important tool for the classroom teacher. Behavioral technology helps teachers design learning environments and maintain settings conducive to productivity. It is also useful in ensuring that each student's accomplishments are noted and appreciated and in avoiding disruption and chaos. Like the behavioral objectives described in Chapter 2b, behavior modification techniques are tools. As such, they are not inherently bad or good; they are simply means of reaching certain outcomes. The value of the outcomes is a separate issue from the value of the tools. We judge tools by how well they achieve; we must judge ends by what is achieved. The two judgments are separate and are based on different criteria.

Ethical Issues in Behavioral Management

Two ethical questions arise about the use of behavior modification. The first is whether we have the right to control the behavior of another person. Many aspects of our environment and the persons in it influence what we do, and influence is a form of control. Economic, social, legal, and familial sanctions impinge on our behavior; if we violate these sanctions, certain consequences will result. Every environment provides consequences, and consequences influence behavior. In most settings, however, we interact with more than one person, and of course we spend time in a variety of settings. Each setting and each individual will affect us differently. Total free will thus may be a myth, but so is total control of one individual over another. Everyone we encounter affects us somewhat; no single person totally dominates us. A classroom teacher who uses behavioral principles to influence student behavior is only one small source of influence in one limited setting. Control of another person is not accomplished with behavior modification. Teachers are hired to teach, to change student behavior through learning. The use of behavioral principles is one means of fulfilling that responsibility.

The second ethical question concerns the ends the tool is used for. Teachers can use their influence positively to encourage individual growth or negatively to inhibit student development. This is a separate issue from the way influence is exerted. In the American public education system, control of the ends rests with the community. School administrators and teachers are hired to promote goals set by the community. The value of the ends is a societal question quite independent of means.

Behavioral Principles and the Individual

Most people accept the premise that schools should promote the growth, development, and accomplishment of each student. In fact, there is ample legislation at both the federal and state levels that seeks to ensure just that outcome. This task is difficult, and we do not necessarily always know the best way to perform it. The use of behavioral principles, however, is one means that can help us reach this goal; there are other means as well, of course. When we use behavioral methods, we examine the behavior and accomplishments of one individual. Each student, not just the few students who always do well, who always perform at the top of the class, can be rewarded for achievements. Does it not seem, then, that behavioral principles can be used as one method of fulfilling our societal goals? With this in mind, the remainder of the chapter shall focus on how to make use of a viable tool.

Recording Data

Of primary importance when you begin to use behavioral principles is the way you will determine whether or not the desired behavior change has been accomplished. In the last chapter we described how the researcher would proceed—by collecting data. The teacher also needs to collect data. Data provide an objective record of behavior. The behavioral scientist examines a data record to determine whether a particular procedure influenced behavior as predicted. The teacher can use similar techniques to reach a similar conclusion. In order to use behavioral technology effectively, one must first determine how to collect data effectively.

Techniques of Data Collection

If data are to be collected, what kind should they be? How should they be recorded? The answer to this question should be obvious by now: data must be collected on behaviors, what the student does. Of all possible behaviors, which should be recorded? When a teacher is working from a set of performance objectives, the behaviors are already specified. You will recall that a performance objective states specifically which performance is of interest (see Chapter 2b). If performance objectives have not been developed or have not been specified for a particular child, then the teacher must specify what performance is to be studied. In the latter case, the teacher must examine what the student is doing or not doing that requires attention. Recall also that to get accurate and reliable data, the acts must be specified in terms of external, observable performances. Failure to do this makes data collection difficult if not impossible.

We often examine student performance in ways less precise than this, getting more global impressions of student behavior. Look at the following examples of reasonable impressions teachers might have of students.

1. "Mary does not seem interested in science."
2. "John disrupts the class and creates trouble."
3. "Kathy doesn't pay attention when I explain an assignment."
4. "Sherry doesn't get along with other students."

These are all conditions a teacher might wish to change. If Mary lacks interest in science, she may not learn important concepts. John's behavior may interfere with his learning and the learning of others. Sherry may suffer from a lack of friendships and social acceptance. There are problems with each of these teacher statements, however. They are conclusions made on the basis of student behaviors, but the behaviors themselves are not described. Behavior change cannot be assessed unless we specify the behaviors in question. The information on operationalizing performance in Chapter 2b describes ways to state outcomes in behavioral terms. The first step in obtaining objective data is thus to identify the target behavior, the behavior one wishes to change, in terms of performance.

Look at a second list of possible teacher statements. These reveal an additional problem associated with inferences.

1. "Dorrie *never* pays attention."
2. "Harry *always* causes trouble."
3. "Marty is *never* in his seat."
4. "Robert is *always* talking."

The statements are all about behavioral strength, how frequently a behavior occurs. They are, however, inferences about strength—subjective conclusions. It is highly doubtful that any child never pays attention, or always fights. Robert might talk a great deal, but not all the time; he has to catch his breath at least occasionally. His behavior may seem incessant more because it irritates the observer than because it is continuous. We need an objective record of how often a behavior occurs to determine whether it changes. The second step in collecting data, therefore, is counting behaviors to get an objective record for use as a basis of comparison.

Counting behaviors to determine their strength can be done in a number of ways, depending on the behavior. In some cases, we are concerned with *frequency*—how often the behavior occurs. In other cases, we are interested in how long a behavior lasts; then a measure of *duration* is required. Whether we are interested in frequency or duration will determine how and what we record.

Frequency recording is very straightforward. Once the behavior is specified, the observer simply tallies each occurrence. This is called *event sampling*. Sometimes, however, a behavior is so frequent that

Daydreaming may be a behavior that a teacher wishes to reduce. In order to determine the effectiveness of a procedure for reducing that behavior, the teacher will gather baseline data, recording the strength of the behavior before instituting a behavioral change procedure.

event sampling presents a problem, requiring so much recording that nothing else can be accomplished. Suppose, for instance, that Robert from the previous example really is a high-frequency talker. Tallying every statement Robert makes could be extremely tedious. In this case, we might want to use a procedure called *time sampling*. With this technique, the period of observation is broken up into short intervals. At the end of each interval, the data collector simply records whether or not the behavior is occurring at that moment. At the end of the observation period, one has a record of the number of intervals in which the behavior occurred, which is a measure of the behavior's strength.

When the duration of a behavior is of interest, the procedure for collecting data is also simple—you time it. Duration recording could prove useful in examining on-task behavior, for example. To take this measure, the teacher gives a student a seatwork assignment and then records the length of time in which the student actually engages in the task before going on to some other activity.

Event sampling, time sampling, and duration timing are not the only possible recording techniques. If a teacher is concerned with a student's performance on spelling or arithmetic tests, for example, simply keeping a record of the number of correct responses is an appropriate recording procedure. If a teacher is bothered by a student's slowness in following directions or moving to the next task, then a measure of *latency* will prove useful. Latency is the time between a cue, such as an instruction, and a response, such as compliance with the instruction. The choice of a specific procedure for data collection depends on the behavior to be studied, and some procedures work better than others. The outcome of applying the procedures, however, is the same: an objective record of behavioral strength.

Collecting Baseline Data

Once a procedure for recording data on a specified performance has been chosen, data collection can begin. The first task is to obtain an objective record of behavioral frequency and stability before the behavioral program is begun. Data collected during this period will serve as a basis of comparison with subsequent changes; it is known as a *baseline*, as mentioned in Chapter 3a. A baseline is essentially a pretest of the level of behavior prior to learning. The length of time for collecting baseline data, like the method of recording it, must be determined on the basis of the behavior in question. You need enough recording time to determine how strong the behavior is and how much it fluctuates.

Consider first a simple personal behavior, such as controlling body weight. With the current emphasis on fitness, many people are concerned with weight loss and dieting. Before starting a diet, however, you need to know how much you weigh. This is simple enough; the scale provides an accurate, if sometimes cruel, objective assessment. However, body weight fluctuates naturally from day to day. Recording your weight just once will not reveal the normal fluctuation. If you start a diet without establishing how your weight normally fluctuates, any weight loss you note might be attributable to the diet, but it could also be a coincidental weight fluctuation. A knowledge of fluctuations occurring before the change plan is begun is needed.

One way to get information on baseline fluctuations is to weigh yourself at the same time each day for one week. When these data are placed on a graph, a picture of stability results. A sample graph is depicted in Figure 3b–1. The graph is an observable, objective record of the level of the performance and of natural fluctuations in that level across time.

The same procedure can be used in the classroom with a particular student behavior. Take, for example, a student who seems uninterested in mathematics. He displays his lack of interest by failing to complete practice worksheets. This behavior could be recorded by observing how long the child works on the worksheets before abandoning them. The teacher would record this behavior for several days when math worksheets were assigned. Again, the result is a measure of the level and stability of a performance. Sample data for this sort of behavior are depicted in Figure 3b–2.

For another classroom example, consider the case of Irvin, who frequently interrupts his teacher when she is teaching. This behavior interrupts the flow of instruction and interferes with the teaching process. What procedures could be used to collect data on Irvin's behavior? Event sampling might be one approach: the teacher could record the

FIGURE 3b–1.   Baseline Data for Weight Control

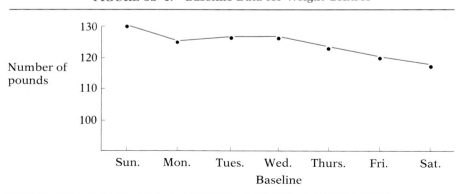

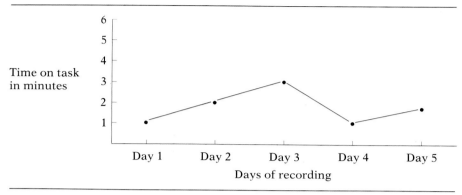

FIGURE 3b–2. Time on Task with Worksheets

frequency of the interruptions. Again, recording should persist over a number of observation periods to obtain an estimate of the behavior's stability. Sample data are given in Figure 3b–3.

The third example pertains to a student having trouble with spelling. Twice a week the teacher gives a spelling test of ten words. The student gets few, if any, of them correct. Two things could be determined by collecting baseline data: (1) how poorly the student is doing, and (2) whether poor scores are general, occurring across word lists, or specific, occurring only on some word lists. The second consideration is one of stability. In this case, the recording procedure would involve tallying success rates; the results could look like those displayed in Figure 3b–4.

FIGURE 3b–3. Irvin's Interruptions

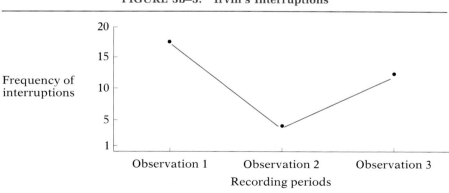

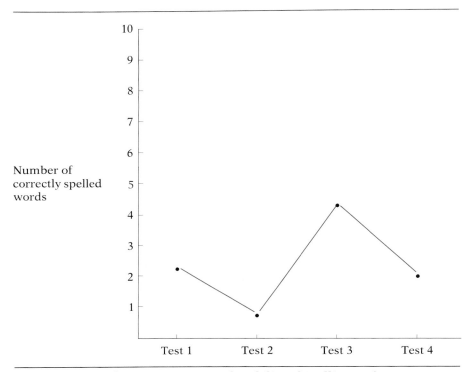

FIGURE 3b–4.   Frequency and Stability of Spelling Performance

You might wonder how one teacher could collect data on every student and still teach. First of all, no teacher can collect systematic data on every student behavior; the procedure has to be reserved for behaviors the teacher feels are important enough to warrant attention. Second, classroom aides or outside observers are often available to assist in data collection. Third, students can collect their own data. A student who displays a problematic behavior is sometimes willing to collect self data and attack the problem himself or herself. One of the authors has seen children with their own data charts taped to their desks willingly monitoring their own performances.

Whether the teacher, an assistant, or the student is the actual recorder, an objective record of significant behavior is obtained. The collection of baseline data yields three important results: (1) the teacher has an objective record of behavioral strength, (2) the stability of performance is established, and (3) the record can be examined for hints about what can be done to alter the situation. At this point it is time to proceed to the intervention phase.

► *ACTIVITY 1.*   Most of us have at least one behavior that we want to change. We might wish to exercise more often, spend more time studying, stop smoking, or lose weight. It is possible to use behavior modification techniques not just on the behavior of others but on our own behavior as well.

Select a behavior of your own that you wish to modify in some way. It could be a response you wish to decrease in frequency (like smoking), decrease in duration (like television watching), increase in frequency (like making nice comments to others), or increase in duration (like studying). State your target behavior in terms of performance. Then devise an appropriate data collection technique. This could be a measure of frequency, as for smoking, or a measure of duration, as for studying. Decide how much time is needed for establishing the strength and stability of the behavior, and then collect baseline data, keeping charts and graphs of what is happening.

One of the things you may discover as you collect data is the phenomenon of *reactivity*. Essentially, reactivity occurs when behavior changes in frequency just as a function of self-recording. That is, behaviors may decrease or increase during a baseline phase before any other intervention is added.

After you have collected your baseline data, make a graph of the results. Keep this baseline for an activity still to come.

► *ACTIVITY 2.*   One classroom behavior that is crucial to learning is whether students stay engaged with learning materials. One cannot expect much learning to occur in the time students spend off task. There are many ways to assess how much time a student spends on a learning activity. The way it is assessed depends on (1) the kind of activity, (2) the age of the learner, and (3) the nature of the educational setting. You would, for example, record different behaviors with high school students than you would with preschoolers.

Identify a learning setting consistent with your own interests. Within the context of this setting, define how you might assess *engaged learning activity*. Then devise a data collection method appropriate to your definition. If you can, do some observing in a setting like the one you identified and try to collect data on at least one student. Finally, evaluate your procedure. Identify its strengths and weaknesses, and describe changes in the technique that might have made it more useful.

Procedures for Increasing Behaviors— The Use of Reinforcement Contingencies

Once a baseline has been established, the change process can proceed. If an increase in the target behavior is desired, reinforcement is the intervention of choice. Positive reinforcement is the easiest, most effective, and generally the best type of reinforcement for use in the classroom, since it requires no aversive stimuli. Moreover, this technique permits the teacher to decide what stimuli will be added as a consequence when the desired behavior is produced.

Even after the target behavior has been selected, several decisions must be made before reinforcement can begin. First, a reinforcing stimulus must be chosen. Second, a schedule of reinforcement delivery must be decided upon. Recall that a continuous schedule increases response rate most quickly. The choice of reinforcers is more difficult. It must be some thing or event (1) that the teacher has the resources and power to deliver, (2) that can be delivered easily when the desired response is produced, (3) that can be delivered immediately following the response, since reinforcement is most effective when it follows the response directly, and (4) that will function as a reinforcer for the particular student. The choice of reinforcer must be based on the characteristics of the student, but classroom research suggests three possibilities: (1) the contingent use of teacher attention and praise, (2) the use of desired activities, and (3) the use of tangible reinforcers like tokens.

The Contingent Use of Teacher Attention

It is often interesting to observe how teachers in the classroom use their most valuable resource—their own attention. In some classrooms, the teacher attends to students who are not performing as desired— those who are not following instructions, who are off task, or who are disturbing others. The attention may consist of reprimands, restatement of instructions, or speaking to the students individually. While off task students are receiving attention, on task, productive students are being ignored. If we assume that teacher attention is a functional reinforcer for the students, what outcome would you predict? Disruptive behavior may very well increase, since it receives teacher attention. At the same time, appropriate behavior may decrease because ignoring behavior places it on an extinction schedule. The situation could become increasingly chaotic, culminating in an unproductive learning environment and an exasperated teacher.

By contrast, a teacher who makes his or her attention contingent upon appropriate responses can create a smoothly functioning learning setting. The amount of teacher attention remains the same—the kind of response that receives attention is what is changed. Reinfor... Johnny when he happens to sit down and do his work is more likely to increase his productive behavior than continually reminding him to return to work when he is doing something else. If we assume, quite reasonably, that children cannot learn when they are not on task, which situation would you prefer to see?

Giving teacher attention for appropriate behavior, coupled with placing inappropriate behavior on extinction as much as possible, can be used to manage the whole classroom as well as individual students. This has been demonstrated by research in real classroom settings. Teacher attention is an almost perfect reinforcer. It costs nothing. It is within the teacher's power and resources. It is delivered easily, and it can be delivered immediately after the desired response is produced.

Suppose a shy child rarely talks or asks questions during classroom discussion. Asking questions is an important information-seeking skill. Reinforcing the shy child with an "I like that question" or "That's a good question" will encourage the child to ask questions more frequently. This is a simple procedure, but it requires that the teacher be attentive enough to note opportunities for reinforcement and deliver it quickly when the child behaves as desired.

When teacher attention is used wisely, attention is provided not only to good students but also to less able students. Recall the earlier example of the student having trouble with spelling. If this student is spelling only one or two words correctly per test, many other classmates will be doing better. In many classrooms, students who spell all the words correctiy are routinely rewarded with good grades, stars, or praise. What of the poor speller? Although the poor speller has a long way to go, he or she may be improving, too. With this method, the poor speller, too, could receive reinforcement for progress. When a poor speller gets three words correct, that is an improvement, and that improvement can be reinforced.

To successfully use teacher attention and praise to encourage appropriate behavior, several conditions must be present. First, the teacher needs a positive valence; that is, teacher attention must be valued. If the teacher is a fear stimulus, punitive most of the time, students may not desire teacher attention. Second, the teacher must be attentive to the individual students, continuously watching for opportunities to reinforce. Third, the teacher should be aware of students' individual needs and goals and the progress they are making. Students who are weak academically should be reinforced for progress. If praise is delivered only for complete success, the weaker student may never get any. If we wish to promote the learning of all individuals, each deserves attention for making gains, however limited they may be.

Teachers and teachers-in-training often ask why students should be reinforced for doing what they are supposed to be doing. How many

ain productive if productivity did not yield positive
least occasionally? How will learners know that their
ed if they are not reinforced? One hopes that learners
id learning reinforcing for its own sake, but it cannot
it they will. Discovering that learning is its own reward
uct of learning.

judgment as to whether teacher attention and praise are
sts with the data. If the target behavior increases, rein-
occurring. If the response fails to increase, it is back to
board to try another approach. You will recall that reinforcement defined in terms of function; the observed function is the
basis for decision-making. Teacher attention will not work for all students under all circumstances, but in many cases it proves to be a
powerful tool.

▶ *ACTIVITY 3.*   Go to a classroom and observe how the teacher
uses attention. Design a category system that will permit you
to note different kinds of teacher attention and different kinds
of student behavior that might receive attention, for example:

	Student Behavior	
	+	−
Teacher Attention +		
−		

Collect data and see if there are any patterns in the delivery
of the teacher's attention. Evaluate your findings in terms of
behavioral principles. Tally the frequency of occurrence of each
of the categories. The + + category would include occurrences
of appropriate student behavior reinforced by the teacher. The
− + would be inappropriate student behavior followed by the
teacher's reinforcement of that behavior, and so on.

▶ *ACTIVITY 4.*   We noted earlier that reinforcement contingencies can be applied to groups as well as to individuals. Teacher
statements to the group can take several forms, but the four
types of interest here are (1) directions, for example, "Turn to
page 53 in your workbooks"; (2) possible reinforcers, for example, "All of you are being very cooperative today"; (3) possible reprimands, for example, "None of you performed well
on this task"; and (4) statements of contingency, for example,
"If you don't quiet down, there will be no recess for any of
you."

With these four categories in mind, make a chart like the following:

	Frequency of comment
Category of comment 1	
2	
3	
4	

Observe in a classroom and record the frequency with which teacher comments fall into these categories. Compare the frequency rates. Are positive comments to the group made often? How would you evaluate these data?

The Premack Principle

To use behavior modification effectively in the classroom, you need to be able to use more than one reinforcer. With some students, teacher attention alone fails to increase responses. With others, it may be effective at first but eventually becomes less so. Other reinforcers must be available. One reinforcer that has been examined under both laboratory and naturalistic conditions is the contingent use of valued activity.

Researchers have found that a high probability behavior, one that a person performs frequently, can be used to reinforce a low frequency behavior. The high-probability behavior functions as a reinforcer and increases the probability of the low-frequency behavior. This finding, known as the Premack Principle (Premack, 1959), states essentially that an activity a person likes can be used to reinforce an activity the person likes less.

Like teacher attention, valued activity can readily be used as a reinforcer in the classroom. It is a reinforcer within the power and resources of the teacher to deliver. It is easily dispensed, it can be employed contingently, and it is effective. Again, however, the individuality of the recipient must be taken into account. One cannot decide beforehand what activity to use as a reinforcer. Since the activity must be valued by the performer, it must be one that the performer, given a free choice, would select. Activity preferences can be established only through observation. Watching a student in free choice situations helps the teacher determine which activities might have reinforcing properties for the student.

An actual case study will serve to illustrate this procedure. The student in question was a fourth grader who was causing his teacher considerable difficulty. He was reportedly rambunctious in class, reg-

Using the Premack Principle, the student completing a less desirable
activity is allowed to participate in a more desirable activity.
The seatwork assignment completed, the student is allowed to play
with a Rubik's cube.

ularly fighting with peers. He spent little time on task and was doing
poorly academically. Apparently, his conduct had resulted in poor peer
relations; he had few friends and was the brunt of much teasing.
Obviously, the situation was a severe one, which took a great deal of
attention and time to change; but an initial plan was designed that
succeeded in turning the situation around.

It was also apparent that the youngster enjoyed one aspect of
school—he liked art. Whenever he was engaged in art activities, his

The teacher had been attempting to deal with the boy primarily
by punishing him: (1) keeping him from valued activities because his
school work was of poor quality, (2) withholding recess and free play,
and (3) scolding him publicly for his poor performance and disruptive-
ness. The situation was becoming worse, so obviously these contingencies were not helping.

It was also apparent that the youngster enjoyed one aspect of
school—he liked art. Whenever he was engaged in art activities, his

inappropriate behavior decreased. This fact was discovered from baseline data. The teacher had, however, forbidden him to work on art because of his otherwise poor conduct. A modification plan was designed in which the contingency was reversed: art activity was used to reinforce and increase his other productive activity. If he spent a given period of time on assigned classwork, he would be allowed to spend a specified period on art.

It did not take long before his on-task performance increased. There were side benefits, too. First, because he was on task more frequently, he had less time for trouble. He was scolded less often. He was happy and active during the art activity, so he fought less, and the teasing of other children decreased. His art work was used to decorate the classroom, so he received additional reinforcement in the form of teacher and peer appreciation of his creations.

Of course, much more needed to be done to stabilize the situation, maintain it, and improve the boy's academic progress, but a positive start had been made by identifying an activity the boy enjoyed and using this activity as a contingent reinforcer. Again, the proof of the plan's effectiveness was in the data.

Every student enjoys doing something. When a teacher discovers one of these desired activities, he identifies a potential reinforcer. If the activity fits into classroom routine, it can be used as a contingent reinforcer. If additional reinforcers are also provided when the child is engaging in the low probability response, the modification plan will be even stronger. In the described case study, the teacher reinforced with attention the boy's efforts to complete his school work, in addition to providing a reinforcing activity. Use of the Premack Principle is compatible with bringing additional reinforcers to bear on a problem.

The Use of Tangible Reinforcers

Tangibles are another type of reinforcing stimulus that can be adapted for use in the classroom. Tangibles are actual things, such as stars, trinkets, or tokens. The child must do a certain amount of work to earn a unit of reinforcement, a tangible. Goals for the amount of work required for reinforcement are set individually for each student. If all students are included, the classroom is operating on a *token economy.*

Tangibles are effective reinforcers, but it is often difficult to establish programs with them. If the tangibles have intrinsic value such as toys, gifts, or food, they are not easy to administer. The program may also be expensive; the reinforcers thus may not be within the teacher's power and resources to dispense. The cost of such programs can come to outweigh their effectiveness.

An additional problem is *satiation.* Satiation occurs when a performer has received so much reinforcement that the reinforcing value of the stimulus is lost. Desired responses will probably fail to increase if the student is satiated, and they may decrease. Although satiation can occur with almost any reinforcer, it happens faster with tangibles. What happens when the student receives enough M & Ms, toys, or gifts? The reinforcer loses its functional value.

A system of tangibles is most appropriate for individuals who are not under strong social control, for whom praise, attention, and the like are not effective reinforcers. When tangibles are used, they are frequently paired with a social reinforcer, such as praise. You will recall from the discussion of secondary reinforcers in Chapter 3a that when a neutral stimulus, such as praise, is paired frequently enough with a functional reinforcer, such as a tangible, the neutral stimulus will acquire reinforcing value. When this occurs, the tangible reinforcer is gradually faded out and the behavior is maintained through social reinforcement alone.

Tokens are another form of tangible, but tokens themselves have no intrinsic value. The procedure is the same. A given amount of work is required to earn a token, and schedules are set individually. Tokens are easier to dispense than other tangibles, and they are within a teacher's power to deliver, but they still present problems. If tokens cannot be exchanged for meaningful, intrinsically valuable back-up reinforcers or reinforcing activities, their reinforcing value evaporates as soon as the novelty wears off. When tangible back-up reinforcers are used, the same problems of satiation and expense occur.

To use token systems effectively, the following conditions should be observed: (1) adequate back-up reinforcers must be available, (2) delivery of tokens should be paired with social reinforcement, (3) satiation must be avoided, and (4) the use of tangibles should be faded out as soon as possible, and reinforcement control should be shifted to a social stimulus. When token economies fail, it is usually because one of these four conditions was not met.

▶ *ACTIVITY 5.*   Return to the baseline data you collected on your own target behavior (see page 97). It is now time to design an intervention plan that you can actually use to change your behavior.

One way to change a behavior yourself is to identify reinforcers you could use in a contingency management situation—that is, you can set a goal for the behavior change and reinforce yourself if you meet the goal. The goals should be reasonable and the reinforcer should of course be something you can deliver. You might wish to set a series of goals and reinforce yourself for meeting each one.

Suppose you wish to increase the time you spend studying

each day. Let us also assume that watching television is an activity you find reinforcing. You could easily establish a contingency between the two events, stating perhaps that you have to study four hours a day before you can watch television. In this example, you would be using the Premack Principle to modify your own behavior.

To begin this activity, (1) make a list of possible (and reasonable) reinforcers, (2) state a goal or a series of goals related to your target behavior, and (3) establish a contingency between (1) and (2).

Then implement your intervention plan. Remember to continue data collection and graph the outcome. When you have finished, evaluate your plan. Did it work? If not, try to figure out why. (Hint: there may have been other events reinforcing the original situation.)

Maintaining Behavior

Regardless of the type of reinforcer chosen, the goal is to make a particular response stable and resistant to extinction. Why go to all the trouble of establishing and applying a behavior change plan only to have the new behavior disappear as soon as the circumstances change? This is a problem of *behavior maintenance,* which is just as important as increasing the behavior in the first place.

You will recall from Chapter 3a that responses are increased most quickly with a continuous schedule of reinforcement, and that extinction is quickest when continuous reinforcement is discontinued. This state of affairs presents the teacher with several dilemmas. First, providing continuous reinforcement is impossible for a classroom teacher who has to divide her attention among thirty or so children. When one is starting a behavior increase plan, one tries to establish the richest, most frequent schedule possible. The teacher must be observant and reinforce desired responses as often as possible. Enlisting the assistance of other personnel and students in the classroom is helpful in this regard.

A second dilemma concerns the fact that a single teacher cannot maintain a rich schedule of reinforcement for a lengthy period, but stopping reinforcement will probably result in a response decrease. What can one do to avoid this? Since extinction of responses occurs much more slowly under conditions of intermittent reinforcement, teachers should switch to an intermittent schedule to preserve desired behavior changes. This is the procedure of *thinning.* Once the desired behavior rate is obtained, the teacher must gradually shift from a continuous to an increasingly thinner schedule. The changeover must be slow, however; rapid changes may lead to extinction.

In maintaining behavior the teacher gets some assistance from the environment. If the student's increased behavior is socially valued, and it is to be hoped that it will be, the student will receive unplanned, or *natural, reinforcement* from others. If a teacher improves a child's interpersonal skills, reinforcement will be forthcoming from the child's peers. If academic skills increase, parents and others may add their reinforcement. The student may even find success intrinsically reinforcing, in which case teacher support will not be as essential. In short, if a teacher can get a positive behavior going, the environment will provide at least some support to help maintain it.

Contingency Contracting

There is no reason for the use of reinforcement principles to be a secretive affair. Reinforcement will work whether or not the recipient understands the contingencies. Frequently, however, the procedure's effectiveness can be improved by enlisting the aid of the performer. When this is done, the teacher and the student form a contract; the reinforcement and the behavior necessary to receive it are specified in advance.

Sometimes a student having trouble in the classroom is no happier about it than the teacher. If the child wishes to overcome the problem and wants reinforcement instead of aversive consequences, a contract worked out between the student and teacher is sometimes an effective beginning. Obviously, the student must understand the arrangement and be motivated to change and cooperate or it will not work.

In a contract arrangement, a motivated student who is old enough can collect data on his or her own behavior. The teacher need not collect data himself, but the teacher must still be observant about behavior change, upholding his end of the contract and delivering reinforcement accordingly. Sometimes students find that having a visible record of their behavior change is reinforcing in itself. If the sight of an increasing frequency rate on a graph is reinforcing to the performer, the teacher has an added source of support for behavior change.

Do Not Forget Recording

In order to objectively determine whether the behavior change plan works, data collection is continued throughout intervention. Since the goal of reinforcement is to increase behavior, the frequency of the behavior should rise. A format for presenting data is depicted in Figure 3b–5. The target behavior in Figure 3b–5 has apparently increased, but one cannot be sure. The change may be coincidental. Before evaluating

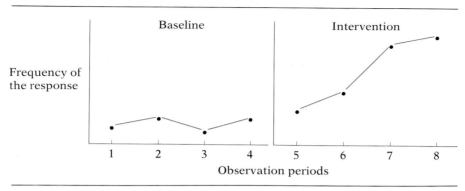

FIGURE 3b–5.   Continuing the Data Collection

the worth of the procedure, a research psychologist would want more information, some sort of proof.

Additional proof can be collected by using the reversal design described in the last chapter. In this procedure, the contingencies are changed and the conditions existing during the collection of baseline data are reinstituted. These baseline conditions are maintained for a period, and then intervention contingencies are applied again. If the intervention increases the target behavior a second time, one can be more certain that the change was caused by the plan rather than by some coincidence. Sample data from an effective plan that has been checked with a reversal design are given in Figure 3b–6.

A classroom teacher may choose not to use a reversal design for several legitimate reasons. In some cases, the teacher is relieved that the situation has improved and wants to leave well enough alone. In other instances, such as when a new skill has been learned and exhibited, it is not possible to return to the earlier situation. In these two cases a reversal design is inappropriate.

FIGURE 3b–6.   Data Collected in a Reversal Design

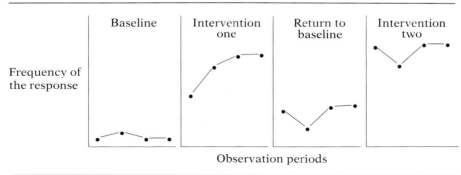

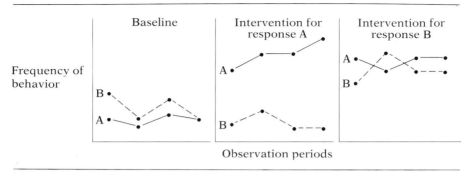

Frequency of behavior

FIGURE 3b–7.   Data Collected in a Multiple-Baseline Design

In situations of this sort, a *multiple-baseline* design is a better technique. In this procedure, data are collected on two or more behaviors, all of which are targeted for increase. After the baseline period, intervention is begun with one of the behaviors. When the first behavior has increased, the intervention is applied to the second behavior. The outcome is similar; results are replicated by using the same intervention twice. In this case, however, the intervention is applied to two separate behaviors, so a return to baseline circumstances is unnecessary. Data collected in a multiple-baseline design would be graphed as depicted in Figure 3b–7.

A teacher's decision about whether to replicate results will depend on the circumstances. The researcher must demonstrate the effectiveness of procedures; the teacher also may wish to.

Increasing Low-Frequency Behaviors

To use positive reinforcements, a response must be performed. Behavior cannot be reinforced unless it occurs. This presents a problem when the target behavior is nonexistent, offering no opportunities for reinforcement, or very infrequent, offering few such opportunities. To be able to apply reinforcement, a procedure is needed to elicit the response in the first place.

One approach that can be used with low-frequency behaviors is the operant procedure of *shaping*. Shaping involves applying reinforcement contingencies in accordance with gradually changing criteria. Rather than just reinforcing the desired response, successive approximations of the target behavior are reinforced. As the performer begins to roughly approximate the target behavior, the criteria for reinforcement are gradually changed; closer approximations of the final response are required before reinforcment is delivered. The intervention continues in this fashion until the target behavior itself is produced. From that point onward, only the target behavior is reinforced.

Suppose a teacher has a young student who is socially isolated. When the intervention begins, the child fails to interact with other students, initiates no interactions with the teacher, and remains physically isolated, staying in a back corner of the room. The teacher wants to increase the child's interaction, but opportunities for reinforcement are rare with a child so isolated. A shaping procedure is called for in this situation. To use shaping, the teacher needs to operationally define three things: (1) the child's current behavior, (2) the final performance goal of the intervention, and (3) the steps or behavioral increments between (1) and (2).

By observation the teacher discovers that the frequency of the child's verbal interaction is zero and that there is a low frequency of physical approach behavior; the child occasionally leaves the back corner and moves closer to other children. This response is far from the target behavior, but it is a gross approximation of full interaction. Once baseline data have been collected on physical approach behavior, the teacher begins to reinforce the approach responses with attention. If attention functions as a reinforcer, the frequency of approach responses will increase; if not, another reinforcer must be selected. Once the behavior has been increased and stabilized, the criterion for reinforcement is changed. The teacher might decide to reinforce only when the child is within two feet of another and looking at the other child. When this behavior has been increased and stabilized, the criterion is changed again, and so on.

The elements of the shaping procedure are as follows:

1. Specify existing behaviors.
2. Establish the goal behavior.
3. Delineate intermediate behaviors between the starting point and the goal.
4. Initiate reinforcement contingencies just slightly above the person's current level of performance.
5. Gradually change the behavioral requirement for reinforcement as each of the steps specified in (3) is attained, increased, and stabilized.

This procedure is sometimes slow and time-consuming, but it is effective if properly applied. Shaping was used in the study described in the Research Report on pages 72–74. Some cautions about its use should be noted, however. The behavior initially reinforced must be a likely event; if the step is too far from existing behaviors, there may be no opportunities for reinforcement. For the same reason, the increments between steps must be gradual. Progress is fastest when a continuous schedule of reinforcement is used, but once the target behavior is attained the schedule must be thinned to ensure resistance to extinction.

Decrease Procedures

In managing their classrooms, teachers are concerned not just with increasing appropriate behaviors but in decreasing inappropriate ones. In these cases, the decrease procedures of extinction and punishment are used to meet behavioral goals.

Extinction

The simplest and most effective procedure for decreasing a response is extinction, removing the reinforcers that have sustained the behavior in the past. No aversive stimuli are required; one must simply remove all reinforcement. This decreases the rate of the response, but the speed of the decrease depends on past reinforcement history. Although extinction can be managed well in the laboratory and its effectiveness is well documented, it is not easy to use this technique in the classroom, for several reasons.

First, the sources of reinforcement that are sustaining the behavior must be identified, and there may be more than one. Some sources of reinforcement, such as teacher attention, may be under the teacher's control. Such factors as peer attention may not be, however. A student who clowns in the classroom and disrupts the flow of learning will probably attract teacher attention, although it may take the form of a reprimand. At the same time, however, clowning attracts peer attention, laughter, and perhaps approval. If these sources of attention function as reinforcers, the behavior will be maintained. The teacher has direct control over her own attention, but it is much more difficult to control reinforcement from peers. Unless all sources of reinforcement are identified and controlled, extinction of the behavior is highly unlikely.

Second, extinction is not a rapid process even when reinforcement from all sources can be terminated. If the behavior has been maintained on an intermittent schedule, as most behaviors in the natural environment are, the response rate will decrease slowly. Three characteristics of the extinction process uncovered through laboratory research deserve mention. First, when a behavior is placed on extinction, response rates tend to accelerate before they decelerate; the situation gets worse before it gets better. Second, after the behavior has begun to decrease, it sometimes accelerates briefly a second time; this is called *spontaneous recovery*. If extinction conditions continue, however, the rate of response decreases to prereinforcement levels. Third, extinction is slower when the performer lacks other means of obtaining reinforcement. People work for reinforcement; if there is only one avenue of obtaining it, that avenue will be pursued.

These three factors present problems for those who wish to use extinction procedures. Extinction requires patience, perseverance, and vigilance. A simple example will illustrate the personal stamina required. One of the authors has an overabundance of dogs, who prefer the warm indoors to the more rugged conditions of the back yard. One of these dogs signals his desire to come inside by throwing himself against a glass door. This response produces a loud, irritating bang. Letting the dog in after this response would reinforce it. Unfortunately, in the past the response has been reinforced all too frequently. Armed with determination and behavioral tools, the author has on several occasions tried to put the behavior on extinction by ignoring it and not letting the dog in. As is typical during extinction, the behavior initially increases in frequency and sometimes in intensity. At this point, it is a tossup as to which element in the situation will wear out first: the dog, the behavior modifier, or the glass door. Most of the time, it is the modifier. The result of this lack of persistence on the author's part is a virtually unextinguishable behavior. Every time the dog's behavior has gotten him into the house it has been reinforced. Since reinforcement has been on an intermittent, thin schedule, any extinction process begun at this point would be extremely slow.

To give another example, consider the familiar scenario of a mother and her toddler in the supermarket. The child asks for candy, cookies, and other treats, but the mother nobly attempts to ignore the child. When the child's demands grow louder and more frequent, however, the mother gives in, fearing that other shoppers will think her a poor parent. The child quiets down, but if the mother wishes to extinguish the behavior in the future it will take longer, requiring more patience and greater perseverance. Two reinforcement principles are operating here: the mother's compliance response has been negatively reinforced (Can you identify the contingency?), and the child's demanding response has been positively reinforced. Moreover, the child's behavior was reinforced on an intermittent schedule. If extinction is attempted in the future, it will be harder to accomplish.

Similar problems face classroom teachers who wish to use extinction procedures. If the behavior has been maintained for some time on an intermittent schedule, extinction will be slow. If, in addition, the behavior is irritating and difficult to ignore, the teacher may be tempted to give in. Even one lapse will worsen the situation, however.

Extinction can be helpful with low-frequency, low-strength behaviors that have not occurred often enough to have entrenched reinforcement histories. If a fairly novel response pops up and receives no reinforcement, it may be quickly abandoned. If a typically well-behaved student has an off day and rudely interrupts the teacher's instructions to the group, ignoring the interruption may be all that is needed to extinguish it. The same response from a student who often interrupts and who has been reinforced with attention for interrupting will not be extinguished as rapidly, however.

In short, a teacher who chooses to employ extinction to decrease behaviors should take the following findings into account:

1. All sources of reinforcement must be identified.
2. All reinforcement must be terminated.
3. Responses previously reinforced on an intermittent schedule will decrease more slowly than others.
4. Weak responses decrease more rapidly than entrenched responses.
5. Extinction proceeds more slowly when alternative responses are not available.

Combining Procedures

To expand on the fifth point in the preceding list: Extinction is more rapid when another response is available. If a desired alternative response is reinforced, the response targeted for extinction will decrease more rapidly. If, in addition, the response selected for reinforcement is incompatible with the one selected for extinction, the process will be faster still.

This point can be illustrated with another case study. A high school teacher was troubled by a student who whispered his contributions to class discussions. This was a problem because the other class members, unable to hear the student's questions and comments, became inattentive, and because the teacher had to stand near the student to hear what he said. This restricted the teacher's mobility and access to other students.

To rectify the situation, a dual procedure was employed. The teacher withdrew her attention from the student's whispered comments. She did not approach the student physically, and she failed to respond to his whispered queries. At the same time, she always responded to comments the student made in a normal conversational tone. The whispering was rapidly extinguished because the student had an alternative way to get the teacher's attention. Moreover, whispering and speaking in a normal tone are incompatible; they cannot be done simultaneously.

Time-Out

A different decrease procedure is difficult to classify in terms of the behavioral principles at work. This procedure, *time-out,* is viewed by some as a special case of extinction (Sulzer-Azaroff & Mayer, 1972); it might also be considered a form of punishment.

In time-out, a child who produces an undesired response is placed in circumstances where it is impossible to earn reinforcement. Time-out, then, is time out from reinforcement. For example, when Tommy throws a temper tantrum (*R*), he is sent to his room (time-out). When Susie misbehaves in the classroom (*R*), she must stand outside the room for ten minutes (time-out). In extreme cases, children who misbehave are put in an area specially prepared for such circumstances, a time-out room.

Time-out can be effective, but is easy to abuse. First, to be used effectively, the child should be removed to the time-out area unemotionally; otherwise, punishment rather than time-out is operating. Second, the individual should be subjected to time-out only for a brief period. The child should be readmitted to the original setting as soon as the undesired response has ceased. If Tommy is sent to his room for a tantrum, in order to reinforce an acceptable response incompatible with tantrums he should be allowed to return as soon as the tantrum ceases. Isolating him for the entire evening seems harsh, and interrupting normal social interchange keeps him from learning appropriate social functioning. One hears numerous time-out horror stories about children put in closets or locked in bathrooms and forgotten. Clearly, application of time-out procedures can be punitive, aversive, and nonconstructive.

Time-out may fail if the setting the child is placed in proves to be reinforcing. Being sent to one's room may be quite interesting if one has lots of toys to play with. Sitting in the hall outside the classroom can be entertaining. In one instance, an aggressive twelve-year-old girl

Time-out procedures can be used with children showing unacceptable behaviors. The child is placed in a situation where he cannot earn reinforcement for his behaviors. The time-out should be brief and the child should be returned to the classroom as soon as the unacceptable behavior ceases.

Scenario Suggestion

Without actual data collection, it is hard to determine both the extent of the disruption in Mr. Bench's classroom and the contingencies maintaining the disruptive behavior. In all likelihood, however, the clowning behavior that seems to initiate the disruption is maintained by student attention, the positive reinforcer.

Mr. Bench could alleviate the situation by reinforcing behavior incompatible with clowning rather than attending to the disruption. A first step would be to physically separate the two instigators, perhaps placing them so that they are not in close proximity. In this way it will be more difficult for one youngster's misbehavior to serve as an antecedent stimulus cue for the other's misbehavior. Then Mr. Bench could reinforce, most likely with teacher attention, on-task behavior in the two youngsters. Since on-task ac-

tivities and clowning are incompatible, increasing the frequency of the former will by necessity decrease the frequency of the latter.

Should an incident occur even under these circumstances, Mr. Bench might reinforce other students for not attending to the instigators. If student attention has been maintaining the clowning, that is, serving as a reinforcer, stopping that attention amounts to placing the clowning on extinction.

Of course, to be certain that these plans are in fact effective in decreasing the disruptive incidents, Mr. Bench must keep records. He must collect objective data. Mr. Bench may wish to try additional methods as well to create a smooth-running classroom; but the use of a few behavioral techniques first may alleviate the situation enough to restore some order and increase learner productivity. It is a good first step.

---

had a marvelous time in a time-out room systematically shredding the hollow-core door. When time-out procedures are reinforcing, the behavior that earned time-out will increase rather than decrease.

Punishment

Punishment, as you already know, is an effective decrease procedure when it is applied immediately, consistently, and with sufficient intensity. It is easy to think of examples of punishment. Spankings, scoldings, removal of privileges, grounding, and withdrawal of affection are punishing contingencies most of us have been exposed to at one time or another.

In using punishment in the classroom, a number of factors must be considered. Ethical and legal restrictions limit the type of punishing stimuli that can be employed. Logistical constraints restrict the immediacy and consistency with which one can administer punishment. The side effects of aggression and avoidance, if exhibited, can unduly disrupt the flow of instruction. One wonders if punishment is worth the trouble when procedures such as extinction produce the same result less aversively.

When punishment appears appropriate or is the only option available, take into account the following points:

1. Low-frequency, less-well-entrenched behaviors decrease more rapidly under conditions of mild punishment than do entrenched behaviors.
2. Success occurs more rapidly when alternative behaviors are available.
3. Like extinction, punishment is most effective in combination with the reinforcement of an incompatible behavior.
4. Individuals habituate or become accustomed to frequent punishment, something that makes it less effective.
5. Punishment fails to teach other appropriate and reinforceable responses.

With these points in mind, it may be advisable to use punishment only for responses that cannot be altered with other approaches. For example, one might use punishment with behavior that could harm the performer or others. One probably would not use extinction to reduce aggressive behavior toward peers, for instance.

You will recall that punishment, like other operant procedures, is defined functionally; if the behavior does not decrease, punishment is not occurring, regardless of the teacher's intention. Often, negative forms of attention such as scoldings or reprimands are assumed *a priori* to be punishing stimuli. This is not the case if subsequent behavior does not decrease, however.

▶ *ACTIVITY 6.* Now that you have completed this chapter, let us see how well you can apply that knowledge in a problem-solving situation.

The Case. Michael is a ten-year-old boy who frequently behaves inappropriately in the classroom. He is rambunctious, spends little time on task, and is consequently not achieving very well. You, the teacher, are exasperated with Michael. In the past, whenever Michael was off task, you have (1) scolded him, (2) kept him from recess, or (3) made him sit in the hall. His rambunctiousness continues; in fact, it has increased.

The Solution. (1) Identify one behavior to focus on. (2) Define the behavior in terms of performance. (3) Identify events that might be maintaining the behavior at its present level. (4) Suggest a possible intervention strategy. (5) Outline a procedure for finding out if the intervention strategy worked.

Summary

In this chapter, we have described applications of behavioral principles in the classroom. The bulk of our discussion centered on the increase procedures of reinforcement rather than the decrease procedures of extinction and punishment. Perhaps this reveals a bias. A classroom is an environment designed for learning, growth, and the development of competence. These outcomes presuppose that children will acquire new responses, behaviors that are adaptive. Reinforcement contingencies are procedures for promoting the acquisition of responses. Naturally, as new adaptive behaviors are learned, maladaptive behaviors must be abandoned; hence, decrease procedures have been discussed as well. When decrease procedures are used, however, coupling them with increase procedures ensures that a discarded response can be replaced by a more valued one.

Every teacher wishes to create a classroom environment that facilitates learning. Behavioral principles are tools a teacher can use to reach that goal. To the extent that the application of these principles decreases chaos and disruption, gives children opportunities for success and accomplishment, and ensures that each child's successes are noted and reinforced, they are a highly useful tool for classroom and instructional management.

Social learning theory is one approach to learning that has a P in the B = E × P equation. This theoretical perspective lies somewhere between the perspective of radical behaviorism (Chapters 3a and 3b) on the one hand and the cognitive perspective (Chapters 5a and 5b) on the other. We examine the social learning perspective in the next pair of chapters.

In Chapter 4a we describe the learning system proposed primarily by Albert Bandura. This is an explanation of behavior that focuses on learning through imitative rather than direct response consequences. In order to explain imitation we must account for the cognitive processes (P variables) that permit individuals to observe one another's performance and incorporate the information into their own behavioral repertoire. How that might occur is described in Chapter 4a.

Learning through imitation has clear applications to the classroom; the teacher often functions as a skill demonstrator while learners assume the role of observers. The effective uses of social learning principles in the classroom are described in Chapter 4b.

Chapter 4a

Social Learning Theory: An Interactive Approach to Learning

Introduction

To many people, radical behaviorism is an elegant, parsimonious, and straightforward explanation of human learning. With this theory it is not necessary to make assumptions and inferences about unobservable mental events, and hypotheses need contain propositions about observable events only. The very characteristics that give behaviorism its strength and rigor, however, are viewed by others as limitations. Critics contend that behaviorists neglect people's internal cognitive activity and thus fail to fully explain the learning process. Those of a less behavioral orientation feel that information processing capacities of the individual, as well as environmental contingencies, are worthy of study. These psychologists wish to put the *P* back in the equation.

Many theorists prefer an *interactionist* approach to learning over that of radical behaviorism. From an interactionist perspective, people's actions reflect a variety of factors acting together. Some of these factors, or causes of behavior, are qualities of the person, and some are aspects of the environment. The product of interest—human behavior—is the result of both kinds of forces operating together. Learning, for example, can be seen as a performance resulting from the action of (1) the external forces operating around a person, the stimulus environment, and (2) the person's information processing capabilities. In an interactionist approach, we consider the contributions of both sources.

An Example of an Interactionist Approach

Social learning theory, advanced by Albert Bandura (1969, 1971, 1977) is one interactionist explanation of learning. Bandura stresses the reciprocal relationship between people and their environments; *reciproc-*

ity implies that influence flows in two directions, not just one. Environmental contingencies do influence people and exert control over behavior, but the individual can also exert control over the environment and alter these contingencies. Each influences the other. In Bandura's scheme (Bandura, 1974), the individual is thus quite active, not just a reactor to environmental stimuli. People actively process and mediate information coming from the environment and use that information to guide their produced behavior, which behavior in turn alters the environmental contingencies.

Social learning theorists propose that one major way people acquire information about the environment and learn new behavior is by observing others, a process called *vicarious learning*. These others are *models*, which can be actual people (for example, live performance), symbolic models (such as written accounts of a performance), or even sets of instructions (compressed accounts of a performance). After we are exposed to models performing behavioral sequences, we *imitate* them. Learning, then, occurs as a result of imitation.

The suggestion that learning occurs through imitating others is not a particularly profound proposition. Parents, teachers, and virtually everyone else who interacts with other people has observed imitation. People are social beings who live and raise children in social settings. Social living has an adaptive value, and it seems reasonable that one of its adaptive features is the possibility of learning not just through trial and error, but by watching the trials and errors of others. The contribution of social learning theory is not merely its suggestion that imitation is a learning process, but its explanation of the way the process of imitation occurs. Studies of imitative learning reveal the variables that affect whether a specific individual will imitate a particular model. As you will see, social learning theory is not a monkey-see, monkey-do explanation of learning. We are not thoughtless imitators, we are *selective* imitators, and it is this selectiveness that must be addressed and explained.

Social learning theory has all the essential elements of an interactive explanation: (1) environmental stimuli, of which a model is one type, are in a functional role; (2) the information-processing capacities of the person are considered; and (3) the reciprocal relationship between the person and the environment is taken into account. Moreover, this theory is directly relevant to education, since most of what occurs in a classroom is explicitly or implicitly based on modeling principles.

Scope of the Research Base

Like behavioral theory, social learning research is empirical; it attempts to find functional, cause-and-effect relationships between independent variables and subsequent behavior, relying heavily on observable data. Research studies of imitative learning, particularly as it relates to children, are numerous. There are many studies in which social or affective behaviors have been altered through modeling procedures. Bandura (Bandura & Menlove, 1968), for example, conducted a study with children who had a pet phobia. These youngsters displayed fear and avoidance of pet dogs and failed to interact normally with them. When the children were exposed to fearless models who did interact with the animals, the children's approach responses increased, while their responses associated with fear decreased. Models have also been instrumental in helping children to be less impulsive (Ridberg, Parke, & Hetherington, 1971), and to increase their risk-taking behavior (Montgomery & Landers, 1974). Children have even learned how to make sophisticated moral judgments by observing models who demonstrated mature ethical reasoning (Bandura & MacDonald, 1963). Observing models does not always lead to a positive behavioral change, of course. Many studies have shown that children can acquire such antisocial behaviors as physical aggression if they observe models who demonstrate aggressive behaviors (Bandura, 1973; Liebert, Neale, & Davidson, 1973).

The effects of modeling on children's behavior are not limited to the acquisition of social behavior. Modeling is useful in promoting cognitive behavior, too. For example, the number of sophisticated questions children ask increases after they are exposed to models who display advanced question-asking skills (Henderson, Swanson, & Zimmerman, 1974; Swanson & Henderson, 1977). Children have even learned complex mathematical skills from watching models use these skills successfully (Zimmerman & Rosenthal, 1974).

These examples demonstrate the many applications of social learning research to the behavior of children. Because such a broad range of behavior is found in the classroom, modeling is a potentially important source of influence for teachers.

How Imitative Learning Occurs

To explain the imitative learning process, social learning theorists consider the person and the environment as causes of behavior. The social learning person is an information processor who observes a multitude of models and uses the information acquired to direct his or her behavior. The social learning environment, like that of the behaviorist, contains stimuli that will strengthen and weaken those behaviors when they are produced. To take both the person and the environment into account, we must look more closely at what learning entails.

Bandura contends that learning is a two-step process. First, people *acquire* a behavior, become capable of it; second, they may or may not *perform* it (Bandura, 1969). The separation of acquisition and performance into distinct stages of learning differs from the strict behavioral

Teachers are models for students. The teacher may model appropriate academic behaviors, as in a science experiment, to facilitate student learning.

view. Behaviorists essentially divide behaviors into those that are learned, performed, and can be objectively observed, and those that are not performed. Bandura views this as a somewhat simplistic division, since all persons know how to perform certain behaviors that for various reasons they do not perform. Most of us, for example, have fairly clear ideas about how to steal a car, cheat on an examination, or physically hurt another person, but few people actually produce those behaviors. Logically, behaviors can be regarded as falling into one of three categories: (1) acquired responses performed with some regularity, (2) acquired behaviors that are not actually produced, and (3) responses that are not performed because they have not been acquired. These three categories allow us to deal separately with the processes of acquisition and performance.

In a classic study of young children who were learning new responses from observation, Bandura demonstrated the validity of the acquisition-performance distinction (Bandura, 1965). He showed children a film of a model who exhibited a sequence of rather novel aggressive responses. Some of the children saw the model rewarded for this behavior, some saw the model punished, and some saw the model receive no consequences at all. Then, as a post-test, each child was placed alone in a playroom where free play could be monitored. Although the children were not instructed to imitate the model, those who had seen the model receive reinforcement imitated the aggressive responses, and they did so more frequently than the other children. One might conclude from these performance differences that this group of children had learned more than the others. Apparently this was not the case, however. A second post-test was conducted in which all the children were offered incentives to reproduce what they had observed the model doing. All of the groups could reproduce the modeled sequence; the performance differences disappeared. The children, even those who produced no aggressive response in the first post-test, had all learned the behaviors equally well. The discrepancy between the results of the two post-tests supports the idea that learning is a two-stage process. Stage 1 concerns what is acquired, whereas Stage 2 focuses on what is performed; the two are not invariably the same. Even observers who do not actually imitate a model may still have acquired or learned the model's behaviors; other factors can affect the production of them. Acquisition seems to be a function of the information provided by the model and what the observer does with that information.

There is additional evidence to support the notion that imitation involves a person's capacity to process information. There is, for example, the process of one-trial learning. We have all on some occasion duplicated a complex behavior that was new to us after seeing it performed only once or twice. When Tad Pole learned to water ski, for example, he watched someone else water ski and heard an explanation of the model's behavior. The modeling sequence worked as a successful teaching approach, and the first time he tried it Tad duplicated the model's complex motor behavior. In a study from the research literature, a group of children observed a model placing blocks of wood in order from longest to shortest (a mathematical skill called seriation). After watching the model perform this novel behavior only a few times, the children duplicated the performance on their first trial (Rosser & Brody, 1981). Obviously, the young observers acquired a great deal of information from just a few examples, information that enabled them to reproduce the task in one trial.

Another phenomenon that indicates the complexity and informative value of models is *deferred imitation*, instances of imitation that occur some time after the imitator has observed a model perform. If Tad had had to wait until the day after he watched his instructor water ski before he got a chance to try it himself, he would have exemplified an instance of deferred imitation. In fact, many imitative responses are first performed long after the behavior has been observed. The cognitive, information-processing activities of the observer must be considered to explain such events as one-trial learning and delayed imitation.

Both of these phenomena require that an observer watch a model, but what is watched must also be stored and later recalled.

Acquisition is the process of making a response part of one's behavioral repertoire, of learning how to do something. This involves an interchange between the person and some informational aspect of the environment. Performance is the process of producing a behavior one has previously acquired—actually emitting the response. This two-stage breakdown is depicted in Figure 4a–1.

The Acquisition Stage

Let us first examine the process of acquisition, the way observers use models as sources of information to add new behaviors to their own behavioral repertoires. Consider some examples:

1. A remarkably naive person approaches a soft-drink machine for a drink, but he lacks the knowledge necessary to get the machine to deliver. What to do? Our thirsty observer watches as an unwitting model approaches, inserts coins, presses buttons, and extracts the desired product.
2. A French chef demonstrates the preparation of a five-course French meal for a group of motivated onlookers. The modeling performance takes two hours and involves assembling the ingredients, preparing several dishes, and describing how the food should feel, look, and taste. This performance is so well coordinated that all the food is ready at the same time.
3. A preschool teacher sorts blocks of various shapes into separate boxes containing squares, rectangles, and triangles. He is trying to teach his class shape concepts. To be sure they understand, the teacher repeats the sorting performance several times, naming the shape of each block as he drops it into the appropriate box.

You can see from these examples that a model's performance of a behavior can contain a large chunk of information with many components. At the minimum, modeling usually involves some sort of demonstration that is often accompanied by *verbal explanation* (symbolic information). Demonstrations can vary in length. The use of a soft-

FIGURE 4a–1. The Two Stages in Learning

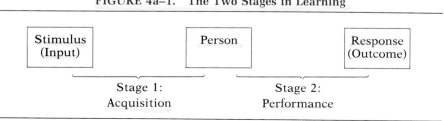

Behaviors may be acquired through observing a model. Deferred imitation occurs when the behavior is performed after a period of time has elapsed and the model is not present. Children frequently model adult behaviors in their play activities.

drink machine can be modeled very quickly, but demonstrating the preparation of a feast can take hours. Regardless of the length, some of the model's actions will be crucial to the observer's ability to repeat the performance, but others will be irrelevant. The observer's task, then, is really not a simple one. Our brains do not function like television cameras—we do not unselectively record every aspect of a situation and later recall it in full detail. We would sometimes like to, but it is beyond the abilities of most of us. When you read a chapter in a book such as this, for example, you do not usually memorize the chapter in precisely the form it is written. Rather, you must be selective, focusing on what you perceive as important and dismissing what appears to be less crucial. The same is true when we observe the performance of a model. We sort out the relevant features of the model's actions and distinguish them from the irrelevant features. Furthermore, we must boil down the entire performance into a simpler description, one containing only those elements of the performance that are important for later duplication.

Social learning theorists recognize the cognitive complexity involved in watching a model and selectively extracting information necessary to repeat the modeled behavior. To acquire the critical information while discarding the noncritical, we must perform three important cognitive activities: (1) selectively attend to what is observed, (2) code the information in a readily available form, and (3) store the code in memory for later retrieval. These three acts are the cognitive processes of *attention, coding,* and *retention.*

Our attention plays a crucial role in determining what we will acquire from observing others. Potential models surround us all the time, but we do not attend equally to everyone's behavior. There are several reasons that certain models draw our attention. Their personal characteristics may attract and interest us, or their behavior itself may stand out in some way. We attend closely to others simply because they are around us frequently and we see their behavior more often. Parents and, of course, teachers are the adult models most children have extensive contact with, and they are frequently imitated models. Certainly these people can possess characteristics, such as nurturance, that make them attractive to children. Some models draw attention simply because of the manner in which the performance is presented. Television and film models, for instance, are highly effective in capturing the attention of viewers simply because of the form of presentation (Bandura, 1977).

Although attention is a necessary prerequisite for learning from others, it is not sufficient to ensure acquisition of behavior. Viewers must also *remember* what they observe if it is going to affect their own productions later. Since it is impossible to remember every facet of the model's performance, the observer must compress the information into some simpler form, a form that can be remembered.

There are essentially two ways to compress behavioral information: (1) form a clear picture or a visual image of what the model did, or (2) generate a verbal description. Either coding process enhances recall. In the seriation study mentioned earlier (Rosser & Brody, 1981), the children were assisted in learning how to order different-length sticks by being given a verbal code: "Things are in order when they go like stairs." This sort of coding makes complex information simpler, and simpler units are easier to remember than complicated ones.

Recall is further enhanced by another process, rehearsal. Practice solidifies both observations and previous codings. One study of mathematical learning in young children found that overt motor rehearsal is much more effective in the acquisition of new skills than careful viewing alone (Swanson, Henderson, & Williams, 1979). Overt rehearsal is not always necessary, however; covert, mental rehearsal can also be effective (Bandura & Jeffrey, 1973).

It seems, therefore, that acquisition, learning a response from watching a model, is a cognitive process, one that depends in large part on the observer's abilities as an information-processing system. The acquisition process can be conceptualized as depicted in Figure 4a–2.

The Performance Stage

Once a behavior is acquired, certain factors influence whether it will be performed. One obvious factor is whether the observer is physically capable of reproducing the behavior; if not, performance cannot occur. A one-year-old infant who observes a model riding a bicycle will not imitate the modeled behavior because the infant lacks the necessary physical capability. Similarly, demonstrating printing to a child who cannot yet hold a pencil will not produce results. There are simply physical limits to what a person can do.

Production will also be limited if the observer lacks the skills necessary to reproduce the modeled behavior. A preschooler who has not yet learned to differentiate long and short sticks cannot be expected to order a set of sticks from longest to shortest; an architecture student cannot produce competent designs if the student has not learned to draw to scale; and a third-grade child will not master multiplication if addition is still a problem. Imitation will not occur in these cases with even the most perfect models. Limits in prior learning or prior skills can preclude the production of observed responses.

Assuming that there are no physical restrictions, that prerequisite skills have been learned, and that the response has indeed been acquired, what then influences performance? This is where reinforcement comes in. People tend to imitate when they expect reinforcement, and they do not imitate when they expect punishment. This is the motivational component of social learning.

People's expectations of reinforcement can be learned, of course, through past experience. Observers who have been reinforced for producing matching responses in the past are more likely to imitate in the future; those who have been punished for imitation imitate less frequently. This kind of contingency and effect on performance can be explained in terms of the operant principles discussed in Chapter 3a. Research indicates, however, that direct, external contingencies are not the only means by which people develop expectations of reinforce-

FIGURE 4a–2.   Components of the Acquisition Phase of Learning

	Step 1		Step 2		Step 3
Model (Input) ⟶	Selective attention	⟶	Coding	⟶	Retention

ment. Individuals also learn to anticipate reinforcement contingencies by observing what happens to the model. Response contingencies of this sort are known as *vicarious consequences.*

Watching a model receive reinforcement for a performance leads the observer to expect reinforcement for matching the model's behavior; this is called *vicarious reinforcement.* The process works in much the same manner as direct reinforcement, but in this case the probability that a response will be performed is altered before it is produced, not after. This is a truly adaptive feature of social living; one can learn which behaviors are valued and reinforced by watching what happens to others, thereby avoiding trial-and-error learning. What is perhaps even more advantageous is that one can avoid reproducing behaviors for which the model was punished. The probability of a person's reproducing a behavior is reduced by the expectation of punishment. This is called *vicarious punishment.* Vicarious punishment works in the same general way as direct punishment, but again the probability of production changes before the punishment contingency is experienced. Vicarious punishment probably helps all of us avoid a lot of unpleasantness as we learn. Vicarious consequences thus serve a useful informational function; we learn what to expect by observing the experiences of others.

As you can see, reinforcement is relevant to Bandura's conception of learning, but we have two basic differences from the Skinnerian approach. First, reinforcement is functional with respect to *performance* and *performance processes;* the response is acquired in the first place through cognitive operations. Second, direct reinforcement is not always necessary—vicarious reinforcement can serve the same function, perhaps more expediently.

The Basic Elements of Learning from Models

It may be helpful at this point to summarize imitative learning processes and emphasize some important points. Learning can be accomplished by observing others, through the process of imitation. The learning process actually has two stages: (a) *acquisition,* which is cognitive in nature and involves attention, coding, and retention; and (b) *performance,* which depends on the person's physical abilities and skills

FIGURE 4a–3.   **Components of Learning Through Observation**

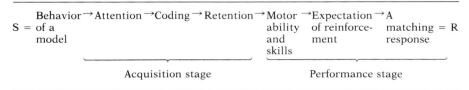

as well as his or her expectation of reinforcement. In imitative learning, actual trial-and-error experience with direct consequences is not necessary; vicarious consequences can serve the same function. This general system is diagrammed in Figure 4a–3.

Types of Modeling Effects

Examine the following examples:

1. Gordy Gourmand is having a meal with a friend in a restaurant. The main part of the meal is completed and Gordy is feeling full and satisfied. The waiter approaches and asks if he wants dessert. Now, Gordy has not been thinking particularly about dessert, but his friend places an order for a piece of rich, thick, creamy chocolate pie. Gordy orders one, too; his behavior has been affected by a model.
2. A college class is listening to an especially boring and tedious lecturer in a large auditorium, and students are getting restless. Suffering from intense boredom, one student close to the front gets up, gathers her supplies, walks down the aisle, and promptly leaves. The lecturer continues; nothing happens to the woman who left. Soon, several other people beat a hasty retreat—imitation again.
3. At a gathering in the home of an avid nonsmoker, one of the guests makes an unfortunate error in judgment and lights up. The host immediately launches into a discourse on the evils of smoking and the way it infringes on the rights of others, much to the humiliation of the smoker. Another smoker quickly puts his cigarettes back in his pocket. This person's behavior has been affected by modeling. A third smoker, however, thoroughly angered and disgusted, launches a verbal counterattack while busily puffing away. This smoker is imitating the first smoker, not the second.

Performance Effects

These examples of imitation share some important features. In each case, a behavior was altered, elicited, or inhibited by the behavior of another person. In addition, all of the behaviors affected were actions the observers were already capable of performing; they were previously acquired behaviors. The examples demonstrate not the acquisition of previously unlearned behaviors but changes in the likelihood of a performance resulting from the actions of a model. Gordy Gourmand is fully capable of ordering pie; the model simply acts as a cue or reminder of that capability. The students in the dull lecture know how to walk out of the room; they simply refrain from doing so until they see a model leave. The smoker who put his cigarettes back in his pocket learned that his smoking behavior would be badly received by observing what befell a peer. We can refer to these examples as *performance effects*. In each case, the probability of a performance was affected by modeled information; new behaviors were not learned.

There are differences between the examples, too. In Gordy's case, his friend's behavior simply acted as a cue, a reminder, or an *elicitor* of a behavior. This is an example of the *facilitative effect* of imitation. The consequences of a response were not involved in this case—eating and enjoying the pie were not observed. The model's behavior simply triggered a similar behavior in an observer. We thus see that models can have a cueing, or eliciting, effect on the behavior of another person.

In the second example, we have a different effect. Walking out in the middle of a lecture is considered unacceptable behavior in most academic settings; it is likely to be construed as rude or unstudentlike. This, then, is an example of a *negatively sanctioned* or possibly punishable behavior. When a model leaves and fails to be punished, however, the observers learn what consequences they can expect for themselves; the model may also have a cueing effect. This is an example of the *disinhibition effect* of modeling. When people observe a model behaving in a way that is often punished, and the model is not punished or even receives positive consequences, the likelihood of imitation increases. Response consequences and expectations of consequences are involved in this type of imitation. This is one of the explanations offered to account for the fact that viewing violent television content increases aggressive behavior in some viewers (Bandura, 1973). It has also been used to explain mob behavior during which usually lawful individuals

Riot behavior often results from the disinhibition effect of modeling. Observing a model perform an illegal behavior without punishing consequences may precipitate other students' participation in the illegal behavior.

engage in unlawful behavior. Vicarious consequences are a part of this modeling effect.

The third example also involves expectations of response consequences, but in this case expectations of punishment were created when the model's behavior met with aversive consequences. Only a rare and foolish observer would imitate a behavior that he has just seen a model punished for. This demonstrates the *inhibition* effect of modeling; the modeling inhibits the observer because of the consequences.

These performance effects are certainly relevant to a classroom situation, as will be explained in the next chapter. They bear particularly on classroom management; but they really entail no new learning. Known responses are elicited or inhibited, but the observer acquires no new skill or novel response.

Acquisition Effects

There are two types of imitative phenomena that do reflect the acquisition of previously-unlearned responses. These are the *modeling effect* (Bandura, 1969) and the acquisition of *rule-governed behaviors* (Rosenthal & Zimmerman, 1978; Zimmerman & Rosenthal, 1974). Both explain how models serve as sources of information for adding new behaviors to the observer's abilities. Accordingly, these two explanations involve the processes of attention, coding, and retention discussed previously as components of the acquisition phase of social learning.

Researchers studying the modeling effect focus primarily on the acquisition of single behaviors. When a parent attempts to teach a young child how to tie a bow, for instance, the parent demonstrates bow tying and the child attempts duplication. If the child produces a satisfactory imitation, he or she has acquired a new behavior through the modeling effect. Similarly, a swimming instructor may wish to teach students in a swimming class the butterfly kick. After the instructor demonstrates the correct form and gives the students paddleboards, they try to duplicate this novel response. Again we have a modeling effect. Examples of vicarious learning in the natural environment are easy to think of.

In academic learning, however, we are not usually concerned with teaching single, isolated behaviors. More generally, we are interested in helping children acquire the concepts or general rules involved in some kind of academic skill. Modeling processes can do this, too, but the process is slightly more complex.

The term *rule-governed behavior* usually refers to a group of specific behaviors that differ in a number of ways but adhere to a common rule. Some examples will clarify this point. Creating a simple declarative sentence is a verbal behavior. Simple sentences of this type differ in a number of ways. They are composed of different words and differ in meaning and content, but they have in common a certain form: For

Research Report

One effect you have read about in this chapter is the inhibition effect of observational learning. This effect is evident in situations in which imitation is reduced as a result of watching a model receive punishment for a response. That is the focus of this study.

Several points about this investigation encouraged us to include it in this chapter. First, of course, it illustrates a learning principle. Second, it exemplifies the paradigm, the procedures researchers employ in their examination of the social learning phenomenon. Third, it demonstrates that research is systematic, not haphazard; for this study did not take place in isolation. It was part of a series of studies. All of the studies in the series began with similar situations, but in each study a different variable was examined. The results of each study increased our understanding of the learning process just a bit. More important, the entire body of research results tells us a great deal about the role of inhibition in the course of socialization.

This study used a toy-play prohibition paradigm also used in a number of earlier studies (for example, Walters & Parke, 1964). In this paradigm, individual children are placed in a room with a set of attractive toys and an unattractive stimulus, like a thick book without pictures. Each subject is left in the room for a time with essentially two activity choices: (1) play with the toys, or (2) examine the boring book. Just before being left, however, the child is cautioned in one way or another not to play with the toys. Then the children are unobtrusively observed to see if, in fact, they touch the toys and how long they play with them.

In our sample study, the investigators wished to discover whether prohibition (warning about toy playing), observational learning (watching a model punished for toy playing), or both together suppressed behavior most effectively. They hypothesized that modeling would be effective with or without

prohibition. Kindergarteners and first graders took part in this study.

The modeling stimulus was a videotape in which a child was depicted in the toy-play setting. The child-model received the warning and was left alone. In the tape, however, the model played with the toys, was caught at it, and received a spanking as a result. Half the subjects observed this tape prior to their sojourn in the room; the other half did not. In each of these two groups, a third of the subjects received a mild warning about toy play, another third got a strong warning, and the remaining third were not warned. The children's behavior in the toy-play room was then observed. The investigators recorded the subject's behavior immediately after the treatment (video model condition plus warning condition). A week later they placed the subjects in the toy-play room a second time and again observed what they did. This second data collection point was undertaken to determine whether the treatment was durable. The data collected on both occasions was the amount of time spent in toy play.

Essentially, the data revealed that prohibition significantly decreased toy play. Children who received a strong warning played with the toys less than did the other subjects. Viewing the videotape also substantially reduced toy play. When prohibitions were mild or absent, however, modeling made the most difference; children who had received a strong warning were already sufficiently inhibited. During retention testing, toy play in general increased, but the effects of observational learning and the prohibitions were still apparent, especially among the first graders.

As you probably anticipated, the study was effective. It showed both the effect of prohibitions and the inhibition effect of modeling.

Zimmerman, B. J., & K. Kinsler, Effects of exposure to a punished model and verbal prohibitions on children's toy play, *Journal of Educational Psychology*, 1979, 71, 388–395.

the most part, each sentence has a subject, a verb, and an object. The common form of the different sentences is an example of a rule. Young children produce sentences of this type long before they go to school and long before they can explain what a simple declarative sentence is. When children create simple sentences they have never heard before but which are in the correct form, they are performing a rule-governed behavior.

We might also consider the example of a conceptual rule you learned in Chapter 3a, the concept of positive reinforcement. Recall that the specific stimuli that function as positive reinforcers can vary. They can be such things as food or grades, such events as a desired activity, or a behavior of another person, such as a smile. The stimuli used as positive reinforcers differ in many ways, but they share two common characteristics—they follow a behavior and they serve to increase the behavior. This feature is the rule that defines the concept of positive reinforcement. When you can produce a novel example of positive reinforcement, you demonstrate that you, too, have acquired the rule.

Social learning theorists interested in cognitive development and cognitive learning have shown through research studies that children can learn rules, not just isolated behaviors, from observing models. Many of these studies have been conducted in the same manner. First, a child is exposed to a model performing a rule-governed behavior; most often, the model demonstrates the behavior a number of times. Then the child is given an opportunity to duplicate the behavior and display knowledge of the rule. The experimenter does not wish to see if the child has simply acquired the specific behaviors observed; the acquisition of the rule is typically the concern. To differentiate rule-learning from specific response-learning, the experimenter asks the child to perform the task in a slightly different way or with materials different enough that the child cannot simply mimic the exact model behavior.

In one such study, Papago Native American preschool children were taught to ask questions by watching models (Swanson & Henderson, 1977). While the child observed, the model was given a picture and began to ask many questions about it. The questions were composed of different words and were about different things in the picture, but they all began with *why*, or *how come*, or *what would happen if*. After the modeling was finished, the observer-child was shown a different picture and asked to pose questions about it. The questions differed from the model's in content, but most of them started with *why*, *how come*, or *what would happen if*. Surprisingly, these were question forms the children had not produced during the pretest. The study provided empirical evidence that a rule-governed behavior can be acquired from models.

In the process of abstracting rules from watching models, the

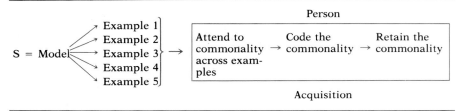

FIGURE 4a–4.   **Acquisition of Rule-Governed Behaviors**

learner attends to the common rule, codes it, and remembers it. The learner must, of course, see more than one example, so with this modeling paradigm a number of models are used. One model may demonstrate the behaviors several times, or several different models may be used. The observer then (1) attends to the regularity across all the exemplars, (2) codes the regularity, not the specific behaviors, and (3) retains the constructed code. When observers imitate in the rule-learning paradigm, they perform according to the rule in a slightly different situation. The materials, the setting, or some other feature is varied to avoid straight mimicry.

Figure 4a–4, which is a variation of Figure 4a–3, shows how the system for learning rules is slightly different from the system for learning single behaviors. Social learning theorists have demonstrated in a variety of research studies that modeling is a powerful device for facilitating the acquisition of rule-governed behaviors. Language rules, mathematical rules, and other conceptual rules have been taught to children with this approach (Rosenthal & Zimmerman, 1978; Zimmerman & Rosenthal, 1974).

Summary

In this brief discussion of social learning and imitation, we have merely scratched the surface of many important and relevant topics. The characteristics of models themselves, for example, are very important in determining whether imitation occurs. A considerable range of behaviors are potentially amenable to alteration by modeling. Emotional and intellectual behaviors can be changed through the process of imitation. Children acquire prosocial and even antisocial behaviors through observing the various models they encounter either inadvertently or by design. What we have attempted to do in this chapter is to explain the basic principles involved in learning through imitation and present what is essentially an interactive explanation of the learning process. In doing so, we have tried to stress a number of key points.

First, learning is a two-stage process that involves *acquiring* a behavior and *performing* a behavior. Second, the acquisition process is

New Directions in Research

Social learning theory has influenced many aspects of psychology in addition to learning psychology. You will encounter it again in the chapters on motivation (10a) and on social behavior (13a). In the last few years, however, this perspective has had tremendous impact on the subject of cognitive development (Zimmerman & Rosenthal, 1974; Rosenthal & Zimmerman, 1978).

Imitation is proposed as the mechanism by which children make cognitive progress in the course of development (Rosenthal & Zimmerman, 1978). To support this contention, researchers must show that behavior change from observing models influences the kinds of competencies that are of interest to developmental psychologists (Kuhn, 1975; Brainerd, 1978). They have done this. Temporal stability of the change must also be achieved; and it has. Most important, the behavior change must be more than specific to an individual matching response. This latter concern reflects an interest in *generalization* across behavioral classes associated with developmental change.

Social learning theorists interested in developmental phenomena conduct studies

demonstrating that imitation is not a mimicry process. What children learn from models generalizes across tasks that were never actually observed (Rosser & Brody, 1981). Apparently, learning from models is a *constructive activity* (Rosser & Horan, in press) in which children combine information from diverse models (Brody & Rosser, in press; Brody & Henderson, 1977) and put it together in a new way. Research suggests that what is acquired from the observation of models is a product of both the new incoming information and what they already know (Rosser & Horan, in press). Modeling information therefore interacts with existing developmental competence (Zimmerman & Jaffee, 1977), existing cognitive structures.

Future research in the social learning tradition will need to show how this interaction takes place. In order to accomplish that feat, more attention must be paid to the cognitive processes of the observer, not just the informational characteristics of the modeling. We might therefore see social learning theory moving further away from a behavioral orientation and toward a more cognitive one. It will be something to continue watching.

a *cognitive* one that depends on (a) selective attention, (b) coding of essential modeled information, and (c) retention of that information. Third, performance, unlike acquisition, depends on the abilities of the observer and whether reinforcement is expected for producing a modeled behavior. We can classify the behavioral results of watching a model into a number of descriptive categories, including (a) facilitative effects, (b) disinhibition effects, (c) inhibition effects, (d) modeling effects, and (e) acquisition of rule-governed behaviors.

Modeling is directly relevant to the activities of teachers. Students are very likely to imitate teachers whether it is desired or not. In the next chapter, we will present some examples of how you as a teacher can use modeling principles effectively to meet your educational goals and the needs of your students.

TEACHING SCENARIO

If students were all alike, teaching would be an easier, if less interesting, profession. Students are not all alike, however. They differ in background, prior experience, disposition, strengths, and weaknesses, so another challenge facing virtually all teachers is meeting diverse needs, or individualizing instruction. The individualization of instruction, like maintaining classroom order, requires multiple techniques. Some suggestions for ways to accomplish the goal can be derived from social learning principles.

In Mr. Perrault's fifth grade classroom the thirty students vary greatly in ability, background, and academic achievement levels. Mr. Perrault would like to individualize instruction more and meet the needs of all the students better, but he is finding this difficult to do in view of the group's heterogeneity. How might Mr. Perrault use modeling principles to achieve greater individualization under these circumstances?

Chapter 4b

Modeling in the Classroom

Introduction

The research information and psychological theory presented in the last chapter summarized what we know about modeling processes. The evidence indicates that models are powerful sources of information who can affect our behavior. Adults constantly encounter various types of models who alter their behavior to different degrees and with different results. Children are exposed to numerous models in their environments, too. They have models in their peer groups, their families, and even in the media. The language children use, their tastes in clothes, and their preferred activities can all be influenced by models. Recall the multitude of miniature Darth Vaders who emerged on Halloween night following the success of *Star Wars* and *The Empire Strikes Back*. Many teachers have encountered parents disturbed by the colorful epithets children may have picked up from peers—language not modeled at home. Or consider the sometimes remarkable uniformity in a group of teenagers who must have something or do something because "everybody's doing it." Models in the family and elsewhere in the environment contribute to such behaviors as these. From a vicarious learning viewpoint, the classroom is an important part of a child's environment because children spend a great deal of time there. Moreover, the school setting provides a variety of models. In any school there are peers, older children, school personnel, characters in books and media, and, of course, teachers.

Examples of imitation in the classroom are abundant. One obvious example from informal observation is that a teacher who relies on sarcasm to control behavior may find that students eventually became sarcastic themselves. You may have observed young children playing school; the youngster in the teacher's role will often repeat with un-canny accuracy the verbal behavior of a previous teacher: "Stay in your seats until you finish your work!"

Children extract behavioral information, develop expectations about response consequences, and learn new skills and competencies from many of the individuals they encounter in the classroom. Teachers who understand social learning principles can put that understanding to use in determining what modeled information will influence student observers. They can also use planned modeling sequences in direct teaching. On the other hand, teachers unaware of the psychological principles involved in vicarious learning may inadvertently allow or even promote modeling effects detrimental to students. They also miss a valuable teaching technique.

In this chapter we discuss just a few of the many possible applications of social learning principles. In some cases, these applications involve merely being aware of behavior being modeled in the class-room. Other applications involve deliberately using modeling princi-ples to structure the learning process.

The Teacher as a Model

Whether or not you actually plan it, as a teacher you will have a considerable influence on your students in both their academic learning and in the way they develop as they mature—not responsibilities to be taken lightly! Of course, teachers are not the only source of learning. There are other models, other sources, over which teachers have little or no control. Teachers generally have little influence on the child's environment outside of school; but within the classroom teachers can control at least one major source of modeled information—their own behavior.

As a child, one of the authors recalls being admonished by her father to "Do as I say, not as I do," in the hope that she would not acquire undesirable habits. As he discovered, however, children are likely to imitate adults' actions despite verbal commands to the con-trary. The crucial implication here is that teachers, as adult models, should be keenly aware of what they do. Do the behaviors modeled by the teacher exemplify the behaviors expected of the children? For in-stance, if a teacher expects students to persist with difficult tasks, does the teacher himself model persistence? If one goal of education is for students to enjoy reading good literature, does the teacher display a positive attitude toward reading? Does the teacher model appropriate language and social behavior as well as considerate interpersonal be-havior? Awareness of your own actions becomes critical when you realize that the behaviors you model may influence other people's behavior.

The teacher, as a model, displays a positive attitude and enjoyment of reading good literature. The student observers who model this behavior will also be likely to enjoy reading good literature.

An unaware teacher could accidentally teach social behaviors and attitudes we would rather students did not acquire. Teachers who are arbitrary or unfair in disciplinary matters may vicariously teach unfairness. Teachers who are intolerant of ethnic and racial differences may encourage similar intolerance in their students. Those whose behavior toward the handicapped child is marked by impatience, exasperation, or discomfort may teach students to interact similarly with exceptional children. Unless a teacher is a virtual saint, he or she should be deliberately aware of the behaviors being modeled in order to avoid inadvertent, accidental modeling.

Research suggests that teachers possess many attributes that influence vicarious learning. First of all, a teacher is a highly visible person to whom learners are constantly exposed. Second, in the classroom the teacher controls the available resources and is a major source of reinforcement. Third, the teacher is frequently viewed as competent and capable, and a certain amount of prestige goes with the position. These are all attributes that contribute to a model's effectiveness (Bandura, 1969, 1977). Because teachers are powerful models, the type of behaviors they model are very important.

The research literature provides us with even more evidence of how a teacher's behavior might influence children. It has been noted, for example, that females achieve less well than males in mathematics (Maccoby & Jacklin, 1974). This is a highly complex issue, but females' reluctance to attempt mathematical activities may be due in part to the influence of teachers (Fox, Fennema, & Sherman, 1977). If a female student is frequently exposed to teachers (particularly female ones) who dislike or fear math or who are uncomfortable with it, the teachers may inadvertently model behaviors reflecting those sentiments. The learner may vicariously acquire the same attitudes and not pursue math further.

We can also find research examples of the way adult models can influence children's social behaviors. In one empirical study (Bandura & MacDonald, 1963), it was shown that models affect the maturity of children's moral reasoning. Children exposed to models displaying high levels of moral reasoning and justice were influenced to do likewise. Children exposed to less sophisticated models had lower levels of reasoning, even when the reasoning modeled was lower than the children's usual level. If mature reasoning is desired in students, it must be modeled by adults.

By using their knowledge of psychology correctly, teachers can use modeling to have a beneficial influence on learning outcomes. Obviously, much of our behavior is inadvertent, and often we are even unaware of it. It would be unreasonable to expect anyone to exercise direct, careful control over every behavior he displayed. Certain behaviors are more important than others, however, and these behaviors can perhaps be deliberately controlled. How would one go about this process?

A teacher must first identify the specific social and affective student outcomes he considers important. Fairness, thoughtfulness, cooperation, and consideration are qualities most people agree are important and desirable. There are many others, of course. The first step, regardless of the particular goal, is to identify the outcomes one considers critical and wishes to influence.

The second step is for the teacher to examine his or her own behavior. Are the desired behavioral outcomes ever displayed so that students can observe them? Are behaviors contrary to the goals ever exhibited? Comparing one's own behavior with behavioral goals for students can be accomplished through introspection or feedback from peers. To be even more systematic, one could observe videotapes of oneself in the classroom. It is the process that is important, not the means.

The third step is to ensure that one's behavior is consistent with one's goals. This step, although important, is quite difficult. It requires continued effort. We should strive for congruence even if we never fully reach it.

▶ *ACTIVITY 1.*   Social learning researchers have recently examined the way children acquire appropriate social and interpersonal behaviors from observing the behavior of models. This will be discussed in much more detail in Chapters 13a and 13b. You now know enough about vicarious learning to begin observing the influence of socially appropriate models, however.

To begin this activity, you need to do two things. First, you must select a desired social behavior, and second, you need to select an educational setting in which this behavior would probably occur. Some examples of acceptable social behavior are cooperating, sharing, and lending assistance. Of course, you will need to define the behavior operationally (see Chapter 2b). Any setting in which a teacher is interacting with a group of students in something other than a lecture situation would be appropriate—a sports activity, small group discussion, or laboratory class, for example.

Having developed an operational definition of your target behavior and having found a setting where the behavior is likely to occur, set up some time periods for observation. More than one time period is needed in order to assess the stability of behavior (remember Chapter 3b).

Observe and record instances of your target behavior modeled by adults and performed by the students. You could arrange the data in a table like the following:

Observation Period	Frequency of the behavior	
	Adults	Students
#1		
#2		
#3		

Evaluate the data you have collected in relation to what you know about social learning principles. Keep your data and operational definition; you will need them for an activity to come.

Classroom Management and Vicarious Consequences

In Chapter 3b, we gave examples of the way teachers use direct reinforcement principles to manage student behavior. The use of positive reinforcement to increase desired outcomes with individual students was described at some length. In those examples, however, we described only the *direct* implementation of behavioral contingencies with individuals. Whenever reinforcement is delivered in a situation where others can observe it, the recipient's behavior may be affected through direct reinforcement, and that of others may also be affected through *vicarious reinforcement*. Observers of the contingency learn what they can expect if they behave in the same way. When a teacher directly reinforces one student, the others are developing expectations about reinforcement and are learning which behaviors will lead to reinforcement for themselves.

The use of reinforcement procedures thus serves double duty: (1) it affects the behavior of one individual directly, and (2) it affects the behavior of observers vicariously. This gives teachers all the more reason to be thoughtful and prudent in the use of reinforcement. Consider, for example, the situation in which a teacher often attends to a rambunctious pupil who has discovered that his obnoxious behavior attracts the teacher attention he desires. The unfortunate teacher may create an unpleasant classroom situation if he or she fails to alter this pattern. First, the negative behavior of the particular student will increase if the teacher's attention truly serves as a reinforcing stimulus. Second, the other students will witness this increase in undesirable behavior. Third, the teacher is inadvertently delivering an unfortunate piece of information to all the observers: Naughty behavior captures teacher attention! The teacher may subsequently find that not one but several individuals are misbehaving.

Another example involves a residential treatment center for emotionally disturbed children where one of the authors once worked. One behavior problem in this setting was that children often ran away. These excursions were seldom lengthy; children usually returned promptly. Unfortunately, once the child was returned, he or she was usually greeted with a great deal of staff attention. There was one unforeseen outcome: after one child ran away, a number of others ran away. Observers had vicariously learned that a brief escape brought attention as a side benefit. Regardless of one's opinions of such child behavior, it caused management problems.

On the more positive side, a teacher who can use reinforcement principles effectively gets an added bonus. Not only will the target individual's behavior be brought in line with educational goals, but the behavior of others may also be affected positively. Whenever reinforcement principles are applied to an individual, information is conveyed to observers.

A reinforcement plan is often a private contract between a student and a teacher. In such cases, the plan is based on individual needs and goals. Sometimes, however, a goal is suited to the group as well as to the individual. A knowledge of the principles of vicarious reinforcement may alter the manner in which a teacher reinforces desired behavior. The statement "I like the way you pay attention!" conveys more information to others than a simple smile. "I like your careful attention to detail on this project!" is more informative than a simple high mark. "Your questions are thoughtful and provocative!" is more informative than a simple "Good!" In short, the informational aspects of reinforcement are important, especially when the content is conveyed to a group, not just an individual. If you want the group to get the message, deliver reinforcement with that in mind.

The influence of the information transmitted in behavior management brings up another issue—the use of punishment. Punishment may decrease the behavior of the punished person; it also tells observers which behaviors are not approved. When we use physical punishment, however, we deliver a potentially damaging piece of information. The possible disadvantages of physical punishment were already described

Teachers frequently attend to the misbehaviors of students with little attention to acceptable behaviors. If attention is a reinforcing stimulus, then an increase in misbehaviors is likely to result.

in Chapter 3a. Social learning theory adds another item to that list: The use of physical punishment to control behavior can model aggression. The punisher demonstrates the effectiveness of aggressive behavior in controlling the behavior of another person; this is unfortunate, regardless of the punishment's other effects. Physical punishment is not often used in school settings; this is yet another reason for keeping its use to a minimum.

This discussion was intended to highlight the informative value of classroom management procedures. Since vicarious learning occurs in every group setting, the informative function affects not just individual recipients but observers of the process as well. When using reinforcement principles in the classroom, therefore, (1) consider the informational value of the procedures; (2) try to select procedures that will be informative to others as well as to the individual addressed directly; (3) avoid procedures conveying information that conflicts with educational goals; and (4) particularly avoid such procedures as physical punishment that might inadvertently promote unacceptable behavior.

▶ *ACTIVITY 2.*   Observe instruction in a small group setting where teachers and students interact. This might be a reading group, a small group discussion, a team sport, or a laboratory class. In the group setting, students will make responses and the teacher will have the opportunity to react to them. Your task is to focus on *positive* teacher statements, those that indicate approval of the student response. Develop a classification system for the teacher statements that includes at least three categories: (1) statements that indicate approval but provide no information about the act approved (for example, "Good job"), (2) statements that indicate approval and refer vaguely to the act approved (for example, "I like the way you played today"), and (3) statements about the specifics of the act (for example, "Your presentation was excellent because you articulated your phrases so clearly").

When you have recorded these types of responses, evaluate your record from the perspective of vicarious learning.

Utilizing Models for Academic Learning

The power of models is not restricted to influencing social behavior or to creating expectations of consequences. Modeling can also be used to teach academic skills directly. Teachers model cognitive performances all the time because they *demonstrate* academic competence. Demonstrations are more effective, however, if modeling principles are taken into account.

When we teach academic skills, we are often trying to teach a general way of behaving. In other words, we hope the learner will be able to apply the acquired knowledge in a variety of situations. If we are teaching high-level question-asking, we expect the student to learn to ask such questions generally, not just during one specific discussion. If we teach a young child how to measure things or tell time we want the skills to *generalize* across settings. Generalized rules can be taught with models, just as specific responses can be.

To teach a cognitive skill with modeling, the behavior must be modeled more than once. Otherwise, the learner may learn to apply the response in only one isolated situation. If you are teaching single-digit addition, you want the child to be able to successfully add any set of numbers. If you modeled addition with just one problem, the student might learn only that problem—an outcome that would be too specific. To teach colors to preschool children, you might demonstrate color labeling with blocks. You want the child to recognize colors wherever they are encountered, however. For the children to acquire generality, you must model correct color identification many times with different materials.

Suppose we wish to teach three-year-olds the difference between square things and round things, a shape discrimination. We hope that after the modeling the child will be able to sort a variety of objects into the two classes. First, we model the behavior. Starting with a pile of paper cutouts, we place them in two groups, one item at a time. The model must be sure the child is attending, of course—without attention we get no acquisition. Second, we take a group of blocks and repeat the sorting with them. The procedure continues with many different kinds of objects. The important thing is that the modeling occur many times with many objects. If the instruction is successful, the child should be able to reproduce the task. We know the child has acquired a rule-governed behavior from observing a model when he or she can correctly sort independently.

An older group might be instructed in the operation of long division. To model long division, a teacher would demonstrate the process a number of times; he or she would not expect the students to acquire the operation after just one example. Demonstrating a procedure a number of times is another example of multiple modeling. In a high school chemistry class, an instructor may wish to teach the learner to balance chemical equations; only a naive instructor would expect the students to learn the skill after seeing it demonstrated just once. To ensure acquisition the instructor would demonstrate many balancing problems. It is easy to think of other classroom examples in which teachers behave in exactly the same way.

In learning rule-governed behaviors, a student will need to observe a number of different examples of the application of the rule. The examples should vary in some way so that the derived rule will be applicable to a wide range of contexts.

In the study on question-asking described in the previous chapter, researchers modeled more than forty questions for learners before they expected a performance. This is fairly characteristic of the number of modelings used in research.

In addition to being *redundant,* the examples modeled should *differ.* It would be foolish to just do the same example many times; not enough information would be conveyed. If you modeled ordering many times but only on problems containing three sticks, the learner might learn to order those three sticks, but not four or five, and no other objects.

Similarly, you cannot teach long division by doing the same problem over and over again. Each modeled example in the series should differ, but the particular skill involved should be held constant.

The modeling we have described so far involves demonstrating skills. A learner's performance can be improved by including verbal information along with the performance. This can be done in two ways. The model can (1) verbally describe what he or she is doing, or (2) state a verbal rule. The two procedures can be used together, of course. Using either one will yield better results than silent demonstration alone. Verbal information directs attention to important aspects of the model's performance. It also serves as a source of even greater redundancy.

In the ordering task described earlier, the model always described the measuring strategy of comparing two sticks: "I'll push them together and see which is longer. This one is longer so I'll put it here." This verbal mediation accompanied the motor performances of comparing measurements and placing the sticks in the correct order. Children failed to learn generalized rules when the verbal mediation was eliminated (Rosser & Brody, 1981). Mathematics instructors verbally explain how to solve math problems as they demonstrate correct solutions. English teachers describe how to construct outlines as well as produce them, and creative writing teachers explain how to construct short stories and also have students read them.

In addition to directing attention, verbal mediation of a model's performance helps the observer *code* the behavior. In fact, verbal mediation is a verbal code, one that is provided by the model rather than constructed by the observer. Aspects of modeling that assist this coding process facilitate the acquisition process.

Verbal coding is easier when the teacher provides *verbal rules*, expressions that capture the essence of a correct performance. Such statements as "*i* before *e* except after *c*" and "things are in order when they go down like steps" are rules of this sort. The research literature is full of examples in which verbal rules strengthened the modeling treatment.

The following, then, are general rules for the effective use of modeling in instruction.

1. Give many examples of the desired performance.
2. Use different examples to demonstrate the performance.
3. Use examples consistent with the rule to be learned.
4. Demonstration is more effective when verbal mediation is provided.
5. Providing verbal rules yields stronger performances than demonstration alone.

Another aspect of effective modeling for academic learning involves the learner rather than the teacher. This aspect is *enactment* or *active rehearsal.* The teacher can set up the modeling sequence in such a way that the observer has an opportunity to match the model's performance. Matching of this sort yields several benefits. First, learners are more likely to pay attention if they realize they are expected to perform as well as observe. Second, students who are actively involved may be more engaged than those who are simply passive recipients of information. Third, if students are performing the task, the teacher can easily check to see if they have acquired it. If the observers cannot match the model's performance, the modeling sequence may be lacking an important facet. It may need to be modified or repeated. Fourth, when children are responding actively, they can be directly reinforced for successfully matching the modeled performance. This will encourage the individual learner and help motivate the others. Research studies of modeling routinely include active matching (Zimmerman & Rosenthal, 1974); the technique has proven more effective than direct observation alone (Swanson, Henderson, & Williams, 1979; Swanson & Henderson, 1977).

Active rehearsal is common in the classroom. In the past, for example, class periods in high schools were sixty minutes long. Forty-five minutes of direct instruction were frequently followed by ten or fifteen minutes of enactment. The last part of the class gave students a chance to practice or rehearse what they had observed. Lab classes in the sciences can serve the same purpose: material demonstrated in class is enacted in the lab. Learners need to act as well as watch. Building enactment into one's lesson plans is consistent with sound social learning principles.

In the case of younger children, enactment should immediately follow demonstration. Delaying practice may demand too much of a child's attention and memory. With very young children, modeling and practice, to be most effective, should proceed on a trial-by-trial basis. The model performs a simple task and the child matches the performance. This alternating trial procedure continues until the modeled skill has been mastered. In short, although enactment is basic to all learning from models, the specific procedures employed will depend on the age and skill level of the learners.

▶ *ACTIVITY 3.*   When researchers use modeling as an instructional procedure, they typically follow this format: (1) demonstration and modeling, (2) opportunity for a matching response, and (3) reinforcement for the matching response. This format is easy to use in the laboratory, but using it in the classroom is more difficult. Moreover, opportunities to use each of the three components vary from one teaching situation to another. Opportunities for matching and reinforcement for matching, for example, are more common in small-group instruction than in lectures.

Choose an age group and a subject matter that interest you. Arrange to observe the group being taught in two of the following settings: (1) a tutorial, that is, one-on-one instruction, (2) a small-group setting, (3) a large-group setting. Tally the frequency of each of the components of modeling, using this format:

		Components of modeling		
		Demonstration	Matching	Reinforcement
	Tutorial			
Group format	Small-group format			
	Large-group format			

After collecting data, evaluate the three formats in terms of social learning principles. What learning outcomes would you predict? How would you reorganize the teaching?

Other Sources of Modeling in the Classroom

The teacher is, of course, not the only model students see in the classroom. Two other sources are (1) peer models and (2) symbolic models depicted in media.

Peers have some definite advantages as models. First, they are personally similar to the student observers, and research indicates that similarity is an important model characteristic (Bandura, 1977). Second, teachers can reinforce peer models for performing desired behaviors. Tutoring, in which a skilled student serves as a model for a less skilled student, is one technique that encourages learning through modeling.

Models need not exist in the flesh; symbolic models in books, on films, and on television are a rich source of behavioral information. In the classroom the teacher may not have the time or the opportunity to demonstrate every behavior he or she wants to encourage. This limitation does not extend to symbolic models, however, and symbolic models as well as live ones can affect behavior. The wise teacher will use such sources. Behaviors described in text, demonstrated on film, or depicted on television can serve as models for both social and cognitive learning.

Scenario Suggestion

Data from social learning research has revealed that modeling is more effective when the model and the observer share similar characteristics. Apparently, observers attend to what a model is doing when they perceive the model as like themselves, performing some behavior of which they too are capable.

In the case of Mr. Perrault's problem with individualizing, this research finding suggests the possibility of using *peer models* as an adjunct in instruction. Peer modeling is one form of *peer tutoring* that might be effective in individualizing instruction and meeting the needs of more students in a heterogeneous group.

For some activities, Mr. Perrault could break the students into small groups or pairs. One member of the pair, a student who has already mastered the particular content, serves as the model for another student who has not. The roles could change, a student serving as a model in his or her strong areas and an observer in a weaker area. Most students will thus fill both roles as activity and focus change.

Both observers and models will benefit. Those who will be models get the benefit of Mr. Perrault's attention when he prepares them for the tutoring role; the observers receive individualized instruction. Since the students themselves move between tutoring and observing, in the end they get the benefit of both.

During the peer modeling sessions Mr. Perrault can move about the room, reinforcing the efforts of both the models and the observers. Everyone will benefit, regardless of ability level, and Mr. Perrault will be handling his large group both efficiently and individually.

Any group of students in a classroom exhibits strengths that a wise and creative teacher can harness to individualized instruction. The teacher need not be the only individual occupying the teaching role. Peer tutoring is but one example of building on student strengths for the benefit of both the group and the individual. Moreover, if you think about it, this certainly is an economical solution to a pervasive and recurrent problem.

One of the authors was involved in television research in which models on videotape facilitated the development of cognitive skills in young children. The various materials, models, and situations presented in this manner held children's attention and helped them learn effectively (Henderson, Zimmerman, Swanson, & Bergan, 1974; Henderson & Swanson, 1977, 1978). When television modeling is used, a variety of models can be depicted in a short time. We used several adult models, peer models, puppet models, and cartoon models—all within a span of ten minutes! Moreover, we used a lot of stimulus items, many drawn from the natural environment. A live teacher can do the same thing, but it takes more time. The teacher can encourage enactment and reinforce correct matches, however; television is limited in this respect. Certainly one reason "Sesame Street" is effective and interesting to children is its use of modeling. A teacher can use symbolic models to augment and enrich the live modeling available in the classroom.

▶ *ACTIVITY 4.*   Recall the social behavior you selected and operationally defined in a previous activity (page 141). Resurrect that operational definition in order to assess the behavior's frequency in sources of symbolic modeling.

Interview students in an age group that interests you (your peers, perhaps). Find out their favorite reading materials, television programs, or movies. Select one of these symbolic sources and go through it. How often was your target behavior modeled in the source?

Summary

We have suggested a few current applications of social learning principles. Modeling is such a pervasive influence in our lives that you can undoubtedly think of many others. In this chapter we focused on only three: (1) the personal behavior of the teacher as a model source for social or affective behavior, (2) the use of reinforcement contingencies in changing group behavior vicariously as well as influencing the behavior of individuals directly, and (3) the deliberate use of modeling sequences in instructional design. Other applications are also possible.

Modeling is pervasive. Teachers are models, regardless of the other roles they fill. Knowledge of social learning principles is therefore critical to the educational process.

From social learning theory we move to those perspectives on the learning process that place primary emphasis on P variables. These include the cognitive learning approaches and information processing. Many elements of cognitive psychology have influenced the American psychological scene for some time, but in recent years this sector of psychological thought has come to the forefront. Individuals embracing this theoretical perspective are leading a renewed research interest in cognitive phenomena, including perceiving, thinking, comprehending, and problem-solving.

In Chapter 5a we review the historical evolution of contemporary cognitive psychology and establish the basic premises of a cognitive approach. You will, however, encounter many of these concepts again in subsequent chapters (for example, in Chapters 11a and 11b as well as 12a and 12b). The major point in this chapter and in chapters to come is that the person is an active processor of environmental information. It is thus impossible to understand and to explain human performance without understanding human information-processing principles.

In Chapter 5b we consider implications of cognitive learning theory for educational practice. Here you will be exposed to yet a different perspective on the learner. This different perspective reiterates an important point: There are multiple perspectives on human learning, multiple implications for educational practice, and hence multiple teaching methodologies.

Chapter 5a

Cognitive and Information-Processing Approaches to Learning

Introduction

The American branch of psychology has never been particularly unified. Throughout the brief history of the discipline, various theories of behavior, of learning, and of psychological phenomena in general have coexisted, as they do today. The rise of behaviorism from Watson and others to the radical behaviorism of Skinner and the cognitive behaviorism of Bandura is only one of several theoretical themes. Another theme originated in assumptions different from those of Watson and culminated in an alternative explanation of the learning process. This set of views is represented in cognitive psychology and information-processing theory.

Cognitive psychology evolved less straightforwardly than behavioral psychology, and the two schools of thought part ways on a number of points. For one, the assumptions that form the foundations of cognitive psychology differ from those of behaviorism. Second, these assumptions lead to a different set of questions about behavior and about learning. Third, cognitivists have tackled the problem of theory-building differently. Whereas behaviorism is a single theory used to explain broad categories of behavior, cognitive psychology is a conglomeration of smaller theories, each of them applicable to a subcategory of behavior with elements in common. The focus of one cognitive theory may be perception, of another, memory, and of a third, verbal learning. A grand scheme or global theory does not yet exist. Instead, we have a diverse package of explanations, each somewhat limited in scope. Fourth, unlike behaviorism, cognitive psychology has no single individual as its primary spokesperson. There is, rather, a list of players who share a common concern: the role of the person in the learning process. In the $B = E \times P$ equation, cognitive psychologists tell us about *P*.

We will examine some of the major premises of cognitive theory in this chapter. We will begin by contrasting it with behaviorism, emphasizing the different assumptions of the two approaches. Then, by examining two historical approaches, those of the gestalt psychologists and of Tolman, we will exemplify the evolution of those assumptions into psychological theory. Contemporary views, represented by the work of Bruner and Ausubel, will be used to demonstrate the applicability of cognitive psychology to learning and to the educational process. Finally, we will briefly introduce information-processing theory.

This discussion hardly exhausts the contributions of cognitive psychologists, however. You will encounter the perspective again and again in the text. In Chapter 6a, the contributions of Jean Piaget, a cognitive developmental psychologist, are introduced. In Chapters 11a and 12a, cognitive theory again surfaces in the context of concept learning, problem solving, prose learning, and imagery. Even this only scratches the surface of a branch of psychology that is currently flourishing.

A Contrast of Approaches to Learning

The cognitive and behaviorist approaches to learning may be thought of as the end points of a continuum (Figure 5a–1). At one end of the continuum is Skinner's radical behaviorism, in which behavior is regarded as a function of the stimulus situation and the environmental consequences of behavior. At the opposite end of the continuum are the

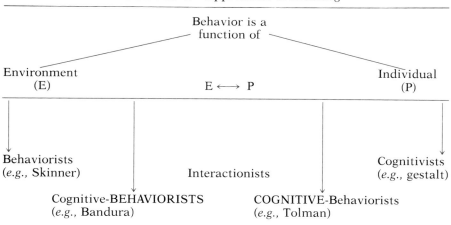

FIGURE 5a–1. Approaches to Learning

cognitive psychologists, who see behavior as a function of the person. In this view, the individual is an active processor of information, and behavior is determined by (1) the way the person perceives a situation, (2) the manner in which the perception is represented internally, and (3) the relationship of the perception to past experiences stored in memory.

There are a number of interactionist approaches that may be thought of as falling between the two end points of the continuum. Advocates of interactionist perspectives consider both environmental contingencies and the cognitions of the individual represented in memory to be important determinants of behavior. Interactionists may be primarily behavioristic in orientation and give secondary importance to cognition (cognitive BEHAVIORISM), or they may consider cognition the primary determinant of behavior while agreeing that some principles of behaviorism are also important (COGNITIVE behaviorism). Although the positions of those at the end points of the continuum are fairly clearly established, the positions of the interactionists vary greatly.

Interactionism ($B = E \times P$) such as that associated with social learning theory represents a blending of the two extreme positions; but the different assumptions of those who emphasize P and those who emphasize E can be expressed most clearly by contrasting the end points. To provide a framework for understanding cognitive theory, therefore, we will contrast the behaviorist and cognitive views of the person, the processes involved in learning, and the outcomes of learning.

Contrasting Assumptions: The Learner

One major difference between the behaviorist and cognitive perspectives concerns their views of the nature of the learner. Behaviorists see the individual as essentially passive; it is the stimuli in the environment, including the consequences of behavior, that shape a person. Cognitive psychologists, on the other hand, maintain that man is innately active when interacting with the environment. Not only does the stimulus affect the learner; the learner, through stored past experiences, affects the stimulus. On one occasion, a person may respond to the sight of food by eating it, but when the individual is not hungry, he or she may ignore the food. Humans react to the same stimulus in different ways at different times.

Consider the implications of the cognitive assumption. The nature and meaning of an environmental event can vary from person to person depending on the circumstances and the individual's history. When we wish to know how the environment appears to different persons, we must deal not with one environment, one stimuli, but many environments and many different stimuli. Behaviorists can view the environment objectively—the same environment can be described in the same way by two observers. Cognitivists, however, must view the environment subjectively; one person's view of the environment will be essentially different from another person's view.

Contrasting Assumptions: The Process

Although behaviorists might agree that some process occurs inside the individual during learning, they adhere strictly to the tenets of empiricism and refrain from speculating about the nature of that process. They focus instead on the observable elements of the situation, the antecedent and consequent events surrounding a response, which occur in a temporal sequence. Cognitivists, however, focus primarily on the internal process that occurs in the individual between the stimulus and the response. As a result they ask different kinds of questions about the learning process. Cognitivists are not concerned with the kind of consequent events that strengthen or maintain a response; they want to know what the person is doing when he or she acquires a response. Because it is impossible to look within a person and directly observe what is happening, a cognitivist must depend on inference, which the faithful behaviorist is loath to do.

Contrasting Assumptions: The Outcome

The two groups of theorists also have different conceptions of the product of learning. Behaviorists maintain that learning consists of building associations between stimuli and responses. Cognitivists describe the product of learning as a change in a person's cognitive structure, his or her mental picture of the world based on past experiences. These past experiences have been built into an extensive network of categories and relationships between categories. When we experience something new in our environment (the thing to be learned), it is incorporated into this cognitive structure. During the process of incorporation, the thing we are learning may be changed to fit our cognitive structure, or we may modify the cognitive structure to incorporate that new thing.

To give a simple example, suppose a young child has attached the name *dog* to the family pet. According to the child's cognitive structure, a *dog* has certain characteristics—four legs, a tail that wags, ears on top of its head, a bark, and so on. When the child encounters a neighbor's pet that has many of the same characteristics, the child promptly labels that pet a dog, too. Suppose, however, that the neighbor's pet makes a different noise: "meow." The child would then either change the characteristics of her *dog* category to include "it barks or meows," or she would form a new category. If another observer is present and says "No, that is not a dog, that is a cat," then the child would have a name for the new category. As the child has more experiences, animals may be categorized as *pets* or *non-pets*, and the *pets* category will be further subdivided to allow for other different kinds. The cognitive structure decreases the number of specific connections the child must learn. The category of *dog* has certain characteristics—it may include poodles, Labradors, St. Bernards, and other breeds. Without the cognitive structure, the child would need to learn a specific connection between each breed and the generic term *dog*.

Our cognitive structures (pictures of the world) are organized through our interactions with the environment. To understand how a cognitive structure is organized, we may either examine our own minds directly or we may consider the world around us. Three aspects of our cognitive organization become apparent. First, our cognitive structure is composed of a large *number* of categories ranging from very broad categories, such as *plants* or *animals*, to narrow categories, such as *my best friend* or *paramecia*. The broad categories have different kinds of objects in them; we group them together to simplify our picture of the world. The narrow categories are usually parts of larger categories. *My best friend* is a part of a larger category of *friends*, and *paramecia* are part of the larger category *one-celled animals*. Nothing in our world is entirely unique; everything fits into some category.

The second aspect of the organization of the cognitive structure is that it operates according to a set of *rules*. These rules may take the form of *distinctive features*, which when applied to a new object permit us to fit it into an already-established category. In the preceding example the distinctive features of dogs were that they had four legs, tails that wag, ears on top of their heads, and so on. For the child in the example, however, these features were not distinct enough to preclude miscategorization.

The third aspect of cognitive organization is that there are *relationships* between the objects in one category and between objects in different categories. Butter is thus related to bread, milk, the color yellow, and cholesterol, to name but a few relationships. It would be difficult, if not impossible, to think of a part of the world that is not related in some way to other parts of the world.

Cognitive psychologists contend that learning occurs when there is a change in the cognitive structure, not when there is a change in the frequency of a response, as behaviorists would have it. Changes may take place in several different ways. New categories may be added by either incorporating a number of existing categories into a wider category or by broadening a category that already exists. Learning would also take place when new relationships between existing categories were discovered, or when the rules defining a category were refined or changed.

Almost all cognitive theorists hypothesize that people possess some sort of cognitive structure or similar mental framework. In very young infants, the cognitive structure may be fairly simple, but through experiences with the environment the structure rapidly elaborates and expands. By the time the child enters school, the cognitive structure has many categories, and numerous interrelationships have been established. Education, then, is designed to further expand and elaborate the cognitive structure.

Suppose a certain learner is faced with a novel problem. What process might he or she use to solve the problem? A behaviorist would probably say that the learner would respond in a way that had previously led to reinforcement in similar circumstances. Depending on the similarity of the novel stimulus to stimuli associated with past learning, the child would probably make a previously reinforced response. If the situation were dissimilar from past experiences and failed to correspond to a previously reinforced behavior, the learner would resort to a trial-and-error procedure, trying one response after another until one of them was reinforced.

Cognitivists might not completely disagree with this interpretation, but they would include an additional variable: The child's ease in solving the problem would depend upon how it fit his or her cognitive structure. If the problem in its existing form failed to fit the structure, the child would not be able to solve it. Because the learner is an active being, however, the child might be able to restructure the stimulus situation in a different way so that it could be solved more easily. To a behaviorist, the explanation depends upon past history, whereas the cognitivist's explanation depends upon the current structuring of the problem.

To summarize: Behaviorists and cognitivists differ in their views of the learner, in their emphases on variables, in their descriptions of the products of learning, and in the roles they ascribe to past experience and current situations. Now that differences have been explained in general, we can examine the different approaches to learning put forth by specific theorists.

Historical Approaches

Although the two historical approaches we will discuss are no longer compelling forces in American psychology, we will review them briefly in order to give you a background for considering present-day cognitive psychology. Many modern positions trace their roots directly to these historical perspectives; hence past work and contemporary work share a common theme. Interestingly enough, the early varieties of behaviorism were already established as viable explanations of learning before the work of either the gestaltists or Tolman became known.

The Gestaltists

Current cognitive theory may be traced most directly to the contributions of a group of German psychologists: Max Wertheimer, Kurt Koffka, and Wolfgang Kohler. Although their theorizing began early in this century, the gestaltists did not influence American psychology strongly until the late 1920s and early 1930s after the behavioristic approach was well entrenched. The German psychologists' approach was well received by those who felt that human behavior differed from subhuman behavior, that because humans had the ability to think, learning involved more than response frequency changes. Even today, many if not most educators are more comfortable with a cognitive approach that emphasizes the active role of the person.

The gestaltists were primarily interested in the way people perceive the stimuli around them. They considered learning to be secondary to perception: If the learner perceives the learning situation easily, then learning will occur. If learning fails to occur, it may be necessary to restructure the environment. One of the tasks of the teacher, according to this viewpoint, is to organize the situation so that the learners can easily incorporate the material to be learned into their store of experiences.

To a gestalt psychologist, perception is subjective. People perceive environmental stimuli differently. While some people planning a picnic may see a cloudy sky as a threat, others may see the beauty of the clouds, and weathermen may see the clouds as indications of a change in the weather. Not only do different people perceive the same stimuli differently, but the same person may perceive the same stimulus differently at different times. Optical illusions (Figure 5a–2) illustrate differences in visual perception. Is the drawing on page 160 of a beautiful, young girl or an unattractive, old woman?

In the same way, people may perceive words or statements differently. Consider the statement "John got even with Monica." This could mean that John repaid Monica with a like action or that John reached the same level as Monica.

A person's perceptions of the environment depend not only on individual aspects of the environment but on how these aspects fit together or are related. Organization, then, also influences perception. Consider the shapes in Figure 5a–3. These shapes might be described as "A parallelogram with two tall narrow rectangles and two shorter narrow rectangles." Describing them sequentially, we might say, "One tall narrow rectangle next to a short narrow rectangle, then a parallelogram, a short narrow rectangle, and another long rectangle." Both descriptions describe the stimuli adequately.

Figure 5a–4 presents the same stimuli in a different organization. A person describing this organization of the shapes will probably describe the whole—"This is a table"—rather than the individual shapes.

FIGURE 5a–2.   Optical Illusion—An Old Woman or a Young Girl?

Although the figure does not depict a table drawn in true perspective, the representation is close enough that the drawing may be classified as a table. The way stimuli are organized, then, affects the way we perceive them.

The experiments of the gestaltists cast some doubt on the behaviorists' notion that learning occurs in small, incremental steps. In one typical experiment, a chimpanzee was put in a cage and some food was placed outside the cage out of the chimpanzee's reach. The experimenters had put sticks in the cage that could be used to rake the food to within the chimpanzee's reach. Initially, the chimpanzee used the sticks to bang on the cage bars, or threw them at the food. Once the chimpanzee perceived a stick as a rake, however, the stick became a sought-after tool used to rake the food in.

Perhaps the most dramatic of these experiments involved a problem mastered by a chimpanzee named Sultan. In this investigation, the food was placed too far from the cage to be reached with a single stick. The process of learning to reach the food was slow, but it was eventually accomplished when the chimpanzee joined two sticks together much as a jointed fishing pole is put together. The first joining

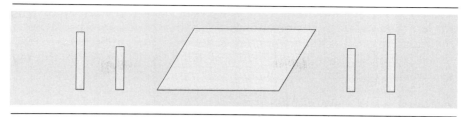

FIGURE 5a–3.　Organization of the Elements in a Table

of the sticks appeared to be almost accidental; it occurred when two sticks happened to be placed approximately end to end. The chimpanzee was then able to perceive the relationship and use the two sticks as a single tool to reach the food (Bower & Hilgard, 1981).

The process of perceiving relationships is termed *insight*. Insight occurs when an individual reorganizes the situation in such a different way that a solution becomes evident. Sultan had an insight when he observed that the two sticks could be made into one long stick.

Insight has been called the "aha!" experience. Cartoonists illustrate it by drawing a light bulb over a character's head. When a learner is faced with a problem, the solution may come all at once, not as the result of a gradual accumulation of associations, as behaviorists explain learning.

The gestaltists' contributed laws of perception in addition to those that have been described (for example, Koffka, 1935; Bower & Hilgard, 1981). Although gestalt psychology ceased to be a distinct approach in the 1940s, elements of the approach are evident in current cognitive theories that deal with perception, organization, and memory (for example, Asch, 1969; Bower, 1970; Tulving, 1968).

Gestalt psychology had its greatest impact on our understanding of the nature of stimuli and the role of insight in learning. Stimuli could no longer be considered to be objective, perceived as the same by everyone; instead, they had to be considered subjective, "stimuli as

FIGURE 5a–4.　The Elements of a Table Organized into a Whole

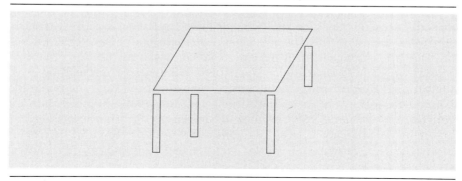

perceived by the individual." The gestaltists' demonstrations of insightful learning raised questions about the behaviorists' interpretation of the learning process. It appears that rather complex problems are sometimes solved not through a series of trials and errors but through suddenly recognizing relationships after reorganizing the problem.

Tolman's Sign Learning

The theory of Edward C. Tolman is also a cognitive approach. Although Tolman endorsed the behaviorists' methodology, he disagreed with their conception of what people learn. Unlike the behaviorists, who believe that people learn contingencies between stimuli and responses, Tolman maintained that people learn cognitions or cognitive maps. We have illustrated the difference between learning S–R connections and learning cognitive maps in the following anecdote.

> Mr. Brown is staying in a hotel on his first visit to a city. He wishes to go to a particular restaurant to eat, so he asks the desk clerk how to get there. The clerk gives the following directions: "Go left two blocks, turn right and go three more blocks, and then turn left and go one more block." Mr. Brown proceeds to the restaurant following these directions, has his meal, and is ready to return to the hotel. If he has just learned S–R connections (Left—2 blocks, R—3 blocks, and L—1 block), he may have trouble returning to the hotel. That pattern will not guide him back. If he has actually learned where the restaurant is in relation to the hotel, however, he can retrace his steps or even take an alternate route back to the hotel.

Tolman would argue that we do not perform behaviors like robots; we learn means-end relationships. Our initial experience of a situation sets up certain expectancies, which we use to guide our actions in the future.

A second major premise of Tolman's theory was that behavior is purposive, directed toward some goal. The goal may be getting an *A* in a course, securing food, or discovering a solution to a problem. Behavior is always intended to approach something or get away from something. A statement of what a person is trying to do would indicate his behavior better than a description of his particular actions.

According to Tolman, we can understand behaviors only by looking at sequences of behavior in their entirety. Behavior is more than the sum of a series of S–R connections. S–R theorists believe that all behaviors are composed of atomistic S–R connections, just as chemists break compounds into their constituent elements. Tolman, however, maintained that when the S–R connections are combined, the behavior is more than the sum of its parts, just as a compound is more than its constituent elements. We cannot understand the characteristics of water by considering it simply a combination of oxygen and hydrogen atoms. When we examine water, we can feel its wetness, its fluidity, and its other physical characteristics. Likewise, solving a problem involves more than discovering a series of S–R connections. Various relationships, combinations, and interactions of elements may also be discovered.

Another characteristic of behavior, according to Tolman, is that it is flexible. Most of the time, behavior is not predictable. We do not know exactly what responses a person will make in the next instant. Except in the few cases of reflexive behavior, such as the salivation of dogs at the sight of food in Pavlov's experiments, responses to stimuli are varied. Consider, for example, the behaviors of students at the end of a testing session. When the instructor says "Stop. The time is up. Hand in your papers," students respond differently. Some respond to the stimulus as directed, but some quit working and begin to review their answers, some begin to answer questions randomly and hurriedly, and for others the stimulus words do not seem to register at all.

Stimuli, according to Tolman, are signs, not elicitors of responses. Pavlov's experiments with dogs may be explained not in terms of connections between *UCS* and *CR* but in terms of meaningful signs. The sound of the bell became a signal that food was coming. The sign created an expectancy in the dog, and this expectancy was followed by salivation. According to this interpretation, stimuli are signs that the learner follows to a goal. The learner is learning meanings, not associations.

Tolman was ingenious in designing experiments to test his hypotheses about learning. His experiments on latent learning will serve as an example. These experiments showed that an animal can learn by exploring a maze even in the absence of reward or reinforcement. In this experiment (Tolman & Honzik, 1930), three groups of rats ran a maze under different conditions. Group I rats were always reinforced for running to the goal box. Group II rats were never reinforced for running to the goal box. The critical Group III rats were not reinforced for the first ten days, but they were reinforced for running to the goal box beginning on the eleventh day. The results showed that Group I rats steadily decreased their numbers of errors over the seventeen days. The errors of Group II rats decreased slightly, but not nearly at the rate of Group I rats. The number of errors for Group III rats was similar to that of Group II rats for the first ten days, but when reinforcement began, the number of errors for this group dropped below the number for Group I rats. The researchers concluded that while Group III rats were not being reinforced, they were indeed learning the map of the maze simply by exploring. The introduction of reinforcement permitted the latent learning (the learning that occurred during exploring) to be expressed in behavior; thus the rapid decrease in errors.

In summary, Tolman emphasized that all behavior is purposive, that organisms learn cognitions or cognitive maps, and that behavior is flexible. Following the gestalt approach, he hypothesized that stimuli serve not as elicitors of actions but as signs that set up expectancies about what will follow.

This discussion of the gestalt and Tolman approaches may give you a better notion of the differences between behaviorists and cognitivists. Two more current cognitive theorists who have had significant impact on education are Jerome Bruner and David Ausubel. Like other cognitive theorists, their formulations are not designed to comprehensively explain all learning.

Current Theorists

The two theorists we have chosen to represent contemporary cognitive theory, David Ausubel and Jerome Bruner, represent broad segments of cognitive theory. Their theories, which are similar in some respects, have broad implications for educators.

Ausubel

David P. Ausubel is an educational psychologist. This differentiates him from theorists who are primarily psychologists but whose theories have been translated from the realm of psychology into educational practice. From Ausubel's viewpoint, the primary subject matter of the educational psychologist is meaningful verbal learning and retention and the variables associated with this kind of learning. Schools, of course, concern themselves with meaningful verbal learning; Ausubel's work has been devoted to exploring different ways to make meaningful verbal learning more efficient.

Ausubel maintains that learning may be classified on two different dimensions, as represented in Figure 5a–5. The first dimension is the manner in which the content is assimilated by the learner, either receptively or by discovery.

In reception learning, the subject content is presented to the student in final form. The usual textbook or college lecture, for example, presents material in final form. The learning involves no discovery on the part of the learner. To learn the material, the learner must incorporate it into his existing store of learning, his cognitive structure.

In discovery learning, the content to be learned must in part be discovered by the learner before it can be incorporated into his cognitive structure. Discovery learning is a two-phase process. The first step is organizing the problem, relating the elements of the problem to the existing cognitive structure. This must be accomplished before the second phase, which is the discovery of the desired end product, the means-end relationship or some other answer to the problem. When this has occurred, the content can be assimilated as it is in reception learning.

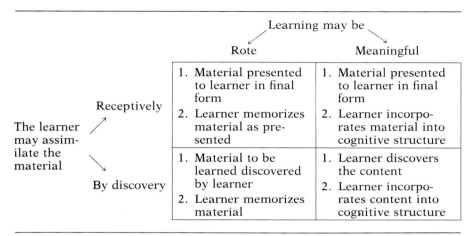

	Rote	Meaningful
Receptively	1. Material presented to learner in final form 2. Learner memorizes material as presented	1. Material presented to learner in final form 2. Learner incorporates material into cognitive structure
By discovery	1. Material to be learned discovered by learner 2. Learner memorizes material	1. Learner discovers the content 2. Learner incorporates content into cognitive structure

FIGURE 5a–5. **Types of Learning**
(Based on Ausubel & Robinson, 1969)

The goal of most classroom instruction is reception learning. Although discovery learning sometimes occurs in the sciences and other courses, it is primarily contrived rediscovery of known propositions. Learning such concepts as *animal* or *democracy* by discovery would be a time-consuming process. To reach the solution to any problem, however, a sufficient store of prior knowledge is necessary. Ausubel argues that the most efficient means of transmitting this store of knowledge is through reception learning.

Reception learning has frequently been criticized because it is confused with the second dimension of learning: Learning may be either rote or meaningful. The confusion stems from the notion that all reception learning is rote and that all meaningful learning occurs by discovery. Ausubel maintains that the two dimensions, reception/discovery and rote/meaningful, are independent. His position is that both discovery and reception learning can be either rote or meaningful (Ausubel, 1961).

Learners who have had training in the scientific method may, for example, be able to state the steps of the scientific method by rote. If learners have not learned the steps meaningfully, however, they will not be able to apply the scientific method. The multiplication tables may be and often are learned by rote, but to use them in solving problems they must be learned meaningfully. Many students learn the mechanics of solving equations in algebra by rote but cannot explain why they perform the functions as they do.

The prerequisites of meaningful learning are presented in Figure 5a–6. The basic requirements are (1) the material to be learned must be potentially meaningful, and (2) the learner must intend to incorporate the material meaningfully. The learner's purpose is thus a prime

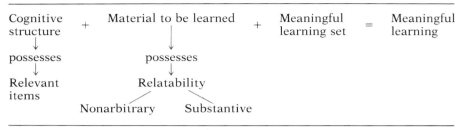

FIGURE 5a–6. Conditions for Meaningful Learning
(Adapted from Ausubel & Robinson, 1969)

factor in meaningful learning. All students have taken courses that seemed irrelevant to their current needs. In such courses, much of the material is learned by rote. Students may be able to fashion correct answers without relating the material to other aspects of their cognitive structures.

The anecdote of the school visitor told by William James on page 150 of his *Talks to Teachers on Psychology* (1899) illustrates the fact that students do learn by rote.

> A friend of mine, visiting a school, was asked to examine a young class in geography. Glancing at the book she said: "Suppose you should dig a hole in the ground, hundreds of feet deep, how should you find it at the bottom—warmer or colder than on the top?" None of the class replying, the teacher said: "I'm sure they know, but I think you didn't ask the question quite rightly. Let me try." So taking the book, she asked: "In what condition is the interior of the globe?" and received the immediate answer from half the class at once: "The interior of the globe is in a state of igneous fusion."

The students had learned the material by rote. For learning to be meaningful, learners must intend to relate the material to their existing cognitive structures.

The potential meaningfulness of material depends upon two factors: (1) the material must possess logical meaningfulness, and (2) relevant ideas must be available in the learner's cognitive structure. To be logically meaningful, material must be nonarbitrary and substantively relatable.

All material to be learned is arbitrary insofar as the names of concepts are arbitrary. What we mean by nonarbitrariness, however, is that material must be consistent with what is already known. Consider as an example of arbitrariness a child learning how to decode the spelling *ough* in words. Given the two words *through* and *though*, the learner must arbitrarily learn by rote which sound goes with which combination of letters. Add to these such words as *rough, bough,* and *cough* and you can see that each different word must be learned as a discrete entity; they thus involve rote learning. A child who has learned the concepts of *rectangle* and *square*, however, could nonarbitrarily incorporate these into the broader classification of *quadrilateral*, since the qualities of *four-sided figures* would fit with the learned concepts of *rectangle* and *square*.

The substantiveness of subject matter implies that it could be stated in different ways without changing its meaning. The definition "An equilateral triangle is a triangle with three equal sides" might be rephrased as "If a triangle has all its sides equal, then it is an equilateral triangle." By changing the order of the words, we did not change the meaning; the statements are equivalent.

Although tasks in school learning are nearly always substantive, substantiveness may be lacking in some laboratory tasks, such as learning a list of nonsense syllables. Telephone numbers or license plate insignia often lack substantiveness and must be learned by rote. If, however, some relationship between the numbers or symbols can be discovered, the task of learning and retaining the information is easier.

The second aspect of potential meaningfulness is that relevant ideas must be available in the learner's cognitive structure. We are concerned here with the experiential backgrounds of learners, their

Children are taught the Pledge of Allegiance during their first year of school. Since the words in the Pledge are not relatable to their cognitive structures, the students learn the Pledge by rote.

stages of development, intelligence, or age. Content must be learned by rote if learners have not had experiences to which they can relate it. This was the case with *igneous fusion* and *interior of the earth.*

For meaningful learning to occur, therefore, the material must be logically meaningful, the learner must intend to incorporate the material into his cognitive structure, and appropriate elements in the cognitive structure must exist to which the new material may be non-arbitrarily and substantively related. If any component is lacking, the material, if learned at all, will be learned by rote.

Bruner

Jerome Bruner's writings (Bruner, 1957, 1960, 1966; Bruner, Goodnow, & Austin, 1956) have covered a wide range of topics, including perception, conceptualization, human development, and instructional theory. Although these writings have not been integrated into a single cohesive learning theory, Bruner has contributed greatly to educational practice. In this section we will focus on Bruner's description of learning as a cognitive process. Some of his other ideas will be explored in later chapters.

Two basic assumptions underlie Bruner's approach to learning. The first is that the acquisition of knowledge is an interactive process. In opposition to the behaviorists, Bruner believes that learners interact actively with the environment; changes occur not just in the environment but in the person as well. The second assumption is that a person constructs his knowledge by relating incoming information to a previously-acquired store of information—the person's model of the world. Bruner's inner model closely resembles Ausubel's cognitive structure. Each learner's model of the world is unique. As we come to know different aspects of our environment, we build them into a structure or model that allows us to group certain things together or build relationships between known things. This model permits us to develop hypotheses, to fit new knowledge into our structures by broadening them or developing new structures or substructures, and to develop expectancies about what will occur.

We have illustrated these different abilities in Figure 5a–7, which represents part of a model of the world with which most of us are familiar. Let us assume that a thing we are unfamiliar with is introduced into our environment. Being curious, we want to incorporate this thing into our structure, to code it into our system. As we observe the thing, we note that it can move itself. One hypothesis might be, "If an organism moves by itself, then it is an animal." In our model of the world, we already have some characteristics of animals, so we can check other characteristics of the thing to see whether our hypothesis is true or not. If the thing matches other defining characteristics of

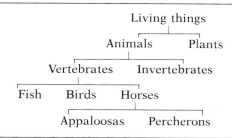

FIGURE 5a–7. A Hierarchical Arrangement as Part of a Cognitive Structure

animal, we can fit it into that category rather than the *plant* category. Upon further observation, we may deduce that the thing has a spinal column, so we can assign it to a more restricted category, that of *vertebrate*. As we developed our model, we assigned certain critical attributes to each category. By checking the attributes of this new thing against the attributes of the previously established categories, we can eventually place the thing in the *horse* category. If it fails to fit any of the specific classifications of horses (Appaloosa, Percheron, and so forth), we will have to add a new category to accommodate it.

According to Bruner, learning involves connecting things that have similarities into a structure that gives them meaning. In the process of living—interacting with the environment—people develop inner models or coding systems to represent the world as they know it. We might think of this structure as a kind of giant filing cabinet, one with many drawers and many files in each drawer. Humans have the capacity to develop this filing cabinet and retain the entries for long periods. Referring to Figure 5a–7, we see that one file might thus be labeled *living things* and have drawers labeled *plants* and *animals*. Each of these drawers would have a number of files, and each file would be further subdivided. If this were all there was to the filing system, however, the structure might be rather sterile, but in this giant system we have many cross references that interrelate the files to create a very complicated series of connections. When you read the word *horse*, for example, many different ideas may come to mind—an image of a specific horse, a horse in a circus, cowboys, farms, horsing around, and so forth.

Bruner's approach to learning might be described as a categorization approach. Bruner assumes that all our interactions with the world involve categories necessary for human functioning. Without categories we would have to have a separate file drawer for each object, thing, and idea in our experience. Categorization simplifies the complexities of the environment.

It is through our categorical system that we are able to recognize new objects. Because new objects possess similarities to objects already

in our coding system, we can classify and attribute certain characteristics to the new things or ideas. In fact, if we encounter a new thing
and cannot categorize it in some way, we cannot identify it, cannot
place it in our filing system.

Central to Bruner's approach is the concept that categorization
allows us to go beyond the information given. We identify objects by
associating them with a class. When we classify an object, we imbue
it with a whole set of properties, critical attributes, and relationships.
We do this through inference, discovering more than we directly perceive from the object itself.

This coding system facilitates learning and retention. The more
complete the coding system is, the easier it is to assimilate new material. Very young children have coding systems made up of rather
discrete units. With further experiences in the environment, however,
their systems become much more complicated, and as a result they
can incorporate more complex material. The coding system facilitates
retention; often, one needs only to recall a general category in order
to recall a specific item in that category.

In summary, Bruner maintains that learning involves developing
categories and a coding system. The various categories relate to one
another in such a way that each individual has his own unique model
of the world. In this model, new learning may be incorporated by
changing the model. This is accomplished through changing the categories, relating the categories in some new way, or adding new categories.

An Information-Processing Approach

One rather new development in cognitive psychology is the information-processing approach to learning. This perspective derives its metaphor for the person from computer technology and systems theory. It
has thus developed along with our increasing sophistication in data
processing. Like cognitive psychologists, information-processing theorists have investigated many diverse aspects of cognitive functioning,
including meaningful verbal learning (for example, Ausubel, 1978),
problem solving (for example, Greeno, 1978; Simon, 1980; Vinacke,
1974), imagery (for example, Kosslyn & Shwartz, 1977; Shepard &
Podgorny, 1978; Paivio, 1971, 1975), and inferencing (Reder, 1979;
Spiro, 1977a & 1977b). This work is discussed in more detail in Chapters 11a and 11b and 12a and 12b. The common feature that unites the
broad spectrum of studies and investigations is the general thesis that
the computer is an appropriate analogy for human thought and cognition and thus for learning.

The Basic Analogy

The computer has been described as a giant brain. Conversely, the brain may be thought of as a minicomputer. Experiences in programming computers to perform complicated manipulations have led to insights useful in generating hypotheses about how the brain functions. Information-processing theorists take the view that humans and computers do the same kinds of thing. They differ, of course, in *hardware,* the structures through which information is managed, but they may not differ much in *software,* the procedures or programs used to manage the information. Essentially, these theorists begin with the assumption that the human mind and the computer *function* similarly.

The operation of a computer may be divided into three suboperations. First there is the input phase, in which the punched cards or magnetic tapes are registered. For the learner this step corresponds to perceiving and registering external stimuli, such as sounds or sights. The second aspect of computer operation is the program. During this phase, input is recorded in a computer language, reorganized, collated, and stored. In learners, this corresponds to encoding the stimuli, organizing the information, and recording it in a storage system. In the third suboperation, output, information from the preceding manipulation is printed or displayed. In learners, a physical, written, or spoken response may be considered output.

Equating the two kinds of processing systems yields some interesting implications. We can, for example, program a computer to process information in a certain way and get a product, a certain kind of performance. We can then give humans the same kind of input and compare the human performance with the computer performance. If the output is similar, we might infer that the computer program accurately represents what the person did. In another instance, we might have a hypothesis about the procedures people use to learn or to solve problems. We could develop a computer program based on that hypothesis and try it out to see if it works efficiently and productively. In this case we would be simulating human action with computer action. Both kinds of investigations are based on the premise that we can use the computer as a model of man.

A Linear Model

Computer programs are very complex because we must tell the computer what to do at every single step; nothing can be taken for granted. To devise programs, we must map out all the stages information must pass through to achieve a desired performance or output. Information-processing theorists have also tried to map out the stages associated with human performances.

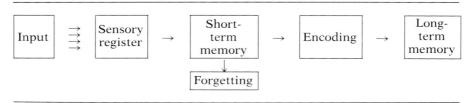

FIGURE 5a–8.   An Information-Processing Approach

Human maps can be general or very specific, restricted to a single type of information. One of the more common maps is a linear one that represents the stages information passes through from input to storage in memory. Many other maps and elaborations of this basic map are being developed all the time. The one we describe will give you an idea of what this perspective is all about. A linear model of an information-processing system is diagrammed in Figure 5a–8.

Sensory Register.   At any given time, many external stimuli impinge upon a person's senses. A student in a classroom faces a multitude of stimuli—a teacher, a textbook, bulletin boards, students, and many others. All of these stimuli may be recorded in the sensory register. This is a nearly literal record of the sensory image; the information is not recognized, categorized, or identified until it passes through the sensory register. The sensory register accepts all information, but it keeps it only briefly, usually less than a second. Then the information either decays spontaneously, or new information from the senses erases what was there previously. Both the durability of information in sensory information storage and the capacity of this storage have been extensively investigated (Sperling, 1960).

The function of the sensory register is to retain information long enough for the person to selectively attend to it and transmit it to the next stage of memory. From the multitude of images in the sensory register, the individual selects certain images to pay attention to.

Short-Term Memory.   To be learned, information from the sensory system must move along the path to the short-term memory. The short-term memory is a special type of memory that holds recently registered information acquired through the sensory system. Short-term memory is used for storing information that we wish to retain for only a few seconds. Telephone numbers are retained in short-term memory from the time they are looked up until they are dialed, for example. Similarly, short-term memory is used for retaining a lecturer's statement until it is recorded in a student's notes.

Short-term memory can retain material for only a brief time without active rehearsal. The capacity of short-term memory is limited, too. New stimuli entering the short-term memory will replace what is already there. The telephone number you looked up may be replaced by other information if someone asks you a question before you dial the number. Most of us have faced gaps in our notes that occurred when a lecturer proceeded to a new bit of information before we had recorded an earlier statement.

Because of this limited capacity, much of what is registered in the short-term memory is promptly forgotten. This serves a good purpose, however. If we did not rapidly forget information in our short-term memories, our minds would be hopelessly confused. Retaining important information is crucial to learning, but much of what we take into our short-term store is irrelevant and should be forgotten.

People can retain information in the short-term store if they rehearse or practice it. By continually repeating the telephone number, we can retain it for a longer period of time. Craik and Watkins (1973) labeled this operation maintenance rehearsal. We may also rehearse new information through the process of elaborative operations. This process involves connecting new material with past learnings either by giving the new material meaning or through imagery. The telephone number 325–1011, for example, could be retained by using this mechanism: $3 + 2 = 5$, $5 + 5 = 10$, and 11 follows ten. If information is neither rehearsed nor elaborated, it is lost from the short-term memory in approximately fifteen seconds.

Long-Term Memory. To retain information for a longer period of time, it must be transferred from short-term to long-term memory. To be transferred, the information must be encoded. Encoding may begin in the short-term memory when the individual rehearses or elaborates the incoming stimuli. With further rehearsal, the information stored briefly in the short-term memory is transferred to the long-term memory, where it may be retained for hours, days, weeks, or perhaps forever. Rote learning typically involves transference to the long-term memory by rehearsal; material is represented in storage essentially as it was presented. This kind of learning might be used to learn the multiplication tables, the spellings of certain words, or the names of the presidents.

More typical of meaningful learning is the elaborative operations process. Through this process we attempt to relate the new information to past experiences previously stored in long-term memory. If we can fit the information into an established category, change a category to include the new information, or relate the information in some other way to our existing memory stores, we are more likely to retain it in long-term memory.

Research Report

Today's investigators in cognitive psychology, particularly information-processing theorists, use experimental methods as sophisticated and complex as any in the discipline. This is a result of the nature of the subject matter—the workings of the human mind, which is also very sophisticated and complex. As you know, mental processes cannot be directly observed, a fact that poses a scientific and methodological problem for cognitive psychologists. Investigators must draw inferences about unobservable processes from performances that are directly observable. In order to meet the criteria of good science, the process of drawing inferences, however, must be precise and specific. Another individual looking at the research outcome should draw the same inference. The research selection chosen for this chapter illustrates the way inferences can be precisely drawn through the use of careful logic and careful methodology.

In cognitive psychology, investigators must begin by generating a model, through their own logic or with computers, that represents some aspect of cognitive processing. If the model accurately reflects human activity, the investigators should be able to use it as a basis for making predictions about patterns of human activity. The next step is to collect data on actual subjects and see if the data correspond to the predictions. The model is then revised to reflect conclusions drawn from the data, new pattern predictions are made, and the process continues. Each study, then, is one element in a program of systematic research designed to create successive approximations of aspects of human thought.

In our research selection, the investigators examined the processes involved in moving information from short-term to long-term storage. It had been generally accepted that information is held in short-term memory by means of rehearsal. Rehearsing or repeating information maintains it for a longer period so that it can be transferred to long-term stor-

age. It follows logically from this model that an item of information held in short-term memory for a longer period than some other item is more likely to be rehearsed and thus more likely to be recalled from long-term memory. If one applied this logic to the recall of information presented in list form (called serial learning), one would expect information at the beginning of a list to be recalled better than material at the end; the former was around longer for rehearsal. In previous research, this negative recency effect for list learning had been empirically observed (Craik, 1970).

This hypothesis was tested in the present experiment. The investigators needed (a) a list of information items, (b) a way to determine that the items got into short-term store—an immediate recall task, and (c) a way to tap whether the items got into long-term store—a delayed recall task. They also had to control (d) the length of time each item was maintained in short-term store and (e) the rate at which the information was presented. According to the model, items that were held longer—that is, with more intervening information—should be recalled better, and items presented more slowly should be recalled better, too, again because of the time factor.

The task involved presenting subjects with lists of words. In each list there were certain critical words that began with a particular letter. The subjects were instructed to monitor the lists and report the last word in the list that began with the specific letter. Since the subjects did not know how many critical words would be presented, they would have to rehearse each one until the next was presented. The critical words were randomly spaced throughout the list with a different number of irrelevant words intervening between them. A critical word followed by many irrelevant words would thus be rehearsed longer than one followed by just a few. This was referred to as the *i* value of the critical word. Short-term recall was tapped by having subjects report the last critical word in each list. To tap long-term recall, subjects were given an unexpected test in which they were asked to recall as many words as possible from all the lists. The prediction (from p. 601):

> Presumably if time in short-term store predicts long-term store retrieval, then final recall performance should increase directly with the number of items monitored during the retention of the critical words, and inversely with presentation rate.

Fifty-four subjects, undergraduate psychology students, heard twenty-seven lists of twenty-one words. The critical words, the presentation rates, and the number of items between critical words were varied under experimental control so that the effect could be monitored and examined. A total of eighty-one critical words were presented to each of the subjects. The critical words were of two types: (1) reported words, the last critical words in each of the twenty-seven lists, and (2) replaced words, critical words in some other position. The short-term memory task

data (recall of last critical word) and long-term memory task data (recall of as many words as possible) were also collected.

The data on the short-term task indicated almost perfect performance: no subject made more than two errors. The average score was 26.2 correctly-reported words. The long-term recall data are presented in the table. The critical information that the investigators found with the long-term recall task was that reported words were recalled more often than replaced words, even though the latter were in short-term memory for a shorter time. Moreover, *i* value had no effect, despite the fact that critical words with high *i* values should have been rehearsed for longer periods.

Since these findings were inconsistent with the model's predictions, they led to the revision of the model. The investigators concluded that neither the amount of time in short-term store nor the amount of rehearsal is critical to recall. It is, rather, the type of rehearsal that is important. You will learn much more about this type of processing model in Chapter 12a.

Craik, F. I. M. & M. J. Watkins, The role of rehearsal in short-term memory (Experiment 1). *Journal of Verbal Learning and Verbal Behavior*, 1973, 12, 599–607.

Summary of Long-Term Recall Data from Craik & Watkins, 1973

TABLE 1 Percentage Recall as a Function of Experimental Condition, *i* Value, and Presentation Rate

Condition	Presentation rate	0	1	2	3	4	5	6	8	12	Mean
Replaced	Slow	12	13	22	10	21	19	19	18	19	17
	Medium	10	15	22	12	14	19	09	12	11	14
	Fast	14	07	11	06	06	14	09	16	15	11
	Mean	12	12	19	10	14	17	13	15	15	14
Reported	Slow	19	20	20	20	31	39	22	26	28	25
	Medium	20	22	19	19	31	26	20	28	20	23
	Fast	26	15	22	26	20	31	19	11	20	21
	Mean	22	19	20	22	28	32	20	22	23	23

(Column group header over 0–12: *i value*)

To illustrate the two ways we transfer information to long-term memory, consider how people learn the concept of *rhombus*. The rhombus (☐) is defined as "an equilateral parallelogram usually having oblique angles." To store this information in long-term memory, a student might write out the definition and repeat it word for word many times. With adequate rehearsal, even a very young child could remember this definition, but he might not attach meaning to it unless the individual words were already meaningful to him.

To learn the definition meaningfully, a student would have to relate the new concept to past experiences already stored in the long-term memory. If the student had already learned the concept of *parallelogram* or *square*, for example, he or she might attempt to incorporate the concept of *rhombus* by relating it to one or both of these concepts. The student might further divide the concept of *parallelogram* by establishing a category *equal-sided parallelograms*, which would include the rhombus. Or, comparing the rhombus to a square, the student might conceive of a rhombus as "a square that doesn't have all the angles equal," or more simply, "a squooshed-down square." Thinking of it yet another way, a student who had a category of *four-sided figures* that already included parallelograms, rectangles, and squares could incorporate rhombuses by adding another division to that category.

Retrieval

The final stage of the information-processing paradigm is retrieval. Retrieval entails making learned material available and using it. Retrieval is often equated with making an overt response; indeed, to make overt responses, people must retrieve something from their long-term memory. Cognitive processes, such as performing addition problems, also entail retrieval.

Frequently, the search-and-retrieval process is not evident in overt responses—the information is used internally. In the example about learning the rhombus meaningfully, the learner would have to retrieve the concepts of *square, parallelogram, angles, equality,* and so forth. We use search and retrieval in problem-solving, reasoning, and categorizing new information. Although we can only draw inferences about this process, since it is not directly observable, it must occur; otherwise, each new bit of information would represent a discrete category in our long-term storage, and our memory systems would become overloaded.

Failures in Production: Forgetting. What happens when the memory system fails? People may be unable to recall previously learned material because they have forgotten it or because they cannot retrieve it. Forgetting is caused by the passage of time or the interference of competing responses. Some theorists argue that forgetting is a function of the time between the original learning and the attempt to recall. Mem-

In order to spell a word correctly, the student must retrieve the information from his long-term memory. A misspelled word may result from the information never having been stored or from the inability to retrieve the information that was learned.

ory traces, like handwriting on a piece of paper, fade. If not used, the memory traces will fade so much that they cannot be recalled at all.

A more popular theory suggests that interference from competing responses causes forgetting. According to this explanation, forgetting entails two different processes—*retroactive inhibition* and *proactive inhibition.* Retroactive inhibition occurs when new learning interferes with previously learned material. Learning vocabulary words of a second foreign language, for example, may interfere with a person's ability to recall the vocabulary of a foreign language learned previously. Proactive inhibition occurs when original learning interferes with the recall of subsequently learned material. If you are introduced to someone who closely resembles a long-time friend, you may call the new acquaintance by your friend's name.

Failure to recall may also result from an inability to retrieve. The memory traces may be present in a person's long-term memory, but at a particular time or under certain circumstances the person may not be able to recall them. Many of us have at some point been confronted with a test question we know the answer to but cannot answer during the test period. After the test paper is handed in, however, we remember the answer immediately.

Failure to retrieve may result from several conditions. It may be that the information learned was never fully registered in memory, never consolidated with other memory traces. Or when it was encoded the information may have been distorted in such a way that it is not available for retrieval. Categorizing information erroneously may also make retrieval impossible.

Methods of increasing the availability of information stored in the long-term memory will be explored in Chapter 5b. Information that cannot be retrieved is useless; for education to be effective, both teachers and students should be aware of methods that ensure that learned information will be available.

Our discussion of information-processing does not fully describe the complexities of the approach. The sequence of processing is not truly spatial; this is just a way of describing the changes that occur and the durability of the material over time. Input, program, and output are not independent; in actuality, there is a great deal of interaction between these steps. When a person sees the printed word STOP, for example, he searches his long-term memory for a match in order to recognize the symbol. Retrieving the information from long-term memory then facilitates the encoding process, which is begun in short-term memory. The interactions are complicated, but the movement of new information to long-term storage can be expressed as the kind of temporal sequence we have described.

Summary

Cognitive theory offers a view of the learning process different from that of the behaviorist. Based on the premise that man is active rather than passive, this theory suggests that behavior is largely determined by the way the person perceives the environment and how these perceptions relate to the previously-established cognitive structure.

Historically, much of current cognitive theory has its roots in the work of the gestalt psychologists and Tolman. The gestaltists emphasized that learning depends upon the individual's perception of the stimuli rather than an objective representation of those stimuli. The way the stimuli are organized also influences learning, they believed. A third gestaltist contribution was the idea that insight is a phenomenon of learning. Tolman contributed the idea that cognitions are the product of learning and that these cognitions are more than a summation of *S-R* connections. His view that behavior is molar, purposeful, and flexible has influenced subsequent learning theory.

The more current approaches of Ausubel and Bruner reflect not only theory but theory applied directly in the classroom. Ausubel's delineation of the factors that precipitate meaningful learning focuses attention on the individual's past experiences as represented in the cognitive structure, on the materials to be learned, and on the student's intent to learn. Bruner's approach postulates that learning chiefly involves developing categories and building relationships among these

New Directions in Research

Suppose a person is presented with a learning task or a problem that is new to him or her. In order to complete the task, the person will need to attend to and abstract the essential information given in the task, perhaps retrieve relevant information from memory, and develop a strategy for reaching a solution. The research we discussed in this chapter bears on how information is encoded and stored, and on how it is retrieved. How does the person acquire the capacity to control all these components of the cognitive system and use them in a productive manner?

In recent years many cognitive psychologists have focused their attention not only on what we learn and what we know, but on how we come to know that we know (Brown, 1975). There is thus a growing interest in strategies of knowing, including: (1) how we acquire the capacity to accurately predict our own performance, (2) how we learn to recognize when we need to retrieve information from memory, and (3) how we acquire retrieval strategies (Markman, 1973; Brown, 1978; Flavell & Wellman, 1977). This is the topic of *metacognition*, learning how to know. It involves the self-regulation and con-

trol of cognitive processes in such a way that we can utilize them efficiently when we need to. Some have proposed that this self-regulative capacity may be the fundamental difference between the experienced and the naive learner (Brown & Deloach, 1978), the successful and the unsuccessful student.

The acquisition of metacognitive strategies has implications for the cognitive development of children (Flavell, 1970, 1971, 1976b; Flavell, Friedrichs, & Hoyt, 1970; Flavell & Wellman, 1977) for learning in classroom settings (Brown, 1978) and even for learning from text (Brown & Smiley, 1978). This research focus and its relation to educational matters is exemplified in the work of Ann Brown (Brown, 1975, 1976, 1978; Brown & Campione, 1977; Brown & Deloach, 1978; Brown & Lawton, 1977; Brown & Smiley, 1978).

The outcome of these investigations, as they continue, is changing our conceptions of the learning process. Indeed, they may change our very notions about the nature of intelligent behavior. The acquisition of metacognitive strategies is a topic to watch.

categories. The individual's system of categories represents his view of the world.

Information-processing theory attempts to explain learning through an analogy between human mental processes and computers. This approach has been instrumental in encouraging investigations of memory and memory processes. Investigators from this perspective are currently studying how information is stored, the duration of memories, and the processes used in retrieving information from memory.

Although there are commonalities among the cognitive approaches, no single theory truly represents the cognitive approach as a whole. Cognitive theorists have tended to investigate discrete aspects of learning phenomena. Current studies focus on concept learning, learning from prose, learning of spatial relations, and discrimination learning; these topics will be discussed further in later chapters.

TEACHING SCENARIO

Few, if any, teachers become excited by a group of passive learners even when order exists, instructions are followed, and all looks smooth on the surface. Most teachers are happiest when they see enthusiasm and interest exuding from the learners in their charge. Student enthusiasm is probably a reinforcer for the majority of educators. It denotes motivation, involvement, interest, and a payoff for instructional effort. Attaining that level of participation, however, is one of the challenges of teaching.

Ms. Feldman is currently teaching a unit on the Civil War in her eighth grade history class. The students seem bored and unresponsive; they are neither asking good questions nor responding well to her questions. She is finding the lack of student participation disheartening and discouraging; moreover, she worries about the students' test performance under these conditions of lack of involvement. Is there some way Ms. Feldman can increase the relevance of her instruction, increase student interest, and perhaps increase learning of the material as well?

Chapter 5b

Classroom Application of Cognitive and Information-Processing Theories

Introduction

"This just doesn't make sense to me." "I've gone over and over this material and I just can't remember it." "Why do we have to learn this stuff?" "This is too hard!" These and similar statements may be heard in classrooms nearly every day. What are the students really saying? The teacher may view students who make these statements as lazy, incapable of learning, or troublemakers. The students, however, may actually be trying to tell the teacher about stumbling blocks to learning and retention. These stumbling blocks may be student characteristics or behavior, or they may result from the teacher's behavior.

The educational process involves transmitting information, skills, and attitudes to the learner. The transmitter may be a teacher, a medium, such as a textbook or film, or some combination of the two. In the primary grades the major transmitter is the teacher, but as students progress through school, textbooks and other media are used more frequently.

The primary goal of education is for students to meaningfully incorporate information, skills, or attitudes into their cognitive structures. Through the process of incorporation the information is made available for use in future learning, problem-solving, and adapting to the environment.

For convenience, the factors that influence this process will be presented in four categories—learner characteristics, events preceding learning, events during learning, and events following learning. The categories are not discrete in that at every stage learner characteristics interact with the events of learning. In addition, some of the events, although specified at one time, may also occur at other times. Teachers may, for example, use questions to facilitate learning by asking them before the learning begins, as a kind of recitation during the learning, or as practice following learning.

Learner Characteristics

For meaningful learning to occur, the cognitive structure must contain information with which new material may be linked or into which it may be incorporated. Students vary greatly in the quantity and quality of previous knowledge they bring to a learning situation. This prior knowledge influences whether new information is incorporated and whether it is incorporated meaningfully or by rote.

It is self-evident that first graders possess less prior knowledge than seventh graders. Other things being equal, the greater the prior knowledge the greater the probability that the cognitive structure will include links to which the new information may be connected.

Even in a single class, however, the teacher finds diversity in students' cognitive structures. Since it is impossible to get inside the heads of the students to examine their cognitive structures, how can the teacher determine whether the students possess the links necessary to incorporate the new material? The teacher must rely mainly on inference for guidance.

This inference may be drawn from studies of children and adolescents that provide general descriptions of children's cognitive abilities at various ages. In the fourth section of this text (Part IV), we discuss some of the learner characteristics that affect learning. Among these characteristics are age, intelligence, past achievement, and sex. The Part III chapters provide some general guidelines about the kinds of previous experiences children have generally had, the kinds of information or skills appropriate for children with those experiences, and children's cognitive abilities. Many of you will also take a course in child or adolescent psychology that will cover the characteristics of learners of various ages in much more detail. The teacher should apply these guidelines cautiously because they are general and describe the characteristics of groups. The characteristics of individual children may deviate considerably from the typical group characteristics.

To determine whether a specific child possesses the prior knowledge and skills needed to undertake a new learning task, teachers may question students about the ideas needed to learn the new material. This may involve a written test or oral questioning. To use this approach successfully, the teacher must know what prior knowledge and skills are needed for incorporating the new material.

To learn long division, for example, a host of prior skills are necessary, including multiplication, subtraction, and borrowing. A teacher might determine the students' readiness to learn long division by testing these skills. Teachers who have been teaching the same students for some time will probably be able to judge the adequacy of prior knowledge from their past performance. In that case, a test of prior knowledge might be unnecessary.

What about the student who lacks the prior knowledge needed for incorporating the new information? One of two things will probably occur. It is to be hoped that students who lack the needed prior knowledge will be able to acquire it before being presented with the new information. Special remedial help from the teacher can be used to build the needed information into the cognitive structure. If the new information is presented without the prior knowledge, however, it will either not be learned or it will be learned by rote. Rote learning may enable students to answer test questions asking for verbatim responses, but it is not meaningful learning and thus is of little use for the learner outside the testing situation.

▶ *ACTIVITY 1.*   Interview three teachers, one each at the elementary, junior high, and senior high levels. Ask each of them the following questions:

1. "How do you determine whether or not your students are ready to undertake a new learning task?"
2. "Assuming that not all students are ready for a new learning task at the same time, what provisions do you make for children who are not ready?"
3. Compare the answers you received with those of four other members of your class. Do you see any differences or commonalities among the responses of teachers at different grade levels?

Events Preceding Learning

The events that immediately precede an act of learning can have an important influence on how easily students learn the new material and how well they retain the new learning over time. These prior events include reminding the students of relevant knowledge, providing organizing structures, and suggesting appropriate strategies for students to use in learning the new information.

Reminding Students of Prior Knowledge

If the teacher has decided that students have attained relevant prior knowledge, the incorporation of the new material can be facilitated by activating the prior knowledge—bringing it into the students' consciousness. Students must retrieve from their cognitive structure the relevant information to which the new information will be related.

Reminding the student of prior knowledge may be as simple as reviewing the material covered on the previous day. A lesson on multiplying two-digit numbers might begin with a review of multiplication of one-digit numbers. To help students understand the branches of the federal government, the teacher might remind them of previous knowledge of the branches of state or local government. Reviews of this sort actually serve two purposes. First, they bring to consciousness relevant ideas that facilitate the incorporation of the new material. Second, rehearsal of previous learning strengthens the learning and improves long-term retention.

At times, students may need to recall prior knowledge from subjects other than the one of immediate concern. To solve physics problems, students may have to recall the solutions of mathematics problems from previous courses. Student understanding of a work of literature may be improved if students recall the history of the period during which the work was written. Integration of knowledge across subject matter provides a more cohesive cognitive structure, a more complete and integrated picture of the world.

Providing Goals or Objectives

We advocated in Chapter 2b that to guide student learning teachers formulate performance objectives. It has been well established that stating student goals either as objectives or prequestions based on objectives before presenting new material enhances relevant learning (for example, Gagne & Rothkopf, 1975). Stating goals apparently improves both long-term and short-term retention (Duell, 1974; Peeck, 1970).

You will recall from the discussion of memory in the preceding chapter (Chapter 5a) that much of the information that enters short-term memory is promptly forgotten. When students read a textbook or listen to a lecture, some of the material is relatively unimportant to learning, and some is completely unnecessary. Giving students prequestions or objectives helps them determine which ideas or concepts the instructor considers most important. The students can then focus their efforts on encoding the important ideas or concepts and attempting to integrate them into the cognitive structure.

This greater retention of question-relevant or objective-relevant learning often occurs at the expense of incidental learning, learning not specified in the objectives. This implies that objectives and prequestions alter the students' reading or listening behaviors. A student may, in fact, read or listen to the material only to answer the prequestions or meet the objectives. Information that fails to answer a question or meet an objective is either not attended to or is not encoded into long-term memory.

Students may be given several different types of prequestions. Some require that the students construct their own answers, while others require that students recognize a correct answer from a list of possible answers. Prequestions that require students to construct answers seem to be more effective than those that require students to select a correct answer, as in multiple choice or true-false items. Questions or objectives that call for such higher-level behaviors as understanding, analysis, or evaluation seem to prompt more thorough study than factual questions or lower-level objectives.

The fact that students retain information better when they have been given objectives seems to reflect differences in students' purposes. According to Ausubel (1961), the learner must have an intent to incorporate the material meaningfully in order to learn meaningfully. Students can read or listen to lectures without incorporating information into their cognitive structures, or they may learn by rote what they read or hear. Most students have taken courses that seemed irrelevant to their current needs. It is possible to get a good grade in such courses by memorizing certain key concepts and ideas without attempting to understand the material or incorporate it meaningfully into one's cognitive structure. If a student wishes to use the information in future courses, in an occupation, or in solving life's problems, however, he will make a greater effort to incorporate the material into his cognitive structure and make connections with previous learning. Craik and Lockhart (1972) have proposed that information can be processed at different depths, and that the choice of depth is determined by the learner's intent or purpose. Processing at a shallow level entails very little incorporation into the cognitive structure, while deep-level processing involves relating the new material to the cognitive structure as completely as possible. Material that is processed more deeply is retained longer than information learned less deeply.

Advance Organizers

Ausubel (1978) has proposed that advance organizers increase the retention of learned material. An advance organizer is a kind of mental device for incorporating more detailed and differentiated material into one's cognitive structure. It is presented prior to the new material. As we have described it, the cognitive structure includes specific concepts that may be incorporated into more generalized categories; these, in turn, may be incorporated into some superordinate category (refer to Figure 5a–6, p. 166). The advance organizer is comparable to a higher-order category that provides a general framework for incorporating the specific aspects of the material to be learned.

The function of the advance organizer, according to Ausubel, is "to bridge the gap between what the student already knows and what he needs to know before he can successfully learn the task at hand" (Ausubel, 1978, pp. 171–172). An advance organizer, then, is related to prior learning and is stated in familiar terms. It provides a framework for anchoring the new learning by relating it to previous categories or by providing new categories in which it may be included. The advance organizer is more general, inclusive, and abstract than an overview or summary that is at the same level as the new material.

The concept of the advance organizer seems to be in opposition to the usual method of presenting material. Traditionally, teachers and textbooks have presented material in a hierarchical pattern, going from the simplest material to the most complex or comprehensive. Ausubel's proposal seems to reverse this process, providing a comprehensive framework at the beginning and then proceeding to the specific. The goal is the same: an organized body of knowledge that is integrated into a whole.

Several researchers have investigated the effectiveness of advance organizers. Barnes and Clawson (1975) concluded after reviewing studies of advance organizers that their benefit to learning and retention remains unproved. This conclusion was based on a comparison of the numbers of published studies that showed a significant positive effect with those that showed no significant effect or a negative effect. Using a different form of analysis and a greater number of studies, Luiten, Ames, and Ackerson (1980) found that advance organizers improve immediate recall of the material learned and that the advantage increased with retention over longer intervals. The advantage was found across all grade levels from primary through college and in many different subjects. This latest evidence seems to indicate that advance organizers do promote learning and retention and that teachers should use them to help their students incorporate new material into their cognitive structures.

Suggesting Appropriate Strategies

Before presenting material, a teacher may suggest certain strategies that students can use to increase learning and retention. These strategies might include note taking, use of imagery, self-generated questions, or overlearning. These and other strategies will be discussed in the next section of this chapter on student behaviors that facilitate learning during the learning act.

Events During Learning

To learn, a student must attend to the information or stimuli being presented, retain it in short-term memory, and encode it for storage in long-term memory. For learned material to be useful, the learner must be able to retrieve it from long-term memory. Retrieval depends upon the number of different paths by which information can be accessed and how permanently the material is stored. If the material can be retrieved only by one path and that path is blocked, the material cannot be obtained. If information can be retrieved by a number of paths (deeper-level processing), routes of access will be available even when one path is blocked.

The aspects of the learning process we will discuss in this section are attention and a broad group of behaviors termed *mathemagenic behaviors*. Mathemagenic behaviors are acts that facilitate the encoding of material into the cognitive structure and make it available for future retrieval.

Attention

It is a rather self-evident truism that "if you don't pay attention, you won't learn." Attending to the appropriate stimuli in a learning situation is a prerequisite for learning. In any classroom learning situation, a number of different stimuli are present—the teacher, textbooks, bulletin boards, noise in the halls, and other students, to name but a few. Students can consciously control their attention to focus on the task at hand. Attending to some stimuli involves shutting out certain other stimuli and focusing on the selected stimulus. A student's attention may thus be concentrated on the teacher's statements or on reading a textbook. All students know, however, that it is possible to read a passage from a book or listen to a lecture and not remember any of the stimuli presented. This outcome indicates a lack of attention.

Even though students can consciously control their attention, certain aspects of the stimulus situation encourage attention. In order to encourage students to attend, a good teacher will develop a repertoire of behaviors.

The teacher may focus students' attention through the use of manding stimuli. Mands are verbal statements that have a probable consequence attached to them (Skinner, 1957). "Pay attention to this." "This is a very important idea." "Notice the difference between . . ." are statements of this sort.

A teacher can also focus attention by changing the pitch or volume of his or her voice or by changing the rate of presentation. A teacher who normally speaks in a soft voice may get the students' attention by speaking more loudly or changing pitch. Conversely, a teacher can gain attention by speaking more softly. Gestures or movements may also be used to secure attention. A sudden or abrupt change in the stimulus situation can change students' attentiveness. When student attention tends to be unfocused or when the teacher desires to change activities, a simple off-on flick of the light switch can be used as a signal for students to refocus their attention.

The materials students use in learning can also include attention-getting devices. A teacher constructing a worksheet that includes both addition and subtraction problems might use plus and minus signs of different colors or exaggerated sizes to get students to perform the correct function.

Textbook writers focus attention on aspects of their texts by using such devices as underlining, boldface type, and italics. They may also enclose certain definitions or concepts in boxes. Textbook writers and editors use these techniques to focus students' attention on important ideas.

In general, we might conclude that novel stimuli or stimuli that stand out in some way tend to attract attention. Any attention-getting device loses its effectiveness when it is not used sparingly. The teacher who says too often, "This is very important," will find that students fail to respond by attending. Similarly, when too many words are italicized or underlined, the device loses its effectiveness for drawing attention.

Mathemagenic Behaviors

Mathemagenic behaviors are those that give birth to learning (Rothkopf, 1965, 1970). They are behaviors that students can perform in order to encode information into their cognitive structures and to make it available for retrieval. When we teach students mathemagenic behaviors, they are learning how to learn. As we mentioned earlier, teachers may suggest that students use these behaviors, but they are often initiated by the students themselves. The purpose of the behaviors is to encourage the students to participate actively in learning. Active interaction with the learning materials increases learning and retention.

Recitation.   A technique often used to increase learning and retrievability is recitation, in which the students produce a response to questions that have been posed. Recitation may take many forms. The most common form of recitation occurs when a teacher asks questions of a class or of an individual student. Questions interspersed throughout textbooks or at the ends of chapters also require recitation. A third type of recitation, self-recitation, occurs when a student produces both the question and the response. After reading a section of a chapter, a student may construct a question about the passage and then answer it.

Active recitation increases learning and retention. Recitation allows the students to rehearse the learning and rephrase the learning in their own words, leading to deeper processing of the information.

Most studies have shown that active recitation does increase learning and retention (for example, Gall *et al.*, 1978). To actively construct an answer to a question, the student must retrieve from memory. The search through memory for the correct response may help strengthen learning and retrievability by activating the pathway to the desired information. The search may also give the student an opportunity to form new associations in his or her cognitive structure.

Teacher questions serve a number of purposes. They give students a chance to practice or rehearse the learned information. ("What were the names of Columbus' three ships?") Questions can also encourage deeper processing of information. ("Why is the bat not classified as a bird?") The teacher can use questions to focus a child's attention. (To Daisy, who is not attending: "Daisy, what did I just say were the four nutritional groups?") In addition, asking questions gives teachers an opportunity to reinforce correct responses.

Studies of question-asking in the classroom reveal that teachers vary greatly in the number and types of questions they ask and in the ways they ask for responses to questions. Teachers may ask no questions at all, as in a lecture, or as many as 150 per hour, the number found in a review of studies of recitation (Gall, 1970). The evidence seems to indicate that more frequent questioning leads to higher student achievement (for example, Dunkin & Biddle, 1974).

The types of questions teachers ask are often divided into two categories: low-level questions and high-level questions. More precise classification is possible through the use of the *Taxonomy of Educational Objectives Handbook I: Cognitive Domain* (Bloom, 1956). The taxonomy presents a classification scheme in which questions are categorized in terms of the student behaviors required to answer them. The taxonomy is arranged in a hierarchy proceeding from simpler to more complex behaviors.

The first category in the hierarchy includes questions of knowledge, which are low-level questions. Knowledge questions require that the student recall or recognize an idea or phenomenon learned about during instruction. Remembering is the process by which such questions are answered.

Although knowledge is an important outcome of education, teachers normally want the students to be able to use their knowledge. Teachers determine whether students can use their knowledge by asking higher-level questions. The succeeding categories of the taxonomy cover increasingly complex behaviors. To answer questions in these categories, students must recall knowledge and use such additional processes as comprehending, applying, analyzing, synthesizing, or evaluating.

The major categories of the taxonomy are presented in Table 5b–1. We have briefly described the types of student behaviors required for answering the questions in each category. To illustrate the types of behavior required, we have included two sample objectives and two sample questions that teachers might ask for each category. To provide a greater range of illustrations, we have given objectives and questions on a number of different topics and courses.

Classroom recitation questions normally fall in one of the first three categories. The majority are in the knowledge category. The Gall *et al.* review (1978) revealed that sixty percent of teachers' questions required the students to recall facts, while only twenty percent required higher-level responses. The remaining twenty percent were procedural-type questions.

The three higher-level categories, analysis, synthesis, and evaluation, are more often used for examinations or class projects than for class recitation because of the time required to answer them. Low-level questions may reflect the goal of amassing a great quantity of information. Questions that reflect higher-order thinking are perhaps aimed at more thoroughly integrating the learning into the cognitive structure. A knowledge of factual information is a prerequisite to integration, of course, so the acquisition of factual information must be assured before integration-type questions are asked.

Researchers are also interested in knowing which students are asked to respond to questions. Classroom practices vary among teachers. Some may ask questions in a serial fashion so that each student has an opportunity to respond. Other teachers consistently call on those who raise their hands, or, in some cases, those who do not raise their hands. A study by Brophy & Evertson (1976) revealed that more able students are called upon more frequently than less able students. In a review of studies, Gage and Berliner (1979) concluded that patterned questioning is better than random questioning for young children. They also concluded that in order to give all students a chance to respond, teachers should call on volunteers less than ten to fifteen percent of the time.

Textbooks also vary in the number and types of questions asked and in the placement of questions. Textbook authors frequently concentrate on low-level questions, but some ask for responses that require integration, inference, and evaluation. In selecting textbooks a teacher might profitably examine the level of questions asked.

Studies consistently indicate that generating one's own questions as one reads leads to greater learning and retention (Frase & Schwartz, 1975). To generate questions, the student must actively interact with the material being presented. He or she must pause frequently during reading to construct questions, a strategy that requires recalling what was read, and then respond to the questions. Then the learner assesses the adequacy of his or her response and decides what to do next— review, reread, or go on to the next passage.

Note-taking.   Another behavior for increasing learning and retention is note-taking. Students are frequently encouraged to take notes during lectures, and they may use the same strategy when reading. Note-taking offers two advantages. First, the notes serve as external storage of information. Second, note-taking encourages the encoding of information so that it is easier to retrieve.

Notes, as external storage information, are used to review for tests. Reviewing notes improves achievement on tests even when the test and review are separated in time (Carter & Van Matre, 1975). Reviewing notes also involves rehearsing already-learned material, a kind of overlearning that tends to make memories more permanent. The review can increase the number of connections between the new material and that already stored in the cognitive structure. This tactic increases the number of different paths by which information can be retrieved.

The influence of note-taking on encoding seems to depend upon the

TABLE 5b–1. Taxonomy of Cognitive Outcomes

	Class	Student behaviors	Sample objectives	Sample questions
1.00	Knowledge	Recall facts Recall definitions Recall ideas	1. The student will name at least five generals who led the Confederate Armies during the Civil War 2. The student will define the terms *force, mass,* and *acceleration*	1. Who were the three leaders in the development of gestalt theory? 2. What do we call the event that follows a response and increases the probability that the response will occur again?
2.00	Comprehension	Giving descriptions Stating main ideas Comparing	1. The student will define *ecology* in his or her own words 2. The student will translate three metaphors from *Huckleberry Finn* into ordinary English	1. Give an example of vicarious reinforcement. 2. What is meant by the saying, "Don't count your chickens before they are hatched"?
3.00	Application	Applying techniques to solve novel problems	1. Given a behavioral description of a novel event, the student will specify the antecedent and consequent events that control the behavior 2. Given a novel problem, the student will use the appropriate trigonometric function to solve the problem	1. The mean of distribution is 50 and the standard deviation is 4. Compute the z score equivalent of a score of 56. 2. What force is generated by an object weighing 30 grams moving at a speed of 20 cm/sec?

4.00	Analysis	Identifying motives and causes Making inferences Identifying parts of a whole and their relationship	1. In the accompanying advertisement, distinguish the statements based on fact from those that are emotional in nature. 2. Identify the three main arguments in the editorial entitled "U.S. Ally Given Poor Deal."
		1. Given a journal article, the student will differentiate the facts from the inferences in the discussion section of the article 2. After observing a ten-minute debate, the student will detect fallacies in the arguments	
5.00	Synthesis	Combining elements to solve a problem Making predictions Producing an original communication	1. Plan a unit of instruction for a subject you will be teaching, incorporating principles of learning, motivation, and retention. 2. Develop a plan for teaching principles of learning to elementary school teachers in an in-service program.
		1. The student will effectively present an extemporaneous speech that includes all important elements 2. The student will construct an objective examination when presented with a table of specifications	
6.00	Evaluation	Giving opinions about issues Judging the validity of ideas Judging the merit of a problem's solution	1. Given two opposing viewpoints of the cause of the present inflation, evaluate the viewpoints in terms of adequacy, soundness, and rational argument. 2. Recent studies have indicated that coffee may be a cause of cancer. Evaluate three of the studies in terms of the criteria of good research.
		1. The student will compare the theories of Skinner and Bandura in terms of their adequacy in explaining affective, cognitive, and motor learning 2. Given two alternative strategies for solving a discipline problem, the student will apply principles of learning and behavior to select the best strategy and defend the choice with appropriate arguments	

Note-taking in a lecture situation requires the student to be active.
The note-taking may lead to deeper processing of information,
and the notes provide an external storage of the information for
later review.

type of notes taken. A study by Bretzing and Kulhavey (1979) required high school students to take notes from a prose passage. Four groups of students were told specifically what kinds of notes to take; the fifth group read the passage without taking notes. The directions for note-taking were as follows: Group 1, summarize the ideas from each page after reading the page; Group 2, paraphrase the important ideas from each page while reading the page; Group 3, take verbatim notes of the important ideas while reading; and Group 4, copy all words beginning with a capital letter. The researchers hypothesized that Groups 1 and 2 would process the information more deeply and relate it in more ways to their cognitive structures. Their hypothesis was substantiated—members of these groups performed better on an achievement test than members of Groups 3 and 4. Interestingly, the verbatim group performed no better than the group that only read the passage.

Note-taking that requires students to relate new material to their existing cognitive structures increases retention. Writing verbatim notes is time-consuming and seems to provide little or no improvement over reading material without taking notes.

A behavior similar to note-taking is highlighting or underlining passages in textbooks to aid learning and retention. This may also encourage the learner to interact more with the material: the student must attend to the material closely enough to distinguish the more important ideas from the less important. The effectiveness of highlighting or underlining for encoding may be questionable, since the practices are similar to the verbatim condition in the Bretzing and Kulhavey study. These practices may, however, draw the student's attention to important ideas during review.

▶ *ACTIVITY 2.* Observe a teacher in a classroom and record the number of questions he or she asks. As you are recording, write down as many of the questions as possible. Later, classify the questions according to Bloom's taxonomy and compare your results with classmates. Are there differences among teachers in the number of questions asked, or in the levels of questions? Do your findings correspond in any way to grade level?

During another observation, observe the way the teacher asks for student responses to questions. Is the question-asking patterned or random? Does the teacher call on volunteers or on nonvolunteers? Do all children have an equal chance to respond? Does the teacher reinforce correct responses? What does the teacher do when an incorrect response is given?

▶ *ACTIVITY 3.* Select a passage from a book about a subject you are relatively unfamiliar with. Read the passage and take notes on it as you would if you were trying to learn the information for a class. Construct a series of open-ended recall questions that tap the important ideas in the passage.

Using a set of fellow students, do the following: (1) Give one third of the students just the passage and instruct them to read it but not to take notes. (2) Give the second third the passage and your notes. Instruct them to read both the passage and the prepared notes, but not to construct their own notes. (3) Give the final group the passage and tell them to read it and take notes on it. Finally, give all the students your open-ended recall test. Which group appears to remember the most information?

If you are brave, you could repeat this activity using a lecture instead of a passage. The effect may be even more pronounced.

Overlearning. Overlearning occurs when a task is learned to mastery and the learner continues learning beyond the initial mastery stage. Overlearning improves student recall of the material learned. This greater retention is evident immediately after learning and over extended periods of time.

In studies of the effects of overlearning, time has been the variable used to determine amount of overlearning. If it took a learner an hour to master a task and he spent an additional thirty minutes studying, this would be fifty percent overlearning. Spending an additional hour beyond initial mastery would be a hundred percent overlearning.

Studies consistently show that overlearning improves retention over the levels found after initial mastery alone. The increase in retention shows diminishing returns, however. A hundred percent overlearning shows less increase over fifty percent overlearning than fifty percent overlearning shows over initial mastery (Krueger, 1929). These diminishing returns are probably due to the labor and boredom involved in overlearning. After a task is mastered, the learner is ready to proceed to new tasks; continued practice may become tedious and reduce the attention given to the task.

Overlearning may improve retention by increasing the number of connections between the new material and that learned previously. It is also possible that overlearning improves recall by strengthening the initial associations. When overlearning is so extensive that little searching is necessary for retrieval, responses may be almost automatic.

Imagery. The encoding process of a student who is reading a textbook or listening to a lecture may be facilitated if the student constructs a mental picture or an image of the information. To form an image, the student must actively attend to the material being presented; this in turn requires that the student relate new information to that already in his cognitive structure.

The effectiveness of the imagery strategy depends upon the material being presented and the student's developmental level. Depending on how concrete or abstract the information is, some materials are easier to image than others. Information about concrete objects is easier to image than abstract information. A cylindrical object rolling down an inclined plane may easily be imaged. Abstract words without concrete referents, such as *justice* and *democracy,* make imagery more difficult.

Giving students instructions on imaging strategies increases learning and retention (Kulhavy & Swenson, 1975). Constructing the image seems to provide more pathways for the information's retrieval.

The ability to image appears to be a function of development. Children younger than eight or nine use no imagery in learning, and attempts to teach them the strategy have proven ineffective (Dunham

& Levin, 1979). After age eight or nine, however, studies have shown differences in both immediate and delayed retention between children who image and those who do not.

Instead of depending upon the learner to construct an image from verbal descriptions, the teacher can provide external imagery in the form of a picture in a textbook or a schematic drawing. Television or other media may also be used. In a study of fourth graders, Peeck (1974) found that recall was better when text was accompanied by pictures than when learners were given text alone. The improved recall was found after both one day and one week.

Imagery may give students a second way to encode information. Paivio (1971) has suggested that students store verbal information in one storage system and pictures in a second. This strategy creates more paths by which the information can be retrieved and thus improves retention over time. You will learn more about the effects of imagery in Chapters 12a and 12b.

> ► *ACTIVITY 4.*   List between fourteen and twenty nouns that name concrete objects. The words should represent real things (*dog, orange*) but should not be related. Select two groups of fellow students. Instruct one group to listen to the words and try to remember them. Read the list and then have the students write in the correct order as many words as they remember. Instruct the second group to form images between pairs of words as they hear them (for example, a dog with an orange in its mouth). Then read the list again and have these students write the words in the correct sequence. Which group does better?
>
> If some students in the first group recall the word list accurately, question them about the strategies they used. Anything interesting?

Mnemonics.   Mnemonics are strategies designed to improve memory through the use of a coding strategy external to the material being learned. Instead of learning the number of days in each month—January has thirty-one, February has twenty-eight or twenty-nine, and so on—most of us were taught "Thirty days hath September, April, June, and November . . ." Many students learn the trigonometric functions by learning the name of the Native American tribe—SOH-CAH-TOA. *Every Good Boy Does Fine* and *F-A-C-E* are mnemonics familiar to beginning music students.

Mnemonics seem to be effective for learning sequences, and they

Scenario Suggestion

Work by cognitive psychologists tells us that students learn most effectively when they are actively involved in the learning process. Apparently, Ms. Feldman is not achieving this active involvement. Perhaps she is depending too much on a lecture presentation that predisposes the students to a passive mode of participation.

In order to increase active learning, Ms. Feldman needs to design activities that encourage deeper involvement than lectures do. She might try breaking the class into small discussion groups, where an issue already presented in a lecture can be debated by the students who in turn prepare a summary of their discussion. Another idea, though it requires more preparation, is to have the groups reenact, within a gameboard format perhaps, a specific incident of historical significance. The historical facts could be incorporated into the activity as the students recreate the events in a meaningful way.

Still a third idea is to have a debate in a role-playing session in which individual students assume the identity of key historical figures—the generals, the abolitionists, the slave owners, and so forth. The students would then need to research their roles in or-

der to express accurately the positions of the figures they represent, thereby making the researched material their own.

There are many other possible activities that might be planned. The key is the active participation of class members. The formats suggested here encourage involvement with the material, making it one's own. Content may take on new meaning and importance for the students, for they will be expressing it in their own way, in their own words. Improved test performance could be a side benefit as well.

In the teaching scenarios of this section we raised four major issues facing educators: (1) assessing and reporting student progress, (2) maintaining classroom control, (3) individualizing instruction in accord with student characteristics, and (4) generating student enthusiasm and motivation. We presented hypothetical situations articulated to these issues and offered possible suggestions for dealing with those dilemmas. These scenario themes cut across a variety of educational topics, however. You will encounter these themes again. Scenarios still to be considered will differ, as will scenario suggestions, but the same or similar themes will reemerge.

---

may be used to increase retrievability. Very elaborate strategies to improve memory have been formulated. Although such elaborate strategies have been proven effective, they have been used primarily by memory experts in the entertainment field.

Mnemonics can be used to improve recall, but they should be used with caution. It may be less efficient to construct a mnemonic and commit it to memory than it would be to spend the same amount of time on the material to be learned. Some students use mnemonics to learn lists by constructing acronyms from the first letters of the concepts or terms included in the list. Morris and Cook (1978) found that first letter mnemonics do not facilitate the learning of new lists of concepts, but they seem to be effective for remembering the order of a set of concepts or terms already known.

Events Following the Learning Act

After initial learning has been completed, various actions can be taken to increase retention. Practicing the information appears to be crucial to increasing the probability of retrieval. Practice can take many forms: rereading, review by the learner or through questions from the teacher, testing, or any other activity in which the student must interact with the learned information. Additional practice may strengthen the retrieval pathways or increase the number of connections to previously learned information. The effectiveness of practice may be influenced by its timing and the conditions under which it occurs.

Some laboratory studies indicate that the greatest percentage of forgetting occurs during the first twenty hours after learning (Ebbinghaus, 1913). This may be due to intervening activities or incomplete encoding at the outset. To decrease this initial forgetting, recently learned material should be practiced within twenty-four hours of the initial learning. A common teaching practice is to briefly review what was taught the preceding day before introducing a new lesson. Subsequent periodic reviews will strengthen retrieval pathways further.

Giving students opportunities to practice under a variety of conditions should increase their retention. The greater the variety of conditions, the more connections are formed with the existing cognitive structure. Mathemagenic behaviors such as active self-recitation and imagery may also strengthen retrieval pathways and increase the number of connections.

Summary

The behaviors of both teachers and students influence the ease with which material is learned and the efficacy with which it is retrieved. Teacher practices that facilitate learning include (1) being aware of student characteristics that affect learning, (2) reminding students of prior knowledge relevant to the new material, and (3) providing goals, objectives, and advance organizers. Teaching students such strategies as note-taking and imagery should also facilitate learning and retention. Students should be encouraged to recite what they have learned, practice it, and overlearn material to increase their retention.

The processing of information and the acquisition of information from a variety of stimuli are popular topics in contemporary cognitive psychology. A great deal of research by both psychologists and educators is now focused on these aspects of cognition. They will be discussed in more depth in Chapters 12a and 12b.

PART III

Focus on the Person: Development

PEOPLE inevitably vary; no two individuals are alike. Accordingly, learners differ in many ways, and these individual differences are crucial to the teaching-learning process. If people are not all alike, we cannot expect them all to respond in the same way to a particular activity or teaching approach in the classroom. Each individual comes equipped with a unique set of attributes, experiences, abilities, and other characteristics that interact with what happens in the classroom. These attributes are *person characteristics,* another type of P in the equation $B = E \times P$. They play an important role in what the individual learns as a result of the educational process.

Because development is an important factor in individual differences, we have made it the focus of the next section of the text. Children differ in their levels of development, and these differences affect both what they can learn and the way they learn; this in turn affects teaching strategies. A knowledge of development processes is thus very relevant to teachers, as it is to parents, social workers, and anyone else who works with children.

We have chosen to examine closely two aspects of development: (1) the development of cognition and (2) the development of language. These abilities are obviously relevant to education. Moreover, as we discuss them we will present the work of another set of major theorists and introduce you to yet another branch of the discipline—developmental psychology.

As we proceed from birth to adulthood we change physically, socially, emotionally, and intellectually. Our cognitive capacities evolve over time. This evolutionary process has implications for learning and instruction, because to some extent developmental processes affect what can be learned and how best it is learned.

In Chapter 6a we examine cognitive development during the maturing years. How does the individual think at one, at ten, at fourteen? We have chosen to address this question by describing how the great Swiss psychologist, Jean Piaget, conceptualized intellectual growth. Piaget has had a dramatic and profound influence on developmental psychology and in many ways has altered our views of the growing person. His insights into children are fresh and fascinating.

If Piaget has affected the psychological community, so too has he influenced education. It is that influence we examine in Chapter 6b. You will, however, reencounter Piaget in later chapters, including Chapter 7a and Chapter 13a.

Chapter 6a

Cognitive Development

Introduction

Four-year-old Johnny is anticipating an airplane trip. Johnny's mother and father wish to make sure that the flight is an exciting and unthreatening experience for him. To prepare him for his adventure, they have taken trips to the airport to familiarize Johnny with planes, terminals, and all the other features of that setting. Johnny has watched planes take off and land, and he has observed the loading and unloading of passengers. When departure day arrives, however, Johnny is agitated and upset. His parents attribute the upset to excitement, but Johnny's behavior worsens as boarding time approaches until finally he cries and refuses to board the plane. When asked why, he replies, "I don't want to go. I don't want to get smaller." Johnny has watched planes take off, has noted that they apparently decrease in size as they rise into the air, and is quite convinced that a similar fate awaits him.*

As an adult acquainted with a variety of visual phenomena, you know that perceived size and distance are related to each other. As a result, you may find Johnny's remark humorous. How did you learn the relationship between size and distance? You acquired this physical information through your experience, which Johnny has not had time to equal. Information that an adult takes for granted is not necessarily part of a child's reality. Youngsters are not merely miniature adults with the same world view as fully-matured individuals. Obviously, they are smaller and younger, and they know less than adults, but they apparently think and perceive the world differently, too. Adults seem to know this intuitively on the basis of their experiences with children.

*The anecdote is based on one reported by K. Campbell during a class discussion.

It is not so common to know just how children do view the world, nor do we necessarily know why they view it as they do. Personal recollections of childhood tend to be too idiosyncratic, cloudy, and distant to provide us with an explanation.

A knowledge of child development is important to those concerned with teaching, for the obvious reason that most teachers face classrooms of children. The children's developmental level will largely dictate what they need to know and the way they can best acquire that information. Teachers must adjust their instructional methods and their expectations to the maturity of the learners.

The field of developmental psychology is a branch of the discipline that focuses on the changes associated with growth. Originating in rather informal child study, it has more recently evolved into a systematic examination of the processes associated with sequential changes in human abilities (Wohlwill, 1973). The purposes of this examination have been (1) to devise theories of developmental change, (2) to identify the causes of change, and (3) to meaningfully describe the sequence of change. The hope, however, is not just that these discoveries will help us understand children, but that we will also learn something about ourselves as a species.

Philosophical and Psychological View of Children

Interest in children and in human growth is not restricted to psychologists. Parents and prospective parents need to know about children, as do teachers. Legislators need developmental information in order to design laws to protect children from abuse, neglect, and unfavorable influences. Television programmers, advertising people, clergy, social workers, and movie makers are all interested in children, whether their purpose is to entertain them, protect them, or help them. Concern for children is a broad social issue, not a narrow scientific one.

People's attitudes toward the social issues related to children tend to be rather subjective. As members of a particular society, we have strong feelings about our young and are concerned with the direction of their growth, since the children of one time become the adults of the next. How could one approach such a topic in a totally objective way? Our subjective interest originates in social attitudes toward children and in the value we place on them socially, emotionally, and even economically. These values have changed throughout history, but concern for children and even their education has always been an important social issue. The styles in which children have been educated, and for that matter whether they have received formal education at all, reflect changing values and philosophical views of their place in society.

Developmental psychologists and educators are not immune to the influences of social context. They, too, have socially derived attitudes about children, which affect how and what they choose to study about them. Moreover, these philosophical biases and values have been incorporated into scientific theories of child development.

This blending of philosophy and science is evident in the ideas of early developmental psychologists, whose philosophical positions were reflected in their scientific statements. One of these investigators, G. Stanley Hall, was heavily influenced by Darwin and the accompanying biological determinism possibly implied by an evolutionary perspective. To Hall, child development was primarily a process of biological unfolding predetermined by genetic make-up. Hall also assumed that the unfolding maturation of the individual mirrored the evolution of the species. For Hall and his immediate successors, the purpose of child study was thus to describe and catalogue the maturational changes both in behavior and physical structure that accompany an increase in age, and to give to their accounts the overall flavor of biological determinism.

John B. Watson, on the other hand, was a strong environmentalist. Watson's general position was also reflected in his statements about children. He is reported to have claimed that, given appropriate control of the environment, he could determine what kind of adult any infant would become. Obviously, since Watson offered environmental determinism, he and Hall expressed opposing views.

Biological and environmental determinism as philosophical views did not originate with Hall and Watson. Watson's position is not unlike the philosophy advocated by John Locke in the seventeenth century. Locke proposed that a newborn child is like a blank slate, or *tabula rasa*, which is written on by experience and sense impressions. Accordingly, Locke recommended that rewards and punishments be used prudently to form the developing child into a socialized, civilized adult. Locke also had his antithesis—Jean-Jacques Rousseau, the French philosopher. Rousseau depicted childhood as a naturally good state, arguing that children who were let alone would automatically mature into moral adults. He regarded civilization and particularly formal socialization as destructive to this natural unfolding process. These philosophical theories, which emphasize our earlier point that views about children reflect views about the nature of mankind, have influenced modern scientific approaches to study of the child.

A View of the Child in Modern Developmental Psychology

In contemporary approaches to child development, neither the pure, hard-line positions of Hall and Watson nor the philosophical arguments of Locke and Rousseau are explicitly stated. Modern approaches do, however, reflect the thinking of these earlier theorists. The ethnological perspective, for example, emphasizes species characteristics as determinants of behavior in a manner reminiscent of Hall (Achenbach, 1978). Behavioral perspectives, on the other hand, stress the importance of environmental variables, as did Watson and his predecessor, Locke (Bijou & Baer, 1967).

Some analysts divide today's developmental paradigms into two categories that can be traced to views represented in philosophy since the Renaissance or even earlier (Reese & Overton, 1970). One category includes *organismic* approaches to development. Organismic models emphasize biological factors, the growing person as a developing organism, and the whole person as a complex, indivisible system. In this view, development progresses through stages, and the general sequence of development is fixed, though it may be modified to some extent by environmental forces.

The other category includes *mechanistic* approaches. Here, the analogy for the person is a machine made up of discrete parts. As the machine is developed, more parts may be added, but the nature of the machine itself remains the same. According to this view, stages are basically irrelevant because behavior change progresses quantitatively—more and more parts are added in a continuous fashion. Behavioral development is not fixed; rather, it progresses in response to environmental demands.

In this modern dichotomy, Rousseau's views coincide with organismic models of development, whereas Locke's are echoed in mechanistic models. Philosophy, and therefore social values, are reflected in scientific theories and research.

Organismic Approaches.   This dichotomy of models is reflected in what investigators choose to study about children and the way they conduct their research. Organismically-oriented psychologists are likely to examine (1) stages of development, (2) sequences of growth, and (3) the child functioning as a whole in a complex environment. They tend to deemphasize the effects of environmental factors on behavior. With this general orientation in mind, psychologists plan their investigations, decide what data to record, choose situations in which to collect data, and draw data-based conclusions.

Reflecting the biases of its model, organismic developmental research tends to be *descriptive;* child behavior is described as a function of maturity. Researchers observe child abilities associated with specific age levels and try to explain them. Sometimes this is done through *longitudinal studies* in which one group of children is observed on repeated occasions as the children grow older. Differences in the children's behavior at Time 1 and Time 2 are attributed to their differences in age. Descriptive age-related research can also be conducted *cross-sectionally* by observing groups of children of different ages. Differences in behavior between the groups of children are again attributed to age.

This method was used extensively in past research; today, many psychologists advocate the longitudinal method (McCall, 1977). Developmental psychologists influenced by organismic views are more likely to use these descriptive approaches in a natural setting, such as a classroom, preschool, play group, or family group. The laboratory is less frequently chosen as a research site.

The results of longitudinal and cross-sectional studies provide data about the way children's behavior changes with age. Age is a somewhat unsatisfactory variable, however, since it represents only the passage of time, and this factor alone fails to explain why an event occurs. Rather than concluding that changes in age cause changes in behavior, investigators ask why behavior changes with age. This question cannot be answered well with descriptive methodologies. Age does index a host of other changes going on within the individual, such as physical ones, neurological ones, and experiential ones. These changes may be causative; age *per se* is not.

Theories of child development that grow out of age-related descriptive research usually propose that some internal change associated with age is actually the cause of development. Important internal sources of behavior that may be responsible for change include biological forces, cognitive structures, and other factors. Such internal constructs as these, however, must be inferred rather than observed. Because age is an important index of internal changes it is used as a basis for drawing inferences.

Mechanistically Based Research.   Psychologists who use a *mechanistic* model ask different questions and study children differently, too. Stages of development, for example, are of less interest to a mechanistically inclined investigator. Instead, the mechanistic psychologists examine the way a feature of the environment or a particular experience affects the behavior of children of different ages.

The research approach best suited to mechanistic studies is the experimental paradigm described in Chapter 2a. In this paradigm, investigators design experiments in which children are exposed to a controlled stimulus event, and the resulting changes in the children's behavior are observed and recorded. The conclusions about cause and effect emphasize the role of the environment in development. Drawing unambiguous conclusions about cause requires the experimental rigor best achieved in the laboratory.

Experimental child research has predominated in the American psychological literature for about the last ten or fifteen years, overshadowing the descriptive variety (McCall, 1977). Much has been learned about child behavior through the use of this approach. More recently, however, the paradigm has been criticized as inappropriate, since much of it is laboratory based; critics say it may reveal relatively little about the natural course of development. Nevertheless, laboratory studies have increased our knowledge of children, contributed to the growth of developmental theory, and helped developmentalists become more sophisticated in their investigations.

Models and Theory.   It is from research in child development that developmental psychologists build their theories. There are both organismically based and mechanistically based theories (Reese & Overton, 1970). They differ dramatically in focus, content, explanation, and the aspects of development given priority. In this chapter, we have selected one theory to discuss in some detail, that of Jean Piaget (Flavell, 1963). This choice is made for a variety of reasons. First, Piagetian theory examines children's *cognitive* and *intellectual* development, which makes it especially germane to classroom learning. Second, intellectual development is given priority over other aspects of development in this theory. Third, educators have been greatly influenced by Piaget's observations about children and have incorporated his thinking into curriculum design. Finally, the Piagetian approach has generated both controversy and research. In some way it has influenced what virtually all developmental psychologists choose to investigate.

Basic Components of Piagetian Theory

The Swiss developmentalist Jean Piaget (1896–1980) wrote prolifically for sixty years about children's cognitive development. He and such collaborators as Barbel Inhelder investigated children's thinking and produced many insightful observations upon the way youngsters build their ideas about physical reality, mathematics, number, space, and other phenomena (Gruber & Voneche, 1977). Adults have constructed ideas about the physical universe that can be represented by formal mathematics; children have no such view of the world. Discovering the nature of children's view of the world and describing the way the misconceptions of childhood evolve into sophisticated adult thinking were the major thrusts of Piagetian work.

Trained originally as a biologist, Piaget refocused his attention on children and their cognitive development, but he carried his biological background into this new area. Biological organisms adapt to their environments; humans are biological organisms, of course, and we adapt through our intelligence. It is the intellectual adaptation of the developing person that Piaget described.

Content and Method

Piagetian developmental theory is an example of *interactionism*—both personal characteristics and environmental events are considered important sources of behavior. The theory is also an example of *structur-*

alism because it includes a depiction ˙of the structure of human cognition (Gardner, 1973; Gruber & Voneche, 1977). Many of Piaget's ideas about children and his style of studying them are characteristic of the organismic model of man described earlier. His work reflects aspects of Rousseau's philosophy, too (Brainerd, 1978). Piaget preferred to classify his work as *genetic epistemology,* the study of the growth of knowledge. Since children are the containers in which concepts and knowledge develop, they logically became the subject of his inquiry. Again, it seems that Piaget's attempts to understand children were at least in part a reflection of his desire to understand our species.

For Piaget, genetic epistemology was concerned with reasoning, thinking, and the development of thought. More specifically, he focused on reasoning about physical reality, a topic that has interested philosophers for hundreds of years. His choice of logical thought as a topic is exemplified even in the titles of his books: *The Child's Conception of Physical Causality* (1927), *Construction of Reality in the Child* (1954), *The Early Growth of Logic in the Child* (Piaget & Inhelder, 1964), *The Child's Conception of Space* (Piaget & Inhelder, 1956), and others.

You encountered the term *cognitive structure* in Chapter 5a. Piaget

The clinical method was recommended by Piaget for determining the cognitive ability of the learner. Whether the child gets the right answer or not is not as important as the clinician's skillful questioning in determining how the child arrived at the answer.

The child's ability to conserve volume can be measured by the Piagetian task. If the child is able to conserve, she will declare that the volume remains the same regardless of the shape of the container.

chose to describe the sequential changes in cognitive structure that occur throughout childhood. Recall that an internal construct such as this cannot be directly observed. How, then, can it be described? Rather than being observed, cognitive structure must be inferred. To draw inferences researchers must use methodologies that yield clues about internal processes. These clues are observable behaviors, ones that permit the investigator to ask, "What must the child's thinking be like if he behaves in this way?"

Piaget's investigative tactic was to encourage the child to act on some problem so that he could infer the thinking behind the child's action. He called this approach the *clinical method*. He sometimes also used naturalistic observations as the basis for inferential clues. Often the child was given a problem to solve, and the investigator elicited not just the child's strategy for solving the problem, but the child's explanation of the solution as well. Both types of information reveal something about the child's cognitive structure.

In one study, for example, an experimenter presents a four-year-old with two identical glasses of juice filled to the same level and placed next to each other. The dialogue between the experimenter (*E*) and the child (*S*) might go as follows:

> *E:* Do these glasses have the same amount of juice, or does one have more?
>
> *S:* They're the same. They're both this tall (with accompanying gesture).

Then the experimenter pours the contents of one glass into a tall, thin glass. Since the second glass is smaller in diameter than the other two glasses, the liquid rises to a higher level. The child observes this transformation, and questioning continues:

> *E:* Now look at these two glasses. Do they both have the same amount of juice?
>
> *S:* No.
>
> *E:* Does one glass have more? Or are they the same?
>
> *S:* This one—more. (Pointing to the thinner glass)
>
> *E:* How do you know?
>
> *S:* It's tall. The juice is this tall!
>
> *E:* But look, I can pour it back again (*E* returns the juice to the original container.)
>
> *S:* Now it's the same . . . It was more.

The child solved the problem, provided an explanation, and produced a sample of observable behavior. Why has the child solved the problem in this manner? An older child or an adult would not behave in this way, but, interestingly enough, this is fairly typical of a four-year-old's reply. How must the child be thinking in order to reach this outcome? In the clinical method, this type of behavioral sample is used to infer characteristics of the child's reasoning, the state of the child's cognitive structure. This style of inferencing is represented in Figure 6a–1.

There are some interesting features about the role of the experimenter in the example. First, the experimenter is actively involved in the task, questioning the child, probing for more information, and even challenging the child's answers. This involvement is designed to obtain as much information about the child's thinking as possible. Second, the experimenter's behavior is flexible. Depending on the child's particular responses, alternative questions and probes are used. In a sense, the child, not the adult, directs the process. Third, only a few children

FIGURE 6a–1. Style of Inferencing Appropriate to the Clinical Method

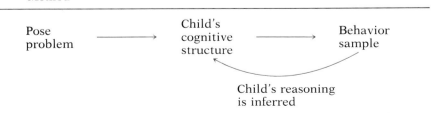

are typically included in one experiment, but these few are examined individually with extensive questioning.

The tasks have some interesting features, too. Review the example and recall the anecdote that opened this chapter (p. 203). In each case, appearance and logical necessity are in conflict. The plane appears to decrease in size, but adults know that this is logically impossible. The juice in the thin container appears to increase in quantity; but since nothing was added, we know there is not more. Adults base their solutions on logic, not appearances; we know from logic which elements in the environment remain constant during change. A young child, however, is unable to call on logic for an answer, so he thinks the appearance of change is change. Many Piagetian tasks pose a contradiction between appearances and reality. A child who has developed a mature style of thinking will solve the problem logically, but a less mature child cannot.

In order to describe a child's cognitive structure, the experimenter needs samples of behavior that reflect the cognitive structure. Moreover, in order to provide useful clues the samples must distinguish between styles of thinking. Piagetian methodology is well suited for obtaining behavior samples that meet these two requirements.

Method and Theory

The clinical method provides clues for inferring the child's mental processes. One clue, however, can be used in a number of ways. The interpretation of behavioral clues depends on the characteristics of the interpreter as well as on the clues themselves. To understand Piaget's inferences we must remember his background, his interests, his goal.

First, recall that Piaget was trained as a biologist, and, in biology, species characteristics take precedence over the characteristics of individuals. Second, remember that he classified his theory as an epistemology, a philosophical topic. Philosophies emphasize characteristics of mankind rather than differences between individuals. It thus appears that Piaget was interested in man as a species and the growth of knowledge in the species. This is not, then, a theory about individual differences in intelligence; it is a search for generalities about human thinking and human growth across individuals.

A researcher's desire to favor either generalities or the characteristics of individuals will affect his style of inference. To illustrate, suppose we have two six-year-old children, Patricia and Wayne. Both children are tackling the problem of ordering a group of sticks of varying lengths from shortest to longest. We watch the children struggle with the task, observe their strategies, question them about the outcomes, and then give them a second group of sticks to add to the arrays they have constructed.

We end up with two behavior protocols. The more verbal child,

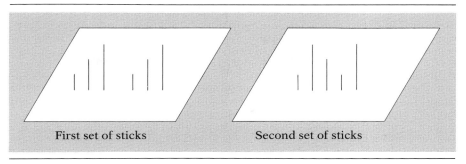

First set of sticks   Second set of sticks

Patricia's Protocol

Patricia, produced a stream of conversation, giving each stick a name and telling a story as she worked at the task. She built two uncoordinated series of sticks, each with its own story. When the second set of sticks was presented, she placed them randomly on the table and smiled with satisfaction at having completed her task. Wayne, on the other hand, remained silent throughout his performance. He concentrated intently on ordering his first set of sticks, working with great difficulty and becoming agitated. When presented with the second set of sticks, he sighed, piled them on the table, leaned back, and refused to play with us any more.

Depending on our initial biases, we will compare the protocols and draw different inferences. If we assume that children's behavior is a product of idiosyncratic experience and genetic make-up, and that Patricia and Wayne differ in these respects, then we would expect their performances to reflect their uniqueness. We would emphasize differences: (1) Patricia described, Wayne did not verbalize; (2) Patricia was pleased with her performance, Wayne appeared frustrated; (3) Wayne built a series of four and a series of two; Patricia built two series of three sticks each. Through our task we collected and compared data and drew conclusions about the differences we observed. If we continued in this manner with more children, we would be on our way to building a mini-theory about children's seriation performances. If we

Wayne's Protocol

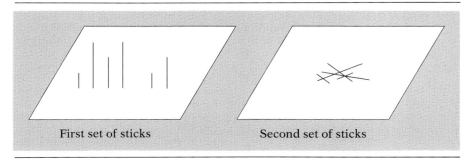

First set of sticks   Second set of sticks

continued to emphasize differences in performance and proficiency among children, the resulting mini-theory would be one of individual variation similar to psychometric notions of intelligence (Chapter 8a).

If we began our analysis of the protocols with another set of assumptions, however, the outcome would be different. This time let us assume that children's performances are mostly a function of developmental maturity. Since both Patricia and Wayne are six years old, they are probably at about the same developmental level. In this case, we would emphasize the commonalities in the protocols: (1) Both children produced two uncoordinated series, (2) neither child was able to place all six sticks in one final series, and (3) neither child was able to insert the second set of sticks. Again we have collected and compared data and drawn conclusions from it, but this time our conclusions depict generalities, not differences. If we extended the work, the resulting mini-theory would emphasize trends across children, not individual differences among them.

This second intellectual route shares characteristics with Piaget's style. Rather than noting variations from a theme, investigators seek universals in child functioning, a theme consistent across individuals. This search for theme is one way to build social science theories (Diesing, 1971), and it is consistent with the Piagetian approach.

The two tactics in our example resulted in different outcomes, ones that fit the initial assumptions. Where do those initial assumptions come from? They derive from the theorist's philosophical model of man. To understand what Piaget said about children, you must understand his initial assumptions.

Theoretical Assumptions

By extrapolating from Piagetian writings we can identify assumptions and themes that tie together specific aspects of this view of child behavior. The first theme is biological. Members of a species share common features, such as morphological structure. An organism's physical form gives it a limited range of behaviors that it can use to adapt to the environment. Organisms that belong to the general class *birds* have the morphological feature *wings*. The feature common to members of the human species is intelligence. This feature permits the behavior of reasoning, and it is through reason that people adapt to the environment. Flight is a biological adaptation; reason is a psychological adaptation. Theorists who stress a biological theme assume that the two kinds of adaptation are of the same nature.

A second theme concerns whether the organism adapts actively or passively. Piagetians assume that people are active. They interact with the environment, act on it, change it, and change themselves, too. Theorists who have a passive view of man assume that people act only in response to environmental pressure. By contrast, Piagetians assume that humans have a biological drive to adapt—to search out contact with the environment, initiate action, and come away with new behavioral adaptations.

Intellectual adaptation involves constructing knowledge. From each interchange with the environment, people acquire new knowledge and, subsequently, new behaviors. The person with increased knowledge continues to engage in environmental exchanges, an activity that creates additional adaptations. As a result of this host of encounters, people enlarge their knowledge structures.

What a person can and will do in a particular encounter with the environment depends on the state of this previously-acquired knowledge. A book, for example, is a piece of the environment. Children of various ages can interact with the book, but their interactions will take different forms depending on their developmental levels. An infant is liable to grasp the book, push it, or suck on it. A two-year-old might pull on the pages, carry it around, throw it, or drop it. A four-year-old might sit with the book, leaf through it, and look at the pictures. A six-year-old will try to read it. The same object is acted on in each exchange, but the actions are different. The determining factor behind the actions is developmental level.

We can summarize the themes in Piagetian theory as follows:

1. Humans are biological organisms that, like other organisms, adapt to the environment.
2. The drive to adapt is an innate biological motive, a species characteristic.
3. In accordance with this drive, humans play an active, dynamic role in the adaptation process.
4. One important form of human adaptation is intellectual.
5. The outcome of a specific adaptation depends on the current state of the person's intellectual structure, which has been created through past adaptations.

The biological theme, the importance of action, and the primacy of structure are critical factors. These statements, then, are the assumptions that guide investigations and conclusions about human development. They are assumptions because they cannot be proven objectively. They are, rather, the *givens* from which further testable statements are generated.

Components of the Theory

To fully understand the course of development, we must know (1) the end product of development, the nature of mature intellect; (2) the initial state, the characteristics of young, undeveloped intellect; and (3) the rules of the transformations that link infant and adult. These elements, depicted in Figure 6a–2, were all dealt with by Piaget.

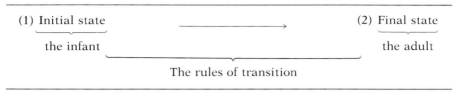

FIGURE 6a–2.   The Three Parts of Developmental Change

The adult intellect is capable of a variety of mental actions, including (1) the manipulation of language in oral discourse, writing, and reading, and (2) the formal manipulation of abstract symbol systems, such as those found in mathematics, chemistry, physics, and propositional logic. Armed with these intellectual tools, adults reason about hypothetical circumstances, mentally conduct experiments and test hypotheses, and solve problems with a minimum of trial and error. Infants, on the other hand, have none of these representational capabilities. If thought is comprised of language, symbols, and logic, and infants possess none of these tools, how do infants think? Infants can use only their senses, perceptions, and limited physical capabilities. Nevertheless, they mature into adults who can use formal representational tools. The transformation takes time, and as it is occurring, a series of intermediate tools are employed.

Stages and Transitions.   Piaget divided the sequence of development into a series of periods. Each period is characterized by the use of a certain type of primary intellectual tool. Since the tools vary according to period, children's ability to reason varies, and the outcome—knowledge—varies, too. Piaget's stages reflect these differences in developing children's thoughts, knowledge, and actions.

The four periods and the approximate age ranges associated with them are:

1. The sensorimotor period   0–2 years
2. The preoperational period   2–6 years
3. The concrete operational period 6–12 years
4. The formal operational period   12–adult

Each period is characterized by a certain style of thinking and interchange between the person and the environment. At each level, children interact with other people and with things in the world and as a result acquire knowledge that prepares them for future interchanges. This knowledge is acquired gradually and sequentially as children mature. The knowledge acquired in the early stages prepares the individual for the next stage; each stage builds on its predecessor. Development thus progresses in a fixed order; stages cannot be skipped, and the order cannot be altered. Each stage is also marked by certain specific accomplishments that allow the person to move on to new intellectual challenges.

Structure and Stage. Stages are defined in terms of the cognitive structure, or *schemes*, that people use in order to think and solve problems. Schemes are action routines or behavioral programs, both mental and physical, that are used to discover the environment. They are essentially characteristic ways of behaving that are used to explore, manipulate stimuli, and discover how the world works. Infants, for example, have a sucking scheme. When a baby encounters a physical stimulus, he or she is likely to suck it whether the stimulus is a breast, bottle, toy, or the baby's own hand. This action program can be applied to a wide variety of objects in order to obtain information about them. The infant will find that breasts and bottles produce nutrients when sucked and that toys and hands do not. The infant's action schemes are coordinated into more complex routines to create new schemes. The sucking scheme, for example, can be combined with the grasping scheme. The infant might encounter a toy, reach for and grasp it (application of grasping scheme), and then pull the toy toward his or her mouth and suck on it (application of sucking scheme). The infant has created a new, more complex scheme that can be applied to a range of other environmental stimuli.

Toddlers, armed with the action schemes acquired during infancy, have more sophisticated routines for interaction, routines that increase their range of exploration. Preschool-age children, for example, can understand verbal symbols, talk, run around, and use their other motor abilities. They use these new abilities and programs to learn even more about the physical and social world.

School-age children have developed even more sophisticated programs, further increasing their range of interactions. They now possess mental as well as physical action sequences. Children at this level have developed operations, which are acquired mental action programs that can be used to solve problems with concrete objects. Together, the individual operations form an integrated set of coordinated mental schemes that Piaget described in terms of mathematics and logic. Equipped with operational tools, school-age children use their intellects to solve a wide variety of physical problems and to learn about reality in ways impossible for younger children. Unlike Patricia and Wayne, school-age children can order a set of sticks of varying lengths and insert another set of sticks in the ordered array. When questioned, they also know that if a blue stick is longer than a red stick, and the red stick is longer than a black stick, then the blue stick must also be longer than the black stick.

Adolescents are even better equipped. Their mental action schemes are fully symbolic, coordinated, and integrated. Not only can they solve problems encountered in the real world, they can mentally create hypothetical problems, apply their mental programs to these problems, and solve them. In short, they can act on a purely symbolic mental level, something younger children cannot do. Like school-age children, adolescents can solve seriation problems, but they can do so without concrete objects. Given only the symbols A > B and B > C, they easily conclude that A > C.

The defining attribute of each period of development is mental structure. Children in the various stages use different mental structures, which evolved from previous stages. With each transformation, new experiences are possible. New knowledge is constructed from these experiences.

The development of the intellect is thus a type of metamorphosis, one somewhat analogous to the biological metamorphosis that occurs during the life cycle of the butterfly. Beginning as an egg, the creature that will develop into a butterfly first emerges as a caterpillar. As a caterpillar, the creature adapts to the environment by feeding voraciously on the leaves of plants. After a certain period of the caterpillar stage, when enough gardens have been consumed, the caterpillar spins a cocoon and transforms itself in form and behavior. From the cocoon emerges a butterfly, a creature obviously different in structure from its earlier form. Its behavioral adaptation has changed, too; for its brief life the butterfly feeds on the nectar of flowers.

The evolution and transformation of the human intellect is not as dramatic as the transformation of the caterpillar, but there are similarities. Structure is a defining characteristic of both. Sequential transformation of structure over a developmental cycle occurs in both. It is impossible to find an adult butterfly that has not served its preparation time in the earlier stages, just as it is impossible to discover a mature intellect that has not accomplished the tasks of earlier stages.

The Means of Progress.   So far we have described the end state of development, the initial stage, and the benchmarks recognizable along the way. A complete theory of development must also explain the rules of change, the way movement from one level to another occurs. Piaget's explanation of *structure* describes the form of the intellect. His *periods* are developmental benchmarks. His description of *function* is an explanation of the means of change.

Function is the general manner in which the organism interacts with the environment across developmental periods. According to Piagetians, a person adapts to the environment and meaningfully organizes the outcome of these adaptations. Piaget assumed that, rather than unsystematically receiving sense data, people organize sense data into coherent pieces of information. Knowledge does not exist within sense data, it is created from sense data by the person. Function is the means by which the construction process, the metamorphosis between raw data and understanding, is accomplished. The organism plays an active role in this construction; it does not merely passively receive information.

In order to understand the idea that knowledge is constructed rather than perceived, imagine that you are standing on a set of straight railroad tracks that go off into the distance. If you look toward the horizon, the tracks appear to get closer and closer together. Your senses tell you that the tracks in the distance actually are closer together than those you are standing on, but you know that that is not the case. You have constructed a concept of parallelism that overrides immediate sense data. Moreover, you did not learn about parallelism just from looking at railroad tracks. Your knowledge goes beyond your perceptions. Function is the means by which you developed that knowledge.

The function process has two parts, *organization* and *adaptation*. People engage in both processes in all developmental levels, so function, unlike structure, is not stage-specific.

Adaptation consists of two subprocesses, *assimilation* and *accommodation*, which complement each other and occur simultaneously in any adaptive act. Given a scheme or program, a child can apply it in one of two ways. In assimilation, the form and sequence of the scheme remain unchanged. Old programs are applied to new stimuli in basically the same fashion. The objects acted upon can vary, can be familiar or unfamiliar, but the general form of the scheme remains constant. Infants put everything in their mouths; children learning to count count everything; budding engineers take everything apart. Same scheme, new stimuli.

An infant who has constructed and integrated the grasping and sucking scheme, for example, can apply that scheme to a wide variety of specific objects. Balls, bottles, blankets, and toes can be grasped, drawn to the mouth, and sucked. These objects are *assimilated* to a general scheme of action. The program is constant; the objects the program is applied to vary. To give another example, suppose a toddler has acquired knowledge of the class *dog*. He or she knows that dogs are playful little creatures that one can play with, pet, pull on, and so forth. When encountering a *dog* the toddler is likely to engage in a similar pattern of behavior. New stimuli, new dogs, can be assimilated into the old program.

Reality imposes certain limits, however, on how new stimuli can be treated. Bottles produce food when sucked; blankets do not. Cocker spaniels are safer to play with than Doberman pinschers. Behavior must be adjusted to adapt to the unique characteristics of the particular stimulus. The dog lover must adjust his or her behavior, approaching and playing with cocker spaniels but avoiding snarling Dobermans. When behavioral routines must be changed to adapt to new stimuli, we are dealing with accommodation. The scheme must *accommodate* to the environmental demands.

With a few exceptions, acts of cognitive adaptation involve the simultaneous occurrence of assimilation and accommodation. It is through this dual process that cognitive progress is made; programs are accommodated and new events are assimilated to these programs. As a result, our cognitive structures elaborate, becoming increasingly complex and sophisticated.

To adapt, an organism must have an existing structure that can be accommodated to new encounters or that can assimilate them. Structure and function, then, are interrelated in producing the child's observable behavior; behavior is, in turn, the evidence of structure and the result of function. The interrelationships between the major components of the theory—structure, function, and behavior—are depicted in Figure 6a–3.

When accommodation and assimilation occur in complementary fashion, the child and his environment are in balance, or *equilibrium*. Assimilation allows the child to approach new stimuli as old ones were approached and to interact with them; through these interactions accommodation occurs, and differences in new stimuli are taken into account as well. When they are in balance, the child's programs help him explore and discover the world. As children accumulate more experience, however, they sometimes encounter contradictions suggesting that their set of tools is not totally adequate. Then the child enters a state of *disequilibrium*. To achieve equilibrium again the child will have to reassess and perhaps reorganize his tools. This is the process of *self-regulation*.

Suppose, for example, that a boy of kindergarten age is sitting on the floor with a cup of five marbles. He places the marbles in a row and counts them. Then he rearranges them in a circle and counts them again, and subsequently repeats the process with a square, a triangle,

FIGURE 6a–3.   **The Interrelationships of Structure, Function, and Behavior**

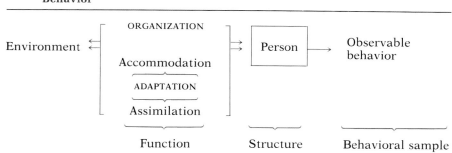

and a long, spread-out row. Each count yields the same outcome—five. This situation appears to be a contradiction; the spatial arrangements are different, but the counting acts are the same. How can the child integrate the elements of sameness and difference into a single unit that explains both? To deal with the apparent contradiction, some cognitive reorganization will be necessary. Experience leads to dis-equilibrium; in order to regain equilibrium a better set of mental tools must be constructed. This, then, is how developmental progress takes place.

Stages and Developmental Tasks

According to the Piagetians, the basic components of development are *structure*, the tools of the child's thoughts; *function*, which relates these tools to the environment; *equilibration*, which explains movement to more advanced levels of adaptation; and *content*, the behavioral man-ifestations associated with progress. For the most part, Piaget examined children's reasoning about physical reality, so most contents are be-haviors that reveal this reasoning. At each developmental level, young-sters use their available tools to acquire some concepts about physical reality, building upon and elaborating notions acquired earlier. Because the accomplishments of different stages are related, in order to under-stand the development of later stages we must begin with the tasks faced by the infant.

The Accomplishments of the Sensorimotor Period

The major task infants face is the discovery of some basic information about the environment. This must be accomplished through the use of rather limited tools—unsophisticated motor abilities, a handful of re-flexes, a fairly sensitive perceptual system, and a drive to know. Using these tools, children discover during this first period (1) that they live in a world of objects, (2) that they, too, are objects in the world, (3) that physical objects have an existence independent of themselves, and (4) that there are relationships between objects and between action and objects.

A critical concept acquired during this time is *object permanence*, the notion that physical objects continue to exist independent of the person (Piaget, 1954). If you take a toy from a young infant and hide it beneath a cover, the child will probably not try to retrieve the toy even if it is within reach. To an infant, an object that is no longer in view no longer exists. By age two, however, the child will be able to retrieve the toy, even if you hide it under a blanket, put a box over the blanket, and move the box to a new location. The concept of object permanence develops gradually during the intervening period. At the first level,

According to Piagetian theory, the infant discovers
reality through physical manipulation of objects.
Through this manipulation, the infant learns to
differentiate herself from other objects in the
environment and learns the properties of
these objects.

infants know that objects exist only when they can perceive them. At
the second level, infants tie objects to past actions with these objects.
If a past action made a disappearing object reappear, the action will
be repeated for the same purpose. Perhaps this explains a baby's delight
with peek-a-boo games in which a caretaker's face appears and reap-
pears, to the accompaniment of chuckling and arm swinging. Children
at the third level will retrieve a hidden object if they observed it being
displaced, removing any impediment and recovering the item. If a
small toy is moved twice, however, placed under a blanket and found,

then placed under the blanket and subsequently placed in a closed hand, the infant will search under the blanket, even though he observed the second displacement. The infant associates the object with his last search behavior, not with the hider's last displacement behavior. Having reached the fourth level, youngsters can handle double displacements if they are both actually witnessed, but they cannot manage what is called invisible displacement. Finally, at about the end of the sensorimotor period, the child can skillfully handle all these adult tricks and retrieve objects through a series of visible and invisible displacements.

Retrieval behavior is a revealing clue to a child's thought processes. We can infer that a child who finds an object he cannot see must know that the object exists. If the child can figure out the location of an object following invisible displacement, he must be able to mentally represent the object. Mental representation is the type of internal thought crucial to further cognitive development. The attainment of object permanence is thus an important cognitive benchmark, one that permits additional intellectual growth.

A growing infant acquires its knowledge of objects by experimenting with them. Objects are grasped, sucked, thrown, kicked, held, and manipulated. Physical actions are the means by which reality is investigated. Infants often repeat their actions in order to solidify their budding knowledge. A parent, for example, may be mildly irritated when toys placed in a playpen are quickly pitched over the rail and pitched out again as soon as they are replaced. The infant, however, is exercising its throwing scheme and discovering the attributes of objects; they crash, bounce, bang, and so on. Physical action produces an outcome. Through physical experimentation, the infant learns a principle of cause and effect—the origins of a young scientist, perhaps.

When armed with a Piagetian perspective, watching the behavior of sensorimotor children can be very interesting. At this level, children's thoughts are expressed as physical actions because they possess no alternative internal forms. The author once observed a toddler in a setting that was decidedly unchild-proof. The room contained a glass coffee table that was invisible to someone two and a half feet tall. The child bumped into the table, much to her surprise. How could something that did not appear to exist cause a bump? A contradiction. The child began acting on the glass table—feeling it, banging it, licking it, and so on (applying old schemes to a new stimulus—assimilation). Through this activity she apparently discovered that she could see through this obviously solid object. How can one see through a solid thing as if it were not there? A second contradiction. Further experimentation followed. The child collected knickknacks from other parts of the room, carted them to the coffee table, held them beneath it, and peered down through the top (new routines adapted to the special attributes of glass—accommodation). The child used her physical actions as a tool to discover something about the characteristics of glass.

By the end of the sensorimotor period, developing children know a great deal about (1) objects, (2) cause-and-effect sequences, and (3) the results of actions and physical experimentation. In addition, they can use some internal representations, or *symbols*. They can mentally represent absent objects. By age two, for example, most children can use language to some degree, and language is a symbol system. They can also engage in imaginative play in which one object is used to symbolize another. When they have reached these milestones, children are ready for the next period of cognitive accomplishment.

The Accomplishments of the Preoperational Period

Children from two to six years are usually described in terms of the abilities they lack rather than the abilities they demonstrate (Flavell, 1963; Gelman & Gallistel, 1978). They are physically proficient, and they are accomplished verbalizers, but they still have misconceptions about physical reality that surprise most adults.

Piaget revealed preschool children's misconceptions through a series of tasks that distinguish preoperational thinking from the thinking of older children. The most famous of these tasks were the conservation problems (Piaget, 1954). The episode with the juice glasses, described previously, is one example of a conservation task.

Some conservation tasks tap *identity conservation*. In one such task, a ball of clay is presented to the child. Then the clay is transformed, rolled into a sausage shape. The child must determine whether a change in quantity accompanied the perceptual change. The preoperational child will insist that it has, even if the sausage is returned to its ball shape. There is a contradiction inherent in the child's solution, of course, but the preoperational child neither recognizes nor deals with this contradiction.

In tasks that tap equivalence conservation, two equal quantities are presented to the child, and one of the quantities is then transformed. The child must determine whether after the transformation the two quantities are still equivalent. Again the preoperational child will say that the initial equivalence was destroyed even after a reversal of the transformation has been demonstrated.

Other tasks are used to test conservation of other dimensions, including number, volume, weight, and mass. Regardless of the dimension being tested, the child's task is the same: to preserve the initial equivalence in spite of a perceptual transformation.

Preschool children's failure on conservation tasks reflects certain qualities of their thinking. First, they ignore contradictions. Second, their thinking is dominated by perception, since the appearance of change is regarded as actual change, even when it is logically impossible. Third, children at this level seem to lack understanding of reversibility, the notion that every operation has a reverse operation that will cancel it. Fourth, preschool children fail to realize that changes in one dimension are compensated for by opposite changes in another. Juice poured from a short, wide glass into a tall, thin one rises to a high level, but it also becomes narrower. The two changes balance each other.

Another group of tasks taps the child's reasoning about class membership (Inhelder & Piaget, 1964). Suppose you present a child with a group of blocks in two colors, ten red ones and three blue ones, and ask, "Are there more red blocks or more blocks?" You are asking about class membership across a hierarchical relationship, as diagrammed in Figure 6a–4. To answer correctly, the child must compare a subclass with the general class. Logic dictates that the general class always be larger than the subclasses that make it up, but this is not apparent to preoperational children. They will tell you there are more red blocks even after counting the red ones, counting all of the blocks, and being asked the question a second time. The outcomes of the two counting acts are not coordinated, and contradiction is again ignored.

A third type of task is designed to tap children's ideas about spatial relations (Piaget & Inhelder, 1956). In this task, Piaget and others (Laurendeau & Pinard, 1970) presented children with a model of a miniature landscape containing three distinct mountains. The child is seated on one side of the model and asked to predict how the landscape would look from the other sides. The child demonstrates his or her knowledge by selecting one picture from a set in which all the views are depicted. Preoperational children typically point to the picture that coincides with their own perspectives. This choice is seen as indicating the child's egocentrism, his inability to understand that there can simultaneously be several perspectives of the same thing.

It is from these tasks and many others like them that the preoperational child's thought processes have been inferred. The qualities of thinking identified through this procedure include: (1) failure to deal with logical contradictions, (2) failure to coordinate hierarchical rela-

---

FIGURE 6a–4.   The Class Relationships in a Class Inclusion Problem

General class
All blocks

Sub-class ←   +   → *Sub-class*
Red blocks   Blue blocks

tionships among classes, (3) dependence on perceptual information, (4) failure to understand the operations involved in compensation and reversibility, and (5) pervasive egocentrism. Perhaps now it is clear why little Johnny assumed he would shrink when he took off in an airplane.

The Accomplishments of the Concrete Operational Period

Concrete operational children can use many of the tools of adult logic. They can solve conservation problems and explain their judgments. As egocentrism wanes, they learn to predict the perspectives of others. They can successfully manipulate and coordinate classes and perform seriation tasks correctly. Not only can concrete operational children solve tasks correctly, they can provide explanations consistent with the rules of logic. They are thus logical thinkers, but their logical thinking is successful only when it is tied to the concrete world. They can solve problems logically if the problems are tied to real objects or events.

To understand the logical limitations of concrete operational thought, compare the operations of algebra and arithmetic. Algebra represents in formal and abstract terms the same operations children learn with number symbols. Most children in this stage cannot handle algebra, however. To children in this period, the symbol 2 has a concrete referent, two objects. Symbols with concrete referents can be manipulated and acted upon; the relations between them have meaning. What is the referent for the symbol *a* in an algebraic statement, however? Any number? This symbol is not a concrete entity in the real world, so it is more difficult for children at this level to cognitively act on. Or suppose you show a concrete operational child the following statements:

1. All sheep are green.
2. George has a sheep.
3. Is George's sheep green?

The answer will most likely be, "Of course not, everybody knows sheep are not green!" The concrete operational child can use logic to solve problems, but only when the problems are based in concrete reality.

The Accomplishments of the Formal Operational Period

When children move from the sensorimotor to the preoperational period, they become capable of making mental representations, and their thoughts are no longer tied to their own physical actions. With the move from the preoperational to the concrete operational period, thought is freed from dependence upon direct perception. In the final step, on the way to formal thinking, thought dispenses with the constraints of physical reality and becomes abstract, symbolic, flexible, and logical.

A formal thinker can deduce on the basis of the givens that George's sheep must be green; the fact that sheep are not green in reality is irrelevant to his conclusions. Formal thinkers can manipulate symbols that have no external, concrete referents; they are thus capable of algebra as well as arithmetic. Thinkers at this level can also grasp simultaneous perspectives of the same phenomenon. Perhaps this is why debate teams are found in high schools but not in elementary schools.

In Piaget's view, the formal operational child thinks like a scientist. Suppose, for example, that Ernestine Engineer is given four beakers containing different chemical solutions, all of which are colorless and

At the formal operational level, the student develops formal patterns of thinking and is able to think logically, rationally, and abstractly. The science laboratory experiment provides the student with the opportunity to hypothesize, to test the hypotheses in a logical way, and to reach conclusions.

Research Report

As we noted earlier in the chapter, to study the growth of logic in children Piaget used the *clinical method*. This method is unlike the experimental methods preferred by most American psychologists because it is flexible and unstandardized across subjects. When Americans were discovering Piaget in the early 1960s, therefore, many investigators conducted *replication* studies in which Piagetian ideas about childen's thinking were reexamined with more standard psychological methods. The purpose was to determine whether the original results would be found again under more controlled circumstances. The study we selected for this chapter is one such replication study.

In Piagetian theory, successful performance depends on a person's ability to apply a scheme or logical structure to the solution of problems. The problems may vary, but the underlying knowledge needed to solve them is basically the same. You might expect, then, that once a child has constructed this basic knowledge, he or she would be able to apply it equally well in all contexts. In other words, once children attain operational thought, they should solve all operational tasks equally well. This does not seem to be the case, however. Many investigators, including Piaget, have noted the occurrence of *horizontal decalage*—uneven performance on tasks related to the same logical structure.

Decalage is evident in conservation tasks. The basic logic—the fact that transformations in perceptual form are unrelated to changes in amount—is common to all conservation problems. The concept of *amount* varies from task to task, however: children can be asked to conserve number, mass, volume, and so on. It seems that it is more difficult to conserve relatively abstract dimensions, such as volume, than it is to conserve less abstract ones like number. A horizontal decalage thus exists for conservation.

Piaget predicted an age-related sequence among conservation tasks. Mass can supposedly be mastered by seven- to eight-year-olds, weight can be mastered by nine- to ten-year-olds, and volume by eleven- to twelve-year-olds. Replication studies suggest, however, that volume may be a more difficult dimension, one not mastered by most children until adolescence.

Using group tests, Elkind examined adolescent subjects' responses to conservation problems in mass, weight, and volume. Subjects were presented with two identical balls of clay and asked a series of four questions. The first tapped knowledge of the initial identity: "Do both balls contain the same amount of clay?" The second question called for a prediction: "Suppose I made one of the balls into a sausage, would the two . . . still contain the same amount of clay?" The third question was asked after one ball was actually formed into a sausage: "Do they both contain the same amount of clay now?" Finally, an explanation of conservation was required. These questions were repeated with *weight* and *volume* substituted for *amount*. To pass each task, the subjects had to respond correctly to all four questions on a given dimension.

From the data analysis, volume proved to be a much more difficult dimension than amount or weight. In fact, only the oldest subjects mastered conservation of volume.

This study supports the existence of horizontal decalage for conservation. It also points out that cognitive development occurs within stages as well as across stages, since all subjects were of formal operational age. Even in a stage theory like Piaget's, development can be seen as a gradual process in which new competencies emerge continually.

Elkind, D. Quantity conceptions in junior and senior high school subjects, *Child Development*, 1961, *32*, 551–560. (a) odorless; an eyedropper; a flask for combining the chemicals; and a chemical that when added to a certain combination of the others will turn it green. A number of different combinations are possible (if you are formal operational, you can figure out how many). A concrete operational child would proceed by trial and error. Not Ernestine. She first determines all the possible alternatives and systematically combines them until she identifies the correct solution. This, then, is the final stage of cognitive development.

Research in Reaction to Piagetian Theory

An enormous amount of research has been generated by Piagetian theory. There are probably few developmental psychologists who have not in some way adjusted either their thinking or their research as a result of his work. Some of the research was designed to replicate Piaget's study (Elkind, 1961b). Not all psychologists agree with Piaget's analysis of the process of development, however. Investigators who question his findings have tried to produce disconfirmatory evidence.

Criticisms of Piagetian work come from a number of different perspectives. There are those who think young children are much more capable than Piaget claimed, that Piaget estimated children's abilities too conservatively (Borke, 1971, 1975; Bower 1971). Others suggest that Piagetian tasks are too complex, noisy, and imprecise to reveal what young children think (Flavell, 1976a). Many of these investigators offer procedural and methodological criticisms of the means by which Piaget drew his conclusions. Others suggest that alternative theories explain children's produced behavior better—more parsimoniously and more elegantly.

Some critics question the tasks Piaget used to elicit behavioral samples from which inferences were drawn. The tasks are typically very complex, a fact that opens the door to questions about the reasons the child fails. Does failure indicate a misconception of reality, or could it instead suggest that the child's difficulty was in understanding what was asked of him, or that the child had problems remembering (Bryant & Trabasso, 1971)?

Many criticisms of task complexity concern the language used by the experimenter (Siegel, 1978). In a conservation task, for example, the presentation of the problem employs such relational words as *same* and *more* (Griffiths, Shantz, & Siegel, 1967). When the child chooses an incorrect relational term, what does that indicate? It could mean that the child really thinks the quantity changed with the perceptual transformation, but it could also mean that the child failed to understand the quantity terms in the same way an adult would (Donaldson & Balfour, 1968). When the child fails, it is impossible to determine the specific cause of the failure. An ample body of research evidence suggests that failure may result from problems with language (LaPointe & O'Donnell, 1974); when the language of the tasks is significantly altered, different performance patterns are found (Braine, 1959; Mehler & Bever, 1968).

A second language problem is the Piagetian requirement that a verbal explanation be given along with correct performance as proof of understanding. A young child may solve a problem correctly but be unable to explain his or her solution. In short, the child may know more than he or she is capable of verbalizing. The Piagetian requirements for success are then biased against less verbal children and children from different cultural and language groups (Henderson & Swanson, 1978; Swanson & Henderson, 1979). They thus provide overly conservative indications of intellectual maturity.

The tasks can be too complex for young children in other ways, too. The three-mountain problem that taps visual perspective-taking, for example, is a very difficult task. To succeed, the child must (1) perceive the three-dimensional landscape, (2) understand that he or she must decipher the other views of the landscape, (3) determine the view from each position, and (4) select the match from a set of pictures. Failure is considered evidence of egocentrism. What if the child does not understand the task? When the child fails, again we do not know why. When the task is changed just a bit, young children are much more successful than Piagetian theory would predict (Shantz & Watson, 1971; Borke, 1978; Horan & Rosser, in press).

Another body of Piagetian-instigated research that raises questions about the theory is training experiments. The basic rationale of a training experiment is that if children can learn to succeed on a selected task before it would be expected developmentally, it would indicate that learning rather than development is the important intellectual process (Brainerd, 1978). If learning is the key, then we don't need to put forth a separate theory to explain development *per se;* we already have learning theories.

Conservation is a target of many training studies. Children have been trained to conserve through the use of reinforcement (Butcher & Schneider, 1973), through modeling (Zimmerman & Rosenthal, 1974a), and through social interaction training (Murray, 1972). Seriation has been similarly trained in preoperational-aged children (Swanson, Henderson & Williams, 1979; Rosser & Brody, 1981; Horan & Rosser, in press), as have many other skills (Zimmerman & Rosenthal, 1974b; Brainerd, 1978).

Another problem relates to the use of a stage construct to explain development. Proving the existence of stages of development poses logical and methodological problems. Many feel that Piagetian work has been unable to overcome those problems, and specifically that children's performances do not really occur in a stage-like progression.

New Directions in Research

In the past, Piagetian research has tended to follow one of two courses. First, using variations of the original tasks, some investigators examine performance on those tasks as a function of age. These investigators follow essentially the same procedures as Piaget and his collaborators but with methodologies characteristic of American psychologists. A second alternative is to relate performance to variables other than age, such as stimulus factors (Odom, 1978), task demands (Borke, 1978; Siegel, 1978), or specific learning experiences (Brainerd, 1973, 1978; Rosser & Horan, in press; Zimmerman & Rosenthal, 1974b). The first course is basically developmental; the second is experimental and based on learning theory.

In the last few years a third alternative has emerged—treating task performance as an incidence of problem-solving. Then the outcome is explained on the basis of information-processing principles rather than developmental ones (Farnham-Diggory, 1972; Klahr & Wallace, 1976).

One interesting and rather unique feature of the information-processing approach is that one must specify in considerable detail both (1) what the task demands are and (2) what the performer must do. As a result we end up with an analysis of the steps required to solve the problem successfully. The investigator tries to assess not just the final outcome but the steps that allow progress toward the outcome. Studies based on this approach yield much greater detail about what is happening in cognitive development. Moreover, the theoretical models built from this detail have greater specificity and greater precision than does the original Piagetian one.

You will find examples of the information-processing approach to cognitive development in the work of David Klahr (Klahr, 1976, 1978; Klahr & Siegler, 1976; Klahr & Wallace, 1976), Robert Siegler (Siegler, 1976, 1978a, 1978b), Rochel Gelman (Gelman, 1972; Gelman & Gallister, 1978), and many others (Trabasso, Isen, Dolecki, McLanahan, Riley, & Tucker, 1978). It is one of the most promising new directions in research.

This criterion is particularly relevant to the period of formal operations. Apparently, many adults fail to perform formal operational tasks even though they are considerably older than twelve. Moreover, formal education affects the performance of these tasks, a fact that again raises questions about the relation between learning and development. Although the answers are not all in, the use of stages to explain development rather than just to describe it remains a problem for Piagetian theory (Ault, 1980).

Conclusions from Empirical Research

Sometimes research raises more questions than it answers. One must sort out the relevant from the irrelevant criticisms. Some research indicates that children can pass Piaget's benchmarks at earlier ages than Piaget's theory suggests. This criticism is largely irrelevant. The sequence of development is more important to the theory than the approximate ages associated with success on the tasks, and the general sequence has not been comprehensively challenged. Even task variation studies really challenge the age issue more than they do the sequence issue.

Training research similarly raises more questions than answers. The fact that a particular skill can be trained in the laboratory fails to indicate how children acquire the competence naturally. Moreover, the learning that results from training may be very specific rather than a generalized change in a child's manner of behaving (Beilin, 1978). Piaget was interested in very broad, generalized styles of behavior and the way these styles evolve and change. Furthermore, he was concerned with the organized system across skills, not the individual skills themselves. It may be that training research and Piagetian research actually address different aspects of child thought. There is much debate between proponents of training studies and more classic Piagetians (for example, Siegel & Brainerd, 1978; Zimmerman, Beilin, Whitehurst, & Brody, 1978); the final results are not yet in.

Piagetian theory is not the final word on child development, but it has revolutionized the way we view developmental phenomena. In the future, more research will be conducted, more will be revealed about children's thinking, and the theory will probably be refined. That is the nature of science. Nevertheless, it is at present the most comprehensive and provocative approach we have.

Summary

In this chapter, we have discussed the way children develop intellectually and construct knowledge of their world. They *adapt* (through *assimilation* and *accommodation*) to their environment and *organize* information procured through their interactions. On the basis of adaptation and organization, children build cognitive *schemes*, organized patterns of behavior. These schemes are integrated into a *cognitive structure* that determines a child's behavioral abilities. Although adaptation and organization continue throughout one's life span, structures change qualitatively with development.

The kinds of structures children possess at different ages determine their *stages* of development. These stages are the *sensorimotor, preoperational, concrete operational,* and *formal operational* periods. Roughly tied to age, the stages occur in fixed *invariant sequence* for all children. At each stage children possess certain tools of thought that are revealed in their approaches to logical problems, the *content* of thought.

Function, structure, content, and stage are the major components of Piagetian theory. Through these constructs Piaget explained the way young children gradually create their knowledge of reality and evolve into logical, competent adult thinkers. Explanations concerned with learning, social learning, and information-processing have been offered as alternatives to Piagetian theory. Regardless of continuing debate, Piaget had a tremendous influence on the way we think about children. His impact has been felt not just in psychology but in education as well. This is the topic addressed in the next chapter.

TEACHING SCENARIO

Two themes identified in previous scenarios were (1) individualizing instruction and (2) generating enthusiasm. Our next scenario incorporates both. Developmental level is one of the personal dimensions that teachers need to take into account; that is, they must adapt instruction to the individual maturity of their learners. Moreover, from a Piagetian perspective, when the adaptation occurs appropriately the learners are more likely to be engaged, active, and involved. Engagement is motivating. Instructional design with developmental differences in mind predicated on increasing engagement may be similarly motivating.

Mr. Ramirez's first grade class recently took a trip to a natural history museum. One of the displays the children observed was a large pendulum in motion; they were fascinated by it. At the time they saw it, many of the youngsters questioned Mr. Ramirez about the pendulum—how it worked, what controlled its speed, and so forth. While he tried to answer the questions as best he could at the time, Mr. Ramirez recognized that for the most part his verbal explanations were meaningless to the children.

Now he wishes to take advantage of the children's natural curiosity and spontaneous interest in the pendulum. He wants to plan instructional activities to elaborate on the children's museum experience. What might be a good approach?

Chapter 6b

Cognitive-Developmental Theory: Implications for Practice

Introduction

In reading the last chapter you may have noticed that many Piagetian tasks are of a mathematical or scientific nature. If you assumed that Piagetian notions have influenced math and science curriculums, you were correct (Varma & Williams, 1976). It would also have been correct to assume that Piaget's interpretation of young children's behavior has affected preschool programs (Kamii, 1972). You were mistaken, however, if you concluded that Piaget, the prolific writer, wrote extensively about educational practice. He did not.

Piaget's relative silence on educational practice is a reflection of his interests. Piaget created the philosophy of *genetic epistemology,* a far-reaching examination of the growth of knowledge. He focused on the global organizing principles of human thought, not the particulars of instruction. Epistemological issues may also focus on the individual, of course, but not in the same manner as an educator would (Guadia, 1977). The teacher wants advice on how to teach Susie to multiply, how to present physics principles to Brent in a meaningful way, how to explain geometric proofs so Margie can see the logic of them. The educator needs specific direction for promoting the intellectual progress of individual learners. Piaget focused less on the individual than educators do.

Many educators profess to subscribe to a general Piagetian philosophy, and many write about educational applications. Classrooms have been reorganized along what are presumed to be Piagetian guidelines. New, supposedly Piaget-derived curriculum materials have been designed, and suggestions abound for improving instruction in accordance with Piaget's theoretical perspective (Guadia, 1977). While all is supposedly based on the work of Piaget, little of it was specifically recommended by him, since he said little about education in general and even less about specific issues (Groen, 1978). What should be discussed, then, in a chapter on the educational applications of Piaget?

We could take a liberal stance, as some writers have done, and describe innovations derived from the Piagetians regardless of whether they have much basis in the theory. We have instead chosen the conservative route, for two reasons. First, it may be intellectually dishonest to present applications as Piagetian when they may not be. Second, we prefer to remain close to the intent of Piagetian theory. As for application, therefore, we present what we see as Piaget's broad impact in two general areas. The first relates to his influence on the process of instruction. The second is his impact on subject-area content.

Piaget's Impact on Process

Educators can benefit greatly from the increased understanding and sensitivity to children that comes with knowledge of cognitive development. Armed with a Piagetian perspective, you will find that children's activities are more enjoyable and definitely more interesting. Their solutions to problems and even their failures become clues to use in deciphering their thought processes.

To develop this kind of sensitivity to children's thinking, you must watch them, interact with them, talk with them, and listen to them. By doing so you will gain personal insight into the phenomena Piaget described. Moreover, you will learn through firsthand observation how you as a teacher can facilitate development. There are a number of ways to gain this sensitivity.

> ► *ACTIVITY 1.*   The first way, of course, is to learn from reading. Such books as Margaret Donaldson's *Children's Minds* (1978) and Singer and Revenson's *How a Child Thinks* (1978) come to mind. These books are written with warmth and understanding and provide a good start. For those interested in the formal aspects of the theory we suggest John Flavell's *The Developmental Psychology of Jean Piaget* (1963), a similar compression by Ginsburg and Opper (1969), or Gruber and Voneche's *The Essential Piaget* (1977). The truly ambitious can inspect any of the books written by Piaget himself.
>
> ► *ACTIVITY 2.*   Examine a current mathematics or science series aimed at children in elementary school. Determine whether the series suggests that concrete objects be used in

teaching. Do you see evidence of actual instruction in the concepts of conservation, seriation, or classification? When you examine teaching materials and instructor's manuals, you may find ample evidence of Piagetian impact on content and instruction.

▶ *ACTIVITY 3.*   One of the most instructive things you can do to understand Piagetian theory is to actually try some of his tasks with children. Attempting a task with an individual child and eliciting the child's reasoning will concretely demonstrate what you have been reading about. Choose a child in an age range that interests you. Adapt one of the following tasks for the child and try it out. Pay attention to what the child says as well as to the performance.

1. Seriation (ages four to nine): Assemble a set of ten sticks graduated in length by about half-inch intervals. Separate the sticks into two sets. The first set should include the even elements of the ordered array (second longest, fourth longest, and so on), and the second set the odd elements. Give the child the first set and instruct him or her to put them in order. Record what the child does. Then give the child the second set to insert into the first set, and again record the child's action. Four- to six-year-olds should be able to manage the first set, but they probably will not be able to manage the insertion task. Note the child's strategy. Concrete operational children generally use some strategy of systematic comparison; less competent children proceed by trial and error.

2. Coordination of perspectives (ages six to ten): Assemble eight identical items into two sets of four each. Arrange the first set in a diamond shape on a table top. You and the child sit on one side of the table. Have a friend sit first to your right, then across from you, and finally to your left. At each position, ask the child to build a display with the second set of items that will show how your friend is seeing the display. Six- to eight-year-olds will have some problem with this. You may find that the child can manage the vertical relationship better than horizontal ones and the horizontal position better than the others. The youngest children will probably build displays that match what they see rather than what your friend sees. This is evidence of egocentrism.

3. Conservation (ages six to fifteen): Look back at the Research Report in Chapter 6a, p. 228. Adapt these conservation tasks and attempt them with your subject. You will probably find

that the child is correct some of the time but not all of the time. This unevenness is called *horizontal decalage.*

4. Hypothetical reasoning (age ten and up): Create a series of statements that begin with an arbitrary premise. For example:

   a. All oak trees have purple leaves.
   b. This is an oak tree.
   c. The leaves on this oak tree are _____?

   Present queries of this sort to your subject. After each answer, ask "How do you know that?" The individual who can reason hypothetically will deduce the correct response from the initial premise. The concrete thinker will appeal to reality: "Oak trees do not have purple leaves."

These activities will give you a chance to observe at firsthand the phenomena Piaget describes and to understand them more fully than you could through reading alone. They may also make you more sensitive to elements of child thought that are easily overlooked, a sensitivity that will help prepare you for further formal aspects of instruction.

The Relationship Between Learning and Development: The Notion of the Match

When looking for Piagetian instructional implications, we must first examine how Piaget envisioned the relationship between learning and development. Learning is the change process we normally associate with instruction; development is the larger process of change. How are the two change processes related?

From a Piagetian perspective, development is a more general process than learning, and it plays a more important role. Learning is a subordinate process restricted by developmental level. This is most clearly stated by the theorist himself:

> I think that development explains learning, and this opinion is contrary to the widely held opinion that development is the sum of discrete learning experiences. For some psychologists development is reduced to a series of specific learned items, and development is thus the sum, the cumulation of this series of specific items. . . . In reality, development is the essential process and each element of learning occurs as a function of total development, rather than being an element which explains development. . . .
> (Jean Piaget quoted in Ripple & Rockcastle, 1964, p. 8)

This quotation illustrates some very important points about Piaget and education. First, he tells us that development and learning are not the same process. The alternative position to Piaget's suggests that development is simply a learning program stretched out over time. This view translates directly to educational practice: Employ learning principles to design a better, more efficient program. Development can be speeded up through learning. This view is in direct contrast to that of Piaget. Piaget informed us that learning is dependent on development rather than the cause of it. We cannot increase a child's rate of development by concentrating on the child's rate of learning.

This raises another issue that has attracted the interest of educators: Can we accelerate development itself? There is no clear-cut Piagetian response to this "American question," as Piaget facetiously referred to it (Guadia, 1977; Gruber & Voneche, 1977). It may be best to respond to questions about developmental acceleration, compressing the time it takes to make cognitive progress, with another of Piaget's often-quoted comments:

> We know that it takes 9 to 23 months before babies develop the notion that an object is still there when a screen is placed in front of it. Now kittens go through . . . it in three months—so they are six months ahead of the baby. Is this an advantage or isn't it? We can certainly see our answer in one sense. The kitten is not going to go much further. The child has taken longer, but is capable of going further so it seems to me the nine months were not for nothing. (Jean Piaget quoted in Elkind, 1969, p. 321)

We may infer from this statement that the rate and speed of development should not be tampered with by applying learning principles or by trying to affect developmental processes directly. The sequence of cognitive development is fixed, and movement through the sequence takes time. If development limits learning, and by implication developmental processes should not be accelerated, what are we left with in terms of instructional advice?

Some have suggested matching materials and teaching techniques with developmental level—that is, we let development dictate learning rather than attempting the reverse. Preoperational children, for example, need to learn about the environment through actual physical activity, the manipulation of objects. To teach these children about the characteristics of objects and procedures for grouping or classifying them, the matching theory approach suggests that they be given real objects to manipulate. Teaching activities that permit children to group objects, pick them up, feel them, and move them around would be preferred to just giving them verbal instruction about classification. In designing activities for preoperational children, therefore, many school programs emphasize experience with real objects in order to help children construct concepts about object qualities.

Young children develop their cognitive ability through the manipulation of concrete objects. The kindergarten classroom will have many manipulables, such as building blocks, which will provide opportunities for children to experiment and to discover relationships between objects.

For another example, recall that the concrete operational child can solve logical problems using concrete objects but not with abstract symbols. To teach arithmetic concepts, a teacher might accordingly provide real objects. Counting strategies, part-whole relationships, fractions, even addition and subtraction can be demonstrated with things as well as symbols. Many current mathematics series initially depict these operations with real objects drawn from the child's environment as a prelude to the use of numerical symbols. This is another example of matching materials with developmental level.

Both of the activities given as examples would help the child acquire knowledge within a stage rather than encouraging movement across stages. Piaget proposed that development is uneven within each stage. Children who have constructed schemes for problem-solving cannot routinely apply the scheme successfully across all situations and materials. As mentioned on p. 238, this unevenness across contexts within a stage is called *horizontal decalage*. Children need to have experiences that allow them to apply newly developed schemes to a wide variety of circumstances. Providing practice with a routine can help the child generalize the routine across new situations and materials.

The occurrence of horizontal decalage has been documented in research on conservation (Reese & Lipsett, 1970). It has been noted, for example, that children usually conserve number before they conserve volume, mass, or weight. Similarly, children can generally order stimuli on the basis of length before they can order on the basis of weight (Baylor & Le Moyne, 1975). In both cases, the general scheme is part of the child's cognitive structure but it has not been extended across a variety of stimuli. Giving the child an opportunity to actively exercise a developing scheme can facilitate growth and development within a period.

Learner Activity

Another assumption basic to Piagetian theory is that of the *active organism*. As described in the preceding chapter, Piaget believed that people seek contact with the environment and act upon it to adapt and to construct knowledge. The acquisition of knowledge should thus not be perceived as a passive transmission of information from teacher to learner. Social transmission obviously plays a role in adaptation, but it is not synonymous with it. The didactic approach of simply explaining or telling a concept to a learner will not ensure understanding.

Suppose you wish to teach a toddler about the geometric form *square*. You could provide a verbal definition of square: a four-sided figure in which all the sides are of equal length and all the angles are 90°. This verbal description includes all the critical information about the concept; but if a youngster initially knew nothing about squares, would this socially transmitted definition enable the child to recognize one? Probably not. The child needs to see squares, draw squares, sort squares out from other shapes, build squares from strips, and so on. Notice that all the verbs used here are active—they describe physical behaviors other than listening.

The same principle would hold if you were teaching beginning chemistry students about the outcome of mixing an acid and a base. Describing the result would be insufficient. Students need to see and experience the outcome, probably through conducting an experiment. A laboratory assignment not only teaches the scientific method (as explained in Chapter 2a), it gives students a chance to interact directly with a feature of the environment.

Most instructional activities involve social transmission, of course. Teachers provide labels for the concepts and phenomena, and they provide feedback as well; but verbal description alone is usually insufficient. For young children to acquire knowledge they must be active, and the activity should be physical.

As learners become older they can be given mental as well as physical activities. In the course of your education, for example, you have probably had to read much difficult material. It is sometimes possible to read passively—your eyes follow the sentences, you understand the words, but you do not really comprehend the content. There are a number of devices that can help you learn verbal material, including (1) *paraphrasing* the material in your own words, (2) *constructing* a written outline, (3) *writing* brief summary paragraphs, and (4) *explaining* it to another person. Each of these procedures involves *construction* because you translate the material into a form that is meaningful to you, a form consistent with your own cognitive structure. Each also requires an active performance. Active involvement in the process of acquiring knowledge is not just for young children.

Piaget's theory is not the only one that considers activity important. Piaget is unique, however, in suggesting that social transmission without action is nonfacilitative and in arguing that there is no equivalent substitute for action.

Equilibration

For children to make cognitive progress, they must be able to recognize and coordinate contradictions. Learners need to experience situations that cannot easily be dealt with by means of the knowledge they already possess. Such circumstances present a challenge—they cannot be solved automatically or by rote. Challenge is motivating and engaging, and it requires active participation from the learner. If a problem is far beyond a child's knowledge and tools, however, its difficulty may be overwhelming or perhaps even unrecognized. The optimal level of challenge encourages learners to make cognitive progress; they must examine the process of solution and reach a new level of equilibrium. Problems that are too easy are not engaging; those that are too difficult are solved superficially or not at all. An intermediate level of challenge is best.

Consider, for example, a conservation of number task. Two rows of five pennies each are lined up in front of a three-year-old. One row is lengthened, and then the child is asked to judge the equivalence of the rows. This problem is way beyond the skill level of a three-year-old. Children of this age cannot recognize its difficulty and logical contradiction. They solve the problem within the limits of their existing cognitive tools, perhaps quickly losing interest. Five-year-olds, however, behave differently because they are proficient with counting and transitional with respect to conservation. Five-year-old Frankie may vacillate in his responses, sometimes saying that the longer row contains more, sometimes that the shorter row does. He may count, change his mind, and eventually reach the correct solution. Transitional children do recognize the contradiction and the problem's difficulty level.

The principles of motor operation may be learned more rapidly by
actually working on a motor than by reading about the operation
of a motor.

Their attempts to rectify the discrepancy involve cognitive reassess-
ment and will probably sustain their motivation and interest. Seven-
year-old James will solve the problem, think you are foolish to ask,
and quickly lose interest in the obvious.

Tasks that facilitate cognitive process or, in Piagetian terms, encourage a new level of equilibration, must be at that middle level—
challenging but not totally unmanageable. Problems that are replica-
tive and too easy overemphasize assimilation. Problems that are too
hard, that are simply mimicked or imitated without understanding,
stress accommodation. Those in the middle involve the equilibration
process that is central to Piaget's concept of cognitive progress.

Tasks of intermediate difficulty may cause cognitive conflict, an
awareness of momentary disequilibrium. Out of this awareness we get
motivation, persistence, and progress without needing to provide external support. Theoretically, this conception of the growth of knowl-

edge makes a great deal of sense. In practice, identifying the optimal challenge is much more difficult, but it is an instructional goal worth striving for.

▶ *ACTIVITY 4.* One of the ways we supposedly learn is by coordinating contradictions. Contradictions will not, however, be recognized if the individual is developmentally unready for it. One way to examine contradiction is to have a child make an erroneous prediction and then show the child the actual outcome. The child's attempt to deal with the contradiction between the prediction and the outcome can demonstrate the equilibration process. Select one of the following tasks, give it to a child of the appropriate age, and observe how the contradiction is managed. If the child fails to recognize the contradiction, you will observe no cognitive conflict in the child's attempt to coordinate the two elements. If the child recognizes the contradiction, cognitive conflict will be evident.

1. *For young children.* Give the child a conservation of number task. After the child makes a nonconserving judgment, ask him or her to count the two rows. After the child has counted, ask for an explanation of how one row can have more if they both contain the same number. Give the child a second conservation of number task. After the child makes a judgment, ask for another explanation. See if the child's performance has changed from his or her first one.
2. *For five- to eight-year-olds.* Obtain two identical beakers (*A* and *B*) and one beaker (*C*) that is taller and thinner than the others. Fill *A* and *B* to the same levels; leave *C* empty. Show the child the three beakers. Explain that you are going to pour the water from *B* into *C*. Ask the child if *C* will have less than, more than, or the same amount of water as *A* after you have poured. Then ask the child to show you how high the water will come up in *C*. (The nonconserver will not recognize the difference in level but will probably predict that *C* will contain the same amount.) Pour *B* into *C* behind a screen, then remove the screen and show the *C* beaker. Now ask again if *A* and *C* have the same amount. Nonconservers will have a conflict problem because they did not expect the height of the water in *C* to increase. Ask for an explanation, and note how the child coordinated the prediction with the observation.
3. *For adolescents and older.* Show the subject a beaker of water

and a small ball of clay. Ask what will happen if you drop the ball in the beaker. Most children of this age will correctly predict that the ball will sink. Perform the action. Then remove the clay ball and describe how you are going to flatten it out into a pancake shape. Most will predict (incorrectly) that it will float. Flatten the clay and perform the act, but be careful not to turn up the edges of the clay. Ask the person to explain the contradiction.

Summary of General Implications

Piaget's theory has several implications for educational practice. Teachers can match materials and outcomes to developmental levels, encourage active learner involvement, and choose tasks that will facilitate equilibration; but teachers can do none of these things unless they are sensitive to students' levels of development. A teacher must be able to determine a child's cognitive level and anticipate where the child is going as well. Sensitivity is also necessary for knowing what sort of resolvable conflicts can be presented to increase motivation. A knowledge of Piagetian theory, then, is indispensable if its wisdom is to be applied in the classroom.

Specific Applications of the Theory

There are many specific applications of Piagetian theory to educational practice. Piagetian notions have been incorporated into assessment devices that identify cognitive readiness (DeMao, 1977), assist in clinical diagnosis (Poulsen, 1977), and measure developmental progress. Piaget's theory has also influenced the design of tests used to assess particular concepts, most notably conservation (Goldschmid & Bentler, 1968). Additionally, some programs geared for perceptually handicapped learners and the mentally retarded (Magary *et al.*, 1977) draw their impetus from his thinking. Most of these programs, however, involve adaptations of general developmental principles to individual differences and remediation. These Piaget-derived devices often end up being used to identify individual characteristics and remedy problems in much the same way that psychometric intelligence tests have been used for decades.

Some educational innovations are geared to all children, not just exceptional ones. These innovations involve applying Piagetian notions about matching the active learner and equilibration to educational planning and curriculum design.

Impact on the Learning Environment

A number of experience-based instructional programs have been built on the Piagetian assumptions that (1) people are self-motivated to adapt to the environment, (2) learners must actively participate in learning, and (3) knowledge must be constructed rather than received. In general, these programs try to insure that learning is based on activity of some sort.

In an extreme form, the teacher in an experience-based program serves as a facilitator rather than an instructor. The teacher designs activities that allow the individual child to choose learning activities suited to his or her individual preferences and needs. Open classrooms, interest centers, and the like are based on assumptions that learning tasks should be learner-directed and activity-based. It is assumed, on rather dubious ground, that children will automatically choose activities that are appropriate for themselves, that they will pursue them for the necessary amount of time, and that they will understand content more deeply than they would with adult-structured direct teaching.

The basic ideas behind this type of learning environment do seem consistent with Piagetian theory, but the practical application of the ideas may or may not be consistent. It is difficult to design and manage learning environments that are totally experience-based. Whether the desired learning occurs in these settings is a debated issue. The long-range outcome of experience-based instructions remains to be seen.

Impact on Curricula

In addition to total learning environments, certain specific content areas have felt the impact of Piagetian theory. In mathematics, for example, the same general themes arise: (1) the mathematics learner is perceived as a constructor of mathematical principles, (2) instructional sequences are planned around the learner rather than around the content, and (3) mathematical operations are examined as analogues of physical actions.

When we consider students as constructors of mathematical principles, we must allow them to find their own mathematical truths. Teachers cannot simply pass on established rules and expect children to comprehend them adequately. In classrooms influenced by Piagetian notions, drill and memorization would be favored less than active problem-solving as an instructional approach. The manipulation of concrete materials would take precedence over paper and pencil exercises with symbols. Discovery of mathematical principles through active manipulation is preferred to direct instruction. These Piagetian innovations have influenced the means, the process through which mathematical information is learned.

Piagetian theory has also influenced the content of instruction. Whenever a teacher wishes to teach a concept to learners, he or she will probably organize and sequence the material on some logical basis. In mathematics instruction, this can be accomplished in many ways. First, one could let the formal structure of mathematics dictate the sequence. This procedure, the type of organization a mathematician might use, served as the basis for some innovations in mathematics instruction in the 1960s. Alternatively, the teacher could organize mathematics instruction in accordance with its sequence of historical development. The assumption here is that the intellectual evolution of the content is the logical sequence of simplest to most complex. Piaget cautioned against both of these organizational approaches (Piaget & Inhelder, 1956). He pointed out that the way a child constructs knowledge is not necessarily consistent with either historical evolution or content as viewed by an adult mathematician. Instead of imposing interpretations on the child, we need to directly examine the way the child develops mathematical knowledge and gear instruction to this sequence.

The Piagetian assumption that instruction should be organized around the learner rather than around content is currently influencing mathematics instruction (Beilin, 1976). Putting this assumption into practice is not easy, however. We do not necessarily know the natural sequence of development for all aspects of mathematics; there is even debate about such basic principles as the development of number concepts (Brainerd, 1973a; Gelman & Gallister, 1978) and notions of space (Martin [ed.], 1976; Kapadia, 1974). The process of organizing mathematics instruction around the learner has begun, but it is far from finished.

A final Piagetian influence on mathematics instruction involves the way we view mathematical operations. One can conceive of them as *rules* that simply need to be learned or socially transmitted. No doubt most of us learned our arithmetic facts this way. Mathematical operations can also be viewed as analogous to physical actions (Lamb, 1977). Many of these actions are conducted at the mental level, but some have comparable physical equivalents.

This idea can be illustrated with an example. The operation of simple addition is the action of combining two sets, so that we know that the set of two twos equals the set of four.

$$2 + 2 = 4$$

We can return to the original state by the reverse operation of subtraction.

$$4 - 2 = 2$$

Scenario Suggestion

Developmental psychologists tell us that young children need to be physically active with the content of their environment—experimenting, discovering, behaving like young scientists. Mr. Ramirez could take advantage of the children's interest in the pendulum phenomenon and create activities that permit this kind of active experimenting.

He might create an interest center, for example, where mini-pendulums could be made and played with. Using a set of small weights and strings of varying lengths, children could make pendulums and observe their action. They could be encouraged to experiment by observing the motion differences that result from varying the length of the string. They might also be encouraged to describe what they see and to hypothesize about the cause of these events.

The childen are too young to derive from these experiences a full understanding of pendulums, but through active experimentation they will learn something, within developmental limitations, about this aspect of their physical environment. What they do acquire and discover for themselves will be more meaningful, more theirs, than Mr. Ramirez's well-intentioned verbal explanations could be.

Learning occurs constantly, not just within scheduled times and specific locations. Many times the environment provides an event or a phenomenon that triggers interest, that generates a desire to learn more. The wise teacher takes advantage of these times, takes advantage of the spontaneous interest of learners. Mr. Ramirez has the opportunity to do just that.

Subtraction is an operation or action that reverses or negates addition, the first operation.

We conduct these operations on a mental level by manipulating symbols without much thought or effort. Young children lack adult tools, however, and they cannot perform the function in the same manner; but there are equivalent operations at the physical level. Buttoning is negated by unbuttoning; building a tower is negated by disassembling it. Spreading out a row of blocks is negated by pushing them back together.

Piaget views mental action and physical action as to some extent isomorphic. If children develop knowledge first physically and then mentally, it follows that a physical analogue could be used as the first step in teaching mathematics operations.

All these innovations in teaching mathematics are predicated on general themes abstracted from the theory. The learner must be active in the construction of knowledge. Instruction should match the natural sequence of the growth of knowledge. Viewing mathematical procedures as mental actions that have analogies to physical actions follows from the theory, too. Whether these ideas will have a widespread influence on practice remains to be seen.

Summary: A Cautionary Note

Although many of these innovations are currently in practice, questions about their fruitfulness remain. The general Rousseauian flavor of the assumption that natural, unorganized learning is better than the formal variety, for example, has been questioned and criticized (Brainerd, 1978). Some contend that organizing on the basis of content is more efficient than basing structure on nebulous notions about a natural sequence. Others more directly challenge the existence of natural sequences (Martin [ed.], 1976).

The more general predictions and recommendations—learner involvement, learner action, and equilibration—would be advocated by many theorists as well as Piaget, at least in their behavioral manifestations. At present, there is clearly a Piagetian philosophy regarding epistemological issues, and there is a Piagetian developmental psychology, but there is no Piagetian science of instruction. Perhaps the most important implication of Piagetian thinking for teachers concerns sensitivity to children and the way they think. Without this, how could one even begin to teach?

In the last set of two chapters we examined developmental aspects of cognition. In the next set we look at a closely related phenomenon, the development of language. Language may truly be mankind's greatest accomplishment; it is surely one of the most complex. In Chapter 7a we present information about how language develops, how psychologists attempt to explain it, and what the general benchmarks of linguistic growth are. The relationship between language and cognition is also considered.

Language is the medium for the exchange of cognition and knowledge in the classroom. In fact, linguistic competence in learners is the province of virtually every teacher, regardless of subject matter. The ramifications of that fact are explored in Chapter 7b.

Chapter 7a

Language:
Development, Learning,
and Thinking

Introduction

In any classroom, regardless of the students, teacher, location, or subject matter, you will observe the use of language. Teachers direct student behavior and communicate information through language. Students interact with each other and with the teacher through conversation—oral language. Instructional materials present information and teach concepts through prose—written language. Student learning is assessed with language on examinations. In fact, it is almost impossible to envision an educational setting not based on the use of language. Language is not the only communication system people use, but it is an extremely pervasive one.

Language is one of man's major accomplishments, one that in many ways differentiates human beings from other animals. Could a politician survive without language? Highly doubtful. Could we learn from the experience of others without language? Only from those in our immediate environment whose conduct we could actually observe. Could we think without language? Many believe we could not. This highly complex human behavior serves as a basis for so many human activities that it may be considered the most important human accomplishment, perhaps an indispensable one.

What is language? Human language is a complex communication system that is representational. It is a system of arbitrary signs shared by the members of a language community. The system is representational in that its signs stand for aspects of reality. It is arbitrary because these signs have no particular natural relationship to the phenomena they symbolize. The word *dog* represents a particular class of animals, but the relationship between the word and the animal is an arbitrary, symbolic one. For all speakers of English, however, the arbitrary symbol represents essentially the same thing.

All human groups possess language. No matter how primitive a cultural group may seem from a material or technological standpoint, each has a complex language system that is neither primitive nor simple. Language is a *species-uniform* characteristic. Moreover, except in cases of severe abnormality, all growing children acquire the language of the culture they are raised in. Language is acquired rapidly, with most children mastering its fundamentals by age five or six. Although languages vary in a great many respects, children learning them pass through many of the same stages of development.

How do we explain the origins and development of this complex human accomplishment that cuts across cultural differences, that is critical to many activities, and that human cognition itself may depend on? Psychologists from diverse theoretical perspectives have tried to explain it—one can hardly offer a comprehensive theory of human behavior without including this most human of behaviors. Educators and developmental psychologists also investigate its origins, since language may be crucial in fostering intellectual growth and learning. In addition, linguists, anthropologists, philosophers, and others attempt to comprehend this universal human attribute.

The existence of language can hardly be explained without considering the way it develops in children. Just as Piaget studied growing children in order to pinpoint the origins of thought, many psycholinguists study children in order to find the roots of language. In this chapter we shall discuss some of the basic characteristics of language, highlight the developmental sequence of language acquisition, and present the theories that have been offered to explain this phenomenon. In conclusion, we shall discuss the relationship between language and thinking.

The Study of Language Acquisition

Language is a *rule-governed* behavior. In any language, a set of rules specifies ways to put sounds together in order to produce meaningful utterances. Most of the sentences we speak are governed by these rules, but it is highly doubtful that any one of us could actually list them all. Although we may not be able to verbalize language rules, we generally perform in accordance with them, speaking and writing grammatically correct sentences. Since people's language performance exceeds their ability to explain their performance, it has been described as an *intuitive* behavior. We can do it even though we are not sure how we do it.

Language is both a *receptive* and a *productive* system. We process linguistic information that comes from others, and we produce linguistic information as well. Producing sentences is considered a creative act, because most of the sentences a person constructs are novel. The number of rules in a language is finite; there are a limited number of grammatical rules for sentence construction. The number of words in a language is also finite, as is witnessed by the fact that they can be catalogued in dictionaries. The number of sentences that can be created with finite rules and finite words is virtually infinite, however. Competent speakers of a language can both produce and comprehend an unlimited number of sentences, many of which they will not have encountered before.

Language, then, is a creative, productive system governed by rules. Adults engage in this rule-governed behavior routinely; infants are totally incapable of doing so.

The Basic Elements of Language

A language has three major elements: (1) a *linguistic* system, which includes the rules for producing and arranging sounds, (2) a *semantic* system, which specifies the relationship between linguistic signs and their referents in the environment, and (3) a system of *pragmatics*, which governs the way language functions in communication. Linguistics emphasizes the structure of language, semantics the meaning of language, and pragmatics the use of language. The relationship between these aspects is depicted in Figure 7a–1.

A language's structure consists of (1) a sound system, or *phonology*, (2) a system of rules for combining sounds into meaningful units, a *morphology*, and (3) a system of rules for combining words, a grammar or *syntax*. The basic sounds in a language are *phonemes*, which are essentially the vowel and consonant sounds from which words are constructed. Any single language consists of only a small subset of all the sounds that can be made with the human vocal apparatus. Some sounds are phonemes in one language but not in another. A glottal stop, for example, is a phoneme in many American Indian languages but not in English. Phonemes are arranged in *morphemes*, which are similar to words but not synonymous with them. Morphemes are the smallest units of sound that carry meaning. The word *book* is a single morpheme,

FIGURE 7a–1. **The Components of Language**

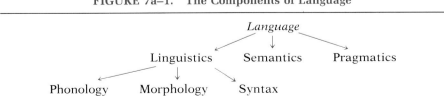

but the word *books* is two morphemes; the final *s* in the word also carries meaning, since it tells us that the referent is more than one book.

In order to form meaningful sentences, words are put together on the basis of *syntactical rules.* One aspect of English syntax that is important to the communicability of sentences is word order. Not all languages place the same emphasis on word order that English does. Compare these two sentences:

1. The baby likes mother.
2. Mother likes the baby.

These sentences differ in meaning only because the words are ordered differently. Examine the following pair:

1. The cat ate the mouse.
2. Mouse the cat ate the.

One is meaningful and one is not, simply because the word order of the second sentence fails to follow the rules of English syntax. Because order is so important in English, it often becomes the focus of child language studies. Investigators also examine children's phonemic development, the order in which specific morphemes are acquired, and the sequence in which various sentence forms appear.

How Language Is Studied

From the point of view of a psychologist, studying language acquisition is not easy. The dependent variables, language production and comprehension, are complex and multifaceted. Since virtually all children acquire language naturally, the usefulness of the training paradigm is limited. Moreover, in order to describe and explain the development of language a researcher must be familiar with both language systems and psychological processes. This combination of skills is encountered infrequently.

Language is extremely complex. Even to objectively describe language systems, people must have a great deal of training and become specialists. These specialists are called *linguists;* they map, analyze, dissect, and describe the formal structures of language systems. They study grammars—sometimes the grammar of a single language or a related group of languages, sometimes universal grammars common to all languages. Traditionally, linguists have focused on language for its own sake, considering the content as an organized set of elements and rules quite independent from the users of the language. Even this is a difficult task, so intricate that no one has yet accurately and completely described the linguistic content of a single language.

In examining a language system a linguist may disregard the psychological involvement of the user. To the psychologist, however, the relationship between the language and the user's psychology is the primary concern. The psychologist wants to know how people use, develop, and learn language. The language user is the focus. We cannot explain human behavior if we ignore the behavior itself, however. Recently, a hybrid field has developed that combines a knowledge of psychological principles with a knowledge of linguistics. Researchers in this field, the *psycholinguists* and the *developmental psycholinguists,* have combind expertise from two disciplines in an attempt to determine how people acquire competence in a complex rule-governed behavior.

Even when armed with interdisciplinary knowledge, researchers who want to study language face a number of scientific and logical problems. Is it best to study the content in the natural environment or in the laboratory? With normal populations or abnormal ones? Can animals serve as subjects? The goal is to describe and explain the acquisition of language. To reach this goal, researchers need to discover the sequence of development and identify the variables that cause it.

The longitudinal methodology described in Chapter 6a is particularly appropriate for this goal. This paradigm can be used to collect descriptive information about sequence. Descriptive methodologies are correlational, however, and as such they cannot help us identify causal variables. The laboratory analogue so useful in other child development research presents problems, too. It is virtually impossible, for example, to find biologically normal persons of an appropriate level of maturation who are ignorant of language and who could be trained in language rules. Where could you find a control group who has not already learned the target behavior? Problems such as these restrict the usefulness of laboratory research.

Laboratory studies are conducted, however. Sometimes the subjects in these experiments are children who do not spontaneously use language in a normal way, perhaps because they are physically handicapped or autistic, or because they have been severely deprived. These children are typically given a training program based on one or more learning principles. If their language improves, we can conclude that learning contributes to language development. Unfortunately, these children are usually so different from normal children that generalizations must be limited. Even if abnormal children do acquire language in the laboratory when learning principles are used, we cannot be sure that the same thing happens with normal children in natural settings. The populations and the environments differ too much.

Primates are used as subjects in other laboratory research. Like human subjects, primate subjects are exposed to language and sometimes given direct training. Sign language is used, since nonhuman primates have vocal structures different from those of humans. There is evidence that primates can learn to use language (Gardner & Gardner, 1971). The sequence in which their language develops is not unlike that of young children (Brown, 1973). Much of this research is fascinating, and it has captured the attention of the scientific community and the press. Through it we do gain insight into the nature of language, but again direct generalization to normal children is limited.

Other laboratory approaches to language investigation use normal children as subjects; for example, investigators can design training research to teach children a specific language rule. They select a rule associated with children who are older than the experimental group and at a higher developmental level. It is assumed that, since speech forms consistent with the rule are nonexistent in the experimental children's spontaneous speech, the children have not yet acquired the rule. If the training procedure works and subjects produce the target speech forms, we have evidence of the importance of learning principles in language acquisition. This type of research has been conducted with many language forms, including acquisition of the passive (Whitehurst, Ironsmith, & Goldfein, 1974), sophisticated question-asking (Swanson & Henderson, 1977), and the use of longer and more complex sentences (Zimmerman & Rosenthal, 1974b).

Unfortunately, even this solution is less than ideal. How do you determine that a child in the experiment had not already acquired a specific linguistic form? The child may have acquired a form before training without having expressed it. When the use of a linguistic form increases after training, it is possible that the training program simply elicited the desired response rather than taught it.

Because of these various investigative difficulties, language research usually employs more than one method. Information from different kinds of studies is used as the basis for explanations. The most frequent approach, however, is naturalistic observation with small numbers of children (as in Brown, 1973). It is evidence from this type of study that has provided the foundation for what we know about the sequence of language development.

A Description of Language Development

The Preverbal Period

During the first year of infancy, children produce no words or sentences, but they do vocalize. Infant vocalizations seem to develop in certain stable sequences during this prelinguistic period: not only do infants babble, there is regularity in their babbling. During the period before actual words are produced, a period that covers most of Piaget's sensorimotor period, children produce certain vocalizations that psycholinguists have divided into three categories (Siegel & Cocking, 1977).

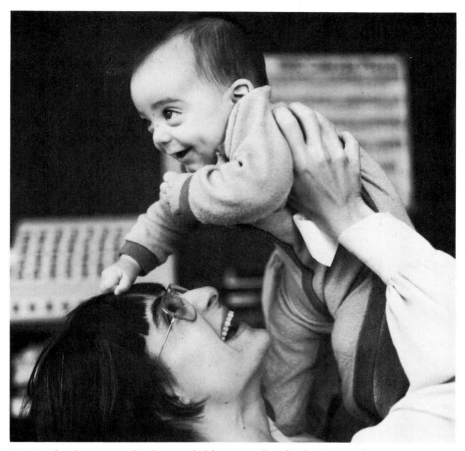

During the first year of infancy, children vocalize by fussing and babbling. Although formal speech is absent, infants can communicate thoughts and emotions through these vocalizations.

The first category includes vocalizations that seem to be organically based. These are the fussing, crying, respiratory sounds, and the sounds that accompany feeding. The second category contains cooing and babbling vocalizations. These are not true linguistic forms, but they are more word-like than those in the first category. In those babbles a much broader range of phonemes is expressed than will be used in whatever language the child will soon learn. Some of them resemble specific language phonemes, but many of them do not. The third category includes the vocalizations that closely resemble the phonemes in the language that the child hears daily.

Developmentally, the organically based sounds generally appear first. They subsequently decrease as babbling sounds increase. Then, at about six to twelve months, the vocal patterns change. Speech-like babbles increase while non-speech-like sounds and the frequency of babbling in general decrease. Just before the baby begins to utter actual words, babbling almost completely disappears.

The preverbal period is important because it may provide clues about the origins of language. Perhaps babbling comes to more closely approximate true speech as a result of acoustical input from the environment. Although this so-called babbling drift seems like a reasonable hypothesis, it is as yet unsubstantiated (Siegel & Cocking, 1977). We do know that young babies can distinguish the different phonemes they hear (Bower, 1977; Eimas, Siqueland, Jusczyk, & Vigorito, 1971) but how incoming sounds influence infant vocalizations is not clear.

A less environment-oriented approach explains babbling as a biological and organic phenomenon. It has been noted, for example, that both hearing and deaf infants babble; and in fact, differences in their babblings are indistinguishable during the first six months of life. The fact that deaf infants cannot base their babbles on what they hear argues against an experiential origin for babbling. Moreover, early babbles are unlike adult phonemes (Ervin-Tripp, 1966; Lenneberg, 1964) and unlike the language the baby will eventually learn. They are thus not imitations of perceived sounds.

The vocalizations an infant makes before six months of age include the sounds of all the world's languages, so any infant could learn any language. After six months, babbles become less flexible. Older babies babble the phonemes of the particular language they hear, and the foreign sounds drop away. Without exposure to speech sounds from the environment, however, true language fails to develop (Bower, 1977).

First Words

Infants utter their first true word when they are about a year old. Most children accomplish this feat between the ages of ten and thirteen months and by about fifteen months have a vocabulary of ten words. A child's first words are much more phonetically restricted than babbling is. They often consist of a one- or two-syllable consonant-vowel combination, such as *dada*. The consonants tend to be sounds produced near the front of the mouth: /p/, /b/, /d/, /t/, /m/, and /n/ (linguists express sounds within slash marks).

A child's first words are used in isolation. Most children acquire about fifty words before they begin putting them together. Even though they are uttered singly, these words serve as more than labels. This early vocabulary typically contains words that are the names of things (for example, *ball*), names of people (for example, *Mommy*), and action words (for example, *give*), and the child uses them to communicate rather than merely at random (Dale, 1972). Children's use of words, even when used one at a time, seems to convey thoughts and content that an adult would express with a sentence. One-word speech is hence called *holophrastic;* this term indicates that a single word may function for a child as an entire sentence does for an adult.

From One Word to Two

When the child is about eighteen to twenty months old, two-word combinations, or *duos,* appear. Roger Brown calls these early multi-word utterances *Stage I language.* Although Stage I language is simpler than adult speech, there are some resemblances. Some kinds of words, such as nouns, adjectives, and verbs, are used frequently; other kinds of words (for example, articles, conjunctions, prepositions, and the like) are used infrequently or not at all. Young children produce unadorned word combinations without the subtle intricacies of adult speech. These early combinations have been characterized as *telegraphic speech* (Brown & Fraser, 1963), since the minor intricacies are omitted just as they would be in telegrams. They may (1) describe actions, as in *Daddy go,* (2) describe the attributes of objects, as in *big dog,* (3) claim possession, as in *my shoe,* (4) or perhaps give commands, as in *give ball.* Moreover, these sentences may be inventive in ways that are atypical of adult expression. A child who watches the door close, for example, may comment with *all gone outside.*

By around age two or two and a half, children's multi-word sentences increase in length, and three- and four-word utterances are created. Most of these sentences are in one of the following forms: (1) agent-action-object, such as *I see truck,* (2) agent-action-location, such as *daddy sit chair,* or (3) agent-action-object-location, such as *Mommy take doggie home.* In these sentences meaning is conveyed primarily by word order, since the finer modifications of speech are missing. Interestingly enough, young children acquiring English make few mistakes in normal word order. They make errors and use words incorrectly, but their speech is understandable and communicates effectively in the context it is used in.

Stage II Speech

At the age of two and a half to three years, children begin to flesh out their simple sentences, adding the grammatical touches that make their sentences more precise. The little words—prepositions, conjunctions, articles, and the like—are added. Prefixes and suffixes that clarify stem words appear, too. Brown (1973), who has studied the development of child language extensively, refers to this as Stage II speech. This is a period of *modulation of meaning.*

Brown examined the sequence in which his young subjects acquired fourteen of these common morphemes, endings, and minor func-

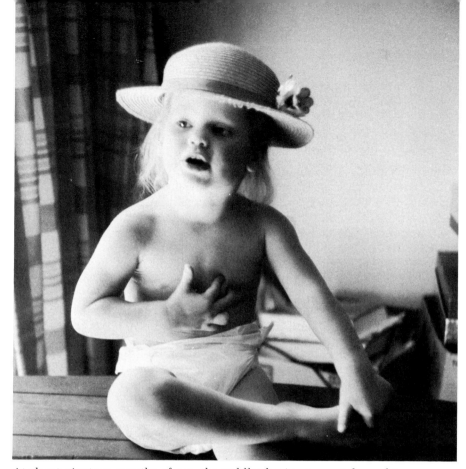

At about nineteen months of age, the toddler begins to use telegraphic speech—two- and three-word combinations for expression. "Me go" may mean "I want to go," "I went," or "I am ready to go."

tion words that clarify sentence meaning. These data are summarized in Table 7a–1. He found variations in the age at which the children added these niceties to their utterances. The sequence of acquisition, however, was surprisingly consistent. Others (deVilliers & deVilliers, 1973) confirmed the general sequence with additional subjects; Brown used a sample of three children. While the rate of language acquisition varies greatly, the order in which children acquire the rules of language seems quite uniform.

Children who are in the process of acquiring these grammatical rules sometimes overgeneralize and use them inappropriately (Dale, 1976). For example, they may *overregularize* verb endings, applying the past regular rule to irregular verbs. *It broke* becomes *it breaked*, or *I went* is overregularized to *I goed*. This may occur for a time even when a child has previously used the irregular form correctly.

Even after acquiring the fourteen morphemes, young children have a way to go before their speech matches that of an adult. They must learn to form questions with *who, what, why, when,* and *where,* and to change the word order accordingly. They must also learn to use auxiliary verbs and to deal with negation. Later, clauses are added as sentences increase in complexity and length, and the use of the passive increases. By the time children go to school, they are proficient speakers. In just four years, children progress from the preverbal stage to become skillful users of language who make infrequent errors. This dramatic accomplishment requires a psychological explanation.

Theories of Language Development

Consider the factors that must be accounted for in a comprehensive explanation of language development: (1) the universality of language in all human groups, (2) the universals and similarities in language development across linguistic groups, (3) the rapid development of language, and (4) the uniformity of the sequence of development. When we find such uniformity across individuals, we might logically conclude that language is a biologically determined aspect of being human; but languages also differ greatly, and we learn only that language we are exposed to. In addition, in order to acquire language children must be exposed to it, and the process takes time. Experience must thus play a role as well.

Theories of language development and language acquisition place different emphases on the environment and on biology. As in other aspects of child development, the *empiricists* look for causal variables

TABLE 7a–1. **Grammatical Morphemes in Order of Acquisition**

Morpheme	Example
1. Present progressive	runn*ing*
2. In	*in* box
3. On	*on* table
4. Plural	three *toys*
5. Past irregular	it *broke*
6. Possessive inflection	Adam'*s* ball
7. Uncontractible copula	There it *is*
8. Articles	*a* cat
	the toy
9. Past regular	Adam *walked*
10. Third person regular	She run*s*
11. Third person irregular	He *has*
12. Uncontractible auxiliary	This *is* turn*ing*
13. Contractible copula	*That's* book
14. Contractible auxiliary	*I'm* walking

Adapted from Roger Brown, *A First Language: The Early Stages* (Cambridge, Mass.: Harvard University Press, 1973, p. 274).

in the environment, whereas the *nativists* examine biological factors. A third group, the *interactionists,* considers the influence of both forces. No one has yet developed a completely satisfactory explanation, but a number of attempts have been made.

Levels of Language

Part of the problem in building language theories is that language is more than what we hear. In the 1950s Noam Chomsky (1957) noted that there are two levels of language: (1) the *surface structure,* the string of utterances we actually hear, and (2) the *deep structure,* a more fundamental level concerned with the meaning of these utterances. The two structures are not necessarily synonymous. Consider, for example, the following sentences:

1. John hit the ball.
2. The ball was hit by John.

The meaning conveyed, the deep structure, is the same; the form of the sentences, the surface structure, differs. Competent speakers perceive that the meanings are the same despite the surface differences. Look back at the list of acquired morphemes in Table 7a–1 (p. 261). There are at least three rules that involve adding an *s* to the end of a word: the plural, the possessive, and the third person regular. All three sound the same, but the meanings differ. Even a single sentence can be ambiguous and have more than one possible meaning or deep structure. Consider, for example, *The ducks are ready to eat.* The difference between the two structures is even more obvious in children's language. The surface structure *Mommy shoe* could mean several things on the deep structure level: (a) *those are Mommy's shoes,* (b) *Mommy, put my shoes on,* (c) *Mommy has shoes on,* and so on. A child who uses this utterance in a number of different contexts would be displaying greater knowledge of deep structure than the surface structure would indicate.

If the surface structure and deep structure were identical, ambiguity and synonymity would not exist. Since they are different, theories of language development must (1) describe them both, (2) describe the origins of them both, and (3) describe the relationship between them.

Behavioral and Social Learning Perspectives

In traditional psychological approaches, language is examined as a learned behavior acquired through experience. Since behaviorists prefer to deal with observable events, they emphasize surface structure—produced verbal behavior and the way it is used. Since deep structure is not directly observable, it must be inferred from surface structure. Defining language as a verbal behavior like any other behavior places it in the category of responses that are acquired, maintained, and increased through learning principles. According to this view, children imitate the speech of those around them. They are reinforced for appropriate responses and either punished or ignored for inappropriate responses (Staats, 1968; Skinner, 1957). It is assumed that children's speech comes to resemble the speech they hear through imitation, selective reinforcement, shaping, and discrimination learning.

If language is not differentiated from other behaviors as a response class, then what we know about the acquisition of other responses generalizes to language. In his book, *Verbal Behavior* (1957), Skinner eloquently presents this view, analyzing language and the way it might be brought under stimulus control. Empirically demonstrating that children learn language through reinforcement and imitation presents a problem, however.

Because reinforcement is defined functionally, it is impossible to determine which verbal responses have been reinforced after the response has been acquired. You can make logical guesses, but you cannot draw functional conclusions. To demonstrate function, the experimenter must control the delivery of the reinforcer and make it contingent on response production. We cannot do this with normal children developing in the natural environment and acquiring language at a rapid rate. It has been done with children who have severe language problems, but this raises the generalization issue discussed previously.

One could assess the behavioral view by observing normal children. If we assume that favorable parental reactions, such as "Good" and "That's right," serve as reinforcers and that unfavorable responses are punishing, we might be able to determine whether any relationship exists between parental reactions and child language. We would expect: (1) that language forms used frequently by parents would be common in children's responses because of imitation, (2) that language responses received favorably would be used frequently, and (3) that punished responses would be used infrequently. One might also expect language development to vary greatly in children because of differences in their environments. Investigations along these lines would not prove the behavioral view, but they would lend credence to it. The reason such studies would not constitute proof is that reinforcement and punishment are defined in terms of a behavioral effect. Positive and negative comments may not in fact serve reinforcing and punishing functions.

In a 1973 study, Brown failed to find evidence that the order of morpheme acquisition in children corresponded to the frequency of the morpheme in parental speech. Moreover, although he did find individual differences in rate of language development, the sequence of development was quite consistent, even though his subjects came from diverse backgrounds. Examinations of parental reinforcement practices do not support a behavioral view, either. It appears that parents reinforce children for speaking truthfully, not for correct syntax (Brown &

Hanlon, 1970). If correct syntax fails to draw favorable reactions from parents, then perhaps syntactical rules are not acquired through reinforcement alone.

Social learning theorists stress that imitation is the important process in language acquisition (Zimmerman & Rosenthal, 1974b; Whitehurst, 1978). They point out that models provide many examples of appropriate speech. Children observe this use of language, abstract the language rules, and then use the learned rules to guide their own behavior. This is an example of the acquisition of rule-governed behavior through observational learning that was described in Chapter 4a. Note that reinforcement is not required, just exposure to models who produce language. Investigators have used this approach to teach a wide variety of syntactic rules to children (Zimmerman & Rosenthal, 1974b; Henderson, Swanson, & Zimmerman, 1974; Swanson & Henderson, 1977), so its effectiveness is empirically well documented.

Social learning research has failed to impress psycholinguists for a variety of reasons. First, children rarely imitate sentences much more complex than those found in their spontaneous speech (Ervin, 1964; Bloom, Hood, & Lightbrown, 1974). Moreover, when children do imitate, they tend to leave out aspects of language associated with levels more advanced than their own (Dale, 1976). A Stage I child asked to repeat *I can see the two doggies* may say, *I see doggie*. Second, social learning studies tend to use children of kindergarten age or older who did not use a particular language form in a pretest. We cannot assume, however, that a child who did not use a certain language form has no knowledge of the form. Modeling may simply elicit the form; a new rule may not have been acquired in the experiment.

Many investigators feel that behavioral and social learning approaches fail to fully explain why children acquire language from experience. Moreover, these approaches lack explanations for the rapidity, universality, and uniformity of sequence characteristic of language development. These perspectives may explain certain learning mechanisms, but they fail to explain the whole story. Nevertheless, it seems plausible that learning principles play a role. Why else would children learn a specific language, the one they hear modeled?

Nativist Views of Language Development

In the 1950s and 1960s such linguists as Noam Chomsky who possessed sophisticated knowledge of formal language systems took issue with traditional empirical explanations of language development. They made two points. First, because of its complexity and the fact that it has two levels, language is unlike other behaviors. Deep structure, the meaning level, is critical to an understanding of language; examining surface structure alone neglects the heart of language. Second, Chomsky argued that children acquire language at an age when they are intellectually incapable of other cognitive skills. How could children display amazing competence with language and at the same time general intellectual incompetence? It seems unreasonable to conclude that language is simpler than other intellectual endeavors. Apparently, the acquisition of language was a special case, a unique behavior. To Chomsky, explanations based on learning theory were totally inadequate.

At the same time that the psychological community was listening to Chomsky's ideas about language development, the influence of Piaget's writings was also being felt in the United States. Piaget described the child from infancy to about age six as intellectually limited; this perspective was consistent with that of Chomsky. The stage was set for viewing language development as something quite special.

Chomsky (1965) reasoned that children use language competently at an early age essentially because they do not have to learn it. Rather, they possess an innate understanding of some aspects of language. This innateness hypothesis (Dale, 1976) suggested that a large part of a child's knowledge of language was an inborn biological characteristic. What did this innate understanding consist of? Chomsky believed that the content of deep structure was a grammar, not the grammar of a specific language, but a universal grammar. Such an innate grammar would contain language rules common to all languages. If we could specify what these grammar universals were, we would know the extent of children's innate knowledge. Language researchers subsequently began searching for the language universals.

In this view, the child's task in developing language proficiency is much simpler than other perspectives suggest. The child has a head start and already knows something at birth. Essentially, the child must learn to match utterances heard, surface structure, with his existing deep structure. Chomsky proposed that humans possess a *Language Acquisition Device* (*LAD*) that enables them to deal with language. The *LAD* is like a language processor in the human brain that transforms surface structure to deep structure and vice versa. So equipped, a child can rapidly learn the specifics of comprehending and producing a particular language.

The idea that the capacity for language is a uniquely human attribute with a biological basis is the crux of the nativist view. Since neurological maturity and language maturity were no doubt related, others (for example, Lenneberg, 1964, 1969) examined evidence about the brain and brain development. The fact that language development was found to be highly correlated with both age and motor development gave credence to this pursuit. Neurological structures seemed to be the place to search for the origins of language.

There are problems with this theoretical position, however. First, the proposed constructs, deep structure and the *LAD*, are not directly observable, so they remain hypothetical. Second, identifying language universals fails to reveal their influence on language learning; this connection also remains hypothetical. Third, we still know very little about the functioning of higher brain centers. Until we do, the nativist position remains a logical but to some extent unsubstantiated perspective on language development.

An Interactionist Perspective

There is another perspective on language development, but it is not as well defined as either the behavioral or nativist theories, and it is associated with more than one primary spokesperson. We describe it as an *interactionist* perspective for two major reasons. First, many of the conclusions imply that language develops from the interaction of the organism with the environment (Clark & Clark, 1977; Ervin-Tripp, 1973). Second, this position has many points in common with Piaget's work in the area of cognitive development, and Piaget's theory is also referred to as interactionist (Gruber & Voneche, 1977).

The empiricists have avoided having to develop a construct of language structure by focusing on verbal behavior, but the nativists emphasize this construct. Nativists assume that a child's language structure exists in essentially its final form when the child is born. Interactionists also address the structure issue, but they view its origins differently. According to interactionists, structures emerge during the course of development; at birth they are nonexistent. It is through experience that children build a system of knowledge about language; they are *active constructors* of the language structure.

Piaget described the way children build cognitive structures through adaptations from experience. Interactionists say that a similar process is used to build a knowledge of language. Experience and adaptations based on experience are important to both views. Cognitive development runs a similar course for all children, despite individual differences in experience and environment; language development seems to follow a general sequence, too. How can we explain the generality across individuals? We can assume that human infants have a certain uniform style of processing environmental information and extracting relevant principles or rules that are then used as a knowledge base. Regardless of whether the content the child acts on is cognitive content or language content, the child constructs a system of knowledge in accordance with universal organizing principles. If children share a general tendency to organize information along certain lines, they should evidence a similar consistency in their behavior, in this case, their produced language.

This notion of an emerging language structure common to the whole species raises an additional question. What is the basis of these organizational tendencies? The basis could be *syntactic,* along the lines of the universal grammar proposed by Chomsky. It could also be *semantic*, related to the meaning of events. Finally, it might be *cognitive—* that is, the development of language knowledge could be related to the construction of more general cognitive knowledge (Dodd, 1980; Siegel & Cocking, 1977).

Whatever the basis of the organizing tendency, if children actively build their knowledge of language they construct rules, refining and elaborating them as they develop. One would expect, then, that children's use of language would be rule-governed. In fact, many studies indicate that child language is rule-governed (Dale, 1976). Child rules and adult rules differ, however. Logically, then, the interactionist perspective seems to have promise, even though the theory has yet to be clearly delineated

We have a long way to go before we really understand language development in children. Since language is a form of information, we need to know more about the way people process information. To learn about information processing, we must learn more about how the brain functions. Finally, because language tends to be the form in which we present and mediate cognitive information, we need to know more about the relationship between language and cognition and the way they develop.

Language and Thinking

When we think, we are acting on a mental level; we represent events or things in our environment and then manipulate these representations in some manner. Perhaps we simply reflect on them, recalling in representational form events we experienced earlier. Then again, we can solve problems by transforming our mental representations into new outcomes. In both cases, thought involves the use of internal representations, or symbols. What form do these representations take? Are they synonymous with language? If so, is thought possible without language? Are young children capable of thinking before they develop the ability to use language?

The relationship between language and thought has long been a subject of interest. Anthropologists, linguists, philosophers, and psychologists all have something to say about the relationship between the two processes. Some have proposed that thought and language are synonymous (for example, Watson, 1924). Others have suggested that the two are highly interdependent (Vygotsky, 1962), or that accomplishments in one are reflected in the other (Piaget, 1972; Chomsky, 1968). As adults, we may intuitively feel that our own thoughts seem to be verbal much of the time, a kind of talking to oneself. Moreover, we may find ourselves hard pressed to think without using language.

Developmental psychologists also address the issue of representations, since young children lack the language facility of adults. Jerome Bruner (1966), for example, suggests that children represent their world in three kinds of thought. The first is the *enactive mode,* in which thought is the equivalent of physical action performed on objects. Enactive thinking resembles Piaget's sensorimotor thought. The second form, *iconic thought,* is essentially pictorial. Information is represented in mental images. The iconic thinker is tied to perceptual experience. His thinking is dominated by perceptual features similar to the notions of the preoperational child. The third form is *symbolic thought,* thinking with an abstract symbol system independent of immediate perceptions. Language is this kind of symbol system.

Bruner contends that children develop from the enactive stage to the iconic stage and finally to the stage in which a truly symbolic mode of thinking becomes the most prevalent. Symbolic thought is flexible and abstract, disengaged from immediate perceptual experience. In the same fashion, Piagetian theory suggests that the developing child moves from sensorimotor to operational thought; the latter is also flexible, abstract, and distinct from perception. The theorists agree that children achieve symbolic thought at about the same developmental level; the use of language follows the same pattern as the development of symbolic thought. Is language use, then, a reflection of the growth of thinking, or does thinking mature because the child acquires language?

Does Thought Reflect Language?

One of the facets of culture that anthropologists study is language. Each cultural group has a unique linguistic system that can be analyzed, dissected, and described just as Chomsky attempted to do with English. Anthropologists tend to study social groups physically and culturally removed from western European influence, however. The differences between these languages and European languages are often remarkable and surprising (see Dale, 1976, for examples). Phonology systems, syntax, and even the semantic categorical systems vary considerably. A Westerner encountering these very foreign-sounding systems of expression would probably be impressed by the differences rather than by any underlying similarities that might exist.

Benjamin Whorf and Edward Sapir (Whorf, 1956) were anthropologists who noted these dramatic differences, primarily as a result of studying American Indian languages. They observed not just syntactic differences—that is, varying approaches to grammatical construction—but also semantic differences. In their exotic language samples they found that there were different kinds and numbers of categorical terms. Categorical terms serve as the basis for classifying things and events. Differences in classification words could imply different ways of examining and organizing reality. English, for example, contains the word *bird,* which denotes a general class of animal. Several South American Indian languages have no equivalent term (Dale, 1976). Could this suggest that experience is organized differently depending on the language's categorical system?

Whorf and Sapir concluded that language does determine thought (Whorf, 1956) and proposed two related hypotheses. The first concerns *linguistic determinism,* stating essentially that all higher levels of thinking are dependent on language, which in turn determines thought. The second concerns *linguistic relativism,* which suggests that people who speak different languages perceive and experience the world differently, too. These two ideas, which became known as the Whorfian hypothesis, implied that we can think only in the terms our language provides. Language not only determines thought, it limits it.

This hypothesis, however, remains without empirical support. Certainly languages differ, but the meaning of these differences in relation to perception and thought is not clear.

Others similarly acknowledge the importance of language to thinking, without viewing it as a limiting force, however. The Russian psychologist, Vygotsky (1962), for example, proposed that speech and thinking are originally independent in the developing child; at about age two, however, the two become blended and interdependent, thereby altering the child's behavior. Language becomes a tool that assists the child in classification, reasoning, and concept development that might otherwise be impossible. Bruner (1966) also believed that language is a key to thought, especially because the use of a symbol system frees the individual from the dominance of immediate perception. With language, thought transcends appearances and time and allows us to represent experiences, internally transform them, and communicate them to others in ways otherwise impossible.

Perhaps when children acquire words and develop competence with language, they increase the proficiency of their thinking as well. Language may provide a means for cognitive activity and problem-solving that encourages cognition to grow in new ways. Language structure may even function as the organizer for other cognitive accomplishments (McNeill, 1970).

Does Language Reflect Thought?

There is one major psychological position at odds with the view that language permits thought. This is the Piagetian perspective. As Piaget states it,

> . . . linguistic progress is not responsible for logical or operational progress. It is rather the other way around. The logical or operational level is likely to be responsible for a more sophisticated language level. (Piaget, 1972, p. 13)

Research Report

Young children are competent language users. They can construct sentences according to a variety of syntactical rules and they possess sizeable vocabularies. They may, however, not use words in the same manner as adults do. A word's meaning for a child may differ from that for an adult. A case in point is children's understanding of relational terms such as *more, same,* and *less.*

Children's comprehension of relational terms is important to those interested in both language and cognition. Development psycholinguists, for example, may wish to determine the order of acquisition of these terms. Since quantity terms are involved in cognitive tasks such as conservation, the concepts are relevant to cognitive-developmentalists as well. One might very well ask whether or not there is a relationship between comprehension of the linguistic forms and logical competence.

Investigators looking at language development have noted some curious findings with respect to relational terms. For example, *more* appears frequently in young children's speech (Bloom, 1970). One might conclude, therefore, that young children understand both *more* and by implication *less* also. Apparently this is not the case. Donaldson and Balfour (1968) noted that three- and four-year-old children do not correctly understand *less*; they treat it as a synonym of *more.* Others (Harasym, Boersma, & Maguire, 1971) found that children's failure to differentiate the two terms was associated with performance on conservation tasks. In our research selection for this chapter, David Palermo evaluated the robustness of these findings and extended the investigation across materials, contexts, and age range.

Two experiments were conducted. In the first, children between three and five served as participants. Their understanding of the terms *more, same,* and *less* was assessed with both discontinuous and continuous quantity. For discontinuous quantity, children were presented with two wooden apple trees on which apple shapes could be at-

tached. Comprehension of the relational terms was assessed by manipulating the number of apples on the trees. Children were asked to *put* more apples on one tree than another, *point* to the tree with more, *predict* which would contain more, etc. Through these sorts of probes comprehension of more, same, and less was accomplished. (A similar procedure with glasses of liquid was used to evaluate the concepts with continuous quantity.)

Findings indicated that *more* was a relatively easy concept; even young children understood its meaning. Most of the older children understood *same* as well, but only about half of the younger children did. *Less* was the most problematic; only about one third of the children demonstrated a grasp of this relational concept.

Using the same materials, kindergarten, first, and second grade children were assessed in the second experiment. A semantic differential technique was also employed. This rating device allows a person to rate concepts along a bipolar dimensional scale. More and less are bipolar terms to someone who understands them and would be rated that way; but young children with incomplete understanding might rate them differently. Findings suggested that even children as old as seven tend to confuse *more* and *less.* Moreover children respond to *less* as if it were *more.*

In general, then, this piece of research reiterates and extends earlier findings. Why development proceeds in this fashion, or the role knowledge of language might play in other quantity tasks is not clear. We can be fairly certain, however, that language comprehension and performance on cognitive tasks is related somehow. Moreover we must be cautious in judging children's comprehension of specific terms. Apparently we cannot assume that children understand all words in the same way that adults do.

Palermo, D. S. More about less: A study of language comprehension. *Journal of verbal learning and verbal behavior,* 1973, *12,* 211–221.

Language is thus a reflection of the growth of logic and thought, not the cause of it. If there is a common sequence in language development, it may be attributable to underlying generalities in the course of cognitive development.

For Piaget, the basis of logical thought is not language but action. The child physically acts upon objects in the environment and through these actions comes to *know* about objects and the relationships between them. Words or signs subsequently become attached to these *known* objects and relations. The label does not give the event meaning, however; it is prior understanding of the events that allows the word to have meaning. From this perspective, thinking is quite independent of language (Piaget, 1967; Furth, 1966). One could depict the Piagetian position on the sequence of thought and language as follows:

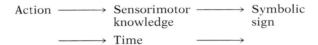

Is there empirical support for this statement? There is some, but it is primarily descriptive and correlational. It reveals no causal connection between thought and language. The evidence cannot demonstrate that cognitive development determines language development, even though some have interpreted it that way (Furth, 1970).

An examination of children's first words, for example, reveals a preponderance of the names of things that children can act on in their environment (Dale, 1976). *Shoes* and *socks* are common words in these early vocabularies; *pants, mittens,* and *diapers* are not. The child can act on the former more easily than the latter. Labels of common items small enough for the child to manipulate physically also appear frequently in early speech, labels like *clock, blanket, key,* and *ball*. Labels for bigger, more complicated items (tables, stoves, windows) and labels for large objects that are simply there (tree, park) are virtually nonexistent. This finding is consistent with a Piagetian perspective; the things children come to know through their own actions are the things they attach labels to. Although this evidence is suggestive, it is far from conclusive.

Before a child can know and therefore label an object, he might logically be expected to have attained the concept of object permanence discussed in Chapter 6a. Until children understand that an object has a separate and independent existence that is constant across time, they would need no sign to signify it. Corrigan (1978) examined the correlation between the attainment of object permanence and early language development. Generally, she found no obvious match between the stages of object permanence and use of language until the final stage (that is, when the child can manage double displacements). At that time there is a large increase in total vocabulary and in the use of labels for objects not present. The first use of words to label nonexistence (for example, *all gone*) and reoccurrence (for example, *more*) occurs at the same time.

Parallels between linguistic and cognitive sophistication have also been observed with older children. Children who can conserve, for example, use quantity terms in different ways from children who cannot (Sinclair, 1967). Conservers use comparative terms (*bigger, smaller*) and coordinate dimensions (*thinner, taller*). Nonconservers do not. The Piagetians have interpreted this observation to mean that linguistic

Many of a child's first words represent objects that she has manipulated by herself. A child will be more likely to use such words as "socks" or "shoes," rather than "shirt" or "pants," since the former can be self-manipulated from an early age while the latter require assistance.

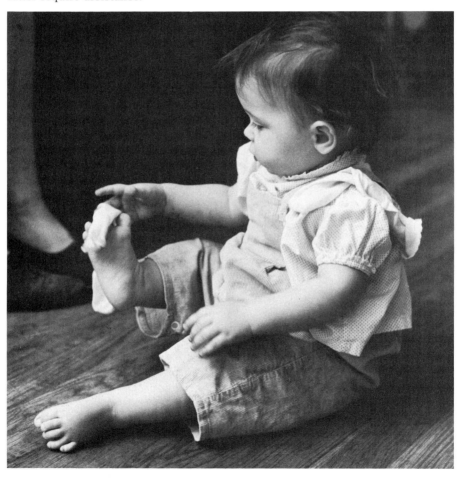

New Directions in Research

In recent years research in children's development of language has mushroomed. The multitude of studies reflect a variety of interests, a variety of new directions. Syntactic development, semantic development, and the relation of language to cognitive development all continue to attract the attention of empirical investigators (Bowerman, 1976; Clark, 1973; Cromer, 1974; Miller, Chapman, Branston, & Reichle, 1980; Moore, 1973). Selecting one example of an important new research direction is not easy. The one we have selected is different from most of the content included in the chapter and serves to reiterate the breadth of topics addressed by language researchers.

Language has sound, form, structure, and meaning; but language also serves a purpose. People use language within a social context to accomplish some end, to serve some function (Halliday, 1975). Language, then, is *functional*; the use of it is *pragmatic*. The developing child must learn not only the rule system for forming linguistic phrases but the rule system for using those phrases. One of the new directions in research is based on a functionalist view of language. It involves the study of language in context, and particularly how children develop competence in language use (Bates, 1976a; 1976b; Bates & McWhinney, 1979; Ochs & Schieffelin, 1979).

The basic premise underlying this research approach is that the structure of language cannot be understood independent of the context in which it is used (Naremore, 1982); we must focus on what we do with language. With application of this research to children, we see interest in what children know about the rules of language use (Hymes, 1971), how they use language in exchanges (Cook-Gumperz, 1981; Ervin-Tripp, 1976; Shields, 1978), and how they use it in conversation (Dore, 1979; Dore, Gearhart & Newman, 1978).

In some ways this body of investigations reflects a broad concern reflected in other aspects of language research as well: concern with the psychological reality of language. Language is something people produce. While linguists may choose to focus on the structure of the product, psychologists want to know about the nature of the producer.

---

sophistication increases with the development of logical thought. A correlation fails to demonstrate which comes first, however.

Investigators have tried to determine the connection between language and thought with a variety of studies. Some have conducted investigations with deaf children to see if non-language-users can solve logical problems (Youniss, Furth, & Ross, 1971). The results indicate that deaf and hearing children have comparable reasoning abilities. Others train children in language skills and subsequently assess their cognitive performance. Sinclair (1967), for example, taught nonconservers to use the relational terms important to a certain conservation task; the verbal training did not improve conservation performance. Some similar studies, however, indicate that cognitive performance does improve (LaPointe & O'Donnell, 1974). The evidence remains equivocal.

Another body of recent research has tackled this issue in a rather intriguing fashion. In these studies the experimenter tries to find language tasks and reasoning tasks that are based on parallel rules. The rule frequently chosen is reversibility, the understanding that an operation can be undone by applying the opposite operation. Conservers, for example, know that the initial state and the final state in a conservation task are equivalent; they understand the notion of reversibility. One equivalent language structure involves comprehension of the passive. *The dog bit the cat* and *The cat was bitten by the dog* are equivalent sentences, although the order of the elements is reversed. The second sentence, the passive, can be transformed into the first, however, by rearranging it and changing the verb form. Which comes first: Must children understand reversibility in a general cognitive sense before they display an understanding of the reversibility of language? Some investigators conclude that operational performance is a prerequisite to linguistic performance (Furth, 1970). Others assert that the two are interdependent (Beilin, 1976). Still others find little evidence of a correspondence (Scholnick & Adams, 1973), and there is also evidence that linguistic competence comes first (Moore & Harris, 1978).

One can conclude only that the empirical evidence is ambiguous. The Piagetian position that language reflects thought has little more support than the Whorfian hypothesis that language determines thought. In all probability, the relationship between language and thought is a complex one. It is very likely that the two processes are interdependent.

Summary

Language is a complex rule-governed behavior that growing children master quickly during their first five or six years of development. Beginning with single words, which emerge about the end of the first year of life, children acquire language in an orderly sequence despite differences in background, experience, and even the particular language mastered. They initially use words one at a time. Subsequently, they learn to use words in simple combinations (*Stage I*), and then they learn the modulation of meaning (*Stage II*).

A number of theories have been offered to explain the way language development takes place. *Empirical* theories emphasize the child's experience and the processes of imitation and reinforcement. *Nativist* theories stress species characteristics, humans' inborn biological capacity to acquire language. *Interactionists* take into account both experiential factors and the inborn style of processing language information that human beings seem to possess.

Although we have presented current information about language development and related it to cognition, researchers are presently conducting research that will change the state of our knowledge. Our current knowledge is a bit sketchy, diverse, and not yet well integrated. Language development is a popular topic that attracts a great deal of interest, however. Theoretical improvements are undoubtedly forthcoming.

In the meantime, teachers will continue to use language with students and will attempt to foster verbal skills. So even if the state of the art is not what we might wish, we must apply what we do know. This application is the topic of the next chapter.

TEACHING SCENARIO

Our scenario is a variation of a topic raised in Chapter 6b. We again consider the challenge of designing instruction with developmental principles in mind, with increased engagement as a side benefit, and with productive learning as a goal.

It is early fall and Ms. Henderson is designing a nature unit for her kindergarten class. Her plans include teaching the children something about the growth cycle of trees and thus the changes associated with autumn. She knows there are also many new words associated with these natural phenomena—color words, shape words, texture words—that she would like the children to acquire. What sorts of experiences can she plan that would assist the children's vocabulary growth about these aspects of the season?

Chapter 7b

Fostering Language Growth in a Classroom Environment

Introduction

Verbal abilities are critical for communication with others, for scholastic achievement, and for professional success. In many ways, schooling depends on language and verbal skills. Direct teaching of verbal literacy takes up a large part of the school day. Verbal information-seeking skills that help students direct their own learning are also taught in the schools; these skills also depend on language. In addition, teachers use language to assess academic progress. Even the standardized aptitude and achievement tests used to evaluate individual and group progress depend on language. Students who cannot process verbal information or who cannot display their knowledge verbally are in trouble. They may even be judged intellectually incompetent.

Teachers often hear students complain that they knew a concept tested on an examination but were unable to express their understanding; yet if a learner cannot demonstrate what he or she has learned, how can the teacher decide whether learning actually occurred? The acquisition of language skills is thus a direct concern of virtually all teachers, not just teachers of reading and English.

Two categories of verbal skills are particularly relevant to formal education. The first includes expressive competencies and communication skills, both oral and written. In the second category are skills that assist in obtaining information, such as reading and questioning skills. Because both types are necessary in order for a student to profit from formal instruction, both are of direct concern to teachers. Teachers will wish to facilitate the development of these skills, since without them students will lag in overall cognitive accomplishment.

Language Diversity in the Classroom

Psycholinguists are attempting to build a general theory of language development, so they emphasize similarities in development across children. Teachers are more apt to be concerned with the range of individual differences they encounter among children. Students vary greatly in language proficiency. There are obvious differences in vocabulary, fluency, syntax, and frequency of verbalizing; some children talk a great deal, others very little.

The variability found in the classroom is due partly to differences in student backgrounds. Early language development, which occurs before the child enters school, is influenced by the child's family environment. The extent to which verbal skills are fostered in the home varies from family to family. In some homes, language skills, expression, and even reading are encouraged before children come to school. Other children may not even be familiar with the alphabet. Families place different priorities on verbal skills, and these priorities are reflected in differences in the children's linguistic behavior.

Children's cultural and socioeconomic backgrounds also vary. Since our society is becoming more pluralistic, cultural differences among children in the classroom are increasingly common. Many teachers encounter learners whose first language is not English, a fact that makes variations among children even more pronounced.

In short, the teacher is faced with a wide variety of individual differences, including differences in general verbal proficiency and in cultural, linguistic, and familial backgrounds. It is not easy to facilitate the development of verbal literacy skills in such a setting, but the effort is vitally necessary.

General Themes from the Psychological Literature

You know from reading the last chapter that opinions about the development of language are very diverse. We cannot delineate one set of clear principles for teachers to use in fostering language skills. Nevertheless, the classroom teacher needs guidelines. How can we resolve this dilemma? We must attempt to extract some basic principles from psychological research.

First, let us summarize what a child entering school will probably be able to do. Most children will be verbal (though not necessarily in English), will have a sizable vocabulary, and will be able to form a range of sentence types. Children's expressions may not be complex, precise, or elaborate, but they will be adequate. Teachers rarely have to teach language skills from scratch. Rather, they must elaborate and expand on the skills the child has already developed. Elaboration in-

Language differences may be a reflection of cultural or ethnic differences. Teachers frequently encounter children whose first language is not English. Bilingual education programs recognize these differences and provide appropriate experiences for children whose native language is not English.

volves (1) increasing vocabulary, (2) refining the precision and communicability of expression, (3) increasing fluency, and (4) increasing the production of language consistent with overall intellectual development. The emphasis on elaboration is the same for all children in the classroom, from the youngest to those in the final stages of formal schooling.

Implications from a Learning Perspective

General learning theory suggests that reinforcement procedures are one means of increasing children's use of language. Student expression and attempts at expression can often be increased if they are reinforced. Moreover, modeling procedures can help elicit student verbalizations and expand the range of sentence types children use (Bandura & Harris, 1964; Carroll, Rosenthal, & Brysh, 1972; Harris & Hassemer, 1972;

Liebert, Odom, Hill, & Huff, 1969). The importance of modeling is also reflected in the finding that adult *expansions* of child-produced sentences encourage more elaborate expression (Dodd, 1980). An expansion is an adult restatement of a child's sentence that increases the sentence's complexity. A child might say, *Look at the picture. It's a horse.* An adult might respond by saying, *Yes, isn't that a lovely picture of a big, brown horse?* The adult's sentence is longer, includes more vocabulary, and has a more complex syntax. Expansions seem to have an effect on child utterances. The principles of both reinforcement and imitation can thus be used to strengthen linguistic behaviors and increase their range.

To encourage imitation, teachers can model complex sentence structure in their own verbal behavior. This tactic is similar to that used in social learning research (Zimmerman & Rosenthal, 1974b; Henderson, Swanson, & Zimmerman, 1974). Imitation is more effective, however, when the student observers also participate, actively generating their own matching sentences (Swanson & Henderson, 1977). Modeling can thus serve as a cue to help the child produce complex sentences, which can then be further strengthened through reinforcement.

The teacher, then, serves as a language model. Whether the target behavior is some aspect of syntax, overall sentence length, or the use of descriptive words, modeling is a powerful tool in changing behavior.

► *ACTIVITY 1.*   You can observe language modeling, imitation, and expansion by watching and recording interactions. The best way to do this is to tape-record conversations, transcribe them, and then analyze them. Select one of the following settings and collect a language sample of an interaction.

1. *Adult and young child.* Give a child and an adult a task to do (for example, looking at a book together) so that they have something to interact about. Collect a language sample that includes both the adult's and the child's part of the interchange. Check the transcript for evidence that the adult (a) reinforced the child's use of language and (b) expanded the child's sentences. Check to see whether the child (a) imitated the adult's language, (b) repeated words first introduced by the adult, and (c) asked any questions.

2. *Peer-peer and peer-younger child interactions.* Select a child in an age range that interests you. Have the child teach a task or game to (a) a peer of the same age and (b) a younger child. Collect language samples on the target speaker in both situations and compare the two records. See if the target speaker adjusted his or her verbal behavior to the

listener. You might compare the two records for (a) amount of explanation, (b) sentence length, (c) amount of repetition, (d) use of questions, and (e) use of explicit directions. You will probably find that the target speaker intuitively adjusted his or her language with the listener in mind.

3. *Teacher and students.* Observe a tutorial session between a teacher and a student or students. Collect a sample of teacher and student language. Compare the two records for (a) amount of verbalization (who talks more), (b) sentence length and complexity, and (c) sophistication of vocabulary. Check also to see if the teacher (a) uses cues to elicit student talking, (b) reinforces student expression, and (c) asks questions that call for an extended verbal reply.

Implications from a Developmental Perspective

Although learning theory provides hints on ways to encourage language development, we can also look to the cognitive perspective for ideas. Piagetian theory, for example, suggests that physical action is the basis of knowledge, which is in turn reflected in language. Children use words and expressions for phenomena they have actually experienced. Accordingly, teachers may wish to provide physical activities along with verbal descriptions, especially with younger children. A description of the action of a pendulum, for example, may be more meaningful if the student builds a pendulum and watches it work. Encouraging learners to physically experiment with objects while one describes the action and its result can increase linguistic abilities.

For a word or expression to have meaning, the learner must establish the connection between the thing or event and its linguistic symbol. The principle of association, pairing a referent and its symbol, is important in learning language (Dodd, 1980) and it is included in some form in many psychological theories. When teaching children label learning, it is advisable to have at hand the object the label is attached to. In addition, letting the child handle the object permits the child to feel, see, and otherwise perceive its attributes, an activity that may help the child represent the attributes with words.

▶ *ACTIVITY 2.* Language symbols are more meaningful when they are associated with the concepts and elements they represent. Accordingly, many teaching activities involve combining language and physical activities to demonstrate the connection. Choose one of the following settings and perform the task indicated.

1. *The young child.* Observe a preschool teacher and a young child doing a task together. See if the teacher introduces new words and labels while the child is interacting with novel materials. Does the teacher encourage the child to describe the characteristics of the materials, the activity, or both? Does the child repeat any of the newly introduced language?

2. *The elementary age child.* Such terms as *more, less,* and *greater than* are very important in describing and understanding quantitative relationships. Design some activities that would allow you to observe children's use of quantitative terms on different dimensions (for example, number, length, and amount).

3. *Older children.* Select a science class in a junior or senior high school. Observe while the teacher demonstrates a laboratory task and the students conduct the demonstrated experiment. Check for the following: (a) Does the teacher pair demonstration with descriptions of the event? (b) Are the students encouraged to describe the experiment, either orally or in writing? (c) Are new terms and expressions introduced during the activity? (d) Does the teacher circulate while students are active and provide verbal information about the experiment? You may be surprised to see how much language students learn while being instructed in other subjects.

Language and Action

Whether one bases language learning on active discovery, reinforcement, or imitation, children must have a chance to practice language skills and try them out. Opportunities to practice language can be added to almost any activity. If students are to be actively involved, they must be given opportunities to talk. The flow of language cannot be just from the teacher to the students. Students must produce language and reformulate thoughts in their own words. Listening and sometimes reading can be passive verbal activities. If we wish to ensure that they are active, other elements must be included. Note taking and worksheets, for example, increase students' engagement and also increase comprehension and recall of material (Redfield, 1980). Paraphrasing is another technique for increasing engagement.

In general, instructional plans that encourage students to use their developing linguistic tools and practice language forms should enhance development and proficiency. Teachers can build activities that encourage verbalizing and writing into almost any instructional area. If one assumes that verbal skills are crucial to intellectual endeavors, one wonders why in so many classrooms it is the teacher who talks while the students are required to be silent.

The Special Case of Seeking Information: Question-Asking Skills

Many educators regard the ability to ask questions as an important skill in what is called learning to learn (Henderson & Swanson, 1977). This is a basic intellectual activity because it permits children to obtain information from their environments and to play a role in directing their own learning (Henderson & Garcia, 1973; Henderson, 1975). Children who can ask a variety of questions can obtain information when they want and need it rather than having to wait for adults to provide it. Psychologists and educators concerned with the linguistic and intellectual development of children contend that question-asking is very important in intellectual life (Cazden, 1970) and central to all problem-solving (Blank & Covington, 1965). Accordingly, teachers who wish to increase students' intellectual competence must also be concerned with this linguistic skill.

Question-Asking and Development

Although the developmental literature indicates that questions of varying types play an important role in intellectual functioning, some categories of questions are more sophisticated and develop later than others. The forms of questioning that appear later are the ones that yield more information from the environment. Ausubel and Sullivan (1970) indicate that forms of questioning that appear early in development ask for names of objects and persons (for example, *What is that? Who is that? Where did they go?*). Questions that call for causal explanations occur later (for example, *Why does it rain? How come snakes don't need legs? What would happen if we ran out of oil?*). Piagetian investigators (Piaget, 1955) also found that causal questions are scarce in the verbal productions of young children. These kinds of questions procure a lot of information for children and may help them broaden their knowledge base (Cazden, 1970). Since the ability to ask questions about causality is generally considered to be critical to the intellectual growth of children, teachers should try to facilitate the growth of this ability.

Several investigators have tried to increase question-asking in school-age children. Torrance (1970), for example, found that opportunities to manipulate objects increased question-asking in six-year-olds. Blank and Covington (1965) found that increasing question-asking in sixth graders increased their participation in class discussions and helped them solve problems on a science achievement test. Others increased questioning with techniques involving novelty and uncertainty (Berlyne & Frommer, 1966). The use of modeling procedures also seems to work (Rosenthal, Zimmerman, & Durning, 1970; Zimmerman & Pike, 1972; Henderson & Garcia, 1973; Henderson, Swanson, & Zimmerman, 1974).

Student questions are important not just in gaining information but in getting the teacher's attention as well. Students who ask good questions have several advantages: (1) they obtain information at the time they need it, (2) they influence instruction by letting the teacher know what still needs to be explained, and (3) they receive individual teacher attention.

A teacher trying to encourage students to ask questions about causality is actually striving to meet two goals that require different means. The first involves learning the linguistic form—how to put words together correctly. The student must learn the forms of causal questions (*why, how come,* and *what would happen if . . . ?*) as well as the order of words in the rest of the sentence. Teaching the linguistic

Children can be encouraged to ask questions by being presented with an ambiguous situation. The teacher is holding a picture representing a situation that might have a number of different interpretations. The children may discover the correct interpretation by asking questions.

form can be accomplished through modeling, practice, and the reinforcement of questions children do produce.

The second goal is to relate questions to problem-solving. When
children have learned how to produce questions, they need to be able
to use them to acquire needed information and solve problems. In
addition to modeling, teachers can use game-like situations to increase
the productive use of questions. Students could, for example, be presented with an incomplete or ambiguous stimulus, such as a confusing
picture, a black box, or a magic trick. The student's task would be to
figure out the situation, to solve the problem by asking questions. In
these game-like situations, high-level questions will obtain more information than low-level or repetitive ones. The child who produces high-
level questions will be reinforced by the information received as well
as for producing the questions.

▶ *ACTIVITY 3.*   Observe a lesson in a classroom setting. Record the frequency and type of questions asked by both teachers and students. Examine your record for the following: (a)
Does the teacher use cues to promote student questions? (b)
Do students often produce sophisticated questions? (c) How
does the teacher respond to student questions? (d) What type
of questions does the teacher use more frequently, high-level
questions that call for elaborate answers (for example, *why*
questions) or simple questions (for example, *what* questions)?

Question-Asking and Cultural Differences

Question-asking abilities vary across groups of children as well as
across individuals. Investigators have noticed, for example, that children from lower socioeconomic groups ask fewer questions than their
middleclass counterparts (McCarthy, 1930; Davis, 1932; Rosenthal,
Zimmerman, & Durning, 1970). Moreover, children from culturally
different backgrounds ask fewer questions than other children (Martin,
1970; Swanson & Henderson, 1977; Henderson, Swanson, & Zimmerman, 1974). If culturally different children fail to indicate their information requirements to the teacher, their educational needs may easily
be overlooked. Teachers need to be sensitive to these issues if they are
to meet the information needs of all their students. Special provisions
may be required to encourage inquiry skills in special populations who
do not spontaneously produce a lot of sophisticated questions.

An example drawn from the social learning literature will illustrate
how this can be accomplished. The Papagos are a group of Native

Americans who live in the southwestern United States near Tucson, Arizona. Papago children generally ask very few questions in settings where they interact with or are observed by Anglos (Henderson & Swanson, 1974). However, the majority of the schools that the children attend are run by Anglos and employ Anglo teachers. Traditionally, the Papagos preferred to obtain information through observation and imitation (Joseph, Spicer, & Chesky, 1949); the use of direct questions was considered rude or in poor taste. Some cross-cultural investigations, however, have suggested that as societies become more complex, instruction depends less upon showing and more upon telling out of context (Bruner, Olver, & Greenfield, 1966). They reason that as opportunities to learn *in situ* diminish, *why* questions become an important means of dealing with the environment. It appeared that many Papago children were at an educational disadvantage, since question-asking was being modeled infrequently for them.

Interested Papago parents wished to change this situation and encourage question-asking skills in their children. Accordingly, a research training project (Henderson & Swanson, 1977) was conducted in which question-asking was the target behavior. The project primarily involved showing modeling sequences to the children on videotape. Question-asking skills improved remarkably with this brief instruction. A sample script follows (Swanson & Henderson, 1977, pp. 349–350).

Margie: Laura and Norbert, look at this picture. (Hold up picture.) Ask me some questions about this picture. (Zoom in on picture but include parts of the characters.)

Laura: *Why* does the man look scared?

Margie: Good question! Because he's falling off his horse. Ask another question.

Norbert: *How come* he isn't using a saddle?

Margie: Good question! Because he likes riding bareback. Ask another question.

Laura: *What would happen if* he fell into the cactus?

Margie: I like that question! The cactus spines would hurt him. You both ask such good questions! You will be so smart when you grow up.

Norbert: That's right. We will learn a lot if we ask questions.

In sequences like the following, distinctions between questions and nonquestions are reviewed. Pat is a Papago woman. Rabbit is a human in costume.

Pat: Now, I'm going to say some things and you tell me if what I say is a question.

Rabbit: Okay.

Pat: Listen (pause). Why do you live in the desert?

Rabbit: Yes—that's a question.

Pat: How do you know?

Rabbit: Because it starts with a question word . . . and because I can make an answer . . . I live in the desert because I like it.

Pat: Good! Listen again. Why do rabbits run away from coyotes?

Rabbit: Yes—that's a question.

Pat: How do you know?

Rabbit: Because . . . it started with a question word . . . and I can make an answer. Rabbits run away from coyotes because they're scared.

Pat: Very good! Listen again. Coyotes are very smart.

Rabbit: No—that's not a question.

Pat: How do you know?

Rabbit: Because—it didn't start with a question word . . . and it doesn't have an answer.

The following sequence, excerpted from the final tape, used as its stimulus a poster of a very complex scene depicting girls playing a Papago game involving the use of a ball and some ribs from the skeleton of a saguaro cactus that are used as sticks in the game. The poster was so complex that it suggested almost limitless possibilities for question-asking.

Pat: Ask a question about this picture.

Rabbit: How come those girls have those saguaro ribs?

Pat: Good question! Because they are playing a Papago ball game.

Rabbit: Why are they swinging the sticks?

Pat: I like that question. Because they are trying to hit the ball.

Rabbit: Why is that girl's hair sticking up?

Pat: Very good question! Because she is running fast.

Rabbit: What would happen if the girl tripped on the stick?

(Zoom out to medium close up.)

Pat: Good question. She would probably fall down. You ask good questions, Rabbit. You are so smart!

(Clapping and cheering from background)

▶ *ACTIVITY 4.*   Examine the script modeling question-asking skills. Note examples of (a) modeling the linguistic form, (b) reinforcement of the linguistic form, (c) direct instruction, and (d) tying questions to the production of information.

Language as a Symbolic Mediator

In the last chapter we also discussed the relationship between language and cognition. Although opinion varies greatly about the precise function of language in thinking, symbolic representation apparently does play a role in the process. To solve a problem or acquire a concept, we must represent the elements involved, and words are one tool for representation.

To learn concepts we must learn to classify things or events on the basis of relevant characteristics (see Chapter 11a for a more complete discussion). The elements in a class are grouped under word tags or labels. The label serves as an abstract symbol of the class and is therefore a useful tool in categorization.

Problem-solving involves altering or transforming one state of affairs into a different state of affairs. Transformations can occur on the representational as well as the physical level. Again, words serve as the basis of the representation. A child who has language skills has an easier task than a child who lacks them.

In the absence of representational tools, a concept learner or problem-solver must depend on immediate perceptual information, which may be misleading. Suppose a child is presented with a series of objects found in the home or classroom. Some are toys, such as blocks, balls, and games, and some are tools, such as keys, a screwdriver, and a can opener. In each set, the objects differ but share a common feature, their function. A child who must depend on perceptual information will attend to easily perceived visual differences rather than less-easily-perceived functional differences.

Young children often use perceptual information to their cognitive disadvantage, even when they have other strategies available to them. Some children may be able to represent things with language but fail to do so spontaneously. Teachers can facilitate cognitive performance by encouraging children to represent things mentally rather than relying on a perception strategy. This has been demonstrated with conservation, for example. In one study (Bruner, Olver, & Greenfield, 1966), nonconservers were prevented from being misled by perceptual clues. When the conservation problem was presented to the subjects, the transformation of the initial equivalence was described to the children but conducted behind a shield. Children had to predict, in the absence of perceptual information, the outcome of the transformation. Most children who were initially nonconservers correctly predicted the final equivalence of quantity. They relied on symbolic means of problem-solving because the perceptual means were removed and they thus performed on a more sophisticated level.

Teachers can facilitate the cognitive performance of learners by helping them develop language mediators and by encouraging them to use symbolic representations they have already learned but do not routinely use. To do this, the teacher must use a lot of language and encourage the child to do likewise. Verbal interaction between student and teacher should facilitate the use of language in cognitive performances. Moreover, discussions of what children see and experience provide the children with explicit terms to use in storing the information acquired.

Even when children can solve problems correctly, follow rules in cognitive performance, and classify on the basis of abstract dimensions, they are not always able to explain their performances, even their correct ones. By interacting with the child, the teacher can help the learner to make *implicit* understanding *explicit.* Asking the child *how do you know that?* or *why did you do it that way?*, for example, encourages the child to express what he or she knows. Once expressed, the knowledge has been formally represented, and it can be stored, recalled, and used again with similar problems in the future. This is one example of metacognitive skills discussed in Chapter 5a.

Language, Thinking, and Teacher-Pupil Interactions

Whether we look to cognitive development theory or perspectives on language development, many psychologists emphasize the constructive nature of knowledge and language acquisition. Children construct on the basis of their experiences and then act in accordance with them. Verbal interaction is one form of experience that can facilitate cognitive constructions on the child's part. Many instructional methods involve verbalization, but not all facilitate constructive activity equally. One obvious example is *lecturing.* In a lecture format, the instructor imparts verbal information, so the technique is a social transmission process. If the students understand the lecture, they can learn a great deal of information. Lecturing, however, does not necessarily encourage active learning for all students, so it may not help some students construct knowledge.

A second form of verbal instruction is actual verbal interchange between student and teacher. Throughout this chapter we have emphasized two-way interchange as a means of facilitating language skills. Interchange in a tutorial relationship does encourage active learning. In this format, teachers can increase pupils' information-seeking skills by eliciting questions from learners. Problem-solving strategies used by students can also be formalized through verbal interaction. By questioning students, teachers force learners to express internal mediation explicitly and to reflect on mental events. All of these outcomes increase explicit knowledge of cognitive acts, provide practice in important expressive skills, and give teachers an opportunity to reinforce lan-

Two-way interchange between an adult and child can facilitate language skills through the use of a question-answer format. Questions posed by the adult should require more than one-word responses so that the child will develop the ability to express thoughts completely.

guage performance. Moreover, students engaged in verbal interchange with a teacher will probably pay more attention to the teaching activity; it is harder to be passive under such circumstances. Because it reflects principles of both cognition and language development, the verbal interchange method is therefore a commendable one.

▶ *ACTIVITY 5.*   Verbal interaction can take a variety of forms, depending on the classroom, the age of the learners, and the preferences of teachers. With young children, for example, a tutorial style is probably more typical, whereas the lecture method is a common format with older learners. The following activities provide opportunities to compare verbal interaction styles. Select one of them.

1. Choose a subject area that interests you and observe several classrooms in which the subject is being taught. Look for differences between classrooms in the verbal interaction used in the teaching style.

2. Identify one classroom in which the lecture method is used and another in which two-way interchanges are more common. Observe learners in the two classrooms to see if their behavior differs.
3. Examine a set of instructional materials and choose one principle to teach. Design two sequences that could be used for teaching the principle, one based on the lecture method, the other on interchange and questioning methods.

Teaching the Linguistically Different: Bilingual Education

Teachers not only encounter differences in overall verbal proficiency among children, they must also teach children from different linguistic backgrounds. Students may speak a form of nonstandard English, such as Black English (Dillard, 1972), or they may come from homes where English is spoken infrequently. The language skills of these children differ from the language of the educational system. Some researchers have found that language differences coincide with social and economic class differences (Bernstein, 1960, 1961). The language styles of the poor have often been judged to be less effective for academic learning (Hess & Shipman, 1968).

In the 1960s, children from economically impoverished environments were often described as culturally disadvantaged and in need of compensatory education to catch up with their middle class peers. Federally funded preschool programs, such as Head Start, were designed around this objective. Some educators believed that the primary basis of the apparent disadvantage was a linguistic one (Bereiter & Engelmann, 1966) that would impair future cognitive accomplishments. Early instruction hence often focused on this so-called intellectual deficit in language skills.

The use of such terms as *culturally disadvantaged, deficit,* and the like in reference to differences associated with socioeconomic status, race, or culture is less common today (Henderson, Zimmerman, Swanson, & Bergan, 1974). They have been replaced with the more neutral term, *culturally different.* Children may differ in primary language when they enter school, but language differences are no longer thought to coincide with cognitive impairment. Linguists tell us that all languages are complex, including nonstandard dialects like Black English (Labov, 1970, 1973). Accordingly, we should not make comparative judgments about the intellectual sophistication of different languages, nor should we assume that non-English-speaking children are intellectually impaired.

When a child comes to school without competence in English, however, numerous problems may develop. Imagine the shock to a young child of entering a new environment in which he cannot understand, communicate, or express his needs. To make things worse, if instruction is solely in English, he is not going to learn much either. Unless some special provisions are made, the non-English-speaking child may become emotionally traumatized by formal schooling and will probably not remain in school very long.

The United States has always contained many people who speak differing languages, and if anything the number and diversity of non-English-speaking persons is increasing. In the past, however, the overriding emphasis was on *assimilation*, the acquisition of the English language along with American values and attitudes at the expense, if necessary, of ethnic tradition and identity. Cognitive accomplishments went by the wayside in favor of instruction in English. Until they mastered English, children had little opportunity to learn material in other subjects; hence, non-English-speaking children fell behind academically.

One of the authors has heard numerous horror stories from students who were punished at school for speaking their primary language, in this case either Spanish or Papago. Not only could these children not communicate with teachers or their English-speaking peers, they were prevented from communicating freely with each other. From experiences of this nature, many of these students even lost proficiency in their first language.

More recently, the strict assimilation approach to the education of children from different linguistic backgrounds has been criticized. It is detrimental to children emotionally, it impairs their sense of ethnic and cultural identity, and it is academically unsound. Most educators now recognize the virtue and necessity of cultural pluralism, which must be respected in the schools.

The former emphasis on assimilation has given way to bilingual and bicultural education. The specific form of bilingual education program is determined by the needs of the particular community and the diversity of the individuals it serves. Most include instruction in English but provide instruction in other subjects in the primary language as well. As a result, children are less likely to fall behind academically while they develop skills in English. Schools often employ bilingual teachers in the early grades or use bilingual teacher aides to provide individual help. To avoid underestimating intellectual competence, formal intellectual assessment may be conducted by bilingual examiners. These programs are undoubtedly an improvement in the educational approach, and they are based on considerable empirical support (Perl & Lambert, 1962).

Scenario Suggestion

Language in the classroom goes beyond simple communication between teachers and students. Learners need new language experiences. They need to extend their linguistic skills, acquire new words, elaborate on forms available to them, and thus increase their range of expression. Instructional formats are adaptable to those ends.

Children will acquire words more readily for those objects and events that they come to know through their own experience and activity. Ms. Henderson needs to engage her youngsters with these objects and events and introduce the new words within the context of personal experience.

Ms. Henderson could plan a nature walk around the school grounds, where the children can observe the plants she describes and collect specimens, like leaves, for exam-

ple, in the course of their walk. Once back in the classroom, children could mount the leaves, feel them, describe them, and group them on the basis of similarity. While the children are ordering their specimens, Ms. Henderson could introduce the new shape, texture, and color words while the children have the leaves before them as external referents.

Children can also be encouraged to describe their finds, and when they use the new words, Ms. Henderson could reinforce them or perhaps even write the words so that they can see what the words look like. Because the children are experiencing the referents of the words rather than learning them arbitrarily, the words are more likely to be meaningful. These additions to their vocabulary may be thus more permanent as well.

Conclusion

Language is the medium of formal education, and fostering verbal skills is a critical means of promoting academic accomplishment. The classroom teacher is in a position to model language skills and to encourage student use of language and expression. Through verbal interaction between teacher and student, the development of linguistic competence that begins in early childhood can be continued in the classroom. The importance of these skills to general academic success, to representational thinking, and perhaps even to eventual professional accomplishment cannot be overestimated.

PART IV

Focus on the Person: Attributes and Characteristics

IT HAS LONG BEEN recognized that individual human differences may affect the outcomes of the learning process. These differences—individual characteristics, attributes, or traits—provide another type of P in the equation $B = E \times P$. Achievement results from the interaction of instruction and the set of characteristics the learner brings to the instructional setting. We emphasized this point in Chapter 2a. We pointed out a set of variables—attribute variables—that were crucial to the understanding of causal sequences. In fact, there is a research tradition in psychology with an emphasis on precisely this issue: aptitude treatment interaction, or *ATI* research.

In the next section we examine two important attributes that educators have always considered relevant to the learning process: *Intelligence* and *motivation*. Many view achievement and success in school as dependent on these factors. In the past both attributes were classed as *traits*, characteristics in which individuals differed and whose differences could be measured. Not infrequently, traits were viewed as immutable, a view leading to a focus on whether a person possessed them rather than on the nature of the traits themselves.

Psychology is changing, however; so too are our ideas about what constitutes intelligence and motivation. In the chapters to come you will learn both about traditional views of these important individual characteristics and about emerging contemporary views as well.

Intelligence! Everyone has some preconceptions, some intuitive notions about it. Our society places high value on it. What is intelligence? How does it function? How do we identify it when we encounter it? Piaget treated it developmentally; cognitive psychologists try to figure out how it works; psychometricians measure it.

For years psychologists have discussed, defined, debated, and deciphered intelligence. The measurement of it is big business. We thus give it considerable space in this book. In Chapter 8a we present both the traditional and contemporary views of intelligence from a theoretical perspective, describing its historical origins and evolution as a psychological construct. From the theoretical issues emerges an application that directly affects education—the measurement of intelligence that is so pervasive in our school system. Concepts underlying the measurement process are presented in Chapter 8b.

Surrounding these topics with respect to both educational and psychological concerns is considerable controversy. This is a controversy spawned not just by a narrow academic focus but by widespread social and political interest. It is hoped that from a study of this pair of chapters you will come to appreciate why this should be the case.

Chapter 8a

Theories of Intelligence

Introduction

Of all the controversial issues in contemporary education, one of the most prominent is the issue of mental ability testing (for example, Cronbach, 1975). The assessment of intelligence is a widespread practice in public schools—in fact, it is pervasive in our society in general. In the course of your education, your intelligence has probably been assessed at least once, and perhaps more than once; and somewhere in your educational records there is a number that is supposed to reflect your ability. There is little doubt that the use of measurement devices to assess mental functioning is a prevalent educational practice. In fact, the practice may be more widespread now than ever before in the history of formal psychometric testing.

Test scores are used in educational and vocational decision-making in a number of ways. Some of the decisions based at least in part on intellectual assessment are included in the following list:

1. Evaluation of students for placement in special education programs
2. Diagnosis of learning and psychological problems
3. Identification of exceptional individuals
4. Selection and placement of individuals in the armed forces
5. The evaluation of the worth of publicly funded education programs like Head Start
6. Evaluation of applicants for university programs and graduate schools
7. Job selection and promotion

This list is far from exhaustive. Clinicians and counselors use intelligence tests in clinical practice, researchers use them in empirical investigations, and educators use them for a multitude of purposes.

Although the measurement of intelligence is widespread and entrenched in our society, it is certainly not uniformly accepted. Political action groups argue that mental assessment is a tool of class and racial oppression. Others criticize mental assessment devices for bias and ethnocentrism, and in some areas the courts have even restricted the use of intelligence tests (Salvia & Ysseldyke, 1978). While defenders of the tests attempt to counteract the multitude of attacks (Jensen, 1980), debate over testing continues to rage (Cronbach, 1975; Bersoff, 1973). The assessment of intelligence is undeniably a hotly debated social, political, educational, and psychological issue.

Why all the controversy? It is because whatever merits these devices may have, and they have many (Bersoff, 1973), the outcomes associated with their use are sometimes politically inflammatory. Special education programs for the educationally disadvantaged, for example, contain a disproportionate number of children who are poor, non-Anglo, or non-English-speaking. The same groups are underrepresented in advanced educational programs, perhaps because they failed to meet the selection criteria. In addition, periodically a rather unreliable and controversial finding resurfaces in the psychological literature, in the press, and even on television: blacks tend to score lower on intelligence measures than whites (Herrnstein, 1971; Jensen, 1968, 1969, 1970). In a country whose philosophical roots are based on a concept of equality, these outcomes raise issues of conscience.

As a citizen and a teacher, it is inevitable that you will repeatedly encounter the debate over intellectual assessment, and you may take a side. To evaluate and understand this topic and the debate that surrounds it, however, you need a thorough grounding in the subject matter. Accordingly, we will cover the assessment of mental ability extensively, discussing (1) the interpretation of the measures themselves—Chapter 8b, (2) individual and group differences on these measures—Chapter 9a, and (3) their impact on educational practice—Chapter 9b. These three chapters focus on the tests *per se*, their uses, and the outcomes of use.

Intellectual assessment is based on three factors: theoretical notions about intelligence, our understanding of the human mind, and assumptions about the nature of intellectual functioning. These conceptions have evolved and changed during the relatively long history of the testing movement, and they have influenced the way we used tests in the past, ways we use them now, and ways we will use them in the future. It is hence at theory and the evolution of theory that we begin.

Historical Overview

Most of us have some vague notions of what intelligence is. We informally evaluate people's intelligence all the time. The statement "Harry is really bright" is more likely to be construed as a compliment than "Harry is really dumb." We also compare people on the basis of mental ability: "Harry is a lot smarter than Richard." We probably base these judgments on a set of behaviors that we intuitively associate with intelligence, for example, learning speed, memory, logical thinking, and the ability to figure things out. Most modern devices for measuring intelligence base comparisons of individuals on the same sort of behaviors we use to make intuitive comparisons, although tests are far more precise. In tests, the behaviors are assessed through performance on individual questions, or items; the set of items together provides an index of intelligence that permits one to make individual comparisons.

The idea of obtaining a measure for the purpose of comparing and ranking people's intelligence began with Francis Galton in the latter part of the nineteenth century. Galton's tests, however, were very different from the tests used today. This early psychometrician was greatly influenced by Darwin and the notions of inheritable individual differences and survival of the fittest (Nunnally, 1967). Galton thus designed items that he thought would be sensitive to these individual differences. Consistent with the theoretical ideas of his time, however, Galton sought to measure intelligence by tapping the molecular level; that is, he measured physiological responses, such as acuteness of vision and the ability to discriminate tones and differentiate colors. Today we do not think of these kinds of behaviors as representing intelligence, and items of this sort are not typically included in modern intelligence measures. Galton's tests, then, are only of historical interest, although some of the Darwinian themes in Galton's work are still relevant for contemporary assessment and contemporary theories of intelligence.

One theme common to Darwin and Galton that has influenced all theoretical work in testing up to the present is emphasis on quantifiable differences between individuals. Different people given the same task are likely to perform the task with varying degrees of proficiency. When degree of proficiency can be quantified—that is, stated in numbers—the performances of different individuals can be compared. One can conclude that person *A* is better than person *B* at the assigned task if *A* gets a quantitatively higher score. The notion of quantifying individual differences, an important contemporary theme, originated in Galton's early work.

A second theme that began with Galton and continues today is the use of statistics to quantify and compare human performances. With his younger associate, Karl Pearson, Galton pioneered many of the statistical procedures used in measurement today. Galton therefore influenced not just the purpose of assessment, which is identifying individual differences, but the methodology of assessment as well.

Mental testing as we know it, however, really began with the work of Alfred Binet around the turn of the century. Binet was charged with determining which French school children would profit from formal schooling and which would not. Like Galton, Binet was thus interested in judging performance proficiencies and using them to compare individuals. Unlike Galton, however, Binet did not measure molecular responses. Instead, he focused on performances more directly associated with schooling, such as memory, thinking, problem-solving, imagination, and comprehension. Binet's test items resemble those used today. The items were consistent with Binet's theoretical notions about what intelligence is:

> It seems to us that in intelligence there is a fundamental faculty, the alteration or lack of which is of the utmost importance for practical life. This faculty is judgment, otherwise called good sense, practical sense, initiative, the faculty of *adapting* oneself to circumstances (Binet & Simon, 1905, as cited in Jensen, 1980, p. 141; emphasis ours).

Although Binet used different kinds of items than Galton did, some of his assumptions were the same: (1) individuals differ on measures of functioning, (2) people can be compared using these measures, and (3) a person's level of proficiency can be quantified. The index of quantification later applied to the Binet-type tests is the familiar *intelligence quotient*, or *IQ* score (Nunnally, 1967).

In addition to continuing the themes that began with Galton, Binet made two other assumptions: (1) intelligence is related to educational promise, and (2) intelligence measures can be used for predicting educational success and for selecting individuals for educational programs. The Binet tests established a conception of intelligence and a use for measures of intelligence that are still current (Salvia & Ysseldyke, 1978). The themes and uses of the tests were transported to the United States in 1916, when Louis Terman revised and extended Binet's tests into the Stanford-Binet intelligence scale, a form of which is still used today (Terman & Merrill, 1973).

It is an interesting historical oddity that one of the people who worked in the Binet laboratories was Jean Piaget (Gruber & Voneche, 1977). Like other associates in the laboratory, Piaget was interested in mental functioning. He administered tests and watched children handle the items. Like Binet, Piaget stressed the idea that *adaptation* is crucial to intelligence, but Piaget built a theory of intelligence very different from Binet's and very different from the conception of underlying modern assessment. Instead of emphasizing individual differences, Piaget's theory stresses human universals, and Piaget found meaning in errors rather than proficiency rates. How can similar sets of information result in two such different conceptualizations of human cognition? To answer that question we must look carefully at the assumptions and themes that began with Darwin and Galton, flourished with Binet, and permeate contemporary testing.

Psychological Constructs, Traits, and Trait Theories

The purpose of psychological study is to explain human behavior and human functioning. In Chapter 2a we discussed the many activities that further the process of explanation—establishing cause-and-effect relationships, accumulating accurate descriptive data, and so on. These are activities related to data. Data alone fail to provide a complete and full explanation, however. Even when a great deal of data is compressed, explanation and understanding remain elusive; something is needed. This additional necessity comes from the theory side of science in the form of theoretical constructs.

What Is a Psychological Construct?

A *construct* is a kind of concept, an abstraction that helps us to explain observed phenomena. When used in conjunction with an observed data-based relationship, the construct can help clarify the relationship's meaning. Some constructs you are already familiar with are Piaget's scheme (Chapter 6a), Chomsky's Language Acquisition Device (Chapter 7a), and the concept of cognitive structure (Chapter 5a). Each construct helps explain events—the cognitive development of a child, rapid language acquisition, and learning and retention. Intelligence is also a construct.

Although constructs can help us understand the events we observe, they are abstractions and as such are not directly observable. Constructs are created by scientists. Cognitive structure, for example, is an abstraction. We cannot directly see a person's cognitive structure; we can only hypothesize that some such element must play a role in thinking. Because they cannot be observed, constructs are hypothetical, abstract concepts. Useful constructs help increase the explanatory power of psychological theory, but the fact that they are not observable means that some subjective interpretation plays a role in their development. The interpretation comes from the theory builder, not the observed data *per se.*

Some constructs represent hypothetical structures presumed to exist within the person. Schemes and the Language Acquisition Device are constructs of this type. Other constructs represent processes that cannot be observed, such as the abstraction of rules from models. Still others represent amounts of an unobservable characteristic that people are thought to possess. Constructs of this type are called *traits;* intelligence is a trait construct.

Traits are used to explain individual differences. Differences in people's behavior are attributed to differences in the amount of a trait they possess. "Susan does better in school than Sherry because she has more motivation." Here motivation is treated as a trait used to explain educational success. (You will learn more about this trait in Chapter 10a.) "Harry learns more rapidly than Steve because he is more intelligent." Intelligence is a trait used here for explanation and comparison. Finally, "Pat will succeed in graduate school because she is so bright." In this statement, a prediction is made on the basis of the amount of a trait a person presumably possesses. Herein lies the common theme of Galton, Binet, and contemporary measurement.

Since traits are unobservable, they must be inferred. We must find behavioral clues that can be used to make inferences about traits. The process is diagrammed in Figure 8a–1. When inference proceeds in this fashion from behavioral clue to underlying trait, the behavior is functioning as a sign, an indirect manifestation of another characteristic (Kratochwill, 1980). To use behavior signs this way, we must accept a number of assumptions about the relationships between behavior and traits.

Assumptions Behind the Measurement of Traits

Since traits are hypothetical and unobservable, they cannot be measured directly. We must posit that there is some observable feature related to the underlying variable, the trait, and then tap the trait indirectly by measuring the observable feature. The observable feature and the trait are not the same thing, of course, but we must presume they are related. The observable feature is some subset of behaviors; the trait is some quantitative characteristic. We therefore measure traits, including intelligence, indirectly rather than directly.

FIGURE 8a–1. Using Behavioral Clues as Signs of an Underlying Trait

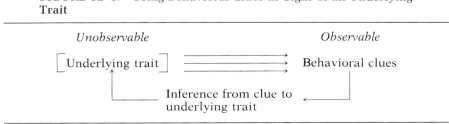

Indirect measurement, the use of behavior to infer underlying characteristics, is common in psychology. Piagetian developmentalists infer a child's operational level from the child's performances on cognitive tasks. Many clinical psychologists infer personality structure from the personal and social behaviors individuals exhibit (Mischel, 1968). The method is similar to the one used by physicians to make medical diagnoses. A physician collects data on the patient's symptoms and infers from them their underlying cause. Indirect assessment is thus rather like *diagnosis*; it has even been referred to as the medical model (Bandura, 1969).

Two issues arise in indirect assessment. The first involves choosing the best set of symptoms or behaviors to draw inference from. This issue involves no challenge to the assumption of indirect measurement; it relates, rather, simply to doing it better. The second issue does question the assumptions of indirect measurement. Many individuals (for example, Bijou & Peterson, 1971) do not accept behaviors as signs of anything else, preferring to treat them as *samples* of what a person can do. This orientation is consistent with the behavioral perspective (Kratochwill, 1980). Data from intellectual assessment devices can be used both ways, but traditionally it is more typical to draw inferences about traits from the tests, especially in the schools.

With such traits as intelligence, the amount of the trait possessed may also be inferred, following the legacy of Binet and Galton. Traits are then conceptualized as quantitative in nature so that measures of traits can be scaled and individual performances can be located on the scale on the basis of how much of the trait is detected.

An analogy may clarify this point and pinpoint some problems associated with the approach. When you wish to determine the amount of oil in your car, you look at the dipstick because you cannot directly see the oil in the engine. The dipstick reading indicates the amount. The fact that you use the dipstick reading to decide whether to add oil indicates that you believe the reading is accurate. If you doubted the accuracy of the reading, however, you could conceivably disassemble the car or drain out the oil and actually check the amount. In this manner, you could confirm that the dipstick reading reflected the actual oil level. With human traits, indirect readings are obtained by measuring behavioral signs. Human beings, however, can not be disassembled—we cannot, so to speak, drain out the oil—so we can never directly check the match between the *assessed level* of the trait and the *actual level*. Just as the measurement of the trait is indirect, the match between actuality and assessment must be determined indirectly. The existence of the trait, its quantitative nature, and the relationship between trait and behavior must thus be considered assumptions rather than facts.

Since we began by reviewing the controversy about intelligence testing, one might wonder if part of the controversy evolved from challenges of the assumptions underlying trait measurement. Are the assumptions underlying intellectual assessment useful? Has adherence to these assumptions hindered or advanced the development of theories of intelligence? Are the assumptions a subject of the current debate about mental testing? We will return to these questions later.

Measurement Technology and the Assessment of Intelligence—in Pursuit of a Better Dipstick

In the past fifty to sixty years a whole branch of psychology closely identified with education has developed, and this branch focuses directly on the issue of measurement. Those who work in this area, the psychometricians, have evolved a technical sophistication in measurement procedures and methodologies that is truly impressive. Expanding the method pioneered by Galton and his associates, experts in measurement have created tests for just about every human characteristic imaginable. These are the *standardized tests*, which include ability and intelligence tests. Each test has certain defined uses and mathematical properties based on the research and data analysis behind its creation. The tests themselves and their statistical characteristics will be discussed in Chapter 8b, since the mechanics of measurement are not a direct theoretical concern. The purposes and aims of measurement technology are, however, of theoretical concern; moreover, the development of the technology certainly played a role in shaping our theories of intelligence.

Identifying Appropriate Signs

Constructing an intelligence test begins with generating a set of items. The items are the signs, the indirect manifestations of other characteristics. A person's performance on all the items represents how much of the trait the person possesses. Which items, which signs are the best indicators? Galton used molecular, physiological signs; Binet used molar, school-related signs. A test-maker's conceptualizations of intelligence guides his choice of assessment items. In a sense, then, each intelligence test is a different operational definition of the construct of intelligence. In fact, some have concluded that intelligence is defined by what the intelligence test measures (Boring, 1923); each test, then, is a kind of definition of the construct. Accordingly, the tests themselves are theoretically very important.

The prototype for contemporary intelligence tests is the Binet Scales. The Stanford-Binet (Terman & Merrill, 1973) revision of the original scale is still a widely used individually administered instrument. Consistent with Binet's original conception, the items used in

The Stanford-Binet Intelligence Test was the prototype for the development of a large number of intelligence tests. The test is administered individually by a trained clinician in a standardized fashion. Some tasks require the child to manipulate objects; other tasks require verbal responses.

this and similar instruments tap behaviors that are molar, related to school settings, and what we might describe as cognitive in nature. They provide a sample of the individual's cognitive functioning. There are a variety of individually administered tests that include scales for children and adults, such as the Wechsler scales (Wechsler, 1955, 1967, 1974). There are group tests (Kuhlmann & Anderson, 1963), tests with a variety of sub-parts (*PMA*, Thurstone & Thurstone, 1962), and many others. All have unique features that reflect differences in the theories of intelligence they are based on. They have a number of similarities as well.

Since the relationship between the sign and the underlying trait is an important part of indirect assessment, the selection of items is determined largely by the way the trait is conceptualized, the so-called trait theory. One might envision the trait as a single characteristic best reflected on a single scale, or one might consider the trait to actually be a set of related traits that represent multiple characteristics. The items are chosen in accordance with the preferred theory. This difference is illustrated in Figure 8a–2.

It is not enough simply to state a trait theory; one must test it. On the basis of the trait theory, one predicts what the patterns of performance data should be like if the theory is accurate. To test the theory, the measure is administered to a number of people and the data are examined to see if they are consistent with the predictions. With a single-dimension theory, for example, one would predict that each item, each behavior sign, is related to the trait. If this is found to be true and the trait underlies the production of the signs, all the items should be related to each other as well. If, on the other hand, a multiple-dimension trait theory is used, items associated with T1 in the diagram (Figure 8a–2) should be related, as should items associated with T2 and with T3. The relationships between items in different dimensions, however, should show a weaker association than items within a single dimension. To test a trait model, therefore, one examines the way the items associate when the test is administered to individuals. Consistencies between actual data and predictions would tend to substantiate the trait theory, as would recurring patterns.

Measurement specialists have developed statistical procedures for examining the association between items that reflect the trait theory. Factor analysis and other correlational methods permit psychometricians to examine (1) the mathematical relationships between the items in a test, and (2) the manner in which the items group together. Although the actual mathematical procedures are highly technical, some of the notions behind the procedures are not.

Essentially, if mathematical assessment indicates that two items

FIGURE 8a–2.   The Relationship Between Conceptualization of the Trait and Items Used

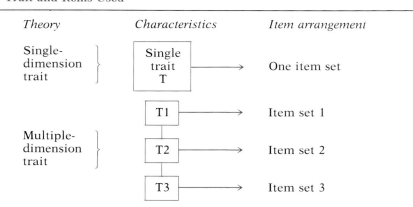

are closely associated, we presume they are measuring the same underlying entity. If no association is evident, then the items are probably not tapping the same trait. If we administer a large set of items, we can subsequently group those that are closely associated. Out of the original set, then, we get groups or subsets of related items. Each set represents an indirect assessment of a single entity. If the item sets are then repeatedly administered to large numbers of people, and if each new collection of data yields the same patterns of item relationships, we have evidence of the robustness of the test and the integrity of the original trait conceptualization that led to the generation of the items. The test itself, once it has been checked out and evaluated in this manner, becomes the set of appropriate signs with which to tap the trait or traits.

The items included in any published, standardized test have been scrutinized in this fashion for their mathematical associations with other conceptually related items. In addition, items included in tests must discriminate between people, that is, ideally they should separate individuals who possess a lot of the trait from those who possess less. In practice, this means that people must get different scores on the test so that comparisons are possible. At the very least, then, an intelligence test is a set of items (1) that are related to each other mathematically, (2) that reflect an underlying trait theory, (3) that discriminate between individuals who possess more or less of the trait, and (4) that yield a quantitative score indicating the amount of trait possessed. Each test is actually a theory of intelligence. The current diversity of tests suggests diversity of theory. It should be noted, however, that the assumptions about indirect assessment of traits through items are a common theme.

Different Theories, Different Tests, Different Dipsticks

As measurement technology grew more sophisticated and as machines for processing data became available, psychometricians were able to use mathematical techniques in new ways, beyond those conceived by the genius of Galton and Pearson. One outcome of increased technology was the development of *factor analysis*. Essentially, factor analysis allows one to determine how items fit together mathematically. Using factor analysis, one can compress large amounts of complex data into a less complex representation of the data. The representation captures the important mathematical relationships of the raw data that were undetectable until the data were simplified. This is done by extending the correlational techniques discussed earlier, which involve (1) identifying items that share a mathematical association, (2) grouping items that share associations along one dimension, and (3) identifying the minimum number of dimensions that will account for all the items.

The dimensions around which the items group, or *load,* are called *factors;* the relationships between the dimensions comprise a *factor structure.* The loading of items on factors is associated with a mathematical quantity, a number, and the factor itself is a mathematical abstraction. Factor analysis, then, is a parsimonious mathematical distillation that results from compressing large sets of data.

During the course of the psychometric movement, a number of theorists have proposed alternative theories of intelligence based on the different factor structures that emerged from the compression of data. One of the original theories was proposed by the Englishman Charles Spearman (1927), who really laid the foundations for factor analysis. Spearman proposed two dimensions or factors to account for individual differences in intelligence, a general factor (g) and specific factors (s). G represented a general ability associated with a wide range of intellectual performances, whereas s represented factors that varied from test to test. The general factor was the important one for Spearman, whose explicit conceptualization of intelligence was essentially that it was a single major trait, not unlike the one implicit in Binet's work. Not everyone thought that Spearman's solution reflected the actual data patterns, however.

In the 1920s and 1930s, methods of factor analysis developed to even greater levels of sophistication. This paved the way for even more sensitive and detailed examinations of individual differences in intelligence and for the testing of more elaborate factor structures. One factor analytic investigator, L. L. Thurstone, isolated a number of factors that he called the Primary Mental Abilities. These included verbal comprehension, word fluency, number, spatial relations, associative memory, perceptual speed, and reasoning. For Thurstone, unlike Spearman and Binet, intelligence was a multi-dimensional trait represented best by a multi-dimensional factor structure. It seems that the more this route was pursued, the more factors emerged from analysis. The culmination seems to have been Guilford's (1967) work. He identified 120 factors comprising intelligence.

Evaluation of Factor Analysis, Methodology, and Intelligence

From the preceding discussion, you can see that data analysis by different investigators yielded different factor structures, which are essentially different theories of intelligence. In our examples, which hardly exhaust the list, Spearman emphasized a single general factor, Thurstone seven factors, and Guilford 120. Which of these approaches is the best alternative? This question is not easily answered, but it may be useful to evaluate different methodologies, their meanings, and the relationship between method and theory.

What Factors Are and Are Not. As noted earlier, the detection of factors, factor structures, and factor loadings is a mathematical process. Factors have weights rather than names; they are extracted from data, not from insight into the workings of the mind. The psychological meanings and the names of factors are added by theorists; they are not inherent in the numbers themselves.

This state of affairs presents a couple of problems. First of all, factor structures are not unique solutions. In other words, given the same set of scores or numbers, factor analysis can yield different patterns of loading. Since more than one mathematical solution is possible, more than one interpretation is possible and more than one theory is possible. The *methodologist* as well as the *methodology* is thus involved in the solution. Second, since factors are only quantitative entities, they may or may not be psychologically relevant to what occurs inside an individual's head. Tying the factor to an internal process or structure again involves drawing inferences about internal characteristics (traits) from observables (factor loadings). This is depicted in Figure 8a–3. Compare Figure 8a–3 with Figure 8a–1 (p. 302). The words are different, but the styles of thinking represented in the diagrams are exactly the same. Accordingly, the assumptions underlying the styles of thinking must be the same, too.

When factors derived from the compression of vast amounts of data are used to describe a test's characteristics, the technique itself presents no particular problems. We draw no inference about unobservable traits when we describe interrelationships between items. In fact, presenting factor analysis data clarifies test characteristics. Problems do arise, however, when inferences about underlying psychological constructs are drawn from factors. When a theorist gives a factor a name, he or she moves one step from description to inference. When the theorist further contends that the factor represents something within the individual, he or she takes a second step. This second step cannot be independently verified and remains an assumption, even if the same factor structure is found in subsequent examinations. It is important to remember that factor solutions do not necessarily prove

FIGURE 8a–3. Using Factor Structure Clues as Signs of an Underlying Trait(s)

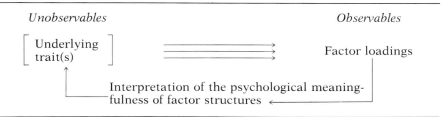

the existence of the internal structure of psychological processes (Lohman, 1979a); they therefore do not necessarily prove the construct of intelligence either.

The Relationship Between Technology and Theory. Each psychological approach is accompanied by a characteristic method or tool that permits investigators to collect data and test theory. Certain hypotheses can be examined better with some tools than with others. Piaget's clinical method, for example, is uniquely adapted to a cognitive developmental perspective. Computer modeling works well with information-processing theory. Longitudinal studies are appropriate for examining children's language development within a nativist framework. Psychometric techniques permit the development of assessment devices. Moreover, we evaluate tools on the basis of how well they help us test psychological theses; that is, on the basis of their effectiveness, not on the basis of what we use them for. The use is evaluated separately (recall the discussion in Chapter 2b about performance objectives as tools).

Sometimes, however, we lose sight of the fact that tools and uses are separate entities that must be evaluated separately. Theories and the technologies they spawn are closely related, and separating them can be difficult. Many critics contend, for example, that Piagetian methods predispose certain outcomes consistent with the theory (Siegel & Brainerd, 1978), and that the use of laboratory experiments to some extent determines that certain kinds of cause-and-effect relationships will be detected (McCall, 1977). The same potential problems exist with measurement technology. Have sophisticated measurement methodologies and methodologists diverted our theories of intelligence through an excessive concern with psychometric aesthetics (Bersoff, 1973)?

Psychometric technologies are tools, and highly useful tools at that, but interpretations of the data discovered with the tools are only as good as the assumptions on which the interpretations are based. If these assumptions are faulty, the most sophisticated, elaborate tools will fail to overcome the problem. Despite changes in technology, the assessment of intelligence is still based on the trait (or traits) construct of intelligence. The measurement and quantification of traits, even through factor analysis, has maintained our focus on individual differences and intra-individual differences in a style similar to that chosen by Galton and Binet. It still amounts to the pursuit of a better dipstick. There may be other ways to conceptualize intelligence, other courses that are not fraught with the same controversy. The assumptions underlying trait measurement with both intelligence and other characteristics are today definitely under fire (Mischel, 1968, 1973; Kratochwill, 1980).

The Benefits of a Trait Approach.   The outcome of decades of work in indirect measurement is twofold. First, psychologists have created a wide variety of standardized tests that measure everything from intelligence and ability to achievement, interests, and values. The methods used in the assessment of intelligence became the prototype for measuring other characteristics, so we now have tests for just about any attribute you can name. These tests serve as the basis of *normative* evaluation. Because of the precise nature and careful methodology of standardized test construction, published tests provide us with *norms*. Norms will be elaborated upon in Chapter 8b, but essentially they allow us to compare individuals on an attribute dimension. It is the process of drawing comparisons with normative data that is involved in making decisions on the basis of assessment procedures.

The second outcome is the field of differential psychology. This aspect of the discipline focuses directly on the way individuals and groups of individuals differ. These differences will be elaborated in Chapter 9a. Understanding and documenting individual and group differences in any precise way, however, would be impossible without the careful, sophisticated work of psychometricians and their products, standardized tests.

The Origins of Intelligence and the Importance of Context

The use of indirect measurement is so widespread in psychology and education that most of us accept the procedure with little question. It may not be the only route to follow, but it is pervasive in professional and lay thinking, and it does yield useful results. It would seem, then, that despite the debate, thinking about human characteristics in terms of trait constructs is commonplace. If, for the moment, we accept the assumption that traits are the underlying causes of observed behavior, then the next question is, how do individuals come to possess traits?

The Nature-Nurture Controversy

You have already read our theoretical discussion of the origins of language and cognition (Chapters 6a & b and Chapters 7a & b), both of which are related to intelligence. A central issue in these discussions was whether language and cognition are attributable to biological processes, the environment, or both. The same question arises with the trait of intelligence—does intelligence arise from biology or from experience? This is the nature-nurture issue.

With language and cognition, those who accept nature as the major

Although monozygotic twins are similar in measured intelligence, differences have been found. Their intelligence scores may be similar, but identical twins frequently behave differently on the same tasks.

force (for example, Chomsky) look to biological structures or processes that explain universals common to all individuals. The trait of intelligence, on the other hand, is supposed to explain differences of functioning between individuals. If individuals differ in behavior, and if biology is assumed to contribute to those differences, then it is probably *specific biology* rather than general species characteristics that is the culprit. Specific biology is genetic inheritance.

At various times in the history of psychology, majority opinion has considered genetic inheritance the primary cause of behavior (Galton and G. Stanley Hall held this view, for example). Sometimes advocates of this position have advanced as evidence the close association noted between intelligence test scores and degree of genetic relationship (Burt, 1966). Monozygotic twins, for example, whose genetic structures are identical, are highly similar in measured intelligence. The farther apart the genetic relationship, the less the resemblance in intellectual functioning (Jensen, 1968). On the other hand, even identical twins do not behave in exactly the same manner; differences do exist. All members of a family do not have the same *IQ*, and *IQ* relationships are stronger when individuals share a common environment as well (Er-lenmeyer-Kimling & Jarvik, 1963). Furthermore, research done in the 30s, 40s, and 50s demonstrated that measured intelligence is far from stable and that *IQ* score changes tended to coincide with dramatic changes in the environment and in experience (Skeels & Dye, 1939; Skodak & Skeels, 1949; Skeels, 1966; Klineberg, 1935). The picture is far from clear, but today most thinkers would not attribute intelligence to a single cause like biology, although they would acknowledge that inheritance probably plays some role.

Measurement and the Causes of Intelligence

The nature-nurture debate has special relevance for detected group differences in intelligence (see Chapter 9a) and for compensatory and special education (see Chapter 9b). The debate also raises some interesting issues with regard to trait measurement. If intelligence is related to genetic inheritance, for example, is it possible to measure the innate part uncontaminated by other factors? What is the appropriate dipstick to use? If experience is an important factor, do intelligence tests reflect some people's backgrounds better than other people's? As you can see, questions about possible causes have a direct bearing on the way the trait is conceptualized and especially on the way it is measured.

By the time a person can be assessed intellectually with any degree of precision, the person has both a specific inheritance and a specific history. We cannot separate the two in any direct way, so all that the measure can detect is the product of the interaction. If we want a common scale for the purpose of comparison, which is what we do with trait constructs, a problem results.

Context and Items. The score on an item in an intelligence test is part of the index for the amount of the trait supposedly possessed. The item serves as a sign, and the form of the item is the *context* for producing the sign. Psychometric trait theories assume that traits are stable and consistent, that they do not vary substantially across time, place, or setting (Kratochwill, 1980; Mischel, 1973). Items and their contexts do vary, however. It follows, then, that if scores vary that variation must be due to changes in context. Since it is impossible to assess a trait without an item, it is impossible to remove the influences of context. Furthermore, if context is related to background, history, and experience, it is impossible to obtain a measure of intelligence that does not reflect those influences. We cannot, therefore, measure so-called innate intelligence.

This problem can be illustrated as follows. Suppose that two people take the same test and get different scores. Suppose also that these two people come from different backgrounds, so they view the item, the context, differently. Is the score difference then due to context differences or to differences in the amount of the trait possessed? The Wechsler Adult Intelligence Scale (Wechsler, 1955), for example, has a subscale called *Information* that taps people's ability to extract information from their experience. One of these items is, "Who wrote Faust?" The ability to extract information from experience is presumed to be a characteristic that is independent of the experiences a person has had. A person who came from a home in which literature was discussed, however, would be more likely to answer this question correctly than would a person from a home where discussing literature had low priority.

It has long been recognized that intelligence tests might be biased against people with certain backgrounds or experiences because of item context. Social class and cultural differences have been suggested as possible sources of bias, resulting in a call for what was called fair testing that is based less on context (Davis, 1949; Eells, Davis, Havighurst, Herrick, & Tyler, 1951). Subsequently, so-called culture-fair intelligence tests such as the one constructed by Cattell (1950; Cattell & Cattell, 1960, 1963) were created. Unfortunately, culture-fair tests apparently do not work very well, especially for predicting school achievement (Salvia & Ysseldyke, 1978); they may even be more biased than the tests they sought to replace (Jensen, 1971). Arguments about possible test bias and the use of tests with culturally different populations continue, therefore (Cleary, Humphrey, Kendrick, & Wesman, 1975; Jensen, 1980), and the issue of context remains unresolved.

Context and Controversy. You may now be able to see why controversy about intelligence testing is so pervasive. Trait constructs and trait measurement yield quantitative scores that are used to compare and rank individuals. Some individuals, and perhaps some groups of individuals, are invariably going to be classified as less competent than others. When rank is further used to select some people for special attention and exclude others, the basis for effective discrimination is created, regardless of the merits and accuracy of the selection decisions. The notion of differentiating people, however, is inherent in the conceptualization of intelligence as reflected in intellectual assessment. Perhaps we should reexamine that notion.

True Scores, Errors of Measurement, and Context

From a psychometric perspective, the score (X) a person receives on a test has two components. One of those components is the *true score* (T); T supposedly reflects the amount of the trait the person possesses. The second component is *error* (e). Error exists because indirect measurement that uses behavior as signs is an imperfect means of assessing a trait. Thus $X = T + e$. Psychometricians attempt to make e as small as possible by standardizing tests, selecting item signs carefully, and meticulously evaluating the properties of the test. These procedures greatly reduce *e*, but they never eliminate it completely. Because of *e*, people's scores vary somewhat from time to time, test to test, and setting to setting. This variance is attributed to the lack of perfection in measurement procedures, not to fluctuations in the amount of a characteristic a person possesses.

If for a moment we reject the assumptions of trait constructs, then variations in an individual's scores reflect not error but actual differences in performance that coincide with changes in context. In fact, where errors due to context would ordinarily be a nuisance, in this situation they would be important; the residual commonality (*T* in the former equation) may not even be the focus. When we suspend the idea of a true score, however—when we no longer assume that test scores tap a trait—we are no longer using indirect assessment. We are no longer ascribing to the dipstick theory of measurement. Instead, we are considering how behavior changes with circumstance, and circumstances are theoretically irrelevant to traits.

Suspending our assumptions about traits is a break from the traditions of Galton, Binet, Spearman, Thurstone, and many other giants of psychology, but a number of authorities are currently advocating this course (Mischel, 1968, 1973). It may change our very notions of intelligence.

A Reevaluation of Trait Measurement

Earlier in the chapter (pp. 302–303) we asked a series of questions about the assumptions behind mental ability testing and the way those assumptions are related to sociopolitical controversy. We can now, on the basis of the preceding discussion, reevaluate those questions.

1. *Are the assumptions underlying intellectual assessment useful ones?* This depends on the purposes of assessment. The assumptions of trait measurement are extremely useful in detecting individual differences. Had these assumptions never been accepted, it is unlikely that standardized testing would ever have flourished. For certain kinds of decisions, a knowledge of individual differences is important because it helps us to predict how people will behave in the future. In addition, whenever educational, vocational, or other resources must be allocated to some students but not to others, it seems wise to be able to identify the people most capable of benefiting from the resources. In many respects, trait assessment procedures allow us to identify these individuals.

On the other hand, trait constructs are not very useful for conceptualizing intelligence as a process; an analogy with oil reserves fails to take process into account. The assumptions lack the power to help us understand the operations involved in intellectual behavior. Moreover, although trait assessment is useful for diagnosing individual differences, it tells us little about how to alter, change, or ameliorate those differences. *IQ* scores provide little direction for remediation and intervention.

2. *Did adherence to these assumptions hinder or assist the development of theories of intelligence?* Again, the answer is both. The assumptions furthered the psychometric movement, theories of individual differences, and trait theories of intelligence. There may, however, be other equally worthwhile ways of conceptualizing intelligence that require different assumptions. Adhering too closely to one set of assumptions can prevent the development of alternatives.

3. *Are the assumptions related to the current debate about mental testing?* Very definitely. Trait measurement stirs controversy because it involves ranking and comparing individuals and because it is possible that tests are biased against particular individuals and populations. When test outcomes influence decisions about people's futures, controversy is unavoidable. Even though the testing movement has supporters who argue eloquently that the tests are unbiased, or who attribute bias to other factors (Cleary, Humphrey, Kendrick, & Wesman, 1975; Jensen, 1980), the controversy is likely to continue.

There is little doubt that we need standardized intelligence tests, but it is equally certain that we must pursue alternative routes as well.

Alternative Approaches to Intelligence

When one of the authors was growing up, her father steadfastly refused to reveal the *IQ* scores his children had received on tests given in the school systems. Although he knew the scores, he reasoned quite directly that "*IQ* is as *IQ* does." This rather folksy dictum expresses assumptions common to two alternatives to intelligence of more recent vintage than the trait variety. These approaches represent a break with traditional psychometric evaluation, but they may help us understand intelligence in new ways.

Behavioral Assessment

Behavioral assessment involves a number of different measures and techniques used by clinicians and psychologists to evaluate behavior (Kratochwill, 1980). The techniques, although varied, reflect certain common themes. First, they all represent a break with the underlying assumptions of trait measurement (Nelson & Hayes, 1979). In behavioral assessment, measurement is not indirect. Overt behavior is of interest in and of itself, not as an indicator of an unobservable variable. Second, behavior is treated not as a *sign* but as a *sample* of what the person can do in a particular setting (Salvia & Ysseldyke, 1978). Third, context, the situation in which the sample is gathered, is an important focus rather than merely a source of error (Bijou, 1976).

If one considers the acquisition of behavior samples in context to be important, one must collect more than one sample in more than one context. Accordingly, psychologists with this orientation collect numerous behavior samples using observation, interviewing, and even traditional tests. Some of the samples come from artificial settings, such as those associated with formal testing; others come from more natural situations in the classroom, home, or workplace. The data, then, consist of a range of samples gathered in a range of settings.

This approach to assessment is consistent with a behavioral perspective, and you will recall from Chapter 3a that behaviorists are uncomfortable drawing inferences from behavior about unobservable causes. Behavior samples are thus not used to assess a trait, which is by definition an underlying variable; the samples are simply considered indicators of how the person can be expected to perform in similar circumstances.

Proponents of behavioral assessment (for example, Kratochwill, 1980) note that this alternative provides more information than traditional procedures. Since the behavior samples are not reduced to a single number, a score, they reflect the person's performance in more detail. This richness of detail is helpful in planning educational intervention (Carver, 1974; Nelson & Bowles, 1975) and remediation designed to meet the needs of the individual. Many of these data collection procedures are bulky and awkward, however, and they can be expensive. Furthermore, they often lack the precision of psychometric instrumentation. Obviously, they are useful for intervention strategies, but they are less useful for normative comparison.

Theoretically, because behaviorally oriented psychologists are loath to draw inferences, they refrain from using data to build constructs. Behavior samples are thus not used as a source of a theory of intelligence; rather than replacing trait theory, behaviorists avoid theory as such. If we wish to examine an alternative theory of intelligence, we must look elsewhere. In terms of the dictum "*IQ* is as *IQ* does," behavioral assessment focuses on the *does*, the overt manifestations of intelligence.

Process Approaches

An alternative theory of intelligence is developing in what you might consider a very unlikely quarter—the field of computer science. Specialists in computers have designed programs that model the mental processes involved in thinking and problem-solving. The computer serves as an analogue for the *process* of human thought. This is the field of *artificial intelligence*, which is contributing greatly to changes in the way we conceptualize intelligence and the human mind.

Research Report

In the last ten years researchers concerned with intelligence and aptitude have changed the approach and the focus of their investigations. Global or even specific descriptions of individual differences are no longer of primary interest. The present concern is about what the individual is doing when solving an intellectual problem—that is, the information-processing strategies used. Identification of the information-processing strategies makes it possible to relate them to ability measures, to instruction, and to outcomes in a much more informative manner than was ever possible with the traditional trait approaches. The research example selected for inclusion in this chapter reflects this contemporary focus.

The intellectual problem studied in this investigation was a type of reasoning task. Essentially, the tasks followed this pattern: "John is taller than Bill; Bill is taller than Pete; who is tallest?" Two relational pieces of information are given; the task is to infer the third. No doubt a variety of solution strategies are possible—some spatial, some verbal, some combinations of the two, and even an algorithmic one. In the last one, the linguistic surface structure of the problem itself is used to make a choice. The strategy chosen may influence the time taken to solve the problem. Moreover, the strategy an individual uses most efficiently may be related to his own pattern of abilities, prior experience and training, or a combination of the two. Essentially, then, solving these problems probably reflects aptitudes of the individual and the strategies chosen as well.

The researchers investigated how efficiently college students could solve this variety of reasoning problem. In addition, they wanted to find out whether strategy instructions (training) would affect efficiency, and whether outcomes would be related to the subjects' patterns of spatial and verbal abilities. They also wished to test mathematical models representing the nature of the information-processing itself in order to determine whether the model was a good fit to what subjects actually did.

When the focus of an investigation is *efficiency* rather than accuracy, one looks at how long it takes to respond. This is a measure of *latency*. The dependent measure in this study was latency in seconds.

A hundred and forty-four undergraduates solved a set of these reasoning problems. They were divided into three groups: (1) untrained subjects, who received no strategy instructions for solving the problems; (2) visualization subjects, who were instructed to try to visualize the relationships presented in the problem; and (3) algorithm subjects, who were taught a strategy that utilized the sentence structure of the information to reach a solution. Subjects were also given verbal and spatial ability tests.

Subjects in the algorithm group solved the problems much faster than did either the untrained subjects or the visualization subjects. The latter two groups of subjects performed with essentially equal speed. The algorithm strategy was thus the most efficient one, and it was easily trained.

Using sophisticated mathematical modeling techniques (which are beyond the scope of this presentation) the investigators were able to reclassify subjects in terms of strategies they actually used in solving the problems. This, then, allowed them to examine the relationship between strategy use and spatial and verbal ability. As you might expect, efficient use of (1) a linguistic strategy was correlated with verbal ability, (2) a visualization strategy was correlated with spatial ability, (3) a mixed strategy was associated with both verbal and spatial ability, and (4) an algorithm strategy was only marginally associated with either of the ability measures.

Intelligent behaving, as tapped by these reasoning tasks, is a complex process affected by both ability and by the strategy used. Strategy in turn can be affected by training. Moreover, these investigators have demonstrated that by using powerful new mathematical tools we can learn a great deal more about the processes involved in intelligent behavior. This is a great improvement in specificity over a trait approach.

Sternberg, R. J., & E. M. Weil. An aptitude x strategy interaction in linear syllogistic reasoning, *Journal of Educational Psychology*, 1980, 72 (2), 226–239.

Trait Versus Process.   Trait approaches to intelligence, particularly those developed from factor analytic studies, treat the mind as a reserve of separate quantities. The focus is not on what the person does with the quantities at a mental level, but on specifying and measuring these quantities. This leads to a conceptualization of the mind as compartmentalized and fragmented, like a spice rack containing jars filled to different levels. We can specify that person *A* possesses more of one kind of spice than person *B,* but not how person *A* uses the spice to create an outcome. Trait approaches neglect to take process into account.

In the last few decades, cognitive psychologists have been investigating the processes of human thought, the mental actions involved in cognition. The consensus today seems to be that the mind is best represented as an integrated, holistic network of action. This view is inconsistent with factor analytic notions; the spice rack analogue is not a good metaphor for this conceptualization of the mind. Spice racks have contents; thought involves processes. These investigations have yet to coalesce into a formal theory of intelligence, but this style of theorizing represents a break with traditional assumptions, approaches, and models of the mind.

Directions for the Future.   As those involved in computer science, cognitive psychology, information-processing, and for that matter development (Piagetians also represent the mind as consisting of integrated networks of action) share ideas more extensively, new conceptualizations of intelligence are bound to develop. We will have new theories of intelligence that will reflect basic assumptions different from those of earlier theories. Darwin, Galton, and Binet may have begun the process of defining intelligence, but they would probably not recognize the direction it is taking today. The task is incomplete, but we can offer predictions about what theories of the future will probably be like:

1. New theories will emphasize the processes involved in intelligent action.

New Directions in Research

While measures based on trait conceptions of intelligence continue to be used widely in the schools, they are not the focus of contemporary investigations in intellectual functioning. There is, at present, less concern with *who has how much?* and more with *what is it?* (Resnick 1976). In recent years many psychologists have rejected the trait approach to intelligence. Rejection of the Galton view and the psychometric view of the nature of intelligence requires that something new be provided with which to replace it. Here we find, as we have before, that it is those investigators working within the information-processing perspective who are supplying the possible replacements (Glaser, 1981; Sternberg, 1977).

Newer developments are reflected in studies of human problem-solving (Greeno, 1978; Newell & Simon, 1972), which is a kind of intellectual functioning, while other studies reflect the impact of artificial intelligence (Miller, 1978). A common feature of both of these approaches is an emphasis on detail. They are both concerned with specifying clearly and precisely what is involved in in-telligent behavior by use of a detailed delineation of process.

The fundamental building block of many information-processing approaches to thinking and intelligent behaving is the elementary cognitive process (Greeno, 1978; Newell & Simon, 1972; Sternberg, 1977). Interest in the components of aptitude has grown rapidly in recent years (for example, Brown & Burton, 1978; Pellegrino & Glaser, 1979; Snow, Frederico, & Montague, 1980), and moreover, the information is of importance to educators (Glaser, 1981). The focus of contemporary research is on process, but process is not well tapped by instruments designed to assess traits.

Sooner or later, these newer conceptions of intelligence will begin to have a broad impact on our assessment of intelligence as well as our understanding of it. With more modern testing models (Hively, 1974; Lord, 1980; Bergan, 1982) and sophisticated methods for handling data (for example, Joreskog & Sorbon, 1979), the intelligence tests of the future will look quite different from the ones in wide use today.

2. New models will be integrated, not compartmentalized like the models associated with factor analysis.
3. New tools, such as the computer analogue, may replace psychometric methodologies.
4. New constructs that are not necessarily quantitative will replace the trait construct.

These future developments will surely prove exciting and may change the way we view ourselves. It seems evident that the combined force of sociopolitical controversy, behavioral psychology, computer science, and a resurgence of interest in cognition will challenge the very basis of trait theory and indirect trait measurement. This is for the future, however. For now, testing is with us, and it will remain with us for some time.

Summary

Theories of intelligence began with the work of Galton in the nineteenth century, continued with Binet, and were elaborated on by the factorialists from the 1920s to the 1960s. The original theory and subsequent elaborations reflected a Darwinian theme of individual differences that has pervaded the psychometric movement since it began. According to this theme, intelligence is a trait (1) that could be measured, (2) that could be quantified, and (3) that varied from person to person. The theme that led to normative evaluation was based on assumptions about the relationship between traits and observable behavior that are entrenched in our society.

More recently, challenges from a variety of quarters have raised doubts about that pervasive theme and the assumptions behind it. As a result, new ways of conceptualizing and measuring intelligence are emerging, but a new theory of intelligence is only now beginning to evolve.

TEACHING SCENARIO

A scenario theme raised in Chapter 2b was the problem of communicating educational progress to parents, students, and others in a way that is meaningful. Most times, however, educators transmit more than information about class progress. In the majority of school systems, students encounter periodic, regular examinations with a variety of standardized tests. Tests yield data about student attributes, primarily in the form of standard scores. These data constitute another set of information that must be communicated.

Explaining test results to parents and students is not always a straightforward matter. First, the numbers themselves can be meaningless and ambiguous when taken out of context. Second, test scores can affect the way we feel about ourselves, the way we gauge our chances for success, and what we decide to do in the future. Communicating this information is not a challenge to take lightly.

Ms. Young is a school counselor in a large junior high school. The ninth grade students have all recently been assessed on a battery of ability tests. The test data are to be communicated to the students and used for counseling purposes in helping the students plan their high school programs.

Ms. Young has the responsibility of communicating the results of the tests and advising a group of the students on program planning. She knows the students should be informed, and she wishes to pass on the information in a way that is both meaningful and informative. At the same time, she does not want to discourage students who did less well than others, to limit the motivation of those who fell short of expectations, or to offer premature barriers on the students' future educational planning. What is the best way to proceed?

Chapter 8b

Measurement of Ability and Achievement

Introduction

Although the arguments regarding the administration and use of standardized testing are well known, their impact on school practices has been relatively slight. A recent survey of sixty-eight school districts revealed that every system had a standardized testing program. The average number of tests administered by each school system each year was five (Sproull & Zubrow, 1981). The great testing debate has apparently not affected the administration of tests, although it may have had an influence on the interpretation and use of test results.

The kinds of standardized tests administered most often are ability and achievement tests. Ability tests are tests of intelligence, scholastic aptitude, or academic potential. Achievement tests measure student accomplishment in various subjects.

Since standardized testing is still widespread, you will almost certainly take part in some aspect of the testing process. Teachers are occasionally involved in the selection of standardized tests. In some schools, teachers may be expected to administer and score such tests. It is very probable that you as a teacher will see the data derived from the test and will be required to interpret the results for personal use as well as for students, parents, and the public.

In this chapter, we will present information that will help you interpret standardized test scores. We will also discuss the basic qualities of a good test. Because test scores may be reported in a number of different ways, we will present some statistical methods that will help you understand the way scores are derived and interpreted. Finally, we will consider some frequently used intelligence and achievement tests and the uses of test results.

Standardized Tests and Measurements

To find out how students differ in ability or achievement, teachers can use a variety of methods and procedures. Such information can be obtained with teacher-made tests, observations of behavior, and class recitations. Standardized tests are another procedure for measuring individual differences. Standardized tests differ from other tests in several ways. They are constructed by professional test developers with the help of experienced item writers and editors. The items on standardized tests are administered to groups before they are published. This provides information for revising the items, selecting items of appropriate difficulty, and constructing scales for interpreting scores. The directions for administering and scoring the tests are clearly specified so that the scores of individual students can be compared with those of larger groups.

Standardized tests are used for measurement, and they also may be used to make evaluations. Although the terms *measurement* and *evaluation* are often used interchangeably, the two processes are different. *Measurement* is the process of quantifying the amount of a given trait a person possesses. *Evaluation* is the process of systematically collecting and analyzing data in order to make a decision. The score a student receives on a standardized test is a measurement. The score may then be used to make a decision about the student; this is evaluation. In this chapter we focus primarily on measurement; the uses of the test results, which may involve evaluation, will be elaborated upon in Chapter 15.

Characteristics of Good Measurement

If you were to examine the two large volumes of Buros' *Mental Measurement Yearbook* (1978), you would find that there is a large number of tests designed to measure ability and achievement. Some of these tests provide excellent measurements, others are satisfactory, and still others are poor instruments for determining individual differences.

Teachers may or may not be involved in the selection of tests, but if you are involved you will want to choose the best test available. What considerations guide a teacher or school administrator in selecting a test to measure individual differences? For tests to be useful, they must meet certain criteria. Two qualities of tests that are considered important are validity and reliability.

Validity

Test validity is an important characteristic. A valid test is one that measures what it is supposed to measure for a specific group or individual. If we are interested in measuring arithmetic achievement, then the test must measure that rather than reading achievement or science achievement. A test that is valid for measuring third grade achievement would be invalid for measuring seventh grade arithmetic achievement. Validity concerns what the test measures and the test's appropriateness for the group or individual who is to be measured. A valid intelligence test measures intellectual behavior, not how well a person drives a car or how a child gets along with his peers. An intelligence test written in English may not provide a valid measure of the intelligence of a child who speaks no English.

There are three types of validity: content validity, construct validity, and criterion-referenced validity. Which of these types is important depends on the type of test and the purpose for which it is being administered.

Content Validity.   Content validity is of major importance in achievement testing. Achievement tests are designed to assess knowledge of a body of material or a list of objectives. To assure that the test is valid, the test maker must be certain that the items actually do cover the content and that the items selected represent the entire range of content or set of objectives.

Suppose a teacher is constructing a test about fractions. In class, the teacher has covered the addition, subtraction, multiplication, and division of both simple and complex fractions. Accordingly, test problems the teacher constructs must deal with fractions, not whole numbers or decimal fractions. The items must include all four operations using both simple and complex fractions. A test that included only addition and subtraction problems would not be valid for this teacher's class. Such a test might have been valid for the group when they had covered only addition and subtraction; however, two questions must be answered in considering content validity: (1) Does the test cover the content that has been taught? (2) Is the test appropriate for this group?

Standardized achievement tests, although they may be technically well written, may not be valid for particular groups or certain individuals within a group. Standardized achievement tests are based on material commonly taught in schools at specific grade levels. A test constructor who wishes to develop an achievement test for third grade arithmetic might, as a first step, find out which textbooks are commonly used in the third grade. An examination of the textbooks would reveal that some topics are common to all of them while other topics are found in only some of them. The test constructor would then construct test items covering the content included by all or most of the textbooks. Subsequently, the test maker might submit these items to a panel of so-called experts and solicit their opinions as to the appropriateness of the items for third graders. If the test items met one or both of these criteria, the test could be considered to have content validity.

This content validity is based on the consensus of the textbooks or the experts. To determine whether the test provides a valid measure of third grade arithmetic achievement for a particular classroom, one would need to determine how well the objectives and content of that class matched those reflected in the test items. A school that did not follow common practices in ordering its arithmetic curriculum might find that a well written test would not be valid for its students.

Construct Validity.   Construct validity is important in the measurement of such personality variables as intelligence, motivation, and self-concept. Construct validity refers to the degree to which a test measures a hypothetical construct. As you will remember from the last chapter, a construct is a formulation used to explain behavior. Constructs, rather than being directly observable, are inferred from observable behavior.

A test designed to measure a construct is dependent upon the validity of the construct itself. When it was observed that some students learned faster, learned more, and retained learned information better than others, the construct of intelligence was developed to explain these differences. If the construct is valid, a test will possess construct validity insofar as students who score higher on the test actually do learn faster, learn more, and retain learned information better than those who score lower on the test.

Establishing construct validity is a lengthy process requiring many research studies. The technical manual that accompanies the published test provides a report on its construct validity that defines and describes the construct to be measured and reports the research evidence that supports the test.

Criterion-Related Validity.   Criterion-related validity refers to how well the test measures either current or future performance. This kind of validity may thus be of two types, concurrent or predictive. When we have another measure to which we can compare test scores, we may establish validity through concurrent measurement. Suppose a test constructor has developed a new intelligence test. One way of validating it would be to compare the students' performance on the new test with their performance on a previously validated intelligence test, such as the Stanford-Binet. If student scores were quite similar on the two tests, the test maker could claim validity on the basis of the already established validity of the Stanford-Binet.

The difference between concurrent and predictive validity is the time between the administration of the test and measurement of the criterion. Aptitude tests are validated on the basis of how well they predict future behavior. The Scholastic Aptitude Test (*SAT*) is administered to high school students to predict how well they will perform in college. Studies show that students who get high scores on the *SAT*

The Scholastic Aptitude Test is administered annually to high
school juniors and seniors. The results are used by colleges for
determining admissions, for placement in course sequences, and for
awarding scholarships.

tend to have higher grade-point averages than those who score low.
The scores from the *SAT* can thus be used to predict college grade-point
average.

Reading readiness tests are administered to kindergartners or beginning first graders to predict their performance in first grade reading.
Algebra aptitude tests are used to predict student performance in first-
year algebra. Tests of clerical and mechanical aptitude and other abilities are used to predict occupational success. All of these tests depend
upon predictive validity.

For both concurrent and predictive validity, the relationship between test performance and the criterion determines the test's validity.
The relationship between test scores and criterion is never perfect,

however, so predictions are less than perfect. The closer the relationship between the test and the criterion, the more accurate the prediction and thus the more valid the test.

Reliability

A second characteristic of a good test is reliability. A reliable test is one that yields consistent results. The results of a test given to a group of students on Monday, for example, should be the same as the test given on Tuesday. The student who scored highest the first day should also score highest the second day; the second highest the first day should score second highest the second day, and so on for the entire group (see Test I, Table 8b–1). If this was the case, we would have a perfectly reliable test. Perfect reliability is difficult to come by, however.

The rankings for Test II and Test III in Table 8b–1 reflect lower reliability. The reliability of Test II is fairly good, since students tended to have the same rank on the second administration as they did on the first. The reliability of Test III is very poor, since some who ranked high on the first scored high on the second and some scored low. The inconsistencies indicate low reliability.

Factors Affecting Reliability.   Several factors can affect the reliability of the test. Some are inherent in the test itself, some involve the conditions of the testing situation, and some are concerned with characteristics of the individual. One factor of the test itself that affects reliability is the length of the test. A test consisting of two questions will not be as reliable as one of fifty questions. Other things being equal, the more questions asked the more reliable the results. Item quality

TABLE 8b–1. **Rankings Showing Different Relationships**

Test I		Test II		Test III	
Day 1	*Day 2*	*Day 1*	*Day 2*	*Day 1*	*Day 2*
1	1	1	3	1	6
2	2	2	1	2	10
3	3	3	4	3	3
4	4	4	2	4	8
5	5	5	6	5	7
6	6	6	7	6	1
7	7	7	5	7	4
8	8	8	9	8	9
9	9	9	10	9	2
10	10	10	8	10	5
Perfect relationship		High positive relationship		Little or no relationship	

also affects reliability. Ambiguous or poorly stated items lower the reliability, inasmuch as the same person could interpret the questions differently on different days.

The conditions of the testing situation also affect reliability. Students tested in a hot, crowded, humid room would probably do less well than they would in a more comfortable atmosphere. Such distractions as excessive noise could also affect student performance.

Variations in the individual from day to day and moment to moment can affect the reliability of tests as well. A temporary physical or mental condition may affect a student's performance. Anxiety, fatigue, or an illness, such as a cold or headache, may lead to an unreliable measurement, as may momentary variations in recall or attention. Luck in guessing may also be a factor. Some days it seems that our guesses are a hundred percent correct; on other days, our luck deserts us completely.

As you can see, test reliability is affected by a number of factors. Any factor that causes a student's performance to differ from his or her true level of achievement is a cause of unreliability.

Reporting Reliabilities.   Most test manuals that accompany standardized tests report the test's reliability. It may be reported in terms of a reliability coefficient, a standard error of measurement, or both.

Reliability Coefficient. A reliability coefficient is a statistic that reflects the degree of relationship between two measures given to the same individuals. If a test is administered first on one day and again on the next, the relationship between the two scores can be calculated. This measure of relationship is the reliability coefficient. It may vary from .00 (no relationship) to 1.00 (perfect relationship). Most standardized tests of achievement and intelligence have reliability coefficients of .90 or higher, which means that the measurements obtained from the tests are quite consistent, and student performance changes little from one testing situation to another. Tests of personality often have lower reliability coefficients than do tests of achievement and intelligence.

The reliability of a test becomes important when decisions are made about students on the basis of a single test score. Basing a student's course grade on a single examination or determining whether to place a student in a group from the results of a single test are risky when the test used is unreliable. The student may be misclassified or given too high or too low a grade only because the test was unreliable.

Standard Error of Measurement. The score a student receives on a test is composed of two parts, a *true score* and an *error score*. The error part of the score comes from the unreliability of the test, and it may either increase or decrease the true score.

Obtained score		True score		Error score
X	=	T	±	E

On a perfectly reliable test, a person's obtained score would exactly equal his true score: E would be 0. No test is perfectly reliable, however, so there will always be an error component. The score a person receives on a test is thus an estimate of the true score. The higher the reliability, the less the error and the more accurate the estimate.

The standard error of measurement is a measure of the amount a person's score might vary from his obtained score as a result of the unreliability of the test. When we take into account the standard error of measurement, the score a student receives on a test is considered to be not a fixed value, but the midpoint of a range into which the person's true score is likely to fall.

Suppose, for example, that an intelligence test was administered to two students, Grace and Charlie, on the same day. Grace's raw score (number of items correct) was 45 and Charlie's raw score was 40. Considering these scores alone, an observer might judge Grace to be more intelligent than Charlie. Assume, however, that the standard error of measurement on the test was four points. The formula given previously in this section can be used to estimate the true scores.

	Obtained score		Error score		True score
	X	±	E	=	T
Grace	45	±	4	=	41–49
Charlie	40	±	4	=	36–44

We can now see that the ranges of the students' scores overlap, so in actuality there may be no difference in their intelligence. Because of the test's unreliability, on a second testing Charlie's score might surpass Grace's.

One might wonder what the chances are that a person's score will fall within the range given in the estimated score. According to measurement theory, if one standard error of measurement (*SEM*) is added to and subtracted from a person's obtained score, the chances are approximately two out of three that the range will include the person's true score. To be more certain that the range includes the true score, we must increase the range.

	Likelihood that the range will include the true score:
Obtained score ± 1 SEM	2 chances out of 3
Obtained score ± 2 SEM	95 chances out of 100
Obtained score ± 3 SEM	997 chances out of 1000

This discussion of reliability and standard error of measurement is designed to alert you to the fallibility of test scores. Because of unreliability, we must think of the obtained score as an estimate of the true score. The accuracy of the estimate depends upon the reliability of the test. The manual that accompanies a standardized test usually includes a standard error of measurement value.

▶ *ACTIVITY 1.*   Obtain a manual for the administration of either the Wechsler Intelligence Scale for Children—Revised (*WISC—R*) or the Wechsler Adult Intelligence Scale—Revised (*WAIS—R*). Read the first three chapters of the manual.

1. What is the author's construct of intelligence?
2. What types of validity are reported?
3. What are the reliabilities and standard errors of measurement for the Verbal *IQ*, Performance *IQ*, and the Full Scale *IQ*?

A Little Bit About Statistics

Some of the measurement concepts we will discuss will be more meaningful if you understand some basic statistical concepts. *Statistics* are terms used to describe a group of measurements. The measurements themselves are considered raw scores. Numbers of items answered correctly on a test, heights of individuals, or the amount of time different students spent on an assignment would all be raw scores. We use statistical methods to bring order and meaning to these scores. Consider, for example, the test scores received by thirty students on a sociology test. Table 8b–2 is a display of the scores as the teacher recorded them. Because the scores are unordered, it is difficult to derive much information from them.

One way to organize the scores in order to get more information from them is to construct a frequency distribution, a list of all the

TABLE 8b–2. **Test Scores of 30 Students**

25	28	21	38	28	23
32	25	27	31	26	27
40	16	28	30	22	32
18	32	31	34	20	31
19	34	36	29	39	36

TABLE 8b–3. **Test Scores Arranged in Frequency Distribution**

Score	Frequency	Score	Frequency
40	1	27	2
39	1	26	1
38	1	25	2
37	0	24	0
36	2	23	1
35	0	22	1
34	2	21	1
33	0	20	1
32	3	19	1
31	3	18	1
30	1	17	0
29	1	16	1
28	3		

Median = 28.5
Mean = 28.6

possible scores between the highest and lowest scores students received. The number of people who received each score is tallied and recorded next to the score, as illustrated in Table 8b–3. The frequency distribution permits us to see the way the scores were distributed over the entire range. By doing a little addition, for example, we find that fifty percent of the students had scores between 27 and 34. Only five persons scored above 34, while ten scored below 27.

Central Tendency Measures

A number of other statistical procedures can be used to convey information about scores. We might, for example, be interested in the group's average score. The term *average* has different meanings, however, and different types of average scores are computed in different ways.

Median.   The *median* of distribution is a type of average in which the scores are separated into two equal parts. The median is the point that separates the upper fifty percent of the scores from the lower fifty percent. It is computed differently depending on whether the total number of scores is odd or even. If there is an even number of scores, the median is the number halfway between the two middle scores. If the number of scores is odd, the median is the middle score of the distribution.

In our sample of the sociology test scores, there are thirty scores. This is an even number, so the median falls between the two middle scores, the fifteenth and sixteenth. Counting up the frequency column, the fifteenth score is 28 and the sixteenth score is 29, so the median (halfway between the two scores) would be 28.5.

Mean. A second and perhaps more common type of average is obtained by adding all the scores and dividing by the total number of scores. This statistic is called the *mean* of the distribution. In our example, we would add 40 + 39 + 38 + 36 ... + 15 and divide by 30. The mean of the distribution is 28.6, very close to the median.

Knowing either the mean or median of a distribution permits one to describe a person's score. Billy's score was 38; he was above the average, both the mean and the median. Sam's score was 22; he scored below the average. Mike scored 16; he was below average also. As you can see, Sam and Mike can be described with the same term, but their scores were different. To better differentiate their scores, we must consider another kind of statistic.

Standard Deviation—A Measure of Variability

The second type of statisic is a measure of the way the scores in a distribution vary. The measure of variability used most often is the *standard deviation*. The standard deviation tells us how far the scores vary from the mean of the distribution. If the scores are all very close to the mean, the standard deviation is small. If they deviate widely from the mean, the standard deviation is large.

To learn the exact procedure for calculating the standard deviation, you can refer to any beginning statistics text. A short-cut method that provides an excellent approximation (Sabers & Klausmeier, 1971) of the exact standard deviation has been devised by Davenport (1971).

$$\text{S.D.} = \frac{1.8 \,(\text{sum of the high fifth} - \text{sum of the low fifth})}{N}$$

To calculate the standard deviation for our sample data in Table 8b–3, add the highest fifth of the scores (40 + 39 + 38 + 36 + 36 + 34 = 223) and the lowest fifth of the scores (16 + 18 + 19 + 20 + 21 + 22 = 116). The difference between the two sums is 107.

$$\text{S.D.} = \frac{1.8 \,(107)}{30} = \frac{192.6}{30} = 6.4$$

The standard deviation can be used to describe how far above or below the mean a score falls. Billy's score was 38, which is 9.4 points above the mean. Dividing this difference by 6.4, we see that Billy's score is 1.8 standard deviations above the mean. Sam's and Mike's scores, which were both below average, can be converted in the same way to see how far below average they were.

$$\text{Sam's score} = \frac{22 - 28.6}{6.4} = -1.0 \quad \text{Mike's score} = \frac{16 - 28.6}{6.4} = -2.0$$

Sam's score was 1 standard deviation below the mean (indicated by the negative sign), whereas Mike's score was twice as far below the mean—2 standard deviations.

Standard Scores

The converted score that represents how far above or below the mean a score falls in standard deviation units is called a *standard score*. The basic standard score is called the Z score, which we calculated for the three scores of 38, 22, and 16.

$$\text{Z score} = \frac{\text{Raw score} - \text{Mean}}{\text{Standard deviation}}$$

The Z score is only one of a number of standard scores, but it provides the basis for all the other scores. When scores are converted to Z scores, the mean of the distribution is 0 and the standard deviation is 1. Other standard scores derived from raw scores have different means and different standard deviations. The Wechsler tests, for example, report *IQ*s as standard scores with a mean of 100 and a standard deviation of 15. A Wechsler *IQ* would be derived by using the formula IQ = 15 (Z score) + 100. The *T* score is another commonly used score, with a mean of 50 and a standard deviation of 10. To calculate a *T* score, multiply the Z score by 10 and add 50. A comparison of commonly reported standard scores is shown in Figure 8b–1.

Another frequently used standard score is the stanine. Stanines are derived by dividing the distribution into nine parts. The score is reported as a single digit number with 9 being the highest score and 1 the lowest score. The mean of the stanine distribution is 5, and the standard deviation is 2. The ranges of the stanines are also shown in Figure 8b–1.

The Normal Curve

When measures are taken of a large number of individuals, the scores may fall in a normal distribution. The distribution of intelligence test scores and achievement test scores for large numbers of people is normal. The normal curve is pictured in Figure 8b–1. The scores are represented along the horizontal line; the height of the curve represents the number of persons who received each score.

Normal score distributions have certain known characteristics:

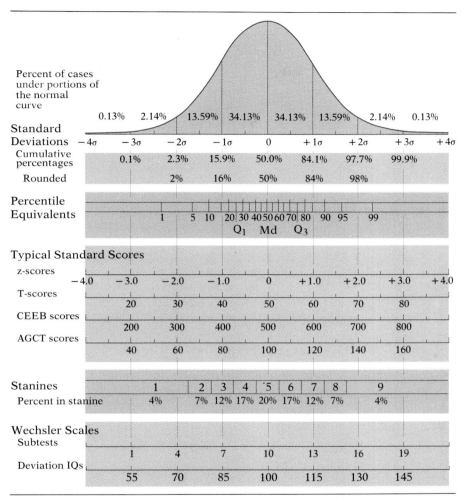

FIGURE 8b–1.   Test Score Interpretation of the Normal Curve Distribution

(From the *Test Service Notebook* 148 of the National Psychological Corporation, 1980)

1. The mean and median of the distribution are at the same point, which is also the score corresponding to the highest point on the curve.
2. For all practical purposes, the range of the scores is between ± 3 standard deviations for the mean.
3. Specified proportions of the scores fall between any two points in the distribution.
   Approximately 68 percent of the scores fall between ± 1 S.D.

Approximately 95 percent of the scores fall between ±2 S.D.
Approximately 99.7 percent of the scores fall within ±3 S.D.
4. The percent of scores falling above or below a particular point in the distribution can be calculated. Referring to Figure 8b–1, we can see that fifty percent of the scores fall below a Z score of 0. With a little calculation (50 percent + 34 percent), we find that 84 percent fall below a Z score of +1, or a Wechsler *IQ* of 115. To find the percent of the scores that fall above or below a point that is not in even standard deviation units, you must refer to a normal curve table, which can be found in statistics or measurement textbooks.

▶ *ACTIVITY 2.*
    Use the following twenty scores for these activities.

40	48	40	36
42	36	33	44
38	41	50	45
45	40	47	50
42	39	45	33

1. Construct a frequency distribution.
2. Calculate the median and the mean.
3. Calculate the standard deviation.
4. What are the Z scores corresponding to 48, 40, and 36?

Other Derived Scores

By converting raw scores to standard scores, we are attempting to obtain a meaningful interpretation of a raw score. Other derived scores can also be used to render a score meaningful.

Percentile Ranks. As we discussed, the median is the point below which fifty percent of the scores fall, and eighty-four percent of the Wechsler *IQ* scores fall below 115. A type of derived score that gives the percent of scores below a certain score is called the percentile rank (*PR*). To find the *PR* of a score, we determine the percent of scores that fall at or below that score. If the *PR* of Tom's score is 45, this means that 45 percent of the scores were equal to or lower than the score Tom received.

Age and Grade Equivalents. Mental Age and Grade Equivalents are other derived scores. Although the use of these derived scores can lead to misconceptions, they are often used to report standardized test results. The median is the statistic used to derive age and grade equivalents. Suppose we administer an achievement test to a large group of

TABLE 8b–4. **Determining Grade Equivalents**

Score		Grade Equivalent
58	(actual)	5.0
57		4.9
56		4.8
55		4.7
54		4.6
53		4.5
52		4.4
51		4.3
50		4.2
49		4.1
48	(actual)	4.0
47		3.9
46		3.7
45		3.6
44		3.5
43		3.4
42		3.3
41		3.1
40	(actual)	3.0

third, fourth, and fifth grade children in September, and medians for the grade levels are 40, 48, and 58 respectively. The grade equivalents of the three scores would be 3.0, 4.0, and 5.0. The grade equivalents for the scores falling between these points would be derived by interpolation (Table 8b–4). In this example, three grade equivalents were empirically determined; the others represent a kind of guess based on the premise that growth in achievement is fairly uniform throughout the school year. Extrapolation is used to extend the grade equivalents for the scores that are below 40 and above 58. These guesses are even riskier than the interpolated values.

Age equivalents are determined in much the same way as grade equivalents. The difference is that the median scores for certain chronological ages are used instead of the grades in which the students are enrolled. Age equivalents are reported in years and months; 8–4 thus means eight years and four months.

The Measurement of Intelligence

The many concepts and definitions of intelligence are reflected in the multitude of intelligence tests that are available. Buros' *Tests in Print* (1974), a compendium of all published tests, lists more than 250 standardized tests of intelligence or scholastic ability. These include tests of general ability, tests of specialized abilities, group tests, individual tests, and tests that represent a wide variety of constructs of intelligence. We will limit our discussion to two individual tests and some of the more popular group tests.

Individual Intelligence Tests

The individual intelligence tests are designed to be given by an examiner specifically trained to administer them and interpret their results. The questions asked on the individual tests may closely resemble those asked on a group test. The advantage of the individual test is that the examiner can observe the examinee's performance better in a one-on-one situation. The examiner may note evidence of anxiety, restricted attention span, or verbal deficits, for example. This information may be useful in interpreting the test results and planning learning activities for the student.

Stanford-Binet.   *The Stanford-Binet Intelligence Scale* consists of a series of questions grouped by age levels from age three to Superior Adult. The questions asked cover vocabulary, verbal absurdities, numerical questions, following directions, and repeating digits and sentences as well as other content and skills. There are six questions at each age level. The score is determined by the number of questions answered correctly beyond a base age level, the highest age level at which all questions are answered correctly. The score is represented in terms of years and months of mental growth—the child's Mental Age (*MA*). To administer the test to a child who is chronologically ten years and one month old (*CA* = 10–1), the examiner might begin testing at the nine-year level. If the child answered all the questions correctly at that level, the examiner would proceed to the ten-year level. Suppose the examinee misses one question at that level and gets five correct. Then the nine-year level would be considered the basal age. Suppose that subsequently the child gets three items correct at the eleven-year level and misses all questions at the twelve-year level, at which time the test is concluded. For each question answered correctly beyond the basal age, the child receives two months' credit, a total of sixteen months. Adding the sixteen months to the basal age, we see that the child's Mental Age is ten years 4 months (*MA* = 10–4). The child answered the same number of questions correctly as the average child of *CA* = 10–4.

Given the child's chronological age, the *MA* can be converted to an intelligence quotient (*IQ*), which represents the ratio of the *MA* to the *CA*. Until the 1960 revision, the *IQ* was computed with the formula *IQ* = *MA/CA* × 100. With the 1960 revision, the score was converted to a standard score with a mean of one hundred and a standard deviation of sixteen. Even though the procedure for determining the *IQ* has changed, the *IQ* is still interpreted as a ratio of mental age to chronological age. The child in the previous example had a *CA* = 10–1 and an *MA* = 10–4. Calculated according to the formula, his *IQ* is approximately 102. (The standard score conversion yields an *IQ* of 100.) On this test, the child's score was about average. If the standard error of measurement is considered to be five and we use the calculated *IQ* of 102, we could say that there are two chances out of three that his true *IQ* is between 97 and 107.

The Wechsler Tests.   The growth in the popularity of the Wechsler tests can be attributed to several factors. Different tests have been constructed for different age levels—*WPPSI* (CA = 4 to 6), *WISC—R* (CA = 6 to 16), *WAIS—R* (CA = 16 and over). The different tests permit the examiner to ask more questions than are asked on the Stanford-Binet. Wechsler divided the questions into two major sections—one series of subtests provides a Verbal *IQ* and another series of subtests provides a Performance *IQ*. The subtests in the verbal and performance sections may permit more substantial clinical interpretation of an examinee's performance than can be obtained from the Stanford-Binet.

Each subtest of the Wechsler tests consists of a series of questions of the same general type. The subtests are administered in a standard order. The examiner keeps asking questions in each subtest until the child misses a series of questions or until the subtest is completed. The subtests for the WISC—R are described briefly in Table 8b–5.

TABLE 8b–5. Subtest Descriptions of WISC—R

Verbal scale

1. General Information—Questions that ask for information generally acquired without specific training.
2. General Comprehension—Questions that attempt to determine a child's understanding of the occurrence of events.
3. Arithmetic—Questions asking for solution of verbal problems.
4. Similarities—Questions on understanding commonalities between concepts.
5. Vocabulary—Items requiring definitions of words.
6. Digit Span—Repetition of a series of digits as stated by the examiner, or in reverse order of the presentation.

Performance scale

1. Picture Completion—Asks that the examinee detect what is missing in a series of pictures of objects.
2. Picture Arrangement—A series of pictures like frames of comic strips must be rearranged in order to tell a story.
3. Block Design—Examinee arranges blocks in a design that matches one presented by the examiner.
4. Object Assembly—Pieces of a puzzle are to be arranged to make a familiar object.
5. Coding—Examinee translates digits into a code according to a prescribed key.
6. Mazes—Examinee traces way out of mazes.

Combining the scores from the subtests yields a Verbal *IQ* and a Performance *IQ* for each student. The Total *IQ* is based on all subtests. The *IQ*s are standard scores with a mean of 100 and a standard deviation of fifteen.

The Total *IQ* and Verbal *IQ* of the Wechsler tests correlate well with the Stanford-Binet, a fact indicating that they measure similar abilities. The relationship of the Performance *IQ* to the Stanford-Binet is somewhat lower, a fact that means the performance subtests measure some different abilities than the Stanford-Binet does.

Group Intelligence Tests

The administration and scoring of group intelligence tests require no formal training, so these tasks often fall to the classroom teacher. The directions to the examiner are stated very explicitly in the test manual, and they should be followed exactly as stated. The major tasks of the test administrator are reading the directions to the examinees, answering questions before beginning the test, and abiding by the time limits. Scoring keys are provided for checking the examinee's responses, and tables for converting raw scores to a derived score, such as Mental Age, Intelligence Quotient, or percentile rank, are given in the test manual. The time allotted for administration of the test is usually between twenty minutes and an hour.

Group tests are not as reliable as individual tests. Because they require less time for administration and require no specially trained administrator, the group tests are commonly used for large-scale intelligence testing programs. Students who score low or high or students who have special problems (reading disability, blindness, deafness) may then be given an individual test.

There are far more group intelligence tests than there are individual tests, and they represent a wide variety of constructs of intelligence. We will briefly describe just three commonly used tests. More extensive descriptions of these and other intelligence tests can be found in Buros' *Mental Measurements Yearbook* (1978).

Otis Quick-Scoring Mental Ability Tests. Forms are available for grades one to sixteen. The test yields verbal, nonverbal, and total *IQ*s.

Lorge-Thorndike Intelligence Tests. Forms are appropriate for grade levels one to twelve. The scores are converted to nonverbal and verbal *IQ*s.

California Tests of Mental Maturity. This is a widely used test that yields scores representing a variety of factors. Subscores are calculated for eight factors including logical reasoning, spatial relationships, numerical reasoning, verbal concepts, memory, language total, nonlanguage total, and total *IQ*. *CTMM* is one of the best instruments for discerning intra-individual differences.

The Distribution and Classification of Intelligence

The distribution of the Wechsler and Stanford-Binet Intelligence Quotients follow the normal curve, as you can see by referring to Figure 8b–1 (p. 335). The mean *IQ* is 100, and approximately fifty percent of the population have measured *IQ*s between 90 and 110.

Wechsler (1955) has presented a classification scheme for intelligence test scores (Table 8b–6). These are not diagnostic labels, and they are not universally accepted. Our knowledge of the standard error of measurement raises questions about the propriety of placing people in different categories on the basis of a one-point difference in *IQ*.

Uses of Intelligence Test Scores

Intelligence test scores are used, among other things, for placing students, for predicting future achievement, and for giving educational guidance. Used judiciously with an understanding of the tests' limitations, a knowledge of student intellectual ability can be helpful in the pursuit of each of the following purposes:

1. *Grouping.* Placement of students can occur within a classroom as well as between classrooms. Although wide-scale homogeneous grouping is uncommon today, teachers still group students for instruction within the classroom, and sometimes special rooms or programs in regular classrooms are provided for the learning disabled, the retarded, and the gifted. Intelligence test results can be used as one of the criteria for determining group membership or adjusting programs for individual students. They should never be used as the only criterion, however.

2. *Prediction of achievement.* To the extent that intelligence tests measure the abilities required for scholastic achievement, their scores may be used to predict achievement. Since many intelligence tests are verbally oriented and measure the ability to work with abstractions

TABLE 8b–6. Wechsler Intelligence Classifications

IQ	Classification	Percent included
130 and above	Very superior	2.2
120–129	Superior	6.7
110–119	Bright normal	16.1
90–109	Average	50.0
80–89	Dull normal	16.1
70–79	Borderline	6.7
69 and below	Mentally defective	2.2

(words, numbers), predictions can be made for subjects that require these abilities. Past achievement, however, has been shown to be a better predictor of future achievement than intelligence tests (Bloom, 1976). Achievement in such subjects as art, music, or physical education, which requires no verbal ability or ability to deal with abstractions, may show little relationship to intelligence.

3. *Educational planning.* Intelligence test scores can be used by counselors to help students plan current and future educational programs. To discourage or encourage a student to enroll in a course or college solely on the basis of an intelligence test, however, is a questionable if not an unethical practice. As in student placement, an intelligence test score is one bit of information that can be considered in helping students set realistic educational goals.

Cautions Regarding Intelligence Test Scores

The banning of intelligence testing in some states and school districts has resulted from the misuse of test results. Misuse may result from misconceptions about intelligence, including those listed below.

Norm-referenced measurement compares an individual's performance with that of a group of students. Criterion-referenced measurement answers the question: "Can a student perform a particular task?"

1. One common misconception is that everyone has a particular *IQ*, that the number is the person's intelligence, and the number is unchangeable. As we know, the *IQ* is nothing more than a measure of a person's performance on a certain set of questions on a particular day at a particular time under one set of conditions. A change in any one of these circumstances would probably result in a different *IQ*.

2. A second misconception is that intelligence is the major determinant of school achievement. Teachers who believe this tend to pigeonhole students, assuming that a student with an *IQ* of 100 will do *C* or average work and that one who has an *IQ* of 120 or above will do *A* work.

This misconception is closely related to the concept of the self-fulfilling prophecy proposed by Rosenthal and Jacobson (1968). According to this notion, students achieve at the level expected of them. If a student is considered to have average ability, the teacher will expect average work from the student. Questions have been raised about the design and analysis of the Rosenthal and Jacobson study, but others have found that teacher expectations do influence student achievement (Baker & Crist, 1971). The role of teacher expectancies will be elaborated in Chapter 10b.

The Measurement of Achievement

Achievement can be measured with a variety of procedures, including formal procedures, such as teacher-made tests and standardized tests, and less formal means, such as classroom recitations. In this section we deal with measuring achievement by means of standardized tests; teacher-made tests and other measurement procedures will be discussed in Chapters 14 and 15.

Two Types of Tests

Most of the standardized tests used to measure achievement are norm-referenced tests (*NRT*). Norm-referenced tests compare one examinee's performance with the performance of others on the same test. The group whose performance serves as the basis for comparison is called the norm group. Individual scores are considered in relation to the norm group's performance. If the average of a group of third graders on a particular test was 25, and Bill scored 28, Bill was above average compared to that norm group. We could also convert Bill's score to a percentile rank on the basis of the norm group. If his score surpassed seventy percent of the scores of the norm group, his percentile rank would be 70.

The score on a norm-referenced test is always compared with the performance of some group. Bill's score could be compared with those of the rest of his class, all third grade students in the school, or all third graders in the state or the nation.

Norm-referenced tests are used to measure growth in achievement. Scores on tests given at the beginning and end of the school year provide information about student gains during the year. Norm-referenced tests are also used for placement and for determining who will be admitted to college. The College Entrance Examination Board (*CEEB*) and the American College Testing Program (*ACT*) are norm-referenced tests used frequently to determine college admissions. The results of these tests may also be used to place students in advanced or remedial courses.

An alternative to norm-referenced testing currently being emphasized is criterion-referenced testing (*CRT*). Criterion-referenced testing, as the name implies, relates the student's performance to some absolute criterion. The student either meets the criterion or does not.

Criterion-referenced measurement developed as a corollary of performance objectives. Performance objectives usually include a criterion used to determine whether a student has met an objective. One objective might be: "The student will correctly solve 8 out of 10 two-digit multiplication problems." Using criterion-referenced measurement, the student's performance would be compared with "8 out of 10." If the student solved eight, nine, or ten problems correctly, he met the criterion; if he got seven or fewer correct, he did not. With *CRT*, all students may meet the criterion or no one may meet it. A student's rank in the class does not affect criterion-referenced measurement.

Criterion-referenced measurement is helpful in that it shows what the child is capable of doing. Norm-referenced measurement tells where the child stands in a group, but it does not tell specifically what skills or knowledge he has attained. Performance on criterion-referenced measures depends on not only what was taught, but on the criterion chosen by the teacher. Different teachers may choose different criteria.

Standardized criterion-referenced tests have not received the acclaim that standardized norm-referenced tests have, but in classroom testing, criterion-referenced tests are often preferable to norm-referenced tests. For a teacher to plan a student's educational program, he or she must know what skills and knowledge the student has already mastered, and criterion-referenced tests can offer that information.

Norm-Referenced Achievement Tests

It is common practice in most elementary schools and some secondary schools to give one or more standardized achievement tests each year. The tests may measure achievement in a single subject or in a particular skill, such as reading or mathematics, or they may consist of a battery of tests covering a wide range of skills and content.

The task of administering achievement tests and scoring and interpreting the results may fall to the classroom teacher. In order to get meaningful scores, the teacher must follow the instructions given in the examiner's manual exactly. These instructions include the directions to the students, provide time for students to ask procedural questions, and state the time limits for each test.

At the elementary school level it is common practice to administer a battery of tests at least once a year. The tests may take several days to administer. Tests should be chosen on the basis of content validity appropriate for the school. Three commonly used test batteries are the Metropolitan Achievement Test (*MAT*), the Stanford Achievement Test (*SAT*), and the Iowa Tests of Basic Skills (*ITBS*). The measures provided by these tests at the intermediate elementary level are shown in Table 8b–7. As you can see from this table, the tests have certain elements in common and certain differences as well. All tests include measures of reading, mathematics, and language achievement, although different subtests may be used to derive these measures. The *SAT* and *MAT* include subtests for measuring science and social studies achievement. The *ITBS* is unique in providing subtests for assessing the study skills of map reading, reading graphs and tables, and the knowledge and use of reference materials. For a more thorough discussion of these and other achievement tests, the student should refer to the *Mental Measurements Yearbook* (Buros, 1978).

Less frequently, batteries of tests are administered in secondary schools. Because of the variety of courses and programs at this level, the tests consist of measures of generalized content or skills. High school teachers generally prefer to use tests on such specific subjects

TABLE 8b–7. Comparison of Subtests of Three Achievement Batteries

Metropolitan Achievement Tests	Stanford Achievement Tests	Iowa Tests of Basic Skills
Reading Total	Reading Total	Vocabulary
Word knowledge	Reading comprehension	Reading comprehension
Reading comprehension	Word study skills	Language total
Language	Mathematics Total	Spelling
Spelling	Concepts	Capitalization
Mathematics Total	Computation	Punctuation
Computation	Application	Usage
Concepts	Spelling	Work study skills
Problem-solving	Language	Map reading
Science	Social science	Graphs & tables
Social Studies	Science	References
		Math Skills Total
		Concepts
		Problems

as biology, first-year algebra, or French as standardized measures of achievement.

Norms and Their Uses.   As you know, the raw scores students receive on achievement tests are converted to percentile ranks, standard scores, or grade equivalents. The choice of which of these scores to report depends on what the results are to be used for, as described below.

Percentile Ranks. For reporting achievement to parents and students, the percentile rank is the preferred score. The percentile rank is easy to interpret, and it provides a measure of the student's status. If possible, the student's score should be reported as a percentile band that takes the standard error of measurement into account. Instead of reporting a score as PR = 65, it might be reported as the percentile rank between 62 and 68.

Standard Scores. These scores are used primarily with test batteries in order to compare student achievement across different subtests. This is possible because the same norm group was used for the entire battery, and the standard scores have common means and standard deviations. Drawing comparisons across tests based on different norm groups is a highly questionable practice.

Grade Equivalents. Grade equivalents are a ready means of measuring the growth of knowledge at least within the grade levels included in the norm group. If tests are administered yearly or at the beginning and end of the same year, the difference in grade equivalents provides a measure of student growth for that year. If a student has a grade equivalent of 2.7 at the beginning of the year and of 3.7 at the end of the year, he or she has attained a year's growth in a year's time, as would be expected.

Use of Achievement Test Results

The results of achievement tests are used by a variety of different groups: administrators, teachers, students, parents, and student personnel workers, such as guidance counselors and school psychologists. Each of the groups uses the results for a different purpose.

Central office administrators, such as superintendents and directors of instruction, often scan test reports for the purpose of comparison (Sproull & Zubrow, 1981). They may compare current results with past results, or different schools in the same district. Comparisons across curricular areas may lead to revisions of a curriculum throughout a school district. Low performance in reading, for example, might lead to the implementation of a new curriculum designed to improve reading scores.

Teachers may also be evaluated on the basis of their students' achievement scores, either formally or informally. Although the use of

Scenario Suggestion

Whatever Ms. Young decides to say to her students in interpreting tests results and advising them on their high school programs, there are several things she must keep in mind, several points she needs to make. Primary among them is that the standardized test data represent only one sample of behavior collected within a specific context. One test score is not a definitive indication of the way an individual might perform in another context.

Ms. Young might begin her explanation by explaining that norm-referenced assessment yields ranked position of a student's score with respect to a norm group; it fails to reveal specifically what the student can or cannot do. Interpreting the data historically, she might add that in the past, persons who have received similar scores have tended to succeed in situations a, b, and c, while experiencing more difficulty in situations d, e, and f. She should be careful to note, however, that predictions hold for groups, not for individuals, because important factors like motivation, desire, and effort remain unassessed and thus are not reflected in the test score data.

With the context set, Ms. Young must then figure how to report the score itself in a meaningful way. The standard score will probably not mean much to a ninth grader. Reporting the scores in stanines or percentile ranks could be more relevant. However, Ms. Young must remember that test scores must be examined within the confines of test reliability, the standard error of measurement. Rather than reporting test score data, which has the appearance of absolute measurement, Ms. Young might wish to express the scores as ranges, the score ± at least one standard error of measurement. This minimizes the appearance that assessment is a matter of certainty, which would be an unfortunate and erroneous conclusion.

The most important thing for Ms. Young to remember in her discussion is that these students are only in the ninth grade; their futures are far from sealed. The circumstances of their lives and their experiences will change in high school. Doors need not be prematurely closed to them, options prematurely cut off—certainly not on the basis of test data alone. Part of her responsibility to report in a clear and meaningful way is making certain that consumers of test information understand the context of assessment and the effect of context on a sample of student behavior.

test results for this purpose is questionable, it undoubtedly occurs. Decisions about firing teachers, giving tenure, and granting merit salary increases have been made on the basis of achievement test results. Test results may be used as one bit of information for making teacher evaluations, but they should not be the only criterion. Factors other than a teacher's effectiveness influence student performance on achievement tests.

Building principals may use test results for the same purpose as central office administrators—comparing their schools to others in the district, comparing teachers within their schools, and comparing different curricular areas. Recently, principals as well as teachers have been concerned with minimum competency testing. The rationale behind this movement is that all students should meet minimum standards of competence in basic skills, either at different grade levels or before graduation. The results of standardized achievement tests are used to determine whether the student has mastered the minimum standards of his or her grade level. Students who fail to meet minimum levels may be retained at grade level, denied a diploma, or placed in remedial programs. These practices are all of concern to the building principal.

Teachers use test results in a variety of ways (Salmon-Cox, 1981). The predominant use is to confirm or supplement teacher judgment. Teachers believe that they know their students' abilities; test results tend to confirm their estimates of students' achievement. Teachers also use test results to guide instruction. This process resembles the curriculum revisions conducted by administrators, but it is at the classroom level. Finally, teachers may use achievement test results in order to group students for instruction. Once again, this use of tests tends to confirm information from other sources, such as classroom performance and observation.

Summary

Selecting a good measurement instrument is the first step in determining individual differences. The measurements must be as valid and reliable as possible. If the test is not valid, it will not be measuring what we want it to measure. An unreliable test will provide scores with a large error factor.

Statistical methods are techniques used to give meaning to raw scores. Constructing a frequency distribution and calculating central tendency measures and the standard deviation are methods that provide us with the basis for interpreting test results.

The two basic types of standardized tests are ability tests and achievement tests. Ability tests are designed to measure intelligence or related constructs. They may be used for student placement or for predicting future achievement. Achievement tests are used in many ways by administrators and teachers. They serve as sources of information for curricular decisions, teacher evaluations, comparisons, and student placement.

One reason intelligence and ability testing stirs controversy is the use of test data. Tests are tools for assessing and describing individual and group differences. Quantified descriptions are useful for a number of purposes, in research, in educational planning, and in the allocation of educational resources; but quantified group differences are subject to misinterpretation (or at least over-interpretation), and thus can be inflammatory, controversial, and even prejudicial.

The concept of group differences needs to be clearly understood. In Chapter 9a we present some of these group differences. More important, we consider the circumstances under which data on group differences are obtained and the logic underlying their pursuit. Those circumstances and the logic of study affect the meaningfulness of detected group differences and raise cautions about interpretation.

In Chapter 9b we turn to an important application of the identification of individual and group differences—special education. How, in fact, do test data affect educational programming, remediation, and special provisions for the exceptional individual?

Chapter 9a

*Psychological Implications of
Ability Classifications: Group
Differences in Intelligence*

Introduction

Educators and psychologists use ability tests in a wide variety of ways. Educational evaluators sometimes use intelligence tests for judging the effectiveness of entire intervention programs, perhaps comparing the scores students receive before and after attending the program. Evaluators might also compare non-participants and participants in order to determine whether the latter benefited from the program. The use of ability testing in evaluations thus has implications for special educational programming, for legislation, and even for funding.

Ability tests are used to evaluate individuals as well as programs. Assessments of an individual's intellectual and academic progress yield data that may be used to compare the individual with a norm group. Recommendations that the student be given remedial education or be placed in a special program may result. Ability testing hence has important ramifications for special education, in that it may be used to determine the programs that are supported and the individuals who enter them. The issues concerning individual assessment and special education are considered in Chapter 9b.

Psychologists as well as educators are interested in assessing differences in ability. Psychologists, however, typically examine groups rather than individuals, and they attempt to ascertain the group characteristics that coincide with reliable ability differences. Regularly detected individual differences in achievement, personality, and intelligence that correspond with group membership serve as the data base for *differential psychology*—the study of individual differences.

Studies of group differences also have implications for psychological theory, particularly our theories of intelligence. If we find, for example, that males and females or people of different races differ in ability patterns, we need to know why. To find an explanation, we must focus on the origins of intelligent behavior, the causes of it. Psychological studies of group differences have been used in this effort.

In this chapter we shall review the evidence on group differences in ability that coincide with important individual characteristics. The research evidence on this topic is far from clear. Part of the ambiguity stems from the process of any scientific investigation, part from the social implications of the research, and part from the problem of evaluating any group differences. To meaningfully evaluate empirical findings, therefore, we must also present information on the meaning of group differences and the way they are determined.

Group Differences and the Nature-Nurture Controversy

The psychometric movement has shown that individuals differ in aptitude and achievement. Even given the best of opportunities, few of us will achieve the intellectual prominence of an Einstein or a Piaget. Individual limitations in ability, motivation, and interest will restrict most of us. Psychologists are interested in the relation of those limitations to other factors. Do measured individual differences in ability coincide with specific demographic characteristics, such as race, socioeconomic status, and sex? This is the question of concern to differential psychologists. We do not yet understand the causes of intelligence, but some have thought that finding correlates of intelligence might tell us something about its causes. The search for regular associations between group membership and ability has therefore been pursued as one route to the origins of intelligence.

From the study of genetics we know that many physical differences arise from chromosomal factors—biology. Biological sex is an obvious example. Racial characteristics are also associated with genetic make-up, though not as straightforwardly as sex. Historically, it has been proposed that biological factors even have an influence on social class membership. The fact that observed group differences in ability and achievement are associated with possibly genetically linked observed characteristics has led many to ask if ability differences are also associated with biology. This is the familiar nature (biology)-nurture (environment) controversy introduced in Chapter 8a. This controversy has surfaced repeatedly around reported sex-associated differences, race-associated differences, and even social class-associated differences in intelligence and ability.

Discussions of group differences must take the nature-nurture issue into account. Since empirical studies conducted on the subject are often used to support one side or the other, we must evaluate their results and see whether the results affect the arguments in the debate.

We will present the findings about three group differences in ability, those for sex, race, and social class. We present them in that order for a specific purpose. Biological sex has the clearest and most direct link with genetic structure, racial characteristics a somewhat less direct link, and social class the weakest. Yet even with sex, separating the contributing influences of biology and environment is incredibly difficult, if not altogether impossible.

Sex Differences and Cognitive Ability

Biological sex is perhaps the most easily observed human characteristic. Moreover, sex differences have attracted research interest for decades, so the volume of data is impressive. Finally, the means of studying sex differences are typical of those used to study any group difference. A summary of the literature on sex differences thus allows us to exemplify not just the findings of this kind of research, but the methods used and the difficulties associated with these methods as well.

In Pursuit of the Null Hypothesis: The Methods of Study

To understand sex differences in ability, we must consider the way these differences are detected in the first place (Sherman, 1978). To investigate empirical questions, we use a method that is based on a particular kind of logic. The method is better suited to some questions than to others.

To illustrate the logic of the method, consider this statement: "All swans are white." This statement can be disproved by finding a single exception, but it can never be proved because we can never be sure that all swans have been examined. An investigator interested in the color of swans could spend his whole life examining the subject, but he or she could never prove the statement. There would always be a chance that somewhere out there beyond his sample lurked the one black swan that would negate the thesis. If the investigator had access to every swan in existence, proof might be established, but that is a very unlikely state of affairs. The investigator would be more likely to have access to a sample of swans that he or she hoped was representative of the general population of swans.

Suppose that in an investigator's sample, all the swans are white. His or her results would fail to disprove the statement rather than proving it. Critics who believed in the existence of black swans could always question the size and representativeness of the investigator's sample or judgments the researcher made about color. They would also have the option of simply continuing the search.

There is a parallel between the swan search and the procedure used by psychological investigators. Psychologists typically begin a study with a statement that can be disconfirmed but not confirmed. This statement is called the *null hypothesis*. The nature of the mathematics used in analyzing psychological data dictates that the null hypothesis generally take the form of a so-called no difference statement. Suppose a psychologist wishes to investigate whether training improves conservation performance. One group of children would be trained, a second group would not. The null hypothesis states that there will be no difference between the groups. Obviously, if the psychologist thinks training is an important experience, the purpose of testing the statement is to reject it. He wants to disprove the notion that training makes no difference. Suppose, however, that the training actually makes no difference in this one case. Does that prove the null hypothesis? Does it prove that training makes no difference? It does not. It merely remains a statement that the psychologist failed to reject. If the study were conducted again and showed that training was influential, the null hypothesis could be rejected.

When we study group differences, we begin with a null hypothesis. We propose that there are no differences between groups and then set out on a course that may lead us to reject that statement. With a sex-associated difference, we begin by assuming that males and females will fail to differ in some characteristic. When we study the characteristic, we are in a position only to disconfirm the statement. It is empirically impossible to prove that groups are equivalent.

Explanations for the Fail-to-Reject Outcomes.

When psychologists conduct empirical tests, they either reject the null hypothesis as probably false or they fail to reject it. Empirical decisions are always based on probabilities, however, so error is possible. Even when the null hypothesis is rejected, the result is thus equivocal. Sometimes a difference surfaces strictly on the basis of chance; we never know for sure.

When the null hypothesis is not rejected, the reason is even more ambiguous. The hypothesis may reflect the situation accurately, but that is not the only possibility. Perhaps the psychologist, like the searcher in pursuit of swans, failed to select an appropriate sample, or perhaps the study was poorly conducted. Empirical data are typically subjected to a statistical test to determine whether an observed difference has occurred strictly by chance. There are many statistical tests, but all involve a kind of ratio. The numerator of the ratio is the difference detected between groups, and the denominator involves variation due to all other factors. One component of the denominator is degree of individual differences. A second is error, which results from imprecise measurement and improper use of procedures. The ratio takes this general form:

$$\frac{\text{Differences due to group membership}}{\text{Individual differences + Error}} = ?$$

In order to reject the null hypothesis, a large number must result from this ratio. Therein lies the problem. If the denominator is a large number, chances of rejecting the null are low unless the numerator is a very large number indeed. The denominator will tend to be large if (1) there are large individual differences in the characteristic being considered, or (2) if the experiment was conducted in a manner that produced a lot of error.

What does a failure to reject the null hypothesis tell us about sex differences? It could mean that there were large individual differences on the characteristic examined, a circumstance that inflated the denominator of the ratio. Perhaps the experiment was conducted poorly and had a large degree of error, something that again inflated the denominator. We cannot determine whether the null hypothesis reflects the actual relationship between male and female abilities, since other factors can also explain the data. Like the swan searcher, we can conduct study after study, fail to reject the null, and never know when a black swan will swim by.

The State of the Art of Studying Sex Differences.   This problem is reflected in the literature on sex differences. The logic of psychological investigation makes it almost impossible to prove that there is no difference between males and females. This difficulty is complicated by the fact that sometimes differences are found on a given measure, although very often they are not. Another problem is that studies that reject the null are more likely to be published than are studies that fail to reject it (Sherman, 1978). Under these circumstances, interpreting the empirical data base is at best difficult. We may not even have access to abundant data in which the null was not rejected.

Empirical Findings on Cognition and Sex

Sometimes empirical investigations of sex differences reveal differences in the average performance levels of males and females. In these studies, the average level for males is compared with the average level for females. If one is appreciably higher than the other, we have evidence that a sex difference exists. Indices of average level, however, are computed from the distributions of the results of tests on many individuals. As you learned in the last chapter (Chapter 8b), distributions of large

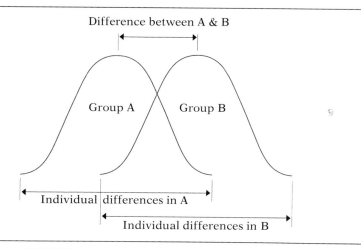

FIGURE 9a–1.   Overlap in Group Distributions

sets of measures tend to look like bell-shaped curves with the average level at or near the center of the curve. This center index serves as the basis of the comparison. Even when a difference is detected there still may be considerable overlap in the distribution as a whole.

Look carefully at Figure 9a–1. The entire distance covered by one of the distributions represents the extent of individual differences; the extent of the group difference is represented by the distance between the peaks of the distributions. Note that the distance for the group differences is smaller than the distance for the individual differences. Figure 9a–1 exemplifies two points about most sex differences findings: (1) the extent of individual differences is typically greater than the extent of group differences even when a group difference is found, and (2) the distributions for females and males tend to overlap.

When we interpret empirical findings, a couple of procedures are used to account for these two points. The first involves examining *effect size,* and the second involves estimating the amount of *variance accounted for* by a particular variable.

In the first procedure, examining effect size, the group difference is compared with estimates of individual variation, the standard deviations of the two distributions. The numerical quantity that results from this operation puts the group difference into perspective. It tells us the size of the difference in standard deviation units. An effect size of 1.00, for example, indicates that the means of the groups differ by one standard deviation. Effect sizes can be computed for individual studies and series of studies; both help put group differences into perspective (Glass, 1978).

The second procedure, estimating the amount of variance accounted for by a particular variable, also yields a meaningful summary quantity. Scores vary, of course, and this variability can be conceptualized as a circle. We wish to figure out what the total variability can be attributed to, what factors account for pieces of the full circle. When we examine sex differences, we can ask: "How much of the total variability in a set of scores can be attributed to sex?" This is represented pictorially in Figure 9a–2. This procedure also places sex differences in context, permitting us to assess whether sex is a large or unimportant factor.

General Intellectual Ability.   Little needs to be said about sex differences in general intelligence; there appear to be none (Sherman, 1978). This lack of detectable differences could be related to the way the variable is measured, however. Typically, when general intelligence tests are constructed and standardized, items that reveal a sex bias, that appear to favor either males or females, are removed from the test. One would hence not expect differences in test scores. There is currently little debate about the conclusion that the sexes perform about the same on measures of general intelligence. This is not necessarily the case when we examine measures of other more specific abilities, however (Sherman, 1978).

Verbal Ability.   Many people assume that females have superior verbal abilities. To put this assumption in perspective, however, we quote Sherman's (1978) recent summary:

> Verbal skill is probably the single most important aspect of intelligence and in this area females are usually conceded to have well-developed powers. Females are generally thought to be verbally precocious compared to males. Males eventually catch up but females are thought to retain a slight edge in all areas of verbal functioning. These generalizations characteristic of Tyler (1965), Maccoby (1966), and Guilford (1967) have been

FIGURE 9a–2.   Variability Depicted as a Circle

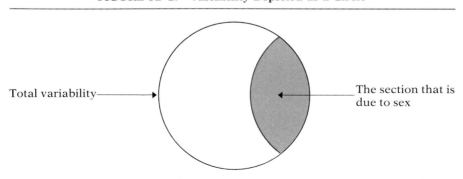

Total variability⟶   ⟵The section that is due to sex

challenged and questioned but still appear valid, *though the demonstrated differences are so small as to be trivial* (Sherman, 1978, p. 39; emphasis is ours).

This very slight advantage for females in verbal skills may be due in part to early language development. Though the data are far from uniform, many researchers contend that girls develop beginning language skills earlier than boys (Harris, 1977; Maccoby, 1966; Nelson, 1973; McGuinness, 1976). This finding may be important. Sherman (1967, 1971, 1978) argues that because of this early advantage, females may develop a preference for verbal problem-solving strategies rather than developing spatial, analytic, or other techniques. Sherman refers to this as the bent twig hypothesis, since it may direct females, at an early age, into a certain style of interaction with the environment. This in turn may explain sex differences noted in other ability areas.

In other aspects of verbal skills, females maintain a slight advantage into adulthood. The effect size reported for this difference is .25 standard deviations—not very large (Maccoby & Jacklin, 1974). Sherman (1978) reports that one percent of the variance in performance on the vocabulary subtest in the 1955 standardization of the *WAIS* was attributable to sex, again not very large.

Mathematics.   When we come to the area of mathematics achievement and ability we find a multitude of contradictory findings and much debate. Few would deny the importance of mathematics for training and employment in most scientific and technical professions. There would also be little argument that women are underrepresented in these fields (Ernest, 1976; Sells, 1976; Fox, Fennema, & Sherman, 1977). In addition, women take fewer advanced mathematics courses than men (Fennema, 1977) and they thus achieve less well in that subject (Maccoby & Jacklin, 1974; Fox, 1977). In fact, Sells (1976) has referred to mathematics as the critical filter that restricts the entrance of women into such fields as chemistry, physics, engineering, architecture, and medicine.

The sex difference in mathematics achievement is detected most easily in adolescence. It is during this period that students decide whether or not to pursue math. Apparently, girls begin dropping out of mathematics about the time geometry would be taken (Fennema, 1977), which is around tenth grade. Recent data, however, suggest that today young women may be staying in mathematics longer (Armstrong, 1979).

Whether the established differences in mathematics achievement are associated with parallel differences in ability is a hotly debated issue. Maccoby and Jacklin (1974) concluded in their comprehensive review that males from early adolescence on display an advantage in

Research Report

One reliably detected sex difference is that associated with spatial ability. As we noted in this chapter, however, spatial ability is a multifaceted phenomenon tapped by a variety of tasks solvable by a variety of strategies. Finding general sex differences in level of performance thus tells us little. In particular, differences reveal no information about the possible cognitive processes underlying those differences.

Kail, Carter, and Pellegrino conducted an investigation designed to examine processing differences between males and females on a spatial task noted for revealing sex-related level differences. These investigators wanted to pinpoint where sex differences would show up so that the meaning of those differences might be clarified.

The target task, an image rotation, is used frequently in spatial ability research. In it, a standard figure is presented in an upright position. Then a comparison figure is presented, but it is rotated a certain number of degrees around a fixed point. The comparison figure is either a match or a mirror image of the original figure; the subject must determine which. The dependent measures are discrimination accuracy rate and response time—that is, the length of time the subject takes to make the discrimination. Investigators examine the changing response time in relation to the number of degrees the comparison figure is rotated. Typically, as the degree of rotation increases, response time also increases (up to 180°), and the relationship between the two forms a straight line. This finding is frequently interpreted as an indication that subjects solve the discrimination problem by mentally rotating the comparison figure into congruence with the standard figure and then comparing them.

Kail, Carter, and Pellegrino examined rotation skills in 104 undergraduate men and women. They used sixteen stimuli. Eight were numbers and letters and eight were let-

ter-like characters from Thurstone's Primary Mental Abilities test (see Chapter 8a). The comparison figure was presented at 0°, 30°, 60°, 90°, 120°, or 150° of rotation, and was either a match or a mirror image. Discrimination accuracy and response time were assessed.

When the comparison figure is presented at 0° of rotation, a mental rotation process is not required. On these problems, therefore, response time assesses the length of time it takes subjects to encode and compare the stimulus and to respond. On the other problems response time assesses mental rotation time as well. The investigators were therefore able to ascertain the aspect of the task in which sex differences would surface: (1) on overall accuracy rate, (2) on the time required to encode and match, or (3) on the time required to encode, rotate, and match.

Men and women failed to differ on overall accuracy rate. There was also no difference in the times required to encode and match. For both men and women, as degree of rotation of the comparison figure increased, so too did response time. The slopes of the lines for men and women did differ, however. The line for women was steeper than that for men. This suggests that women take longer to rotate the comparison stimuli mentally than do men, and the difference between the two rates becomes larger as the degree of rotation becomes greater. Although all subjects performed the task faster with letters and numbers than with the items from the Primary Mental Ability test, the detected sex difference was the same for both types of stimuli.

Apparently, the only significant sex difference was that men mentally rotated the stimuli more rapidly than did women. However, seventy percent of the women had rotation rates comparable to the men's. Only thirty percent of the women were actually responding at a slower rate. The investigators interpreted this finding as an indication that some women, by no means all, may use a different strategy to solve the rotation problem than do men and most other women. The important sex difference is thus not level of ability between the sexes but variability within each sex. In addition, to quote the authors, "Males' superiority on at least this spatial

task seems to be linked to a *single component of processing*" (p. 186; the emphasis is ours).

Kail, R., P. Carter, & J. Pellegrino, The locus of sex differences in spatial ability, *Perception & psychophysics*, 1979, *16* (3), 182–186.

---

mathematical ability as well as achievement. Sherman (1978) disagrees, however (Fox, Fennema, & Sherman, 1977).

Concerning the specifics of mathematics skills, we can conclude that: (1) girls tend to be ahead of boys in counting skills during pre-school years (Maccoby & Jacklin, 1974); (2) prior to high school there are essentially no differences in computational skills (Oetzel, 1966; Fennema & Sherman, 1976); (3) girls score below boys from adolescence on in such aspects as measurement, geometry, variables and relationships, probability and statistics, and consumer math (Mullis, 1975).

The only indices of effect size come from the Maccoby and Jacklin (1974) summary. Sherman (1978) reports that the largest was much less than one standard deviation.

Spatial Ability. If sex differences in mathematics achievement are based on an aptitude factor, that factor might be related to spatial skills—the ability to interpret, manipulate, and transform spatial information. There is evidence that spatial abilities affect success in some aspects of mathematics, such as geometry (Bennett, Seashore, & Wesman, 1974), quantitative thinking (Bennett, Seashore, & Wesman, 1974), and perhaps calculus (Eisenberg & McGinty, 1977). Females are generally less successful than males on measures of spatial abilities (McGee, 1979). Again, these differences are not reliably noted until early adolescence.

There is a problem with these conclusions, however. Many different skills are lumped together under the general heading of spatial abilities. The Piagetian three-mountain task described in Chapter 6a, for example, is a spatial task. So is the ability to mentally unfold a box or to copy a design made of blocks. (The latter is a subtest on the Wechsler Intelligence Scales.) These tasks tap visualization skills. Other spatial tasks involve the ability to distinguish small figures against a complex background, to detect a true vertical, or to rotate a visual image mentally. Obviously, these tasks have some features in common, since they all deal with visual phenomena, but they also differ. Do they all tap the same ability?

Sex differences have been found in mathematics achievement. The causes of these sex differences are not agreed upon. Some argue that experience and cultural expectations are the cause; others maintain that there are biological differences between the sexes.

Some investigators argue that there is not one spatial ability, but a number of them (Lohman, 1979a; McGee, 1979). To interpret data on sex differences with spatial tasks, we should probably consider what kinds of tasks reveal differences rather than lumping them all together. The tasks differ greatly in difficulty level and complexity (Sherman, 1978) and are probably solved with different mental strategies as well (Lohman, 1979a, b).

In order to assess what is called field dependence and independence, frequently two tests have been used (Witkin *et al.*, 1962). In the Rod and Frame Test, the subject is placed in a totally dark room and shown a lighted frame with a line in it. The frame is tilted. The subject must indicate when he or she believes the line is oriented vertically. Many studies, but not all, show that males do better than females on this task (Sherman, 1978). It is assumed that females have trouble disregarding the misleading frame and orienting the line independent of the frame. In the Embedded Figures Test, the subject must disregard a fussy background and distinguish smaller pictures. Success is again assumed to reflect field independence. Sex differences favoring males are frequently but not always found on this test, too (Maccoby & Jacklin, 1974). Differences sometimes show up prior to adolescence, and they correlate with various measures of competence in Euclidean geometry (Liben, 1978).

On tests that require visualization skills, a male advantage is detected in early adolescence (Maccoby & Jacklin, 1974). Sometimes differences favoring males are also found on Piagetian-type spatial tasks (Tuddenham, 1970) and tasks requiring the mental manipulation of three-dimensional forms (Fairweather, 1976). Preadolescent differences are rare, however (Rosser, Horan, Campbell, Mattson, Mazzeo, & Swarner, 1980).

The effect size of sex-associated differences in spatial abilities is generally reported as about .40 standard deviations (Maccoby & Jacklin, 1974). The amount of variance accounted for by sex varies from study to study. The highest amount reported is about five percent (Sherman, 1978). It seems reasonable to conclude that males do better than females on spatial tasks, but not generally until adolescence.

Interpreting Detected Sex Differences

After identifying the cognitive differences related to sex, we face an even trickier task—explaining them. What causes males and females to differ in the skills examined, biology or experience?

A Biological Base for Sex Differences.   The biological explanations are highly technical and beyond the scope of this book. There are two that may explain the empirical findings, at least in part. The first suggests that some specific cognitive abilities are carried as recessive genes on the X-chromosome. If this is true, males, who have just one X-chromosome, would display the characteristics more often than females. Males would need to inherit just one recessive gene in order to display the ability, whereas females would need to inherit two, something that would be less likely. Stafford (1972) has offered this explanation for the biological transmission of both mathematical problem-solving abilities and spatial abilities.

If this explanation held, we could predict what proportions of males and females would display superior abilities. The explanation could then be tested by comparing expected proportions with actual proportions in a sample of males and females. Stafford (1972) contends that his data correspond to the expectations for quantitative reasoning, but others disagree (Sherman, 1978). Bock (1967) and others (Hartlage, 1970; Bock & Kolakowski, 1973) report a good fit for spatial abilities, too, but again contradictory evidence and convincing alternative explanations can be found. This hypothesis may have some merit, but judging from the extent of the current controversy it would be premature to suggest that it is the sole explanation. When we consider that spatial skills involve different abilities, furthermore, it seems unreasonable to assume a direct connection between a set of abilities and a single gene.

A second biological explanation concerns brain lateralization. The brain has two hemispheres, which are thought to have different functions. The left hemisphere is associated with verbal and analytical tasks and the right with spatial tasks. Lateralization is the term used to refer to the dominance of one hemisphere over the other. A number of theories propose that the process of lateralization differs for males and females and that these differences are reflected in different abilities and skills. Data on these theories is still forthcoming, so it is probably too early to make judgments about them.

A Socialization Base for Sex Differences.   Whatever the final decision on the validity of biological explanations, they present a problem. Current data show that sex differences in ability fail to appear until adolescence. By that time, a child has had from ten to twelve years of experience and socialization, and the two sexes have been socialized differently. Adolescent girls and boys therefore differ in both biology and experience; it is extremely difficult to isolate the effects of each of the two causes.

Growing children are socialized into sex roles. These roles are sets of primarily implicit expectations about the behavior, activity preferences, attitudes, and values of the two sexes. Parents treat male and female children differently even as infants; teachers treat boys and girls differently; and peer influences are different, too (Sherman, 1978). In short, sex-role socialization from a very early age is virtually unavoidable.

Sex-role socialization influences cognitive behavior and expectations as well as social and personal behavior. One obvious example is that achievement is emphasized more for males than for females. Less obviously, mathematics is stereotyped as a supposedly male domain (Fox, Fennema, & Sherman, 1977). Girls may not be expected to do as well in mathematics, and many are actually anxious and frightened about it. Some contend that spatial ability is also sex-typed as a male domain, whereas reading is considered a feminine domain (Stein & Smithells, 1969).

The socialization hypothesis has logical appeal, but research support for this view tends to be weak. Most of the research is correlational; investigators have attempted to find a correspondence between sex-role attitudes, sex-stereotyped judgments, and measures of cognitive achievement. Correlational data can establish only the existence of a relationship between two variables, however, not the fact that one causes the other. Data on attitudes and achievement do show correlations (Sherman, 1978) but it is difficult to draw conclusions from this data. For the socialization hypothesis to become more than a hypothesis, we need a lot more information.

The solution to these issues will probably involve isolating the contribution of both biological and experiential factors. At present, we simply are unable to do this. We do know, however, that even when sex differences are detected they are small, certainly smaller than individual differences. Certain males have marvelous verbal abilities and certain females become brilliant mathematicians. There are female architects and male poets. In general, the range of individual differences is much greater than the range associated with sex differences.

Racial Differences and Ability

Detected ability differences associated with race are at least as controversial as those associated with sex. The reasons for the controversy are similar, too. Sex is linked to genetic structure; so are physical racial characteristics. The possibility that ability is associated with genetic endowment is again an issue.

Isolating the Role of Genetic Factors

We have the technology to examine chromosomal structure directly, so we know the relationship between chromosomal structure and biological sex. Racial characteristics, however, are associated not with chromosomes, but with the genes carried on the chromosomes. Genes can be examined only indirectly. We examine the proportion of individuals who display a given characteristic (phenotype) and infer actual genetic make-up (genotype). Since we use inference rather than direct examination, isolating the biological contribution to the subtle characteristics associated with race is a difficult process that yields equivocal results.

Most studies of racial difference examine general intelligence measures and compare black and white group differences. Unlike the findings for sex differences, findings for racial differences in intelligence are consistent. In most studies, the mean for blacks is about ten to twenty *IQ* points below the mean for whites (Jensen, 1971). This is an effect size of approximately 1.0, depending on the intelligence measure used. As with other group differences, however, the two distributions overlap, and the range of individual differences within one group exceeds the range of differences between groups.

What do these differences mean in the debate about biological determinism? Some observers believe the observed differences have a hereditary cause (Shuey, 1966); others explain the difference in terms of environmental influences (Klineberg, 1963). How can the same data be interpreted in two diametrically opposed ways?

The influences of heredity and biology are perfectly confounded—they cannot be separated. It is impossible to remove one of the influences and determine the role of the other. Investigators must try to separate the two by indirect means. One procedure used involves a mathematical heritability statistic (Jensen, 1969). This procedure attempts to separate the role of each factor through mathematical manipulation. The technique has been widely criticized as inappropriate and misleading (Crow, 1969). A second procedure involves equating or matching individuals on the basis of experience. In this approach, black individuals are matched with white individuals on the basis of some experiential indicator, such as social class, family income, or parents' education. It is assumed that black and white individuals who belong to the same social class have experienced similar environments. When differences favoring whites are found (Jensen, 1969), it is thus assumed that the differences are not just experiential.

Reflect on this assumption a bit. In the United States, pervasive racial discrimination has existed for a very long time. How can the environments of white children and black children possibly be equated? A middle-class black family and a middle-class white family may have identical incomes, but members of the black family may be restricted as to where they can live and what activities they can be involved in. They may have been excluded for generations from a variety of social experiences. Members of the family will probably have experienced systematic political, social, and educational discrimination. It is virtually inconceivable that the children of the two families could be legitimately equated on the basis of experience.

If sex influences socialization, it seems likely that race does, too. There is ample evidence, for example, that when educational opportunity is changed, when the environment is changed, black children make considerable gains in *IQ* scores (Klineberg, 1935; Lee, 1951).

A related explanation for the differential performance of black and white children revolves around the issue of test bias (Reschly, 1979; Kratochwill, Alper, & Cancelli, 1980). Black children may bring different experiences to the testing context, so test items and the norms based on the items may lack a match with their experiences. In short, traditional tests may be experientially or culturally loaded. If so, the norms would reflect the cultural loading, and comparisons with the norms could be misleading; they might even discriminate against the non-white or minority group child.

Many propose that detected group differences would look quite different if traditional tests were renormed (Alley & Foster, 1978; Sattler, 1974), if pluralistic norms were developed (Mercer, 1971, 1973), or if culture-fair tests were used instead of the standard ones. A number of individuals contend, however, that the traditional assessment instruments are not unduly biased (Jensen, 1980), or that tests developed to be culturally fair are not particularly useful for many purposes (Salvia & Ysseldyke, 1978). It is clear, however, that changes affecting motivation in the testing session or that alter item content do correspond with changes in performance (Kratochwill, Alper, & Cancelli, 1980).

Whether or not one believes tests are biased against minority children, we know that test performances fluctuate across contexts. Accordingly, it seems a bit risky to infer an unvarying biological cause to a performance when the performance itself is not constant. If biology, a genotype, plays a role, we are not going to detect it simply by examining test scores that at best reflect only phenotype, and an unstable phenotype at that.

Hereditarian Views and Educational Opportunity

In addition to scientific and logical problems associated with the view that intelligence is hereditary, there are potential political and social ramifications as well. If we assume that biology determines ability and that biology cannot change, the next logical step is to assume that we can do nothing about racial differences in ability. This assumption could lead us to accept racial *IQ* differences and to abandon efforts to do anything about them. Abandoning these efforts might be considered a denial of educational opportunity. Equality of opportunity is an explicit social value in our society, of course, and schools are supposed to reflect social values. Attributing differences to the environment is a more optimistic route. Unlike heredity, environments are not fixed; they can be changed and enriched to provide greater opportunity. This approach is consistent with our professed societal values.

Social Class Differences in Ability

Social class membership is another characteristic associated with differences in performance on intelligence and achievement tests. In fact, the correlation between social class and intelligence has been reported to be about .30 (Havighurst, Bowman, Liddle, Matthews, & Pierce, 1962). This correlation indicates that social class accounts for about nine percent of the variance in intelligence scores. In this case, it is children from low-income families who do less well on measures of intelligence and achievement.

The values and activities of the home environment vary across different social classes, and it is in the home that much of a child's socialization takes place. In the home, for example, children are exposed to occupational models, language models, and personal models, each of which influences the child's behavior and values. The values of home and school are probably more consistent for children from middle-class than from low-income families (Swanson & Henderson, 1976). This inconsistency for values of low-income children is even more pronounced when income differences are compounded by cultural differences. Children from low-income families may thus be at a disadvantage in the school environment, where assessment takes place.

Here again we may be dealing with a mismatch between a child's experience and the context of assessment, including both the test items and the atmosphere. When social class differences are compounded by language differences, the use of language in assessment becomes a very complex issue (Garcia, 1972; Sattler, 1974). Even when a child's primary language is not an issue, cultural context, learning strategies, and value systems may be mismatched (Alley & Foster, 1978).

Cultural differences are not the only source of problems in the interpretation of social class differences. Even when obvious language and cultural differences are unapparent, research suggests that eco-

The environmentalist viewpoint has spurred many school preparatory programs, such as Head Start, for children with disadvantages resulting from varying social and cultural backgrounds.

New Directions in Research

Because of contemporary changes in conceptions of the nature of intelligence, we also see changes in views of individual differences. The older literature on individual differences depended heavily upon traditional assessment devices, intelligence and aptitude tests, to index those differences. When the assessment devices are challenged, therefore, so too are the findings obtained with those devices. How differential psychologists will meet these new challenges remains to be seen.

For a while it appeared that a promising direction was to examine the interactions between individual differences in aptitudes and alternative instructional strategies. This aptitude-treatment interaction literature, or *ATI* research, is certainly a refinement within the bounds of differential psychology, but to the extent that it depends on traditional assessment procedures even *ATI* research is subject to considerable challenge (Bracht, 1970; Cronbach & Snow, 1969; Resnick, 1976). Until we derive a new and accepted method of tapping this construct we call intelligence, it is hard to predict future directions in the study of individual differences.

Of one thing we can be fairly certain: New methods for assessing individual differences will reflect the impact of work in cognitive psychology. Whether these newer measurement devices derive from cognitive developmental theory (Green, Ford, & Flamer, 1971; Pinard & Sharp, 1972; Tuddenham, 1971), or focus on information-processing strategies (Carroll, 1976), or depend on elementary cognitive processes (Bergan, 1982), they are certain to differ from the trait-based ones. As the measures change, so too will our descriptions and explanations of individual differences.

nomically disadvantaged children dislike both evaluation (Labov, 1970; Zigler, Abelson, & Seitz, 1973) and the testing setting (Johnson, 1974; Labov, 1970), so they cannot be expected to be motivated to perform at their best levels. Test performances may thus yield inaccurate estimates of what children can really do (Reschly, 1979). Again, the fact that context changes are associated with performance fluctuation makes it very risky to draw connections between assessment outcomes and actual ability.

Whether detected social class differences in intelligence are a function of testing itself or a result of the effects of poverty, the differences are not immutable. The goal of such educational programs as Project Head Start is to break the cycle of poverty in which children from low-income homes grow up and establish low-income homes of their own. Poverty and educational disadvantages are eliminated only with difficulty, however, since social, political, and economic factors are all intertwined with education. Poverty is a complex problem affected by all of society's institutions; schools cannot be made the only instrument of social change.

Schools and educators must not deny individuals the opportunity to advance and change, either. Many children from low-income families do get an education, do join the ranks of the economic middle class, and do achieve as well as their middle-class counterparts.

Conclusions and Summary

In this chapter we have summarized the general findings about differences in ability associated with sex, race, and social class. We have also discussed the way these differences are detected and interpreted. Regardless of the demographic variable considered, the variable is an attribute variable and cannot be manipulated; hence we cannot identify a causal relationship between sex, race, or social class and the measured outcome, intelligence. Data on group differences are correlational, and statements about cause cannot be made on the basis of correlation. This body of research thus really tells us little about the causes of intelligence.

This paucity of evidence makes evaluating and interpreting group differences in ability a difficult task. When you must evaluate and interpret them, it is important to recall the following facts:

1. The range of individual differences is always greater than the range of any group difference.
2. Demographic variables seldom account for much of a noted variation in measured ability.
3. The distributions of the scores of different groups always overlap; sometimes they overlap a great deal.

Experience and environment play an important role in most aspects of human behavior. These factors are malleable, not fixed. Accordingly, it seems logical to believe that human behavior is also malleable, susceptible to change.

TEACHING SCENARIO

Again we raise the important theme of providing for individual differences. Special education involves individualizing instruction for the exceptional person; it is a means of adjusting the school setting in accord with a learner's special needs. There are a number of possible approaches that share common threads. First and foremost, special education is adaptive education; it is instruction adapted to the individual.

When Mr. Keppler first assumes his duties as a fifth grade teacher in a new classroom, he finds he has three students with various learning problems who have been mainstreamed into his classroom. For part of the day these students leave his supervision and work with a special education resource teacher who gives them special assistance. Mr. Keppler is concerned first with understanding the nature of the children's education problems, which is not yet clear to him. Second, he wants to make certain that what he does in the regular classroom is consistent with and supportive of the efforts and objectives of the resource teacher. What is the best way to achieve this consistency?

Chapter 9b

Providing for Individual and Group Differences: Special Education

Introduction

Individual differences are a fact of life. In fact, recognition of and concern with differences are so ingrained in our culture and social system that we scarcely know how to think in terms of other characteristics. The use of norm-referenced assessment is equally ingrained in our culture, especially in our educational system. These tests are used for a variety of purposes, as we indicated in Chapter 8a. We still use them for at least one of the purposes for which Binet originally developed them—the identification of individuals who will profit from formal education. More recently in the United States and elsewhere, they have been used for an additional purpose—the identification of individuals who need remedial education. An entire branch of education has developed around the more recent use, the branch known as special education.

Special education is an area fraught with political, judicial, sociological, and educational controversies well beyond the scope of this text. Much of this controversy concerns three issues. First, the identification of students who need special education through traditional assessment may be discriminatory (Kratochwill, Alper, & Cancelli, 1980). Second, norm-referenced assessment, while useful in a psychometric sense for detecting individual differences, is not as useful for measuring educational gain (Carver, 1974). Third, there is a lack of consensus about the methods of educational remediation that are both equitable and effective. None of these issues is strictly educational; all are political as well. How can we understand this topic and the controversy that surrounds it?

We have chosen to divide our discussion of special education into two sections. In the first, we will examine the way students who need special educational services are identified. In the second, we will cover the special programs offered to those identified. We cover these processes separately because they involve somewhat different issues.

Identifying Special Needs

The primary method for identifying children who need special education is through formal assessment with standardized psychometric instruments, particularly intelligence tests. Data from intelligence tests, specific ability tests, achievement tests, and personality measures provide much of the basis for decisions about remediation plans, special provisions, and special class placements. This use of tests raises a number of questions about the traditional psychometric model. The most important questions concern (1) the validity of the instruments used for this kind of decision-making, and (2) the specific validity of the tests for use with special populations, particularly ethnic groups.

General Validity of the Psychometric Model

Traditional psychometric instruments are for the most part based on a trait model (see Chapter 8a). This means they are designed to detect the amount of ability an individual has in comparison with others. Data from these instruments reveal a person's rank compared with a reference group, but they fail to reveal the student's particular type of competence or the reasons he or she achieved a certain rank.

The *IQ* score is a standardized index that indicates a student's placement in the range reflected in the normal curve (see Chapter 8b). Moreover, it is a global index of functioning. A global index cannot, however, be used to determine specific intellectual strengths or weaknesses or to determine the specific intellectual skills that need remediation. In fact, intelligence tests do not yield information that can be used to describe accurately what a child can or cannot do, what the child can or cannot learn, or what the teacher should do as a result. In short, these measures are gross estimators of functioning, and they are not prescriptive. One may classify a child's score in terms of its position on the normal curve, but this classification indicates nothing about what special education services a child may require.

Because the amount and variety of information yielded by intelligence tests is limited, formal evaluation of children invariably involves other measures as well. To assess learning disorders, for example, one might use tests of perceptual motor functions or psycholinguistic devices, such as the *Illinois Test of Psycholinguistic Abilities*. To assess social and personal adjustment, one might use projective tests or other personality trait instruments. Most of these devices are, like intelligence tests, based on a trait model. Recently observational methods that are not based on a trait model and are not norm-referenced have been gaining in popularity (Kratochwill, 1980). These may also be used in assessment.

The first step in evaluating and identifying a person who might need special educational services is typically a referral from a teacher, parent, or other adult concerned with the child's functioning. The reasons for initial referrals vary, but they are usually based on informal observation in the classroom or the home. Probably the most frequent reason for teacher referral is problematic behavior in the classroom, either behavioral, social, or academic.

If it seems warranted, the student is subsequently examined by a school psychologist or other educational specialist who has extensive training in evaluation procedures. It is the specialist who conducts a formal assessment with a battery of devices. The outcome of the formal evaluation and the recommendations of the evaluator and others serve as the basis for further decisions.

The Outcome of Evaluation. Once a student has been assessed and the data have been evaluated, he or she may be given a label, such as *gifted, mentally retarded, learning disabled,* or *emotionally disturbed.* The student may also be recommended for special programming or placement in a special class.

If the use of a psychometric model is controversial, the decision to label or place the child is even more so. It has been suggested that giving a child a label, especially one that denotes limited capacity, may lead to lower expectations for and different treatment of the child. These lower expectations may function as a so-called self-fulfilling prophecy (Rosenthal & Jacobson, 1968). Furthermore, people who are labeled often dislike their labels (MacMillan, Jones, & Aloia, 1974). The effects of labeling on performance are far from clear (Ysseldyke & Foster, 1978; Yoshida & Myers, 1975; Meyers, Sundstrom, & Yoshida, 1974), but the issue has been a subject of concern, and recommendations have been made to minimize the risks (Reschly, 1979).

Because of the potential problems in the assessment, diagnosis, and remediation of educational problems, most school districts are extremely careful in their evaluation procedures. Most establish clear policy guidelines, and the process involves a number of individuals, including specialists. Careful records are kept, conferences are held, and capriciousness is avoided as much as possible. In the past, judgments about educational problems and needs may have been subjective. Today the situation is marked by caution. Evaluation continues to be a much debated topic (for example, Kratochwill, Alper, & Cancelli, 1980; Kratochwill, 1980; Salvia & Ysseldyke, 1978), but it remains part of the contemporary educational scene.

▶ *ACTIVITY 1.* To learn how special education decisions are made in your community, interview a school official involved in the process. This might be a director of special education services, a school psychologist, or a school principal. Find out how the decision-making process is conducted, including (1) who is involved, (2) what evaluation instruments are used, (3) how the process is recorded, and (4) what the steps of the process are.

When you have identified the assessment instruments used, go to Buros' *Mental Measurements Yearbook* (1978) and read the summaries and critiques of those instruments. Then answer the following questions: (1) Does the school use referenced instruments exclusively, or others as well? (2) Does evaluation include direct observation in the classroom or home environment? (3) Are decisions based on data from many techniques or just a few?

Evaluation of Special Populations

Traditional testing models come under the greatest fire when they are used with ethnic minorities. In some cases, this use has led to a call for a moratorium on certain standardized tests (Cleary, Humphreys, Kendrick, & Wesman, 1975) and recommendations that they not be used with black children (Williams, 1970). One argument in this debate is that such testing violates the civil rights of the ethnic minority child (Williams, 1971). Since a disproportionate number of minority children receive aversive labels and are placed in special classes, it is argued that they are denied equal educational opportunity.

In Chapters 8a and 9a we raised the issue of the possible bias of psychometric tests with ethnic minorities. The possibility that tests may be biased has led to an interest in nondiscriminatory assessment techniques (Kratochwill, Alper, & Cancelli, 1980). These approaches include Piagetian-based assessment procedures (Laosa, 1977; Struthers & DeAvila, 1967; DeAvila & Harassy, 1975), learning potential approaches (Kratochwill, 1977), criterion-referenced assessment (Mercer & Ysseldyke, 1977), and direct observational assessment (Jones, Reid, & Patterson, 1974). Although these approaches also present problems, they are not based on the trait model and lack reliance on normative comparison. As a result, many believe they are less discriminatory than traditional instruments (Mercer & Ysseldyke, 1977) and more likely to lead to unbiased decision-making.

Much of the impetus for the development of nondiscriminatory assessment procedures derives from legislation and judicial decisions.

The Civil Rights Act of 1964 and the Education of All Handicapped Children Act of 1975 (*PL* 94–142) have had an especially strong influence. School districts jeopardize their federal funding if they fail to comply with the antidiscrimination provisions of the Civil Rights Act, and *PL* 94–142 includes guidelines for nondiscriminatory assessment.

Such court cases as *Lau* v. *Nichols* (1974), *Diana* v. *California State Board of Education* (1970), and *Guadalupe* v. *Tempe Elementary School District* (1971) have called attention to the bilingual issues in assessment and the placement of disproportionate numbers of non-Anglo children in classes for the mentally retarded. Others, such as *Larry P.* v. *Riles* (1972), have dealt with the possible cultural bias of tests against black children. These and other judicial decisions have resulted in greater caution in classifying students, especially those from ethnic minorities, on the basis of traditional assessment. Some court decisions have directed that alternative strategies of assessment be used, and even that the number of placements be reduced (Oakland & Laosa, 1977).

▶ *ACTIVITY 2.*　Continuing your interview from the first activity (see p. 374), find out if there are any minority or special groups represented in the schools in your community. Find out what additional assessment procedures are used with non-English-speaking children, with ethnic minorities, or with low socioeconomic status children. Does the school district use bilingual examiners? Compare the assessment procedures used in these special cases with your earlier findings.

Quite obviously, the use of assessment procedures for identifying students in need of special educational programming is a complicated matter. While we wish to provide the services that are necessary, we do not wish to discriminate against members of certain groups and deny them educational opportunity. Achieving both goals is difficult. Identifying students who need services is one major problem; providing the services is the next.

Providing for Individual Differences

Since we acknowledge individual differences, those of us in education must adjust educational programs to provide for them. There have been many attempts to do this in the history of education, some successful and some less so. No single adjustment has proven effective for all students. The current practice is to use a combination of approaches.

The practices used fall into three main categories. The first involves varying the time students are given for completion of an educational program. The second attempts to reduce the variability of the student population by grouping students into smaller instructional units on the basis of ability or some other characteristic. The third approach is based on the notion that teachers will always be confronted with individual differences in the classroom; they must thus make provision for these differences in planning the regular instructional program.

Varying Length of Time in School

The usual practice in education is to admit children to school on the basis of chronological age. Many states and school districts set time limits for the age of school entrance. The age is normally five years for enrollment in kindergarten and six years for enrollment in first grade. After entering school, the child is expected to spend the next twelve or thirteen years in the school system and eventually graduate from high school. This lockstep kind of educational program, one grade per year, may, however, be too slow for some students and too fast for others. Schools that recognize this have attempted to provide for different rates of learning by varying the time the student is given to complete school.

Acceleration.   Acceleration allows some children to move through the educational system at an earlier age or in a shorter time than other children. Acceleration practices include early school admission, skipping grades, early admission to college, and allowing high school students to take college-level courses.

Early admission to school is not practiced widely because of state and local school district age requirements. Schools occasionally make exceptions for children who are unusually intelligent and socially mature. Children admitted early are usually within six months of the age requirement, however.

Skipping grades involves eliminating one year or one semester in a student's school program. The practice of skipping grades is limited, since teachers and parents often question its advisability. Their reservations concern the problem of the child's making the social adjustment to an older age group and the fear that the student will not learn certain skills normally taught in the year skipped, both of which might affect future school achievement. Contrary to popular belief, however, children who have skipped a grade have been shown to be equal or superior in social adjustment to those who are not accelerated. Those who skip a grade can normally acquire any missed skills with little, if any, assistance from the teacher.

Many secondary schools permit students to graduate after they have successfully completed a specified number of units of credit. A

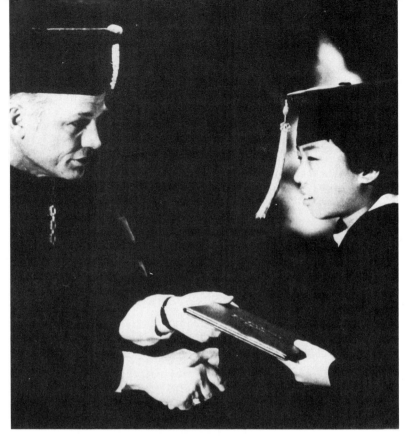

Acceleration is one of the program adjustments provided for meeting the needs of gifted students. The gifted child who is accelerated moves through an educational program in a shorter time by means of early admission, skipping grades, or enrolling in a greater number of courses than the normal child.

gifted student may enroll in more courses per year than the average student and so graduate in a shorter time.

Some secondary schools provide for the gifted by offering college-level courses in high school. Students who complete these courses and successfully pass the examination may receive college credit. This keeps the student with his age mates during the secondary school years and thus reduces the fear of social adjustment problems that might result from early admission to college.

Colleges sometimes provide for intellectually superior students by admitting them without requiring a high school degree. One such program was developed by Stanley (1977) at Johns Hopkins University. Stanley selected a small group of students aged thirteen to fifteen who showed remarkable mathematical achievement and enrolled them in the Mathematics Department of Johns Hopkins University. All of these students adjusted quite well to the program socially, and their performances in college-level classes were at the honors level.

Evaluation of Acceleration.   Intellectually superior students whose school program is not adjusted in some way will waste a great deal of time. The gifted learn faster and apparently achieve at a much higher level than is typical of their classmates. Regular programming might lead to boredom, lack of interest, and low motivation. Acceleration provides the students with an intellectual challenge more congruent with their abilities.

Acceleration allows gifted children who plan a professional education to complete their requirements earlier and become independent at an earlier age. Without acceleration, gifted students may spend their first thirty years in education programs. Reducing the education time not only leads to earlier independence, it gives such children a longer productive time in their chosen professions.

The primary objection to acceleration seems to be the adjustment problems that may occur when the child leaves his or her own age mates and becomes involved with an older group. There is no concrete evidence that this problem exists, however; in fact, most studies show equal or superior adjustment in these children.

Slowing the Pace of Schooling.   If the gifted child can proceed through school in a shorter time, then the child who learns at a slower pace may require a longer time to complete schooling. Retention at grade level was common during the late nineteenth and earlier twentieth centuries. Students who had failed to master the skills or content necessary for succeeding at the next grade level were simply retained for an additional year or more in the same grade.

During the 1940s and 1950s there was a considerable decrease in the number of students retained at a grade level for a second year. This decrease may have been due to several factors. First, research studies showed that students who were retained in a grade achieved no better than comparable students who were promoted to the next grade (for example, Coffield & Blommers, 1956). A second factor was the increased concern of the school for the total child. Students were retained because of deficits in academic achievement, but schools began to focus on noncognitive outcomes of education. The negative effects of retention on retained students' self-concepts, the social adjustment problems of placing retained children in a younger group, and the effect of failure on the children's school motivation raised questions about the desirability of the practice. It became more common to promote children in order to keep them with their age mates.

The decrease in the number of students retained at grade level does not mean that the practice has been eliminated. As long as our educational system requires that students acquire certain skills and content before moving to the next grade, some students who learn at a lower rate will not be promoted.

The recent competency-based educational programs that have been mandated by legislation in many states may actually increase the number of students retained at grade level. The rationale for competency-based education is that all students should meet certain standards upon completion of certain grades. Those standards are usually in the basic skills—reading, language arts, and mathematics. The points at which competence is judged vary from state to state. Some states assess competence just once, in twelfth grade for high school graduation; others measure competence at a number of grade levels (for example, three, six, nine, and twelve).

Competence is usually assessed with a test, either a local or statewide test or a nationally standardized test. Students who fail to meet the criteria must be enrolled in programs designed to remedy their deficiencies. Few states have attempted to prescribe remediation procedures, so local school districts determine the means for remediation. Among the possible provisions are summer remedial programs, special remedial classes during the regular school year, and retention at grade level. Since the programs were established only within recent years, it is too early to determine whether they have affected the number of students retained at grade level.

An Alternative—The Nongraded School. One educational approach that attempts to provide for individual differences without the disadvantages of acceleration or retention is the nongraded school. Although considered by many to be an innovative approach, nongraded schools preceded the graded system and were prevalent in one-room rural schools.

Nongraded schools provide a vertical arrangement rather than the usual horizontal one. Instructional groups that include students of different ages are organized in one or more curricular areas. Assignment to groups is based on the students' past achievement and present developmental needs. Nongraded classes are more common in the elementary schools than in middle or secondary schools and more usual at the primary level (grades one through three) than at the intermediate level.

In a nongraded school, students are placed in groups for instruction on the basis of past achievement, ability, and readiness to learn a particular content or skill. The groups are normally arranged in such curricular areas as reading, mathematics, and language arts. The groups are flexible in that a student may be assigned to one level for reading, a different level for mathematics, and a third level for language arts. There is also mobility within curricular areas. A student having difficulty with a learning task may be reassigned to a lower level to gain some prerequisite skills or knowledge, and a student showing a spurt in achievement in a certain area may be moved to a

The non-graded school provides for individual differences by placement of students in instructional groups on the basis of past achievement, ability, or readiness, rather than placement according to chronological age.

higher level. Student placement in a group is based on the premise that the student will both find a challenge in the group and also be able to succeed at that level. The program of the nongraded school is planned so that students can complete the program at their own pace. The emphasis is on student success in mastering content and skills.

Evaluations of nongraded schools have failed to show that they are superior to graded systems. Although proponents claim that the students are happier and more motivated and that they have more positive attitudes toward school, these claims have not been supported by empirical evidence. Achievement test scores sometimes favor the graded schools, sometimes the nongraded. In many cases, there are no achievement differences.

The lack of clear evidence that one system is superior to the other may be due in part to the different kinds of nongraded programs. Otto & Sanders (1964) proposed that for a school to be truly nongraded, a great many changes are necessary—in administration, teacher attitudes and practices, instructional materials, and even the basic philosophy undergirding the elementary school. Undoubtedly, many schools have inaugurated so-called ungraded programs that involved few changes other than the formation of groups. Teachers still use the same texts, the same curricular guides, and the same methods of instruction. Unless educational practices and procedures are thoroughly revised, few differences will result, since good teachers in graded classrooms develop procedures to provide for individual differences, too.

Individually Guided Education (IGE).   The *IGE* approach developed at the Wisconsin Research and Developmental Center (Klausmeier, Rossmiller, & Saily, 1978) is a nongraded approach to individualized learning programs for students. *IGE* is a multiunit plan appropriate for a school or school district. Using this approach, an elementary school enrolling about 600 students might be divided into four units. In each unit one teacher would be designated unit leader. Each unit would also include from three to five staff teachers, instructional and clerical aides to assist the teachers, and approximately 150 students. The students in each unit are grouped by age—Unit I, four to five years; Unit II, six to nine years; Unit III, eight to eleven years; and Unit IV, ten to twelve years. Note that there is some overlap of years—placement in units takes such factors as social maturity, intelligence, and past achievement as well as chronological age into account.

The unit leader and the teachers work cooperatively. Each teacher's strengths and weaknesses are considered in the assignment of tasks. One teacher's major role might be to create and organize learning materials. Another especially proficient with small-group instruction might be given that responsibility. A third might specialize in evaluation. The emphasis is on a team approach and cooperative planning.

The instructional programming model used in *IGE* is shown in Figure 9b–1. The steps for implementing the program are prescribed. The first step, formulating educational objectives, is a responsibility of the principal and unit leaders, who draw on parents, instructional specialists, and other resources as needed. When the educational objectives have been delineated, decisions are then made concerning the objectives to be attained by each unit. These objectives become the focus of the educational programs of each unit. The third step is to determine the entry level characteristics of each student. Once this has been accomplished, instructional objectives are set for each child for short periods of time. Step Five is the actual instructional process, which is planned cooperatively by the teachers. After instruction the student's attainments are assessed and judgments are made about proceeding to the next objective or taking other actions if the objectives were not met.

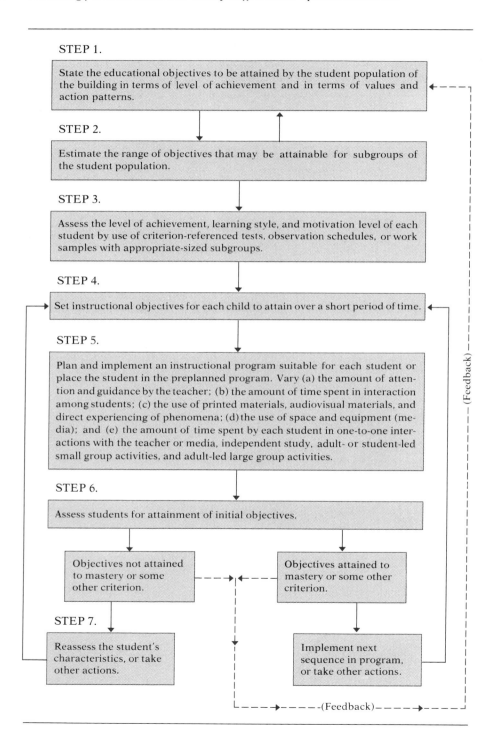

STEP 1.

State the educational objectives to be attained by the student population of the building in terms of level of achievement and in terms of values and action patterns.

STEP 2.

Estimate the range of objectives that may be attainable for subgroups of the student population.

STEP 3.

Assess the level of achievement, learning style, and motivation level of each student by use of criterion-referenced tests, observation schedules, or work samples with appropriate-sized subgroups.

STEP 4.

Set instructional objectives for each child to attain over a short period of time.

STEP 5.

Plan and implement an instructional program suitable for each student or place the student in the preplanned program. Vary (a) the amount of attention and guidance by the teacher; (b) the amount of time spent in interaction among students; (c) the use of printed materials, audiovisual materials, and direct experiencing of phenomena; (d) the use of space and equipment (media); and (e) the amount of time spent by each student in one-to-one interactions with the teacher or media, independent study, adult- or student-led small group activities, and adult-led large group activities.

STEP 6.

Assess students for attainment of initial objectives.

Objectives not attained to mastery or some other criterion.

Objectives attained to mastery or some other criterion.

STEP 7.

Reassess the student's characteristics, or take other actions.

Implement next sequence in program, or take other actions.

(Feedback)

(Feedback)

The primary emphasis of *IGE* is to allow students to work at their own pace in an environment in which each student can be successful. Students move through the units at different rates. The success of such a program is based on several key variables, including (1) adequate specification of objectives, (2) knowledge of student characteristics, and (3) organizing a group of teachers and aides who will cooperate to make each unit function smoothly.

Reducing Variability Within Groups

A second major approach used to provide for individual differences is homogeneous grouping—reducing the variability among students in a group, or grouping students on the basis of common characteristics. Reducing variability does not itself provide for individual differences, but it does narrow the range of student differences, an arrangement that is helpful in planning instruction.

The age limits established for school entrance attempt to reduce variability on the basis of chronological age. Other variables may also be used for grouping, either separately or in conjunction with age. These include the cognitive variables of intelligence and achievement, physical variables, and social and emotional variables.

By reducing the range of individual differences, homogeneous grouping helps the teacher provide instruction appropriate for the group. Homogeneous grouping does not eliminate individual differences; it simply reduces their range.

Ability Grouping. Ability grouping involves assigning students to classes on the basis of intelligence, achievement, or teacher judgment. The rationale is to give the teacher a homogeneous group of students so that instruction, materials, and activities can more easily be planned to fit the needs of all students. A teacher faced with a heterogeneous group may tend to aim instruction at the group's average level, so superior students may be bored and slower students may be frustrated. If the classes are formed so that groups consist of either superior students, average students, or slower students, it should be possible to design more appropriate instruction, since the range of abilities is smaller.

Ability grouping may involve grouping students who fall at the extremes on the cognitive variables (the gifted and the retarded) or grouping in a number of categories (gifted, above average, average, below average, and retarded). Students may be assigned to groups on the basis of one criterion or several. The criteria used most frequently

◀ FIGURE 9b–1. **Instructional Programming Model in IGE**
(From Klausmeier, 1978)

include achievement, intelligence test scores, teacher judgment, and reading ability.

Opinions about ability grouping vary widely. Teachers as a group favor ability grouping, although most prefer to teach the average or above average groups. Parents' and students' opinions vary depending on the group the student is assigned to. When students are assigned to the superior groups, their opinions tend to be favorable, but those assigned to the slower groups tend to react unfavorably.

Some of the arguments for and against ability grouping are given below.

Pro	*Con*
1. It allows students to progress at their own rates with students of similar ability.	1. It is undemocratic and unrealistic to group students on the basis of their ability. They need to learn to adjust to and associate with students of all levels of abilities.
2. Students are more likely to be challenged to do their best in a group commensurate with their abilities.	2. Students of lesser ability may profit from participating in learning experiences with those of higher ability.
3. The methods and materials used are more appropriate to the entire group.	3. True ability grouping is impossible because of test unreliability.
4. Providing for individual differences is very time-consuming for the teacher.	4. Teachers may assume the class is homogeneous and neglect students whose abilities are more varied.

The evidence regarding the effectiveness of ability grouping is inconclusive (Esposito, 1973). The evidence is slightly in favor of grouping for the academically talented. For the average and below average, the results are mixed—negative effects are found in slightly more than half the cases. Ability grouping is more successful when materials, objectives, curriculum, and teaching methods are modified in accordance with group abilities. As was true with nongraded schools, instituting ability grouping without changing instructional programs provides little improvement over heterogeneous grouping.

Special Classes.   Although it is economically infeasible for small school districts, large school districts often provide special classes for the gifted. The children are grouped by grades, and a special enriched curriculum based upon the students' needs and interests is provided. Students are encouraged to explore topics and subjects omitted from the regular curriculum, but the students are not accelerated in grade placement. In secondary schools, gifted students may be assigned to honors sections that go beyond the regular curriculum. These students are often grouped in college preparatory courses, which serve roughly the same purpose.

Special classes for the mentally handicapped are also provided by most school districts. The profoundly or dependent mentally handicapped children normally attend schools other than public ones. These individuals may receive some training through private agencies, state institutions, or private schools. Provisions for educating the trainable mentally handicapped (*TMH*) in the public schools have evolved over the last twenty to thirty years, however.

Educational programs for the trainable revolve around developing self-care skills, assisting the child's socialization in the home and neighborhood, and, if possible, teaching the child skills that could be used to produce an income, in the home or some other sheltered environment. Given the opportunity, these children may develop a wide range of skills. The academic skills normally taught in schools are inappropriate for the trainable, except at a very low level. The reading ability of these children will be limited. They may learn to recognize their names, a few words and phrases that will help them function in society, and street and bus signs. They are given no formal instruction in arithmetic, but they may learn certain quantitative concepts, such as *more, less, larger,* and *smaller.* They may also learn to count to ten and write these numbers. Most of the training, however, revolves around self-care activities—personal hygiene and the practical arts of cooking, cleaning, gardening, and other household tasks. Older children may be taught skills that could be used in highly routine occupations.

In the decades before the 1970s, the educable mentally handicapped (*EMH*) were generally taught in special classes by teachers with specialized training. The number of students enrolled in each class was kept relatively small. The curriculum was adapted to the slower rate of learning typical of these children. Since the passage of PL 94–142, the number of special classes for the educable mentally handicapped has decreased. The educational goals for these children remain similar whether they are in special classes or not, however.

Education programs for the *EMH* include the traditional subjects of reading, writing, and arithmetic, some work in such subjects as science and social studies, and regular programs in art, music, and physical education. *EMH* children can learn to read at between the second and fifth grade levels. In arithmetic, achievement will reach the level of the child's mental age or grade equivalent; a child with a mental age of ten, for example, might achieve at the third or fourth grade level. The programs are designed to emphasize skills that will be useful to the child.

Junior and senior high special classrooms focus on prevocational and vocational training. Although students may receive some further training in academic skills, the emphasis is on preparing the child for the world of work through classes in occupational exploration, shop, home economics, and occupational information. Part-time work experiences are often built into secondary school programs.

Perhaps you can see why members of minority groups are upset that their children are often disproportionately represented in *EMH* programs. Since *EMH* programs typically lack academic orientation and emphasis on the skills needed for further academic education, any misidentified or misplaced children are denied educational opportunity. The debate is fueled by the possibility that assessment procedures are discriminatory and result in the misidentification and misplacement of minority children.

Other Special Groups.   Groups may be formed on the basis of handicapping conditions other than mental retardation. Throughout the history of special education students with different handicaps have been grouped for special education. Visual or auditory impairments, learning disabilities, and behavior disorders are among the conditions that have led to the formation of special groups.

Visually Impaired. The partially sighted and the blind were originally educated in residential schools. Since the 1950s, however, most visually impaired children have been enrolled in local school programs. One provision made by the local schools has been the formation of special classrooms with specially trained teachers.

The educational problems of the visually impaired are centered around (1) restriction due to their inability to see objects, and (2) restriction in experience due to limited mobility.

Most of the educational adjustments designed to alleviate these problems involve the materials provided for learning. The visually impaired develop cognitive abilities at the same rate as sighted children, and their school achievements are comparable when adequate provisions are made for appropriate learning materials. In the classroom, large-print books may be provided for the partially sighted, and Braille or talking books may be provided for the blind. To increase visually impaired students' knowledge of objects, teachers may make greater use of verbal descriptions and concrete objects that blind students can explore by touch. With appropriate materials and greater use of verbal description and instructions, the educational progress of the blind or partially sighted child differs insignificantly from that of the sighted child (Kirk & Gallagher, 1979).

Hearing Impaired. Like the visually impaired, hard-of-hearing and deaf children were originally educated in residential institutions. Although some local school programs for the hearing impaired have been established, a smaller proportion of deaf children are enrolled in these programs than is true for the visually impaired.

The hard-of-hearing child may require only minor modifications in education programming. The use of hearing aids and auditory training in detecting speech sounds may help the hard-of-hearing child proceed through a regular program. Giving the student a seat where he or she can hear the teacher and using the chalkboard or overhead projector to give instruction will also facilitate learning. Children who have a more severe hearing loss may encounter the same learning problems as the deaf.

Deaf children, especially those who are congenitally deaf, have great problems in securing an education. Congenitally deaf children fail to learn to speak through normal channels, and the development of speech and language is a lengthy process. Since much school learning depends upon the acquisition of language and speech, deaf children are often several years behind their age mates in educational achievement.

Learning Disabled. Children with specific learning disabilities have a wide range of learning problems. A learning disability is indicated when there is a discrepancy between a child's ability and his achievement. The discrepancy is usually in only one or a very limited number of areas of functioning and thus indicates no general retardation. A child of average or above average intelligence who fails to learn to read, who has delayed speech, or who lacks the ability to retain what he or she has learned may be considered to have a specific learning disability.

The educational adjustments made for the learning disabled are as diverse as the disabilities themselves. A child who has a learning disability in reading requires an educational program different from the program needed by one with a perceptual motor disability. Language disorders and visual-perceptual deficiencies also require different types of adjustments. A survey of the types of disabilities and the educational adjustments made for them has been provided by Kirk & Gallagher (1979).

Behaviorally Disordered. A number of behaviors may be classified as disordered, including extreme hostility, maliciousness, persistent disobedience, hypersensitivity, and extreme shyness. The various behaviors may be classified into two broad categories—aggressive behaviors and withdrawn behaviors. Special provisions are required in educational programs for the behaviorally disordered when the behaviors significantly interfere with the child's own development, the lives of others, or both.

Because behavior disorders are so diverse, the educational procedures used to assist children who suffer from them cannot be explained here in detail. One of the more successful approaches involves the use of behavior modification techniques, which were described in Chapters 3a and 3b. In this approach, the teacher specifies exactly which behavior or behaviors are maladaptive, determines what conditions led to the behavior, and then changes the antecedent or consequent events to modify or alter the behavior.

Evaluation. The use of grouping as a means of providing for individual differences has been without uniform success. Studies show conflicting results, perhaps because of the number of variables that may influence the outcomes of such studies. The teacher, the materials and facilities used, and the type of educational intervention could all influence the results. The efficacy of special class placement is also a subject of debate. Some studies indicate that the procedure is unsuccessful (Kirk, 1964; MacMillan, 1971), but these studies have methodological problems, so the picture is far from clear. Although educators may have strong opinions about the strengths or weaknesses of grouping, there is little conclusive evidence to support or condemn the practice.

Mainstreaming. One major factor that has affected grouping in traditional segregated special education classes is the implementation of the Education for All Handicapped Children Act (*PL* 94–142). This law, sometimes called the mainstreaming law, states that handicapped children should be educated in the least restrictive environment. The environments that may be used for educating handicapped children, from least to most restrictive, are as follows:

1. Regular classroom
2. Regular classroom with supplementary instructional services
3. Regular classroom with part-time special class
4. Full-time special class
5. Special schools in public school systems
6. Residential, hospital, or total care settings

The law requires that handicapped students be educated with children who lack handicaps insofar as the conditions of the handicapped students allow. Those with less severe handicaps are normally placed in one of the less restrictive environments. As a result of this law, the regular classroom teacher may have a greater range of individual differences in the classroom than was usual in the past.

PL 94–142 also provides for individualized programs. Each handicapped child must have an Individualized Educational Plan (*IEP*). The plan is formulated with the child's parents and includes (1) a statement of the child's present level of educational performance, (2) a statement of goals for the child, both long-term and short-term, (3) a statement of the educational provisions to be made for the child, including where the child will be placed and what services will be provided, and (4) a statement of what evaluation procedures will be used and specifically when evaluation will be carried out.

Whether mainstreaming will result in better education for handicapped children than the special classroom remains to be seen. The requirement that an *IEP* be provided for each child encourages teachers to focus attention on specific needs of individual children and educa-

Individual differences may be physical as well as intellectual.
Mainstreaming of special students has increased the
range of individual differences among students in a class.

tional programming to meet those needs. It is to be hoped that the
regular classroom teacher who is responsible for planning and execut-
ing the *IEP* will come to more fully appreciate the individual differences in all children in the classroom.

▶ *ACTIVITY 3.*   Continuing your interview (p. 375), find out
what kinds of services are provided for special education in
your community. Check to see (1) whether special classes are
available and, if so, for whom, (2) whether resource teachers
and resource rooms are used, and (3) whether there are special
facilities outside the public school.

Once you have identified the special resources provided in
your community and its school system, arrange to observe in
one or more of the settings. Pay particular attention to (1)
classroom structure, (2) instructional methods, (3) teacher-
pupil ratios, and (4) use of such additional personnel as aides.

Providing for Individual Differences in the Regular Classroom

Most classroom teachers at both the elementary and secondary school levels teach heterogeneous groups of students. As we have noted, there are intra- and inter-individual differences even in homogeneous groups, and the teacher must take them into consideration in planning educational programs. Good teachers have always recognized and attempted to provide for individual differences in some way, either within the class or through the use of support personnel. The approaches a teacher may use in the classroom resemble those described previously—grouping, individualized learning programs, or the assistance of specialized personnel.

Grouping Within the Class

The practice of grouping by ability within the classroom has a long history. Almost everyone is familiar with reading groups, for example. The class may be divided into groups on the basis of past reading achievement or teacher judgment. Different tasks, assignments, worksheets and other materials, and instructional procedures are provided to meet the needs of each group. The purpose is the same as for ability grouping between classrooms—to reduce the variability of the students being taught at one time.

Children are grouped for instruction in subjects other than reading, although that may be the area in which the practice is used most frequently. Groups can be used in almost any subject—mathematics, science, language arts, or social studies. At the secondary level, homogeneous groups may be formed for instructional purposes within a heterogeneous class.

Most of the same arguments can be made for or against grouping within classes as were made for ability grouping between classes. The evidence concerning the effectiveness of grouping within the class is also inconclusive.

Individualized Instruction

Since the 1960s a variety of individualized instruction programs for students have evolved, including the Personalized System of Instruction (*PSI*), the Individually Prescribed Instruction (*IPI*), and the previously mentioned Individually Guided Education (*IGE*). The Keller plan that has been adopted in many college courses and the mastery learning approaches of Carroll (1963) and Bloom (1976) use many of the same procedures. These approaches differ in some respects, but they have certain features in common.

The most successful individualized instruction programs are those that have been developed and implemented in entire schools, but the procedures may also be adapted by an individual teacher for a single classroom. Most of the individualized programs have all or most of the following elements:

1. The content of the curriculum is broken down into a number of units. At the elementary level, each unit would be quite brief, requiring perhaps one hour for the entire unit. At the secondary or college level, the units would be somewhat longer, perhaps requiring one or more hours a day for one to three weeks.
2. The objectives are stated clearly for each unit, usually in terms of what the student should be able to do at the end of the unit.
3. To determine their standing in a particular content area, students are given pretests.
4. Each student is given a unit of material and instructions designed to help each one reach unit objectives.
5. A student works on the unit either alone or with others who are working on the same unit.
6. Upon completing the unit, the student is given a test, which is scored as soon as possible. Students who meet the criterion are assigned the next unit. Those who fail to meet the criterion are assigned additional activities, after which they are given a second form of the test. This is repeated until the student meets the criterion.

At the elementary level, individualized instruction may be used for just one subject, such as reading, or for all skill and content areas. At the secondary school and college levels, individualized instruction may be used for single courses or for sequences of courses in a curricular area.

The primary advantage of individualized instruction is that it permits students to move through a program at their own pace. With this approach it is unnecessary to hold back the high-achieving student, and the slower student can work at a level at which success is likely. Since students are expected to master the content of one unit before proceeding to the next, when they are faced with new tasks they should already have mastered subordinate skills. Records of the units a student has completed can be given to subsequent teachers so that they will know where to resume instruction.

A frequently cited disadvantage of individualized instruction is that it involves a monumental amount of clerical work. Keeping records of the units each student has completed, scoring tests, and issuing new units for thirty students in three or four curricular areas would require most of the teacher's time. Even a secondary school teacher who taught one subject to approximately 150 students a day would find little time for other activities. To alleviate this problem, some schools employ clerical aides or even use computers to help with record keeping.

In individualized instruction approaches the teacher serves more as a diagnostician and instructional facilitator than as a traditional information dispenser. After the units have been formulated the teacher's primary duties are to diagnose student performance, discern learning problems, and provide remediation.

The procedures for individualized instruction listed above are consistent with those of the *IEP* requirement of *PL 94–142*. The objectives for handicapped children may not be exactly those designated for the student's grade level, but they will be similar to objectives from either above or below that grade level.

Other Resources

The classroom teacher may use other resources in the school or community to help provide for individual differences. Tutors, itinerant teachers, and resource rooms may be used to relieve some of the burden.

Tutors.   Some schools employ teacher aides to help the teacher in the classroom. Others use volunteers from the community who devote some time each week to assisting teachers. Teacher aides often work with students who have learning problems, usually under the teacher's direction. The teacher aide may also relieve the teacher of some clerical or supervisory duties so that the teacher will have more time for tutoring students with learning problems.

Tutoring a student normally involves remediating learning problems. Remediation may include providing instruction in missed skills or knowledge or correcting errors in previous learning. The key steps to follow in remedial tutoring are to (1) diagnose the problem, (2) determine appropriate procedures for remediation, (3) apply the procedures, and (4) evaluate the effect of remediation.

Diagnosing the problem is the responsibility of either the teacher or a specialist, such as a school psychologist or expert in a particular subject matter. Most aides lack the skills necessary for diagnosis. A diagnosis may be made on the basis of observations of the student or through more standardized measures, such as diagnostic tests. For remediation to be successful, it is crucial to determine specifically what errors the student is making or what skills he is missing.

Developing the remediation procedure depends upon accurate diagnosis and a knowledge of instructional techniques. No single technique can be used for all learning problems. Planning a procedure that will correct past deficiencies and maintain the student's interest requires ingenuity and creativity.

If the remediation procedure is stated specifically enough, the procedure can be applied by a teacher's aide or volunteer. Students can

---

Scenario Suggestion

Children who receive special education services, such as Mr. Keppler's three students, have usually been evaluated by educational specialists within the school system. Typically, each child will have been seen by a school psychologist who will have observed, interviewed, and perhaps conducted individualized testing. In addition, other personnel, including regular and special education teachers, will also have been involved. In most cases these specialists will have prepared formal evaluations of each student's abilities and progress. The outcome of the evaluations may be used to formulate an *IEP* (Individual Educational Program) for the student, with prescriptions for special assistance.

To best understand the educational needs of his students, Mr. Keppler should meet with the psychologist (or other evaluator) and the resource teacher to find out what is being done and why. In this way Mr. Keppler can discover the objectives of the resource teacher and the activities he or she provides for the student. Then Mr. Keppler can augment these activities with others that support and agree with the student's individualized objectives. Consistent programming among all professionals involved will result.

Since individualized instruction is based on adaptation to the individual, the teacher must learn as much as possible about the individual and his or her special educational needs. Most psychologists and educators feel that such knowledge comes through access to many samples of the person's behavior. No one index clearly indicates what a person can or cannot do or which instructional circumstances yield the best outcome. Individualizing instruction depends on knowledge of the individual; that knowledge comes with multiple samples of behavior.

---

also be used as tutors at this stage, although the teacher should be careful not to exploit students.

It is the evaluation that determines whether the remedy worked. If the child has learned the skill or no longer makes the errors, the remediation was successful. If the tutoring was unsuccessful, then the entire procedure must be reexamined for errors in diagnosis, and new remediation procedures must be implemented.

Itinerant Teachers. Itinerant teachers have been specially trained to work with students who have learning problems or require specialized attention. Speech clinicians, remedial reading teachers, teachers of the gifted or learning disabled, and other special education personnel may be employed on an itinerant basis. These specialists are usually responsible for several schools and move from school to school as needed. They serve as resources for the regular classroom teacher, providing services that the regular teacher may not be able to provide because of lack of training, experience, or time.

Itinerant teachers may take children who need special help from the classroom for short periods of time on a regular basis or as necessary. They may also help the classroom teacher plan appropriate instruction or provide special materials. The frequency of the itinerant teachers' meetings with a student or a teacher is determined by the needs of the situation. An itinerant teacher may meet with a student every day for remedial reading, or two or three times a week for speech correction. Meetings to provide a teacher with materials may be necessary only occasionally.

Resource Rooms.   The resource room is an alternative for students who need more extensive programs than itinerant teachers can provide. Students may be assigned to a resource room for part of the day but spend the rest of the day with their regular classmates. Students in resource rooms are taught by specialists trained to deal with a specific type of exceptionality.

Summary

Schools use a number of methods to provide for individual differences. These include varying the length of time that students are in school, grouping, and provisions for exceptionalities in the regular classroom. Each method has its advocates and critics, but no one method has been proven to be better than the others.

Regardless of the measures taken to reduce individual differences, students will differ in every classroom. The teacher's attempts to provide for these differences may have far-reaching effects on students. Those who disregard individual differences will find that many students are bored or frustrated. Teachers should attempt to meet the needs of every student, even though this is a goal that is rarely attained.

Motivation is a psychological construct that, like intelligence, has great relevance to education. Many times teachers express frustration when encountering unmotivated students, or they desire means for increasing motivation in their charges. What is motivation? A trait? A process? An outcome of experience?

In Chapter 10a we present the theoretical basis for approaches to motivation and provide you with a sense of the historical tradition behind the concept. Interestingly enough, you should see parallels between the evolution of the psychological concept of intelligence and that of motivation. In contemporary perspectives neither is viewed as a trait; originally, both were. In Chapter 10b we exemplify the application to classroom practice of current notions on motivation.

You have already encountered a great deal in this text, both theoretically and in application, about motivation. Though we did not explicitly state it, our discussions of behaviorism (Chapter 3a) and behavior modification (Chapter 3b) have direct bearing on this topic. What is the motivated person except the individual who persists in tasks without obvious external reinforcement? A person functioning on a thin reinforcement schedule, one who finds knowledge of results reinforcing, or one capable of self-reinforcement, is going to appear highly motivated. What you learned in Chapters 3a and 3b therefore has direct bearing on the next set of chapters.

There is yet another tie to your past reading. Chapter 10a concludes with a discussion of self-efficacy and motivation; Chapter 10b includes the applications of self-efficacy in the classroom. The major proponent of the self-efficacy construct is Albert Bandura, whom you encountered in the context of social learning theory (Chapters 4a & 4b). You have thus already been exposed to many aspects of motivation; these chapters continue past threads.

Chapter 10a

Motivation

Introduction

To explain a behavior, one must be able to identify the factors associated with variability in the behavior. What factors are associated with academic achievement? As we have already explained, past experience and intelligence are two factors that account for some of the variability in an individual's performance. There is still a great deal of unexplained variability in academic achievement, however. One factor that is a persistent concern of teachers is motivation. When we listen to teachers discussing students, we find that much of their concern revolves around the motivational aspects of behavior. We might hear such statements as "Kids just aren't motivated to do school work" or "Johnny spends most of the day daydreaming and doesn't get his work done."

Although motivation is a real concern to teachers, psychological interest in motivational processes has been a rather recent development compared with the interest accorded such topics as learning and intelligence. As with other psychological investigations, studies of motivation have yielded a variety of explanations about its origins and effects. This is because motivation, like intelligence, is a construct. As a construct it is not directly observable; it must be inferred. Drawing inferences involves the creativity of scientists and results in alternative theories. It is these theories that are the focus of this chapter.

Historical Overview

There are some interesting similarities between the history of intelligence theories and the history of motivation theories. Galton and Darwin influenced motivation theory, too. The early hypothesis that motivation is innate and instinctual (James, 1890) is reminiscent of

Galton's approach to intelligence. With the rise of behaviorism, the instinct hypothesis was replaced by the notion of primary drives, which were considered to be universal in all species, consistent with the Darwinian theory of evolution. These primary drives were assumed to arise from something needed for survival. We thus have a hunger drive, a thirst drive, and so on.

The primary drives of animals could be manipulated in the laboratory. Among humans, however, these drives were fairly likely to be satisfied, and it was assumed that another set of drives, called secondary drives, were in operation. These drives were thought to influence behavior in much the same way as the primary drives.

Once the idea of secondary drives was introduced, attempts were made to catalogue them, a procedure similar to discovering the factors of intelligence. A number of lists were generated, some of which had elements in common, others of which had rather unique elements. As the length and number of lists increased, the approach lost the parsimony that was characteristic of lists of primary drives.

One natural outcome of the construction of lists of secondary drives was the attempt by psychometricians to measure amounts of motivation. We would not only find that people had different amounts of motivation, but that people might be motivated primarily by needs that could be considered individual traits. A person thus might have a strong need for affiliation, dominance, achievement, or aggression. The trait that received the most emphasis and provided the basis for much current theorizing was the need to achieve (McClelland, Atkinson, Clark, & Lowell, 1953). The trait approach itself was useful chiefly for descriptive purposes. It did little to explain the variability of human behavior.

Subsequently, researchers began to examine the way traits interact with situational variables to determine behavior. What variables could be used to explain why a person with high achievement needs would make a great effort in some situations but little effort in others? This question has been the focus of such theorists as David McClelland and John Atkinson. Their work and that of other contemporary motivation theorists reflects the impact of cognitive and social learning theorists. They believe that a person's willingness to undertake and persist at a task is determined in large part by perception of past and present situations.

Cognitive factors (perceptions) thus predominate in the attribution theory of motivation (Weiner, 1972). A person's perceptions of the causes of success and failure influence his or her future behavior. These perceptions are a result of the way the person processes information from the environment. Bandura's (1977) self-efficacy approach is another current motivation theory that has arisen from social and cognitive learning theory. There is thus a trend away from the trait approach toward approaches based on interaction between the individual and the environment. We have seen this trend in many of the topics we have examined.

Motivation and Related Constructs

Motivation is the factor in behavior that initiates and directs activity and sustains it over a period of time. All behavior is motivated—studying, daydreaming, watching television, eating, moving, sleeping, and so on. Although we cannot observe motivation directly, we can draw inferences about the motives that might be operating.

Consider the inferences made about motivation by the parent of a newborn infant. The infant wakes from a nap and initiates an activity—crying. The crying could stem from a number of different motives—hunger, thirst, lack of comfort, or something else. If the parent suspects that the infant is hungry, giving the infant food should decrease the crying.

Needs and drives are additional constructs related to motivation. Drive is primarily a behavioristic construct. It is used to denote the impelling force behind behavior. In the above example, the infant's behavior might be said to result from a hunger drive.

Others might say that the infant's behavior arises from a need—the need for food. Needs were originally considered to be deficiencies in an individual that impelled him or her to act. As we shall see later, it is now believed that needs may arise out of deficiencies and out of growth. These needs then become reasons for behavior.

Since motives, drives, and needs are all based on inferences, different observers may interpret the same phenomena differently. The differences arise from a number of factors. First, different motives may give rise to the same behavior. The infant's crying may result from hunger or from discomfort due to a wet diaper. Similarly, two students may work on a homework assignment for different reasons, one hoping to get an *A* and the second hoping to escape the teacher's displeasure. Second, the same motives may be reflected in different behaviors. One student motivated to gain the teacher's attention might try to make the honor roll; another might misbehave in the classroom. Third, it is likely that many behaviors result from a combination of motives. We go to work each day for a number of reasons—to make money, to achieve certain goals, to gain prestige, and so on. As you can see, these factors lead to a rather muddled picture of motivation. We now turn to the theories of motivation, theories that attempt to make sense of the muddle.

Instincts as Motives

Although most present-day psychologists reject the idea that man is born with instincts, until the advent of behaviorism the idea was widely accepted. Swayed by the Darwinian theory of evolution, psychologists such as William James hypothesized that much behavior was caused by instincts universal within species. James (1890) defined instinct as the capability to act to bring about a certain outcome without foreseeing that outcome and without having been taught the capability. He believed that the uniqueness of human behavior was due to the greater number of instincts that man possessed. Long lists of instincts were developed. James, for example, believed that man had natural instincts for climbing, imitation, pugnacity, sympathy, hunting, acquisitiveness, modesty, shame, love, jealousy, and parental love.

The view that instincts were innate and universal qualities removed the issue of motivation from the realm of education. If instincts were unlearned, schools were not responsible for developing them. Instincts that were favorable to the school and society in general would be permitted to flourish. Bothersome or unfavorable instincts were to be thwarted. Many educators contended that the best procedure for curbing instincts was punishment. The schools thus very early assumed the task of subduing inappropriate instincts by punishing the behavior that reflected them. There was little emphasis on developing climates in which students could learn more appropriate behavior. Unfortunately, even though the idea of instinctual behavior is no longer accepted, teachers still devote a great deal of time and attention to restraining undesirable behavior rather than focusing on efforts to create conditions that will encourage positive behavior. Since students are expected to behave properly, they may not be reinforced for good behavior. Bad behavior immediately draws teacher attention, however, usually in the form of a negative reaction.

When behaviorists abandoned the notion of instinct, they began to consider the other factors that might motivate behavior. Being behaviorists, they were interested primarily in observables. The procedures they developed to increase and decrease motivation involved manipulating observables, changing environmental stimulation.

Drives and Homeostasis

The drive theory of the behaviorists hypothesized that drives could be increased or decreased by creating certain conditions in the environment. Humans, like subhumans, require certain conditions for survival. When these conditions are unmet, disequilibrium, or a lack of homeostasis, results. The organism is then impelled to seek equilibrium, to bring itself into balance. Food, for example, is necessary for survival; by withholding food the researcher can increase an animal's hunger drive. The hungry animal will attempt to reduce that drive and bring itself back into a state of equilibrium. This came to be known as the *drive reduction theory* (Dollard & Miller, 1950; Hull, 1952). Whenever a drive was produced by withholding food or water or by inflicting pain, the organism was impelled to act in such a way that the drive would be reduced. This idea fits very well with the concept of reinforcement, which was presented in Chapter 3a. A reinforcer was defined as anything that would reduce a drive. For reinforcement theorists, therefore, drives were necessary in order for learning to occur.

Primary and Secondary Drives

The drives manipulated in the laboratories of the behaviorists were those assumed necessary for survival. These are *primary drives*. Extending the concept of primary drives to explain all human behavior presented a problem, however. The primary drives of humans are frequently satisfied. What, then, was the motivation for human behavior? The drive reduction theory had to be extended to include *secondary drives*, learned drives that were subject to the same laws of learning as any other human performance. As conceptualized, secondary drives were not directly involved in meeting the needs of survival.

Unfortunately, the behaviorists never clearly established how these secondary drives are learned or how many secondary drives there are. One hypothesis was that secondary drives are established through classical conditioning procedures. An infant who is having its hunger needs satisfied, for example, may simultaneously be touched, talked to, and cuddled by its parents. The secondary drive for these loving reactions would be established through pairing. The problem with this explanation is that it would permit almost any kind of related stimuli to become the source of a secondary drive. If loud noises always accompanied the child's satisfaction of his hunger drive, would this create a drive for hearing loud noises?

At first, the drive reduction theory was a parsimonious, closed system. Create a deficiency in the individual; this will spur him to act in some way. If the action is desirable, provide reinforcement. In this manner the person will move toward a state of equilibrium, a desirable state. The secondary drive concept was open-ended, however. How many secondary drives were there? Were drives general or specific? Do we have one general hunger or a number of hungers for specific foods?

Classification of Needs

When the drive reduction approach was carried to its limits, it proved to be an unsatisfactory way of explaining motivation. An alternative approach was needed. One approach that gained some popularity involved formulating *needs lists*. Some were armchair lists; others were

Among the hypothesized universal needs is the need
for love. The infant's need for love may be satisfied
by holding, cuddling, and other physical actions.

based on psychometric or other experimental procedures. The lists
varied in length, specificity, and derivation. We will present two of
these approaches, those of Maslow and Murray.

Maslow's Needs Hierarchy

Maslow (1954) proposed a hierarchical list of human needs (Figure
10a–1). He assumed that needs lower on the hierarchy had to be at
least minimally satisfied before the higher needs arose.

The four lower levels of needs result from deficiencies. These deficiencies create tensions within the individual, who then acts in such a
way as to reduce tensions. The most important needs are at the base;
these are the kinds of needs the behaviorists classified as primary. The
safety needs are the needs to feel secure and safe and the need to know
that physiological needs will continue to be satisfied. When these needs
are at least minimally met, then the social needs of belonging and
esteem become the motivators.

The three upper levels of the hierarchy, intellectual achievement,
aesthetic appreciation, and self-actualization, are termed being needs,

or growth needs. These needs are different from the deficiency needs in that they fail to decrease with satisfaction. In fact, the opposite is true. Satisfying the being needs increases them; knowledge leads to a desire for more knowledge. The needs are constantly renewed. People who reach the apex of the hierarchy, self-actualization, continue to seek self-fulfillment and to attempt to become all that they are capable of being.

Maslow's approach has been criticized on a number of points (Smith, 1969). Although the system appears parsimonious, it lacks the ability to reflect with complete accuracy the way people behave. Most of us move freely both up and down the hierarchy, motivated by different needs at different times. We may forego the physiological need for food in order to accomplish a task, to belong, or to be loved. In times of stress, even the need to know and understand may be neglected in order to feel safe and remove the stressful condition. Maslow's hierarchy also seems to be value laden; it is considered better to be at the higher levels of the hierarchy. Self-actualization seems to be the supreme goal for everyone, although Maslow felt that very few people ever reach that level.

Maslow's approach did focus teacher attention on some important concerns. A student who comes to school hungry, ill, or suffering from parental abuse is unlikely to be highly motivated to know or to understand. If a classroom atmosphere is threatening, in order to meet their safety needs students may develop what is called school sickness or school-phobic reactions. Providing students with opportunities to belong and to gain self-esteem as well as esteem from others are important considerations in planning classroom activities.

FIGURE 10a–1. Maslow's Needs Hierarchy

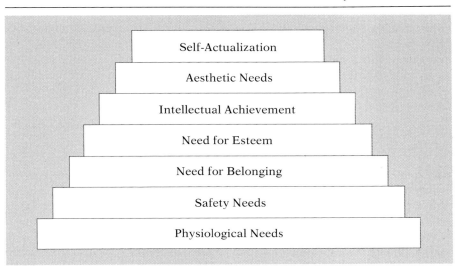

Self-Actualization

Aesthetic Needs

Intellectual Achievement

Need for Esteem

Need for Belonging

Safety Needs

Physiological Needs

Murray's Need System

H. A. Murray (1938) developed one of the more extensive needs classifications. Although he proposed no hierarchy, he included two primary classifications. *Viscerogenic* needs were physiologically based, the equivalent to Maslow's physiological needs. The *psychogenic* needs were learned tendencies to react in certain ways; they thus represented individual traits. Although each individual possessed certain tendencies, Murray felt that factors other than needs would also influence whether a behavior would occur.

Murray proposed twenty-eight psychological needs, including the need for play, the need to achieve, the need for autonomy, and the need for affiliation. Murray avoided considering this an exhaustive list of all human needs; he proposed it primarily to encourage research.

The theory forbore from assuming that all needs were represented in all people. It did suggest, however, that people differ in the strengths of their needs. Some people thus might have a great need to achieve, while others would have a strong need for affiliation or dominance. Researchers, especially the psychometricians, focused initially on determining who possessed which needs and to what extent. Personality tests were developed to try to assess the strength of the various individual motives.

Murray himself, borrowing from Freudian psychology, developed the Thematic Apperception Test (*TAT*) to measure individual differences in motivation. In this test, subjects are shown a series of ambiguous pictures and asked to write or tell stories about the pictures. It is assumed that the subjects project their own thoughts or needs upon the people in the pictures. The strengths of a person's needs is quantified by identifying common themes across a series of pictures.

Perhaps because of unsuccessful experiences with measures of other traits, the movement toward measuring motivation proceeded little beyond the *TAT*. Of the needs Murray listed, the one that has been measured most successfully is the need for achievement. This need has been investigated rather widely. A number of theorists have used Murray's conception and measurement of this need as a springboard to further research.

Achievement Motivation

Much of the research on the need for achievement has been accomplished by David McClelland and John Atkinson and their colleagues. Like Murray, they believe that motivation is learned and that it exists in different strengths in different people. Atkinson (1957) proposed that need achievement (*nAch*) scores derived from the administration of items like those on the *TAT* indicate the strength of the achievement motive. The motive itself is conceptualized as a relatively stable tendency for an individual to strive for success.

Although the motives underlying behavior may be stable, a person behaves differently when confronted with different tasks. This apparent inconsistency occurs because the underlying motive is only one aspect of the motivation in a particular situation. Two other factors that influence a person's tendency to undertake a task are the expectancy of success and the incentive for success. Together, these three factors—motive, expectancy, and incentive—are assumed to combine multiplicatively to determine the person's total motivation for the task.

Tolman was the first to introduce expectancy as a variable in the explanation of behavior (see Chapter 5a). An expectancy is a cognitive anticipation derived from external stimuli. If one performs an act and a certain consequence follows, then a cognition is formed for that relationship. The strength of the expectancy can be determined by the subjective probability that the consequence will follow the act. If in the past a student attended every lecture and read the textbook and received an *A* on a test, the student would expect to receive another *A*

Individuals with a high achievement motivation will persist at a task for a long period of time. Achievement motivation may be exhibited in a variety of ways, such as athletics, academic endeavors, and musical accomplishments.

for performing the same behaviors. If the student performs the behaviors again but fails to receive an *A* this time, then the probability of receiving an *A* on a third test would be reduced. We develop expectancies about the results of our actions on the basis of past experiences. These then become a factor in future behaviors.

An incentive is the value placed upon success. A person may value succeeding at a very easy task only slightly, but succeeding at a very difficult task may have great incentive value. The incentive is the complement of the expectancy for success. In another form, this can be stated *incentive = 1 − expectancy of success.* If the expectancy of success is low, the incentive value is high. The product of expectancy and incentive is greatest when the probability of succeeding is fifty percent.

According to this theory, the manipulable aspects of motivation are the expectancies and the value of the incentives. Since a person's expectancies are the result of past experiences, a person who has a history of success at a particular task will believe himself likely to succeed on similar tasks in the future. If the probability of success is high, the incentive is low, and consequently the person's tendency to undertake the task may be low. Given that *nAch* is stable, a person would have the greatest motivation for tasks of intermediate difficulty in which the product of expectancy and incentive values was greatest.

Motivation to Avoid Failure

Further examination of the behavior of people faced with a task reveals that motivation is composed of two factors—motivation for success (M_S) and motivation to avoid failure (M_{AF}). Motivation to succeed is the same as the motivation to achieve discussed in the preceding section. The motivation to avoid failure is also viewed as a relatively stable trait; it has been measured by the Test Anxiety Questionnaire (Mandler & Sarason, 1952). The strength of one's tendency to avoid failure also results from the product of three factors—the motivation to avoid failure, the expectancy of failure, and the incentive value of failure (guilt, shame, ridicule).

The resultant motivation is the difference between the motivation to succeed and the motivation to avoid failure. In an unconstrained situation in which the person can choose to perform or not perform a task, if $M_S > M_{AF}$, the person will attempt the task and may persist for a long period, depending upon the difference between M_S and M_{AF}.

Achievement Differences and Behavior

Much of the research on achievement motivation has dealt with individuals' choices of activities in a constrained situation in which they must perform a task but are given a choice of activities. Such studies (for example, Atkinson & Litwin, 1960) show behavioral differences between high M_S individuals and high M_{AF} individuals. If the strength of M_S is greater than the strength of M_{AF}, then the person will choose an activity of intermediate difficulty. Individuals whose M_{AF} is greater than M_S, however, tend to choose either very easy or very difficult tasks. In these two kinds of tasks the anxiety associated with failure is minimized. Failure at very easy tasks is unlikely and failure at difficult tasks can be attributed to the task rather than to the individual. One may even gain social approval by attempting very difficult tasks despite failing at them.

The theory has been applied to some school-related research problems. Isaacson (1964) examined the college courses chosen by students whose $M_S < M_{AF}$ and whose $M_{AF} < M_S$. Consistent with the theory were the findings that students whose M_S exceeded M_{AF} chose courses of intermediate difficulty. Students whose M_{AF} exceeded M_S tended to choose very easy or very difficult courses.

Mahone (1960) examined the relationship between choice of occupation and motivation to succeed or to avoid failure. Students with different motivations were asked their choice of occupation. Trained clinical psychologists then rated the realism of the students' choices on the basis of academic performance, college entrance scores, and other data. The results showed that the great majority of students whose $M_{AF} < M_S$ were realistic in their choice of occupations; the occupations they chose matched the judgments of the psychologists. Most students whose $M_S < M_{AF}$ were unrealistic, choosing occupations either above or below their abilities.

O'Connor, Atkinson, and Horner (1966) examined the differential effects of achievement motivation and ability grouping in the schools. Sixth grade students were assigned to homogeneous-ability classrooms and their M_S and M_{AF} were measured. It was assumed that the tasks assigned to the different ability groups would be more nearly of intermediate difficulty for all group members than would be the case in heterogeneous classrooms. The results supported the prediction that students high in M_S would show greater interest and achievement when grouped by ability. No effect on achievement was reported for students who were high in M_{AF}, but there was a significant decline in interest in school work when these students were assigned to homogeneous-ability groups.

Achievement Differences and the Effects of Success and Failure

According to the achievement motivation theory, success and failure should affect students who are motivated to succeed differently from the way they would affect students motivated to avoid failure. Following a review of studies in achievement motivation, Weiner (1972) concluded that students with high resultant motivation ($M_S - M_{AF}$), showed increased motivation following failure and decreased motivation following success. Conversely, if the resultant motivation was low, success led to increased motivation and motivation was inhibited following failure. These results indicate that some failure is beneficial for students who are highly motivated to succeed. Continued failure, however, would probably lead to a decrease in motivation. The teacher's decision to fail or not to fail a student is difficult to make because its effects depend upon the predominant motive guiding the student's behavior.

The theory of achievement motivation assumes that there is a trait or several traits that interact with cognitive factors (expectancies and incentive values) to produce motivation. According to this view, the traits of motivation to succeed and motivation to avoid failure are learned. They are affected by early experiences and they remain relatively stable over time. A more current approach to motivation, attribution theory, is also concerned with motivation for achievement. This perspective views motives as more alterable, the result of the individual's processing of information.

The Attribution Theory of Motivation

On the basis of earlier work by Rotter (1966), Heider (1958), and others, Weiner has developed an attribution theory of motivation. This approach is a distinct shift in that it avoids assuming that motivation is a trait within the individual. Instead, actions are based on a person's perceptions of the causes of success, failure, or both. Motivation can be changed by altering those perceptions.

Although Weiner's theory has changed over time, the basic notion is that "the search for understanding is the (or a) basic 'spring of action'" (Weiner, 1979, p. 2). Much of human behavior is thus directed by our need to know or understand. This need to know or understand often leads to questions, some of which are *attributional* in nature. In the classroom, such questions might include "Why did I flunk that math test?" "Why didn't I get an *A* on the Shakespeare essay?" or "Why did Mary get a better grade than I did?" These are questions of attribution that arise from environmental experiences. The answers we give to such questions may largely determine our motivation to attempt future tasks. We may not consciously ask such questions about every environmental outcome, but we sometimes do, especially when we fail or experience an unexpected outcome.

Students often attribute outcomes to ability (or lack of it), effort (or lack of it), luck (either good or bad), or task difficulty (easy or hard). Other attributed causes are the behavior of other people, mood, fatigue, or attention. The causes to which we attribute outcomes affect our expectancies for the future, our self-esteem, and the judgments we make about others (interpersonal judgments).

The Dimensions of Attribution

Weiner (1974a, 1979) proposed that the attributions that people make for success or failure vary on three dimensions. These dimensions are linked in turn to outcomes likely to influence the behavior of the individual in the future.

The three dimensions are *locus, stability,* and *controllability*. The locus dimension consists of internal and external causes. Internal causes are those within the individual—ability and effort, for example. External causes are those outside the individual, such as task difficulty, luck, and other persons like the teacher, parents, or peers. The second dimension is stability: Are the causes relatively permanent, or do they vary across situations? A person's ability to perform a particular kind of task would be relatively stable, whereas mood and attention would be unstable. Task difficulty would be stable; luck would be unstable. The third category, controllability, concerns whether or not the individual has control of the variable. Effort may be under the person's control, but ability would be uncontrollable. Together, these three dimensions yield eight different types of attributions, examples of which are presented in Figure 10a–2. Student statements corresponding to the attributions are also included.

Of the various causes proposed by researchers (for example, Frieze, 1976), ability and effort seem to be the attributions most frequently cited for success or failure. These are two different dimensions; both are stable and internal, but they differ as to whether control is possible. Effort can be controlled, but ability cannot. In general, we might expect that attributing failure to lack of ability would lead to lower motivation—"I'm just unable to do it." If failure is attributed to lack of effort, however, increased effort might bring success.

Consequences of Causal Attribution

Weiner (1979) contends that each of the three dimensions influences thought and action. Stability influences the way one's expectancies change following success or failure. The locus dimension affects the emotional consequences of achievement, primarily the individual's self-esteem. Investigations of the control factor have focused on the way our perceptions of other people's control of their behavior influences our evaluations of their behavior and our inclination to help them.

Attribution theory casts some doubt on the theory of reinforcement, especially on the dimension of causal stability. Reinforcement theory states that responses followed by reinforcement are more likely to reoccur in the future. Research (Weiner, 1974a) suggests, however, that

Controllability	Stability	Locus	Example	Student statements
Controlled	Stable	Internal	Typical effort	I usually work hard at math.
		External	Teacher behavior	The teacher always presents well-organized lectures.
	Unstable	Internal	Attention	I just didn't pay attention to that section of the chapter.
		External	Unusual help from others	It sure was a good thing that my Dad helped me with that problem.
Uncontrolled	Stable	Internal	Ability	I have always been good in grammar.
		External	Task difficulty	That test was just too difficult.
	Unstable	Internal	Mood	I was really depressed when I took the college entrance test.
		External	Luck	I really lucked out in seeing that in my notes just before I took the test.

FIGURE 10a–2. Attributional Causes
(Adapted from Weiner, 1979)

the effect of reinforcement depends on whether causes are perceived as stable or unstable. If a person perceives success to be caused by stable factors (ability or typical effort), then future success will be anticipated and the behavior will increase. If success is perceived to be caused by unstable factors (luck, help from others), the expectancy of success does not increase. Failures attributed to unstable factors (bad luck, mood, or lack of immediate effort) increase expectation of failure less than failures attributed to stable factors (ability, typical effort, or task difficulty).

The locus of causality seems to be associated primarily with the emotional consequences of success and failure (Weiner, Russell, & Lerman, 1978). Research shows that the dominant emotion connected with success is happiness, while the emotion generally associated with failure is disappointment. Table 10a–1 shows the specific links between attribution and emotion. Attributing success to internal causes generally leads to feelings of pride, competence, confidence, and satisfaction. Ascribing failure to internal causes leads to discouragement, feelings of incompetence, guilt, and resignation. As you can readily see, attributing success to internal factors will increase self-esteem, whereas attributing failure to the same internal causes will lower the person's self-esteem.

Investigations of the control factor have focused on whether or not we perceive other people's behavior as being under voluntary control. The perception affects our evaluations of people's behavior and our willingness to help them. Ickes and Kidd (1976) and Piliavin, Rodin, and Piliavin (1969) found that people were more willing to help others in distress if they perceived the distress as beyond the person's control rather than self-induced. One might be more likely to help a person who has fallen in the street if the fall were due to epilepsy (uncontrollable) than if the fall were a result of drunkenness (controllable). Similarly, a teacher might be more willing to help a child perceived as having low ability (uncontrollable) than one perceived as not trying (controllable). Studies on evaluation of performance and perceived control of causality are of special importance to teachers (for example, Weiner & Kukla, 1970). In one such study, prospective teachers and others pretending to be teachers were given information about students and then asked to evaluate their performances. Although the students performed comparably on an examination, evaluations were influenced more by effort than by ability. Successful performances were rewarded more for good effort than for high ability, and failure was punished more for lack of effort than for lack of ability.

Attribution theory emphasizes the cognitive aspects of motivation. A person's understanding of the causes of success and failure lead not just to changes in expectancies of future success or failure but to emotional reactions as well. Students who attribute lack of success to internal, stable factors are likely to be apathetic, discouraged, depressed, or unmotivated. If failures are attributed to external or unstable factors, students may be led to discover ways to overcome them.

The increased emphasis on the cognitive aspects of motivation has precipitated a more optimistic look at motivation. The trait theory, on the other hand, presents the rather fatalistic view that motivation is a

TABLE 10a–1. Attribution-Emotion Linkages

Attribution	Emotion linkage (success)	Emotion linkage (failure)
Ability	Competence, pride	Incompetence, resignation
Other people	Gratefulness, thankfulness	Anger
Stable effort	Contentment	Guilt
Luck	Surprise, relief, and guilt	Surprise

(Adapted from Weiner, 1979)

factor of personality unlikely to change. According to attribution theory, motivation may be changed by changing perceptions of causality. Bandura has proposed another cognitive approach to motivation, one that is consistent with his social learning theory (Chapter 4a). This theory will be explored in the next section.

Self-Efficacy Theory

Bandura (1977a) hypothesizes that behavioral functioning is largely a result of the person's perceived self-efficacy. Self-efficacy determines whether a coping behavior will be initiated, how much effort will be expended, and how long the coping behavior will be maintained. Self-efficacy, then, has the same characteristics as motivation, as we initially defined it.

Self-efficacy theory is based on the idea that behavior is cognitively mediated. The individual is a processor of environmental information. The processing of information regarding past outcomes determines self-efficacy, which in turn determines behavior.

A primary difference between Bandura's theory and other cognitive explanations of motivation concerns the concept of expectancy. Ban-

When a student has high self-efficacy expectations of her ability to complete a task, she will persist at that task. Self-efficacy expectations primarily arise from past experiences or from observing the experiences of others.

Research Report

In this chapter we have discussed at some length Bandura's self-efficacy approach to motivation. Quite consistently, therefore, we have chosen a self-efficacy study for our research highlight. This study not only exemplifies one operational definition of self-efficacy, it depicts the social learning methodology introduced in Chapter 4a. It is also one piece of a continuing systematic investigation of the concept still being conducted by Barry Zimmerman.

In this study the investigators determined the length of time children would persist on an insoluble task and ascertained whether their degree of persistence could be affected by an adult model's persistence. The children in the experiment were first and second graders. The model in the experiment operated on a puzzle consisting of two interlocking elliptical rings separable if slid carefully in opposite directions. The children's puzzle, however, was a slight variation of the model's, undetectably altered so that the pieces could not be separated.

To establish a baseline for degree of persistence, the investigators first examined the performance of a control group. These subjects were given the task so that it could be determined how long children would spontaneously stay with the insoluble puzzle in the absence of modeling. Unlike the control group, the four experimental groups were first exposed to modeling that varied in two ways: (1) duration of the model's persistence, either high (fifteen minutes) or low (thirty

seconds), and (2) degree of the model's success—success or none. The model accompanied the performance with appropriate verbal comments like "I am going to keep trying; I do not want to give up." After watching the model, these children were given the insoluble puzzle and were allowed to play with it for as long as they wished up to a limit of twenty minutes. The duration of their effort served as the dependent measure.

Children who observed the successful high-persistence model stayed with the task longer than did children in the control group; those who observed the unsuccessful low-persistence model stayed with the task for a briefer time than did controls. Children who saw either an unsuccessful high persistence model or a successful low persistence model lacked any difference from the controls. The investigators determined that both the success of the model and the model's degree of persistence affected performance. They found, however, that "model persistence was twice as influential as model success in motivating children to continue problem solving." (p. 511)

This study, like others in the series, supports the notion that observation of models in the environment may be an important factor in influencing this one aspect of motivation.

Zimmerman, B. J., & R. Blotner, Effects of model persistence and success on children's problem solving, *Journal of Educational Psychology*, 1979, 71, 4, 508–513.

dura suggests that expectancy can be considered in two ways. In Bandura's approach, the achievement motivation theorists' explanation of expectancy is termed a *response-outcome expectancy*. People learn response-outcome expectations by observing the environmental consequences of their own actions or the actions of others. The response-outcome expectation is defined as a person's estimate that a given behavior will lead to certain outcomes. An *efficacy expectation,* on the other hand, represents the person's conviction that he or she can perform the actions that lead to the outcome. A student might expect that studying diligently, doing homework, and taking careful notes during class would lead to an *A* in a course—this would be an outcome expectancy. The crucial question applied to the student's behavior, however, is "How sure am I that I can study diligently, do the homework, and take careful notes?" Individuals may know that responses will lead to predictable outcomes, but if they doubt their ability to perform the responses, the outcome expectancy will fail to influence their behavior.

Perceptions of self-efficacy determine the activities a person will choose to participate in. If, according to an individual's self-efficacy perceptions pursuing a task is unlikely to lead to success, the person will avoid the task. Efficacy expectations also determine how much effort one is willing to spend on a task and how persistent one will be. This does not mean that self-efficacy is the only determinant of behavior; efficacy alone is no guarantee that the task will be undertaken. To perform the task, one must have acquired the necessary skills, and incentives are also important.

According to Bandura, self-efficacy estimates vary on several dimensions: magnitude, generality, and strength. We could determine magnitude by ordering tasks in terms of increasing difficulty. Some people would expect to be able to perform only the simplest tasks (low magnitude); others would expect to be able to handle the most difficult (high magnitude). Expectations also differ in generality. Some expectations are restricted to a specific activity, whereas others are more generalized. The strength variable determines the extent of the coping efforts. If one has a strong efficacy expectation, one will persevere at a task against great odds and in the face of many obstacles. If one has a weak expectation, one will quickly give up the activity when obstacles are encountered.

Sources of Efficacy Expectations

Self-efficacy estimates arise from different sources. They are based primarily on performance accomplishments. The outcomes of previous attempts affect a person's estimates of what will happen in the future. Successfully performing a task leads to an increase in self-efficacy, whereas failure leads to a decrease.

Vicarious experiences, observing models attempting to perform a task, can also influence self-efficacy. Several modeling variables that may affect efficacy expectations have been hypothesized. Models who display effort in completing a task will be more influential than those who solve the task without effort. Efficacy estimates may also be en-

New Directions in Research

Social learning theory again surfaces as an influential source of research and explanation of a psychological phenomenon, this time motivation. In previous research on imitation, investigators have demonstrated the impact of parental models on academic achievement (Henderson & Merritt, 1968; Swanson & Henderson, 1976), but it is the concept of self-efficacy (Bandura, 1977a) that really gives impetus to social learning research and motivation.

Barry Zimmerman at the City University of New York is one person currently utilizing the self-efficacy concept in research on children's motivation within a problem-solving situation (Zimmerman, 1981; Zimmerman & Blotner, 1979; Zimmerman & Ringle, 1981). The research demonstrates the effect models can have in altering children's persistence on difficult tasks and on their predictions of success, both of which are components of motivation. The research is new, a phenomenon studied in the laboratory. It is a thrust of future research to keep track of.

Self-efficacy is a cognitive component of behavior (Bandura, Adams, & Beyer, 1977); its use within the social learning paradigm again demonstrates the cognitive drift in this perspective that was discussed in Chapter 4a. Self-efficacy is not, however, a trait construct, but one that represents the person's ability to process environmental information for use in guiding behavior. It is this information processing theme we see surfacing again and again, in topic after topic.

hanced if the model is similar to the observer. Opportunities to observe several models successfully complete a task may increase the observer's efficacy estimate as well.

Self-efficacy can also be increased through verbal persuasion, especially if aids for performing the task are provided. Verbal persuasion without aids might lead to failure, something that would discredit the persuader.

Of these three methods, performance accomplishments seem to be the most effective. The best technique would be to provide environmental support for successfully completing the task and then gradually withdraw support as the student makes additional attempts. Self-efficacy estimates increase the most when the individual ultimately initiates and completes the task successfully.

Bandura cautions that the effectiveness of these methods will depend upon how the person processes the information, especially information about the causes of behavior. The factors that attribution theorists feel may influence motivation will also affect efficacy estimates. A successful performance attributed to external causes, for example, will do little to change the person's efficacy estimates, but attributing success to internal causes will enhance self-efficacy.

Implications of the Theory

Much of Bandura's research on applications of self-efficacy theory has been conducted with people suffering from phobias, strong specific fears (for example, Bandura, 1977). Applications to school-related activities or school-age childen have been limited. If we assume, however, that school tasks may cause students to doubt their ability, self-efficacy theory seems to be appropriate for examining school motivation.

Two studies examined the effects of a model's behavior on persistence and self-efficacy. Zimmerman and Blotner (1979) conducted a study in which first and second grade children were exposed to an adult model who persisted for either a long or a short time in attempting to solve a wire puzzle. Some children saw the model complete the task successfully; others observed the model fail. Children who observed the persistent, successful model subsequently made a significantly longer attempt to solve the puzzle than did children in the control group, whereas children who observed a model who was neither persistent nor successful made a significantly shorter effort than did the control group children. Observing a model's performance can thus significantly improve or inhibit an observer's persistence on a similar task, even when the model does not closely resemble the observer.

The second study (Zimmerman & Ringle, 1981) examined the way an adult male model's persistence and statements of confidence about his ability to solve the puzzle affected first and second graders' performance on similar tasks. In addition to measuring the children's actual persistence, at various points in this experiment the investigators measured the subjects' self-efficacy estimates. The model's persistence at the task and his statements of confidence significantly increased the children's persistence on the tasks; the model's comments were in fact more effective than the persistence. The modeling significantly affected the children's self-efficacy estimates as well.

Although research on school-related activities is limited, it appears that we may be able to use self-efficacy theory to improve student motivation. As self-efficacy estimates increase, students' willingness to attempt tasks increases, and they spend more time and effort attempting to complete tasks successfully.

Summary

Theorists have developed several different constructs of motivation and motivational processes. There is general agreement that one's motivation initiates and directs one's activity and determines how persistent one will be. The differences that arise concern the origin of motivations, the way they develop, and the way they can be changed.

In the early stages of motivation theory, internal motives were considered. Subsequently, there was a trend toward specifying universal motives, either learned or unlearned. These motives were considered to be traits that tended to be stable over time. More recent approaches suggest that motivation is influenced more by the situation and the way the student processes information. In this view, a student's motivation is influenced by his or her perceptions. Because perceptions can be changed, student motivation is assumed to be more subject to change than was true for the trait perspective. Some methods teachers can use to increase student motivation will be explored in Chapter 10b.

TEACHING SCENARIO

Motivated students are those involved with the learning process, those actively engaged in interacting with materials. Engagement, as you recall, is one of our scenario themes. Any instructional technique that increases activity, increases interaction, and increases engagement may heighten motivation.

Dr. Fuller is charged with designing a mathematics remediation program for high school students who have not achieved well as a result of regular mathematics instruction. The students are self-selected for enrollment in the program, and many of them are female or minority students who have expressed doubts about their ability to master the content.

The major delivery system Dr. Fuller wishes to use is a set of lessons supplemented by video cassettes attached to an interactive computer system. Students can check out the videotapes and the computer exercises as often as they wish until they feel comfortable with the material.

In designing the instructional software, Dr. Fuller wants to be certain that his programming is as effective as possible. He hopes to help the students achieve not only some mathematical competence but a feeling of mastery over the material and thus a desire to pursue mathematics. What techniques might be built into the instruction to achieve these ends?

Chapter 10b

Motivation in the Classroom

Introduction

Motivation seems to be no problem for most students. When the teacher gives an assignment, they begin it immediately, focus on the task exclusively, and persist until they are finished. Students vary greatly, however. Some may be slow to begin a task; others may begin readily enough but become distracted easily. Student motivation may also vary from one course to another. Even within a course, students may pursue certain activities more diligently than others, putting off beginning a term paper until a few days before it is due, for example.

In this chapter we focus on teacher activities that can be used to increase student motivation. Although motivation is considered to be a characteristic of the individual, environmental factors under teacher control are also influential. In the first section, we focus on the radical behaviorist approach. Later sections will be devoted to the more cognitive approaches that emphasize expectancies, goals, and success experiences.

Radical Behaviorist Approach

The radical behaviorist theory (Chapter 3a) refrains from employing the construct of motivation, such a construct being considered superfluous for explaining a person's behavior. In this theory it is considered unnecessary to draw inferences about needs or underlying traits to explain why certain behaviors occur. To adherents of this approach, a motivated student is one who has been appropriately reinforced for the behavior that leads to achievement.

The teacher who uses this approach will determine which behaviors facilitate and which inhibit achievement of course objectives. The teacher's task is to reinforce the desired behaviors and to extinguish those that are undesirable.

Behaviors that would be reinforced include attending to instruction, initiating activity, participating in classroom activities, persisting at task-related behaviors, and completing assignments. These behaviors have already been established in many students; occasional reinforcement of the behaviors is all that is needed to maintain them. In other students, however, the behaviors will need to be established or at least improved. With these students the teacher can apply the procedures explained in Chapter 3b: shaping, appropriate scheduling of reinforcements, the use of tangible and intangible reinforcers, and the application of the Premack Principle.

Consider the case of Jeff, who consistently delays beginning seatwork assignments, such as reading or completing worksheets. Instead of beginning, Jeff engages in a variety of activities, including daydreaming, talking with friends, or wandering around the room. These behaviors usually gain the teacher's attention ("Jeff, take your seat" or "Jeff, get busy."), a response that may serve to reinforce them. Withdrawing teacher attention will lead to a decrease in these behaviors if that is the only reinforcement Jeff is receiving for them. To encourage Jeff to begin work, the teacher can reinforce him when he does begin his assignments immediately. The teacher might also use the Premack Principle by selecting an activity that Jeff prefers to seatwork, such as taking care of the class's pet hamster, and using it to reinforce Jeff for beginning his work.

Skinner (1968) has criticized school practice as being inefficient in that reinforcement is provided too infrequently. Some teachers, for example, only reinforce children for succcessful completion of an assignment, not for the behaviors that led to the completion. Good students who successfully complete assignments may receive good grades, verbal approval, special privileges, or other positive reinforcers, all of which may generalize to the behaviors that led to successful completion. Less able students may not receive these reinforcers, however, even though they too initiate, direct, and persist in achievement-related behaviors. In fact, these students may be punished by losing privileges or receiving low grades and verbal disapproval. Should these punishments generalize to the behaviors the student did perform, the behaviors decrease. The teacher should be aware that a number of behaviors are involved in completing a task. Even though the completed task may not warrant reinforcement, the subordinate behaviors should be reinforced if they are to be maintained.

The radical behaviorist approach involves focusing on the behaviors that facilitate or diminish achievement. Reinforcing the behaviors that lead to achievement will increase them. Behaviors that diminish

Teacher attention can serve as a reinforcer for behaviors that lead
to achievement. To be most effective, the teacher should focus
her remarks on specific behaviors ("I like the way you kept working
at those arithmetic problems") rather than a more general statement
("That's good").

achievement can be extinguished through elimination of the reinforcers
or through punishment.

Expectancies and Motivation

As we discussed in the previous chapter, cognitive approaches emphasize that motivation is influenced by two factors: (1) the person's expectancy of success, failure, or both, and (2) the factors to which the
person attributes success and failure. Expectancies are based on several
factors, including past experiences, the expectations of others, and
vicarious experiences.

Past Experiences

You have probably heard the adage that nothing succeeds like success.
This saying neatly expresses the effect of past experiences on future
performance. Students who have been successful in the past will expect
to succeed in the future. This expectation of success will increase their
motivation. Conversely, those who have repeatedly met with failure on

a task will expect to meet failure in the future and will try to avoid attempting the task.

Expectancies can be changed, but the longer they have been confirmed the more difficult it is to change them. A single success following a long series of failures is unlikely to appreciably change a person's expectation of failure. The success is more likely to be attributed to external factors, such as luck or ease of task, than to internal factors, such as effort or ability. Since luck and task difficulty are uncontrollable, a single success lacks the power to change the student's expectancy of success.

Students who have a long history of failures at a task will have little motivation to attempt similar tasks. The teacher may be able to influence motivation in a number of ways, however, including those listed below.

1. *Provide differentiated assignments.* If the same assignment is given to all students, some will succeed, some will fail, and others will be bored. Assignments should be differentiated so that each student will be challenged but still have a reasonable chance for success. The procedures for *Individually Guided Education* discussed in Chapter 9b can be used to create differentiated assignments.

2. *Use criterion-referenced evaluations.* The nature of norm-referenced evaluation requires that students be compared with each other, so some students will be judged more successful than others. Criterion-referenced evaluation, on the other hand, compares student performance not with the performance of other students but with some attainable criterion. Some students may take longer or have to expend more effort to reach the criterion, but reaching the criterion signifies success for every student.

3. *Redefine success.* Each person has his or her own definition of success. With regard to school achievement, one student might define success as getting the top grade in class and consider anything less to be a sign of failure. Another student might define success as being above average, while a third might feel successful just passing the course. Schools have been criticized for making grades the sole criterion for success. Opponents of grading have argued that success should be measured not in absolute terms but in terms of improvement over previous performance. This would allow everyone to have an opportunity to succeed, the person at the lower end of the scale as well as the person at the upper end.

Expectancies of Others and Motivation

Although past experiences play a strong role in determining future expectancies, the expectations reflected by teachers, parents, or peers may also influence student motivation. These expectations may be stated outright or communicated covertly through different nonverbal behaviors. The behavior of others may affect student behavior by raising or lowering motivation.

Teacher Expectations. The publication of *Pygmalion in the Classroom* (Rosenthal & Jacobson, 1968) focused attention on the effect of teacher expectancies on student achievement. The researchers claimed to have shown in this study that higher teacher expectations for students resulted in greater gains in achievement. In the experiment described, teachers were told that some students' test results indicated that they would show great growth in achievement in the ensuing year. Actually, there were no tests—the students were chosen at random. According to the researchers, the achievement of these students actually did surpass that of comparable students at the end of the year. Even though the study has been severely criticized for methodological and interpretative problems (for example, Elashoff, Snow, & Jones, 1971), it was valuable in focusing attention on the role of teacher expectations on student behavior.

Teachers do form expectations about what students will achieve, although they are rarely based on a single test score, as was supposedly the case in the Rosenthal and Jacobson study. In addition to test scores, previous academic performance, information from other teachers, and observations of the students themselves may also influence teachers' expectancies.

The following model, proposed by Brophy and Good (Good, 1981), explains how teacher expectancies affect student behavior. This model has been used as a guide in research on the influence of teacher expectancy.

1. The teacher expects specific behaviors and achievement from certain students.
2. Because of these varied expectancies, the teacher behaves differently toward different students.
3. This treatment communicates to the students what behavior and achievement the teacher expects of them and affects their self-concepts, achievement motivation, and levels of aspirations.
4. If the treatment is consistent over time, and if the students do not resist or change it in some way, it will shape their achievement and behavior. High expectation students will be led to achieve at high levels, whereas the achievement of low-level students will decline.
5. With time, students' achievement and behavior will conform more and more to the behavior originally expected of them. (Good, 1981)

Teachers may communicate their expectancies verbally or more indirectly through their nonverbal behaviors toward the students. The research of Good and Brophy (1974) reveals some consistencies in the ways teachers behave toward high- and low-achieving students. In accordance with the model, it is hypothesized that these teacher behaviors result from different expectations. The teacher behaviors Good and Brophy describe are as follows:

1. Slow students tend to be seated farther from the teacher or in a large group. They are thus less accessible to the teacher, a fact that probably reduces student-teacher interaction.

2. Because of this lack of student-teacher interaction, teachers pay less attention to low-achieving students in academic situations, smiling at them less often and maintaining less eye contact with them.

3. Perhaps the most notable differences concern the way the teacher behaves toward students responding in the classroom. Compared with high-achieving students, low-achieving students are

   a. called upon less often.
   b. given less time for reporting.
   c. criticized more frequently for incorrect responses.
   d. praised less frequently for correct responses.
   e. praised more frequently for marginal or inadequate responses.
   f. given less assistance for inadequate answers.

These results seem to have implications for student motivation. If low-achieving students are called upon less frequently, they may feel it is less necessary to be prepared. If criticism is more frequent and praise less frequent, the student is discouraged from volunteering and encouraged to be passive.

4. Teachers tend to demand less work and effort from low-achieving students.

These and other studies indicate that teachers do react differently to low- and high-achieving students. We would not expect teachers to treat every student in exactly the same fashion, but teachers must be aware of the effect of their behavior on student motivation and performance.

The effect that a teacher's verbal communication can have on a student can be illustrated with an experience one of the authors had while counseling a high school sophomore. Jim was in academic difficulty in all his high school classes, doing failing or near-failing work even though he was of near-average ability. This had been the pattern throughout most of his school career, although he had managed to earn passing grades so that he had been promoted each year. While discussing the problem, Jim was asked to explain why he thought he was not more successful. Jim responded, "I just can't do it. I'm dumb." When asked why he believed that, Jim related an incident that had occurred seven years before when he was in third grade. "I was having trouble in reading and my third grade teacher kept me after school every day to help me. After several weeks of this, my teacher said, 'I just can't teach you. You are too dumb!' "

Although other factors probably reinforced this belief, this statement must have had great impact. Note that the factor Jim attributed his failure to was stable, internal, and uncontrollable. Jim thus saw no help for the situation; since he was "dumb," additional effort would be unable to affect his performance. One wonders if Jim would have behaved differently if the teacher had attributed the problem to an external cause: "I know you can learn to read. Maybe this book is too difficult." If easier tasks that Jim could succeed at had been introduced and the difficulty level had been gradually increased, Jim's career might have been very different.

Expectancies of Parents and Peers.   Although little or no research has been conducted on the effect of parent or peer expectations on student motivation, these expectancies probably have the same kind of effect as teacher expectancies. There is some evidence that children of parents who expect achievement and demand effort are more motivated to achieve than the children of parents who lack these expectancies (Winterbottom, 1958).

Expectancies from Vicarious Experience.   Expectancies for success or failure may also arise from observations of a model's performance or from others' comments about their experiences. Observing a model successfully complete a task may lead one to an expectancy of success. The effect of modeling on expectancy may be limited, however, by the individual's perception of the similarity between the model's ability and one's own ability.

This is one of the factors in Bandura's self-efficacy theory (Bandura, 1977) discussed in Chapter 10a, p. 416. When one observes a model performing a task, one may develop an expectancy that certain behaviors lead to success. As Bandura points out, however, it is not his expectancy that controls motivation, but the person's perception of his own ability to successfully perform the behavior.

When a student observes an English teacher modeling the diagramming of sentences, for example, the student may fail to develop an expectancy about being able to diagram sentences if the student perceives his or her own ability to be different from the teacher's. If a peer of similar ability modeled the procedure, however, the student might develop an expectancy of efficacy.

Expectancies also arise from what other people relate to us about their experiences with certain courses or subject matter. On every college campus there are some courses that have the reputation of being difficult or challenging and other courses that are considered easy. As these reputations are transmitted to each succeeding group of students, they affect the students' expectations of that course.

Mathematics is an example of a subject that is widely reputed to be relatively difficult. This is probably one of the reasons that enrollment is low in high school and college mathematics courses that are not required. If a child's parents say, "I was never good in math," they may lead the child to expect to do poorly as well. This expectancy may be reinforced by teacher comments. An expectancy of poor performance may lead to low motivation, which in turn leads to poor performance, thereby substantiating the expectancy. The cycle has remained relatively stable over many generations.

Goals and Motivations

Everyone strives for certain goals. These goals serve as motivation to initiate activity and to direct and maintain it as well. Goals can be divided into two categories, short-term and long-term. A short-term goal, such as a desire for food, may be satisfied by stopping for a pizza. A junior high school student's desire to be a physician would be a long-term goal.

Goals also differ in specificity. To satisfy a hunger, one might seek any food or just one specific food. The goal "a college education" is less specific than the goal "a degree in engineering." The more specific the goal, the more direction it provides for activity.

Teacher and Student Goals

The teacher in the classroom should be aware that there are two sets of goals operating—the teacher's and the students'. If the two sets coincide, the classroom will be harmonious, with everyone working toward common goals. Situations arise, however, in which student goals are not in harmony with teacher goals. In such instances the students are often considered unmotivated. They actually are motivated, of course, but toward goals other than the teacher's. Conflict between teacher and student goals often leads to classroom management problems.

Although it is unreasonable to expect the two sets of goals to always coincide, classroom motivation problems may be alleviated if the goals are similar. Different methods, some of which are mentioned in the following list, can be used to help synchronize teacher and student goals.

1. *Cooperative planning.* Although the teacher is ultimately responsible for teaching the content, it may be helpful to involve students in planning activities and schedules. Curriculum objectives may be met in a variety of ways. Allowing students to help in the planning would involve them more directly in the course, a tactic that would probably increase their motivation.

2. *Individualizing goals.* Each student's goals differ in at least some respects from every other student's. Teachers may need to spend time acquainting themselves with the goals of individual students. This makes it possible for the teacher to find opportunities for relating student goals to class goals.

3. *Increasing the relevance of the goals.* Students often lack motivation for school tasks because they cannot see how they are relevant to their goals. Questions such as "Why do we have to study this stuff?" or "Why do we have to do this?" imply that students cannot relate school tasks to their present goals. Attempts by the teacher to relate the goals for each subject to present or future life situations may help students perceive the tasks' relevance.

Performance Objectives

Performance objectives, which were introduced in Chapter 2b, are another method of directing student activity. Performance objectives state a goal, specifying what the student is expected to do, what the content is, and what criterion will be used to determine the acceptability of a student's performance. Providing students with objectives clarifies the activity's purpose and directs student efforts.

The use of computers and computer-assisted instruction can help teachers to individualize programs to fit each student's needs. With appropriate materials, a student can move through a sequence of lessons at her own speed.

Scenario Suggestion

Because Dr. Fuller is using videotapes, he can include human models in the programming. He would do well to utilize models who are like the student population who will be observing the tapes. Learners who see models similar to themselves succeeding on the target tasks are more likely to believe that they too can master the content. They may thus attend more closely to the information and be more apt to attempt the problems.

Dr. Fuller should avoid implying that the content is simple and easily mastered; because of their past experiences, his viewers may not believe him. His models, on the other hand, can note that while the material is difficult, success can still be achieved with persistence. In fact, reinforcement for persistence on difficult tasks can be built right into the tapes.

As to the structure of the content itself, pacing should gradually increase in difficulty, avoiding the necessity for observers to make major conceptual leaps. By gradually increasing complexity, including numerous examples, and providing opportunity for practice, Dr. Fuller should be able to keep the students from becoming lost or frustrated and from giving up. The computer exercises can be programmed according to the same pacing and can be spaced into the video modeling in order to provide practice. The programming can also be of a branching format, using the students' responses on problems to direct them to the next appropriate exercise.

The interactive computer provides other features related to increased motivation. For one, the computer can offer immediate feedback in terms of knowledge of results; computers are even programmable to reinforce. Moreover, since students are interacting with the computer in doing problems and exercises, they are not passive learners. They are engaged in private, working at their own pace, and receiving reinforcement. The combined use of social learning principles, reinforcement principles, and active participation consistent with computer capabilities should affect the feelings of self-efficacy and success of the learners. Motivation should thus also increase.

Changing attitudes toward success with mathematical content is not easily achieved against a history of failure. By using a combination of behavioral and social learning principles in his programming, however, Dr. Fuller may make some inroads into alleviation of the problem.

Consider the following assignments that a teacher might give:

Assignment 1. "Read pages 315–325 in your government book."

Assignment 2. "After you have read pages 315–325 in your government book, you should be able to name the three branches of the federal government and describe the system of checks and balances imposed by the Constitution in setting up the three branches."

Obviously, the second assignment directs student activity much more than the first does. Letting students know the expected outcome of a task can facilitate their achievement.

▶ *ACTIVITY 1.*   The idea for this activity came from an experience that one of the authors had. A junior in high school was enrolled in a required World History course. He was doing poorly in the course and was causing some discipline problems. In a conference with the author, who was serving as principal of the school, the student said he thought the course was a waste of time and he did not see how it would help him to be a better barber, which was his goal. It was a difficult question to answer: What good would it do him?

We frequently tend to think of the value of a subject we teach as related to future courses in public school or in college, but many students, like the young man who wanted to be a barber, have goals other than college. Consider three occupations that require no education beyond high school (for example, service station attendant, typist, homemaker) and provide a rationale for students with these career goals to at least one of the following:

1. Shakepeare's *Macbeth*
2. Geometry
3. American history from 1492–1776.

Summary

The motivation of different students to achieve in school may vary widely, and a single student may be motivated differently in different courses or subjects. To increase motivation, radical behaviorists reinforce the behaviors that lead to achievement and attempt to extinguish those that detract from achievement.

The cognitive and social learning theorists emphasize the roles of cognition in motivation, contending that motivation is determined in large part by student expectancies for success, failure, or both. Expectancies arise from past experiences and from teacher, parents, and peers.

Providing students with goals helps them initiate and direct their activity. Ideally, the goals of the teacher and the students should be in harmony. Creating performance objectives is one means of providing students with goals.

PART V

Focus on Outcome

UP TO THIS POINT we have been discussing the forces that interact in the *process* of changing behavior. The environmental variables (E) and person characteristics (P) that influence the process have been discussed in some detail. We now turn to the outcome of this process, the behavior (B) in the general equation $B = E \times P$.

As we have stressed throughout the book, a produced behavior results from the joint action of environmental events and individual characteristics. There are many different kinds of behavior, of course. We have selected three that are especially relevant to the processes that occur in classrooms. We deal first with *conceptual behavior,* the thinking skills associated with learning concepts and solving problems. Second, we deal with *comprehension.* Since a great deal of teaching involves presenting information to students, knowing how learners process and understand information is very important. Third, we present *social behavioral* outcomes, because the classroom is a social as well as an academic situation. Young people acquire social skills, social competence, and ways of interacting with each other by participating in classroom activities. These outcomes, then, are also important to education.

Finally, we turn to the *measurement* and *assessment* of outcomes, methods of determining when goals have been reached. In the first section of the text, you learned how to set goals, how to phrase them, and how to organize them. In this final section, you will learn how to determine when they have been achieved.

The basic building blocks of knowledge that when combined serve a function in any intellectual endeavor are concepts. The acquisition of concepts, application of concepts, and utilization of concepts in complex problem-solving are basic outcomes of the learning process. All teachers must teach concepts; all learners regardless of level must acquire them for effective academic functioning. What are concepts and how do we acquire them? This is the subject matter of Chapter 11a, which includes theoretical perspectives on the issues, and of Chapter 11b, which encompasses the application of those theoretical principles.

Concept learning has surfaced before in this text, however. Recall the discussion of the acquisition of rule-governed behaviors in Chapter 4a; that process involves concept learning from models. One of Piaget's major investigative thrusts (Chapter 6a) was the development of logical concepts. Words represent concepts, so language development (Chapter 7a) is relevant. Although the titles of Chapters 11a and 11b may sound new to you, by now many of the principles discussed will sound familiar.

Chapter 11a

Concept Learning

Introduction

Imagine, if you can, a person who is unable to classify or organize the events, objects, and activities encountered in day-to-day living. Since no two stimuli are exactly the same, that person would have to react differently to each stimulus that was perceived. This would impose an enormous load upon memory. The person would have to separately classify each apple seen and he would react to them all differently. Similarly, each activity would have to be classified separately. Each of the different ways that people run, for example, would have a different label. The appropriate response to each class dismissal bell (leaving) would have to be learned. Existing under such conditions would be extremely complex.

Human beings can, however, categorize the various stimuli they encounter. Even though no two apples are exactly alike, we can group them together and react similarly to all members of the class. We can specify the attributes of the class *apples,* give the category a name, and respond to all class members in the same way—by eating them. Concepts are the categories we impose on the stimuli in our environment. They provide organizational schemes for assimilating new stimuli and for determining relationships within and between categories.

Concept learning is a principal outcome of education. "The teaching of words, and of the meanings and concepts they designate or convey, is one of the principal tasks of teachers at all levels of education" (Carroll, 1964). Concepts are the building blocks of thinking. They provide the basis for the higher mental processes of formulating principles and generalizations. To solve problems, a learner must know the appropriate rules, and these rules are based on the concepts the learner has attained.

Definitions and Varieties of Concepts

Although psychologists recognize the importance of concepts, a completely adequate definition of *concept* has not been delineated. Dictionary definitions, such as *something conceived in the mind* or *a general or abstract idea* are too broad or too circular to be useful. A definition that involves categories or sets may be more adequate: "Concepts are the categories into which human beings organize all the environmental stimuli which bombard their senses constantly" (Spitzer, 1977, p. 5).

Perhaps no single definition can reveal the richest meaning of *concept* or the variety of concepts that students acquire. Since concepts are internal representations of a class of stimuli, they cannot be observed; they must be inferred from behavior. Even though we can provide a verbal definition of a concept, a definition does not reveal all the relationships between that concept and others.

The variety of concepts we learn is limitless. The concept of *cold* is very different from the concept of *relativity* on a number of dimensions. Flavell (1970a) has suggested that concepts may differ on seven dimensions.

1. *Attributes.* Each concept has a number of different attributes. Examples of the concept must possess the relevant attributes; they include irrelevant attributes as well. Examples of the concept of *table* must have a flat surface and downward extensions that raise the flat surface from the floor. Size and color are irrelevant. Attributes may be physical, such as color, height, or shape, or they may be functional. Concepts may be described in terms of their immediate static properties (perceptible elements) or in terms of nonimmediate transformational properties (what the object could do or become under certain circumstances).

2. *Structure.* Structure concerns the way the attributes are interrelated or combined. Three different concept structures have been described. *Conjunctive concepts* are those in which two or more properties must be present in order for something to qualify as an example of the concept. An actress is *a female who performs in plays.* The two attributes *female* and *performs in plays* must both be present in order to represent the concept of *actress. Disjunctive concepts* are those in which either of two or more properties must be present. The concept of *uncle* is a disjunctive concept. An uncle may be either a brother of one of the parents or a man who is married to a sister of one of the parents. *Relational concepts* specify a certain relationship among the concept's attributes. Social class is an example of a relational concept. Social class is determined by the relation of income, education, occupation, and other factors.

3. *Abstractness.* Concepts may be tangible and concrete, or they

may have no concrete referents and consist of other concepts. A triangle is tangible; courage is more abstract.

4. *Inclusiveness*. This refers to the number of instances the concept includes. To a very young child, the concept of *dog* may refer to one specific animal—the family pet. As the child comes in contact with other dogs, the child's concept of *dog* will be broadened to include more instances.

5. *Generality*. Concepts vary in terms of their superordinate or subordinate position in classification. The concept of *carrot* is subordinate to the concept of *vegetable*, which is in turn subordinate to the concept of *edible plants*. The more general the concept, the more associations can be made with other concepts.

6. *Precision*. A concept's precision concerns whether there is a workable, explicit set of rules for distinguishing examples of the concept from nonexamples. Klausmeier (1977) described four levels of concept attainment, ranging from the concrete to the formal level. Concepts at the formal level are the most precise, since at this level the required attributes of the concept may be defined. We will discuss Klausmeier's levels more completely later in this chapter in the section on concept development.

7. *Power*. The power of a concept is determined by the extent to which people agree that it is important or by the possibilities for future concept acquisition that its attainment permits.

Because there are many varieties of concepts, it is difficult to arrive at a unitary definition of *concept*. According to our definition, a concept is an abstraction that represents a class of objects, events, activities, or relationships that have attributes in common. As one experiences different stimuli, one forms concepts that allow one to group them in some way. Since concepts are abstractions based on experiences, and since no two people have exactly the same experiences, the concepts people form probably differ, too. Even though our concepts differ, they are sufficiently similar for us to be able to communicate by means of the commonly-accepted labels we attach to them. These labels or words are arbitrary symbols used to denote the concepts, which are internal abstractions. The labels themselves are not the concepts. Our concept

FIGURE 11a–1.   Representation of Conceptual Behavior

S	O	R
Environmental input	The concept as abstraction	Naming, classifying, identifying, defining, and so on

of *student* would not change even if we labeled it differently. If we substituted the label *goose* for *student,* we would speak of *geese in the classroom, fighting for goose rights,* or *going to the goose union for a cup of coffee,* but our concept of a student would be the same.

In summary, a concept is a mental abstraction that represents a class of stimuli. We infer that a concept has been learned when the learner is able to perform certain behaviors. Figure 11a–1 illustrates these relationships using the *S-O-R* paradigm.

Acquisition of Concepts

Concepts may be acquired through two processes—concept formation or concept assimilation (Ausubel, 1968). Concept formation is more typical of the acquisition of concepts during the preschool years. It is exemplified by the learning of concrete concepts as described by Gagne

Children's first concepts may come from interacting with objects in the environment. By observing a number of different animals at one time, the young child will be able to determine which attributes are criterial for an animal to be in a particular class of animals.

(1977). Concept assimilation becomes a more prominent means of acquiring concepts during and after the school years.

Concept Formation

Although they may have been modified by later experiences, many of the concepts you have acquired developed very early in your life. By the time children enter school, they have acquired such concepts as *table, chair, run, up,* and many others. These concepts are established primarily through concept formation.

Concept formation is an inductive process. When a child encounters environmental stimuli, he or she abstracts certain properties or attributes that different stimuli have in common. Concept formation is a type of discovery learning. The first primitive abstractions may be attached to a single example of the concept. A child's concept of a ball, for instance, may be attached to a single object—a small, round, red object that rolls. The attributes of that example are hypothesized as representing that concept. As the child encounters other instances and noninstances of the concept, the original abstraction may have to be restricted or broadened in such a way that such attributes as color or size are no longer considered criterial for the concept.

Concept formation follows an example/rule, or *eg-rule* pattern. The learner encounters or is presented with many examples and non-examples of the concept. Through the process of discrimination and abstraction, he establishes a rule specifying the criteria for the concept.

Concept Assimilation

After entering school, children are expected to learn many concepts through the process of concept assimilation. In contrast with concept formation, which is inductive, concept assimilation is deductive. In this process the learner is given the name of the concept and the concept's attributes. The definition may include verbal equivalents one hopes the learner has already acquired. The word *serene*, for example, has such verbal equivalents as *calm, peaceful,* and *unruffled*. If the learner has already acquired these concepts he or she can attach the new word, *serene*, to them. A formal definition of a word indicates commonalities with the concept and differentiates it from other concepts. The formal definition of *steed, a high-spirited horse,* gives it the attributes common to *horse,* but distinguishes it from other horses with the concept of *high-spirited.*

To acquire concepts by assimilation, the learner must have already acquired the concepts embodied in the verbal equivalents or the formal definition. After the definition of the concept is presented, the concept may be illustrated by providing examples or verbal descriptions of examples. This is referred to as rule/example, or *rule-eg*, concept learning. Ausubel (1968) advocates that rule-eg learning be used in expository teaching.

Although both types of concept learning are effective, concept formation is more time-consuming than concept assimilation. Considering all of the concepts students are expected to learn during the school year, the extensive use of the discovery method would be limiting. Proponents of discovery learning contend that concepts learned by the eg-rule method are more meaningful to students than those learned by the rule-eg method. There is no consensus regarding the superiority of one method over the other, however. It is likely that "most school learning of concepts is a process that combines in some way deductive and inductive features" (Carroll, 1964, p. 189).

Theoretical Explanations of Concept Learning

For more than sixty years concept learning has been investigated by psychologists. Most early experimentation took place in laboratories and used artificial concepts, as we illustrate below. Most experiments involved concept formation. The experiments generally involved showing subjects a number of stimuli that had a variety of attributes. The subjects were expected to form a concept that was based on the features of the stimuli.

An early experiment by Hull (1920) typifies one experimental procedure. Hull showed his subjects twelve series of Chinese pictograph symbols, each paired with a nonsense syllable. Pictographs are composed of radicals (patterns of brush strokes) that are combined in specific ways to form a given pictograph character. A radical may appear in a number of pictographs in combination with other radicals. A given radical was always paired with the same nonsense syllable. The subject's task was to associate the nonsense syllable with the radical whenever the latter was presented. First, the subject would be shown the entire series of pictographs paired with the appropriate nonsense syllables. On the next trial, a pictograph would be shown and the subject was to respond with the correct nonsense syllable. Each pictograph was then presented again with the correct response, so the subject learned immediately whether his or her response was correct. The subject would proceed through the series of pictographs in this fashion until he or she always gave the correct response when the pictographs were presented. This procedure became the prototype for many studies. The presentation of one stimulus at a time was labeled the *receptive paradigm*.

A second procedure, the *selective paradigm*, is illustrated in a series of experiments by Bruner, Goodnow, and Austin (1956). The materials in these studies were eighty-one rectangular cards that varied on four attributes: number of borders, objects within borders, color of objects, and number of objects. Each card had one, two, or three borders; the objects within the borders were triangles, crosses, or squares; the color of the objects was green, black, or red; and the number of objects was one, two, or three. Each card differed from every other card on at least one of the attributes.

In the selective paradigm, the subjects were presented with the array of all eighty-one cards and told to discover a certain predetermined concept that described one subset of the cards. The subset might be the cards containing two green objects with two borders. Color, number of objects, and number of borders were thus relevant attributes, whereas the shape of the objects was an irrelevant attribute. These concepts were conjunctive concepts requiring the presence of two or more attributes.

The outcomes of these early studies of concept formation provided evidence about some of the factors that affect concept learning. Even though most of the experiments were carried out in the laboratory, the results have been shown to be applicable to classroom situations as well (Remstad, 1969). Some of these results will be discussed in the following sections.

The psychological orientations of the experimenters influenced the types of factors they investigated. The behaviorists focused on the stimulus elements and the application of conditioning principles to concept acquisition. The cognitivists were more interested in the processing strategies, the relationships between concepts, and the representation of concepts in the cognitive structure.

Behavioral Approaches

To the behaviorists, the basis of concept learning, as with other types of learning, is the association between stimulus and response. The primary difference between concept learning and other types is that the learner, rather than making a single response to a single stimulus, makes a single response to a number of different stimuli. The stimuli differ in some attributes, but they have one or more attributes in common. The learner's task is to associate a single response with the common attributes among the stimuli.

The first step in forming a concept would be to associate R_1 to S_1. Such conditioning principles as contiguity and reinforcement would affect the acquisition of this S-R connection. The learner is then presented with S_2. If S_2 has attributes that are perceptibly similar to those of S_1, then R_1 may be produced. If the S_2–R_1 association is reinforced, then that connection is strengthened. Through associating a number of stimuli that have attributes in common with S_1, the child will learn a common response, which would be considered evidence of acquisition of a concept.

Consider as an example a young child learning the concept of *house*.

The original stimulus might be the child's own house. Through conditioning, the child associates the word *house* with his or her home (S_1–R_1 in Figure 11a–2). As the child encounters other stimuli, perhaps neighbors' houses represented by S_2 and S_3, he or she responds to the similar elements of the stimuli (windows, doors, chimney) with *house*. When the child encounters S_4 and responds with *house*, however, the response is not reinforced. Through reinforcement and extinction procedures (withholding the reinforcement), the response of *house* comes to be associated only with structures that have relevant attributes.

FIGURE 11a–2.   Acquisition of the Concept of House

		R	Reinforcement
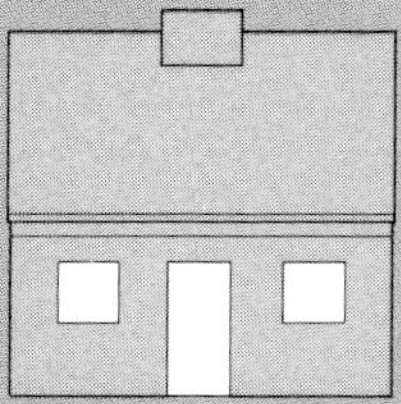	S_1	"House"	Yes
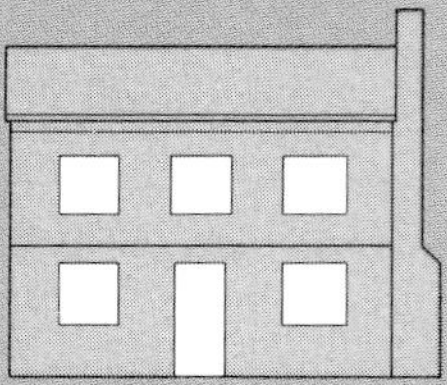	S_2	"House"	Yes
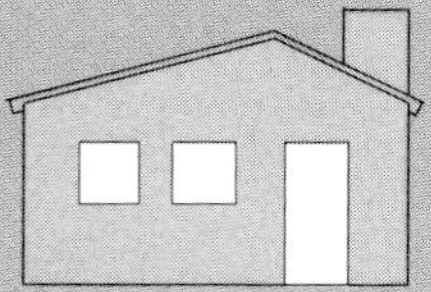	S_3	"House"	Yes
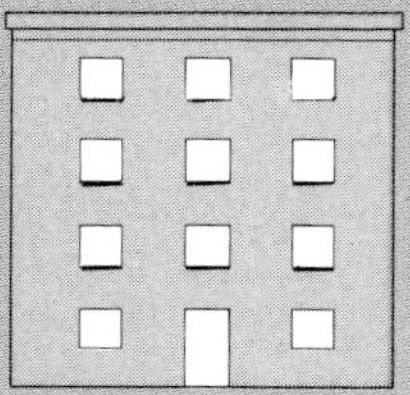	S_4	"House"	No

The conditioning approach may explain the acquisition of some concrete concepts, but it fails to explain the acquisition of abstract concepts or concepts that lack perceptibly similar elements. Consider, for example, the activities of swimming, horse racing, and football. These activities are all represented by the concept of *sports*, but they have few identical or similar elements. The behaviorists might argue that, in this instance, the process involves learning to respond to different stimuli with a common response in accordance with the same principles of conditioning.

When mediating responses are introduced into the *S-R* paradigm, it is a more adequate explanation of concept learning. Mediating responses are the covert associations that occur between the *S-R*, usually signified by *S-(r-s-r-s-)R*. We may associate a number of responses with any single stimulus. *Dog* may thus suggest responses of *friendly, furry, tail, barks*, and so on. When the stimulus *dog* is presented, the stimulus elicits covert responses that lead to covert stimuli. These stimuli are compared to the existing concept of *dog*. If the attributes are in harmony, the response will be *dog*.

To behaviorists, concept learning involves quantitative changes. The changes consist of (1) adding more stimuli to an already-learned response, or (2) increasing the number of different *S-R* connections.

The behaviorists have emphasized the observable aspects of the situation as the critical factors in concept learning. Some studies indicate that concept learning is affected by the following factors:

1. *Dominance of the criterial attributes.* In Hull's (1920) study, the dominance of the radical that was to be associated with a nonsense syllable was varied. When the color of the radical was different from the rest of the pictograph, the association was learned faster.

2. *Patterns of reinforcement and feedback.* Simply exposing subjects to examples of a concept without giving them feedback has little effect on their performance (Bourne, Guy, & Wadsworth, 1967).

3. *Number of positive and negative instances.* Several studies have shown that concepts are learned more readily from positive instances— that is, providing the learner with examples of the concept. Providing the learner with examples that do not possess the relevant attribute tends to sharpen the concepts.

4. *Number of attributes.* The more relevant attributes concepts have, the more difficult they are to learn.

Cognitive Approaches

Cognitive approaches to learning have focused on the process of attaining concepts, on the nature of the concepts, and on the way concepts are represented in the cognitive structure. Although the cognitivists are concerned with the conditions that facilitate concept formation, their emphasis has been on internal processes used in learning concepts.

Two strategies that people use to attain concepts were delineated by Bruner, Goodnow, and Austin (1956) in the series of experiments cited earlier (pp. 438–439). You will recall that the materials used in their studies had four varying attributes—number of borders, shapes of objects, colors of objects, and number of objects. Using the selective paradigm, the investigators found that subjects used different strategies to discover the concept.

Two of the strategies used were conservative focusing and focus gambling. The most reasonable strategy is conservative focusing. After the subject has selected an example of the concept through trial and error, he or she determines the next selection on the basis of that example's attributes. In conservative focusing, the learner varies the next selection by just one attribute. In other words, the next selection has three of the same attributes as the first. To illustrate, suppose the selected example was an object with two borders and two green circles, and the experimenter said that it was an example of the concept. The next selection might be two green circles with three borders. If that is also an example of the concept, the learner knows that number of borders is irrelevant. If it is incorrect, the subject knows that having two borders is a criterion. The next selection would then have two borders and would vary either in number, color, or shape. The process of changing one attribute at a time is continued until all the criteria have been discovered.

In focus gambling, the subject uses much the same procedure except that more than one attribute is changed on the selections that follow the choice of the first example. The subject may vary both number of borders and number of objects. A correct selection provides twice as much information, but an incorrect selection provides little feedback.

The process of acquiring concepts seems to reflect a hypothesis-testing approach (Trabasso & Bower, 1968). Given an example of a concept, the individual hypothesizes that certain attributes of the example are criteria for membership in that category. This hypothesis can be tested with another example. If the second example is negative, the hypothesis is changed in some way. Through a series of such trials, the learner refines his or her hypothesis and finally selects the attributes that are the criteria for the concept.

Studies of concept attainment have revealed several relevant findings, as described below.

1. Conjunctive concepts are easier to learn than disjunctive or relational concepts. Many studies (for example, Neisser & Weene, 1962; Bourne, 1970) have shown that a concept that requires the presence of two or more attributes is easier to learn than one that requires either of two or more attributes.

2. It is easier to learn concepts using the selective paradigm than

the receptive paradigm. The simultaneous presentation of examples and non-examples reduces the demands on memory. When the receptive paradigm is used, the subject is shown an example of the concept, the example is removed, and then another stimulus is presented. The subject must retain the attributes of the example in order to respond to the new stimulus. If several non-examples appear, however, the subject may forget attributes of the example (Remstad, 1969).

Concepts and the Cognitive Structure

In Chapter 5a we discussed cognitive structure as an explanation of what is learned. To the cognitivists, the concepts that a learner acquires comprise a significant portion of the cognitive structure. Concepts are the categories. Each category has a set of rules or features that allow new stimuli to be placed in a category, depending on the way its attributes match the category's rules.

Learning a concept creates a qualitative change in the cognitive structure. Because the various aspects of the cognitive structure are interrelated, the formation of a new concept affects the entire organization.

The emphasis of the cognitive approach is that concept learning depends not just on the stimuli and the way they are perceived but on the person's cognitive structure as well. People acquire concepts only when they already possess relevant knowledge to which they can relate a new concept.

Current Approaches

Since the middle of the 1960s we have seen a shift in approaches to the study of concept learning, especially among educational psychologists. The impetus for this change resulted in part from an article by Carroll (1964), which emphasized the differences between concept learning as studied in the laboratory and concept learning in the schools. Carroll cited the following differences in the two processes:

1. The two types of concepts differ in nature. A concept learned in school is usually a genuinely new concept, not an artificial combination of familiar attributes.

2. Concepts learned in school depend upon attributes that are themselves difficult concepts. Moreover, school concepts are often verbal in nature and cannot be represented by concrete objects.

3. Laboratory studies emphasized the learning of conjunctive concepts, which have been shown to be easier to learn than disjunctive or relational concepts.

4. Laboratory studies, in general, emphasized inductive ap-

proaches to learning concepts, while most concepts learned in schools are learned deductively.

In his article Carroll (1964) illustrated procedures for teaching such concepts as *tourist, longitude,* and *torts.* His approach was based on a combination of inductive and deductive techniques. He suggested that a combined approach might be superior to the use of either approach alone.

At about the time Carroll's article appeared, Gagne (1965) published the first edition of *The Conditions of Learning.* This book provided further impetus for examining learning in the classroom rather than in the laboratory.

According to Gagne, concept learning is one part of a hierarchy of eight types of learning. In this hierarchy, each level of learning is dependent upon the levels below it. Gagne's hierarchy is presented in Table 11a–1. Learning Type 6, concept learning, is equivalent to concept formation. Concept assimilation is considered to be a special type of rule learning, Type 7.

Gagne emphasized that two sets of conditions were necessary for each type of learning to occur—conditions within the learner and conditions outside the learner in the learning situation. Gagne has continued to revise his approach, and in the latest edition of *The Conditions of Learning* (1977) he suggests that the following conditions are necessary for the learning of concrete concepts.

Conditions within the learner: The learner must be able to discriminate between an example of the concept and a non-example. If verbal instruction is to be used, the subject must have previously learned a verbal label. The learner must recall both the discrimination and the verbal label.
Conditions of the learning situation: Verbal cues are the primary means of teaching concrete concepts.

1. An example of the specific stimulus object or stimulus dimension is presented simultaneously with a non-example. In teaching the concept of *circle,* the teacher might present a picture of a circle and a triangle and say to the child, "Show me a circle." If the learner responds correctly, the discrimination has been confirmed.
2. During the generalization phase, the specific example is presented with non-examples—circle-square, circle-rectangle, circle-parallelogram, and so on. In each presentation the teacher asks the child to select the circle.
3. Until this point, the teacher has always presented a circle of the same size and color. Now the size and color of the circles may be varied and presented with non-examples that vary in size—small circle-large square, large circle-small rectangle, and so on. If the child still identifies the circle in each trial, he or she can be assumed to have learned the concept. We can verify the acquisition of the concept by asking the child to identify other examples not previously used, perhaps the head of a thumb tack or the opening in a pencil sharpener.

TABLE 11a–1. Gagne's Learning Hierarchy

Type of learning	*Procedure*	*Example*
1. Signal learning	Classical conditioning	Eye blink to a sound after pairing sound with puff of air to the eye.
2. Stimulus-response learning	Operant or instrumental conditioning	Infant learning to hold a bottle for feeding.
3. Chaining	Series of *S-R* connections	Unlocking a door, which includes (1) positioning the key, (2) inserting the key, (3) turning the key, (4) opening the door.
4. Verbal association	Verbal chains, including naming of objects and connections of words into a verbal sequence	Learning the Pledge of Allegiance
5. Discrimination learning	Producing a different response to similar stimuli	Differentiating a circle and an ellipse
6. Learning concrete concepts	Making a common response to stimuli with similar attributes	Common response *house* given to a wide variety of sizes and shapes of buildings.
7a. Defined concepts and	a. Using previously learned concepts to acquire a new concept	A cousin is the son or daughter of an aunt or uncle.
b. Rules	b. Responding to a class of stimuli with a class of performances.	Distance equals rate multiplied by time.
8. Problem-solving	Combining rules to reach a solution that yields a higher order rule	Discovery of steps in proving a theorem in geometry

4. For a student to acquire a concept, it is apparently necessary that correct responses be confirmed. To facilitate concept learning, several instances that involve the same discrimination should be presented in succession.

Gagne's conditions for learning defined concepts will be presented in Chapter 11b. For now, suffice it to say that the primary condition is that the learner must already possess the concepts that comprise the defined concept to be learned.

Since the 1960s researchers at the Wisconsin Research and Development Center have been conducting extensive investigations of concept learning in the typical classroom situation. The studies have focused on types of concepts and variables that affect concept learning. A model of concept attainment has been developed from these studies. Although it is impossible to discuss all the Wisconsin research, in the next section we present the concept attainment model.

Levels of Concept Attainment

The development of concepts seems to progress through a series of stages. The levels range from merely being able to identify an example of the concept to being able to fully describe the concept's attributes. We do not attain all our concepts at the same level. Most of us could fully describe the attributes of the concept of *book*. Although our descriptions would differ, we could still communicate an adequate definition to another person. We might have attained the concept of *samovar* at a lower level, however. We might be able to recognize a samovar or give a vague description of it, such as "something you heat water in," but this would be insufficient to distinguish that concept from others. You may have found that when someone has asked you your concept of a certain word, you have been able to relate the word to other concepts or use it in a sentence but could not define it formally. We attain concepts at different levels.

Klausmeier (1977) has hypothesized that there are four levels of concept attainment. These levels appear in an invariant sequence. People approach the highest level of attainment at different rates, and some concepts are never attained at the highest level. Different concepts are learned at different ages. From our previous discussion of Piaget (see, for example, Chapter 6a), you know that young children are adept at learning concrete concepts, but abstract concepts, especially complex abstract concepts, are learned later.

As we discussed in Chapter 6a, development involves more than simply acquiring more concepts. New and different constructions are developed. As the concepts at successively higher levels are attained, they are used more effectively in learning principles and in solving problems. The learner may also discover more relationships among the concepts.

Klausmeier's (1977) four levels of concept attainment are the *concrete, identity, classificatory,* and *formal* levels. He applies these levels only to concepts that have more than one example, that have observable examples or representations of examples, and that are defined in terms of attributes. Relational and other concepts may possess only some of these qualities, so they may follow a different pattern of attainment. Many of the concepts taught in schools do satisfy these requirements, however. A description of Klausmeier's four levels follows.

1. *Concrete level.* We may infer that a person has attained a concept at the concrete level when the person recognizes an object encountered previously. A young child who has had an opportunity to play with a toy and makes the same response when he sees the toy again has attained a concrete level concept.

To attain concrete level concept, the learner must be able to attend to the object and to discriminate that object from the surrounding stimuli. In addition, he must represent the object as an image and retain the image.

2. *Identity level.* At the identity level, a person will recognize an object (a) after an interval of time, (b) when the person has a different spatial orientation to the object, or (c) when the object is identified through a different sense modality, for example, recognizing a ball by means of touch as opposed to recognition when seeing it.

In addition to the three operations necessary for concrete level attainment—attending, discriminating, and remembering—the learner must be able to generalize somewhat, to recognize that two or more identical forms of the same thing are members of the same class.

Some psychologists use different terms to denote these two levels of concept attainment. Gagne (1976) uses the term *discrimination* for the concrete level and *generalization of discrimination* for the identity level. Piaget (1970) referred to these two levels as *object concepts.*

3. *Classificatory level.* At the classificatory level, the learner recognizes the equivalence of two different examples of the same class. Although the learner can neither specify the attribute's criteria nor define the word that represents the concept, he can classify examples and non-examples of the concept even when the examples and non-examples have many similar attributes.

The additional mental operation involved in attaining concepts at the classificatory level is generalizing that two or more examples are in some way equivalent. In this mental operation the learner attempts to abstract the qualities that the objects have in common.

4. *Formal level.* For formal level concept attainment, the learner must be able to determine the defining attributes of the concept. We may infer that a learner has attained a concept at the formal level when he or she can name the concept, define the concept in terms of its criterial attributes, discriminate and name the defining attributes, and evaluate actual or verbally described examples and non-examples of the concept.

Klausmeier (1970) suggests that the operations involved in formal attainment may be either inductive or deductive. Inductive operations may be of two types. The first type is equivalent to the previously described concept formation: the learner formulates the rules from encounters with a number of different positive examples. The second type is a hypothesis-testing approach. In this approach, the learner creates a hypothesis about which attributes are relevant, tests the hypothesis against positive and negative examples, and revises the hypothesis as necessary.

The deductive operation resembles concept assimilation, which was described in the previous section. The learner is given the concept name, the criterion attributes, and verbal descriptions of examples. The rules for membership in the category are defined so that the learner can use them to determine whether a stimulus belongs in the category.

In a longitudinal study of concept development, Klausmeier (1977) found that many students had attained the concepts studied—*equilateral triangle, noun, tree,* and *cutting tool*—by the end of kindergarten. Attainment was found to increase steadily throughout the school years.

The Importance of Concept Learning

Early in this chapter we emphasized the fact that concepts provide a framework for making learning more efficient and solving storage problems. Without concepts, each act of learning would be discrete, each stimulus would produce a different response, and it would be nearly impossible to store all the information one had learned. Because we form concepts, we can generalize the attributes of a concept to new instances and classify new stimuli in our stores of concepts. Concepts are the building blocks for higher-level processes. Two higher-level processes that depend on learned concepts are learning principles and rules and solving problems.

Learning Principles and Rules

Rules are relationships between two or more concepts. The acquisition of a concept through assimilation can be considered an example of rule-learning through categorization. The definition of a concept is normally based on a relationship between two or more other concepts. Rules may be used for purposes other than categorization, thus providing the learner with other ways of operating with concepts.

In language learning, for example, one learns rules for spelling, punctuation, sentence construction, and word pronunciation. Mathematics is based on a carefully prescribed body of rules. Defined concepts are important to any course of study; they are often combined into relational rules. The defined concepts of force, mass, and acceleration, for example, are combined in the relational rule *Force = Mass × Acceleration.*

When a student has acquired a rule, we infer that it gives the

Principles express relationships between two or more concepts.
Each of the concepts making up the principle must be understood
by the student to make the principle meaningful.

student a means of responding to a class of stimuli in a certain way.
Learning the rule that *the area of a triangle is equal to half the base times
the height* gives us a procedure for finding the area of the whole class
of triangles. If we use this rule we need not discover the relationship
between area, base, and height for every kind of triangle to learn how
to get its area.

To learn rules, the learner must already know the concepts that
make up the rule. If the learner lacks the concepts included in the rule,
the teacher must make provisions for helping the student acquire the
concepts before or during the rule-learning. If the concepts of the rule
are well established in the learner's cognitive structure, for the student
to acquire the rule it may be necessary only to state it. The rule *Turtles
lay eggs* will be learned easily if the student has already acquired the
concepts of *turtles*, *lay*, and *eggs*. Most kindergarten children know the
concept of *turtle*, but the concepts of *lay* and *eggs* may be less fully
established. If a child's conception of *lay* is restricted to the act of
placing, as in "Lay the book on the table," the child may acquire the
rule incorrectly. Similarly, the child would not grasp the rule if his or
her conception of *eggs* was restricted to the objects produced by fowls.

When a child has not attained concepts that comprise the rule, he
may simply produce a verbal chain, a repetition of a series of words in
a specific order. We could, for example, teach preschool children to say,

when given a cue, "The area of a rectangle equals its length times its width." The fact that a student can state a rule does not, however, mean that he or she has acquired it. To understand the rule, the learner must know the concepts of *area, rectangle, equals, length, times,* and *width.* When a student has failed to acquire the concepts subordinate to the rule, rote learning is the only type that occurs, and this learning has little effect on the learner's behavior. A great many college students can state the rule *"i* before *e* except after *c"* without being able to spell *receive* correctly.

To ensure that a student has acquired a rule, he or she should be given the opportunity to practice it in a variety of contexts. Practicing the rule facilitates retention, and providing a variety of contexts helps the student transfer learning.

Problem-Solving

One major purpose for which we learn rules is to use them in solving problems. Used in this sense, problem-solving involves more than simply applying rules. To psychologists, problem-solving "is a process by which the learner discovers a combination of previously learned rules which can be applied to achieve a solution for a novel situation" (Gagne, 1977, p. 155). Since the learner has not encountered the situation before, direct application of known rules will be ineffective. To solve problems, the learner must form a new combination of previously acquired rules. Through solving the problem the learner acquires something new: a higher-order rule that is based on the new combination and that can be used to solve similar problems. The use of this new higher-order rule to solve problems would be considered application of a strategy, not problem-solving *per se.*

Although much has been written about the need to teach children problem-solving skills, the process of problem-solving is not fully understood. Since problem-solving involves covert thinking processes that are not directly observable and that vary from person to person, it is nearly impossible to specify the procedures involved.

Dewey (1910) offered one description of the sequence of events involved in problem-solving. This sequence, listed below, and similar ones are still cited today.

1. *Presentation of the problem.* The problem may occur naturally (Why won't my car start?), or it may be presented verbally or in writing.

2. *Definition of the problem.* The learner delineates the crucial aspects of the problems, dismissing irrelevant factors and emphasizing those that specify the problem's important features.

3. *Formulation of hypotheses.* Possible solutions are proposed on the basis of the definition of the problem. Some are dismissed, others

are retained. With further examination, one hypothesis comes to be regarded as the most probable.

4. *Verification of the hypothesis.* The probable hypothesis is applied to the problem to determine if it actually is the solution. If it is not, the learner returns to Step 2 or 3 and begins the process again.

Although Dewey's steps may explain the problem-solving process, they are of little assistance to teachers attempting to help students learn problem-solving techniques. Laboratory studies of problem-solving provide some direction, but we must use caution in generalizing the results of these studies to the classroom. As was true of concept learning, the problems used in experiments are generally artificial, not the real problems of everyday life. In addition, the experimenter has more control over complexity of the environment in providing supports for problem-solving than teachers generally have in the classroom.

The laboratory approach to problem-solving can be illustrated with an experiment conducted by Maier (1930). The subject was brought into a room in which two ropes were suspended from the ceiling. The subject's task was to tie the two ends of the rope together. On a nearby table were a few tools, including a hammer and pliers. The subject found through observation, or by actually attempting to reach the two ropes, that they were too far apart to reach at the same time. The subject could use one or more of the tools to increase his or her reach, but this failed to provide a solution. Some subjects never did solve the problem. Others, recalling the principle of the pendulum, tied one of the tools on the end of a rope and set the rope swinging so that both ropes could be reached at the same time and joined together.

Studies such as this have permitted some conclusions to be drawn about the factors that affect problem-solving. To solve a problem, the learner must understand the components of the problem and what the end result should be. The learner must already have attained the concepts that comprise the problem. A knowledge of the goal or end result helps focus attempts to solve the problem.

Recalling the appropriate rules can facilitate problem-solving. In the laboratory example, subjects quickly solve the problem when given the word *pendulum* as a cue. When no guidance is given, the learner must search through his entire store of attained rules for those that might be applicable.

The amount of guidance given to a learner in helping him or her recall a previously learned rule will affect the rapidity with which the problem is solved. One of the authors is reminded of his son's attempts midway through a geometry course to solve the following problem: "Given a rectangle with lines joining the midpoints of the adjacent sides, prove that the figure formed is a rhombus." The only guidance the instructor provided was to say, "You will need to use something

---

New Directions in Research

Closely related to concept learning and equally important to educators is the psychological phenomenon of problem-solving. This topic has recently attracted the attention of investigators with a wide range of interests. Developmental psychologists study problem-solving (Klahr, 1976; Siegler, 1978(a)), as do those concerned with the nature of intelligence (Resnick & Glaser, 1975; 1976) and with artificial intelligence and simulation (Simon, 1976). Problem-solving is directly relevant to educational processes and outcomes as well as to psychological ones, and thus the relationship between schooling and problem-solving is also a contemporary focus (Hill,

1979; Larkin, 1980; Lesgold, Pellegrino, Fokkema, & Glaser, 1978; Reif, Larkin, & Brackett, 1976; Rubenstein, 1980; Simon, 1980).

Current research in problem-solving is based primarily on an information-processing perspective of the learning process (Mayer, 1975; Newell & Simon, 1972; Greeno, 1974; 1976). It has therefore flowered as a research topic as the paradigm has grown in popularity. Problem-solving is not, however, a well-defined, clear research topic with precise operational definitions (Davis, 1973; Resnick & Glaser, 1975). It does, nevertheless, have great vitality. Watch for continued empirical productivity in this area.

---

we learned a long time ago." This clue provided little assistance to the problem-solvers. The problem might have been easier to solve if the instructor had mentioned that congruent triangles were the "something" to be recalled.

Another factor that affects problem-solving is the learner's ability to generate hypotheses. Students who lack this ability are likely to settle on a hypothesis prematurely and try it repeatedly. This is an example of functional fixedness (Duncker, 1945). Flexibility in forming hypotheses appears to be characteristic of good problem-solvers.

Summary

In this chapter we have discussed the importance of concept learning. The formation of concepts allows us to organize and simplify our environment. Concepts are the bases for thinking, for learning rules, and ultimately for solving problems. Without concepts, teaching would be impossible.

The behaviorists and the cognitivists approach concept learning differently. The behaviorist approach emphasizes conditioning procedures, whereas the cognitive approach relates concept learning to the cognitive structure.

Current approaches to concept learning have been developed by

Ausubel, Carroll, Gagne, and the Wisconsin Research and Development Center. These approaches have explicated the different ways in which concepts are acquired, through concept formation and concept assimilation. Gagne and researchers at the Wisconsin Center suggest that concepts can be attained at different levels. Contemporary studies tend to focus much more directly on concept learning in the classroom than the earlier laboratory studies did, although many of the conclusions of classroom studies support results achieved in the laboratory. In the chapter that follows, we will suggest ways of applying the results of these investigations to classroom practice.

TEACHING SCENARIO

Classroom management, another of our scenario themes, involves more than techniques for dealing with misbehavior. Careful instructional design and advance planning are an aspect of management also. When instruction is well planned and thought out, the class work flows smoothly, students are engaged in learning, and misbehavior is less frequent. A smoothly functioning classroom with involved groups of students permits opportunities for reinforcing productive, appropriate behavior, for learning to occur, and for motivation to increase. Effective advance planning is a necessity in order to achieve that outcome.

Ms. Turner is preparing a unit of instruction on fractions for her pupils. Although the students already know something about the concepts of fractions and know how to add fractions with the same denominators, she must teach them addition of fractions with unlike denominators. This latter operation involves the concept of the lowest common denominator, a new concept. What are some procedures Ms. Turner can plan in her instructional unit in order to facilitate concept acquisition?

Chapter 11b

Concept Learning in the Schools

Introduction

Concept learning is a basic outcome of an educational experience. Acquired concepts reduce the necessity for constant learning. Once we have attained a concept, we can use it to learn other concepts and rules. Concepts are the vehicles for instruction. Without concepts, you would be unable to accept verbal instruction from your professors, nor would you be able to read a passage from a text and discern the meaning. Learning from prose entails the use of concepts. This topic will be discussed separately in Chapters 12a and 12b.

At all levels of education, teachers are concerned with the teaching of concepts. Although the levels of concept attainment, the teaching procedures, and the uses for which the concepts are learned may be different at the elementary level from those at the college level, concept learning is important at all levels. Consider, for example, how many new concepts you have formed while reading this book—such concepts as validity, rule-governed behaviors, and reinforcement. You may have attained some of these concepts earlier in other contexts, but they were probably developed further and sharpened as you learned the material in this text.

Teachers face a variety of questions related to the teaching of concepts. The teacher must consider the concepts that should be taught, the level of the concepts students can be expected to attain, and the methods that will be used to teach the concepts.

Determining the Concepts to Be Taught

Information on the concepts that should be taught to students of a particular age or grade can be derived from a number of different sources, including textbook authors, curriculum developers, the teacher's own knowledge and experience, and the learners themselves.

Beginning teachers depend primarily upon textbook authors and curriculum specialists for guidance in deciding which concepts to teach. Authors of textbooks have selected the concepts they believe are appropriate for students in that subject at that particular grade level. Words that represent new concepts are often printed in italics or bold-face print. Some authors preface a chapter with a list of the new concepts, or include questions within or at the end of the chapter that ask students to define the important concepts. The numbers of concepts presented and the adequacy of the explanations or definitions of the concepts vary greatly from text to text.

Markle (1975), in discussing the inadequacies of textbooks for teaching concepts, contends that they often present concepts incompletely, or use other concepts that the student may not know in order to explain or define a new concept. A student's first encounter with the word *tundra* in a geography text, for example, might be "a tundra is a cold, barren land." Since *cold* is a relative term and *barren* may be an unfamiliar concept, the student may not acquire the concept of *tundra* from this description unless the teacher supplements the textbook definition.

Many school systems develop their own curriculum guides that specify the concepts students are expected to learn in each subject at each grade level. The guides may be in the form of performance objectives or simply lists of key concepts.

The teacher's own experiences and knowledge are another source for determining which concepts students should attain. Conceptual abilities must enter into the decision. Piaget's stages, which were introduced in Chapter 6a, provide information on cognitive abilities that may be used to determine conceptual abilities. Elementary school students, for example, more easily learn concepts with concrete referents, whereas students who have reached the formal operations level can learn more abstract concepts.

Students' language development also influences the types of concepts they can learn and the methods of instruction that may be used. The teacher's use of language appropriate to the learner's age is an important consideration in concept teaching. It is not uncommon for beginning teachers to use language that is above the students' level of understanding.

The learners themselves are another source for identifying which concepts may be taught. If we could get inside students to see their cognitive structures, we might be able to locate gaps, inaccuracies, or inconsistencies that would provide guidance. Since that is impossible, we must be alert to student behaviors that indicate that a concept has not been attained. Students frequently indicate the concepts they need to learn by the questions they ask. In the same way, student responses to teacher questions may indicate that they have failed to attain a

Elementary school students learn concepts easier when concrete
examples are used. These students are manipulating Cuisenaire
rods to learn numbers, concepts, and addition facts.

concept or that they have attained it inadequately or incorrectly. Skillful teachers may discover the source of incompleteness or inaccuracy
by asking questions. All learning theories emphasize the important
influence of previous learning on subsequent learning. Allowing students to proceed with inadequate concepts may precipitate learning
problems in the future.

Curriculum guides and textbooks provide a framework for planning
the concepts that are to be taught, and the behavior of the learners
themselves will indicate other concepts. The teacher's own knowledge
of cognitive and language development will provide additional information, not only for deciding upon concepts to teach, but for determining the levels at which we may expect learners to attain them.

▶ *ACTIVITY 1.*   Choose a section of the textbook for a course
you will be teaching or would like to teach. Make a list of ten
words that represent concepts your students will need to learn.
For each concept, develop a definition expressed in language
appropriate for the age level you will be teaching.

Planning Instruction

After selecting the concepts to be taught, a teacher must plan instructional strategies for teaching them. To plan, the teacher must decide what level of concept attainment can be expected of the students. Concept analysis will help the teacher clarify the concept and choose materials for teaching.

Determining Level of Concept Attainment

The level of concept attainment expected of the learner depends upon the complexity of the concept and the learner's level of cognitive development. Some students may learn a concept at the low concrete or identity levels, while others may be capable of attaining the concept at the classificatory or formal level. Consider the concept of *family,* for example. A preschool child may learn the concept of family as "The

FIGURE 11b–1.   Discrimination of Squares Worksheet

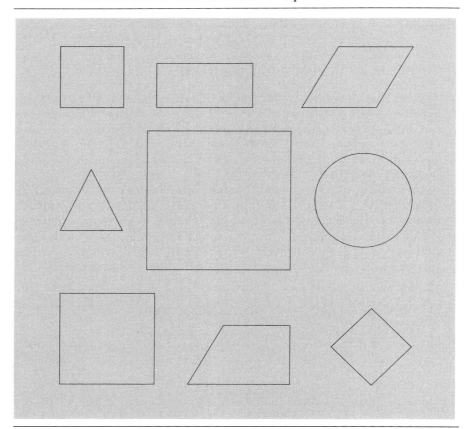

people I live with—father, mother, brothers, and sisters." An older child might develop the concept further: "people who have common ancestors or are united by marriage." The concept may be developed further still as the child learns about plant and animal families, the family of man, or families of curves.

As mentioned, Piaget's stages can guide the teacher in determining expected levels of concept attainment. Many of the concepts learned during the preoperational stage will be at the concrete or identity level. During the concrete operational stage, classificatory level attainment might be expected, at least for concepts that have concrete referents. Formal level attainment can be expected when appropriate instruction is given to students in the formal operational period.

Expected levels of concept attainment are reflected in the objectives set for students. Consider, for example, the following objectives for the acquisition at various levels of the concept *square*.

1. Shown a drawing of a square, the learner will respond "square."
2. Shown a drawing of a square, a triangle, and a circle, the student will select the square by pointing at it.
3. Shown the accompanying figure (Figure 11b–1), the student will circle each of the squares.
4. The student will list the criterial attributes of a square.

These objectives call for different types of evidence about the acquisition of the concept of *square*. Each would be a legitimate objective for students at a certain level of cognitive development. Adequate objectives will specify the behaviors that signify various levels of concept attainment.

Concept Analysis

Concept analysis is a procedure developed to help teachers plan instructional sequences for concept attainment. Techniques of this sort have been developed by Klausmeier, Ghatala, and Frayer (1974), at the Wisconsin Center, by Markle and Tiemann (1970), and by others as well. Although the procedures differ in some respects, certain steps appear to be common to them all.

To conduct a concept analysis, the teacher should take the following considerations into account:

1. The concept's name
2. The concept's criterial and variable attributes
3. The concept's definition
4. Examples and non-examples of the concept
5. The concept's relationship to other concepts

Concept analysis with the concept of *square*, as shown in Figure 11b–2, is illustrated as follows:

1. *The concept name.* Learners can form concepts without attaching names to them, especially at the concrete and identity levels. Very young children make up their own words to represent the concepts they form. After they begin school, however, they are taught the widely accepted concept names. Agreement on the name for a concept permits people to communicate about it.

2. *The concept's criterial and variable attributes.* The criterial attributes are the characteristics of a concept that are essential in differentiating examples from non-examples and in determining whether a new object is an example of the concept. Although all of the attributes

FIGURE 11b–2.   **Concept Analysis of a Square**

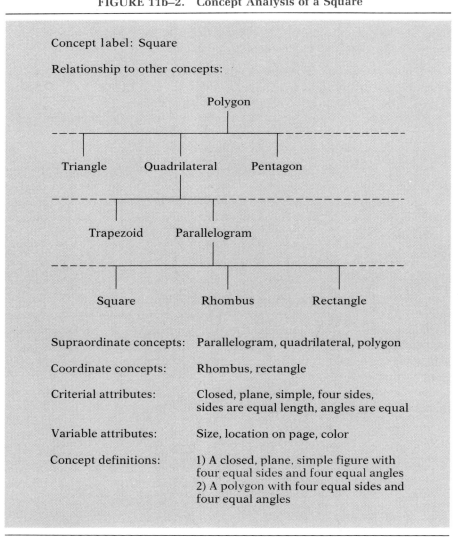

Concept label: Square

Relationship to other concepts:

Supraordinate concepts: Parallelogram, quadrilateral, polygon

Coordinate concepts: Rhombus, rectangle

Criterial attributes: Closed, plane, simple, four sides, sides are equal length, angles are equal

Variable attributes: Size, location on page, color

Concept definitions: 1) A closed, plane, simple figure with four equal sides and four equal angles
2) A polygon with four equal sides and four equal angles

FIGURE 11b–2.   Concept Analysis of a Square (cont.)

Rational set of examples:

Example	Non-example	
☐	▭	(Sides not equal)
☐	▱	(Angles not equal)
☐	⌐	(Not closed)
☐	▭ (cube)	(Not plane)
☐	⊠	(Not simple)
☐	△	(Not four sides)

of a concept may not be taught at every level of attainment, the teacher should be aware of them to assure that examples and non-examples are always differentiated. From the concept analysis of *square* we learn that it has the following criterial attributes: it is a closed, plane, simple figure that has four sides of equal length and equal angles at the intersections.

The variable attributes of a concept are the characteristics that may vary among examples without influencing inclusion in that concept category. The teacher may vary these attributes in the examples used for instruction. Squares, for instance, may vary in size, location on the page, and color.

3. *The concept's definition.* Even though the students may not be expected to learn a concept's formal definition, concept analysis should include a definition, although learners at the concrete and identity levels are not normally expected to be able to define concepts. At the classificatory level the learner may be able to state some of the defining attributes, but not all of them, and generally only the predominant ones. At the formal level students may learn concepts through being provided with the definition. The ability to state the definition may be used as a criterion for a student's having learned the concept.

Concept analysis may yield two different types of definition of the concept of *square*. The first definition is a statement of all of the criterial attributes of *square*. The second uses a superordinate concept, *polygon*, to indicate that the square has all the characteristics of a polygon and to demonstrate the attributes that differentiate squares from other polygons.

4. *Examples and non-examples of the concept.* Listing the attributes of a concept facilitates the development of examples and non-examples. Klausmeier, Rossmiller and Saily (1978) recommend that at least one rational set of examples be developed. A rational set consists of examples of the concept paired with non-examples that lack one criterial attribute. The rational set developed for the square (Figure 11b–2, page 461) lists the criterial attribute missing in each non-example.

5. *The concept's relationship to other concepts: superordinate, coordinate, and subordinate.* For many concepts, we may develop a hierarchy of related concepts that shows how the concept relates to other concepts. Forming a hierarchy may be helpful in instruction. If students have attained a superordinate concept, then instruction may consist of adding the criterial attributes for the concept to be learned. Definition 2 in the analysis is an example of this procedure; it is assumed that students already know the definition of *polygon*. If students have not learned superordinate concepts, a definition that lists the critical attributes would be preferred. To be meaningful, however, each of the attributes must be defined.

Coordinate concepts provide information about related concepts that need to be differentiated either before or after the concept is learned. Showing students how a rectangle with unequal sides and a square are not alike accentuates the criterial attribute of equal sides.

Teachers may not do a formal analysis of every concept they teach, although doing one is recommended. Some analysis of concepts is necessary in order to focus and plan instruction. If the objective is that a student be able to differentiate examples from non-examples, concept analysis will provide illustrations. If the objective is for the student to be able to list criterial attributes, these are noted in the analysis. Providing related concepts, as in the hierarchy, may facilitate subsequent as well as current instruction.

▶ *ACTIVITY 2.*   Choose a concept from the subject you plan to teach and attempt the following tasks:

1. Write four performance objectives that would indicate different levels of concept attainment.
2. Develop three methods you could use to determine whether a student has attained the concept.
3. Try a formal analysis of the concept, following the example given above (pp. 459–463).

Determining Instructional Method

During their first years in school, children learn some concepts through concept formation. When the concepts represent concrete objects or visible attributes, attaining concepts by induction may be appropriate, although time-consuming.

To give an example: Children at the kindergarten level might be expected to learn color concepts. To teach the concept of *redness*, a child might first be presented with a red circle. The first goal would be for a child to respond with the word *red* when the object was presented. To focus the child's attention on the color rather than the shape, other red shapes and objects would be presented that would require the same response, "red." When the child had learned to associate *red* with a variety of red stimuli, the teacher would then pair a red shape with a shape of a different color. The child would be asked to point to the red shape. Other shapes and colors would be presented, always paired with a red shape. When the child consistently chose *red*, we could infer that he or she had acquired a concept of *redness*. To double check, we might ask the child to point out other red objects in the room.

To teach the concept of "equal" the teacher provides a number of eggs and egg cups. The child can discover equality by placing the eggs in the egg cups to see if there is the same number of each.

As children mature, concept formation (inductive operations) decreases and concept assimilation (deductive operations) increases. Many of the concepts learned in school are attained through deduction. The more concepts a child has attained, the easier it is for the child to learn concepts through assimilation.

Concept assimilation involves learning concepts through their definitions. The definition of a concept includes one or more *thing-concepts* and a relational concept. The definition of *coliseum*, for example, is a "large building designed to hold many spectators." The first thing-concept in the definition is *building; designed to hold* is the relational concept; and *spectators* is a second thing-concept. *Large* is a restrictive attribute of the first thing-concept, and *many* is a restrictive attribute of the second thing-concept. The two restrictive attributes are themselves concepts; there are thus actually five concepts in the definition of *coliseum*.

It would be difficult for a learner to learn the concept of *coliseum* through concept formation, since there are few coliseums available to use as examples. Consequently, the concept of coliseum must be learned through concept assimilation. One could use pictures as examples, but pictures give a limited view of the concept; it is doubtful that the full concept is attained this way. A child from the inner city who acquires his concept of *cow* from pictures in his books may be astounded when he sees his first cow.

To acquire concepts by definition, the learner must already have acquired the thing-concepts and the relational concepts. If the learner knows these concepts and can recall them, the acquisition will entail joining the concepts in a prescribed order. If the learner lacks the prerequisite concepts he or she will fail to acquire the new concepts. The learner may learn the definition by rote by simply linking the words together in the prescribed sequence, but if learned in this way the concept's usefulness for further thinking or rule learning will be negligible.

As Carroll (1964) pointed out, learning in school probably involves both inductive and deductive processes. With an inductive process, examples are given before the definition; with a deductive process, examples are given after the definition. To exemplify concrete concepts, the teacher might use the objects themselves, pictures or line drawings of the objects, or other such media as videotapes, motion pictures, or slides. With abstract concepts, the examples are more likely to be verbal.

Let us illustrate the use of both procedures by imagining a fourth grade classroom in which the students are reading a story during language arts. One of the sentences in the story is "Billy's brother showed his *loyalty* to his country by enlisting in the army." The sentence provides an example of a behavior that illustrates *loyalty*. If this is the first time the students have encountered the word, their concept of loyalty might be restricted to a single act, enlisting in the army. Since the children may not encounter the word *loyalty* for quite some time, it might be unwise to rely on concept formation to broaden the concept. The students would have to retain this specific example, recall it when they encountered *loyalty* again, and incorporate the new instance with "joining the army."

To facilitate acquisition of the concept, the teacher might present or elicit other verbal examples that were more closely related to the child's own experiences.

Example 1. Teacher: "Which is the best school in town?"
Student: "Our school."
Teacher: "Why would you say that?"
Student: "Because I like our school. Because the best kids go there."
Teacher: "When you *selected* our school, you were showing loyalty to the school."
Example 2. Teacher: "Suppose someone started to 'pick on' your best friend and you 'stuck up' for him. You would be showing loyalty to your friend."

After presenting these and other examples, the teacher might give a formal definition, such as "Loyalty is being faithful and devoted to a person, government, or organization." Fourth grade children may not have acquired the concepts of *faithful* and *devoted*, so the teacher might have to present simpler explanations such as "You want to help them; you like them." After the teacher explains the formal definition, he or she might elicit further examples from the students to ascertain that they had acquired the concept. Examples illustrating a lack of loyalty could be provided to further sharpen the concept.

Instructional Models

A number of models for facilitating concept teaching have been formulated (Clark, 1971; Gagne, 1977; Klausmeier, Ghatala, & Frayer, 1974; Markle & Tiemann, 1969). Since the models differ somewhat, some are more appropriate than others for teaching certain types of concepts. The approaches also differ in the specificity of their procedures. We will discuss two models, the Gagne model and the Klausmeier-Frayer model.

Gagne's Model.   Gagne's model for concept learning (Type 6) was presented in Chapter 11a. It was exemplified by the first example in this section on learning the concept of redness. A brief summary of the steps is given in Table 11b–1.

Providing students with feedback is an important aspect of this model. The feedback may involve confirming correct responses or correcting the learners' incorrect responses.

Gagne's model for defined concepts includes the following steps:

Step 1. State the general nature of the performance that will be expected of the student when learning is complete.

Step 2. Give the students instructions to help them recall the component concepts that make up the definition.

Step 3. Offer verbal statements that will help students organize the rule.

Step 4. Ask students to provide examples of the concept.

TABLE 11b–1. Gagne's Steps for Concept Formation

Step 1.   Ensure that the student has acquired the concept name and can discriminate an instance of the concept.

Step 2.   Present the student with an example and a non-example of the concept and ask the student to choose the example.

Step 3.   Present the student with an example and other non-examples and in each case have the student select the example.

Step 4.   Pair examples of the concept that have different variable attributes with other non-examples. If the student still correctly identifies the concept, it can be assumed that he or she has acquired it.

Step 5.   Verify concept acquisition by having the student identify examples not included in the learning process.

Klausmeier-Frayer Model. The Klausmeier-Frayer model (Klausmeier, 1976) describes different instructional procedures that can be used to facilitate concept attainment at different levels—the concrete or identity levels, the beginning classificatory level, and the mature classificatory or formal levels. The inductive approach is used more frequently at the lower levels and the deductive approach predominates at the higher levels.

Concrete or Identity Level. At these levels the student is expected to be able to discriminate examples of the concept from non-examples. To help the learner, the teacher will:

1. Present an example or a representation of an example along with one or two non-examples. To teach the concept of *square* we would present squares of different sizes and colors, and non-examples, such as triangles and circles.

2. Give the name of the object and help the learner associate the name with the examples. While pointing to each of the examples the teacher would say, "This is a square." The child would then be asked, "What do we call this?" or be told "Tell me what this is."

3. Provide immediate feedback when the child recognizes examples and gives the correct name: "Yes, that's right. That is a square."

4. Show the child the object later and elicit the response again.

5. Repeat the procedure as needed to be sure the child has acquired and retained the concept.

Beginning Classificatory Level. At this level we expect students to be able to discriminate examples from non-examples and to be able to list and name some of the defining attributes. They may also be able to give an informal definition of the concept.

To help the student attain a concept at this level, the teacher will:

1. Verify that the student has attained the concept at the identity level.

2. Present examples and non-examples of the concept. To teach the concept of *square* at this level, the variety of non-examples might be expanded to include four-sided figures that more closely resemble the square than those presented at the identity level and thus are more difficult to discriminate from a square.

3. Help the student use either deduction or induction to discriminate and name some of the defining attributes. Although we might not expect the student to discover all the attributes of a square, we could present a series of examples and ask, "How are these shapes all alike?" If the student has learned to use a ruler, the teacher might suggest measuring the sides of a square. Given a piece of cardboard with a right angle, the student might be led to discover that it fit each of the square's angles. We would expect a student at this level to learn the defining attributes *four equal sides* and *four equal angles.*

4. Help the learner define the concept in the student's own words. At this stage a definition will probably not be complete or formal, but it should include at least the attributes discriminated in the previous step.

5. Provide other examples and non-examples so that the student can apply the criterial attributes to determine whether the examples represent the concept.

Mature Classificatory and Formal Level. Concepts at this level are often taught with an expository approach. The concept is defined and the attributes are named before the examples and non-examples are presented.

1. Give the concept name and its defining attributes. At the formal level, all the attributes would be included. For the concept of *square*, the attributes of *closed, simple, plane, four equal sides,* and *four equal angles* would be included.

2. Present a definition. As mentioned earlier, the definition may take different forms. One form would be a statement of all the criterial attributes. If the student has attained a superordinate concept, that concept may be used in conjunction with the new concept's restrictive attributes.

3. Present one or more rational sets of matched examples and non-examples so that the student can apply the definition in order to differentiate them. This step is included to determine whether the student has acquired a meaningful definition, not just a verbal chain.

4. Emphasize the defining attributes. Using the rational set, in the examples emphasize the attributes that are omitted from the non-examples. You may also add emphasis through verbal exposition.

5. Provide a strategy for differentiating examples and non-examples of the concept. Textbooks and teachers often overlook the teaching of strategies that students might use to determine whether an object is an example of the concept. One strategy that can be applied to many concepts is constructing a series of questions about the presence or absence of the defining attributes. The attributes of *square* might be checked with the following questions:

    a. Is it a plane figure?
    b. Is it a closed figure?
    c. Is it a simple figure?
    d. Does it have four sides?
    e. Are the sides equal in length?
    f. Are the angles equal?

If all the questions can be answered yes, the object is a square. If any of the questions can be answered no, the instance is a non-example.

As you can see from the models, teaching concepts is not easy. The models may not be appropriate for all concepts. New methods and approaches will undoubtedly be developed as we learn more about conceptual learning.

► *ACTIVITY 3.* Practice applying the methods of concept teaching with the following activities:

1. Choose a concrete concept, such as a geometric shape, and teach it to a preschool child. Keep a record of what you do. After the instruction, determine whether you used concept formation, concept assimilation, or both.
2. Choose a concept to teach by definition. Analyze the subordinate concepts that make up the definition.
3. Choose a concept you might teach and devise a plan for teaching that concept using both inductive and deductive procedures.

Concepts and Transfer

We emphasized earlier the way people use concepts to reduce the complexity of the environment. In this section we will consider the role concepts play in promoting further learning.

Consider the following sentence of nonsense words:

The isoger ilts on the apelo.

This sentence conveys little information to most people. One can understand it, however, if one is given further information: An *isoger* is a bird, *to ilt* is to rest standing on one leg with wings outspread, and an *apelo* is an elliptical decoration on top of a sphere. One could even construct a mental image of the events described in the sentence. This is possible because you had already acquired the concepts of *bird*, *sphere*, and so on. The concepts you had already acquired allowed you to incorporate the new learning.

The attainment of concepts not only facilitates subsequent learning, it provides for extensions of learning. When you learned that an isoger was a bird, you knew immediately that it had feathers, two legs, and two wings, that it flew, and so on. All of the criterial attributes of *bird* would apply to this specific example. Rather than learning the individual attributes of *isoger*, you could generalize your previous knowledge of birds to this new example. This generalization is an example of *transfer*—transfer of the attributes of a class to a specific example. Transfer seems to occur almost automatically. It is possible only because we possess concepts.

Scenario Suggestion

Ms. Turner might begin her preparation by analyzing the concept. She should outline the prerequisite knowledge the students should have for acquiring the concept of lowest common denominator. This analysis would include denominator, prime numbers, common, multiplication of numbers, and adding fractions with like denominators.

Her instructional unit would include an opportunity to review the differentiation of numerators and denominators, as well as adding fractions with like denominators. If she has not already introduced the term "common," after practicing addition of fractions with like denominators, she could then explain that "common" is another word for "like." This could be followed by giving the students pairs of fractions and asking them to tell whether or not the fractions have common denominators.

The next step in instruction would involve the introduction of the measuring of lowest in relationship to common denominator. To facilitate this, Ms. Turner would review the concept of a prime number, allowing the students to factor the numbers into prime numbers.

Examples:

$12 = 2 \cdot 2 \cdot 3$ $14 = 2 \cdot 7$ $32 = 2 \cdot 2 \cdot 2 \cdot 2 \cdot 2$
$18 = 2 \cdot 3 \cdot 3$ $20 = 2 \cdot 2 \cdot 5$ $21 = 3 \cdot 7$

The definition of lowest common denominator could then be given: "The lowest common denominator is the product of the fewest prime numbers which are necessary to include both denominators."

Ms. Turner could then provide some rules for finding a lowest common denominator.

1. Factor the denominators into their prime numbers.
2. Choose the denominator with the greatest number of prime factors.
3. Compare each of the other denominator's prime numbers to the one with the greatest numbers.
   a. If all of the factors are included in the first denominator chosen, then that is the lowest common denominator.
   b. If any different factors are included in these denominators or if any factors are repeated more times than in the first denominator chosen then they must be multiplied by the factors in the first denominator.

Transfer may be either positive or negative. Positive transfer facilitates learning. Transferring the characteristics of *bird* to a specific example is an instance of positive transfer. When previous learning impedes new learning, it is called negative transfer. If we observe a flying animal with wings and other characteristics of "birdness" and conclude that it is a bird when it is actually a bat (a non-bird), we have negative transfer. Negative transfer frequently occurs when the attained concepts are incomplete. In the instance just given, our bird concept was incomplete—birds have feathers, bats do not.

The use of concepts for higher-level operations is known as vertical transfer. As we discussed in Chapter 10a, the learning of rules and principles is based on concept learning. Concept learning, then, is transferred to that higher-level process. A rule or principle relates two or more concepts.

Just as concepts can be transferred vertically to rules or principles, rules and principles can be transferred to other situations at the same level or to the higher process of problem-solving. The rule that "singular nouns require singular verbs," for example, is based on the subordinate concepts of *singular, nouns, verbs,* and *require.* A student who has acquired this rule can use it in a variety of situations, such as writing a term paper, talking, or completing a grammar lesson in which one must choose a singular or plural verb on the basis of the form of the subject of the sentence.

Principles may also be transferred vertically to problem-solving. Although one must possess the relevant rules in order to solve a problem, possessing the rules alone will not assure that the problem will be solved. One solves problems by recalling principles and reorganizing them in new ways.

Summary

Teachers must decide upon the concepts they will teach their students, the level at which students are expected to acquire them, and the method of teaching to be used. The same decisions must be made for rule-learning and problem-solving. A knowledge of cognitive development and language development provides some of the information needed to make such decisions. Concept analyses can be used to plan instruction and to determine whether students have attained concepts at the appropriate level. Concept attainment facilitates further learning through transfer processes.

Concept acquisition is one outcome of the learning process. Understanding information, comprehension, is another. The latter is the subject matter of Chapters 12a and 12b—the way students are able to abstract meaning from instructional material. In Chapter 12a we present the theoretical background and psychological principles involved in comprehension; in Chapter 12b we apply these principles to education.

Comprehension is essentially the cognitive processing of information. You might suppose, and quite correctly, that cognitive learning theory bears on this topic. The learning principles you encountered in Chapters 5a and 5b are reiterated, with elaboration, in the two chapters to follow. Now the target behavior is more specific—the cognitive learning principles involved in the comprehension of prose and the interpretation of visual material.

Chapter 12a

The Comprehension of Information: Learning from Prose and Pictures

Introduction

School learning often begins when students are required to abstract information from instructional materials. Cognitive processes, such as problem-solving, begin with information, but we cannot expect students to solve problems until they have the relevant information at hand. Accordingly, many of the teacher's instructional activities are designed to help learners process and comprehend the information presented to them. As teachers, we expect students to be able to focus on important information, store it, and later recall it. Whenever lectures, readings, diagrams, pictures, or films are presented, we expect students to process the information they contain.

Extracting and recalling important information from materials is called *comprehension*. Comprehending is a cognitive activity that involves processing material mentally in order to grasp its meaning, retaining the meaning in some way, and retrieving the meaning at a later time. The content may be presented in such varied forms as word lists, sentences, prose, pictures, or diagrams; but comprehension of the meaning of these materials is in all cases the essential and desired outcome. How much do we really know about the process of comprehension?

When teachers assign students readings in a textbook and subsequently test the students, they are making a number of assumptions about comprehension. Some of these assumptions are exemplified in the kinds of items included in the test. A teacher may assume, for example, that students will be able to *recognize* the facts and premises in the assigned passages. Teachers also often assume that students will be able to *recall* the content in their own words or to form *inferences*.

Students fail test items, however; they fail to recognize and to recall information presented to them; they fail to comprehend material even when exposed to it. To understand and remedy failures in comprehension, teachers must understand the comprehension process. The nature of this complex process is the subject of this chapter. We turn to the field of cognitive psychology for some illumination of the topic.

The Nature of Psychological Studies of Comprehension

Comprehension of complex materials like prose is a relatively recent focus of psychological research. Few investigations of comprehension were undertaken prior to the 1970s. There are a number of reasons for this, and a number of consequences, too. The reasons are both historical and technological. The results are that there are a number of relatively young competing theories of comprehension and that as yet our understanding of the process itself is rather rudimentary.

Historical Antecedents

Cognitive interests have become a popular focus in psychology only in the last ten or fifteen years. Prior to that time, American psychology was dominated by the behaviorists. As you learned in Chapter 3a, behaviorists are concerned with observable rather than private events, and many of the events in cognition, like comprehension itself, are private events. A mental image is a private event that cannot be observed directly by anyone except the person in whose mind it occurs. Before the late 1960s when imagery work began resurfacing (Paivio, 1969), imagery, because of its private nature, was not really considered a respectable topic for psychological study. There was a fear of returning to the earlier introspective paradigm that the behaviorists had replaced in the 1930s. At any rate, until the 1970s the time was not ripe for the examination of private events. Previously, although cognitive interests had not been totally absent, they were not the main focus of most research psychologists.

Another historical factor that probably delayed psychological study of complex cognitive topics was the respectability of laboratory research. Studies in the laboratory were directed at small units of behavior, perhaps even animal behavior. It was assumed that the experimenter could exercise better control if he or she examined small rather than large units of behavior. Complex human performances were broken down into smaller, more manageable units that could be operationalized more easily than more global performances. Rather than studying the comprehension of prose, which is a very complex behavior, investigators examined people's memory of lists, pairs of words, or pairs of nonsense syllables. Pairs of words are easier to specify, and their presentation can be controlled well in the laboratory. Word pairs can even be presented to subjects with machines; hence the experiments can be clear, precise, and not messy. Prose, on the other hand, is complicated and messy. Interestingly enough, even when mental imagery reappeared as a respectable research topic, it was examined in the context of learning lists and pairs of stimuli. The desire for clean scientific studies with well-defined variables was a dominant value in psychology. Until methodologies could be developed for dealing with messy stimuli and global performances in equally precise ways, the discipline was not ready for the study of complex mental events.

Technological Innovations

A technological advance assisted the cause of cognition. It became possible to use a computer as a model for human thinking. Computer programs can be written as analogues for human mental processes. Computers, like humans, store information in memories and have to retrieve it. With these machines it became possible to objectify cognitive events and make them very precise. Processing no longer needed to be totally private; it could be public in the form of a computer program. Moreover, a computer program of a cognitive process is a kind of operational definition of a global performance, one in which every single step is objectified.

Computers are not the total answer, however. No program has yet been devised for processing language exactly as humans do (Anderson, 1980). The use of computer models does, however, allow for objectivity in attempts to study private mental events; processing is operationalized. Moreover, computers can handle very complex stimulus materials. With these machines complex stimuli can be presented carefully to experimental subjects with the kind of control typical of the laboratory. Computers can even be used to simulate prose processing (Reder, 1979). This new technology has given new hope to those attempting to handle more complicated research problems.

The Basic Orientation

New tools helped fuel new interests, and with them many investigators are now willing to study such topics as text comprehension and spatial processing. The specific questions and styles of these many investigations vary, but a theme emerges across them, one consistent with the theme emphasized in the rest of this book. Many psychologists who study cognition conclude that what a person comprehends depends both on the nature of the material and on what the person brings to the material. In short, the outcome results from the interaction of person and environment. Some researchers focus on the person part, investigating such factors as cognitive structures, schemata, or depth of processing. Others focus on the external part, considering such factors as the structure of the information provided. Most agree, however, that what is comprehended, retained, and later recalled results from the interaction of the two.

The Comprehension of Prose

We process prose passages whenever we hear or read them and are paying attention. We also hope to remember what we hear or read. There is an interesting feature about the way we typically recall information, however. People seldom remember the exact sentence or even the exact words that were presented. You may remember the information in the last chapter, but you probably remember none of the exact sentences. While this may seem obvious, it is an intriguing phenomenon from a psychological perspective. After all, prose information is presented as a series of sentences. Each sentence is internally ordered, and the sentences within a passage are ordered as well. If you were to scramble either the sentence order or the passage order, in most cases the meaning would be lost. It seems, then, that order is very important in making sense of what we read and hear. When we recall the text, however, we may recall neither sentence order nor passage order but still recall the information correctly. A theory that explains comprehension from text must deal with this curious phenomenon.

There is another interesting phenomenon that has surfaced in studies of comprehension and recall. Without realizing it, people sometimes recall from a passage information that was not actually presented there. In such cases, the people apparently draw inferences from the text that was presented. These inferences, if correct, are implied in the text but are not actually stated. The fact that people can confuse what was actually presented with the inferences they themselves drew from the text is another interesting feature that any theory of comprehension must explain.

A third observation about text recall was made some time ago. In the 1930s, Bartlett (1932) investigated what people recalled from text, presenting subjects with a passage they were later asked to recall. His subjects were English-speaking and culturally Western. The passage was presented in English, but it was from a non-Western source. The passage and the subjects thus differed in their cultural perspective. The incidents and events described in the passage seemed strange and different when examined from a Western frame of reference. Interestingly enough, when the subjects recalled the passage they changed the incidents and events, and they changed them in a definite direction— toward a Western perspective. It appeared to Bartlett that recall was

Reading involves the process of encoding the material for later retrieval. Past experience will affect the interpretation and inferences made during the encoding process.

influenced by the reader's perspective as well as by the content of what was read. Depending on the reader's frame of reference, the prose itself, when it is recalled, may be interpreted and altered.

These interesting phenomena—(1) recall of information content without recall of form, (2) recall of inferences confused with presented statements, and (3) recall of information altered to be consistent with the reader—present a challenge to psychologists. How must information be stored for confusions of this kind to occur? How do people integrate new information with information already known? How, too, does the structure of text itself influence the information that is recalled?

Insufficient Explanations

In our attempt to envision what a good explanation of comprehension must encompass, it may be helpful to discuss insufficient explanations, those that fail to account for observations about comprehension. By evaluating inadequate explanations, one can develop a better picture of the kind of explanation needed. We can break comprehension down into three components: (1) *encoding*, dealing with the information at the time of presentation, (2) *memory*, storage of the information, and

(3) *recall*, retrieving the information at a later time. We can examine insufficient explanations for each of these components.

When people hear or read prose, they are exposed to a string of words. The string of words has sound, form, and meaning. If encoding remained at the sound or form level, then meaning might be lost. If only the meaning is encoded, then form might be lost. It appears that we can handle both, depending on the demands of the task. When you read a passage for content, for example, it is easy to overlook typographical errors, misspelling, and similar mistakes; these are elements of form. We can switch gears, however, and attend to form alone when proofreading is our primary task. Typists can, if they wish, type every word and every sentence of a passage while ignoring the meaning of the text. Apparently, people can be flexible when encoding text, attending to form only, meaning only, or both simultaneously. Explanations of encoding that address themselves only to the processing of form would omit an explanation of the flexibility, and they would deal inadequately with our failure to recall verbatim sentences. On the other hand, explanations of meaning alone neglect people's ability to recall form alone, as one might do when memorizing a poem in an unknown foreign language. An adequate explanation requires both.

When encoded information is stored in memory, additional complexities arise. Suppose we memorize a prose passage, storing the sentences verbatim. At the time of recall, we might expect some sentences to be produced verbatim and others to have been forgotten. When people are asked to memorize lists of unrelated words and recall them, they tend to recall words at the top and bottom of the list but to lose words in the middle. Errors are errors of omission. If sentences are stored verbatim, like unrelated words in a list, one would again expect errors of omission, but this is not exactly what happens. There are errors of omission, but there are other kinds as well. One may recall, for example, the gist of a sentence but change the form, or recall an inference that was not actually a part of the list. Conceptualizations that treat sentence memory like word list memory would fail to adequately explain the variety of error types.

Earlier ideas about memory tended to treat it as something static—error was equated with forgetting, and forgetting was synonymous with decay. Some material would be recalled and some lost. The longer the delay between input and recall, the more would be lost. Changes in memory over time were assumed to be changes in amount recalled. Now we realize that information loss is not the only kind of change possible. Remembered information can be transformed, elaborated, or otherwise changed. This was noted by Bartlett (1932) with his adult subjects and by Piaget (Piaget & Inhelder, 1969) with children. Adequate explanations of memory must deal with the *transformation* of information in memory as well as with forgetting.

Memory of a passage might also be viewed as an isolated event, independent of other events. In this view, a passage is read, retained, and retrieved separately from other passages and other previously acquired knowledge. How could an explanation such as this account for the performance of Bartlett's subjects? When remembered events contain something from contexts other than the reading of the passage itself, they cannot be treated as independent events.

The process of retrieval is not simple, either. We might consider recall as a scanning procedure—that is, when a question is asked, we scan our memory files looking for a piece of stored information. If the information is in the file, we can answer; if it is not in the file, we cannot. Consider two questions: (1) Are trees members of the plant family? (2) Do trees eat meat? The answer to the first question is probably stored in memory, since most of us have learned directly that trees are plants. We quickly scan our memory files, find the piece of information, and respond: Yes. Now look at the second question. It is doubtful that we were ever told directly that trees do not eat meat; that piece of information is not stored as such in our memory files. A scanning explanation might propose that we search the files for the answer. Logically, if the answer is not in our files, we should be unable to come up with an answer. Nevertheless, you could probably answer both questions very quickly. Retrieval, therefore, must involve more than mere scanning.

Researchers studying prose comprehension have also noted that recall is influenced by the procedures used to test it. Different kinds of performances are associated with free recall than with probed recall, for example. Retrieval of information from prose, like encoding and memory, is not a simple act.

Requirements for More Adequate Explanations

Explanations of prose processing that could encompass the complexity of the process must have a number of features. They must account for flexibility in encoding information, for example. Conceptualizations of memory must take confusions, alterations, and transformations of encoding information into account. They must account for decay as well. Moreover, an adequate explanation must deal with the interaction that takes place between the processor of the prose and the prose itself.

Memory is at the heart of comprehension. This process exemplifies the need for an interactive explanation. When a person processes prose for later recall, he or she must store information in long-term memory (see Chapter 5a for a discussion of long-term memory). People who read passages, however, already have material from past experiences stored in their memories; their minds are not blank slates as they approach a new comprehension task. A relevant question, then, is how the new information contained in the prose will be incorporated with old information already stored in memory. It might either be added on to the old, or it could be integrated with the old. If memory were simply additive, past knowledge would not necessarily change or be confused with new information. If integration occurs, however, those kinds of confusions are more likely. Since we have empirical evidence of confusions, the view that the new is integrated with the old seems more plausible.

Many modern psychologists concerned with the nature of memory conceptualize it as a network of propositions, a kind of cognitive structure (Anderson, 1980). Information is stored in this network, but so are the relationships between elements of information. Pieces of information form the *nodes* of the network; *propositions* are the relationships between the nodes. Incoming information is fitted into this system of nodes and relationships; the new and old thus become intertwined. When one is asked to recall something, one may produce a mixture of the new and the old. According to this conceptualization, memory is organized. Moreover, this view accounts for the interaction of the person's past experiences (old information) with the experience being processed (new information).

What, then, is the nature of the propositions? Are they verbal material, sentences, words, or something else? The consensus seems to be that propositions are more abstract than verbal material (Pylyshyn, 1973); they consist of the meaning underlying the verbal material, somewhat like the deep structure of language you read about in Chapter 7a. The meaning, not the verbal material itself, is what is stored in the propositional network. Information from a variety of sources—oral language, written language, pictures, and so on—can thus all be stored in the same memory network. Hence we integrate new and old information and information acquired through a variety of channels as well. One need not posit different memories for spatial information, auditory information, and verbal information; all are a part of the same thing.

The view that memory is organized around the meaning of information is also helpful in explaining the errors people make in recalling information. People may recall the gist of a passage, for example, but express it in synonymous rather than verbatim language. Recall of the gist seems logical if we assume that it is meaning rather than precise linguistic material that is stored. Recall of inferences also makes sense, since the person would be recalling relationships constructed when the new information was integrated with the old. These constructions would be added to the information provided.

In short, this explanation for memory suggests that (1) memory is an organized structure of propositions, (2) these propositions are integrated on the basis of meaning rather than on the basis of form alone, (3) new and old information become intertwined in memory, and (4) memory is a construction influenced by both the person obtaining the information and the information presented.

Schema Theory

One theoretical approach that has influenced prose learning research is schema theory (Anderson, R. C. 1978). You have encountered the word *schema* before in the chapter on Piaget (Chapter 6a). There are some interesting parallels between Piaget's use of the word *schema* and its use by prose researchers, but there are some differences as well. Prose researchers conceive of a schema as being a sort of knowledge bundle. On the basis of past experiences, people, in the view of prose researchers, construct schemas of related information that can influence the way they interpret and integrate new experiences. Incoming information, particularly if it is ambiguous, must be integrated with the old information stored in the schemas. Later, when the information is recalled, elements of the existing knowledge and the new knowledge may be confused, a phenomenon supporting the notion that the previously formed schemas influence the interpretation and storage of prose material.

The investigation of prose learning may involve a number of different research approaches. One procedure is to construct an ambiguous passage that is open to more than one interpretation (Bransford & Johnson, 1972); the interpretation selected will depend on the reader's past experiences. Sometimes one can predict that certain groups of people will be more likely to choose one interpretation over another. Ideally, the researcher constructs an ambiguous passage that could be interpreted in two or three ways and proposes hypotheses about the interpretation that will be chosen by people with different experiences. Then researchers design recall tasks that will differentiate people on the basis of the interpretation they select, the differentiation to be consistent with the initial hypotheses. It is assumed that some groups of people have had certain experiences that have led them to construct particular schemas, that others who have had different experiences have not developed these schemas, and that those who possess the schemas will perform differently from those who lack them.

A second approach to tapping schemas also begins with an ambiguous passage. In this case, however, the experimenter manipulates the subjects' access to schemas rather than making presuppositions about subjects' past experiences. A title, picture, or orienting statement accompanying the passage serves as a sort of cue to direct readers to a specific schema (Dooling & Lachman, 1971; Bransford & Johnson, 1972). Titles, for example, could be manipulated so that certain subjects get one title while others get a different one or no title at all. If schemas influence prose processing we would expect different recall

Research Report

Because of the importance of schema theory in contemporary prose learning studies, we have chosen to highlight a schema-based research selection in this chapter. Our selection is an exemplary piece of research for a number of reasons. First, the study is methodologically sound and deals with complex variables in clearly operationalized terms. Second, the investigators have used schema theory to predict behavioral outcomes and have tested those predictions. This is sound scientific procedure. One of the criteria of good theory is usefulness in predicting outcomes in advance, in addition to explaining them after the fact. Thorndyke and Hayes-Roth have tested the predictability of schema theory.

The first step in generalizing predictions that are to be tested is defining the schema construct and its properties. Schemas are clusters of knowledge that represent some general and frequently encountered concept. Schemas are therefore built from past experience with examples of that concept. Schemas, then, stand for and represent those past examples, and they guide the processing of experiences that include new examples of the concept. Schema-related examples share common features even though they may differ in specific details.

The second step is predicting the outcomes of schema use in the recall of information. The logic goes something like this: Any concept example contains both general and unique properties. In a group of schema-related examples, the general properties are redundant information; they are shared and thus replicated across examples. The unique properties or details of each example represent non-redundant information. If a person has encountered multiple examples and thus has built a strong schema, then recall of the general properties of a new example should be high. The same individual may, however, confuse details of the new example with details of previously encountered ones. The recall of detail thus may be low.

The third step is operationalizing these general notions. An example may help here. Look at the following sentences:

1. George Washington was the first president of the United States. He lived in Mount Vernon.
2. Thomas Jefferson was the third president of the United States. He lived in Monticello.

Much of the information in these two sentences is identical, but details differ (that is, the name, the number, the location). Chances are that if you read a set of sentences of this type you would probably remember the general information, but you might confuse the details.

Thorndyke and Hayes-Roth designed a group of stories that were (1) parallel in text structure, (2) on the same topic, and (3) differing in detail. These stories constituted a training package that could be used to create a schema. There was also a target story of the same structure and on the same topic as the training studies. Sentences in the target stories could vary: (1) they could repeat verbatim a sentence from the training stories called repeated sentences, (2) change a detail in a parallel sentence from the training stories called changed sentences, or (3) be unrelated to sentences from the training stories called unrelated sentences.

If a subject were exposed to the training stories, then a schema for this information would be created. The greater the exposure, the stronger the schema. When tested for recall of the target stories, we might expect the following outcomes:

1. The greater the degree of exposure to the training stories (that is, the schema examples) the greater the recall of repeated sen-

tences in the target stories because of the redundancy of information.

2. The greater the degree of exposure to the training stories, the lower the recall of changed sentences because of the competition among details.

3. Recall of unrelated sentences would be independent of the degree of exposure to the training stories, since these sentences are unassociated with either the general properties or the detail of the schema stories.

Fifty undergraduates participated in the study. Treatments varied in terms of the number of training stories that preceded presentation of the target story (one, two, three, four, or eight training stories). When the subjects were tested for recall of the three kinds of sentences in the target stories, the results were consistent with the predictions, thereby providing support for this proposed model of memory schema.

There are two features of this study that we consider especially important. The first is the treatment of schema formation as an independent variable manipulated by the experimenters. Causal statements are therefore possible. The second is the precision of the outcome predictions. This feature is essential for theory testing.

Although we have greatly oversimplified a complex and sophisticated study, we have highlighted some features that make this selection an example of very good science.

Thorndyke, P. W., & Hayes-Roth, B. The use of schemata in the acquisition and transfer of knowledge, *Cognitive Psychology*, 1979, 11, 82–106 (Experiment 1).

performances to correspond to different orienting schemas. This does appear to be the case.

Research based on schema theory makes a strong case for the relevance of past knowledge in the comprehension of prose. It points out the need to understand what the person brings to the situation in which comprehension is expected and to explain the way new information is assimilated to past information. The theory has weaknesses as well, however. First, unlike Piagetian notions of schema, the word as used by these theorists has yet to be precisely defined. Second, the idea that what the person brings to a situation determines what is extracted is not revolutionary or even a particularly novel proposition; Bartlett made it in 1932. We really need a more precise understanding of the way this occurs, and for what reasons. Schema-theory researchers are, however, conducting well-controlled, precise investigations of complex stimuli, such as prose passages, and precise schema models are now being developed and disseminated.

Depth of Processing Models

Another growing avenue of research into prose comprehension focuses on factors in people's prose processing that influence comprehension. At some point, you have probably read a passage or listened to a speaker without being particularly engaged. If asked to recall the information the speaker communicated, you would find it extremely difficult. This phenomenon, which is probably universal, emphasizes an important point about comprehension: different *levels of processing* information may influence what is extracted.

Some investigators (Anderson, 1970; Craik & Lockhart, 1972) have proposed that verbal stimuli, like language, can be processed at different depths. Moreover, the depth of processing seems to be related to later retention. At a superficial level, language is processed not necessarily in terms of its semantic meaning, but in terms of its form. We may, for example, judge whether words are presented in capital or lower-case letters (Craik, 1973). On a deeper level, prose is processed in terms of its meaning, and subsequent recall reflects that meaning. Research findings on these notions of depth of processing (Craik, 1973; Johnson & Jenkins, 1973) generally support the hypothesis that orienting tasks requiring semantic analysis improve attention, at least for single-word stimuli, noun pairs, and sentences.

While schema theory emphasizes what the learner brings to the situation, depth of processing models emphasizes what the learner does in the situation. As you learned in Chapters 5a and 5b, for learning to take place the learner apparently needs to be active and to focus primarily on meaning. Being active may involve paraphrasing material, answering questions, or forming images, but activity of some sort seems to be crucial for comprehension and recall.

The material reviewed so far in this chapter points up the importance of such learner variables as (1) learner activity, (2) past experience, and (3) prior memory structure. Comprehension, like other outcomes, thus seems to result from an interactive process.

Text Structure

Some investigators have examined the other element involved in comprehension, the prose itself (Meyer, 1975). As we noted earlier, the language in sentences and passages has a specific structure. Sentences that violate prescribed structure are not meaningful and probably cannot be recalled, either. Similarly, the organization of passages may influence their comprehension and recall. Intuitively, it seems reasonable to assume that text structure is important, but specifying the organizational properties of comprehensible prose is a difficult proposition.

A number of models on the nature of text structure have been proposed. These are called *text grammars.* Some are based on the semantic representations of prose (Dawes, 1964, 1966) and some on the logical relations in a passage (Crothers, 1972; Frederiksen, 1972). Others analyze text on the basis of the propositions it contains (Kintsch, 1974). These models have generated research on the importance of text analysis and text structure for prose comprehension. It is far from clear which is the most productive model and which corresponds most closely to what goes on in the comprehender's mind.

Pictures and Comprehension

One activity that seems to help learners recall from prose is having them elaborate on the material (Reder, 1979). Elaboration can take many forms, but all of them involve reflecting on the material's meaning. Questions interjected throughout the passage, for example, can focus reflection on the meaning of the material, on what should be inferred from the direct statements, and on the passage's implications. In short, elaboration is any device that encourages the reader to think actively about the gist of the passage. Reflecting on the meaning and implications of a passage may encourage the reader to integrate the new information into the existing memory structure and form associations and relationships between the new and old. These processes increase the number and variety of references that can be used for retrieval.

One type of elaboration procedure that has attracted research interest recently is the use of images and pictures (Pressley, 1976a & 1976b). Along with the prose, readers can be given pictures that depict the gist of a passage, or they can be instructed to form mental images that capture the relevant information. The former is called *imposed imagery* and the latter *induced imagery*. The use of imagery may be helpful for a number of reasons. First, in order to conjure up images of content the learner must actively focus on meaning and deep-level processing. Second, forming an image is a type of rehearsal that leads a person to reflect on the material one additional time. Third, pictures or images provide another source of information. These notions of the way a picture or image may enhance comprehension have instigated a number of research efforts.

Like investigations of other kinds of comprehension strategies, imagery studies did not at first focus on the comprehension of prose. Instead, imagery was examined as a mediator in paired-associate learning. It turned out to be an effective memory device (Paivio, 1969). The body of research on paired-associate learning and serial learning led to theory building in imagery (Paivio, 1971) and to an interest in imagery as a mediator in children's learning as well (Reese, 1970).

Later, imagery as a mediator in prose learning became a popular research topic (Samuels, 1970). In some of that research, children served as subjects and the task was comprehension of oral prose. Pictures—imposed imagery—were the mediators of interest (Lesgold, Levin, Shimron, & Guttman, 1975). The provision of pictures proved to be an effective technique in these kinds of studies. In research with

The use of pictures, illustrations, graphs, and drawings may aid the student in the encoding of prose. The student has access to both a visual representation and a verbal one, which may facilitate retrieval from long-term memory.

children on a sentence learning task, Levin, Bender, and Lesgold (1976) compared a rehearsal strategy with a strategy of providing pictures. They found that children who were shown pictures had significantly better recall than those who were not. This result has been found in other investigations as well (Ruch & Levin, 1977). In short, there seems to be ample evidence that providing pictures assists prose comprehension and recall, probably because they provide the learner with an external memory representation.

Pictures are stimulus features that experimenters can manipulate. Images, on the other hand, are formed mentally. Investigators can instruct a subject to form an image, but they cannot be certain that the subject actually does so, nor can they know the content of the image. Perhaps for this reason, the results of research on the use of induced imagery in improving comprehension are inconclusive (Pressley, 1976a). We do know, however, that young children have trouble generating useful images (Wolff & Levin, 1972; Guttman, 1976).

The equivocal findings on the usefulness of induced imagery raise another set of concerns. What is imagery? How are images represented in memory? What role do images play in cognitive activity?

Spatial Information and Imagery

As we noted earlier in this chapter, information is also presented to learners in the form of visual displays. Sometimes visual displays are used in conjunction with language, as in flow charts. Sometimes they are stylized representations of complex spatial information, like maps. In other instances they represent concepts, as when we present the concepts of fractions with a picture of a cut-up pie. In all cases visual displays are supposed to convey information and assist comprehension.

This form of information appears to have characteristics different from other forms, however. Language, for example, has sequence and temporal order; visual information is organized spatially. Whereas visual information is processed with the eyes, oral language is processed through a person's ears. Does this make the two forms different?

Mental Imagery—What Is It?

Intuitively, most people assume that spatially organized information might be stored as a kind of picture in the head. If you were asked what the United States looks like, for example, you could easily think of a picture of a map. The map is an image that is based in part on past experiences—seeing maps. Once you have this image in mind, you can act on it, you can scan its perimeter, move in for a closeup on one section, or compare two states for similarity of shape. In doing so, you may experience something that appears to resemble seeing. Words and language seem not to be involved in this mental manipulation. Does that mean that imagery is different from other forms of thinking?

Paivio (1971), who is primarily responsible for making imagery a respectable research topic, suggested a *dual processing hypothesis*. His idea is essentially that we have two procedures for processing information, one visual and one verbal. A visual encoding strategy is best suited for spatial information, visual displays, and concrete ideas. The verbal procedure is best for abstract ideas and information sequenced temporally, such as language. In this conceptualization, we have a visual code specialized for spatial memory and a verbal code specialized for temporal memory. Spatial processing, memory, and recall are highly visual in nature. Some even contend that there are separate stores for visual and verbal material (Haber & Erdelyi, 1972).

We can, however, be very flexible in playing with information in our heads. You can generate mental images, for example, for events that you have never actually seen—a fish wearing a suit, a mountain exploding. Or you can take a word, such as *cube*, translate it into an image, act on it by unfolding it in your head, and describe the resulting flattened shape with language. We can also take verbal information and transform it into an image. In view of this flexibility, there have been challenges to the dual-coding hypothesis (Anderson & Bower, 1973).

Since many investigators have found the dual-processing explanation unsatisfactory or at least too limited, investigations into the nature of mental imagery have continued. Some have investigated correspondences between what we can do with imagery and what we can do with our visual system (Kosslyn & Shwartz, 1977; Kosslyn, 1978). Others have considered the correspondence between physical action and mental imagery (Shepard & Feng, 1972). Most of these studies are fascinating, innovative, and clever. They clearly exemplify the methodological sophistication of modern cognitive psychologists.

Regardless of the point of view proposed by a particular imagery investigator, all hold one point in common: A mental image is not simply a picture in the head, a sort of mental photograph. Mental images are *constructions*, not just traces of prior perceptions. As such, they can be generated and used as mediators in problem-solving and in information storage.

Research on Mental Imagery

One body of research on mental imagery examines the correspondence between what we can do with an image and what we would do physically with a real object (Shepard & Metzler, 1971; Marmor, 1975; Shepard & Feng, 1972). Imagine, for example, a cube, and then imagine the cube unfolding. Does the mental unfolding process seem very similar to the process of actually unfolding a cardboard box? In another example, imagine the capital letter *R* and then imagine rotating the letter in a 360° circle. Does the mental rotation of the letter seem to resemble the actual physical rotation of the object? On the basis of personal introspection, these mental processes and actual physical processes seem to be a good fit. Psychologists use the mathematical term *isomorphic* to describe the correspondence.

One research strategy for assessing the isomorphism between physical and mental activity involves inquiring into the time it takes to conduct a mental action on a mental image. It takes longer to fold a flat piece of paper twice than to fold it once. To return to the object example, it takes longer to physically rotate the *R* 180° than to rotate it 10° from an upright position. Researchers interested in this aspect of imagery obtain a measure of reaction time, the length of time it takes a subject to perform a mental action. Using this paradigm, investigators have found that the time it takes to rotate an image is a function of the number of degrees of rotation required; the more degrees of rotation, the greater the reaction time. In fact, on a graph the relationship between the degree of rotation required between 0° and 180° and the reaction time is an ascending straight line (Shepard & Metzler, 1971; Marmor, 1975). Similarly, the time required to fold a flat cube depends on the number of folds required; the more folds, the longer the reaction time (Shepard & Feng, 1972). Hence it seems that mental actions on mental images are similar to our physical actions on real objects.

If images are well suited to the coding and storage of spatial information, one might wonder whether images have spatial characteristics. This question has attracted research interest, too. Kosslyn, Ball, and Reiser (1978) found that more time was required to scan greater distances across visual images. Subjects also required more time to see properties of subjectively smaller images than properties of large ones (Kosslyn, 1975). Distance and size are spatial characteristics in the concrete world; they also seem to be spatial characteristics of images.

Are images constrained by the same limitations as actual vision with the eyes? Current research seems to indicate that the answer is yes. Incoming visual information interferes with visual imagery, for example (Kosslyn & Pomerantz, 1977). Moreover, just as visual acuity is reduced as we observe objects at progressively more peripheral regions of the visual field, mental imagery acuity is reduced when we imagine objects at progressively more peripheral regions of the visual field (Finke & Kosslyn, 1980).

It seems, then, that the nature of mental images, the constraints on them, and the things we can do with them correspond to our physical and visual abilities. Images are not, however, just traces or spatial copies of past visual or physical experiences. We construct them, rather, from information in our memories. The original form of the information from which we construct is a hotly debated theoretical issue (Pylyshyn, 1973; Anderson, 1978a; Kosslyn & Pomerantz, 1977), one that has yet to be resolved.

Imagery in Children

Most of the recent sophisticated research on imagery has been conducted with adults. Much less is known about the imaging capacities of children. We do not yet have a great deal of empirical work on which to base a theory of imagery development. Some literature on prose learning emphasizes the problems children encounter using induced imagery as a mediator; other studies suggest that imagery deficits are a reason young children fail with certain kinds of problem-solving tasks (Dean, 1979; Huttenlocher & Presson, 1973). Our information is still limited, however. In general, the research suggests that children younger than about age eight or nine have difficulty using imaginal mediators. We cannot be sure whether these are results of imaging failures on the child's part or a result of failures in the instructions used to get children to use imagery.

New Directions in Research

One rapidly expanding topic of research in prose learning is the study of comprehension from connected discourse. Many of the investigations into this topic, as we noted earlier in the chapter, are generated from the framework of *schema theory* (Anderson, Spiro, & Montague, 1977; Spiro, Bruce, & Brewer, 1980). Schema theory has not yet evolved into a tight, well-delineated, theoretical system (Thorndyke & Yekovich, 1980), but its current heuristic value for spurring research activity is impressive.

Much schema-based empirical work is being conducted at the Center for the Study of Reading at the University of Illinois by people like Richard Anderson (Anderson, 1977; 1978; Anderson, Spiro, & Anderson, 1978; Anderson & Pichert, 1978), Rand Spiro (Spiro, 1977a; 1977b; Spiro & Tirre, 1980), and many others. The Center produces a great many technical reports for the dissemi-nation of research findings as well as published papers, so the impact of schema theory is widely felt.

Schema-based research has implications for theory in cognitive psychology (Rumelhart & Ortony, 1977) and educational issues as well (Anderson, 1977). Those latter implications include our understanding of the reading process (Adams, 1980; Brown, 1980; Perfetti & Hogaboam, 1975) and of individual differences in comprehension (Spiro & Tirre, 1980; Perfetti & Lesgold, 1978), both of which bear on the teaching of reading. We can see then that the research base has inherent interest for educators and psychologists alike.

No doubt schema theory will continue to generate empirical investigation and will continue to evolve into a more precise explanatory system. Much remains to be done before the latter goal is accomplished. In the meantime, schema theory is a topic to watch.

Piaget addressed the issue of mental imagery in children (Piaget & Inhelder, 1971) and inspired others as well (Wolff & Levin, 1972; Dean, 1976, 1979). Essentially, Piaget treats imagery, like other forms of thought, as a construction of the child. The specific construction arises from the child's physical activity at the sensorimotor level. From physical actions on objects, children develop a knowledge of object relationships. This knowledge is then represented in mental imagery.

Piaget contended that mental imagery is the child's ability to anticipate the outcome of an action on an object or objects. It is mental action rather than physical action, however. Developmentally, the origin and growth of imagery is governed by the same processes as the origin and growth of other mental operations. Imagery is synonymous with coordinated mental action and, as you learned in Chapter 6a, coordinated mental actions of any kind are not theoretically expected before concrete operations.

Marmor (1975) did replicate the findings of adult studies of rotation with children as young as five. She succeeded in getting her subjects to use mental imagery and found the same kinds of results noted with adults: The greater the required mental rotation, the longer it took the subjects to accomplish it. In another study (Brainerd & Huevel, 1974), children were trained to use imagery to anticipate the outcome of unfolding geometric shapes. In both studies, however, physical activity was a training procedure related in important ways to the children's success.

One thing is clear from research with both children and adults. Mental imagery is a construction on the part of the person. Past visual information feeds into the process, as does past physical activity. A generated mental image may, however, be something new, not directly experienced before, that a person creates and utilizes in comprehending, retaining, and retrieving information presented spatially.

Conclusions and Summary

Recall of information is a valued outcome of education. Successful recall, however, is a complex process that involves (1) encoding, (2) memory, (3) retrieval, and (4) comprehension. Modern research in cognitive psychology is making great strides in illuminating these processes for us, leading to the development of models that can represent human processes. At the same time, innovative research paradigms are being created to test hypotheses about mental events. From the empirical outcomes of the research, computer analogues are being designed to simulate human thinking. This is currently one of the most exciting areas in psychology.

The answers being sought about human comprehension are not all in. Much important work remains to be done. Some things are already quite clear, however. The human mind is organized, integrated, and complex, a holistic mental network. The formation of this network is most likely a function of our characteristics as a biological species and our individual experiences. Once again, a familiar theme surfaces: Our performances depend both upon individual qualities and elements of the environment. Comprehension is one outcome that is congruent with this general theme.

Psychological research has identified some of the features of the interaction between the individual and the environment. From empirical results and computer simulations we now have much more sophisticated ideas about human memory than formerly, for instance. We know something about encoding strategies, the nature of mental imagery, and the influence of text structure and prior knowledge, but we have a long way to go. In the next few decades, exciting information will no doubt be generated. More and more knowledge about the way humans interact with their environment and perform accordingly is on the horizon.

TEACHING SCENARIO

In the early grades of school the major responsibility for ensuring active learning and engagement rests with the teacher. As students advance, however, they must assume more and more of that responsibility themselves. By the time they enter college the primary mode of information delivery is via lectures and reading. Whether the student can achieve active involvement under those circumstances will depend on skills acquired earlier.

Mr. Stevens is planning to teach a special summer course in study skills for graduating high school seniors who will be entering college in the fall. He knows that as they move on to college these students are facing a dramatic shift in their education experience. He knows, for example, that they are apt to enroll in large classes where they will be required to assume responsibility for much of their own learning and their own schedule of study. The students must therefore be prepared with skills useful for managing the heavy reading schedule often required of freshmen and likely to aid in promoting self-directed study. What skills might Mr. Stevens emphasize that would meet these objectives?

Chapter 12b

Techniques for Increasing Comprehension in the Classroom

Introduction

In the last chapter we summarized research results and theories concerning the way people process information. Clearly, there is much more to be learned about information-processing, but education must continue even without all the answers, and we must consider the applications possible from research results that we feel fairly certain about. In this chapter we will propose some applications based on recent empirical findings. Interestingly enough, a number of them will sound strikingly familiar. Many of the techniques educators have been using for some time are consistent with recent research results. The match may have resulted from trial and error in teaching, from intuition, or from some other source. Whatever the reason for it, the match exists, so the applications presented in this chapter are far from revolutionary. They are consistent with the knowledge base provided by scientific investigation, however.

Research on comprehension has dealt with prose, induced imagery, and imposed imagery, but findings on these three topics have different implications for practice. Many of the empirical findings on prose and imposed imagery (pictures) have a bearing on practice. This is not the case for investigations of induced imagery. Research on this subject has focused on theoretical questions about the nature of the process, and it would be premature to offer practical recommendations on the basis of this body of research. Accordingly, most of the discussion in this chapter will focus on prose comprehension and the use of pictorial materials.

Information Content and the Fallacy of Assumptions

We noted early in the last chapter that teachers make assumptions about comprehension. One assumption they often make is that if students are motivated to carry out assigned tasks, they will learn. Teachers assume that if students actually read assignments, they will be able to recall the important information. When students do poorly on a test that taps recall, a teacher may attribute the poor results to a lack of motivation, laziness, failure to perform assigned tasks, or simply lack of ability. These elements certainly can affect performance, but it is sometimes difficult to know when they have affected it.

One point made in the last chapter concerned the inherent complexity of comprehension and recall. A number of events can either occur or fail to occur as information is processed. A student may have read assigned material but failed to extract the information to be tested; this is not necessarily a motivation problem. Perhaps the student had trouble retrieving information. A poor performance may be caused by a number of factors rather than one specific factor.

The first recommendation, then, is not to make automatic assumptions about students' comprehension. A teacher may find the content of instructional materials self-evident, but learners who have different schemas and different processing styles may not. Closer attention to both the materials and student processing is warranted before one makes assumptions about the causes of a performance.

The Nature of the Materials: Prose

Since comprehension involves a number of steps, where does one start to examine the process? We can begin by looking at the material, the source of the information the student is to encode and store. With prose, teachers should examine the content, form, and structure of the passages that will be used in instruction.

Prose material has an overall structure. The points to be made are organized in some way. Some of the points will be important, some will be less so, and some will only be implied. Teachers also have ideas about the relative importance of content and implications. It is the ideas that the teacher considers important that are likely to appear on tests. The structure of the text influences the way key points stand out, however (Meyer, 1975). The points the teacher considers important may not be emphasized by the text structure. Key points that must be inferred may be buried in extraneous materials.

It is probably wise to compare the ideas that the teacher considers important with the ideas emphasized by the text. If they differ, students may miss important information. Prose researchers have demonstrated that the placement of a piece of information in the text influences the chance of its recall (Meyer, 1975). In one study (Meyer & McConkie, 1973) it was found that ideas positioned high in the content structure were recalled more often than those in middle or low structural positions. So-called high ideas are those considered important.

Formal analysis of text is a complex process; and opinions about it vary (Reder, 1979). Classroom teachers lack the expertise and the time to formally analyze all the passages they use in the classroom, but it is possible for teachers to inspect prose and compare the author's high ideas with the teacher's expectations. If students recall more of the ideas the author places in high structural positions and the teacher is concerned with ideas the author places in a low position, comprehension problems may result.

Another reason to inspect prose is to identify important information that is implied but not stated outright. Teachers may wish to test student comprehension of implicit ideas, but students may either fail to note implicit ideas or fail to recognize their importance. If the teacher wants students to recall implications and inferences, he or she should stress their importance in class.

Before using prose materials in instruction, then, teachers can identify superordinate and subordinate ideas as well as important implicit information in the text. They can also assess the importance of content and implications. When the text structure and teacher expectations match, the structuring of ideas is consistent, and this makes them easier for students to comprehend. If they are inconsistent, then teachers may wish to augment reading with other activities.

▶ *ACTIVITY 1.*   There are several ways to practice inspecting the structure of textual material. We often construct outlines of passages as we read them, for example. The structure of the outline (major headings, minor headings, and so on) gives you some notion of the content, the relative importance of the content, and the organization of the passage. Select one of the following exercises and practice examining textual structure.

1. Find a prose passage dealing with material you might like to teach a group of students. Identify and list (a) the superordinate ideas, (b) the subordinate ideas, and (c) the important implications.
2. Examine the section "Imagery in Children" (pp. 489–491) in Chapter 12a. Identify what you think are the author's (a) superordinate ideas, (b) subordinate ideas, and (c) important implications. Compare your list with Table 12b-1 at the end of this chapter. Do they match?
3. Choose a passage and outline the important ideas. Have a friend analyze the same passage. Are the analyses similar?

Two-dimensional drawings may not provide an adequate representation of an object for young children. A three-dimensional model or the actual object will provide a fuller representation.

When you have completed your activity you will probably find that mismatches are more likely than matches. Even informal text analysis is very difficult, and more than one outcome is possible. Identification of key points is a function not just of text structure but of the text reader as well. Two readers will not necessarily assess content in the same way. To emphasize certain information the teacher may have to do more than simply present the content. This reiterates an important conclusion: It is unwise to make assumptions about what readers will extract from text. Closer examination and reflection are required.

The Nature of the Materials: Pictures and Diagrams

The content of spatial information must also be examined. We have little information on the way children comprehend spatial information. Research in this topic has tended to focus on individual differences in ability (Lohman, 1979a, 1979b) rather than on process and comprehension. As with prose, it is unwise to assume that students will automatically extract the important information from spatial presentations.

Pictures and diagrams are forms of representation that in some respects resemble language. As representations, they are symbols for events, concepts, or phenomena, and they are subject to interpretation. We have to learn the relationship between the spatial display or symbol and the information conveyed. You know that an arrow ⟶, is the visual symbol for movement in a specific direction. You also know that this symbol ⬡ represents a six-sided, solid, three-dimensional form. Neither the shapes of all six of its sides nor its three-dimensionality are explicitly displayed, however. They are represented symbolically. To adults, the symbol's meaning is clear; to children, it may not be. To give another example: A map is a representation of large-scale space. In order to find one's way with a map, one must translate information depicted in small-scale space to actions in large-scale space. The map itself contains the essential information, but it cannot be assumed that learners will be able to comprehend it because in order to make use of it one must translate the information into a different scale.

Here is a cogent example of children's problems with space. It has been noted that young children do not necessarily perceive the match between a three-dimensional object and its two-dimensional representation (Rosser *et al.*, 1980; Mattson, 1981). Matches of this sort are recognized later in development. Two-dimensional representations of three-dimensional objects may thus not be good instructional devices to use with young children.

Like text, such spatial depictions as diagrams and pictures should be analyzed for their content. Do they communicate the relevant content to students, or does the content need to be explained? Are spatial depictions appropriate for the students' developmental level?

▶ *ACTIVITY 2.*   Select a published series of math or science books for elementary school children and choose some diagrams that represent important content, concepts, or operations. For each diagram, identify the superordinate idea conveyed and note the spatial features that represent that information. Then show your diagrams to some children and ask what they think the pictures represent. Ask them to identify the spatial features that convey the information. Do this for several children of different ages. Compare your analysis with the protocols you collected from the children. Are there discrepancies?

▶ *ACTIVITY 3.*   Draw a map of the layout of a school, and have children of different ages draw school maps, too. Examine their maps for content and distortions. If possible, have the children explain their maps to you, including the activities they perform in the different locations. You will probably find that size distortions correspond to the children's familiarity with various locations and to the value they place on the activities they perform in these locations. Compare the children's maps. Do all the children perceive space in the same way?

Identifying the Information Depicted

Analyzing the form of the information to be used in instruction is one way to identify the author's priorities and compare them with one's own instructional priorities. Noting consistencies in the two sets of priorities can help the teacher (1) select materials that match instructional goals, (2) choose other teaching approaches to emphasize important content, and (3) identify the content to be assessed later. Analysis of the content does not, however, ensure that students will extract information in a particular way. Students may not learn material as the author intended. We must thus consider the learner's abilities and performance as well as the information to be comprehended.

Building on the Learner's Perspective

Students are not blank slates when they encounter new information. Teachers can use this fact to help learners integrate the new information with the old. The teacher can try to plug into the learners' schemas, giving them a frame of reference for dealing with new material. This may be done through the use of (1) titles, (2) orienting statements, and (3) advance organizers.

Titles and Subtitles as Organizational Devices

Titles are used to indicate the content of a passage. Generally, titles are used to state the basic idea of a passage. Subtitles serve the same purpose. Since titles and subtitles precede the material they refer to, they serve as orienters or points of reference for the reader. In fact, listing the titles and subtitles of a chapter enables the reader not only to apprehend the main organizing points, but also to grasp the relationships among those points. Some will stand out as more important, whereas others will be subordinate.

As mentioned previously, outlining is a procedure for organizing titles and subtitles in terms of their importance. The content of paragraphs is also represented in an outline. A paragraph's content is often summarized in the topic sentence, which can be regarded as a sort of paragraph title. Topic sentences are often placed at or near the beginning of the paragraph, again as orienting devices for what is to come. Outlines are helpful in learning, and for that matter in writing prose, because they can be used to organize major ideas and the relationships among ideas.

Providing students with titles and subtitles that break passages into sections on the basis of important ideas is one way to direct their attention as they read. The title assumes a high position in the text structure and provides an organizer for the information that follows. Some texts use subtitles, others do not. The teacher can provide titles and subtitles when they are lacking.

Encouraging the use of outlines by students can assist them in focusing attention on major ideas and organizing ideas coherently. Outlining material that has been read can also assist the student in the recall of learned information.

Teachers may also encourage students to create their own outlines of titles and subtitles. This activity focuses students' attention on major ideas and the way they are organized, and it may improve student recall performances. Titles can also serve orienting functions for diagrams and spatial presentations. A diagram's label provides a frame of reference for the information it contains.

> ▶ *ACTIVITY 4.* List the superordinate ideas and subordinate ideas in Chapter 12a. In addition, outline the chapter by listing its titles and subtitles. Does the arrangement of titles reflect the relationship among ideas?
>
> ▶ *ACTIVITY 5.* Select a passage of expository prose (nonfiction) that contains no subtitles. After identifying the key ideas in the passage, add titles and subtitles. Show some fellow students the titled version and others the untitled version. After they have read it, have them recall the major ideas. Which group did better?

Orienting Statements

Orienting statements may also be used to help students integrate new information. These devices relate new information to information the students already know. When we emphasize the relationships and similarities between the old and the new, the new material is rendered more familiar and easier to assimilate.

Statements such as "This is like _____," "This chapter deals with the same issues as _____," and "The next reading is another approach to the problem we discussed yesterday" serve orienting functions. They place new information in a familiar context.

Another procedure for establishing context is to reiterate a theme common to two pieces of material. Explications of theme can help the reader construct a network of relationships in his or her memory. This chapter, for example, has a theme in common with the introduction to this section: Learning outcomes are a function of person characteristics and environmental factors. The introduction served an orienting function. In most of the chapters in this section, we have reiterated this theme in an attempt to tie the pieces together.

▶ *ACTIVITY 6.*   Recall can be affected by orienting statements and by the reiteration of ties between old and new material. These devices can be used quite easily in instruction. Select one of the following exercises and observe for yourself the effect of these procedures.

1. Select two passages on similar topics. Create an orienting statement that relates the two. Give one person the passages without orienting statements and another person the passages with orienting statements. Then assess your subjects' recall. Did they perceive the relationship between the passages equally well?
2. Select a passage or story designed for children. Develop orienting statements that could be used to tie the passage or story to experiences familiar to children. Give the unoriented passage to one child and the oriented version to another. Did your orienting statements affect the amount and variety of the children's recall?

Advance Organizers

Advance organizers are a type of orienting statement. Since they were presented in Chapter 5b, we will omit a detailed discussion here. As you may remember, they direct the student to the superordinate concept that transcends and encompasses the material to come. They provide a preview of the content to follow, stating the major ideas and showing how they are related to other key points.

The usefulness of advance organizers has for some time been debated in the research literature. It appears now that they do aid retention. In a recent review of the literature on advance organizers, Luiten, Ames, and Ackerson (1980) found that (1) advance organizers are effective instructional devices, (2) they seem to work with all age levels, grade levels, and subject matter, and (3) they are probably most effective when delivered orally. There remain questions about whether the organizer must be provided before the material is read (Gagne & Wiegand, 1970). The position of the organizer may not be as important as its explicitness.

Encouraging Elaboration

The results of empirical study and our own common sense tell us that we remember content better when we think about it. The time we spend reflecting on information does appear to improve recall and retention. The effectiveness of reflection is not simply a matter of time or rehearsal of information, however. It is the manner in which we think about information, the way we elaborate on it, that is important. As you may remember, depth of processing models suggest that recall is better when the learner is active in the processing of information.

A number of procedures, including paraphrasing and the use of priming questions, may be used to increase the amount of students' activity in learning. Both techniques encourage students to think about information and restate it in their own words.

The Use of Priming Questions

Priming questions are queries included in text that require the student to think about the information he or she has just read or is about to read. They may precede the text, coincide with it, or follow it. Their function is to focus the student's attention on the most relevant aspects of a passage. When the student responds to a question, he or she elaborates or at least restates the content. Most important, the reader who answers the questions may process the material at a deeper level as well as review it.

Apparently, priming questions are most effective when they are spread throughout the text, appearing every paragraph or two (Frase, 1970). The type of question is also influential. Improvements in student recall are greatest when high-level questions are used. These questions require that the student integrate or apply the material to a new situation (Watts & Anderson, 1971). The elaboration required of students

Scenario Suggestion

When faced with a heavy reading schedule and a need to comprehend material from that reading, one needs to employ procedures that permit attention to and organization of the main points in some meaningful way. Mr. Stevens reasons that his students need methods for noting major and minor points, for organizing those points, and, most important, for making those points comprehensible.

Highlighting and outlining are two techniques that focus attention on key points in prose material. Retention of key points is augmented by making those points a part of the reader. Mr. Stevens thus offers the following advice to his students and gives them reading in which they can practice these techniques:

1. For each paragraph or section of text, restate in your own words the key idea.
2. Reiterate the subpoints that support or exemplify the main idea.
3. Paraphrase, again in your own words, the essential content of the paragraph/passage.
4. Construct questions related to the main and subordinate points—create your own priming questions.
5. Construct responses, again in your own words, to those questions.

Mr. Stevens reasons that restating major premises of passages in one's own words not only assists in attending to key points but in making content meaningful to the reader. Such tactics should improve both comprehension and retention of the materials. In addition, following the five steps encourages active involvement with the text, since a person cannot read passively and construct paraphrased statements at the same time. Since research in cognitive psychology in general and prose comprehension more specifically suggests the importance of active processing, Mr. Stevens' ideas should prove worthwhile.

▶ *ACTIVITY 7.*   Try one of the following exercises to get some first-hand experience using priming questions.

1. Examine a group of expository passages directed at school-age children. Are priming questions included at the beginning, the end, in the text, or in the margins?
2. Examine passages from textbooks for undergraduate college students. Are priming questions included? Are they low-level or high-level?
3. Select a passage of expository prose in your subject. Construct a set of priming questions for the passage and indicate where they might be located.
4. Construct a set of high-level priming questions for Chapter 12a.

responding to high-level questions apparently improves comprehension.

The Elaboration of Inferences

Drawings, pictures, and diagrams may be used to improve students' comprehension and recall of text, especially when they focus the reader's attention on important aspects of information. Like priming questions, these devices can be used to emphasize key points and encourage elaboration. Since pictures often present the same information as the text but in a different form, they also serve as reiterations of content. Exposing students to the same concept expressed in different forms is a type of rehearsal.

The use of pictures and visual devices is especially useful for young children. External aids may provide them with organizational frameworks they cannot yet generate on their own. In addition, a picture is a concrete representation of content, and young children are developmentally more capable of handling concrete concepts than abstract concepts. Including extraneous pictures simply to make a prose passage more attractive, however, may not improve comprehension very much. In fact, extraneous pictures can draw reader attention away from the important information, a phenomenon that may decrease comprehension. Pictures that inaccurately represent content may have a detrimental effect as well. Nevertheless, the use of carefully chosen pictures to reiterate key features of prose may improve retention.

► *ACTIVITY 8.*   Most current texts, even those for adult learners, include both prose and pictures.

1. Examine texts for a number of grade levels for science, math, social studies, or some other subject. Are pictures used in these books? Does the number used decrease with increasing grade level? Do the pictures make more than one point?
2. Select a prose passage for children that includes pictures as well as text. Identify the key points in the text, and then examine the pictures to see if they are consistent with the key points.
3. Select a piece of expository prose for school-age children. Identify two or three key points in the prose. Describe the way diagrams or pictures might be used to reiterate those points.

Conclusion

The transmittal of information between teachers and students is clearly an important part of the educational process. Information is not always self-evident, however, and the transmittal process is not automatic. A learner's ability to abstract information is a function of the presentation of content and the learner's frame of reference. We need to understand both components and the way they interact.

Teachers can improve comprehension by inspecting the instructional material, by ensuring that the material reflects performance goals, and by emphasizing important information. They can direct student attention to the important content through the use of titles, orienting passages, and advance organizers. Finally, they can provide activities that encourage students to actively process information at the deepest level of comprehension. There are several such techniques, including priming questions, practice with inference, paraphrasing, and elaboration. Most important, in order to facilitate students' acquisition of information the teacher should avoid making assumptions about comprehension and attend to all elements of the process.

TABLE 12b–1.   Major Ideas in "Imagery in Children," Chapter 12a

Superordinate ideas	*Subordinate ideas*
I. Children have more difficulty with imaging than adults do	a. Have difficulty using imaging as a mediator in prose learning b. Have difficulty with problems that require imagery strategies c. Information, however, is limited
II. Until about age eight or nine, children have difficulty using imagery	a. Could be a research artifact
III. Piaget approaches imagery as a construction of the child	a. Originates in motor activity b. Involves the anticipation of action on objects c. Is governed by same process as logical thought d. Cannot be expected prior to concrete operations
IV. Some investigators have replicated adult findings with children by training them with physical action	a. Rotation studies b. Unfolding geometric forms

Social behaviors as well as cognitive skills are developed within the school. After the first year or so, students spend a major part of their day in school, interacting with adults, participating in peer group activities, and learning the rules of appropriate social conduct. Effective social functioning is therefore another important outcome of the educational process, and it is the subject matter of Chapters 13a and 13b.

The psychological perspective on the acquisition of appropriate social skills, which we present in Chapter 13a, has been influenced heavily by two schools of thought. First, the Piagetian approach (Chapter 6a) has served as the impetus for many studies of the topic. Second, social learning theory, too (Chapter 4a), bears on these phenomena. As we review the theoretical underpinnings and the empirical investigation of prosocial behavior, cognitive developmental principles and social learning themes are thus reiterated.

Given the research base on the acquisition of prosocial behavior, how do teachers influence the socialization process? That is the content of Chapter 13b. In that chapter we integrate aspects of a variety of theoretical views and discuss their application to the classroom.

Chapter 13a

Social Cognition and Prosocial Behavior

Introduction

The acquisition of facts, concepts, operations, and problem-solving strategies in academic subjects is an accepted goal of education. Intellectual achievement is rarely the sole product of formal schooling, however. In the classroom children also learn to build friendships with classmates, to form social contracts, to cooperate with each other, and to follow rules. Social skills are thus also an important outcome of education.

Learning social skills is important for a number of reasons. First, a society cannot survive without social order, which is based on standards of conduct and interpersonal interaction. We must be able to form agreements with one another and predict each other's behavior. Without some agreement and standards of conduct, we would have social anarchy. All societies thus have rules that specify acceptable behaviors, such as assisting others, protecting the less fortunate, and behaving morally, along with rules prohibiting unacceptable behaviors like stealing, aggression, and damaging another's property. To become functioning adults, children must learn this rule system. Second, rules are necessary for smooth operation in the classroom, just as they are in the larger society. Respect for the rights of others, sharing, and cooperating are valued classroom behaviors; destruction, aggression, and cruelty are forbidden. Children learn social rules in the classroom as part of their overall socialization for the rules of society. Third, on the more practical side, a teacher cannot teach unless there is some semblance of order in the classroom. If a teacher faced thirty children without establishing standards of conduct, imagine the chaos, disorder, and disruption that would occur. Management of the social system of the classroom is essential for effective instruction.

The next two chapters deal with classroom management, but they differ from the usual treatment of the subject. Discussions about classroom management typically focus on procedures for controlling and eliminating disruptive and undesired behavior in students: (1) how to prevent Johnny from hitting Sarah, (2) how to deal with Terry's stealing, (3) how to handle Sue's yelling and swearing, and (4) how to confront and manage cheating. The emphasis is on getting rid of inappropriate behavior. Procedures for decreasing behavior were presented in Chapters 3a and 3b. The suppression of behavior, however, does not teach an appropriate alternative; it is an unconstructive approach. Accordingly, we have chosen a different tack here: We will focus on the acquisition of positive forms of social behavior. A child who has incorporated a moral and social code of conduct is less likely to steal, physically attack another, or cheat on a test. How children acquire these prosocial competencies and how teachers can promote prosocial development are the focuses of our discussion.

What Is Prosocial Behavior?

Prosocial behaviors are types of responses that a society values. The behaviors considered prosocial vary across specific cultural, subcultural, and historical contexts, but certain themes of conduct are common to most, if not all. Morality, for example, is generally included in this behavior class, as are *empathy, cooperation*, and *altruism*. You are probably familiar with these behavioral concepts. Specifying the exact behaviors that exemplify morality or empathy is more difficult, however. Are you sure you could identify an altruistic act if you saw one? Although most of us feel intuitively that we know what prosocial behavior is, our conceptions of it are imprecise. In fact, the issue of defining these behaviors has attracted extensive discussion and debate (Anderson & Messick, 1974; Wispe, 1972).

We can demonstrate this problem with an example. A teenager on a remote strip of beach sees an adult struggling to swim beyond the breakers. The swimmer appears to be having trouble. Although the teenager is not a particularly strong swimmer, she enters the water anyway and rescues the endangered person at considerable risk to herself. The rescued man is, to say the least, grateful. He rewards the teenager financially and informs the press of the heroic deed; the rescuer is honored by the community, accepts a reward from the victim, and enjoys a brief flurry of public acclaim. Would this incident be an altruistic act, an example of prosocial behavior? Altruism has been defined as consisting of self-sacrificial acts performed without expectation of reward (Mussen & Eisenberg-Berg, 1977). Did our teenager make a self-sacrifice? Did she expect the reward she received? These questions are hard to answer, because they involve motivations and intentions that cannot be observed directly.

Problems with definitions are rarely an issue in everyday conduct. The teenager has performed a good deed and saved another person. Definitions are, however, of concern to psychological investigators who study how and why people acquire prosocial behavior. Psychologists using objective methods must know a prosocial act when they see one, especially if they assume that these behaviors are in some way special and different.

Prosocial Behavior and Psychological Study

The way people acquire the capacity to behave prosocially is a research topic of great interest to psychologists. It is also a focus of debate and differences of opinion, for a number of reasons. First, prosocial behaviors are important for the survival of social systems, so we have an emotional interest in them as well as an objective, scientific interest. Second, children's acquisition of these competencies is of concern not only to psychologists but to parents, teachers, and others as well. Third, prosocial behaviors may be uniquely human acts uncharacteristic of other animal species, so understanding this uniqueness may help us understand something of the nature of human beings.

Psychological investigations of behaviors of broad social interest are influenced by philosophy and by people's attitudes. You will recall that in Chapter 6a we discussed two basic models of man, the mechanistic and the organismic models, which serve as philosophical bases for the study of children's cognitive development. These underlying philosophical views directly influence objective empirical study. The same situation exists with respect to prosocial behavior and development. Two philosophical models have given rise to two approaches to prosocial research and two bodies of empirical evidence. If we wish to understand this important class of behaviors, we need to examine the basis and products of both.

Basic Psychological Questions About Prosocial Behavior

To place the scientific examination of prosocial behavior in perspective, we must examine the questions that generate the studies in the first place. Knowing the questions enables us to evaluate the evidence more effectively.

The Major Question

The main goal of any psychological study is to identify the cause or causes of a class of behaviors. We often ask whether a behavior is the result of external environmental conditions or some internal characteristics or trait of the person. We encountered a similar question in our discussions of learning theory, cognitive development, and language. With respect to prosocial behaviors, we wish to know why people behave positively. Is it because of environmental demands or basic personality characteristics? This, however, is a big question that can be answered neither easily nor directly. To use an empirical approach, we must break the general question into more specific questions that are more amenable to study.

The Situational Specificity Issue.   Is a person's social behavior consistent across situations? Does an honest person behave honestly in every setting, for example? If we answer yes to that question, we would expect that supposedly honest people would refrain from stealing from other people, shoplifting, or cheating on their income taxes. If we

Cheating behavior may be situation-specific or it may be a consistent behavior across situations. If the cheating is situation-specific, changing the factors in the situation that precipitate cheating will eliminate the behavior. The elimination of consistent cheating behavior will require a more extended treatment program.

answer no, we would be unable to assume that a person who refrained from stealing from close friends would also refrain from cheating on taxes. The person's actions would depend on the circumstances. We are asking here about the *situational specificity* of overt behavior—whether a person behaves with any degree of consistency in different situations. Investigators who believe that people are consistent watch the individual for constant factors that transcend situational differences. They look for *person variables* that would explain consistency in behavior. Those who believe that people behave inconsistently, on the other hand, seek to explain the inconsistency by means of *environmental variables* that differ across situations.

One way of trying to gather evidence on the consistency question is to look for a relationship, a correlation, between behaviors assessed in different settings. As you recall from Chapter 2a, correlational information fails to reveal cause-and-effect relationships, but discovering a correlation between two variables is a first step to finding such a relationship. A positive correlation between similar behaviors in different settings is evidence of behavioral consistency even if we lack an understanding of the cause of the consistency.

The empirical literature on consistency in prosocial behavior includes evidence of both specificity and consistency (Mischel, 1968; Rushton, 1976). There are only moderate correlations between different prosocial behaviors (for example, r's = $+.40$). This indicates that there is some consistency but considerable inconsistency as well. All we can conclude from the data is that prosocial behavior is neither totally consistent nor totally random. Unfortunately, this conclusion provides a very unsatisfactory answer to our initial question.

Since we can use the data to support either consistency or inconsistency, the question changes: Is it more important to explain observed consistency or observed inconsistency? We cannot answer this question on the basis of empirical evidence alone because it is a question about philosophical values. Psychologists with organismic leanings examine the consistency component, whereas mechanistically oriented investigators examine the environmental variables associated with inconsistency.

The Uniqueness of the Behavior Issue. Are prosocial behaviors special, different from other behaviors? Those who say yes search for a special explanation of these responses, one that differs from explanations of other behaviors. Those who say no believe that explanations developed from the study of other responses would apply to these behaviors as well. Again, preference is a philosophical decision, not just an empirical one. Preference does, however, influence further investigation.

The Causal Process Issue.   Are prosocial behaviors learned directly? Researchers who answer affirmatively focus their investigations on learning principles that explain the acquisition of the behaviors. These psychologists typically conduct learning studies in which they attempt to teach children to perform prosocially. Those who answer negatively face a second question: If prosocial behaviors are not learned directly, how are they acquired? Most of these psychologists attribute acquisition to developmental processes.

Two Psychological Perspectives

Essentially, we have outlined three questions:

1. Is prosocial behavior consistent or situationally specific, and which is more important?
2. Are prosocial behaviors unique responses that require a unique explanation?
3. Are prosocial behaviors learned directly, or do they develop in a broader context?

The answers to these three questions comprise a set of directives that influence empirical study. In evaluating the research evidence, we must keep the investigator's initial presuppositions in mind. Part of our knowledge base was developed on the basis of one set of answers and part on the basis of a different set.

The Cognitive-Developmental Perspective

In Chapter 6a, you learned about the Piagetian position on the development of cognitive functioning. Piaget had a lot to say about social development as well. In fact, his theory has broad implications about the growth of positive social behaviors, including altruism, morality, empathy, helping, and sharing. These implications have generated a great deal of empirical work. Before we describe the research and the theoretical explanations associated with it, you should recall some basic points about this psychological perspective:

1. It is primarily a developmental approach, one that describes and explains human accomplishments associated with increasing maturity.
2. Behavioral accomplishments reflect the state of developing mental structures. These structures have a pervasive influence on what the child is able to do at any given time.
3. Children's knowledge of their world results from a complex construction process, not from direct learning of facts and rules.

The General Issues

Is prosocial behavior consistent or situationally specific, and which is more important? Internal cognitive structure, a characteristic of the person, is the focus of cognitive-developmental interest. Cognitive structures change with age, but not with situation. At a given developmental level, structures are thus relatively consistent and stable. If structure is regarded as the source of behavior, stable structures should be associated with consistent behavior. Logically, then, it seems that cognitive developmentalists would answer our question by stressing *consistency.*

Are prosocial behaviors unique responses that require a unique explanation? Generally, the answer from this theoretical perspective would be no, since specific behaviors, whether social, affective, or cognitive, all reflect the same underlying mental structures. The structures evolve and change with development. These changes are then reflected in logical, social, and moral reasoning (Piaget, 1950), which are all aspects of overall cognitive functioning.

Are these behaviors learned directly, or do they develop in a broader context? By now you should be able to answer this question easily. Behavior develops in a broad context. Behavioral change occurs not as a direct result of learning but through an equilibration process determined by biological functioning and active interaction with the physical and social environment.

Research on Perspective-Taking

The answers to these general issue questions affect research investigations. Since this system treats cognitive and social development as interdependent, for example, an underlying competence that ties the two classes of behavior together must be found. Why would the behaviors be similar unless there was some basic link between them? The link is the ability to understand another person's perspective and coordinate that perspective with one's own (Piaget, 1932; Bearison & Isaacs, 1975). Logically, it seems unlikely that a person would cooperate, lend support, offer aid, or make a self-sacrifice if he or she lacked understanding of another's needs, point of view, or feelings. This ability, referred to as *role-taking,* is an essential prerequisite to the production of prosocial behavior.

At least two types of role-taking have been identified. The first is *perceptual* role-taking or visual perspective-taking. Piaget assessed this ability with the three-mountain problem (Piaget & Inhelder, 1956). In this task, which you may recall from Chapter 6a, the child is presented with a three-dimensional model of a landscape scene containing three distinct mountains. Sitting on one side and seeing only one side of the scene, the child must predict the way the scene looks from other positions. Researchers have varied the task in a number of ways (Salatas & Flavell, 1976; Borke, 1975), but the problem for the child remains essentially the same.

A second type of role-taking is assessed in connection with socially oriented tasks that tap conceptual role-taking. In these tasks, children are required to predict another person's thoughts and cognitions rather than what the other sees (Chandler & Greenspan, 1972; Urberg & Docherty, 1976). Researchers use a variety of tasks to assess this conceptual ability, including stories (Feffer & Gourevitch, 1960; Selman & Byrne, 1974) and games (DeVries, 1970; Flavell, Botkin, Fry, Wright, & Jarvis, 1968). An experimenter may, for example, tell a child a story in which a character has an experience we commonly associate with an emotional reaction, such as happiness (going to a birthday party), sadness (losing money down a drain), anger (being pushed around by a bully), or fear (encountering a vicious dog). The stories can become quite complex and include a number of characters who experience a variety of different emotions. After hearing the story, the subject is asked to indicate the feelings of the characters. To do this successfully, the subject must place himself or herself in another person's shoes and predict that person's perspective, in this case an emotional one.

Whether the content of the task is visual, social, or cognitive, in order to solve it the child requires basically the same ability. Essentially, the child encounters a problem in which he or she (X) and another (O) experience cognitions that are different or in conflict. If X can still predict O's cognitive state and explain why O is in that state, the child is judged to possess this ability. When the content is visual, success is considered as evidence of projective spatial knowledge. When the content is social or emotional, the tasks assess *empathy*, a prosocial behavior.

Investigators examine these abilities in children to find out when children can demonstrate success and to describe the sequence of children's development. Generally, children are unsuccessful at these tasks until about age seven or eight, when they enter the stage of concrete operations. This delay in success at such tasks is considered evidence of the young child's *egocentrism*, the inability to comprehend the perspective of anyone other than self. Gradually, the child develops the ability to *decenter* and to infer the thoughts of others in a variety of complex situations (Feffer, 1970). It is not, however, until the onset of formal operations in adolescence that sophisticated social perspective-taking inferences appear reliably (Chandler & Greenspan, 1972).

These developmental findings have some dramatic implications. Remember that at least theoretically, role-taking serves as the basis for other forms of prosocial reasoning and conduct. If young children are pervasively egocentric, we cannot expect them to display empathy, altruism, helping, or a host of other desirable qualities. Needless to say, many people find it hard to accept this picture of childhood partly because it often appears to contradict naturalistic observation.. Those who support an innate human empathetic motive (Hoffman, 1977) or those who have observed apparent prosocial behavior in very young children (Borke, 1978) may find the conclusion unwarranted.

A number of investigators have in fact collected data that challenge this theoretical conclusion. Borke (1971), for example, found evidence of nonegocentric behavior even in preschool children when the tasks employed were simplified. Instead of asking children to describe the emotional states of characters in a story, Borke asked them to point to pictures of faces that expressed the possible emotions. Even young children were fairly successful in distinguishing generally happy and generally unhappy affective states. Eisenberg-Berg and Neal (1979) also found evidence of a primitive empathetic reasoning in young children. Studies that support the construct of egocentrism and studies that challenge it, however, often differ in many ways. Different kinds of tasks are used, and some are more complex than others, so their results are not easy to coordinate. In general, children tend to fail on the complex tasks and succeed on the simpler ones.

Since task differences and conflicting results seem to coincide, others have tried to discover whether there are any clear relationships between the various measures that all supposedly tap perspective-taking. Correlations between measures of this ability are typically low (Ford, 1979). Apparently, the research tasks designed to measure empathy actually measure different abilities, and not all measure the same ones. To some extent, this places the construct of egocentrism in question and definitely raises questions about the measures used. Whether or not children display an egocentric orientation seems to depend on the specific circumstances. Could it be that egocentric behavior is situationally specific?

Research on Correspondence

Another way to examine prosocial behavior is to see whether there is an empirical as well as a logical relationship beween perspective-taking and other indices of prosocialness. If empathy truly underlies other prosocial behaviors, such as altruism, cooperation, and sharing, then measures of the first should correlate with measures of the second (see Rushton, 1976, for a review).

Several investigators have addressed the relationship question. Many have found a significant positive correlation between role-taking and moral reasoning (Ambron & Irwin, 1975; Lee, 1971; Selman, 1971; Rubin & Schneider, 1973), and between empathy and cooperation (Marcus, Tellen, & Roke, 1979; Johnson, 1975). Sometimes role-taking correlates positively with altruism as well (Rubin & Schneider, 1973; Krebs, 1975; Buckley, Siegel, & Ness, 1979). Some experimental studies suggest that when children are trained in general perspective-taking, they show a corresponding improvement in other prosocial behaviors, such as sharing (Ianotti, 1978). A positive relationship between perspective-taking and prosocial behavior is not always found, however (Zahn-Waxler, Radke-Yarrow, & Brady-Smith, 1977), and even when it is, the correlations are not very strong (typically $r = .40$ to $.60$). What does this mean?

You may recall that when a correlation coefficient is squared (r^2), the resulting quantity indicates how much variance two behavioral measures have in common. When the correlation between a measure of empathy and a measure of another prosocial behavior is .50, twenty-five percent of the variance is explained and seventy-five percent remains unexplained. In terms of the consistency-specificity issue, then, we see some consistency but a great deal of inconsistency as well. Piagetian theory gives us some idea of the reason we find consistency, but an explanation of the sizable unexplained variability still eludes us. Accordingly, in order to search further for answers we must consider bodies of research conducted by investigators who would respond differently to the three initial questions.

The Learning Theory Perspective

Learning psychologists use different methods to study children's behavior than do cognitive-developmentalists. They may, for example, measure the behavior differently, they usually attempt to train the behavior, and they focus on those aspects of the situation that promote appropriate responses. These techniques differ from the descriptive and correlational methods typically adopted by developmentalists, who relate behavioral change to increases in age and maturity.

The way the behavior is assessed is important because it reveals to us what investigators from the two perspectives are really investigating. If they are actually studying different aspects of behavior, then findings that appear contradictory may not necessarily be in conflict. Cognitive-developmentalists focus on the growing child's reasoning and, to a lesser extent, on performances associated with the reasoning. This choice of focus is a logical one, because in order to describe the internal organization of the mental structures and the accompanying thought processes, one must select a behavior that reveals thinking. A likely candidate for reflecting thought is verbal reasoning. In many studies of empathy, for example, the child is asked to explain how another person feels. Developmental studies investigate less frequently what the child will do as a consequence of the way another feels, but this focus—the child's performance in a given situation—is typical of learning studies. After all, what people reason should be done and what they actually perform do not always match. A person may be able to predict when another needs assistance, but actually providing the assistance is a further step, another behavior. Cognitive-developmentalists and learning psychologists may thus not even be studying the same behavior.

The General Issues

Is prosocial behavior consistent or situationally specific, and which is more important? Mischel (1973) proposes that observed social behaviors should be considered in terms of *person variables*, which may be cognitive, and *situational variables*, which are environmental. Consistency in behavior is attributable to person variables and to similarities across situations. Situation-specific behavior results from differences in environmental settings. Most learning studies try to determine the specific environmental factors that affect behavior or the way certain person variables combine with situational variables to change behavior. In general, however, specificity is the more characteristic target.

Are prosocial behaviors unique responses that require a unique explanation? Behaviorally oriented learning psychologists would answer this question the same way that cognitive-developmentalists would, but for different reasons. Learning principles like reinforcement, extinction, and imitation apply to all operant behaviors. One need not develop a unique set of psychological processes for any one behavior when a general set can apply to all of them.

Are these behaviors directly learned, or are they developed in a broader context? Learning is the mechanism for behavioral change and skill acquisition. Learning is also the mechanism for developmental accomplishments, but the changes we associate with development are less formal and less structured, and they take more time than those we refer to as learned. The same set of psychological principles is associated with both, however.

Learning Research on Prosocial Behaviors

Learning psychologists believe that prosocial behaviors are acquired through socialization. Accordingly, they want to know which specific socialization practices promote prosocial performances. Features of the environment and characteristics of socializing agents in that environment thus become important factors to study. The stimulus features commonly addressed are (1) models, (2) response consequences, and (3) verbal instructions. The relationship between these stimulus features and subsequent behavior is typically studied in a laboratory-like setting where the experimenter has control, in the hope of being able to draw cause-and-effect conclusions about the way a given stimulus affects responding. Most commonly, the behavior in question is

Empathy and cooperation are prosocial behaviors that are valued by
society and encouraged by the schools. Like other behaviors, these
are learned and the same principles of learning that apply to other
types of learning apply to these behaviors.

some performance related to altruism, such as sharing, donating, or
assisting.

Altruism is a logical target behavior. It is valued socially and involves a performance that is observable directly, unlike empathy, which
involves reasoning rather than doing. Even altruism presents some
problems, however. In defining altruism, cognitive-developmentalists
emphasize its self-sacrificial nature; that is, it is not reinforced. In an
operant learning paradigm, however, responses are emitted precisely
because of past reinforcement; the notion that a behavior occurs in the
absence of past reinforcement poses a paradox. Can one truly be certain
that reinforcement is absent, however? The reinforcing stimuli may be
extremely subtle, self-delivered, or expected. A behavior may be on a
thin reinforcement schedule that has made it resistant to extinction,
or altruistic behavior may have become a generalized reinforcer. It is
apparently impossible to prove the presence or absence of reinforcement. Learning-based research avoids this dilemma by selecting narrow definitions based on what most of us would generally accept as
altruistic performances.

In an early study of one aspect of altruism, Fischer (1963) trained preschoolers to share with an unknown peer by rewarding the desired response with bubblegum; this extrinsic reinforcer proved effective. Social reinforcers have also worked with children in other studies of donating behaviors (Bryan & London, 1970). In a more recent study (Hartmann *et al.*, 1976), aversive response consequences were used in order to increase the donating behavior of ten-year-olds. In this study, failure to donate resulted in a fine and an explanation of the contingency. A number of investigators have examined the effects of providing children with altruistic models (for example, Bryan, 1970; Rosenhan & White, 1967; Hartup & Coates, 1967). Most of these studies have been based on the modeling principles outlined by Bandura (1969, 1977b), which were presented in Chapter 4a. When children are exposed to altruistic models, their own donating behavior typically increases. Models are a more powerful source of behavior change than instructions or preaching (Bryan & Walbek, 1970a, 1970b). Whether or not the model is reinforced seems not to be particularly important to the observer's subsequent behavior (Elliot & Vasta, 1970). More important, in some studies the change in children's altruistic behavior seems to last over time (Rushton, 1975; Grusec, Saas-Kortsaak, & Simutis, 1978) and to carry over to settings outside the laboratory (Bryan & Test, 1967).

Although reinforcement and modeling studies both show us that situational demands do affect children's prosocial behavior, a problem remains. For the most part, these investigations take place under laboratory or laboratory-like conditions. The results tell us how the response can be facilitated under similar conditions, but not how children acquire them in the natural course of development. Studies undertaken in nonlaboratory environments are much rarer (for example, Friedrich & Stein, 1975), and their outcomes are less dramatic (Yarrow, Scott, & Waxler, 1973).

Other researchers have tried to investigate the interaction between cognitive person variables and such environmental factors as reinforcement and models. This research is designed to determine whether the child's interpretation of the situation has any influence on behavior. Interpretation is a cognitive event occurring within the individual, not a stimulus event in the environment. It has been demonstrated that interpretation does influence altruistic behavior (Barnett, King, & Howard, 1979; Peterson, Hartmann, & Gelfand, 1977), a fact that reemphasizes the need to examine both the person and the situation.

We have, then, two bodies of empirical literature, learning studies and developmental studies. One body examines prosocial performance and the other prosocial reasoning; we cannot afford to ignore either (Rushton, 1976). To develop a set of guidelines for practice, we must integrate information from the two sources (Rosser, 1981).

Integrating the Empirical Evidence

Taken as a whole, the research literature suggests that the production of prosocial behavior depends upon a number of factors. The subject's developmental level influences the reasoning associated with prosocial responding; such situational variables as models and reinforcement contingencies affect the production of the prosocial act. The child's interpretation of a social event has an influence, too; this last element involves information-processing. All these facets are probably involved in any given prosocial performance.

To demonstrate how each of these elements might be involved, let us return to the example of the teenage rescuer. Before the swimmer could actually react and save the victim, she would have to interpret the event and make some decision. First she would have to observe the victim's struggle and understand that these behavioral cues were signals of distress. This step involves processing and interpreting behavioral information. A young child might not be able to interpret the victim's signals. Second, the rescuer would need to infer the victim's feelings or those feelings she herself would have in the same situation. This involves perspective-taking, and again a younger person might be incapable of the inference. Third, the rescuer must decide on a plan of action, a performance. The act of rescue itself may depend upon past learning. Has the rescuer learned through past instruction, exposure to models, or previous reinforcement that saving the victim is the socially desired thing to do? All three things would need to occur before a prosocial performance could reasonably be expected.

To give another example, suppose that Oliver Oblivious is approaching the entrance to the school. He may enter through one of three doors. At the door to Oliver's far right, a student in a wheelchair is trying to open the door. The handicapped student seems to be having some difficulty, however, and he has dropped his books. Oliver is faced with a choice. He could walk in through the door directly ahead of him and ignore the struggles of the other person, or he could decide to engage in a prosocial response and assist the handicapped person. For Oliver to make the prosocial decision, three things must happen: (1) he must perceive the other person's signals for need, (2) he must understand the perspective implied by the signals, and (3) he must choose to help. Oliver is eight. What do you think he would do, and why?

We cannot conceptualize this process in terms of decision-making. A decision to act depends on steps involving developmental level, information-processing, and past learning history. Each step could affect the final decision. This conceptualization is depicted in Figure 13a–1.

According to this view, prosocial performances are not simple responses. They depend, rather, on several abilities that must occur together. Development, information-processing abilities, and past learning history could all limit people's performance choices. The results of

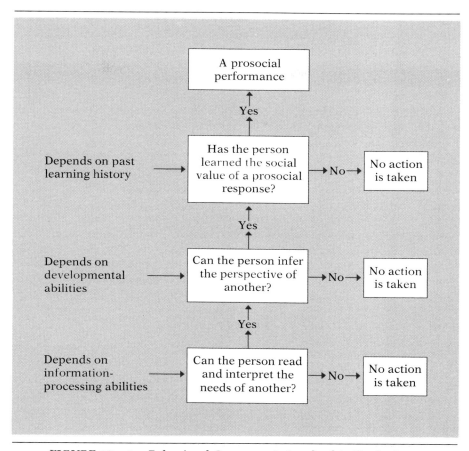

FIGURE 13a–1. **Behavioral Components Involved in Producing a Prosocial Response**

cognitive-developmental studies tell us what reasoning capacities we can expect at any point in the developmental cycle. Learning research findings bear on experiences affecting performance, and research on the interaction of cognitive and situational variables suggests specifics of the decision-making process.

With this conceptualization in mind, let us return to the three basic questions and available empirical data.

The General Issues Reexamined

Is prosocial behavior consistent or situationally specific, and which is more important? According to a decision-making model, both consistency and specificity in actual behavior can be expected. Developmental abilities in perspective-taking are probably age-related and thus would contribute to consistency at the reasoning level. An individual's learning history is a constant that contributes to consistency as well. The cues in the particular situation and the way those cues are interpreted can, however, be expected to vary from incident to incident. When cues and interpretations of cues vary, so does behavior. This explanation, then, fits with virtually all the available data.

Are prosocial behaviors unique responses that require a unique explanation? No, they are like other behaviors associated with decision-making. All behaviors involve interpreting environmental cues in accordance with developmental capacities and past learning.

Are these behaviors directly learned, or are they developed in a broader context? Both. The evidence from developmental studies strongly indicates that perspective-taking abilities are related to general cognitive development. Information-processing capacities are probably related to development as well. The interpretation and reasoning components of prosocial behavior are thus developmental phenomena. Learning-based research clearly tells us, however, that environmental contingencies and general learning principles affect performances. Within the limitations of their cognitive development, children's prosocial behavior is probably determined by learning.

Can Prosocial Behavior Be Influenced?

Learning research indicates clearly that the environment does affect children's prosocial performances. Instructions, reinforcement, models, and directions all have an effect on children's behavior, so these variables are relevant to attempts to change behavior. All these environmental events are sources of information. A child may not know how to use these sources, however. The effect information has on the child's reasoning may vary depending on the child's developmental processes. Moreover, we still lack precise understanding of the link between reasoning and performance. We might be able to alter the reasoning process directly once we understand it more fully. In general, though, our actions as socializing agents play an important role, given the child's developmental limitations. If Oliver had observed his teacher assist those in need, had been reinforced previously for giving help, or had been told about the importance of helping, he would probably open the door for the student in the wheelchair.

The Special Case of Moral Reasoning

The development of moral reasoning in children is also related to prosocial behavior. The moral aspect of behavior has been examined and written about so much, however, that it deserves separate discussion. The same issues surface here: (1) the developmental sequence, (2) the relationship between reasoning and behaving, and (3) the mechanisms of behavior change. Again, the research findings are controversial, but they are already having an influence, warranted or not, on educational practice.

Piaget on Moral Development

Piaget in an early work (1932) turned his attention to the development of moral thought. He distinguished two levels or stages of moral reasoning after examining how children deal with rules and how they judge transgressions. The first is the stage of *moral realism*, which coincides with the preoperational period described in Chapter 6a. Children in the moral realism stage see rules as absolute and unchangeable rather than as the outcome of social agreement. They assume that rules are sacred, that breaking rules results in automatic punishment, and that actions are either totally right or totally wrong. Theirs is a black and white moral system with no grey areas. In addition, young children believe that everyone thinks the same way. This notion is consistent with the assumption of egocentrism. Whether a particular action is judged right or wrong depends on its consequences, whether it violates rules, and whether it is punished.

Suppose, for example, that a subject is presented with a pair of stories. In one story, a child is helping his mother set the table when he accidentally drops a pile of plates, breaking five of them. In the second story, a child who is sneaking a snack in the kitchen knocks one plate on the floor and breaks it. The subject must determine which child has performed the more serious transgression, the worse deed. Children functioning at the stage of moral realism judge the child who broke five plates as the naughtiest. The magnitude of the damage, five broken plates, is the more serious consequence. That the child was trying to help his mother is irrelevant to the moral realist; the intentions behind an act are not considered at this level. To take intentions into account, the child must be able to adopt another's perspective, something that is impossible during the egocentric preoperational period. Since information about intentions is unavailable for decision-making, the decision must be made on the basis of the evidence that is available to the child—five broken plates as opposed to one broken plate.

The second stage in the Piagetian system coincides with the concrete operational period and is called *autonomous morality*, or moral relativism. At this level, children see rules as relative and alterable, depending on the social context. They know that actions must be assessed with the intentions of the actor in mind. Accordingly, more mature children see the child who broke one plate as the naughty one, since his intention was to sneak a snack rather than to help his mother.

Once a child can take another's perspective, information about intention may be used in making judgments.

Movement from the first to the second stage of moral reasoning results from changes in cognitive ability associated with the equilibration process. You will recall that experience is important to equilibration, since it is the source of the cognitive conflict that the child must coordinate. The social experiences of children thus provide fuel for the development of more mature social and moral reasoning.

Kohlberg on Moral Development

Lawrence Kohlberg (1958, 1969) is a cognitive developmentalist who has expanded and elaborated on Piaget's original work. Like Piaget, Kohlberg is concerned with moral reasoning. Kohlberg, however, outlines three levels of two stages each. His sequence of moral development thus has six steps. A child's position in the sequence is determined on the basis of his response to a story about a moral dilemma. In the stories featuring these dilemmas, a character is faced with a difficult moral choice. The child's task is to recommend a decision and, more important, provide a rationale for the decision. The rationale reveals the child's moral reasoning, which can then be categorized.

A typical moral dilemma is included in the story about Heinz. Heinz's wife will die unless she obtains a certain drug; only one pharmacist has the drug. The pharmacist will give Heinz the drug only for a very high price that Heinz cannot possibly afford. Heinz has a problem. Should he steal the drug, or should he let his wife die? Kohlberg is interested not in the decision a child recommends but in the justification for the decision. The child's justification is external evidence of moral reasoning, which in turn reveals cognitive structure.

The first level of Kohlberg's system is the preconventional level. At this level, judgments are made on the basis of external rules—to avoid punishment, or to obtain rewards. Either decision might be made on the basis of preconventional reasoning. In one decision, Heinz would be punished for stealing—recommendation: do not steal the drug. Heinz might, however, also be punished for letting his wife die—recommendation: steal. The defining feature of the preconventional level is the use of avoidance of punishment as a rationale, not the specific recommendation. A child at Stage 2 of the preconventional level would be more inclined to make a recommendation on the basis of anticipated benefits rather than on the basis of avoidance of punishment alone.

At the second level, *conventional morality*, judgments are based on the conventional social order and the expectations of others. At Stage 3, this involves a concern for social approval; at Stage 4, it includes social responsibility. While younger children typically provide preconventional justifications, most adults attain the conventional level (Kohlberg, 1976).

Research Report

For at least the last ten years the major impetus behind research on moral reasoning has been Kohlberg's theory of moral development, which we have discussed in this chapter. Kohlberg's stages of growth are based on a series of moral dilemmas about the conflict associated with possible violation of a prohibition. The dilemmas concern laws, rules, and regulations, and thus tap the reasoning of regulation-breaking. Moral reasoning can, however, involve other varieties of conflicts. Deciding whether to assist another person, for example, is a moral issue; it does not involve the violation of a prohibition. Does prosocial moral reasoning reveal the same stages and rationales found with prohibition-oriented dilemmas?

Eisenberg-Berg chose to examine the development of prosocial moral reasoning. She wanted to determine whether the sequence and content of children's reasoning in response to non-prohibition situations would differ from what Kohlberg had found.

Subjects in the study were 125 boys and girls in the second through the twelfth grades who responded to four stories concerning a prosocial moral dilemma. The stories varied in theme but were similar in conflict. Each involved a setting in which a character had the opportunity to assist another at a net cost to himself or herself. Subjects were asked to decide what the story character should do and to justify the recommendation.

Response protocols were scored with a detailed multi-categorical coding system. The system was similar to Kohlberg's but the categories were weighted equally. In this system of scoring, therefore, no one category was considered more advanced or better than another, an approach that is different from Kohlberg's.

The data analysis procedures used were sophisticated, elaborate, and beyond the scope of this discussion. The full findings were equally elaborate; we shall therefore highlight just a few. First, elementary school children's reasoning tended to be hedonistic; but with increasing age, empathetic reasoning increased. Second, empathy and concern for the needs of others was reflected in much of both the elementary school and high school students' reasoning, including that of the second graders. Third, virtually none of the children verbalized the authority-oriented considerations that would be consistent with Kohlberg's Stage 1.

The author concluded that the early development of prosocial moral reasoning probably differs from that associated with the prohibition type. Moreover, empathetic responding no doubt plays an important role in the development of a prosocial orientation. It is interesting, in this respect, that nearly all students who advocated a non-prosocial story resolution supported it with hedonistic, non-empathetic reasoning.

Eisenberg-Berg, Nancy, The development of children's prosocial moral judgment, *Developmental Psychology*, 1979, 15, No. 2, 128–137.

At the final, *post-conventional* level, moral reasoning is based on an internal set of ethical principles. Few people reach this level. Judgments at Stage 5 are made on the basis of respect for the larger social system and at Stage 6 on adherence to abstract ethics.

Implications and Evaluation

According to Kohlberg, the sequence of moral development is linear and invariant, and it coincides with increasing cognitive maturity. Kohlberg also contends that the sequence is universal, not specific to Western culture. The implications of these assumptions are (1) that moral development moves forward only—people never regress to a less advanced level, and (2) the sequence is the same in all cultures. Furthermore, there is an implicit assumption that moral behavior is based on moral reasoning, but it is reasoning, not behavior, that is assessed.

Empirical evidence raises some questions about the validity of these assumptions. In general, the sequence seems to reflect the evidence, but both stage-skipping and regression to earlier stages have been noted in the research literature (Holstein, 1972; Kuhn, 1976). The universality has also been questioned (Simpson, 1974). Moreover, it seems that very few people ever reach the higher levels of functioning. One might question the validity of a system for representing human behavior that includes categories in which few people can be included.

Others have criticized Kohlberg on methodological grounds (Kurtines & Greif, 1974). Kohlberg works with open-ended verbal protocols. Protocols of this type can be very difficult to code; often, some of the data fail to fit the classification system. When data are uncodable or can be coded in more than one way, problems of reliability and consistency arise. Trying for greater objectivity, Kohlberg has refined his system in recent years (1976), but methodological problems remain. It may be that his stages are evident only when this particular kind of measurement device is used; if so, his stages are instrument-specific. If this is the case, Kohlberg's moral sequence may have very restricted generality. It may be a theory of moral dilemma responses instead of a theory of morality in a broader sense.

Kohlberg's dilemmas are further restricted in generality because they focus on constraints and the morality of constraints—for example, deciding to transgress a rule. Moral reasoning is also involved in selecting prosocial acts independent of specific rules—for example, deciding to help someone when avoiding giving help does not involve breaking a rule, as in the situation that confronted Oliver. Prosocial moral reasoning apparently fails to follow the same developmental course as the constraint-oriented variety (Eisenberg-Berg, 1979; Eisenberg-Berg & Neal, 1979). A theory that fits only one kind of moral reasoning with one kind of assessment device may be of very limited usefulness.

Perhaps the most serious issue is one we have raised before, the relationship between verbal reasoning and actual behavior. As we discovered in our more general treatment of prosocial behavior, these are probably related somehow, but the exact relationship remains unclear.

New Directions in Research

The area of prosocial behavior development is currently very popular. As a result, a number of recent research summaries have been published about the topic (see, for example, Bar-Tal, 1976; Eisenberg-Berg, 1982b; Staub, 1979), and it appears that this research area will continue to be a lively one. What will be the future focus?

It is fairly clear that the role of cognition in behaving prosocially is still a very important research focus in many studies (for example, Krebs & Gilmore, 1982). That role is of interest to those operating from a cognitive-developmental perspective (for example, Turiel, 1978; Eisenberg-Berg, 1982a), and represents the continuation of the research tradition begun in the seventies. There is a possibility

that these contents are attracting the interest of those operating within an information-processing framework as well (Rosser, 1981; 1982).

A recent thrust, with a few past examples, is a move to conduct research on prosocial behaviors not in the laboratory but in natural settings. Rather than employing structured (and perhaps artificial) tasks, investigators want to observe children's prosocial behavior in schools and preschools (Eisenberg-Berg, 1982b; Bar-Tal, Raviv, & Goldberg, 1982). This research, with an emphasis on increased ecological validity, naturalistic development, and other less obtrusive observation procedures, is a direction to watch.

The issue can be raised again with respect to both Kohlberg and Piaget: Does moral reasoning reflect actual moral behavior? Again, we note only a modest relationship (Mischel & Mischel, 1976; Mussen & Eisenberg-Berg, 1977), even for prosocial moral reasoning (Eisenberg-Berg & Hand, 1979). Until more evidence is accumulated and these issues are clarified, we must suspend final judgments.

Summary

To integrate and summarize the information we have presented in this chapter, let us return to the questions we began with.

Is prosocial behavior consistent or situationally specific, and which is more important? We would have to say that both are involved and both are important. Research evidence indicates that there is some consistency, perhaps because of an underlying cognitive process that affects what we do. Cognitive developmentalists suggest that the consistency is due to reasoning, either moral reasoning or perspective-taking. Learning research tells us about the role of environmental variables: reinforcement, models, and instruction. When these variables change, so does behavior, but not like a weathervane in a thunderstorm. Internal processes place constraints on change, but environmental variables contribute to the moderate degree of flexibility in behavior that we observe regularly.

Are prosocial behaviors unique responses that require a unique explanation? Yes and no. Since reasoning is somehow involved in prosocial and moral behavior, these responses are similar in some respects to other cognitive processes. They probably differ from less complex behaviors, however. They may also be uniquely human responses; this issue is still open to debate.

Are these behaviors learned directly, or are they developed in a broader context? Again we must answer both ways. The existence of developmental sequences for perspective-taking and moral reasoning has generally been substantiated by the empirical evidence. A process like equilibration is thus probably involved in acquisition; equilibration involves both experience and the maturation of cognitive structures. Development places the limits on modifiability. Learning research indicates clearly, however, that behavior can be changed through direct training efforts. Learning as well as maturation is involved. To fully understand and hence to facilitate prosocial and moral behavior, we need to account for both sources of influence.

TEACHING SCENARIO

Classroom management, one of our scenario themes, involves promoting appropriate social functioning as well as controlling the antisocial variety. Teachers who can encourage students to act prosocially face a much pleasanter classroom than those who cannot. Prosocial behavior and misbehavior are for the most part incompatible. Increase the former and the latter must decrease.

Ms. Chapman is facing a difficult social situation in her sixth grade classroom. A new student who entered the class at mid-year has not yet gained social acceptance by the majority of the other class members. The problem is not particularly pronounced during class activities, when Ms. Chapman is present, but on the playground, in her absence, it appears that the newcomer is being systematically excluded from the activities of the others. The child is upset by this, as are the child's parents. What might Ms. Chapman do to alleviate the situation and encourage greater social interaction with the new student?

Chapter 13b

Promoting Prosocial Behavior
in the Classroom

Introduction

In the previous chapter we presented the psychological findings on prosocial development. To foster prosocial outcomes in the classroom we must next put this information into practice. Fostering prosocial behavior involves a number of steps. Teachers must determine which behaviors they wish to foster and which psychological principles relate to the desired outcomes. These principles must then be translated into instructional activities. In addition, each of these steps must be modified in accordance with the developmental level of the students, since development is a limiting factor in prosocial activities. When we specify prosocial outcomes, we are deciding on a destination; when we specify procedures, we are figuring out how to get there. The students' developmental level is a constraint imposed on the trip.

Classroom teachers typically have two reasons to be concerned with prosocial behavior. First, moral education is regarded as a teacher responsibility in many schools. Second, for the classroom to run smoothly, people must get along with each other and respect each other's rights and privileges. Respect for others is not automatic, however. The teacher is one agent of socialization who can help students meet these goals.

Regardless of the reasons for emphasizing prosocial education, the teacher's task is basically the same. He or she must specify: (1) product, the desired outcomes, and (2) process, the way to reach those outcomes. The product can be outlined by creating a set of performance objectives for prosocial behaviors. One type of process was presented in the last chapter. This process, which involves decision-making, includes three basic steps: (1) *reading* (deciphering) the situation, (2) *reasoning* about the information noted, and (3) *producing* a prosocial act. This decision-making sequence will serve as our guideline for relating research to practice.

Specifying the Outcomes: Reasons for Focusing on Prosocial Learning

Teachers who wish to foster prosocial growth face a problem very similar to the one faced by psychologists who wish to study it: How can the behavior be defined so that we can recognize it when it is produced? The psychologist tackles the issue by creating an *operational definition* of the behavior. The teacher's creation of performance objectives serves a similar purpose. Performance objectives are operational definitions of outcomes. The first step in fostering prosocial growth is to produce these outcome statements.

Why should teachers outline performance objectives related to prosocial behaviors? There are a number of reasons, best illustrated with situations that might occur in an actual classroom.

Cooperative behavior may result from the exigencies of the situation. Reinforcement of that cooperative behavior will increase the probability of it occurring again.

Emphasizing Perspective-Taking

With the current emphasis on mainstreaming handicapped children, exceptional children will be a part of most classrooms. These children may look different from their peers, may have different needs, and may behave somewhat differently as well. If their classmates are unable to comprehend their special needs or their perspectives, they might behave in ways an adult would find cruel; they might tease the handicapped children, exclude them from activities, or refuse to offer them their assistance. Teachers can prevent social interactions of this type by fostering prosocial behavior.

Similarly, the student population in most urban schools includes children from different ethnic and racial backgrounds. Again, these differences among students could lead to antisocial behavior, including teasing, ostracism, the formation of racial or ethnic gangs, and perhaps even violence. Such antisocial behaviors reflect problems in the larger society, but that does not mean we need to permit them in the schools. Perhaps if students can learn to appreciate the perspectives of others, even those who appear different in some way, the frequency of antisocial behavior will diminish. It is more difficult to be cruel to another person if you can appreciate that person's position, at least temporarily.

Emphasizing Cooperation and Sharing

There are many situations in which people need to cooperate with each other in order to meet life's demands successfully. In families, in the workplace, and in the classroom, the ability to cooperate is necessary for smooth social functioning. Students working on a class project, for example, must cooperate to bring the product to fruition, and lab groups in a science class need to cooperate to finish an experiment. Cooperation even plays a role during games and recreation time. Schools frequently do an adequate job of fostering competition in sports, academics, and other aspects of school life. Cooperation, however, is just as important, and it can also be fostered in the classroom. Accordingly, teachers may wish to design performance objectives targeted at this prosocial behavior which, like perspective-taking, is an important social competence.

Sharing is another prosocial behavior relevant to the classroom. Materials, supplies, and apparatus are frequently in limited supply. There are rarely enough materials for each child to have his or her own set, so materials and supplies must be shared. There may be only one set of blocks in a preschool class, a few Bunsen burners in a chemistry class, or one encyclopedia in a history class. A limited amount of equipment necessitates sharing. Children also share by taking turns at learning centers and by exchanging library books. Students who have internalized this prosocial competence will be able to share materials and privileges equitably.

▶ *ACTIVITY 1.* Observing children in a variety of settings will give you some sense of how often they spontaneously behave prosocially. Start by defining a set of prosocial competencies that you might reasonably expect to see in a school environment, such as sharing materials or cooperating on a project. Armed with your definitions, visit (1) a classroom where joint projects are being conducted (a science class, perhaps), and (2) a playground where group games are being played. Try to observe children both when an adult is present and when one is absent. During your observations, do the following:

1. Note if and when the adults who are present model the prosocial behaviors you have identified.
2. Note whether adults instruct or direct the children to behave prosocially.
3. Record the frequency with which children spontaneously behave prosocially without adult direction.
4. Note whether there is a difference in the children's social behavior in the presence and in the absence of an adult.

Generalized vs. Specific Prosocial Competence

Prosocial behaviors occur in a context, a setting in which a prosocial act is anticipated. Although we may wish children to share, we probably want them to avoid indiscriminately giving away everything they have. Similarly, we may hope that students will understand the perspectives of others, but not to the extent of letting others abuse them. Indiscriminate sharing, altruism, or empathy may be too costly to the child to be considered reasonable behavior. Accordingly, we sometimes hope that a child will learn to behave selectively, depending on the situational context. There are other behaviors, however, that we hope the children will generalize. We may very well want the child to behave morally in all situations, with all persons, whether or not an adult is present, and whether or not a reward is expected. We thus sometimes hope for *generalized* competencies and other times hope for *selective* competencies. The choice depends on both the nature of the behavior and the context in which it occurs.

Performance objectives, as you recall from Chapter 2b, include both performance and context. The context is stated in the *condition* part of the statement. Generalized competencies are expected across

TABLE 13b–1. Performance Objectives for Prosocial Competencies

Prosocial behavior	Condition	Performance	Criterion
Sharing	Given a joint project with another child	the student will share one set of materials	without arguing over ownership
Empathy	When presented with a story involving two protagonists	the student will identify the perspective	of both characters
Moral reasoning	When presented with a moral choice	the student will provide a justification for the choice	at least equivalent to Kohlberg's Stage 4 reasoning
Altruism	When confronted with a child who has no lunch	the student will provide food to the child	by sharing some of his or her own lunch

conditions, selective competencies under only some conditions. Teachers can produce behavioral objectives that relate to both. Examples are provided in Table 13b–1. Conditions place limits on when we can expect to see prosocial behavior; the developmental level limits the types of behavior expected. It would be unreasonable, for example, to expect a six-year-old child to produce moral justifications at Kohlberg's Stage 6 when few adults can do so. Both situational features and development are therefore involved in the production of appropriate objectives.

> ► *ACTIVITY 2.* Produce performance objectives appropriate for adolescents that tap empathy, morality, and cooperation. Specify the condition, the observable performance, and the criteria.
>
> ► *ACTIVITY 3.* On the basis of information in the last chapter (Chapter 13a), produce a series of performance objectives for perspective-taking appropriate for children aged four, six, and ten.
>
> ► *ACTIVITY 4.* Construct a list of six prosocial performances and determine which are reasonably generalized and which are more situationally specific. Identify typical restricting circumstances for the second group. Write objectives that reflect the contextual limitations.

Once the important performance objectives have been described, we turn to the next task: how to attain them.

Outlining the Process

The steps a person goes through before engaging in a prosocial act were outlined in the decision-making flow chart in Figure 13a–1 in the last chapter (see page 521). First, the person must analyze the situation that suggests the need for a prosocial response. This involves attending to the *cues*, the signs that give meaning to a setting. These signs may take several forms. They may be verbal, such as requests for assistance; they may involve interpreting emotions from a person's facial expression; or they may involve situational cues, realizing that a person in a given set of circumstances probably needs assistance. A child who comes from a financially impoverished family, for example, probably will have no money for special purchases. Students are not innately sensitive to these cues; they must learn them from experience. Oliver has to learn to attend to the signals that the student in the wheelchair sends to even realize that the student needs help.

Second, the learner must use the cue information in a reasoning process. The information must be interpreted. Billy, for example, sees a younger child crying because his pet dog has been injured by a car. The presence of the wounded animal and the child's crying are cues that tell Billy about the event. Billy then must be able to reason about those cues to determine how the crying child must feel, or at least how Billy would feel if he were in the same position. Only when Billy can reason about the event he witnessed can one expect him to lend assistance.

Third, after the cues have been read and reasoned about, action can be taken. Billy might comfort the child, call the child's parents, help take the pet to a veterinarian, or do all these things. *Read, interpret,* and *act* are thus the three components of prosocial behavior. The action taken depends on Billy's expectations about what he is supposed to do; these expectations are determined by past learning.

Reading cues, reasoning about them, and finally acting on them are different kinds of performances. Different experiences can be used to foster each proficiency.

▶ *ACTIVITY 5.*   Observe children in preschool or early elementary school. Describe the way the children signal their needs to the teacher and to one another. Identify the signals that appear to be most effective in obtaining teacher assistance as opposed to assistance from peers. Are the same signals used in both instances?

Assisting Children to Interpret Situational Cues

Becoming sensitive to the demands of social situations is probably one of the most crucial elements of general social competence. Whether we are aware of it or not, we adjust our behavior to meet the demands of the situation. Our behavior differs in different settings—at a football game, at a party, in a classroom, at a job interview. A socially competent person adjusts to the demands of different situations. How this process occurs and how we learn to make the adjustments is not totally clear, but it is a recognized component of responsible social action.

We probably learn sensitivity to response demands informally, through trial and error and by watching the behavior of others. Teachers can formalize the process somewhat by calling learners' attention to social signals. This is a problem of discrimination learning—learning to attend to the relevant features of an event while disregarding the irrelevant features. In the case of Billy, the young child's crying and the injured pet are relevant features for giving assistance; the sex of the child and the breed of the dog are irrelevant. Any instructional activity that calls attention to relevant cues helps the learner in this first step along the way to a prosocial performance.

One appropriate technique is for the teacher to call attention to signals for assistance. In the context of reading or telling a story, for example, the teacher can identify the needs of the characters in the story and explain which aspects of the characters' behavior revealed the needs. In the classroom, the teacher could point out the needs of a student and again reveal the behavior that indicated the need. In this way, students can observe the teacher model the use of behavioral information to assess social situations. Essentially, the teacher is thinking out loud so that learners can observe the thinking process.

Another technique is to solicit reasoning from the students themselves and ask them to identify the clues. The teacher can ask the learners to describe the needs of a character in a story and then ask, "How did you know that?" In instances of this sort, the students would be practicing linking signals with emotions. As a prelude to further reasoning, the teacher might ask students to do this sequentially for a series of story characters. Accurate identifications or links could be reinforced, and alternative explanations can be offered for inaccurate identifications. This procedure may also help learners become more conscious of their own thinking processes, a procedure that facilitates the important cognition skill of *metacognition*.

A teacher can describe cue reading or solicit readings from students in a variety of contexts. Stories, classroom incidents, even television can provide situations for practicing the discrimination of relevant social cues. Since this is an important prerequisite to social competence, it is the first step in promoting prosocial performance. The procedure employs many learning devices: (1) directing selective attention, (2) modeling the inferential process of assessing needs, (3) reinforcing competent signal reading, and (4) becoming aware of one's own cognitive processes.

Affecting the Reasoning Process

The child needs to learn to take the view of others, to consider the intentions of others, and to coordinate perspectives with intentions. We know little about these reasoning processes. We do know that younger children have trouble with them, as do many older children. Nevertheless, we have some indication of the way we can influence the processes. The devices we use are similar to those used in cue reading: (1) modeling the reasoning process and (2) eliciting from others their reasoning about intentions.

In the first case, a teacher would model the process by articulating the reasoning he or she engaged in to decipher another's perspective. Or the teacher might provide his or her rationale for a moral judgment, again externalizing the reasoning process. It has been shown that providing a rationale for moral judgments affects the moral judgments subsequently made by observers (Bandura & MacDonald, 1963). Such reasoning and rationale provision can sometimes even affect behavior without the occurrence of an actual situation requiring a moral judgment. By providing a rationale, the teacher gives learners information they can use in making their own prosocial decisions. To facilitate moral reasoning, for example, one might model reasoning one level above students' current functioning level. This can help develop their moral reasoning to a more mature stage.

Another technique supported by empirical evidence is role-playing or dramatic play (Staub, 1971). Although this technique has been criticized, it has proven somewhat effective. In role-playing, learners actually assume or pretend to be a character in a dilemma. By adopting the role of the character, they can come to appreciate the character's perspective. If they subsequently assume the roles of other characters as well, they experience a series of perspectives. If, in addition, the perspectives differ or are in conflict, the player must coordinate them. This conflict or disequilibrium is thought to force the player to coordinate a multitude of perspectives that occur simultaneously. In short, it is a device designed to facilitate the equilibration process that is considered central to development in the cognitive-developmental perspective. The final word is still not in on the effectiveness of role-playing in the coordination of perspectives. It does seem to hold promise for prosocial development, however, and it is currently being used in classrooms.

Finally, teachers can also help children explain and examine their own prosocial reasoning. Prompting children to reason about their intentions has been shown in research studies to be effective (Bearison & Isaacs, 1975). This strategy helps learners become more conscious of their cognitive processes. In addition, asking children to explain the reasoning behind their own prosocial acts, to reason about the positions and feelings of others, and to reason about choices forces them to externalize their internal cognitive process and gives the teacher an opportunity to comment.

▶ *ACTIVITY 6.*   Identify a set of social situations that might occur in a classroom. Some examples are (1) the introduction of a new student, (2) interaction with a handicapped student, and (3) arbitrating an argument between two students.

Having identified your situations, interview youngsters of different ages. Describe your scenarios and ask the children (1) how the characters feel, (2) why they feel the way they do, and (3) what should be done. This should acquaint you with the spontaneous prosocial reasoning of children; if you interview children of different ages, you will probably see developmental differences as well.

Once you have discovered the way children react to your scenarios, describe how you might encourage them to reflect on the characters' perspectives. You might consider (1) eliciting prosocial reasoning, (2) modeling prosocial reasoning, and (3) role-playing.

You could conduct this activity in the same way with a moral dilemma. Examples might pertain to stealing from a classmate, or lying to cover for a friend. With your moral dilemma in hand, complete again the steps in the previous activity.

Promoting Prosocial Action

Learning principles are directly relevant when we wish to influence action rather than reasoning. As we discussed in the last chapter, modeling, reinforcement, and expectations of reinforcement are key variables. Teachers are models and sources of reinforcement, so they are in a position to influence action.

Teachers should pay attention to the prosocial actions students make spontaneously. If these actions are reinforced with praise, recognition, or some other response, the prosocial response will be strengthened. Moreover, when a teacher delivers reinforcement to one student directly, the other students may be reinforced vicariously. Good teachers, then, will watch for opportunities to reinforce prosocial actions.

Teachers can also model prosocial behavior for students. They can behave altruistically, empathetically, and morally. It is important, however, that the modeling be consistent. It is hoped that student observers will abstract a general rule about prosocial action, such as (1) it is good to give to the less fortunate, (2) it is desirable to share and cooperate with others, or (3) we should try to understand the views of others. As you recall from Chapters 4a and 4b, people acquire rules from watching models repeat a performance a number of times. Observers learn consistency across model incidents and use it to guide their own behavior. A student who observes a model perform once will not learn a generalized rule; the modeling must be repeated.

Consistent modeling is important in all rule-governed imitation,

Role-playing provides an opportunity for children to experience another person's perspective. Prosocial behaviors may be related to the acquisition of perspective-taking skills.

Scenario Suggestion

The children in Ms. Chapman's class may be acting in ways an adult would perceive as cruel because they lack understanding of the way it feels to be treated as they are treating the newcomer. Perhaps they lack empathy, or the ability to perceive an event as another would experience it, or an appreciation of the way the newcomer perceives their behavior. Ms. Chapman may alleviate the situation and improve her students' social cognition by helping them assume the perspective of the newcomer.

There are a number of activities Ms. Chapman might plan for helping her students appreciate the perspective of a person left out by others. First, the group could read or listen to stories from the perspective of those left out by others. Second, discussions about the way it feels to be excluded could follow. Third, role-playing activities in which children assume the position of the excluded one can be planned. These activities focus on the *cognitive component* of prosocial behavior, understanding the perspective of another person.

Ms. Chapman also needs to attend to the social behavior of her students as well as their cognitions associated with the behavior. She can reinforce those who spontaneously include the newcomer, play with the new student, or initiate social interchange. The reinforcement will support and perhaps increase the frequency of social interaction.

The situation is not necessarily a simple one, but Ms. Chapman may be able to help immensely by attacking both components of prosocial behavior: (1) the cognitive component, perspective-taking, and (2) the behavioral component, social action.

Note that these activities have a positive focus that permits the teacher to play a reinforcing rather than a punitive role. In addition, the purpose is to increase skills, both cognitive and social, rather than to eradicate responses. Classroom management can be a positive process; it can be constructive. It is thus not very different from any other aspect of education.

---

but it is exceptionally important in attempts to encourage prosocial behavior. If a teacher behaves prosocially sometimes but not other times, students will probably fail to learn the desired behavioral rule. Prosocial behavior often requires the performer to make a sacrifice— some things may be given up, or a personal risk may be taken; it is rarely rewarding in a material sense. Inconsistent modeling can inadvertently provide an excuse for observers not to behave self-sacrificially.

As they model prosocial behavior, teachers can provide a verbal rationale. You will recall that information from observational learning must be stored in the observer's memory in order to affect his behavior at a later time. A verbal rationale helps the observer remember. When a teacher states a rule, such as "We should help people in trouble if we can," or "We should try to share our things with others who do not have them," he or she enhances the learning process. In addition, when

The actions consistent with prosocial behavior are influenced by past learning. Empathetic behavior often occurs as a result of having observed models displaying that behavior.

the teacher articulates the reasoning behind behavior being modeled, he or she reveals to observers the thinking behind the act. Such statements as (1) "I am helping Johnny because he cannot do this all by himself," (2) "Muffy is unhappy today, so I will be especially nice to her," (3) "Gregory has hurt his leg, so I will help him carry his books" explain why the prosocial act is being performed.

In short, then, teachers can help students learn generalized prosocial responses by behaving consistently, by providing verbal rules, and by offering verbal rationales. Interestingly enough, when models are inconsistent or when their preaching fails to match their actions, children tend to learn the modeled or verbalized response that is less prosocial (Bryan, 1970). An attitude of "Do as I say, not as I do" does not work here. Children may disregard the sermonizing and behave in accordance with the example.

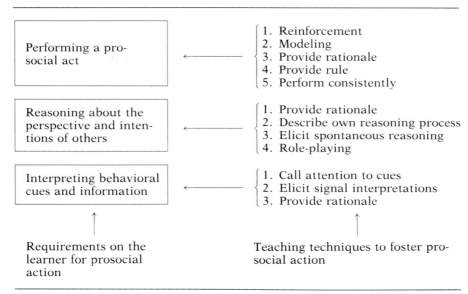

FIGURE 13b–1.   The Relationship Between Student Action and
Teaching Technique

Summary

We have described several ways of encouraging prosocial behavior in
the classroom. Some of the recommendations are designed to influence
information-processing, some reasoning, and some action. The correspondence between the specific recommendations and the decision-
making model is depicted in Figure 13b–1.

By successfully implementing these techniques and encouraging
prosocial behavior, the teacher can make the classroom a more pleasant
environment. At the same time, the teacher is encouraging the important process of prosocial socialization in the larger society.

The processes of learning and development and the types of outcomes of those processes have been discussed in preceding chapters. We turn now to procedures for measuring the outcomes. How
do we know whether students have accomplished the objectives
that have been established? Issues pertaining to this question were
first raised in Chapter 8b where we discussed the use of standardized tests to measure student achievement. Topics from Chapter
8b serve as relevant background for the present chapter, including
content validity, reliability, and criterion and norm-referenced
tests.

In this chapter the emphasis is on teacher-made tests as a
method of measuring achievement of cognitive outcomes. Assuming that appropriate performance objectives have been formulated (Chapter 2b) and instruction and activities have been
planned and conducted for helping the students meet the objectives (Chapters 11 and 12), the culmination of this series of procedures is the construction of an instrument to measure how well
the students have mastered the objectives. Procedures for constructing a content-valid test and using different types of questions are explained and exemplified in this chapter by the construction of a test covering the material in Chapter 3a.

Chapter 14

The Construction of Measurement Instruments

Introduction

To determine whether students are meeting the objectives prepared for the teaching of a particular concept, some sort of measurement or evaluation of student behaviors is generally needed. In Chapter 2b we discussed the construction of performance objectives. Now we are asking how it can be determined whether students have met the objectives. Cognitive outcomes are normally measured with tests. Affective and psychomotor outcomes are probably measured more effectively with controlled observation of performance, or with rating scales or checklists. Since schools focus primarily on changes in cognitive behaviors and on cognitive outcomes, we will focus this discussion on that aspect of achievement and ways to measure it.

The Need for Teacher-Made Tests

Teachers obtain some evidence of student progress in their day-to-day interactions with students. When a student responds to a teacher's questions, for example, the teacher acquires some evidence, at least with regard to the particular question. Student homework assignments provide another bit of evidence, as do teachers' observations of the way students use their time.

These less formal measures are rather unreliable for measuring student progress, however, for a number of reasons. The procedure of asking questions in class is limited, since the teacher cannot ask a question again once a correct response has been given. If different questions are asked, variations in their difficulty level will be a problem. The halo effect, which suggests that judgments of the adequacy of responses are affected by personality variables of the student, is another

Tests provide a more adequate method of measuring achievement than informal observations. All students are faced with the same questions, each student has the opportunity to respond, and a written record of the responses is available.

persistent problem in evaluating oral responses in class. Moreover, the number of questions and responses possible during class time is limited, so every student may not have an equal opportunity to respond. In the same way, student assignments may reflect not just the student's achievement, but also the achievements of parents, friends, or others who might have helped with the assignment. Teachers' observations of the student's use of class time may also be influenced by the halo effect, and in any case it is rather difficult to measure adequately by means of observation alone how thirty or more students use their time.

To obtain a more reliable and valid measure of student cognitive achievement, teachers normally rely on more formal procedures, such as tests constructed for the purpose. Teacher-made tests have several advantages over more informal means of evaluating achievement. First, carefully planned tests contain questions concerning all the outcomes the students should attain. Second, all students are asked the same questions; the teacher thus obtains evidence about every student's performance. Third, the teacher may include questions of differing levels of difficulty, thus allowing the comparison of student performances. Only the more successful students ,will get the very difficult items correct, and the poorer students may succeed only on the easy items. Fourth, a criterion can be established for determining which responses will be considered adequate, a plan that eliminates much of the halo effect.

Measurement Decisions

Teachers who decide to use paper and pencil tests to measure student achievement must answer many questions. Before testing, one must ask:

1. When and how often should I test?
2. What should I test?
3. What kinds of items should I use?
4. How can I write good items?

After testing, the teacher must ask:

5. Were the items appropriate in terms of difficulty and discrimination?
6. How reliable are the scores?
7. How do I evaluate a student's performance on the test?

Frequency and Timing of Tests

There is no single correct answer to the question "How often do I test?" Some teachers prefer to give daily quizzes and perhaps major examinations as well. Others prefer to give just one or two tests during a semester or nine-week period. A frequency between these two extremes is probably best.

Teachers who test frequently—those who give daily quizzes, for example—spend too much time on evaluation, to the detriment of other instructional activities. The rationale used by these teachers is that frequent testing encourages good study habits, since students must prepare daily and cannot postpone studying. This could be an advantage, but the teacher faces other problems. The teacher may spend an inordinate amount of time constructing good items, or, lacking time, the teacher may resort to poorer items, perhaps of a factual type, which are the easiest to construct. Daily quizzes might be better used to focus study, or as topics for discussion rather than for evaluating student performance.

Infrequent testing has disadvantages as well. Foremost is the problem of adequately covering the objectives and content. A teacher cannot adequately cover with a single test the objectives of a nine- or eighteen-week course. The reliability of a single examination covering that much instruction is questionable; chance rather than knowledge may determine the student's score. Another problem is that the fewer tests given to determine a student's achievement, the greater a student's anxiety. Anxiety often leads to poorer performance. In desperation, a student may resort to cheating.

Fortunately, teachers are not completely without guidance in scheduling examinations. The subject matter in most textbooks is divided into logical segments, either units or chapters, that may serve as guides for timing examinations. The teacher's manuals that accompany many textbooks also suggest divisions of the subject matter.

In such courses as mathematics in which material is presented sequentially, early material must be mastered before subsequent material can be presented. Teachers of this type of course will undoubtedly plan tests to determine which students are ready to proceed to the next topic and which need more instruction. Test results may indicate that the entire class needs further learning experiences before proceeding. This feedback function of testing is important. Teachers who test too infrequently may find that they lost many students weeks before, an exigency that makes the process of remediation or reteaching more difficult.

Several factors, then, will determine when tests should be given. One factor is the logical breaks in the subject matter. Tests must be given often enough to cover the content adequately and to determine student readiness for the next topic. Students should be told when a test will be given as soon as a time has been established. There is no good reason to give an unannounced quiz or major examination. When this is done, it is usually as a punishment, and the result is diminished rapport between teacher and students.

What to Test

In a construction project, such as building a house, the builder follows a set of plans, blueprints, or specifications to assure that when the building is finished it will be a complete and suitable dwelling. In the same way, a teacher devising a test must follow some sort of blueprint or table of specifications in order to construct a complete and suitable test. Formulating the test blueprint or table of specifications is the teacher's first step in ensuring that the test possesses *content validity*. A test that has content validity is one that measures what has been taught, what the student is expected to have learned from a period of instruction.

A teacher who has formulated the objectives for a unit of study before beginning instruction has already started a test blueprint. You will recall that objectives consist of two primary components, the behavior expected of the student and the content on which the behavior is to be performed. Below are two examples from test blueprints.

1. The student will be able to list four basic elements of a behavior modification program.

   Behavior: List   Content: Behavior Modification

2. The student will be able to compute the percentage of decrease between original and sale prices of items.

   Behavior: Compute   Content: Percentage

A test blueprint is a matrix composed of the same two dimensions as the objectives—behavior and content.

   To place objectives in a matrix, it is usually advisable to compress the number of behavioral descriptors into broader categories. If this is not done and an entry is included for each behavioral description, the matrix becomes very long and complex. One suggested compression might make use of the elements of Bloom's Taxonomy (1956) or some derivation of it.

Matrix Category	*Sample Descriptor Words*
1. Factual knowledge	1. Define, list, name
2. Understanding	2. Describe, recognize examples of, explain, paraphrase
3. Relationships	3. Compare and contrast, relate, differentiate
4. Ability to calculate	4. Calculate, compute, add, divide
5. Applications to predict	5. Suggest outcomes, determine consequences, forecast
6. Applications to suggest appropriate actions	6. Determine, compare, detect, present
7. Ability to evaluate	7. Evaluate, judge, assess

The content dimension of the matrix can be determined easily from the major divisions of the material to be covered. The chapters in a unit or major headings in a chapter may be used to divide the content.

   Combining the two elements—broad categories of behavior and major divisions of content—gives the teacher a blueprint of the test. The schema for a blueprint covering the present chapter is presented in Figure 14–1. To complete the blueprint, the teacher fills in the cells with the content considered important, as reflected in the unit objectives.

   The teacher then needs to determine how much emphasis to give to each section of the blueprint. This decision is based on the teacher's judgments about the importance of the various parts of the unit of study. The time spent teaching each content segment may be used as a guide for determining the emphasis to be given that part of the test. Suppose that in the preceding matrix, the teacher spent one day on

	A. Need for test	B. Measurement decisions	C. Extended response	D. Restricted response	E. Evaluating the test response
Factual knowledge					
Understanding					
Relationships					
Ability to calculate					
Application to predict					
Applications to suggest appropriate actions					
Ability to evaluate					

FIGURE 14–1.   Schema for a Blueprint for a Test Covering Chapter 14

content *A* and *B*, one day on content *C*, two days on content *D*, and two days on content *E*. The test might then be constructed with one-sixth of the items from contents *A* and *B* (one day out of six), one-sixth from content *C*, and one-third from each of contents *D* and *E*.

The same kind of decision must be made on the behavior dimension. How much emphasis should be given to factual knowledge, understanding of principles, prediction? These decisions will be based on the teacher's judgment about which behaviors are appropriate for the students' developmental level and experiential background.

The completed test blueprint can now guide the teacher in constructing the test. If the test items match the blueprint, the teacher's test will have content validity. The interrelationships between the objectives, instruction, and measurement should be evident. If a teacher has created course objectives, instruction will be planned to help students meet the objectives and the test will be planned to measure how well the students have met them. All the steps in the instructional process will thus be consistent with each other.

Types of Questions

We can divide the types of questions asked on a test into two categories, extended response and restricted response. Extended response questions, such as essay questions, give the student some freedom in organizing and constructing an answer. No single prescribed answer can be expected, although correct answers must contain certain features. This means that essay questions are scored somewhat subjectively; they are thus often called subjective questions.

Restricted response questions are scored objectively. Answer keys can be constructed before the test is administered, so items are easy to score as correct or incorrect. Restricted response questions may be further differentiated into recognition and recall questions. Recognition items include multiple-choice, true-false, and matching questions. The examinee recognizes the correct or best response from a limited number of possible responses. Completion and short-answer questions are recall questions, in which the examinee must recall and write a single word, number, or phrase in response to the item.

Another type of question has elements of both extended response and restricted response questions. To answer this type of question, the examinee must write a longer answer than for a recall type, but the correctness of the answer can be determined easily. Students may, for example, be asked to define words or concepts, to list events, or to give examples of concepts. In each of these situations, the student would give a longer answer than would be needed with a restricted response item. Freedom to respond is limited, however, and for the answer to be judged correct, specific elements must be included. Since they are scored objectively and responses must be specific, we will consider items of this type to be objective. In the discussion that follows, then, these extended short-answer questions, completion questions, and regular short-answer questions will be considered recall items.

Each type of question has its advantages and disadvantages. For some objectives, essay questions are the best way to determine a student's achievement. In other cases, recall or recognition questions may be more appropriate. The teacher may find it beneficial to use the different types in conjunction.

Extended response questions allow students to plan their own answers and express them in their own words. The ability to organize one's thoughts and knowledge and communicate them in writing should be an important goal of education, although it has frequently been neglected. In answering recall items, examinees will have some opportunity to respond in their own words with information recalled from memory. Recall items are considered somewhat more difficult than recognition questions, in which examinees choose from a limited number of alternatives and have no chance to express their own ideas. All types of items can be used to measure the same behaviors, including knowledge, understanding, application, analysis, and evaluation. Most novice test constructors, however, have more trouble constructing good restricted response questions that measure relatively complex outcomes, such as analysis, synthesis, and evaluation.

Students taking an extended response examination spend most of their time recalling the elements that will comprise the answer, organizing these elements, and writing the answers. By contrast, on a restricted response test students spend most of their time reading the questions and thinking of the correct answer. Students who have difficulty expressing themselves in writing normally will do less well on extended response tests, and students with reading difficulties will find restricted response tests more difficult. Since both reading and expressing oneself in writing are important skills, it is probably advantageous to vary the types of questions used.

Because writing is more time-consuming than reading, teachers must normally ask fewer extended response questions than restricted response questions. Extended response tests can thus be constructed more quickly than restricted response tests. The former might require four to six questions, the latter thirty or more. This advantage of extended response questions may be outweighed by the fact that they take much longer to score. Since on extended response questions students are free to express themselves, many different responses will have to be evaluated; differences in adequacy of response, correctness, and relationships among statements contribute to the difficulty of scoring. Restricted response questions, on the other hand, have predetermined correct responses, so scoring is largely a clerical task and can be done rapidly. Responses to recall items will also vary somewhat because of the use of synonyms for the correct answer in completion questions and the variable completeness of answers to short-answer questions.

Because they include fewer questions, extended response tests may be less reliable and accurate than restricted response tests. Longer tests, which are possible with restricted response questions, cover the content-behavior matrix more completely and thus more accurately reflect the student's achievement. Consider the diagrams in Figure 14–2. Each of the two equal squares represents the total content-behavior matrix. The extended response questions are fewer in number, but they are more general. The amount of material they cover may be thus represented by the shaded areas in the left-hand square. Restricted response questions are more specific, but they are scattered throughout the entire matrix, as in the right-hand square. Assume that a student knows fifty percent of the material in each matrix. It would be much easier to miss that fifty percent with the extended response test, since the questions have covered only one-fifth of the possible cells. The restricted response test, in contrast, has questions from each cell, so it includes a greater sample of the total content and thus is more likely to cover the fifty percent that the student knows.

Scoring the responses to essay questions is less reliable than scoring responses to restricted response questions. Since for restricted response questions the correct answers are predetermined, different scor-

Extended response   Recognition response

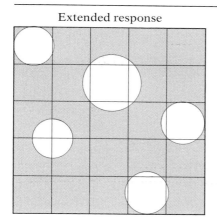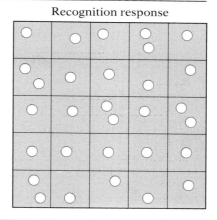

FIGURE 14–2. **Comparison of Content Validities of Two Types of Tests**

ers will judge the correctness of answers in the same way, and the same scorer would score the test much the same way on different occasions. Studies of the scoring of essay examinations, however, consistently show great variability in different teachers' assessments of responses. Writing style, correct grammar usage, misspelled words, and handwriting may influence teachers differently and lead to different scores. Not only do different teachers score differently, but the same teacher may score responses differently at different times (Coffman, 1971). The mood of the scorer, fatigue, and changing standards as scoring progresses may all lead the same teacher to give different scores at different times.

Recognition questions have frequently been criticized because they permit the student to guess the correct answer. While it is true that a student may guess the correct answer without having mastered the material, it would be a rare student who would guess the correct answers to all or even most of the questions. Students normally know something about the questions, so their responses are rarely random guesses. The use of recall items greatly reduces the opportunity for students to guess the correct answer.

A comparable problem with extended response questions is that students may bluff in answering the question. Students with exceptional writing ability can construct responses that may impress the reader even though they fail to answer the question. Writing all around a topic without answering the question is another kind of bluffing. Students also learn to bluff by writing longer answers, since scores are frequently inflated in proportion to the length of response.

Extended Response	Restricted Response	
	RECALL TYPE	RECOGNITION TYPE
1. Students plan their own answers and express them in their own words	1. Students recall and state the answer	1. Students recognize the answer from a limited number of alternatives
2. Student's response may reflect all the relevant outcomes	2. May test all the different behaviors depending on expertness of test constructor	2. May test all the different behaviors depending on expertness of test constructor
3. Student spends time in recall, organization, and writing	3. Student spends time in recall and writing	3. Student spends time in reading and thinking
4. Fewer but more general questions	4. Intermediate number of questions and generality	4. Greater number and more specific questions
5. Great variation in answers is likely	5. Some variation in responses in terms of synonyms, order, and completeness	5. Answers either right or wrong
6. Reliability and coverage of content limited	6. Greater coverage of content than extended response	6. Greater reliability and coverage of content
7. Permits bluffing	7. Little opportunity for bluffing; little chance for guessing	7. Permits guessing

Constructing and Scoring the Extended Response Test

Extended response questions are normally considered easier to construct than limited response questions. Consequently, teachers with little experience in writing tests are likely to select them. Constructing a good extended response test does require thought and preparation on the part of the teacher, however. We can make several suggestions for writing this type of item.

1. Formulate questions that require students to express their command of essential knowledge. Questions should avoid merely asking students to repeat information presented in the textbook or by the teacher. Rather, questions should elicit responses that demonstrate that the student can evaluate the material and understands its implications, its relationships to other ideas, and its applications. Extended response questions may be used most advantageously to evaluate students' attainment of the upper levels of Bloom's Taxonomy (1956), including applications to novel situations, analysis, synthesis, and evaluation.

2. Questions should outline the examinee's task as completely and specifically as possible. A common weakness of extended response questions is that they fail to adequately define the task for the examinee. This leads to a multitude of different answers and approaches to the question. An example of a question that lacks structure (taken from a social studies examination) is "Who was Benjamin Franklin?" The answer to this question could be a single statement or a book. A better item might be "Discuss Benjamin Franklin's contributions to government and science. Include in your discussion the impact of these contributions on present-day society." This question focuses clearly on a specific task and illustrates that it is sometimes necessary to include additional suggestions about what is expected in an answer.

Questions that begin with *who, what,* or *when,* are usually weak. To elicit an extended response it would be better to use such words as *differentiate, explain, discuss, compare and contrast, illustrate,* and *evaluate.* The teacher will probably find it advantageous before the examination to discuss with students what these words mean, or to provide supplemental directions with the questions in order to specify what is expected.

3. It is preferable to construct tests with a number of questions that can be answered briefly. As we noted in the preceding section, one of the major problems with extended response questions is that they fail to cover a large part of the content. Several questions that require briefer responses would increase the content validity and reliability of the test.

4. If students' test performances are to be compared, avoid giving the examinees optional questions. Allowing students to answer three out of five questions has disadvantages. A good student will not benefit from this type of procedure, whereas poorer students will, because a person who knows responses to all five questions will get the same score as one who knows only three out of five. Scores on the examination will be closer together because students will pick the questions they can answer best. This makes it more difficult for the teacher to differentiate student performances. If the questions all come from the test blueprint, in order to assure content validity and reliability all students should be expected to attempt to answer all questions.

5. Test the suitability of a question by asking a colleague to write a model answer to it. This gives the teacher an opportunity to see whether another knowledgeable person interprets the question in the intended way. The teacher might also write an ideal answer and compare it to that of the colleague. This allows the teacher to evaluate the adequacy of the question and make any necessary revisions before giving the test to students.

The quality of an extended response examination depends largely upon the skill of the scorer and the accuracy of the scoring procedure.

Though there are many problems in scoring this type of examination, such as the effect (favorable or unfavorable) of handwriting, the possibility of halo effect, and the difficulty of determining the adequacy and correctness of expression, the scorer can attempt to minimize their effect by following these suggestions:

1. If possible, decide in advance which elements the ideal answer should contain and the point value that will be attached to each element. In constructing the ideal answer, the scorer may state the elements that are crucial for an adequate answer and those that would increase the quality of the answer. Points could then be assigned in accordance with the relative importance of the elements. This method of scoring seems to be most reliable, and it also makes it easy to inform students of the rationale for the points assigned.

Before the actual scoring process begins, the scorer might pick six or eight student papers at random and compare the ideal answer to these student responses. This could lead to revisions in the ideal answer that would provide a more realistic basis for scoring each examinee's performance. Suppose, for example, that none of the students' papers included one or more of the points that the scorer included in the ideal answer. This suggests that the examinees interpreted the question differently from the way the scorer did. If none of the students included ideas the scorer included, deducting points from each student's paper will not help differentiate the students. The selection of random papers may likewise reveal that students included some points the scorer omitted but for which the students should receive credit.

2. If the responses cannot be divided into specific points, it may be necessary to resort to an overall scoring procedure. This type of scoring is more difficult to explain to students and may be less reliable than the point system. Using this procedure, the scorer reads the responses, judges their adequacy, and then groups them in homogeneous piles. There are usually at least three piles—the more there are, the finer the differentiations the scorer must make. After having read the responses once and sorted them into piles, the scorer rereads each pile to be sure it contains homogeneous responses. It is possible to shift one or more papers upward or downward to adjust a pile's homogeneity. If the scorer shifts a number of responses, a third reading might be used to verify that the responses are still comparable.

When the scorer has assured that the responses in each pile are homogeneous, points can be assigned to them. As noted, in this approach to scoring it may be more difficult to justify to the students the assignment of points.

3. Whichever scoring method is used, score the responses question by question rather than student by student. Using this procedure, the scorer would score all the students' responses to the first question, then

all responses to the second question, and so on. The advantage of this method of scoring is that the scorer maintains one frame of reference for scoring each question rather than changing frames of reference for each question, as would be necessary if the scorer read papers student by student. This method also minimizes the halo effect. If papers are read student by student, a student's response on one question is more likely to affect the scoring of the following response.

It is also advantageous for the scorer to shuffle the papers after reading each question so that for the next question the papers will be read in a different order. This distributes the effects of first impressions and fatigue so that these factors do not always influence the scoring of the responses of the same students.

4. Grade the papers as anonymously as possible in order to minimize the halo effect. Have the students put their names on the back of the last page only, for example. A procedure used successfully by one of the authors is to ask students to record their names and a code number on a paper passed around the class during the examination. The students write their code numbers rather than their names on their test papers. The list of names and code numbers is then filed away until all the papers are corrected, at which time the scorer identifies each student's paper.

5. Attempt to minimize the effects of quality of handwriting, grammar, and spelling on the scoring of papers, unless these are specific goals of the course, as might be true in English or Language Arts. Teachers who are aware that these factors may bias the scoring will attempt to disregard them as far as scoring for content is concerned, attending to the content of the response rather than the mechanics of expression.

▶ *ACTIVITY 1.*

1. Construct an extended response question concerning some section of this chapter. Write a model answer for that question.

2. Give your question to two or three other students in class and ask them to answer it. Compare their answers with the model answer, and then respond to the following questions:

   a. Was the question clearly stated? Did you get comparable answers from all students?

   b. Were any elements of the model answer omitted by all students in their responses?

   c. Did any of the students' responses include ideas other than those in your model answer?

Constructing Restricted Response Questions

Restricted response questions can be divided into two categories, recognition items and recall items. Recognition items are those that require the student to choose the correct response from a limited number of alternatives, as in multiple choice, true-false, or matching items. Recall items ask the student to recall a word or phrase, or, with extended short-answer items, a list of names, concepts, or specific facts.

These types of items have often been criticized for measuring only the lower levels of learning, such as factual knowledge. This problem, rather than being inherent in the type of item, is a criticism of the test constructor. As is illustrated in Bloom's Taxonomy of Educational Objectives (1956), restricted response items, specifically multiple choice items, can be constructed to measure all levels of learning outcomes.

Some of our suggestions can be applied to the construction of several types of restricted response questions, others just to one type. In the following sections we focus mainly on the construction of multiple choice items, but brief discussions of other types are also included.

Multiple-Choice Items

It is not easy to construct good multiple-choice items that ask the student for more than factual information. It can, in fact, be very time-consuming. Item writers for standardized tests may produce only two or three usable items in an hour. A teacher who plans to measure student achievement with a multiple-choice examination would be well advised to begin the task quite some time before the date of the test. Some teachers find it useful to keep a supply of three by five index cards and to construct possible test items periodically or daily as instruction proceeds. In this way, by the time the test is needed the teacher will have a pool of items covering the entire content, and it will be relatively easy to select items and put them into a test format. Even teachers with many years of experience find the task of constructing thirty or thirty-five multiple-choice items at one time a grueling experience.

Multiple-choice items consist of two parts, the stem and the options. The stem, which presents the problem to the student, may be phrased as a question or an incomplete statement. The options are the possible answers to the questions or the completions of the statements.

The number of options provided for each question may range from three to five or six, depending upon the teacher's ingenuity in constructing answers that might plausibly be correct. A multiple-choice item with only two options is comparable to two true-false questions on the same topic. Giving more than five or six options leads students to spend a long time in reading. It is better to include more questions with fewer options than a few questions with many options each.

The number of options to be provided for a question is determined by the number of plausible possibilities that can be constructed. If the test constructor can construct only three plausible answers, that is all that should be included. There is no requirement that every item have the same number of options. Including options that no students will choose adds nothing to the worth of the item.

Suggestions for writing this type of item follow.

1. Develop items that measure important and relevant outcomes. Student achievement should be based on the mastery of meaningful ideas or propositions that are relevant to the student's future behavior. Questions that assess rote memorization or specific facts that are irrelevant to the students' future achievement should be eliminated. Laws, principles, and generalizations are more meaningful and more likely to be retained and used by the student in the future. Laws, principles, and generalizations may also be learned by rote, however, so the test constructor should phrase them in novel terms or require the student to apply them to novel situations.

2. Develop items that present a problem clearly to the student. Beginning test constructors may find it easier to phrase the stem in question form in order to be certain that they have formulated a problem. If incomplete statements are used in the stem, they should include enough information to indicate clearly what kind of response is required. Stating the stem as a question helps the teacher formulate homogeneous options.

3. In developing items, beware of including irrelevant clues in either the stem or the options that might indicate the correctness or incorrectness of the options. Grammatical clues at the end of an incomplete statement, such as *an*, which indicates that the correct option begins with a vowel, or a singular verb, such as *is* or *was*, which indicates that the option is singular, may help the student eliminate some answers. Instead, include the relevant verb or article with the option.

Clang associations between the stem and the correct response will also allow some students to choose the right answer by guessing. The following sample question contains a clang association.

A test of intelligence measures

1. personality.
2. manual dexterity.
3. intellectual ability.
4. achievement.

Intelligence and *intellectual* have the same root, a circumstance that might lead a person with no knowledge of the subject to choose that answer.

Even the lengths of the options should be examined. The longest option is often the correct one because more words must be used to qualify or substantiate its correctness.

4. In constructing a set of items, vary the position of the correct response. Unless care is taken in writing items, test constructors tend to place the correct response in one position more often than others. One should attempt to have approximately equal numbers of correct options in each position. Additionally, the positions of the correct responses should follow an essentially random pattern.

5. Include only one answer that experts would agree is correct or best. The directions to the students may be "Choose the correct answer" or "Choose the best answer." Whichever direction is given, include only one response that meets the criterion of *correct* or *best.*

6. Use the options *none of these* or *all of these* sparingly, if at all. When the directions say to choose the best answer, of course, neither of these responses would be correct. *All of these* implies that all options are equally plausible and *none of these* implies that all options completely lack plausibility—possibilities that are highly unlikely.

7. Keep the reading level of items low in relation to the reading ability of the group being tested. Unless one is giving a reading test, students should not be penalized for an inability to read and understand the questions. The reading level of the test should be below the average reading level of the class.

8. Include only as many items as all or almost all the students will have the time to finish. Achievement tests should be power tests rather than speed tests. Allowing students enough time to think through each of the options should also increase the reliability of the measurement. When students lack sufficient time to complete the test, they will resort to guessing, a tactic that introduces error into the test performance. Approximately one minute per question should be allowed for answering fairly complex questions. Students could perhaps be given forty-five seconds for less complex questions.

Other Types of Restricted Response Items

The other types of restricted response items are really variations of the multiple-choice item. True-false items consist essentially of the stem of a multiple-choice item and (a) the correct option if the item is true or (b) an incorrect option if the item is false. A completion item resembles the stem of a multiple-choice item except that the student supplies the correct answer. Matching exercises present a series of multiple-choice items and one set of options for answering the entire series. Following is an example of an exam question written in different ways but measuring the same conceptual knowledge:

Multiple-Choice

A child asks his parent for a cookie. The parent refuses, and the child throws a tantrum. The parent then gives the child a cookie. The tantrum behavior has been

1. put on an extinction schedule.
2. positively reinforced.
3. negatively reinforced.
4. punished.

True-False

1. A child asks his parent for a cookie. The parent refuses. The child throws a tantrum. The parent then gives the child a cookie. The tantrum behavior has been positively reinforced.   T   F

   OR

2. A child asks his parent for a cookie. The parent refuses. The child throws a tantrum. The parent then gives the child a cookie. The tantrum behavior has been negatively reinforced.   T   F

Completion

A child asks his parent for a cookie. The parent refuses. The child throws a tantrum. The parent then gives the child a cookie. The tantrum behavior has been _____.

Extended Short-Answer

Give an example of positive reinforcement.

Matching

Directions: In each of the following, what is happening to the behavior of the child? Match the answers to the questions.

Questions	*Answers*
_____ 1. Giving a child a cookie after he throws a tantrum	a. Positive reinforcement
_____ 2. Spanking a child for whining	b. Negative reinforcement
_____ 3. Teacher quits frowning when the child begins to study	c. Extinction
_____ 4. Teacher ignores a child's behavior	d. Punishment
_____ 5. A child cries and the father stops spanking	

Suggestions for Writing

Because of the similarities of these types of items, many of our suggestions for writing multiple-choice items apply equally to the writing of other restricted items. The test constructor should, however, consider certain specific suggestions for each of the other types:

True-False

1. Avoid lifting statements verbatim from the textbook.
2. For better discrimination, use more false items than true items but not many more.
3. Avoid using such words as *all, always, none,* and *never.* These are usually clues that the item is false.
4. Watch the length of the question. True items are usually longer than false items.

Completion

1. It is best to use one blank per question.
2. If, as in mathematics problems, the answer should be stated in certain units, those units should be specified.

Matching

1. The directions should clearly state the basis for matching.
2. The options presented should be homogeneous.
3. To decrease guessing, allow the examinees to use the options more than once.

Extended Short-Answer

In the question, include information that tells the student what is required for an answer to be considered complete. Compare these two examples:

> *Poor:* List the advantages and disadvantages of group intelligence tests.
> *Better:* List three advantages and three disadvantages of group intelligence tests.

Scoring Restricted Response Items

Scoring recognition items—multiple-choice, true-false, and matching—is a fairly routine task. Before testing we construct a key for the correct answers and then compare student responses with the key. Scoring can be facilitated by using a separate answer sheet for student responses, or by including before the questions spaces on which the students can record their answers.

Scoring recall items—completion and short-answer—is somewhat more subjective and usually takes longer, because instead of answering as anticipated, students may respond with synonyms or words similar to the keyed words. Separate judgments about the correctness of these unexpected responses must be made. The keyed answer for the completion item on page 561, for example is *positively reinforced*. A student might instead choose the response *rewarded* or *given approval*. The correctness of such alternate responses depends on the subjective judgment of the scorer.

Extended short-answer responses may vary in adequacy or correctness, much like extended response items. In order to assign full credit, partial credit, or no credit, the scorer must judge student paraphrasing, grammatical construction, and completeness of response individually.

► *ACTIVITY 2.*
  1. Develop a performance objective for some topic in this chapter.
  2. Construct a multiple-choice item to measure that objective.
  3. Construct at least two other types of restricted response items to measure the same objective.

Evaluating the Test

If one follows a test blueprint when constructing the test, one establishes content validity by adequately sampling the behaviors and the content. Test validity is important in establishing the fact that the test actually measures student achievement.

Student responses on the test can be used to determine the quality of the items and the reliability of the test. Item quality is determined by two factors, item difficulty and item discrimination. An examination of item quality can determine the value of the item for measuring student achievement. Some teachers find it advantageous to keep a file of test items for the courses they teach including the item difficulty and discrimination from previous administrations of items. A record of item quality can help the teacher choose items for future tests. To obtain measures of item quality and discrimination, one uses a set of scored test papers.

Item Analysis of Norm-Referenced Tests

To perform an item analysis on norm-referenced tests, select the test papers of the highest-scoring third of the class and the lowest-scoring third of the class. Use the responses of these students to determine item difficulty and discrimination.

Item Difficulty.   To calculate the difficulty of an item, add the proportions of students in the upper third and the lower third who answered the questions correctly and divide that sum by two.

$$\text{Item difficulty} = \frac{\begin{array}{l}\text{Proportion in upper} \\ \frac{1}{3} \text{ who answered} \\ \text{correctly}\end{array} + \begin{array}{l}\text{Proportion in lower} \\ \frac{1}{3} \text{ who answered} \\ \text{incorrectly}\end{array}}{2}$$

Suppose, for example, that eighty percent of the upper third and forty percent of the lower third answered an item correctly. To calculate the difficulty level, we add .80 and .40 and divided by two; the result is an item difficulty of .60. Difficulty levels can range from .00 (item missed by all students) to 1.00 (item answered correctly by all students).

The optimum difficulty for norm-referenced tests is .50. When items are answered correctly by fifty percent of the students, the total test scores tend to be spread over a large range. A wide spread of scores makes it easier to discriminate among student performances and increases the measure's reliability. Items with difficulty levels of .25 to .75 are considered good items. Very easy items (.75–1.00) discriminate poorly among students, but they may be used to provide successful experiences for the less able students. Difficult items (.00–.25) will not increase the spread of scores appreciably, though they may be used to challenge the highest-achieving students.

Item Discrimination.   A good test item discriminates between those who know the material and those who do not. If we assume that the highest scorers knew the most and the lowest scorers the least, then the discrimination index is the difference between the proportions of high scorers and low scorers who answered a question correctly.

$$\begin{array}{l}\text{Discrimination} \\ \text{index}\end{array} = \begin{array}{l}\text{Proportion of upper } \frac{1}{3} \\ \text{who answered correctly}\end{array} - \begin{array}{l}\text{Proportion of lower } \frac{1}{3} \\ \text{who answered correctly}\end{array}$$

Using the proportions from the preceding example, the discrimination index would be .40 (.80 − .40). This would be considered a good item, one that discriminates well. Discrimination indices can range from

+1.00 to −1.00. An item that has a negative discrimination index is considered a bad item in that it indicates that the lower-scoring students knew more than the higher-scoring students.

The higher the discrimination index, the better the item discriminates. Items with discrimination indices of .40 or higher are considered good items, appropriate for reuse. Items with discrimination indices less than .19 are considered poor. If the discrimination index is between .20 and .39, the item may be used again, but it should perhaps be revised.

▶ *ACTIVITY 3.*   A teacher gives a test to thirty students. Responses for the top ten and the bottom ten students for five questions are:

Item #	Correct responses	
	Upper ten students	*Lower ten students*
1	10	8
2	5	3
3	2	0
4	4	6
5	7	7

1. Calculate the difficulty level and discrimination index for each item.
2. Which is the best item? Why?
3. Which is the poorest item? Why?

Item Analysis of Criterion-Referenced Tests

The procedures for analyzing criterion-referenced measures are less well established than those for norm-referenced tests. Since the expected outcomes of the two types of measures differ, the procedures for analyzing the items differ as well.

Item Difficulty.   The concept of item difficulty has little meaning in criterion-referenced testing. In criterion-referenced measurement, the goal is for every student to meet the criterion, so there would be no difference between the highest and lowest students. If a large proportion of the students misses an item, it might indicate that it is a poor item. It might also mean, however, that the item is good but the instruction was poor; the students may not have learned what was necessary in order to answer the item correctly.

Item Discrimination.   Instead of being concerned with discriminations between high- and low-scoring students, as we were with norm-referenced measurement, in criterion-referenced measurement we are concerned with discriminating between those who have benefited from instruction and those who have not. To establish the discriminating power of an item or group of items, one can administer a pretest of the objectives. After instruction, one would administer the same test or an equivalent one. Differences in individual performances on the two tests would indicate the items' value for discrimination.

Reliability

In our discussion of reliability in Chapter 8b, we emphasized that there is always an element of error in a student's observed score. Measures of reliability are an estimate of the extent of the error. The reliability coefficients of teacher-made tests are lower than those for standardized tests, usually ranging between .50 and .70.

The procedures for calculating the reliability of tests are too complex and varied to consider in this text. The student may refer to any measurement text for a discussion of the procedures used. There are, however, some factors that a teacher may control to increase test reliability. These factors are:

1. *Length of test.* Other things being equal, the longer the test, the more reliable it is.

2. *Conditions of testing.* Reliability can be increased by giving the test in a comfortable environment. The teacher can control such factors as temperature, lighting, and distracting influences.

3. *Condition of students.* Allow enough time for students to prepare for the test in order to reduce test anxiety. Provide alternate times for students whose physical or mental health are not up to par.

Using Test Results for Feedback and Learning

Although many teachers assume that the primary purpose of tests is the evaluation of student achievement, more emphasis should be given to the use of tests for feedback to facilitate student learning as well as to assist in reteaching. To be most effective, students should be given feedback as soon as possible after the test is administered.

Test results tell the teacher whether remedial instruction or reteaching is necessary either for individuals or for the entire group. This feedback is especially important in highly sequenced courses like mathematics. Allowing students to proceed to the next topic when they lack understanding of the first topic will doom at least some of them to failure.

Tests should be considered part of the learning process. Feedback on tests can correct student misconceptions, encourage overlearning, and serve as reinforcement.

Teachers can provide feedback to the students by devoting class time to a review of the questions asked on the test or by holding conferences with individual students. This feedback can be used to correct student misconceptions and to help students discover their strengths and weaknesses on the material covered on the test. Reviewing the test with the students also encourages overlearning of the material, a procedure that improves retention. For some students, feedback serves a reinforcing function, thereby increasing the behaviors that led to successful accomplishment.

During the feedback session the teacher may reteach some of the concepts or skills that the students missed. Student questions about the test problems provide clues for remediating instruction. Emphasizing the positive aspects of the students' performance may improve motivation.

Although the teacher may attempt to emphasize the feedback and learning aspects of the test, students are generally concerned most with knowing what grade they received. Grades and grading, the evaluation of student achievement, will be discussed in Chapter 15.

Illustration of Test Construction

The preceding principles of test construction can be applied to any course or segment of a course. We have chosen the following hypothetical situation to illustrate the application of the principles.

. . .

Professor Harrow is teaching a first course in educational psychology and is using the Rosser-Nicholson text. He wants to determine if the students in his class have mastered the material in Chapter 3a before proceeding to application of this material in class projects. The objectives, test blueprint, and test that follow are limited to the material in the text. In an actual situation, the instructor would undoubtedly include additional objectives reflecting the lectures or other class activities. These objectives would then necessitate changes in the test blueprint and items.

The Performance Objectives

Professor Harrow's instruction was guided by the objectives he developed for this unit. The objectives listed below will be used as a basis for formulating the test blueprint.

1. Describe the events that precipitated the rise of behaviorism.
2. Name at least three proponents of behaviorism.
3. Describe the tenets of behavioral methodologists.
4. Given causes of behavior, determine whether they would be considered behavioral or not.
5. Compare, contrast, and recognize or give examples of the following pairs of terms:
   a) antecedent stimuli—consequent stimuli
   b) unconditioned stimulus—conditioned stimulus
   c) respondent behavior—operant behavior
   d) primary reinforcer—secondary reinforcer
   e) positive reinforcement—negative reinforcement
   f) positive punishment—negative punishment.
6. Define the following terms:
   a) higher order conditioning
   b) self-reinforcement
   c) knowledge of results.
7. Describe the difference between respondent and operant conditioning in terms of
   a) type of response
   b) contingency of stimulus and response
   c) causal relationships.
8. Describe the classical conditioning paradigm.
9. Given an example of classical conditioning, name the UCS, CS, UCR, and CR.
10. Describe the procedure by which a stimulus becomes a secondary reinforcer.
11. a) List the four different schedules of reinforcement.
    b) Describe how extinction is affected if reinforcement has been continuous or intermittent.
    c) Recognize examples of different schedules of reinforcement.

12. Recognize examples of operant conditioning procedures in which the probability of a response would (1) increase, (2) decrease, or (3) not be affected.
13. Evaluate the three methods for decreasing behavior—extinction, positive punishment, and negative punishment.

The Test Blueprint

The content dimension of the test blueprint can easily be divided into the four main segments of the chapter. An examination of the descriptor words of the objectives shows that they can be compressed into five divisions: (1) factual knowledge, (2) understanding, (3) relationships, (4) applications, and (5) evaluation. The test blueprint consists of twenty cells and the objectives can be placed in the appropriate cells. The completed blueprint is presented in Figure 14–3.

Mr. Harrow now must make some value judgments about the amount of emphasis to give to each content-behavior division. He judges the operant conditioning section to be most important, so he allocates fifty percent of the test to that section. Classical conditioning will comprise thirty-three percent of the test and the remaining seventeen percent will be divided between the first two sections.

Considering the educational level of the students, Professor Harrow judges that little emphasis should be given to factual knowledge, only five percent. Forty percent would be devoted to understanding and ten percent to relationships. Since applications will be covered more fully in Chapter 3b and the evaluation will be emphasized after practical application, he allocates twenty and twenty-five percent, respectively, to those areas. The points on the tests will be divided in those proportions, which are indicated on the margins of the test blueprint.

The Test Items

Professor Harrow prefers to use several different types of test items— multiple-choice, completion, true-false, and extended short-answer. Several different approaches could be taken in constructing the items. One procedure would be to develop items covering the behavior-content of each cell. This is probably the best way to ensure content validity. Another approach would be simply to write items as he thinks of them. After constructing a number of items, he would select those that fit the blueprint. This approach would probably entail writing more items than would be used, but that would be advantageous in that it would give him an opportunity to choose the best items from those constructed to use in the test. Mr. Harrow might also have constructed items as the instruction was taking place, so he would need only to choose those items that fit the test blueprint.

The test blueprint is designed to cover the entire content and all behaviors. In most cases, however, the test items will represent only a

	CONTENT				
BEHAVIOR	1. Introduction	2. Under-pinnings of behaviorism	3. Classical conditioning	4. Operant conditioning	
A. Factual knowledge	Obj. 2 Item 6			Obj. 11a	5%
B. Understanding	Obj. 1 Item 11	Obj. 3	Obj. 5a, 5b, 5c, 6a, 8 Items 1, 2, 3, 8	Obj. 5c, 5d, 5e, 5f, 6b, 6c, 10, 11b Items 4, 5, 7, 9, 10	40%
C. Relationships			Obj. 7a, 7b, 7c Items 8, 13	Obj. 7a, 7b, 7c	10%
D. Application			Obj. 9 Item 15	Obj. 11c, 12 Items 14, 16a	20%
E. Evaluation		Obj. 4 Item 12		Obj. 13 Item 16b	25%
	10%	7%	33%	50%	

FIGURE 14–3.   Test Blueprint for Chapter 3A

sample of all the content and behaviors included in each cell of the blueprint. To restrict the length of the test, the test constructor needs to select from each of the cells.

Professor Harrow selected five completion questions (one point each), five true-false questions (one point each), four multiple-choice questions (two points each), and two extended short-answer questions (four points and eight points each). The item numbers are recorded in the appropriate cells of the test blueprint.

The Test Format

The order of presentation of items may be random or systematic. One systematic approach could be to order the items in the same way the subject was taught. This scheme is helpful to the student because it allows the student to consider the items in the order learned and perhaps reviewed. A second systematic approach would be to order the items from easiest to most difficult. This format may relieve test anxiety. Success on the first items may increase the student's confidence in attempting the more difficult items. Since Mr. Harrow has different types of items, he elects to group the items by type and within each section place the items in the same order as the instruction occurred.

An important task remaining is to write the directions for answering the questions. The directions should be clear and concise and should explain the basis for answering the questions, the way the student is to record the answers, and the credit given for each correct answer.

The completed test is shown below.

Test: Behavioral Approaches to Learning

True-False (one point each). For each of the questions, circle the T if the statement is true; circle the F if the statement is false.

T F 1. Food would be considered a secondary reinforcer.
T F 2. The controlling stimulus in operant conditioning is the antecedent stimulus.
T F 3. Higher-order conditioning occurs when a neutral stimulus is paired with an unconditioned stimulus.
T F 4. Positive and negative reinforcement differ in the effect that they have on the probability of a response occurring.
T F 5. If a response is difficult to extinguish, it has likely been reinforced continuously.

Completion (one point each). Write the correct word or words in the blanks in each of the following statements.

6. Three proponents of behaviorism are _____, _____, and _____.
7. Learning to write with a pencil exemplifies _____ conditioning.
8. A stimulus that is followed by an unlearned response is the basis for _____ conditioning.
9. A stimulus is considered to be a _____ if the probability of the occurrence of the immediately preceding response increases.
10. The good feelings that a child experiences when receiving praise for good behavior may become a reinforcer. This is an example of _____.

Multiple choice (two points each). Place the letter corresponding to the correct answer in the blank preceding each question.

____ 11. Psychology was originally the study of consciousness. Which one of the following emphasized the study of the unconscious?
  a. British empiricists
  b. Freud
  c. Watson
  d. Pavlov

____ 12. Tommy is fighting with Billy on the playground. Which one of the following explanations would be proposed as a cause of a behaviorist?
  a. Tommy is innately aggressive.
  b. Tommy feels insecure.
  c. Tommy doesn't like Billy.
  d. Tommy has received peer approval for fighting in the past.

_____ 13. The order of contingencies for the two types of conditioning are
a. respondent, S-R; operant, S-R
b. respondent, S-R; operant, R-S
c. respondent, R-S; operant, S-R
d. respondent, R-S; operant, R-S

_____ 14. Mrs. Rayner's class of third grade children have been assigned a worksheet to complete. The students are working diligently, except Greg, who is interrupting the work of his friend, Brian. Mrs. Rayner frowns sternly at Greg. Greg's behavior would
a. decrease as a result of positive punishment.
b. decrease as a result of negative punishment.
c. increase as a result of positive reinforcement.
d. be unpredictable, given only the above information.

Short answers. Answer the following questions on a separate sheet of paper.

15. (four points) A small child is playing in the yard and reaches to pick a flower, not seeing a bee on the flower. The child is stung by the bee and begins to cry. A few days later, an adult picks a flower and tries to hand it to the child. The child begins to cry. Name the UCS, CS, UCR, and CR.

16. (eight points) A mother asks a counselor for advice on the best procedure for decreasing her child's nail-biting behavior. The mother says that she has thought of three alternatives: (1) slapping the child's hand when the child bites her nails, (2) taking away TV privileges for nail-biting, and (3) ignoring the nail-biting.
a. What kind of decrease procedures are represented by each alternative?
b. Evaluate each procedure for its probable effectiveness.

▶ *ACTIVITY 4.* Since this is Professor Harrow's first experience at test construction, some weaknesses may be reflected in his procedures. The following activities will allow you to apply your knowledge to eliminate some of the weaknesses:

1. Review Chapter 3a in regard to Professor Harrow's objectives. List any additional objectives that you would include and eliminate any of his objectives that you would not deem to be important.
2. Construct a new test blueprint with your revised list of objectives.
3. Examine the test items that Professor Harrow used. Evaluate the appropriateness of the items in terms of matching the objectives and following the guidelines for constructing test items.
4. Professor Harrow did not write items for Objectives 3, 6c, 8, 11a, and 11c. Choose two of these objectives and write appropriate items for measuring student achievement of these objectives.

Summary

Measuring the cognitive outcomes of education provides us with evidence of the student's achievement of course objectives. The teacher must decide how often to test, what to test, and what types of questions to use. The frequency of testing is determined by subject matter divisions, the need for feedback, and adequate coverage of the content. Decisions about what to test are based on the performance objectives; these objectives are the basis for the test blueprint used to construct the test. The decision about whether to use extended response questions, restricted response questions, or both may be based on the kinds of performance expected from the students and the expertise of the test constructor.

There are a number of different guidelines for constructing and scoring different types of items. Extended response questions take a long time to score but can be constructed more easily than restricted response questions. Restricted response questions take longer to construct but are easily scored. The quality of the test depends upon its validity and reliability as well as the quality of the items. Item quality is a function of the difficulty level and the discrimination index.

The procedures outlined in Chapter 14 will provide a score for each student. The next step is to evaluate those scores. To answer the question, "How well did the student achieve the objectives?" requires that the teacher place a value on the score. The evaluations in a large majority of cases take the form of grades. The initial emphasis of the chapter is on the different procedures teachers might use for assigning grades to test scores.

Some outcomes of education are not amenable to measurement by tests. Evaluation of products (e.g., term papers, art work) and procedures (e.g., oral reading, music performance) require different methods. Checklists and rating scales are frequently chosen methods.

In the final section of the chapter, we explore methods for combining measurements and evaluations for periodic summaries of achievement. The periodic summaries are used for school records as well as for reporting to parents, which may take the form of report cards, parent-teacher conferences or narrative reports.

Chapter 15

Evaluation of Student Progress

Introduction

Many teachers consider evaluating student behaviors to be one of the least desirable tasks they must perform. Listening to a group of teachers at grading time, one can discern the anguish, uncertainty, and equivocation that the task arouses. From time to time, articles are published or speeches are made advocating the elimination of the grading or evaluation process. Evaluation of students has been an integral part of the educational process for such a long time that such articles and speeches have little influence, however, except to focus attention on problems of evaluation.

There are several reasons for evaluating students:

1. Evaluation can be used to determine whether a student has met objectives set by the teacher or school.
2. Evaluation can reveal a student's strengths and weaknesses.
3. Evaluation can determine a student's achievement in relation to other students.

The first two reasons are concerned with evaluating students in order to improve instruction. The evaluation provides feedback to the teacher and student about changes in instructional procedures, the need for remediation, possible acceleration, or other adjustments that might help meet the student's needs.

The third reason is concerned with making decisions about the student's future. Evaluations made in the past provide information useful in making decisions about future course placement, college admission, retention at grade level, or selection for honors programs.

Pros and Cons of Grading

Although evaluation may take several different forms in the school setting, it generally involves grading. The pros and cons of grading are debated, sometimes vehemently, by teachers, students, administrators, and parents.

Advocates of grades point out that they serve several useful purposes:

1. Grades are necessary for administrative purposes. Records of student achievement are necessary for placement, for admission to college, and for employment references.
2. Grades provide information for student guidance. Selection of courses, for example, is based in part on information about past achievement. Records of grades also provide information for decisions about attending college or preparing for a vocation.
3. Assigning grades is a convenient method of providing information on the child's achievement to parents and others. Parents want a simple way to interpret their children's achievement. Since grades have been used for many years, parents feel more comfortable with this type of evaluation than with more general statements of achievement. A typical parent question after receiving a narrative report in a letter or conference with the teacher is, "But what grade did my child receive?"
4. Grades may be motivating and may reward student achievement. Students who know they will be evaluated try harder. Grades are immediate, attainable goals. Children and adolescents may find it difficult to work toward remote goals without the feedback provided by intervening evaluation.

Critics of grading, on the other hand, point out problems with the practice:

1. There are no agreed-upon criteria for marks. An *A* in one teacher's class means something different from an *A* in another's class. Different teachers may evaluate on the basis of absolute achievement, achievement in relation to ability, achievement and effort, or achievement contaminated by such factors as attitude, attendance, or behavior in class.
2. Grades are unreliable. Insofar as the methods of gathering information are unreliable, grades are unreliable as well. Poorly constructed tests, subjectivity, and inadequate observations or records of observations lead to unreliability.
3. Grades increase anxiety. Pressure to get good grades can increase student anxiety. In some cases this is beneficial; raising the anxiety

Evaluation by grading may provide more immediate goals for the student and provide for reinforcement of behaviors leading to achievement. Too much emphasis on grades, however, can increase the anxiety of students and lower their performance.

level of low-anxiety students may help them perform at the optimum level. Too much anxiety lowers performance, however.

4. Students become interested in grades rather than in learning. This observation, however, assumes that grades and learning are independent. If testing instruments are designed to reflect course objectives, high achievement will be reflected in good grades. In this situation, a student who works for grades will also learn.

5. Low grades tend to reduce motivation and lead to alienation from school. Students who consistently receive low grades see themselves as incapable. They tend to find other situations that will provide successful experiences. Students who get low grades are more likely to be absent often and to drop out of school.

Both the opponents and proponents of grading have valid arguments for their positions. By recognizing the problems with grading, teachers can attempt to overcome them. Grades, since they are so firmly entrenched in our society, will continue to be part of the evaluation process. The teacher's objective, then, is to provide information as valid and reliable as possible for making evaluations.

What Is Evaluated?

Any student behavior can be evaluated. Teachers' time is limited, however, so teachers must decide how much to evaluate. Certainly, teachers must consider evidence of academic achievement as important to evaluate, since schools are designed to promote academic achievement. Without such evidence, we cannot determine the value of schooling. To evaluate academic achievement one might consider the results of tests and quizzes, homework and seatwork, class recitations, themes, term papers, speeches, group or individual projects, and other evidence.

Since we consider the child's total school adjustment, evidence of personal and social development is also important. Teachers and parents are concerned with whether or not the child is developing good study skills, character traits, and social skills.

The subject being taught or the level at which the teacher is teaching may influence the kinds of evidence used for evaluation. Physical education teachers are concerned with the development of physical skills, coordination, agility, and good health practices. Art teachers may be concerned with the products made by the students, but they will also seek evidence about the procedures used, the development of creativity, and the appreciation of art. Elementary teachers, especially those at the primary levels, are concerned with the basic skills; secondary teachers tend to focus on content rather than skills *per se.*

It is impossible to discuss in this text evaluation procedures for all the outcomes of education. The discussion that follows will be limited to suggestions for evaluating test results, products and procedures, and personal and social development.

Marking Systems

The number of different symbols used for evaluation by teachers and schools varies considerably. In a given system there may be as few as two or as many as a hundred. The argument for using more than two categories is that it permits greater differentiation of students. If too many categories are used, however, whether teachers can reliably ascertain differences between them becomes doubtful.

Two-Category System

This type of system requires the teacher to make only one discrimination for each student: the student has performed either acceptably or unacceptably. The symbols most frequently used are *P* (pass)-*F* (fail), *Cr* (credit)-*NC* (no credit), or *S* (satisfactory)-*U* (unsatisfactory).

Proponents of the two-category system maintain that it reduces competition for grades. They reason that with decreased competitiveness, there is less cheating and anxiety, and students no longer study for grades but for learning. The empirical evidence for such beliefs is meager, however, and some studies have even shown that students in *P-F* courses display decreased motivation for learning and lower achievement (Main & Gallagher, 1972; Hales, Bain, & Rand, 1971).

When a two-category marking system is used, information that might affect a number of educational practices is lost. Criteria for admission to college are difficult to determine, since there is no difference between the top student in the class and a student who barely passes. Other school practices based on differential achievement, such as selection for the honor roll or special programs, are also affected.

Five-Category System

The five-category system is the most popular. This system differentiates students better than the two-category system. The categories are broad enough to permit fairly accurate judgments. The most commonly used symbols are *A, B, C, D,* and *F* or *1, 2, 3, 4,* and *5*.

The five-category system has been in use for a long enough time that parents and students apparently understand the meaning of the symbols. Students' grade-point averages are commonly based on conversion from the five-point scale.

Systems with More than Five Categories

One of the first marking systems contained, at least in theory, a hundred different categories. All evaluations were expressed as percentages, with one hundred percent representing a perfect performance. Some percentage between sixty and seventy-five was considered a passing grade, with scores above that point defining different degrees of acceptability. Percentage scores are easily misinterpreted, and differentiations based on percentages are often greatly exaggerated. A student who has a 90.2 percent average, for example, might be named to the honor roll while a student with an average of 89.8 percent would be considered ineligible. The use of percentage marking systems began to decrease in the 1940s, and today they are seldom used. The influence of percentage marking is still evident, however, in marking systems in which letter grades are assigned on the basis of percentages.

Another system that uses more than five categories is based on the five-category system. In this system a plus or minus sign is added to each of the passing marks. This provides for thirteen different categories, so the teacher must make more differentiations. Although some teachers may collect accurate enough data to make this more refined differentiation, it is doubtful that there is much difference between an *A* − and a *B* + or between a *C* and a *C* −.

Evaluation of Test Results

The method a teacher uses to evaluate achievement test scores will be determined by two factors. The first concerns whether a criterion-referenced or norm-referenced measurement was taken. The second consideration is whether to use absolute standards or relative standards. The two factors are not completely independent. Criterion-referenced measurements are normally evaluated on absolute standards. Norm-referenced measurements may entail either absolute or relative standards.

Evaluation of Criterion-Referenced Measurement

In our discussion of criterion-referenced measurement in Chapter 8b, we indicated that this type of measurement is based on a set of clearly specified objectives that state (1) the desired performance and (2) the criterion for success. Criterion-referenced measures allow the students to demonstrate whether they have mastered an objective or not. Suppose a fifth grade teacher had the following arithmetic objective: "The student will within four minutes be able to write the correct answers to one hundred multiplication facts." To determine whether the student had met the objective, the teacher would provide a sheet of one hundred multiplication facts, ask the student to write the answers, and set time limits. The measure would be evaluated with a two-category system, such as *P-F* or *S-U.*

To report grades to parents, students, and administrators, the teacher would list the objectives of the course and indicate whether the student had met them. Each student's achievement would be evaluated independently—performances would not be compared. This type of reporting is perhaps the most informative in that it specifies exactly what the student has accomplished.

Evaluation of Norm-Referenced Measurement

Norm-referenced measurements may be evaluated using either absolute or relative standards. Absolute standards established prior to measurement specify the criteria for receiving each grade or mark. When relative standards are used, the student's performance is compared to that of a reference group, usually the class in which the student is enrolled.

Absolute Standard. One common type of evaluation that reflects an absolute standard involves assigning letter grades on the basis of the percentage of the items that a student answered correctly. Two frequently used grading systems that assign different numerical values to grades are illustrated below.

	System I		System II
A	= 90–100 percent	A	= 94–100 percent
B	= 80–89 percent	B	= 87–93 percent
C	= 70–79 percent	C	= 80–86 percent
D	= 60–69 percent	D	= 75–79 percent
F	= 59 percent and below	F	= 74 percent and below

The advantage of the absolute standard is that a uniform system is applied to all measurements. The criteria are established in advance, and students are aware of the standards. With this type of grading system, any number of students may receive high grades. If all students score above ninety percent in System I, then all students would receive A's. Conversely, if no students scored above 90 percent, no A's would be awarded.

The distribution of grades depends to a great extent upon the difficulty of the test, which is determined in turn by the difficulty indices of the items that the teacher writes. Very easy items would practically ensure a large number of high grades; a teacher who desired to limit the number of high grades could write very difficult items.

In Table 15–1 the two systems are applied to a set of test scores and the corresponding letter grades are recorded in the first two columns. As illustrated, one point can make a difference between a B or a C. If error of measurement is considered, it is likely that some students will be misclassified when these systems are used.

When the teacher believes that the spread of grades contains too few high grades and too many low, the absolute standards may be compromised in order to adjust the grades. One compromise that teachers make is to consider the top score to be one hundred percent. Other scores are then computed as percentages of the top score, and grades are assigned by using one of the grade-assignment systems. The results of this compromise procedure are illustrated for System I in the third column of Table 15–1.

Relative Standards. Using relative standards, a student's score is evaluated in terms of its rank in the total distribution of scores. Teachers can use many different methods that incorporate relative standards.

Normal Curve Method. The normal curve has been used as a model for evaluating test performance. A certain percentage of scores is assigned to each grade category. The largest proportion would receive C's, with smaller and equal proportions receiving B's and D's and the smallest proportions receiving A's and F's. Different teachers use different proportions. One fairly common distribution allocates grades as follows: the top seven percent would be given A's, the next twenty-three percent B's, the middle forty percent C's, the next twenty-three percent D's, and the lowest seven percent F's.

TABLE 15–1. Different Evaluations of 30 Scores on a 50-Point Test

Absolute				Relative			
System I	System II	Compromise (System I)	Scores	Normal curve	Strict guess	Lenient guess	System- atic
B	C	A	42	A	B	A	A
B	C	A	41	A	B	A	B
B	C	A	40	B	B	A	B
C	D	A	39	B	B	A	B
C	D	A	39	B	B	A	B
C	D	A	38	B	B	A	B
C	D	A	38	B	B	A	B
C	F	B	35	B	C	B	B
D	F	B	34	B	C	B	B
D	F	C	33	C	C	B	B
D	F	C	33	C	C	B	B
D	F	C	33	C	C	B	B
D	D	C	30	C	D	C	C
F	F	D	29	C	D	C	C
F	F	D	29	C	D	C	C
F	F	D	29	C	D	C	C
F	F	D	28	C	D	C	C
F	F	D	27	C	D	C	C
F	F	D	27	C	D	C	C
F	F	D	26	C	D	C	C
F	F	F	22	C	F	D	D
F	F	F	21	D	F	D	D
F	F	F	20	D	F	D	D
F	F	F	20	D	F	D	D
F	F	F	20	D	F	D	D
F	F	F	19	D	F	D	D
F	F	F	18	D	F	D	D
F	F	F	17	D	F	D	D
F	F	F	12	F	F	F	F
F	F	F	11	F	F	F	F

The normal curve method is applied in the fifth column of Table 15–1. This method assumes that scores in the group being measured follow a normal distribution. As we discussed earlier, normal distributions occur only when a large number of people are measured, never with a group of thirty. Teacher-made tests rarely, if ever, yield a normal distribution of scores. Fitting a non-normal group of scores into a normal distribution introduces error into our evaluations. As was true with the absolute standards, the difference between letter grades may be one score point, an eventuality that leads to misclassification of students through measurement errors.

The So-Called Guess Method. The guess method receives its name from the teacher's saying, "I guess I'll give these scores *A*'s, these scores

B's," and so on. In fairness to teachers who use this system, the guesses are not random. They are based, rather, on a preconceived idea of what percentage of students should receive each grade, such as the normal distribution or an approximation of it. This method also uses the natural breaks in the distribution for divisions between grades. Natural breaks are gaps where no scores fall in the distribution. Using natural gaps as division points tends to minimize misclassifications due to errors of measurement.

This procedure seems to work fairly well for some distributions. Using the natural breaks may distort quite radically the percent of students receiving each grade, however. Consider the distribution of scores in Table 15–1. The first break is between thirty-five and thirty-eight. Seven scores were above that break. The teacher must decide whether all seven students will receive *A*'s or whether there will be no *A*'s awarded and those students will receive *B*'s. The same sort of decision must be made concerning the other natural breaks. Two different ways of assigning grades to the scores in Table 15–1, labeled *strict* and *lenient,* are illustrated in the sixth and seventh columns.

This method depends to some extent on the vagaries of the teacher's mood or disposition at the time the grades are assigned. The grades in the sixth column may have resulted from a teacher's idea that the students had not been working hard enough, or perhaps the teacher had an extremely trying and hectic day before assigning the grades. On another day or in another mood, the teacher might have used the grades in the seventh column.

Systematic Marking. In a systematic marking procedure described by Ebel (1979), the average test performance of the class is considered the average grade, and equal intervals are used for each letter grade. For a class of average ability, the median of the class would be the middle of the *C* range of scores. The standard deviation is the interval used to determine the range of each letter grade. The grade of *C* would cover the ranges half a standard deviation above and below the median. The *B* range would extend one standard deviation above the top *C*, and the *D* range would extend one standard deviation below the lowest *C*. Scores falling more than 1.5 standard deviations above the median would be classified as *A*'s, and those lower than 1.5 standard deviations below the median would be *F*'s. For the distribution in Table 15–1, the median is 29 and the standard deviation, calculated by the method described in Chapter 8b, is 8.5. The grade assignments would be:

$$A = \text{above highest } B \qquad = \qquad = 41.75 \text{ and higher}$$
$$B = 1 \text{ S.D. above highest } C = 32.25 + 8.5 = 33.25 - 41.75$$
$$C = \text{Median} \pm .5 \text{ S.D.} \qquad = 29 \pm 4.25 = 24.75 - 33.25$$
$$D = 1 \text{ S.D. below lowest } C = 24.75 - 8.5 = 16.25 - 33.25$$
$$F = \text{below lowest } D \qquad = \qquad = \text{below } 16.25$$

An advantage of this system is that the proportion of students who will receive each grade is not predetermined. Another advantage is that the average performance receives the average grade. Since equal intervals are provided for each grade, the whole distribution has a consistency that the normal curve or guessing methods lack. Using the normal curve method, for example, the difference between the highest and lowest *B* was seven points, whereas the difference between the highest and lowest *C* was twelve points. The systematic procedure makes each grade range represent an equal interval.

The primary disadvantage of this method is that letter grades may differ by only one point, so misclassifications may result from measurement error. This method also requires more calculation than the other methods.

The systematic method of marking was developed to adjust the grading to the level of the class being evaluated. In the preceding example, the class was considered average, so the average grade was

Teachers will need to evaluate products and procedures as well as performance on paper and pencil tests. Rating scales and checklists provide for more adequate evaluation of products and procedures.

a *C*. With classes of higher or lower ability, a different average grade might be chosen. The adjustments to be made for the differing ability levels of classes are described by Ebel (1979).

A perfect grading system applicable to all courses and all students has yet to be developed. In choosing a grading system, the teacher should consider the following criteria.

1. *Fairness*. The grades assigned should be fair to the students. Capricious grading or using grades as a weapon of control leads to poor rapport between teachers and students.

2. *Objectivity*. Grades should be assigned as objectively as possible. When subjectivity becomes a part of the grading system, teacher's biases toward students will affect the grades, which should be reflections of student achievement and unaffected by whether the teacher likes the student.

3. *Defensibility*. At the secondary level of education, students frequently ask the teacher to defend the system of evaluation used. At the elementary level, parents sometimes ask the teacher to explain the evaluation system. An evaluation system that depends on the whims of the teacher is not easily defended.

4. *Minimize misclassification*. Be aware that scores near the top or bottom of a grade range may actually be misclassified. Some teachers add a plus or minus sign to these grades in order to indicate their proximity to the next letter grade.

Evaluating Other Educational Outcomes

Paper and pencil tests are effective procedures for measuring cognitive outcomes. After the third grade, paper and pencil tests may become the primary means of evaluating student achievement. Other educational outcomes are less amenable to evaluation with paper and pencil tests, however. In some classes, for example, students' products and the procedures for completing tasks are important in evaluating achievement. Personal and social development are also difficult to evaluate with tests.

Products and Procedures

Many teachers must evaluate products and procedures. Products that might be evaluated include sculpture, bookcases constructed in woodworking class, themes, and term papers. Oral reading, the use of the microscope, speaking, playing an instrument, using an athletic skill, and driving a car involve procedures that might be evaluated.

Two methods commonly used to evaluate products and procedures are *checklists* and *rating scales*. Published checklists and rating scales are available for some skills and products. Checklists and rating scales constructed by the teacher are, however, more likely to reflect that teacher's objectives and expectations, even though they may lack the technical refinement of the published variety.

Constructing the Instrument. The first task in constructing a rating scale or checklist is to determine the components important for a successful product or procedure. These components will resemble the course objectives and may be based on them. What are the important components? Consider, for example, the procedure of presenting a speech. The important elements might be posture, voice quality, use of gestures, rate of speaking, eye contact with audience, and diction. The elements will vary, depending on the product or procedure.

Students should be told which components will be evaluated. They should also be told if they vary in importance. In evaluating a term paper, a teacher might devise a weighting scheme for the components:

Format	30 percent
Grammar	10 percent
Content	40 percent
Use of footnotes	10 percent
Bibliography	10 percent

Telling the students which aspects will be evaluated and what emphasis will be placed on each of them allows them to work toward meeting the teacher's expectations.

Checklists. If the teacher is concerned only with the presence or absence of a particular component, a checklist is the appropriate instrument. The checklist requires only a yes-no response for each component of the product or procedure. Checklists are especially useful when a procedure can be divided into a series of clearly defined actions or steps. An example of a checklist that might be used to evaluate a person's ability to start and move a car from a curbside parking position is illustrated in Figure 15–1. In using a checklist the evaluator merely checks whether each step was performed or not. Order of performance is important in this example, so the listing on the scale represents that order.

Checklists can be excellent devices for providing feedback to students. When evaluating a complex procedure, it is difficult for an evaluator to remember each component of the performance. Without a checklist or some other record of the components, the evaluation tends to be global: "That was a good job" or "You were OK." With a checklist, the evaluator can provide specific statements about each aspect of the performance.

Rating Scales. For many products and procedures, the evaluator is concerned with the degree of a characteristic or the frequency with which a behavior occurs. Rating scales require a kind of judgment

Student _____   Instructor _____

Date _____

Yes	No		Comments
___	___	1. Check to see that car is in *neutral* or *park*.	
___	___	2. Turn ignition switch.	
___	___	3. Start car.	
___	___	4. Check instrument panel.	
___	___	5. Turn on *turn* signal.	
___	___	6. Depress brake/clutch.	
___	___	7. Shift into appropriate gear.	
___	___	8. Check traffic in front and behind.	
___	___	9. Release brake/clutch.	
___	___	10. Accelerate gradually.	
___	___	11. Turn into correct traffic lane.	

FIGURE 15–1.   Checklist

different from the one required by checklists, not a simple yes-no or present-absent response but a qualitative or quantitative judgment about the product or procedure.

There are a number of different types of rating scales. Three types are illustrated in Figure 15–2, all of them for the purpose of rating the components of a speech performance. With the *numerical rating scale,* the observer circles a number corresponding to a description. To be effective, there must be general agreement about the meanings of the descriptive terms.

The *graphic rating scales* consist of a continuum of descriptive categories. To indicate the ranking for a particular category, the observer places a mark somewhere on a line over the names of the categories. The specificity of the terms used on graphic rating scales varies. Our first illustration uses terms similar to those used in the numerical rating scale. To interpret this type of rating, observers would have to have a common understanding of the meaning of the terms. A better graphic rating scale would include more specific behavioral descriptions at the various points on the scale, as does our second illustration.

FIGURE 15–2.   **Types of Rating Scales**

NUMERICAL RATING SCALE

Directions: Indicate the quality of each aspect of the speech by circling the appropriate number. The numbers represent the following values.

  5—Outstanding
  4—Above average
  3—Average
  2—Below average
  1—Unsatisfactory

1. Use of gestures

  1   2   3   4   5

2. Voice quality

  1   2   3   4   5

GRAPHIC RATING SCALE

Directions: Indicate the quality of each aspect of the speech by placing a check (✔) on the horizontal line in each item.

1. Use of gestures

  _____
  Never   Occasionally   Frequently

2. Voice quality

  _____
  Weak   Average   Strong

GRAPHIC RATING SCALE—BEHAVIORAL DESCRIPTORS

Directions: Indicate the quality of each aspect of the speech by placing a (✔) on the horizontal line in each item.

1. Use of gestures

Never	Seldom; stilted	Occasional and appropriate	Frequent; sometimes inappropriately	Frequent; at appropriate times

2. Voice quality

Weak, squeaky, carries poorly	Moderate but at times weak, carries poorly	Moderate in strength, carries fairly well	Strong but varies toward moderate, carries well	Strong, full, carries well

---

Two types of errors are common in using rating scales, and observers should try to avoid them. *Personal bias* errors occur when a rater tends to rate everyone at approximately the same position on the scale. This obscures differences between individuals. Personal bias errors also make it more difficult to discriminate the strengths and weaknesses of an individual's performance. The second type of error results from the *halo effect*. This occurs when an observer's general impression of a product or procedure influences all of his ratings for that individual. The halo effect may be occurring when all aspects of an individual's product or performance are given high, low, or average ratings. This type of error also tends to obscure any differences present in the procedure or product being evaluated. Rating scales are superior to general impressions because they require that each component be examined. The halo effect eliminates this benefit.

Rating scales can be effective instruments for evaluating products and procedures if the following suggestions are observed.

1. The rating scale should include characteristics that are educationally significant. One can use the objectives for the unit or the course as characteristics.
2. The characteristics to be rated should be observable directly.
3. Students should be told which characteristics of the product or procedure will be evaluated.
4. The number of different characteristics to be rated during one observation should be limited. Products that can be evaluated over a period of time may have more characteristics than a process or procedure that occurs only once.
5. In rating the product or procedure, the observer should be as objective as possible, guarding against personal bias and the halo effect.
6. The descriptors used to designate the points on the scales should be as specific as possible.
7. The student should be given feedback on the rating of the product or procedure.

▶ *ACTIVITY 1.*   Choose a subject and grade level that you might like to teach. Select a product or procedure appropriate for that subject and grade level and develop either a checklist or a rating scale for evaluating the product or procedure. Examples include artwork, speaking performance, term papers, or science experiments. Determine what emphasis would be placed on each element of the evaluation.

Evaluating Personal and Social Outcomes

The personal and social outcomes of education may also be evaluated with checklists or rating scales. Report cards sent home to parents often include a rating of some aspect or aspects of the student's behavior or development. Some schools require that periodic ratings of students be submitted to counselors, administrators, or both.

The major difference between evaluating products and procedures and evaluating personal and social behaviors is in the time of the ratings. Ratings of personal and social behaviors are normally done periodically, at set times, whereas evaluations of products and procedures are done during or shortly after the completion of the task. Ratings done at the end of a period, whether nine weeks, a semester, or a school year, are usually less objective and more subject to rater bias than ratings done shortly after a behavior or performance has occurred.

To decrease subjectivity, the teacher or evaluator should keep records of behaviors that lend credibility to the ratings. Anecdotal records are factual descriptions of meaningful incidents the teacher has observed involving students. Each incident is recorded shortly after it happens. The incidents may be recorded on index cards or in a notebook the teacher can refer to for the periodic evaluations.

An anecdotal record should state specifically what occurred as objectively as possible. Any interpretation or judgment of the occurrence should be clearly separate from the factual report. A sample anecdotal record is presented in Figure 15–3.

One criticism of anecdotal records is that atypical behaviors are more likely to be recorded than typical behaviors, and negative behaviors are recorded more frequently than positive behaviors. To avoid these problems, teachers can establish regular observation schedules to observe different students at set times and thereby record more

---

FIGURE 15–3.   Anecdotal Record

Observer   Mary O'Brien   Date   11/16/82

Student   George O.

During math class, the student teacher returned the homework from the preceding day. George received his paper and immediately hid it in his folder. When Alex asked him what grade he got, George began to cry and asked to leave the room.

Possible Interpretation: George is accustomed to receiving *A* grades. The student teacher had given him a *B* − because of lack of neatness.

---

typical behavior in the anecdotal records. Of course, atypical behaviors may be important, and records of them may tend to counteract some general impressions. Noting that a hostile child has made a friendly gesture or that a normally shy child has volunteered to speak in class may be useful in evaluating behaviors and planning experiences to facilitate social development. It is wise to remember, however, that personal and social outcomes are determined only with difficulty and that subjectivity reduces the reliability of the ratings. The use of anecdotal records and scales of specific behaviors can help reduce subjectivity.

Combining Scores for Periodic Evaluation

Most school systems require that student achievement be formally evaluated at regular intervals, perhaps every nine weeks, every semester, or at the end of the school year. During these periods, the teacher should have accumulated a number of evaluations based on a variety of performances, including tests, term papers or other products, quizzes, class recitations, and homework or seatwork. In determining student achievement, these performances are usually not equally valuable. The teacher must determine the importance of each and the way it will contribute to the mark to be given at the end of the period. The decision should be communicated to the students.

One possible weighting of the evaluation would be as follows:

Class recitation	10 percent
Homework/seatwork	10 percent
Quizzes	15 percent
Term paper or project	20 percent
Test #1	20 percent
Test #2	25 percent

Perhaps the easiest method for weighting the components is to assign points to them according to the degree of their importance. The maximum points for recitation and homework would be ten points each, quizzes fifteen points, term papers twenty points, Test #1 twenty points, and Test #2 twenty-five points. If one wished to use more points, a multiple of these points could be used as long as the percentages remained the same. For instance, one could assign point values of twenty, twenty, thirty, forty, forty, and fifty.

This procedure is illustrated in Table 15–2. The student's mark is determined by the total number of points. One of the procedures of norm-referenced grading could then be used to determine the grade on the basis of accumulated points.

TABLE 15–2. **Student Points for Nine-Week Period**

Student	Class recitation (10 pts)	Homework (10 pts)	Quizzes (15 pts)	Term paper (20 pts)	Test #1 (25 pts)	Test #2 (20 pts)	Total
1. Ronald	10	9	15	18	19	23	94
2. Robert	9	8	13	20	19	25	94
3. Bert	4	5	8	10	18	20	65
4. Polly	5	3	10	8	10	15	51
5. Sue	8	9	12	16	11	16	72
6. Tom	9	10	10	17	14	18	78
7. Carol	10	10	14	19	18	22	93
8. Nan	10	10	15	20	18	24	97
9. Rodney	9	6	13	15	19	18	80
10. Max	7	8	11	14	14	13	67
11. Leo	3	6	8	6	9	10	42
12. Ann	6	5	6	11	8	9	45
13. Lois	8	9	4	10	14	14	59
14. Mary	9	10	12	18	16	18	83
15. Tim	9	9	5	18	18	17	76
16. Sally	9	8	10	17	15	23	82
17. Debbie	10	10	15	20	16	24	95
18. Brenda	4	3	8	9	7	12	43
19. Frank	5	2	6	11	9	10	43
20. Jim	3	5	5	8	10	11	42

A second method of weighting requires that all scores be converted to a common scale. A standard score such as the z score or T score described in Chapter 8b can be used to do this. After the standard score has been computed for each student on each performance, it is multiplied by the appropriate weight, and an average standard score is calculated. If the ten percent weighting is considered the base, the weightings for recitation and homework would be the ratios of the percentages of the contributions of other factors to the ten percent.

Class recitation	1 × standard score
Homework/seatwork	1 × standard score
Quizzes	1.5 × standard score
Term paper or project	2.0 × standard score
Test #1	2.0 × standard score
Test #2	2.5 × standard score

To determine the average standard score, the sum of the products of the weights and standard scores would then be divided by ten. One of the procedures described previously for determining grades for norm-referenced measurement could then be applied in order to compute the cumulative mark. The method is applied to two students' scores in Table 15–3.

This method is more precise than the totaling of points method because the variability of scores is considered in the calculation. The procedure does require more calculations, however, and the results may not differ appreciably from those of the first method.

The cumulative reports of achievement are placed in the student's permanent records and used to determine placement, to guide the student's education, and to inform parents of their child's educational achievements. The last purpose of such reports is the focus of the next section.

▶ *ACTIVITY 2.*   Using the total points for the students in Table 15–2, determine the students' grades for the nine-week period, employing each of the following methods:

a. System I
b. Normal curve method
c. Guess method
d. Systematic method

   Compare your results with other members of the class. You should find agreement for methods a, b, and d, but you may find differences for method c. If you were a teacher, which of the grades would you report? Justify your answer.

▶ *ACTIVITY 3.*   Apply the information and procedures used for determining grades shown in Table 15–3 to two other students' points for the nine-week period. As a class project, each student might choose different students from the list so that composite scores are available for all of the twenty students. If this is possible, share the information and determine grades for the nine-week period by one or more of the methods used in Activity 2.

Reporting to Parents

One of the purposes of evaluation is to inform parents of their children's academic progress. The information communicated and the form of the communication varies from school to school. The communication may be as brief as a single mark, or it may include no marks at all. The

TABLE 15–3. Calculating Weighted Standard Scores

	Class Recitation	Homework	Quizzes	Term paper	Test #1	Test #2
Mean	7.35	7.25	10.0	14.25	14.10	17.1
S.D.	2.34	2.43	3.51	4.32	3.78	5.04
1. Ronald	10	9	15	18	19	23
z score	1.13	.72	1.42	.87	1.30	1.17
2. Robert	9	8	13	20	19	25
z score	.71	.31	.85	1.33	1.30	1.57

Ronald		*Robert*	
$1.13 \times 1 = 1.13$		$.71 \times 1 = .71$	
$.72 \times 1 = .72$		$.31 \times 1 = .31$	
$1.42 \times 1.5 = 2.13$		$.85 \times 1.5 = 1.275$	
$.87 \times 2.0 = 1.74$		$1.33 \times 2.0 = 2.66$	
$1.30 \times 2.0 = 2.60$		$1.30 \times 2.0 = 2.60$	
$1.17 \times 2.5 = 2.925$		$1.57 \times 2.5 = 3.925$	
$\overline{11.245} \div 10$		$\overline{11.48} \div 10$	
$= 1.12$		$= 1.15$	

method of communication may be a report card, a parent-teacher conference, a checklist of accomplishments, a narrative describing the child's progress, or some combination of these.

Single or Multiple Marks

Some reports to parents include a single mark or grade for each class the student is enrolled in. When a single mark is used, it often reflects a variety of evaluations. The mark may signify not just achievement but the teacher's evaluation of the student's attitude, effort, deportment, or absence record as well. A single mark communicates nothing to the parents about the student's specific strengths or weaknesses in courses. The parents' interpretation of the mark may in fact be based largely on their own experiences as students. It may be related only slightly to the behaviors the teacher considered in making the evaluation.

Multiple marks normally convey more information than a single mark. Multiple marks take a variety of forms. In one system, the teacher provides a mark for achievement and another mark for ability or effort. A student may thus receive a letter grade for achievement and some indication of the way the achievement relates to ability (Table 15–4).

Multiple marking systems almost universally include an achievement evaluation. The additional marks may include an evaluation of the skills that led to the overall evaluation or a rating of nonacademic outcomes, such as personal and social characteristics, work habits, or

TABLE 15–4. Achievement and Effort Grading

A—Superior	1. Achieving above level expected for ability
B—Above average	2. Achieving at level expected for ability
C—Average	3. Achieving below level expected for ability
D—Below average	
F—Failing	

B-1 would represent above-average performance that is above the expected level.

D-3 would represent below-average performance that is below the expected level.

deportment. An example of a multiple marks report card is shown in Figure 15–4.

Reports Without Marks

A criterion-based reporting system usually includes no cumulative evaluative mark. Instead, the report includes a list of objectives for each subject at the child's grade level. The report sent to the parents designates the objectives that were accomplished during that reporting period. This information can help the parent see exactly what skills have been attained and what remains to be accomplished.

At the primary level (Grades K–3), teachers often give parents a narrative report or meet them at a parent-teacher conference. For such a procedure, marks need not be assigned, and the parent is informed of the child's academic gains as well as the child's personal and social development. Conferences also make it possible for the child's strengths and weaknesses to be discussed.

Methods of Reporting

Schools use different procedures to make periodic reports to parents. Traditionally, report cards have been the most common procedure. Other procedures are the parent-teacher conference and the narrative report.

Report Cards.   In every school, discussions are held periodically about improving the reporting of student achievement. Teachers as a group express dissatisfaction with report cards because they fail to convey enough information or because they require too much information. This dissatisfaction may be based, at least in part, on the teachers' dislike of judging students. Despite all the dissatisfaction, however, the report card is still the most popular way to report student progress.

The primary advantage of report cards compared to other forms

Name

1st Period Teacher

Grade

School Year

SUBJECT	1st Quarter					2nd Quarter					3rd Quarter					4th Quarter					FINAL GRADE
	GRADE	effort	behavior	tardy	absent	GRADE	effort	behavior	tardy	absent	GRADE	effort	behavior	tardy	absent	GRADE	effort	behavior	tardy	absent	
English																					
Mathematics																					
Science																					
Geography 7th																					
History 8th																					
Electives																					
1.																					
2.																					
3.																					

Grade Key: A = excellent B = good C = satisfactory D = needs improvement F = failing I = incomplete
Comments on reverse side

FIGURE 15–4. Example of Multiple Marks Report Card

of reporting is economy of time. It is relatively easy, after the evaluations have been made, to enter one mark or several.

A disadvantage of the report card is that it tends to be a one-way communication—from the school to the parent. Some report cards do make provisions for parents to write comments to return to the school; in practice, however, parents seldom make comments.

We can make several suggestions to teachers for completing report cards:

1. Marks for achievement should include only evaluations of achievement. This is especially important when single marks are given, but it is also important in other marking systems.
2. Collect enough data to make a reliable evaluation. At the beginning of the school year, determine what evaluations are required on the report card and make provisions to collect related data during the reporting period. If no data are available, it is better not to give a mark.
3. Be as objective as possible in marking. Avoid letting personal likes and dislikes affect your marking. Grades should never be used for punishment.

Parent-Teacher Conferences.   Parent-teacher conferences are a common method of reporting at the elementary school level. The method is used less frequently at the secondary school level, largely because each student has a number of teachers.

Although more time-consuming than report cards, parent-teacher conferences encourage two-way communication concerning the education of children. In conference, one can report on student progress more extensively and interpret goals and procedures to parents more easily.

A parent-teacher conference should be a time for sharing information from both viewpoints. The teacher should report the child's progress, but in addition there should be an exchange of information that might facilitate the child's educational progress. Some guidelines for conferences follow.

1. *Planning for the conference.* For a conference to be successful, adequate preparation is needed. The teacher should have available evaluation reports, samples of the student's work, and statements of objectives. An examination of the child's school records may yield information that can facilitate communication with the parents. If the teacher wants specific information from the parents, a list of questions could be constructed to guide the discussion.

2. *Conducting the conference.* Conduct the conference in a comfortable and private setting. Begin and end the conference on a positive note. Emphasize the positive aspects of the child's achievement, but be

One purpose of evaluation is to inform parents of their child's academic performance. Parent-teacher conferences should be carefully planned to allow for two-way communication regarding a child's achievement.

honest and avoid exaggerating. If negative aspects must be discussed, attempt to enlist the parent's cooperation rather than placing the parent in a defensive position. Spend part of the time listening to the parent; regard the parent as a partner who has something to contribute.

3. *Writing the report.* After each conference, the teacher should write a brief report noting specific information that should be part of the child's school record. Again, objectivity in reporting is the goal.

Narrative Reports. A compromise between report cards and the parent-teacher conferences is the narrative report. With this method the teacher may provide much of the same information that would be provided through a parent-teacher conference. A narrative report permits one to gain no information from the parent, however.

Writing good narrative reports is a time-consuming task, and they often provide little more information than multiple mark report cards. Unless the narrative report is carefully written, parents may misinterpret it. This problem might be avoided in a parent-teacher conference.

A teacher who must write thirty narrative reports at the end of a reporting period will have trouble creating meaningful reports for all thirty students. The narratives may tend to deteriorate into generalized, stereotyped statements of little value.

The benefits of the narrative reports might be greater if they were written as the need arose rather than at the end of a reporting period. Informing the parents of unique aspects of their children's progress or development can be beneficial to both parents and children.

Summary

Evaluating students is never an easy task. Conscientious teachers will expend a great deal of metaphorical blood, sweat, and tears on the evaluation process. Collecting the necessary information, summarizing the information, and arriving at a fair evaluation of each student takes effort, creativity, and time. Regardless of how many people say "Grades are not important," no one, least of all the student, is fooled by such a statement. Grades are important, and the influence of grades on students makes grading a serious task. The improvement of grading and reporting practices should be a prime concern of all those involved—students, teachers, administrators, and parents.

Epilogue

Introduction

How shall we summarize these fifteen chapters, the diversity of content, the variety of theory? What are the major conclusions, the key points we hope you have abstracted from this volume? To summarize the content, to reemphasize these key points, we can reiterate the major themes that were woven through all the chapters. Common threads ran through the research sections, the discussions of psychological theory, the applications, and the activities. These themes constitute a summary and thus are worth restatement.

If you reexamine the theory chapters, the *a* members of each chapter pair, you should note great diversity in psychological theory. There is no one psychological system, no one explanation of human behavior. The different theories depend on the initial assumptions made about the nature of the human organism, the nature of reality. Behaviorism, social learning theory, and information-processing are thus different theories based on different initial assumptions; they are also contemporaneous explanatory systems for human behavior.

Psychology is not yet a discipline advanced to the point where one major theoretical system can successfully replace all members of the competition. It is therefore necessary for the student of psychology to be knowledgeable in more than one theoretical system. Depending on the specific content (for example, learning, motivation, development), the prevailing philosophical assumptions (for example, organismic, mechanistic, interactive), and the accepted analogues (for example, the biological organism, the machine, the computer), the popularity and prominence of any particular theoretical system will shift.

Paradigm Shifts

As philosophers of science have pointed out, scientific systems undergo *paradigm shifts* (Kuhn, 1962). In a paradigm shift, less vital older approaches are replaced by emerging, newer, and less tested systems, until they too run their course. Science and the prevailing scientific research approaches and theories thus change rather than remaining static. In the history of science we see periods of stability when a particular paradigm is entrenched, followed by periods of greater instability as the older ones lose their grip and emerging ones compete for prominence. In the evolution of a science the time of a shift is a time characterized by energy, productivity, excitement, and change.

Psychology is too young a discipline ever to have had only one major paradigm at a time, but psychology is a science and it is presently in the midst of the most dramatic paradigm shift since the 1930s. Along with the prominence of behaviorism, the stability of the 1950s and 1960s has given way, beginning in the 1970s and moving into the 1980s, to the resurgence of a number of competing models. A new paradigm is just beginning to take hold. The face of the science is changing rapidly, and the excitement is intense. It is the themes related to this shift, those portending what is to come, with which we wish to close.

The Themes of the 80s for Psychology

Our summary entails a restatement of these themes. They cut across the theory chapters, they are embedded in the New Directions for Research segments, and they demonstrate our theoretical position. Perhaps they also reveal something of the future of our science.

Theme One: The Prevailing Analogue Is an Interactive One

The prevailing theme in the 1970s and 1980s is an interactive one. That means, as we have stated many times across many chapters, that B = E × P—human behavior is the outcome of environmental forces and personal characteristics acting in conjunction. Popular contemporary theories are those that begin with an interactive model, attempt to account for both experiential and personal variables, and are thus more comprehensive than biological deterministic or strict environmental approaches. Examples of theories that are consistent with the prevailing sentiment and are popular or growing rapidly in popularity include social learning theory (Chapters 4a, 10a, 13a), cognitive-developmental theory (Chapters 6a, 7a, 13a), and information-processing approaches (Chapters 5a, 6a, 7a, 8a, 12a). Those waning in appeal or undergoing change to fit with the current Zeitgeist include trait approaches to intelligence (Chapters 8a, 9a), radical behaviorism (Chapter 3a), and drive approaches to motivation (Chapter 10a).

If you reexamine the sections entitled New Directions for Research, which signal new developments in the discipline, you will see this theoretical shift in action. Research in cognitive behaviorism (Chapter 3a), metacognition (Chapter 5a), self-efficacy (Chapter 10a), problem-solving (Chapters 6a and 11a), and schema theory (Chapter 12a) are examples of research based on an interactive model.

Theme Two: The Prevailing Assumption Is the Active Nature of Man

If the prevailing analogue is an interactive model, the prevailing assumption about the nature of man is that of an active, cognizing organism. Theoretical systems that view the person in this manner are the ones gaining attention. The Piagetian perspective (Chapter 6a), schema theory (Chapter 12a), attribution theory (Chapter 10a), process approaches to intelligence (Chapter 8a), and of course the information-processing paradigm (Chapters 5a, 8a, 11a, 12a, 13a) reflect this shift.

In fact, were we to pick one contender for the primary paradigm of the 1980s, the winner (if perhaps only temporarily, as is the nature of science) would be the information-processing approach. This emerging theoretical system with its computer analogy is consistent with the prevailing assumption about the nature of man, and its heuristic value for generating research is tremendous. While information-processing has yet to coalesce into a unified theoretical system, research based on its ideas is a body of investigation worth watching.

Theme Three: Psychology Is at Its Best When It Is Based in Science

When psychology became an empirical science, it was established as a discipline in its own right. The scientific base, use of the scientific method, and dependence on data for the source of evidence are the hallmarks of integrity that must be maintained across any paradigm shift. We outlined the basics of empiricism in Chapter 2a, but they resurface in every chapter, every Research Report. Psychological theory will be unable to maintain prominence if it is unamenable to test by empirical methods. Like all science, it must lead to the generation of hypotheses; these hypotheses must suggest experimentation. Data must fit with theoretical predictions. Such an empirical value system separates scientific psychology from so-called pop psych.

Psychology in general owes a debt to behaviorism (Chapter 3a) for much of its scientific basis. The insistence on operationalizing variables, emphasizing observables, and demonstrating cause and effect are the hallmarks of behavioral psychology. They are also criteria that have been absorbed into most other psychological systems and investigations as well. We can thank the behaviorists for keeping us honest, for keeping our feet firmly planted in data.

With the paradigm shift will come new methods and techniques for handling data (see, for example, Chapter 2a, New Directions for Research) including such advances as computer simulation. These new methods will not, however, include a desertion of a basic attitude, a desertion of an empirical value system.

Theme Four: The Discipline of Psychology Is the Basis of Educational Practice

Why, in a book directed at those interested in education, have we stressed so much psychology? Our contention is that psychology is the body of knowledge that underpins the practice of teaching. As we stated in Chapter 1, when it comes to human behavior, psychologists study changes in it and teachers direct changes in it. The content of the two disciplines is very similar.

Effective teaching incorporates sound psychological principles. The effective teacher must therefore be conversant with these principles. The knowledge base changes, however, the research changes, and so the principles change. Teachers must become consumers of psychological knowledge who keep abreast of those changes. Otherwise, practice will lag behind discovery.

Implications of the Themes for Educational Practice

If there is no single explanation of human behavior, neither is there one single proven method for dealing with behavior in the classroom. There are alternatives depending on the setting, the individual, the behavior, and of course the teacher. With our Scenarios, our *b* chapters, and our Activities, we have tried to demonstrate what some of those alternatives are, at least from the perspective of psychology. The alternatives and solutions directed at the applied issues also reflect the major themes.

Theme One: Education Is also an Interactive Process

Education involves changes in human behavior; the outcomes of the educational process are thus a function of $E \times P$. The accomplishments of the learner in the classroom reflect personal characteristics, such as developmental level (Chapter 6b), language skills (Chapter 7b), and intelligence (Chapter 8b and 9b), and they reflect environmental factors, such as reinforcement contingencies (Chapter 3b), social learning models (Chapter 4b), text structure (Chapter 12b), and instruction (Chapter 11b). Each source plays a role; the teacher needs to understand both.

Since *E* can vary, and *P* can also vary, teachers need to be adaptable. Instruction and activities must be adapted to the characteristics of the learners. There is no one way to proceed, therefore. Depending on the circumstances and on the students, teachers will have to try different approaches. Adaptability and trying alternatives need not proceed by trial and error, however. The *b* chapters suggest some alternatives predicated on the basis of psychological research. The teacher well grounded in psychology has some basis for selecting alternative approaches vis-a-vis specific circumstances.

The *b* chapters cannot possibly have covered all circumstances that you as teachers will face. They are samples only. The samples do, however, have some common threads:

1. Educational activities have a plan and a purpose. The ends are the changes in student behaviors that are desired.
2. Instructional methods are the means for achieving those ends efficiently and productively.
3. Methods and ends must be adapted to the characteristics of the learners, the person variables.
4. If the ends are not attained, adaptability—a change in method—is required. *P* variables are not under the teacher's direct control.

Theme Two: The Person Is an Active Cognizing Organism

Virtually all psychological theories propose that the person needs to be active. Behaviorists note that in order to experience contingencies an individual must produce responses (Chapter 3b). Social learning theorists talk about enactment (Chapter 4b), as do Piagetians (Chapter 6b) and cognitive psychologists (Chapters 5b, 11b, 12b). The implications? Teaching methods that engage the learner rather than those that encourage a passive stance should prove most productive.

In our applied examples we have tried to stress the active role of the learner. Encouraging the production of questions, for example (Chapter 7b), the use of priming questions and elaboration (Chapter 12b), role-playing (Chapter 13b), interaction with real objects (Chapter 6b), all involve the learner in a very active way. The next thread that crosses the content is thus action:

5. Instructional methods predicated on the active involvement of the learner in instruction are preferable to those that encourage only passive attending.

Theme Three: Teaching, Like Science, Can Be Data-Based

The teacher, like the psychologist, needs to be objective in order to determine when change is accomplished, when ends are reached. Objectivity requires attention to data, the collection of evidence in such a way that informed judgments can be made. The data collection procedures of the teacher may be less formal than those of the scientist, but the purpose is the same: a non-subjective record.

The use of performance objectives (Chapter 2b), careful construction of test and assessment devices (Chapter 14), collection of behavioral frequency data (Chapter 3b), design of an objective grading system (Chapter 15), and other observational procedures are the teacher's data tools. With them, evidence can be procured, progress can be assessed, and adaptations can be made accordingly. Data are not for the laboratory alone. That brings us to our next thread:

6. Wise instructional decision-making is predicated on the collection of objective evidence. Teachers thus need to utilize sound data collection procedures in order to judge progress and to adapt accordingly.

Summary: The Effect of the Paradigm Shift on Educational Practices

If educational practice is predicated on psychological knowledge, and if psychology is in a paradigm shift, will teaching methods also change? Most certainly they will, and in fact they already are changing. Even though practice traditionally lags behind the state of the art in science, the ripple effect still holds.

Theme Four: There Is a Relationship Between Psychology and Education

More recent innovations stemming from paradigm changes in psychology include experiential approaches in preschools and changes in math and science curricula as a result of the Piagetian impact. Schema theory is influencing the teaching of reading. Cognitive psychologists are influencing mathematics instruction and problem-solving approaches. New assessment devices are being designed to reflect our changing notions of intelligence. The changes will no doubt continue.

With change in the state of the art in psychology that is affecting educational practice, teachers who graduate with a set of tools based on the current state of the art will quickly become obsolete unless they too change. They must keep abreast of new developments; they must become intelligent consumers of the psychological knowledge base. Perhaps, then, the best way to end this book is with our final piece of advice, our final statement of a thread:

7. Science changes. Knowledge changes. Practices change. Since teachers are the translators of knowledge, the agents of practice, they too must keep changing.

What does all this translate to? Keep reading, keep learning, keep growing. Learning and growing is not just for children.

Glossary

Ability Grouping A method of organization for instruction in which students with homogeneous ability are grouped together. A common type of ability grouping consists of reading groups within a classroom where students with high, medium, or low reading ability are taught separately.

Ability Tests Tests designed to measure intelligence or potential for academic achievement.

Absolute Standards Used for the evaluation of student performance based on a teacher's judgment of performance without comparison to the group.

Acceleration As used in this context, refers to moving through school at a faster rate than normal. May be accomplished, for example, through early admission or skipping grades.

Accommodation From Piaget, a component of adaptation that refers to activity in which possessed modes of behaving (old knowledge) are altered in response to an environmental demand or to encountering a new phenomenon. The existing cognitive structure is accommodated to the new experience or element.

Achievement Motivation nAch First proposed by Murray and further developed by Atkinson & McClelland. Characterized as a relatively stable tendency for an individual to strive for success.

Achievement Tests Tests designed to measure the academic accomplishments of students.

Acquisition of Rule-Governed Behaviors An imitative learning effect where a new class of behaviors is learned from the observation of a model(s). The behaviors in the class are governed by the same rule; thus the rule is abstracted during the course of the observation.

Adaptation From Piaget, refers to the propensity of the human organism to adapt to the environment and to experience. One of the two invariant functions that characterize man's style of interacting with the environment.

Advance Organizers Introductions to material to be learned which are at a higher level than the material and which provide an ideational scaffold for incorporating the new material.

Altruism A behavioral class referring to those behaviors performed for the benefit of another person without expectation of reward to the performer. This is a controversial behavior to define because intentions must be inferred.

Anecdotal Records Descriptions of behaviors of individuals that may prove useful in evaluation of personal and social development.

Antecedent Event An event that occurs prior to the event we wish to explain. In a temporal sequence $A \rightarrow B$, A is the antecedent event.

Antecedent Stimulus A stimulus that occurs temporally prior to the response, as S followed by R.

Aptitude A potential for development along a certain line or extent that one may be expected to achieve. Scholastic aptitude is the extent one might be able to achieve in school.

Aptitude-Treatment Interaction (ATI) A research approach to individual differences where the effect of an instructional technique is compared across abilities and in which an interaction between an independent variable (treatment) and an attribute variable (aptitude) is expected.

Artificial Intelligence Attempts to model, through the use of a computer, the cognitive processes necessary to accomplish a particular task.

Assimilation From Piaget, a component of adaptation that refers to activity in which possessed modes of behaving (old knowledge) are applied to new phenomena in the environment. The new element is assimilated into the existing cognitive structure.

Attribute Variable An individual characteristic that can vary but is not subject to manipulation within an experiment. These are characteristics that subjects bring with them into the experimental settings, for example, age, sex, ability, and past experience.

Attributes Qualities of concepts that serve to define the categories.

Attribution Theory A theory of motivation that examines a person's retrospective perception of the causes for success or failure.

Autonomous Morality From Piaget, the second stage of moral development coinciding with the concrete operation period; it is a stage of moral relativism. Children see rules as relative and alterable depending on the social context. They also know that actions must be assessed with the intentions of the actor in mind.

Babbling Drift Refers to the hypothesis (primarily unsubstantiated) that the first speech by young children results from a gradual refinement of the babbling evident in the preverbal period.

Baseline A record of the frequency and stability of a target behavior prior to the introduction of an intervention strategy. It is rather like a pretest of response strength.

Behavioral Assessment A measurement or assessment approach in which data is collected on a number of behaviors. These constitute behavior *samples* of the person's capabilities. Typically, assessment would focus on observable behaviors, use direct measurement, and would not use the samples to infer nonobservable underlying entities or constructs.

Behaviorism A theoretical perspective in psychology restricted to the study of observable events. In methodological behaviorism all variables are externalized and defined in terms of observable events, but cognitive, unobservable events are not necessarily ruled out as explanatory constructs. In radical behaviorism, the unit of analysis is the observable operant and consequences. Unobservable, mental events are not considered to be appropriate subject matter for a science of human behavior.

Biological Determinism A perspective on human development that conceptualizes the developmental process as an unfolding, maturational process that is biologically, or genetically, determined or pre-set. Associated with people like G. Stanley Hall.

Bloom's Taxonomy A classification of cognitive outcomes arranged in order of the complexity of process used for answering questions based on these outcomes.

Case Study A research study involving one or a few subjects. It can be either descriptive or experimental but is limited in generalization by the number of individuals investigated.

Central Tendency Measures Statistical terms that describe the center of the frequency distribution and include the median and the mean.

Checklist A listing of all of the important elements that should be included in a performance or product. The evaluator merely checks *Yes* or *No* indicating the presence or absence of each element.

Clang Association A term associated with multiple-choice items in which a term in one of the possible responses is similar to one in the stem. This similarity allows the student to answer the question correctly without having to possess the relevant knowledge.

Class Inclusion The understanding, in class relations, that a subclass is always smaller than and contained within the larger class.

Classical/Respondent Conditioning The learning process, studied by Pavlov and Watson, associated with responding to formerly neutral antecedent stimuli, which acquire eliciting power through frequent pairing with an unconditioned stimulus.

Classificatory Level of Concept Attainment The level at which the learner is able to classify correctly two or more different examples and recognize that they are equivalent. The child who is able to classify an apple, an orange, and a banana as *fruit* exemplifies the classificatory level of concept attainment.

Clinical Method From Piagetian theory, a style of investigation that 1) utilizes few subjects, 2) is non-standardized and flexible, and 3) elicits spontaneous reasoning from subjects. The child's answers influence the direction of questioning. From the child's reasoning, inferences are made to a diagnosis of cognitive structure and level.

Cognitive Behaviorism A branch of behavioral psychology that includes some consideration of internal processing, which affects behavior. This approach adheres to the behavioral model but includes factors other than the observable stimuli and responses, which are the focus of the Radical Behaviorist approach.

Cognitive-Developmental Perspective An approach to the study and explanation of intellectual development associated with Piagetian theory. Basically, the perspective includes an interactive stage model of developmental change in which the development of competence derives from both biological propensity and action within the physical environment.

Cognitive Map In opposition to the behaviorists, who aver that we learn S–R connections, Tolman maintains that we learn cognitions or cognitive maps. These maps guide our behaviors so that we do not perform behaviors in a robot-like manner but have a mental image of relationships, signs, means, and ends so that we can vary behavior according to the needs of the situation.

Cognitive Structure Refers to a person's past experiences and learning with all the interrelationships between them that are stored by the individual.

Cognitivism A branch of psychology focused on the internal processes of the individual that occur between the presentation of the stimulus and the occurrence of the response.

Comprehension Abstraction of the meaning embedded in a set of presented information; sometimes used synonomously with understanding. Generally refers to understanding the meaning of verbal information, prose.

Computer Analogue A model of cognition and cognitive processing that uses a computer representation for human thought. Man is approached as if he functioned in the same manner as a computer does in terms of software.

Concept A category into which one groups objects or ideas with similar attributes. Concepts vary in number of attributes, structures, abstractness, inclusiveness, generality, precision, and power.

Concept Analysis A procedure used in planning instruction of concepts. The analysis includes identification of the critical attributes, definition of the concept, provision of examples and non-examples, and stating the relationship of this concept to other concepts. A concept analysis clarifies the concept and provides the teacher with a format for teaching it.

Concept Assimilation Concept learning that involves learning the word that signifies the concept and being given the rules for inclusion of examples in that concept.

Concept Formation Concept learning that occurs as a result of experiencing examples of the concept.

Conceptual Behavior The thinking skills that deal with the formation of concepts, principles, rule-learning, and problem-solving.

Conceptual Role-Taking The ability to anticipate what a person knows, thinks, or feels about a situation when the perspective of that person differs from self. Derived from Piagetian theory, where it is conceptualized as a development coinciding with concrete operations.

Concrete Level of Concept Attainment When a learner recognizes an object that he has encountered before and acts on that object in a similar way to the first encounter, we may infer that he has attained a concept at the concrete level.

Concrete Operational Period The third Piagetian stage, from approximately 6–12 years. The child in this stage is a logical thinker but is limited to dealing with concrete reality. The child can reason about class and order relations, is a conserver, has decentered, and exhibits understanding of reversibility and compensation.

Concurrent Validity A type of criterion-related validity where the criterion is currently available. A new intelligence test may be concurrently validated by correlating the scores from the test with another test with established validity, such as the WISC-R or Stanford-Binet.

Conditioned Response (CR) A response that occurs after the presentation of a conditioned stimulus. The connection between the stimulus and the response is thus learned. The learning process is classical conditioning.

Conditioned Stimulus (CS) A formerly neutral stimulus that has been paired with an unconditioned stimulus and through this pairing has acquired the power to elicit a response. Responding in the presence of the conditioned stimulus is learned through the process of classical conditioning.

Conjunctive Concepts Concepts where two or more properties must be present in order for an object to be included as an example of that concept.

Consequent Stimulus A stimulus that occurs temporally after a response, as R is followed by S. The consequent stimulus is the effect produced by the response.

Conservation From Piaget, the ability to recognize that changes in perceptual form are independent of changes in quantity, the latter remaining invariant.

Conservative Focusing A strategy used in the selective paradigm for concept learning. When a learner has selected a stimulus that is an example of a concept, he clarifies the concept by proceeding systematically to other stimuli which differ in only one attribute.

Constraint-Oriented Morality Refers to the moral judgment research by people like Kohlberg, where subjects reason about situations requiring transgression of a legal or moral sanction. Thus there is a social constraint present in the situation and the subject must make a reasoned judgment about violating that constraint.

Construct Validity A type of validity that expresses how well a test measures some hypothetical construct that has been operationally defined. Examples of tests that are construct validated are tests of intelligence, motivation, and creativity.

Construct-Psychological An abstract, theoretical concept, which cannot be directly observed. It is a hypothetical abstraction that assists in the explanation of observed phenomenon.

Content Validity A type of validity primarily applicable to achievement tests. A test with content validity includes the behaviors and content that have been taught and that the student has been expected to accomplish.

Context The situation in which a behavior is sampled. In psychometrics, the item is the context, while the behavior is the ability tapped.

Contingency The regular association between events. Usually refers to the regular association between a response and a stimulus in the operant conditioning paradigm.

Contingency Contracting An agreed-upon arrangement in behavioral technology which specifies the behavioral requirements necessary to earn reinforcement.

Continuous Reinforcement A schedule of reinforcement delivery where a reinforcing stimulus follows each and every production of a response.

Conventional Morality The second level in Kohlberg's theory of moral development. Judgments are based on the conventional social order and the expectations of others. There is evidence of concern for social approval and social responsibility. Typical of the moral reasoning of most adults.

Coordination of Perspectives Refers to the ability to balance different points of view on the same phenomenon, i.e., to know that others will experience the phenomenon differently than self if the perspectives are different. In Piagetian theory, coordination of perspectives (or perspective-taking) is tapped with the three mountain problem. Children are generally not successful until the period of concrete operations, when the egocentrism of pre-operational thought is overcome.

Correlational Studies Descriptive studies in which the variables are not subject to manipulation by the experimenter. Such studies reveal the association between variables, i.e., how they covary; but without manipulation a cause-and-effect relationship cannot be established.

Criterial Attributes Those qualities of a concept that are required to be present in order for an example to belong to that category.

Criterion-Referenced Test (CRT) A test that expresses a student's performance in terms of objectives that the student has mastered.

Criterion-Related Validity A type of validity established on the basis of a correlation between test scores and another criterion.

Cross-Sectional Studies An approach to studying development where groups of children differing in age are compared at one point in time. Through cross-group comparisons, age-group differences are detected and conclusions are drawn about developmental processes.

"Culture Fair" Testing Attempts to measure ability in which the influence of past cultural experience is supposedly removed. Thus all cultural groups should approach test items in the same way. Has not proved to be a particularly successful approach.

Decentering The transition from an egocentric orientation to mature perspective-taking. It involves the ability to differentiate the point of view of self from the point of view of others. From Piagetian theory.

Deep Structure The meaning or structure underlying the observed form in a verbal utterance.

Deferred Imitation Imitation by an observer of a model's behavior some time after the behavior occurred. In social learning theory, deferred imitation is used to support the cognitive mediation component of the process. In Piagetian theory, deferred imitation toward the end of the sensorimotor period is used as evidence for the development of the symbolic function.

Dependent Variable The outcome variable, or behavioral effect, in an experiment that reflects changes in the independent variable.

Desensitization A treatment strategy where a maladaptive response is eliminated through exposure to the eliciting stimulus in situations where the response is not possible or has a low probability of production. The association between the stimulus and the response is removed.

Differential Psychology The study of individual differences.

Dimensions of Attribution As proposed by Weiner, the dimensions of attribution are the controllability, the stability, and the locus of control. Attributions may be perceived as under the control of the behaver, stable or unstable, and whether they come from within or from outside the behaver.

Discovery Learning Considered to be the opposite of reception learning. In discovery learning, the learner must discover the content to be learned before incorporating that content into her cognitive structure.

Discrimination Index A quantification of item discrimination derived by finding the difference, among those who answered a question correctly, between the percent of students who scored highest on the test and those who scored lowest on the test. Discrimination indices might range from +1.00 (indicating all students who scored highest answered the item correctly and none of the students who scored lowest answered the item correctly) to −1.00 (indicating the reverse situation). Discrimination indices are computed using the upper and lower thirds of the students.

Disinhibition Effect In social learning theory, if an observer sees a model reinforced or not punished for a negatively sanctioned behavior, there is an increased probability for imitation to occur.

Disjunctive Concepts Concepts in which either of two or more properties must be present. A sister-in-law may be the wife of one's sibling or a sibling of one's spouse.

Drive Reduction Theory An early explanation of motivation indicating that an individual behaved in such a way as to reduce a drive, which for primary drives might result from deprivation or from aversive stimuli.

Dual Processing Hypothesis A hypothesis originating with Paivio and others. The notion here is that concrete and pictorial material is processed differently than abstract and linguistic material. The first is associated with imaginal processing while the second is processed in terms of a verbal code. The hypothesis is controversial and rejected by many cognitive psychologists.

Duos Combinations of single words representing the first "sentences" in the course of language development.

Duration Recording A procedure for recording the strength of a behavior by indexing *how long* the behavior lasts, i.e., how much time it takes for the response to occur.

Effect Size A procedure for comparing the degree of difference between the central tendency indexes of two distributions.

Efficacy Expectation A person's judgment of whether he or she is capable of performing a particular behavior.

Egocentrism The inability to differentiate the perspective of self from the perspective of others. An assumption that everyone sees, knows, and feels the same as self. Derives from Piagetian theory where egocentrism is considered a characteristic of preoperational thought.

Elaboration A rehearsal strategy where ideas or units of information are connected with other ideas, fleshed-out, and made more meaningful.

Empathetic Reasoning The ability to infer how others feel in given circumstances. Generally refers to the cognitive processes (rather than affective ones) involved in the inferential process.

Empathy The ability to comprehend how another person feels. Within the cognitive-developmental perspective, the concern is with knowing how another feels, a cognitive process, rather than feeling what another feels. Sometimes used interchangeably with conceptual role-taking ability.

Empirical Evidence Evidence predicated on the collection of observable, reliable data.

Empiricism A philosophical school of thought derived from eighteenth century British philosophers, which gives rise to science. It is a perspective that stresses the role of the environment and experience in the development of knowledge through sense data. There is a primary emphasis on observation and the collection of data rather than on the spontaneous constructive activity of the mind. When translated into psychology, it is a perspective that emphasizes the role of the environment in learning and development.

Enactive Mode From Bruner, a term that

denotes thought in terms of physical activity. Roughly equivalent to sensorimotor thought in a Piagetian approach.

Encoding In an information-processing approach, refers to the detection and representation of presented information for later processing.

Environmental Determinism A perspective on human development that conceptualizes the developmental process as a product of environmental influence. Hard-line environmental determinism was represented in the position of John Watson. Essentially, development is equated with learning in the behavioral sense. Thus development is explainable via behavioral learning principles.

Epistemology Study of knowledge, a philosophical topic.

Equilibration From Piaget, refers to the self-regulatory process of balancing assimilation and accommodation such that developmental progress is made. Thus it is the means for development and a dialectic solution for bringing opposing forces (or functions) into equilibrium.

Equivalence Conservation Recognition that if two entities are equal, the equality is preserved across any perceptual change in one of the entities.

Error Variability in observed data that results from imprecision in measurement or procedure.

Evaluation The process of systematically collecting and analyzing data in order to make a decision.

Event Sampling Indexing the strength of a behavior by counting its frequency. The behavior is recorded each time it occurs within the specified recording period.

Existing Conditions The initial state of affairs prior to the introduction of a causal event, prior to the manipulation of an independent variable.

Expansion Elaboration of a child's utterance, usually performed by a language model, where the basic ideas expressed by a child are added to, expanded, or elaborated into a more complex utterance.

Expectancy Due to past experiences, a person may have developed a cognitive anticipation that certain results follow. The occurrence of a stimulus or a pattern of stimuli is thus expected.

Experienced-Based Instruction An approach to instruction that emphasizes the child's spontaneous activity in the learning process. While it is consistent with a Piagetian perspective, it is not exclusively a Piagetian technique.

Experiment An investigation of a phenomenon predicated on objective demonstration of an empirical relationship.

Experimental Paradigm An investigative approach borrowed from the hard sciences. Typically this is typified by control, which is possible in the laboratory, of extraneous variables, and experimental manipulation of the independent variable(s) for the purposes of demonstrating cause and effect.

Expository Teaching Teaching that involves the *rule-eg* method. The material is presented to the student in final form. This method is often considered to be the opposite of discovery learning.

Extended Short-Answer In this text, a type of item that requires a specific answer lengthier than the one or two words common for short-answer questions.

Extended-Response Question A question that requires the student to search his store of knowledge and construct a lengthy response, often in the form of an essay.

Extinction A process in which a behavior previously reinforced is no longer reinforced. The behavior will return to its previous non-reinforced level of frequency.

Extraneous Variable A variable present in the experimental setting that may affect the dependent variable but is not relevant to the experimental hypothesis. If extraneous variables are not controlled, confounding occurs and the data obtained becomes uninterpretable.

Facilitative Effect of Modeling In social learning theory, an imitative learning outcome where the behavior of a model cues an observer to produce the behavior. Reinforcement is not necessary and it typifies those situations where the response is already a part of the observer's behavioral repertoire.

Factor Analysis   A statistical procedure for compressing large data sets into simpler, more parsimonious, and more meaningful representations of the data.

Factor Structure   The outcome of factor analysis. A parsimonious representation of large data sets that occurs when the data is compressed with mathematical procedures.

Field Study   A study that takes place in a natural as opposed to a laboratory setting.

Fixed Interval Schedule   A schedule of reinforcement where reinforcement is delivered at set time intervals regardless of the frequency of the response, for example, every five minutes, or every two weeks.

Fixed Ratio Schedule   A schedule of reinforcement where reinforcement is delivered after a set, non-varying number of responses occur, for example, every fifth response.

Focus Gambling   After selecting an example of a concept in the selective paradigm, the learner chooses as the next stimulus an object differing in more than one attribute.

Forgetting   The inability to retrieve previously learned material due to the passage of time or to the interference of competing responses.

Formal Level of Concept Attainment   The level attained when a learner is able to define the criterial attributes of a concept.

Formal Operational Period   The last of the Piagetian stages, beginning at approximately age twelve. Thought is logical, flexible, and fully symbolic.

Frequency Distribution   A listing of the scores or values of data with the number of individuals who received each score.

Functional Fixedness   In problem-solving, when a learner displays only one method of attack and persists with the same method even though it does not lead to success.

Functional Relationship   A cause-and-effect relationship between two variables. Expressed by the equation $y = f(x)$.

Generality of Concept   Refers to position of the concept in terms of the number of superordinate or subordinate concepts. A polygon is more general than a quadrilateral, which is in turn more general than a rectangle.

Genetic Epistemology   The philosophy of the development of knowledge associated with Jean Piaget. Basically, Piaget takes the position that knowledge is constructed on the basis of structural properties and thus emerges gradually. Knowledge is neither innate nor an imprint of physical reality, but the result of an emerging constructive process influenced by both biological and physical characteristics.

Gestalt Psychology   An early approach to cognitive psychology, originating in Germany. Proponents included Wertheimer, Koffka, and Kohler. Their work focused mainly on perception and they felt that whatever facilitated perception would also facilitate learning.

Grade Equivalents   Conversion of a standardized test score to express the median score for students at a particular grade level. A score with a grade equivalent of 4.2 indicates that 50% of the students in the second month of the 4th grade scored below that point.

Graphic Rating Scale   A rating scale where the varying degrees of adequacy or acceptability are indicated by terms describing the performance.

Halo Effect   In the use of rating scales, the halo effect occurs when an individual's performance shows no differentiation in the various elements.

Heritability Statistic   A mathematic procedure that attempts to isolate the amount of variance in a data set attributable to genetic factors.

Higher-Order Conditioning   A classical conditioning process where the stimulus filling the unconditioned role is a learned one which previously acquired its eliciting power through pairing with another unconditioned stimulus.

Holophrastic Speech Early speech in children where a single word is utilized to convey a whole idea, equivalent to an adult's complete sentence.

Horizontal Decalage From Piaget, refers to the unevenness in performance within a developmental stage. It is a descriptive term denoting the fact that the individual has acquired a scheme (knowledge or concept) but has not yet applied it successfully across contexts.

Hypothesis A tentative statement that expresses the expected or hypothesized relationship between two variables. It usually takes the form "If *A*, then *B*."

Hypothesis Testing Approach In learning concepts, the learner appears to be using this approach when he forms an hypothesis about the attributes of a concept, tries this hypothesis on another stimulus, and maintains or revises his hypothesis as a result of confirmation or disconfirmation that the stimulus was an example.

Iconic Mode From Bruner, a thought mode in terms of immediate perceptual input. Somewhat like thought in the form of perceptual images, it is conceptualized as a limited means of thinking exhibited by children in the equivalent of the pre-operational stage of development.

Identity Conservation Understanding that a perceptual change in an object does not affect quantity provided no amount is added or taken away.

Identity Level of Concept Attainment A concept of an object at the identity level is inferred when a learner recognizes an object after an interval of time has elapsed, or when she has a different spatial orientation, or through a different sensory modality.

Imagery, Mental Refers to a cognitive, and unobservable, representation of informa-

tion that is quasi-pictorial and spatial in nature.

Imitation Reproducing the behavior of another individual following observation of that behavior. In social learning theory, imitation is the process of learning from observation. In Piagetian theory, it is an example of accommodation.

Imposed Imagery The presentation of pictures to convey essential information. The picture supposedly serves as a stimulus for a mental picture or image.

Inclusiveness of Concept Refers to the number of instances included in a concept.

Incompatible Behaviors Behaviors which cannot possibly occur together at the same point in time because they are mutually exclusive.

Independent Variable The variable in an experiment whose value the experimenter controls and which subsequently affects the dependent variable. It is the suspected causal variable that causes a change in the value of the dependent variable.

Indirect Measurement A measurement approach in which tasks or test items are conceptualized as "signs" of some underlying entity that cannot be directly observed. From indirect signs, the underlying entity is inferred.

Individualized Instruction Instruction based upon the needs of an individual rather than on the needs of the group. Using individualized instruction, different educational programs would be established for each individual in a group.

Induced Imagery Directions to form a mental picture of presented information in the absence of an external picture of the information. Supposedly the directions serve to induce a mental representation that is quasi-pictorial in nature.

Inductive Process Used in reference to concept learning. This process involves encountering examples of a concept so that the person forms the concept.

Inference Abstracting a logical implication, not actually stated, from a set of presented information. Generally, given *A* and given

B, C must follow logically, but *C* is not stated.

Information-Processing Approach A perspective on human behavior that is rooted in a computer analogy. The analogy is used to represent how a person would receive, store, recall, and act on provided information. Those utilizing this model borrow both concepts and language from computer science.

Inhibition Effect In social learning theory, if an observer sees a model punished for producing a behavior, the probability of imitation is decreased, i.e., the behavior is inhibited.

Innate Inborn or inherited.

Insight The sudden "seeing" of relationships or solutions to problems. Insight normally occurs with an abruptness. Sometimes insight is referred to as the "aha" phenomenon.

Instincts Innate tendencies of organisms to behave in a certain way.

Instrumental/Operant Conditioning The basic learning process associated with radical behaviorism. The essential element is that the production of a response is the outcome of consequences that have followed that response in the past. Consequences alter the probabilities of response production, either increasing or decreasing the probability and therefore the frequency of produced behaviors.

Intellectual Assessment Measuring intelligence, ability, cognitive functioning, etc.

Intelligence Quotient, IQ A measurement index for the amount of intelligence an individual possesses. Originally it was computed as:

$$\frac{\text{mental age}}{\text{chronological age}} \times 100$$

Now it is a standard score with a mean of 100 and indicates the position of the score in a normal distribution.

Interactionism The notion that an event, particularly a human event, is the outcome of several variables acting together. Normally refers to the combined effect of both

person and environmental events on a behavior. Expressed as $B = E \times P$.

Intermittent Reinforcement A schedule of reinforcement in which reinforcement does not occur after every response but only after some level of response frequency.

Intervention A deliberate alteration of the contingencies affecting the production of a behavior; a treatment strategy.

Intuitive Behavior A behavior that a person is capable of doing correctly but is not capable of explaining. Generally refers to language.

Invariant Sequence A sequence of change along a single continuum that can occur in only one order. The developmental stages of Piaget form such an invariant sequence.

Item Analysis Procedures for determining the difficulty and discrimination index for a test question.

Item Difficulty Item difficulty is calculated by using the percentage of the group who answered the item correctly. Item difficulties may range from .00, indicating that no one answered the question correctly, to 1.00, meaning that everyone answered the question correctly. For maximum discrimination and differentiation of scores, .50 difficulty is preferred.

Item Discrimination The quality of an item for differentiating between the students who scored highest and those who scored lowest. (*See* Discrimination Index.)

Itinerant Teacher A teacher with special skills for teaching students with particular and exceptional needs, who may move from school to school to assist in the education of special students. Examples would include teachers of the blind or deaf or speech therapists.

Knowledge of Results An outcome or effect of a response that, according to Skinner, serves as a reinforcer for the response.

Laboratory Analogue Synonomous with experimental paradigm. Refers to a style of research investigation where variables are under the control of the experimenter in order to permit cause-and-effect conclusions. Such control is seldom possible outside of the laboratory setting, hence the name.

Language Acquisition Device (LAD) From Chomsky, an unobservable, hypothetical construct referring to an inborn language processor that permits rapid language development. Chomsky's view is that the child is born with knowledge of universal language rules that permits the processing of surface structure and thus language development at a time when the child is intellectually unprepared to handle other complex cognitive accomplishments.

Language Universals Characteristics of language that are uniform in all languages.

Latency The period of time between the presentation of a cue and the onset of a behavior.

Lateralization The dominance of one brain hemisphere over the other.

Levels of Concept Attainment Levels referring to what the learner is able to do with his knowledge of the concept. A concept, at the lowest level, may only be recognized as something that the learner has encountered. At the highest level, the concept can be named, defined, and verbally described.

Levels of Processing One approach to the encoding of prose information that suggests that what we recall is a function of the degree of processing involved. Recall of semantic material requires a greater degree of processing than the recall of form information.

Linguist A specialist in the structure of language systems.

Linguistic Determinism The notion that language influences, in fact determines, thought and the perception of reality. One aspect of the Whorfian hypothesis.

Linguistic Relativism The notion that languages differ and thus those who speak different languages see the world, i.e., think, differently.

Linguistic System The structure of language, including phonology, morphology, and syntax.

Locus of Causality The attributions of success or failure perceived by a person.

Locus of Control Originally proposed by Rotter (1966) to explain motivation as a function of whether the person perceives results as coming from factors within himself or from factors outside of himself.

Logical Meaningfulness The concept that the material is relatable to the individual's cognitive structure. (*See* Relatability).

Long-Term Memory The third phase in information processing, where material from the short-term memory has been encoded and through rehearsal or elaboration is incognitive structure. (*See* Relatability.)

Longitudinal Studies An approach to studying development where a group of children are observed over time as they grow and age. By repeated observations on the same individuals, conclusions are drawn about developmental processes.

M_{AF} A symbol representing a person's motive to avoid failure.

M_S A symbol for motivation to succeed.

Mainstreaming Provision for the education of handicapped populations, which allows them to be educated in the least restrictive environment, ranging from the normal classroom to institutional confinement.

Maslow's Needs Hierarchy An ordering of human needs starting with physiological needs and extending to the growth needs.

Mean A statistic that gives the arithmetic average of all the scores in a frequency distribution. The mean is derived by summing the scores and dividing by the number of scores.

Meaningful Learning Meaningful learning is learning that is incorporated into the cognitive structure. Learning that is related to past learning is considered to be meaningful.

Measurement The process of quantifying how much of a given attribute a person possesses.

Mechanistic Model An approach to human development based on a machine analogy.

The developmental process is viewed as a result of experience, which can be understood through a reductionistic approach. The basic emphasis is on changes associated with experience and the manipulation of environmental variables.

Median A score in a frequency distribution that divides the frequencies in half. Fifty percent of the scores fall above the median and fifty percent of the scores fall below the median.

Mediators Cognitive processes or behaviors that occur between the presentation of a stimulus and the production of a response.

Mental Events Events that occur on a cognitive level and thus cannot be directly observed at the time they occur.

Mental Testing The assessment of cognitive functioning, cognitive traits, abilities, etc.; measuring those aspects of cognitive behavior that are not directly observable.

Metacognition Knowledge or cognitions about the procedures involved in knowing, retrieving, recalling, problem solving. Knowing how to know, knowing that you know, etc.

Model A behavioral example produced by an individual.

Modeling Effect Acquisition of a novel behavior that occurs as a result of observing the behavior produced by another individual.

Moral Development From Kohlberg and Piaget, refers to the individual's development of the ability to reason ethically about moral situations. Both theorists propose that moral development involves an invariant stage sequence related to cognitive development.

Moral Dilemma Vignettes utilized in moral development research where an individual is faced with a situation of moral judgment between two alternatives. The vignettes are used to tap moral reasoning and reveal the individual's level of moral development.

Moral Realism From Piaget, the first stage of moral development coinciding with the preoperational period. In this stage children view rules as absolute and unchangeable, with automatic punishment for breaking them. Whether a particular action is judged right or wrong depends on its objective consequences, i.e., intentions are not considered.

Morphology, Morpheme The system for combining sounds into meaningful units. A morpheme is the smallest meaningful sound unit in a language.

Motivation A construct for that which causes a person to act, directs that activity, and sustains the activity.

Multiple-Baseline Design A strategy of collecting data in which two or more behaviors are observed and recorded simultaneously. Intervention is sequential across the behaviors in an attempt to obtain replication of an effect across behaviors.

Multiple-Choice Items A recognition type of test question that poses a question or incomplete statement with a number (usually 3–5) of possible answers. The student is expected to choose the correct or best answer from the alternatives.

Murray's Needs System An extensive classification of needs including viscerogenic and psychogenic needs.

Nativism A philosophical and psychological perspective that emphasizes innate, inborn capabilities as opposed to those acquired strictly through experience. The idea that knowledge and behavioral capabilities exist from birth and influence future activity is a major idea in this perspective.

Natural Reinforcers Reinforcers that can be expected to occur in real social settings as opposed to contrived situations.

Nature-Nurture Controversy The debate surrounding the relative contribution of genetic inheritance and experience to some behavioral expression, usually intelligence and ability.

Needs Hypothesized constructs that motivate a person. According to Maslow, needs may result from such deficiencies as the need for food or for love, or they may be such growth needs as the need to know.

Negative Punishment Operant process in which the removal of a stimulus following a behavior decreases the probability of the behavior occurring again.

Negative Reinforcement An operant process in which the removal of a stimulus following a behavior leads to an increased frequency of the behavior.

Negative Transfer The outcome when previous learning impedes subsequent learning.

Neutral Stimulus A stimulus that does not demonstrate a reliable relationship with a particular response. There is an absence of a contingency.

Nodes The elements comprising the propositional network in long-term memory. The propositions involve relationships between nodes.

Nondiscriminatory Assessment Assessment procedures designed such that different cultural groups are not placed in a situation of undue disadvantage.

Norm The average or typical test score for members of a particular group. Norms are often reported in tables for standardized tests that report typical score values for various homogeneous groups, such as grade levels or various ages.

Norm-Referenced Tests (NRT) Tests that express scores by comparing a person's score to other pupils' scores from an appropriate reference group.

Normal Curve Distribution A bell-shaped ideal frequency distribution. Most of the scores fall near the center of the distribution, with fewer scores occurring as the scores deviate from the center.

Normal Curve Method A method of assigning marks in which specified proportions of the group receive each letter grade. A commonly used scale is 7% *A*s, 24% *B*s, 38% *C*s, 24% *D*s, and 7% *F*s.

Normative Evaluation Evaluation based on norm-referenced achievement tests.

Null Hypothesis A statement that can be rejected but cannot be empirically confirmed. In statistics, the null hypothesis typically takes the form of a "no difference" equation, and it specifies the sampling distribution with which observed data is compared. On the basis of data, the null hypothesis can be rejected as an accurate reflection of the state of nature; the alternative outcome is a failure to reject the statement only and does not constitute demonstration of its truth value.

Numerical Rating Scale A rating scale where the varying degrees of adequacy or acceptability are indicated by numbers; a 1 might indicate superior and a 5 might indicate inadequacy, with the numbers 2, 3, and 4 indicating points between these extremes.

Object Permanence The concept that objects exist independent of the perceiver. An accomplishment of the sensorimotor period, it is the cornerstone of symbolic activity and representational thought.

Operant A response that has an effect on the environment.

Operant Conditioning A learning process where the effects of a response function to alter the subsequent frequency of that response. The major learning process in radical behaviorism.

Operationalization, Operational Definition Defining behaviors and variables in terms of how they are to be measured or manipulated within the setting.

Organismic Model An approach to human development based on a biological analogy. The developmental process is viewed as unidirectional, holistic, and a function of biological enfolding principles. Thus the basic emphasis is on changes associated with age.

Organization From Piaget, refers to the propensity of the human organism to organize experience and information into meaningful wholes. One of the two invariant functions which characterize man's style of interacting with the environment.

Orienting Statements A statement, preceding a prose passage, that directs the reader (or listener) to the schema (existing knowledge) relevant to the content of the passage. Titles, for example, can function as orienting statements.

Overregularization   The tendency of young children developing language skills to reg ularize irregular verbs after they have properly used the irregular form in the past. For example, the substitution of "I goed" for "I went."

Paired Associate Learning   A paradigm for studying learning and recall. Typically, stimuli are presented in pairs. They can be pairs of words, nonsense syllables, pictures, etc. To test learning and/or recall, the first member of the pair is presented and the subject must supply its associate.

Paradigm Shift   A gradual change in the commonly accepted method within a science; a change in scientific perspective.

Percentile Ranks   A conversion of raw scores into a number expressing the percentage of scores that fall at or below that score; a score with a percentile rank of 20 indicates that 20% of the scores fell at or below that point.

Performance Objective   A statement of performance in terms of an observable behavior, the conditions under which the behavior will occur, and the criteria necessary to achieve mastery.

Personal Bias Error   In the use of rating scales, an evaluator who tends to rate everyone at about the same place on the rating scale.

Perspective-Taking   The ability to anticipate how an individual other than self perceives a situation. Can involve visual, conceptual, or affective perceptions of another. Comes from Piagetian theory and is not expected as a competence until the period of concrete operations.

Phonology, Phoneme   The sound system of a language. Phonemes are the units of sound in a language that, when combined, form meaningful units.

Positive Punishment   An operant process where the presentation of a stimulus fol lowing a behavior decreases the frequency of the behavior.

Positive Reinforcement   An operant process where the presentation of a stimulus following a behavior increases the frequency of the behavior.

Positive Reinforcer   A stimulus that, when presented after a behavior, serves to increase the frequency of the behavior.

Positive Transfer   The process that causes previous learning to facilitate subsequent learning.

Post-Conventional Level of Morality   The final level in Kohlberg's theory of moral development. Moral reasoning is based on an internal set of ethical principles, which include respect for the larger social system and adherence to abstract ethics. Few people reach this level.

Power of Concept   The agreement of people as to the importance of a concept for future conceptual learning.

Pragmatics   The examination of the function of language and how it is used in the interactive process.

Precision of Concept   A concept is precise insofar as there are explicit rules for distinguishing examples of that concept from nonexamples.

Preconventional Level of Morality   The first level in Kohlberg's theory of moral development. Moral judgments are made on the basis of external rules to avoid punishment or to obtain rewards. Typical of younger children's reasoning on moral dilemma problems.

Predictive Validity   A type of criterion-related validity where the criterion will only be available sometime in the future. The predictive validity of a scholastic aptitude test may be established by correlating the scores with achievement at the end of an academic program.

Premack Principle   A reinforcement contingency in which a high probability behavior *(A)* is used to reinforce a low probability behavior *(B)*. A and B should be empirically determined. Access to *A* is dependent on some level of production of *B*.

Preoperational Period The second Piagetian stage, covering approximately ages 2–6. The child is a symbolizer as reflected in use of language, deferred imitation, and symbolic play. However, the preoperational child cannot override immediate perceptual experience and reason logically about physical phenomena. Thus the child is perceptually dominated, egocentric, and does not understand logical concepts like reversibility, compensation, class relations, and conservation.

Primary Drives Those drives necessary for the survival of the species (e.g., hunger, thirst, sex).

Priming Questions Questions inserted within prose material that encourage the reader to reflect on the meaningful content of the prose passage.

Principle A statement expressing a relationship between two or more concepts.

Proposition The representation of a relationship between elements. Many cognitive psychologists represent memory as a network of propositions.

Prose Connected discourse.

Prosocial Behavior Positive forms of social behavior valued within the social system. These include behavior examples such as altruism, empathy, cooperation, and sharing. A research interest of those operating within the cognitive-developmental perspective.

Psychogenic Needs The 28 needs in Murray's system that were learned, including the need to achieve, to affiliate, to be autonomous.

Psycholinguist, Developmental Psycholinguist The individual who studies language from a psychological perspective, i.e., language as it is produced by people rather than in the abstract.

Psychometric Model A perspective on human ability and behavior that is based on measurement assumptions. Typically these assumptions include the notion that quantitative traits underlie performance, that these traits can be indirectly assessed through measurement procedures, that the resulting assessment can be quantified, and that individuals can be compared on the quantified dimension.

Punishment An operant process where stimulus events following a response decrease the frequency of the response.

Purposive Behavior Tolman's theory that all behavior is goal-oriented and thus occurs as a result of those goals.

Rating Scale A listing of all of the important elements that should be included in a performance or product, with varying degrees of acceptability or adequacy of each element to be checked by the evaluator.

Reactivity The tendency for frequency rates of responses to change as a function of recording them in the absence of other stimulus alterations.

Recall The ability to retrieve information at a later time.

Recall Questions Test questions that require the student to search her memory to determine the answer to a question. Examples are short-answer, essay, and completion items.

Reception Learning Reception learning occurs when the content to be learned is presented in a final, complete form, through lecture, textbook, or other media.

Receptive Paradigm Used in reference to concept learning. This paradigm involves the presentation of one example or nonexample of a concept at a time, and the observer's task is to correctly classify the examples.

Reciprocity Refers to influence that is two-way or reciprocal. Social learning theorists use the word to refer to the notion that while the environment affects the person, the person also affects the environment; thus the direction of influence is reciprocal.

Recognition Questions Test questions in which the answers are provided and the student must determine the correct answer from those given. Examples are multiple-choice, true-false, and matching items.

Rehearsal Repetition of learned material,

called maintenance rehearsal, to increase the length of time a person retains the information.

Relatability In order for learning to be incorporated into the cognitive structure, it must be relatable. Material must be substantive and nonarbitrary to be relatable. Nonarbitrariness means that the material fits with previous learning; substantiveness means that the material can be stated in different ways without changing the meaning.

Relational Concepts Concepts that include or specify a relationship between the concept's attributes.

Relative Standards Used for the evaluation of student performance where the evaluation is based on how the student performed in relation to the group.

Reliability A characteristic of a test that describes how accurately the test measures what it is designed to measure. Reliability may be reported as a correlation coefficient, which is a called reliability coefficient, or as a standard error of measurement, which tells how much error is associated with a person's observed score.

Reliability Coefficient A correlation coefficient established by correlating scores on a test given at two different times or scores on equivalent forms of a test.

Replication A consistently observed cause-and-effect relationship. The finding can be reproduced by another scientist, with other subjects, in another setting. In operant technology, replication must be observed for clear conclusions. In other varieties of research, statistical techniques are employed as a substitute for observed replication.

Resource Rooms Rooms within a school where students with exceptional needs may spend part of the day with a teacher who has specific skills for teaching such students.

Respondent Behavior Behavior that occurs virtually automatically following the presentation of a stimulus. It is the major focus of classical conditioning and is the re-

sponse class studied by Watson and Pavlov.

Response A produced behavior.

Response-Outcome Expectancy An expectancy predicated on a person's knowledge of what is necessary for a particular outcome.

Restricted Response Items Items for which there is little, if any, variability in the correct response. Scoring keys can be constructed before the test is administered since the correct responses are prescribed.

Retrieval The final stage in information processing where previous learning is made available for current use.

Reversal An intervention phase in operant technology where there is a return to the contingencies operating during the baseline phase. Used for the purposes of replication.

Reversal Design In operant technology, an *ABAB* design where *A* represents baseline contingencies and *B* represents intervention contingencies. The functional relationship is demonstrated twice and is thus replicated.

Role-Taking Synonomous with conceptual perspective-taking, i.e., the ability to anticipate the cognitions of someone other than self.

Rote-Learning Learning that is not incorporated into the cognitive structure. Material learned by rote is not related to previous learning.

Rule A form of principle expressing a relationship between two or more concepts.

Rule/Example Concept Learning Another term signifying concept assimilation. The attributes of the concept are defined so that examples may be determined.

Satiation When sufficient reinforcement is received such that the stimulus no longer functions as a reinforcer and the behavior it follows ceases to be affected. Satiation can be a problem with tangible and primary reinforcers.

Schedule of Reinforcement The rate at which reinforcement is delivered.

Schema/Scheme   Used two ways: 1) In schema theory, refers to a "knowledge bundle" derived from prior experience that affects the encoding and recall of new material. 2) In Piagetian theory, refers to an organized sequence of action, physical or mental, that occurs in generally the same form across contexts. Supposedly schemas reflect the individual's structure of knowledge of the world, analogous to a mental or behavioral program. *Schema* usually refers to these sequences in the sensorimotor stage where the sequence is overt and physical. *Scheme* refers to the mental action sequences associated with later developmental stages.

Schema Theory   A loosely integrated theoretical perspective on prose processing. Generally refers to the notion that the encoding and recall of prose is affected by the individual's prior knowledge, or schemas, about the material. Thus what a person comprehends when faced with new material is a product of *both* the new material and schemas derived from past experience.

Scientific Method   A procedure for investigating phenomena that is objective, repeatable, and public. It is predicated on the reliable demonstration of cause-and-effect relationships and derives from a view of the world associated with the philosophy of empiricism. The procedures followed, not the content examined, engender the scientific method.

Secondary Drives   Those drives that are learned and are species specific.

Selection Paradigm   A number of examples and nonexamples of concepts are presented at one time and the observer's task is to discover the concept through selection of examples.

Self-Actualization   Hypothesized by Maslow to be a need to become all that one is able to become, one of the growth needs.

Self-Efficacy   A person's perception concerning his or her ability to perform a task or behave in a particular way.

Self-Esteem   A person's perception of his own worth, value and/or abilities.

Semantic System   The meaning of language, what the linguistic structure represents.

Sensorimotor Period   The first Piagetian stage, covering approximately birth through age two. The child's major mode of functioning is through physical movement and exploration. Major accomplishments during this period are 1) the attainment of the object concept, 2) beginnings of the symbolic function, 3) differentiation of the self from the rest of the environment, and 4) rudimentary understanding of means-ends relationships.

Sensory Register   Incoming stimulation is first recorded in the sensory register. The information is a nearly literal or pictorial record of the sensory image. This information is only stored here briefly before it passes to the short-term memory, where it may be recognized, categorized, or identified.

Seriation   Comprehension of order and ordered relations among elements on a continuous dimension. Being able to order objects into a sequence such that $A > B > C > D$.

Short-Term Memory   The second phase in the information processing system where stimuli, which have passed through the sensory register, are held long enough to be recognized or identified. Material is stored here for only a few seconds before it is either lost or transferred to the long-term memory.

Sign Learning   Tolman's thesis that stimuli are signs, signalling what is to follow, in opposition to the behavioristic idea that stimuli elicit responses. To Tolman, signs create expectancies for outcomes of actions.

Situational Specificity   A lack of consistency in behavior across settings; that is, whether a person produces a given response will depend on the circumstances. Usually refers to the performance of social behaviors.

Social Learning Theory   An approach to explaining learning with an emphasis on learning through imitation. Primary proponent is Albert Bandura. Generally it is proposed that learners observe the behavior of others, cognitively mediate what they see, and imitate the behavior under appropriate circumstances. The acquisition of behavior in this paradigm is explained through contiguity and cognitive mediation. Performance depends on expectations of reinforcement acquired through vicarious reinforcement principles.

Spatial Ability The ability to interpret, manipulate, and transform spatial information.

Species Uniform Characteristic A characteristic possessed by every member of a species (e.g., language) except in instances of gross abnormality.

Specific Biology Genetic inheritance as opposed to general species characteristics.

Specific History Idiosyncratic experience of the individual.

Spontaneous Recovery In the extinction process, after reinforcement has ceased, a behavior may increase to its reinforcement level in the absence of added reinforcement. It will subsequently return to baseline frequency if reinforcement is not forthcoming.

Stage I Language From Roger Brown, the unadorned simple speech evident in early language development. Utterances typically contain more than one word, are rule-governed and meaningful, but are unlike adult utterances. These utterances lack grammatical refinements.

Stage II Speech, Modulation of Meaning The point in language development when children begin to add endings to words and to use the little function words that elaborate their utterances; from Roger Brown.

Standard Deviation A statistic used to describe the variability of a distribution of scores. Variability refers to the scatter of the scores in a distribution.

Standard Error of Measurement A measure of reliability that expresses the amount of possible error that may be reflected in an observed score.

Standard Score A score derived from a raw score so that it can be expressed on a uniform standard scale. The Z score is a simple standard score that expresses how much a score deviates from the mean in standard deviation units.

Standardized Test A test that has been constructed following detailed specifications, where items have been tried out and refined in terms of difficulty and discrimination. These tests are accompanied by a manual giving specific directions for administration and scoring and providing relevant and dependable norms for score interpretation.

Stanine A single digit standard score on a nine-unit scale. The distribution has a mean of five and a standard deviation of two.

Statistics 1) An abbreviation for statistical methods that are procedures for organizing or interpreting data; 2) Terms used to summarize a body of data.

Structuralism A philosophical position in which the meaning of phenomena are derived from their place within a larger structure or system. Implies that individual parts lack meaning outside of their relation to the whole. Associated with a Piagetian perspective.

Structure, Cognitive An unobservable construct referring to the organization of knowledge that an individual possesses. Different models of cognitive structure are possible depending on theoretical perspective.

Substantiveness Material is substantive insofar as it may be stated in different ways without changing the meaning.

Surface Structure The actual words heard in a verbal utterance.

Symbolic Mode From Bruner, a mode of thinking that is representational, i.e., linguistic, and that permits logical deduction and inference beyond immediate perceptual experience.

Symbolic Model The behavior of others depicted in representational form, such as in media.

Syntax The rule system for combining morphemes into meaningful utterances, or sentences; grammar.

T Score A normalized standard score with a mean of fifty and a standard deviation of ten.

Tabula Rasa The idea that the infant is born as a blank slate without innate ideas, and that slate is written on by experience. Associated with the empiricist philosophy of John Locke.

Taxonomy A classification arranged in a particular order.

Telegraphic Speech A descriptive term for early child language. Refers to the phenomenon that young children's first sentences tend to resemble a telegraph message, i.e., the order of words is correct and the nouns and verbs are there, but the little words and endings to words are missing, e.g., "I see truck."

Temporal Sequence A sequence of events that occurs over time.

Test Blueprint A grid of the content and behaviors to be included in a test of achievement. The use of a test blueprint assists in making the test content valid.

Test Matrix (*See* Test Blueprint.)

Text Grammars Procedures for organizing and representing the ideas, semantic units, meaning, or propositions embedded in a prose passage.

Theory An explanatory system for depicting some phenomenon. Scientific theory is based on data and empirical evidence but goes beyond data by integrating evidence and proposing yet-to-be observed relationships. Sound theory must meet a number of criteria; primary among them is the ability to both *explain* and *predict* the occurrence of relevant phenomena.

Thinning A process of gradually reducing a schedule of reinforcement from a continuous to an intermittent one. Functions to increase durability of the behavior and resistance to extinction.

Time Out Placing an individual in a controlled setting where it is not possible to earn reinforcement. May actually be a form of punishment.

Time Sampling A recording method in operant technology where one observes the presence or absence of a target behavior within a specified time interval.

Token Economy A reinforcement system set up on a group basis where tangibles are delivered for meeting response goals. The reinforcers are generally tokens, which can be exchanged for back-up reinforcers. Behavioral goals necessary to earn tokens can be individually set, but typically the whole group will be functioning on the system. A useful operant technique when the group of individuals is unresponsive to social reinforcement control.

Trait A psychological construct assumed to underlie the expression of a set of behaviors. Behavior thus is a reflection of the trait's existence. Typically traits are conceptualized as quantitative characteristics, thus people can be compared (following trait measurement) as to how much of the underlying trait they possess.

Transfer To apply previous learning to subsequent learning. Addition facts that are applied to multiplication problems exemplify transfer.

True Score The component of an observed score that represents the "true" ability.

Types of Reinforcers (social, primary, secondary) Primary reinforcers are those necessary to support life, have intrinsic reinforcing value, and thus function as reinforcers without prior learning. Secondary reinforcers are originally neutral stimuli which acquire reinforcing value through frequent pairing with a primary reinforcer. Social reinforcers are a type of secondary reinforcer supplied by another individual, e.g., hugs, praise, smiles.

Unconditioned Response (UCR) A response that occurs automatically following the presentation of a stimulus. Is thought to be an unlearned, automatic response.

Unconditioned Stimulus (UCS) A stimulus

that automatically elicits a response in the absence of prior learning.

Validity A characteristic of a test describing whether the test measures what it is designed to measure.

Variable A quantity or measurement that can assume more than one value.

Variable Interval Schedule A schedule of reinforcement where delivery of the reinforcement varies around some average interval of time. Behaviors maintained on such a schedule are resistant to extinction when reinforcement is terminated.

Variable Ratio Schedule A schedule of reinforcement where delivery of the reinforcer depends on the frequency of response production. The number of responses required to earn reinforcement varies around some average amount. Behaviors maintained on such a schedule are highly resistant to extinction when reinforcement is terminated.

Variance Accounted for The amount of variance shared by two variables. Computed by squaring the correlation coefficient obtained with the variables.

Verbal Coding In some learning theory, the reduction of a model's behavior into a verbal description of the relevant dimensions of the performance. Can be external and observable or cognitive and unobservable. A hypothesized cognitive mediator in the imitative learning process.

Vertical Transfer If the content to be taught can be hierarchically arranged, vertical transfer occurs when learning taking place at a lower level is used in learning taking place at a higher level.

Vicarious Consequences Consequences that occur to a model and are observed by a learner and affect the probability of the observer imitating the modeled behavior.

Vicarious Learning Learning from observing the behavior of others in the environment.

Vicarious Punishment Punishing consequences for the behavior produced by a model, which function to decrease the probability of imitation in an observer.

Vicarious Reinforcement Reinforcing consequences for the behavior produced by a model, which function to increase the probability of imitation in an observer.

Viscerogenic Needs Those needs in Murray's system that were physiological (similar to primary drives).

Visual Perspective-Taking The ability to anticipate how another individual sees a visual display when that individual is observing the display from a position different from that of the self. Derives from Piagetian theory and is tapped by the three mountain task. Children usually do not experience success on the task until the period of concrete operations.

Visualization Skills An aspect of spatial competency tapped by tasks requiring matching, manipulation, etc., of visual information.

Weighted Standard Score Used for combining scores for periodic evaluation of student achievement. Different tests or performances are converted to standard scores and these scores are given varying amounts of emphasis by multiplying the standard score by a factor indicating the emphasis the evaluator wished to place on that test or performance.

Whorfian Hypothesis One approach to the relationship between language and thought. Essentially this view is that 1) language determines thought (linguistic determinism) and 2) people who speak different languages therefore also think differently (linguistic relativism).

Z Score A standard score that expresses how far a score deviates from the mean in standard deviation units; thus $Z = \dfrac{X - \overline{X}}{S}$. The mean of the Z scores is 0 and the standard deviation is 1.

References

Achenbach, T. M. *Research in developmental psychology.* New York: The Free Press, 1978.

Adams, M. J. Failures to comprehend and levels of processing in reading. In R. J. Spiro, B. C. Bruce, & W. F. Brewer (Eds.), *Theoretical issues in reading comprehension.* Hillsdale, N.J.: Erlbaum, 1980.

Alley, G., & Foster, C. Nondiscriminatory testing of minority and exceptional children. *Focus on Exceptional Children,* 1978, *9,* 1–14.

Ambron, S. R., & Irwin, D. M. Role-taking and moral judgments . . . in five- and seven-year-olds. *Developmental Psychology,* 1975, *11* (1), 102.

Anderson, J. R. Arguments concerning representations for mental imagery. *Psychological Review,* 1978, 85, *4,* 247–277. (a)

Anderson, J. R. Computer simulation of a language acquisition system: A second report. In D. LaBerge & S. J. Samuels (Eds.), *Perception and comprehension.* Hillsdale, N.J.: Erlbaum, 1978. (b)

Anderson, J. R. *Cognitive psychology and its implications.* San Francisco: W. H. Freeman, 1980.

Anderson, J. R., & Bower, G. H. *Human associative memory.* Washington, D.C.: Hemisphere Press, 1973.

Anderson, R. Control of student mediating processes during verbal learning and instructions. *Journal of Educational Research,* 1970, *40,* 349–369.

Anderson, R. C. The notion of schemata and the educational enterprise. In R. C. Anderson, R. J. Spiro, & W. C. Montague (Eds.), *Schooling and the acquisition of knowledge.* Hillsdale, N.J.: Erlbaum, 1977, 415–432.

Anderson, R. C. Schema-directed processes in language comprehension. In A. Lesgold, J. Pellegrino, S. Fokkema, & R. Glaser (Eds.), *Cognitive psychology and instruction.* New York: Plenum Press, 1978, 62–82.

Anderson, R. C., & Pichert, J. W. Recall of previously unrecallable information following a shift in perspective. *Journal of Verbal Learning and Verbal Behavior,* 1978, *17,* 1–12.

Anderson, R. C., Spiro, R. J., & Anderson, M. C. Schemata as scaffolding for the representation of information in discourse. *American Educational Research Journal,* 1978, *15,* 433–440.

Anderson, R. C., Spiro, R. J., & Montague, W. E. (Eds.). *Schooling and the acquisition of knowledge.* Hillsdale, N.J.: Erlbaum, 1977.

Anderson, S. B., & Messick, S. Social competence in young children. *Developmental Psychology,* 1974, *10*(2), 282–293.

Armstrong, J. M. A national assessment of achievement and participation of women in mathematics. Final report to the National Institute of Education on Grant No. NIE-G-77-0061, Education Commission of the States, Denver, December 1979.

Aronfreed, J. Aversive control of socialization. In D. Levin (Ed.), *Nebraska Symposium on Motivation.* Lincoln: University of Nebraska Press, 1968.

Asch, S. E. Reformulation of the problem of association. *American Psychologist,* 1969, *24,* 92–102.

Atkinson, J. W. Motivational determinants of risk-taking behavior. *Psychological Review,* 1957, *64,* 359–372.

Atkinson, J. W. *An introduction to motivation.* Princeton, N.J.: Van Nostrand, 1964.

Atkinson, J. W., & Feather, N. T. (Eds.). *A theory of achievement motivation.* New York: Wiley, 1966.

Atkinson, J. W., & Litwin, G. H. Achievement motive and test anxiety conceived as motive to approach success and motive to avoid failure. *Journal of Abnormal and Social Psychology*, 1960, *60*, 52–63.

Atkinson, J. W., & Raynor, J. O. *Motivation and achievement*. Washington, D.C.: V. H. Winston, 1974.

Ault, R. L. *Developmental perspectives*. Santa Monica, Calif.: Goodyear, 1980.

Ausubel, D. P. Learning by discovery: Rationale and mystique. *Bulletin of National Association of Secondary School Principals*, 1961, *45*, 18–58.

Ausubel, D. P. *Educational psychology: A cognitive view*. New York: Holt, Rinehart & Winston, 1968.

Ausubel, D. P. In defense of advance organizers: A reply to the critics. *Review of Educational Research*, 1978, *48*, 251–257.

Ausubel, D. P., & Robinson, F. G. *School learning: An introduction to educational psychology*. New York: Holt, Rinehart & Winston, 1969.

Ausubel, D. P., & Sullivan, E. V. *Theory and problems in child development* (2nd ed.). New York: Grune & Stratton, 1970.

Baker, J. P., & Crist, J. L. Teacher expectancies: A review of the literature. In J. D. Elashoff & R. E. Snow, *Pygmalion reconsidered*. Worthington, Ohio: Charles A. Jones, 1971.

Baller, W. R., Charles, D. C., & Miller, E. *Mid-life attainment of the mentally retarded: A longitudinal study*. Lincoln: University of Nebraska Press, 1967.

Bandura, A. Influence of models' reinforcement contingencies on the acquisition of imitative responses. *Journal of Personality and Social Psychology*, 1965, *1*, 589–595.

Bandura, A. *Principles of behavior modification*. New York: Holt, Rinehart & Winston, 1969.

Bandura, A. *Social learning theory*. New York: General Learning Press, 1971.

Bandura, A. *Aggression: A social learning analysis*. Englewood Cliffs, N.J.: Prentice-Hall, 1973.

Bandura, A. Behavior theory and models of man. *American Psychologist*, 1974, *29*, 859–870.

Bandura, A. Self-efficacy: Toward a unifying theory of behavioral change. *Psychological Review*, 1977, *84*(2), 191–215. (a)

Bandura, A. *Social learning theory*. Englewood Cliffs, N.J.: Prentice-Hall, 1977. (b)

Bandura, A., Adams, N. E., & Beyer, J. Cognitive processes mediating behavioral change. *Journal of Personality and Social Psychology*, 1977, *35*, 125–139.

Bandura, A., & Harris, M. B. Modification of syntactic style. *Journal of Experimental Child Psychology*, 1964, *69*, 1–9.

Bandura, A., & Jeffrey, R. W. Role of symbolic coding and rehearsal processes in observational learning, *Journal of Research in Personality*, 1973, *26*, 122–130.

Bandura, A., & MacDonald, F. J. Influences of social reinforcement and the behavior of models in shaping children's moral judgments. *Journal of Abnormal and Social Psychology*, 1963, *67*, 274–281.

Bandura, A., & Menlove, F. L. Factors determining vicarious extinction of avoidance behavior through symbolic modeling. *Journal of Personality and Social Psychology*, 1968, *8*, 99–108.

Bandura, A., & Walters, R. H. *Social learning and personality development*. New York: Holt, Rinehart & Winston, 1963.

Barnes, B. R., & Clawson, E. V. Do advance organizers facilitate learning? Recommendations for further research based on an analysis of 32 studies. *Review of Educational Research*, 1975, *45*, 637–659.

Barnett, M. A., King, L. M., & Howard, J. A. Inducing affect about self or other: Effects on generosity in children. *Developmental Psychology*, 1979, *15*, 164–167.

Bar-Tal, D. *Prosocial behavior: theory and research*. New York: Halsted, 1976.

Bar-Tal, D., Raviv, A., & Goldberg, M. Helping behavior among preschool children: An observational study. *Child Development*, 1982, *53*, 396–402.

Bartlett, F. C. *Remembering: A study in experimental and social psychology*. Cambridge, England: Cambridge University Press, 1932.

Bates, E. *Language and context: The acquisition of pragmatics*. New York: Academic Press, 1976. (a)

Bates, E. Pragmatics and sociolinguistics in child language. In D. M. Morehead & A. E. Morehead (Eds.), *Normal and deficient child language*. Baltimore, Md.: University Park Press, 1976. (b)

Bates, E., & McWhinney, B. A functionalist approach to the acquisition of grammar. In E. Ochs & B. Schieffelin (Eds.), *Developmental Pragmatics*. New York: Academic Press, 1979.

Baylor, G. W., & LeMoyne, G. Experiments in seriation with children: Toward an information processing explanation of horizontal decalage. *Canadian Journal of Behavioral Science*, 1975, *7*, 5–29.

Bearison, D. J., & Isaacs, L. Production deficiency in children's moral judgments. *Developmental Psychology*, 1975, *11*, 732–737.

Beilin, H. Linguistic, logical and cognitive models

for learning mathematical concepts. In A. Osborne & D. A. Bradford (Eds.), *Models for learning mathematics*, ERIC Center for Science, Mathematics, and Enviromental Education, College of Education, The Ohio State University, 1976.

Beilin, H. An alternative to social learning theory: Discussion of papers by Whitehurst, Zimmerman, & Brody. *Contemporary Educational Psychology*, 1978, *3*, 27–31.

Bellach, A. S., & Hersen, M. (Eds.). *Research and practice in social skills training*. New York: Plenum Press, 1979.

Bennett, G. K., Seashore, H. G., & Wesman, A. G. *Differential aptitude tests manual* (4th ed.). New York: Psychological Corporation, 1966.

Bennett, G. K., Seashore, H. G., & Wesman, A. G. *Manual for the differential aptitude tests: Forms S and T* (5th ed.). New York: Psychological Corporation, 1974.

Bereiter, C., & Engelmann, S. *Teaching disadvantaged children in the preschool*. Englewood Cliffs, N.J.: Prentice-Hall, 1966.

Bergan, J. R. A domain structure model for measuring cognitive development. Technical report on Grant HHS/ACYF #105-81-C-008, The University of Arizona, 1982.

Berlyne, D. W., & Frommer, F. D. Some determinants of the incidence and content of children's questions. *Child Development*, 1966, *37*, 177–189.

Bernstein, B. Language and social class. *British Journal of Sociology*, 1960, *11*, 271–276.

Bernstein, B. Social structure, language, and learning. *Educational Research*, 1961, *3*(3), 163–176.

Bersoff, D. N. Silk purses into sows' ears: The decline of psychological testing and a suggestion for its redemption. *American Psychologist*, 1973, *28*, 892–899.

Bijou, S. W. *Child development: The basic stage of early childhood*. Englewood Cliffs, N.J.: Prentice-Hall, 1976.

Bijou, S. W., & Baer, D. M. *Child development: Readings in experimental analysis*. New York: Appleton-Century-Crofts, 1967.

Bijou, S. W., & Peterson, R. F. Psychological assessment in children: A functional analysis. In R. McReynolds (Ed.), *Advances in psychological assessment* (Vol. 2). Palo Alto, Calif.: Science and Behavior Books, 1971.

Bijou, S. W., & Ruiz, R. *Behavior modification: Contributions to education*. Hilldale, N.J.: Erlbaum, 1981.

Binet, A., & Simon, T. *The development of intelligence in children*. Trans. by Elizabeth S. Kite. Baltimore, Md.: Williams & Wilkins, 1916.

Blank, S. S., & Covington, M. Inducing children to ask questions in problem solving. *Journal of Educational Research*, September 1965, *59*(1), 21–27.

Bloom, B. S. (Ed.) *Taxonomy of educational objectives: Cognitive Domain*. New York: David McKay, 1956.

Bloom, B. S. (Ed.). *Taxonomy of educational objectives: Affective Domain*. New York: David McKay, 1964.

Bloom, B. S. *Learning for mastery: Evaluation comment 1*, No. 2. Los Angeles: University of California Center for the Study of Evaluation, 1968.

Bloom, B. S. *Human characteristics and school learning*. New York: McGraw-Hill, 1976.

Bloom, L. *Language development: Form and function in emerging grammars*. Cambridge, Mass.: MIT Press, 1970.

Bloom, L., Hood, L., & Lightbrown, P. Imitation in language development: If, when, and why? *Cognitive Psychology*, 1974, *6*, 380–420.

Bock, R. D. A family study of spatial visualizing ability. *American Psychologist*, 1967, *22*, 571.

Bock, R. D., & Kolakowski, D. Further evidence of sex-linked major gene influence on human spatial visualizing ability. *American Journal of Human Genetics*, 1973, *25*, 1–14.

Boring, E. G. Intelligence as the test tests it. *New Republic*, June 1923, *35*, 35–36.

Boring, E. G. *A history of experimental psychology* (2nd ed.). New York: Appleton-Century-Crofts, 1950.

Borke, H. Interpersonal perception of young children: Egocentrism or empathy? *Developmental Psychology*, 1971, *5*, 263–269.

Borke, H. Piaget's mountain revisited: Changes in the egocentric landscape. *Developmental Psychology*, 1975, *11*(2), 240–243.

Borke, H. Piaget's view of social interaction and the theoretical construct of empathy. In L. S. Siegel & C. J. Brainerd (Eds.), *Alternatives to Piaget: Critical essays on the theory*. New York: Academic Press, 1978.

Bourne, L. E. Knowing and using concepts. *Psychological Review*, 1970, *77*, 546–556.

Bourne, L. E., Guy, D. E., & Wadsworth, N. Verbal-reinforcement combinations and the relative frequency of information feedback in a card sorting task. *Journal of Experimental Psychology*, 1967, *73*, 220–226.

Bower, G. H. Organizational factors in memory. *Cognitive Psychology*, 1970, *1*, 18–46.

Bower, G. H. Adaption-level coding of stimuli and

serial position effects. In M. H. Appley (Ed.), *Adaption-level theory.* New York: Academic, 1971.

Bower, G. H., & Hilgard, E. R. *Theories of Learning.* Englewood Cliffs, N.J.: Prentice-Hall, 1981.

Bower, T. G. *A primer of infant development.* San Francisco: W. H. Freeman, 1977.

Bower, T. G. R. The object in the world of the infant. *Scientific American,* 1971, *225,* 30–47.

Bower, T. G. R., & Wishart, J. F. The effects of motor skill on object permanence. *Cognition,* 1972, *1,* 165–171 (second experiment).

Bowerman, M. Semantic factors in acquisition of rules for word use and sentence construction. In D. M. Morehead & A. E. Morehead (Eds.), *Normal and deficient child language.* Baltimore, Md.: University Park Press, 1976.

Bracht, G. H. Experimental factors related to aptitude-treatment interactions. *Review of Educational Research,* 1970, *40,* 627–645.

Braine, M. D. S. The ontogeny of certain logical operations: Piaget's formulation examined by nonverbal methods. *Psychological Monographs,* 1959, *73* (5, Whole No. 475).

Brainerd, C. J. Mathematical and behavioral foundations of number. *Journal of General Psychology,* 1973, *88,* 221–281. (a)

Brainerd, C. J. Neo-Piagetian training experiments revisited: Is there any support for the cognitive-developmental stage hypothesis? *Cognition,* 1973, *2,* 349–370. (b)

Brainerd, C. J. Does prior knowledge of the compensation rule increase susceptibility to conservation training? *Developmental Psychology,* 1976, *12,* 1–5.

Brainerd, C. J. Learning research and Piagetian theory. In L. S. Siegel & C. J. Brainerd (Eds.), *Alternatives to Piaget.* New York: Academic Press, 1978.

Brainerd, C. J., & Huevel, K. V. Development of geometric imagery in five to eight year olds. *Genetic Psychology Monographs,* 1974, *89,* 89–143.

Bransford, J. D., & Johnson, M. K. Contextual prerequisites for understanding: Some investigations of comprehension and recall. *Journal of Verbal Learning and Verbal Behavior,* 1972, *11,* 717–726.

Bransford, J. D., & Johnson, M. K. Considerations of some problems of comprehension. In W. Chase (Ed.), *Visual information processing.* New York: Academic Press, 1973.

Bretzing, B. H., & Kulhavey, R. W. Note taking and depth of processing. *Contemporary Educational Psychology.* 1979, *4,* 145–153.

Brody, G. H., & Henderson, R. W. Effects of mul-

tiple model variations and rationale provision on the moral judgments and explanations of young children. *Child Development,* 1977, *48,* 1117–1120.

Brody, G. H., & Rosser, R. A. The acquisition of multiple modeled information: An error analysis approach to observational learning. *Journal of Genetic Psychology,* in press.

Brophy, J. E., & Evertson, C. M. *Learning from teaching: A developmental perspective.* Boston: Allyn & Bacon, 1976.

Brophy, J. E., & Good, T. L. Teachers' communication of differential expectations for children's classroom performance: Some behavioral data. *Journal of Educational Psychology,* 1970, *61,* 365–374.

Brown, A. L. The development of memory: Knowing, knowing about knowing, and knowing how to know. In H. W. Reese (Ed.), *Advances in child development and behavior* (Vol. 10). New York: Academic Press, 1975.

Brown, A. L. Semantic integration of children's reconstruction of narrative sequences. *Cognitive Psychology,* 1976, *8,* 247–262.

Brown, A. L. Knowing when, where and how to remember: A problem of metacognition. In R. Glaser (Ed.), *Advances in instructional psychology.* Hillsdale, N.J.: Erlbaum, 1978.

Brown, A. L. Metacognitive development and reading. In R. J. Spiro, B. C. Bruce, & W. F. Brewer (Eds.), *Theoretical issues in reading comprehension.* Hillsdale, N.J.: Erlbaum, 1980.

Brown, A. L., & Campione, J. Training strategic study time apportionment in educable retarded children. *Intelligence,* 1977, *1,* 94–107.

Brown, A. L., & Deloach, J. Skills, plans, and self-regulation. In R. Siegler (Ed.), *Children's thinking: What develops?* Hillsdale, N.J.: Erlbaum, 1978.

Brown, A. L., & Lawton, S. The feeling of knowing experience in educable retarded children. *Developmental Psychology,* 1977, *13,* 364–380.

Brown, A. L., & Smiley, S. The development of strategies for studying texts. *Child Development,* 1978, *49,* 1076–1088.

Brown, J. S., & Burton, R. R. Diagnostic models for the procedural bugs in basic mathematical skills. *Cognitive Science,* 1978, *2,* 155–192.

Brown, R. *A first language: The early stages.* Cambridge, Mass.: Harvard University Press, 1973.

Brown, R., & Fraser, C. The acquisition of syntax. In C. N. Cofer & B. Musgrave (Eds.), *Verbal behavior and learning: Problems and Processes.* New York: McGraw-Hill, 1963, 158–201.

Brown, R., & Hanlon, C. Derivational complexity and order of acquisition in child speech. In J. R. Hayes (Ed.), *Cognition and the development of language.* New York: Wiley, 1970, 155–207.

Bruner, J. S. Going beyond the information given. In H. Gruber, K. R. Hammond, & R. Jesser (Eds.), *Contemporary approaches to cognition.* Cambridge, Mass.: Harvard University Press, 1957.

Bruner, J. S. *The process of education.* Cambridge, Mass.: Harvard University Press, 1960.

Bruner, J. S. *Toward a theory of instruction.* Cambridge, Mass.: Harvard University Press, 1966.

Bruner, J. S., Goodnow, J., & Austin, G. *A study of thinking.* New York: Wiley, 1956.

Bruner, J. S., Olver, R. R., & Greenfield, P. M. *Studies in Cognitive Growth.* New York: Wiley, 1966.

Bryan, J. H. Children's reactions to helpers: Their money isn't where their mouths are. In J. Macauley & L. Berkowitz (Eds.), *Altruism and helping behavior.* New York: Academic Press, 1970.

Bryan, J. H., & London, P. Altruistic behavior in children. *Psychological Bulletin,* 1970, *73,* 200–211.

Bryan, J. H., & Test, M. A. Models and helping: Naturalistic studies in aiding behavior. *Journal of Personality and Social Psychology,* 1967, *6,* 400–407.

Bryan J. H., & Walbek, N. Preaching and practicing self-sacrifice: Children's actions and reactions. *Child Development,* 1970, *41,* 329–353. (a)

Bryan, J. H., & Walbek, N. The impact of words and deeds concerning altruism upon children. *Child Development,* 1970, *41,* 747–757. (b)

Bryant, P. E., & Trabasso, T. Transitive inferences and memory in young children. *Nature,* 1971, *232,* 456–458.

Buckley, N., Siegel, L. S., & Ness, S. Egocentrism, empathy, and altruistic behavior in young children. *Developmental Psychology,* 1979, *15,* 329–330.

Buros, O. K. (Ed.). *Tests in print.* Highland Park, N.J.: The Gryphon Press, 1974.

Buros, O. K. *Mental Measurements Yearbook.* Highland Park, N.J.: The Gryphon Press, 1978.

Burt, C. The genetic determination of differences in intelligence: A study of monozygotic twins reared together and apart. *British Journal of Psychology,* 1966, *57,* 137–153.

Butcher, B., & Schneider, R. E. Acquisition and generalization of conservation by preschoolers using operant training. *Journal of Experimental Child Psychology,* 1973, *16,* 187–204.

Carroll, J. B. A model of school learning. *Teachers College Record,* 1963, *64,* 723–733.

Carroll, J. B. Words, meanings, and concepts. *Harvard Educational Review,* 1964, *34* (2), 178–202.

Carroll, J. B. Psychometric tests as cognitive tasks: A new "structure of intellect." In L. B. Resnick (Ed.), *The nature of intelligence.* Hillsdale, N.J.: Erlbaum, 1976.

Carroll, W. R., Rosenthal, T. L., & Brysh, C. G. The social transmission of grammatical parameter. *Journal of Educational Psychology,* 1972, *63,* 589–594.

Carson, T. P., & Adams, H. E. Affective disorders: Behavioral perspecting. In S. M. Turner, K. S. Calhorn, & H. E. Adams (Eds.), *Handbook of clinical behavior therapy.* New York: Wiley, 1981

Carter, J. F., & Van Matre, N. H. Note taking versus note having. *Journal of Educational Psychology,* 1975, *67,* 900–904.

Carver, R. P. Two dimensions of tests: Psychometric and edumetric. *American Psychologist,* 1974, *29*(7), 512–518.

Cattell, R. B. *Culture Fair Intelligence Test: Scale 1.* Champaign, Ill.: Institute for Personality and Ability Testing, 1950.

Cattell, R. B., & Cattell, A. K. S. *Culture Fair Intelligence Test: Scale 2.* Champaign, Ill.: Institute for Personality and Ability Testing, 1960.

Cattell, R. B., & Cattell, A. K. S. *Culture Fair Intelligence Test: Scale 3.* Champaign, Ill.: Institute for Personality and Ability Testing, 1963.

Cazden, C. B. Children's questions: Their forms, functions and roles in education. *Young Children,* 1970, *25,* 202–220.

Chandler, M. J., & Greenspan, S. Ersatz egocentrism: A reply to H. Borke. *Developmental Psychology,* 1972, *7,* 104–106.

Charles, D. C. Ability and accomplishment of persons earlier judged mentally deficient. *Genetic Psychology Monographs,* 1953, *47,* 3–71.

Cheyne, J. A., & Walters, R. H. Intensity of punishment, timing of punishment, and cognitive structure as determinants of response inhibition. *Journal of Experimental Child Psychology,* 1969, *7,* 231–244.

Chomsky, N. *Syntactic Structures.* The Hague: Mouton, 1957.

Chomsky, N. *Aspects of the theory of syntax.* Cambridge, Mass.: MIT Press, 1965.

Chomsky, N. Language and the mind. *Psychology Today,* 1968, *1*(9), 48–51, 66–68.

Ciminero, A. R., Calhoun, K. W., & Adams, H. E. (Eds.). *Handbook of behavioral assessment.* New York: Wiley, 1977.

Clark, D. C. Teaching concepts in the classroom: A set of prescriptions derived from experimental research. *Journal of Educational Psychology Monographs*, 1971, *62*, 253–278.

Clark, E. What's in a word? On the child's acquisition of semantics in his first language. In T. E. Moore (Ed.), *Cognitive development and the acquisition of language.* New York: Academic Press, 1973.

Clark, H. H., & Clark, E. V. *Psychology and language: An introduction to psycholinguistics.* New York: Harcourt Brace Jovanovich, 1977.

Cleary, T. A., Humphrey, L., Kendrick, A., & Wesman, A. Educational uses of tests with disadvantaged students. *American Psychologist*, 1975, *30*, 15–41.

Coffield, W. H., & Blommers, P. Effects of non-promotion on educational achievement in the elementary school. *Journal of Educational Psychology*, 1956, *47*, 235–250.

Coffman, W. E. On the reliability of ratings of essay examinations in English. *Research on Teaching of English*, Spring 1971, *5*, 24–26.

Cook-Gumperz, J. Persuasive talk: The social organization of children's talk. In J. Green & C. Wallat (Eds.), *Ethnography and language in educational settings.* Norwood, N. H.: Ablex, 1981.

Corrigan, R. Language development as related to stage 6 objective permanence. *Journal of Child Language*, 1978, *5*, 173–189.

Craik, F. I. M. The fate of primary memory items in free recall. *Journal of Verbal Learning and Verbal Behavior*, 1970, *9*, 143–148.

Craik, F. I. M. Levels of analysis view of memory. In P. Pliner, L. Kramer, & T. Alloway (Eds.), *Communication and affect: Language and thought.* New York: Academic Press, 1973.

Craik, F. I. M., & Lockhart, R. S. Levels of processing: A framework for memory research. *Journal of Verbal Learning and Verbal Behavior*, 1972, *11*, 671–684.

Craik, F. I. M., & Watkins, M. J. The role of rehearsal in short-term memory (Experiment I). *Journal of Verbal Learning and Verbal Behavior*, 1973, *12*, 599–607.

Cromer, R. F. The development of language and cognition: The cognition hypothesis. In B. Foss (Ed.), *New perspectives in child development.* Harmondsworth, England: Penguin Books, 1974.

Cronbach, L. J. Five decades of public controversy over mental testing. *American Psychologist*, 1975, *30*(1), 1–14.

Cronbach, L. J., & Snow, R. E. Individual differences in learning ability as a function of instructional variables. Final report, Contract No. OEC-4-6-061269-1217, U.S. Office of Education. Stan-

ford, Calif.: Stanford University, School of Education, 1969.

Crothers, E. Memory structure and the recall of discourse. In R. O. Freedle & J. B. Carroll (Eds.), *Language comprehension and the acquisition of knowledge.* Washington, D.C.: Winston, 1972.

Crow, J. F. Genetic theories and influences: Comments on the value of diversity. *Harvard Educational Review*, 1969, *1*, 153–161.

Dale, P. S. *Language development: Structure and function.* Hinsdale, Ill.: Dryden Press, 1972.

Dale, P. S. Hesitations in maternal speech. *Language and speech*, 1974, *17*(2), 174–181.

Dale, P. S. *Language development: Structure and function* (2nd ed.). New York: Holt, Rinehart & Winston, 1976.

Davenport, A. S. Classifications of distributions based on estimates of spread. Unpublished Ph.D. dissertation, University of Iowa, 1971.

Davis, A. Poor people have brains too. *Phi Delta Kappan*, 1949, *30*, 294–295.

Davis, E. A. The form and function of children's questions. *Child Development*, 1932, *3*, 57–74.

Davis, G. A. *Psychology of problem solving.* New York: Basic Books, 1973.

Dawes, R. Cognitive distortion. *Psychological Reports*, 1964, *14*, 443–459.

Dawes, R. Memory and the distortion of meaningful written material. *British Journal of Psychology*, 1966, *57*, 77–86.

Dean, A. L. The structure of imagery. *Child Development*, 1976, *47*, 949–958.

Dean, A. L. Patterns of change in relations between children's anticipatory imagery and operative thought. *Developmental Psychology*, 1979, *15*(2), 153–163.

DeAvila, E. A., & Harassy, B. E. Piagetian alternatives to IQ: Mexican American study. In N. Hobbs (Ed.), *Issues in the classification of exceptional children.* San Francisco: Jossey-Bass, 1975.

DeMao, V. L. Piagetian assessment of reading readiness. In J. F. Magary et al. (Eds.), *Piagetian theory and the helping professions.* Los Angeles: University of Southern California Bookstore, 1977.

deVilliers, J. G., & deVilliers, P. A. A cross-sectional study of the acquisition of grammatical morphemes in child speech. *Journal of Psycholinguistic Research*, 1973, *2*, 267–278.

DeVries, R. The development of role-taking as reflected by behavior of bright, average, and retarded children in a social guessing game. *Child Development*, 1970, *41*, 759–770.

Dewey, J. *How we think*. Boston: Heath, 1910.

Diana vs. California State Board of Education. No. C–70 37 RFP, District Court of Northern California (February 1970).

Diesing, P. *Patterns of discovery in the social sciences*. Chicago: Aldine-Atherton, 1971.

Dillard, J. L. *Black English: Its history and usage in the United States*. New York: Random House, 1972.

Dodd, D. H. Language development. In R. L. Ault (Ed.), *Developmental perspectives*. Santa Monica, Calif.: Goodyear Publishing, 1980.

Dollard, J., & Miller, N. E. *Personality and Psychotherapy*. New York: McGraw-Hill, 1950.

Donaldson, M. *Children's Minds*. New York: W. W. Norton, 1978.

Donaldson, M., & Balfour, G. Less is more: A study of language comprehension in children. *British Journal of Psychology*, 1968, *59*(4), 461–471.

Dooling, D. J., & Lachman, R. Effects of comprehension on retention of prose. *Journal of Experimental Psychology*, 1971, *88*, 216–222.

Dore, J. "Conversational acts and the acquisition of language." In E. Ochs & B. Schieffelin, *Developmental Pragmatics*. New York: Academic Press, 1979.

Dore, J., Gearhart, M., & Newman, D. The structure of nursery school conversation. In K. Nelson (Ed.), *Children's Language Vol. 1*. New York: Gardner Press, 1978.

Duell, O. K. Effect of type of objective, level of test questions, and the judged importance of tested materials upon posttest performance. *Journal of Educational Psychology*, 1974, *66*, 225–232.

Duncker, K. On problem solving. *Psychological Monographs*, 1945, *58*, 270.

Dunham, T. C., & Levin, J. R. Imagery instruction and young children's prose learning: No evidence of support. *Contemporary Educational Psychology*, 1979, *4*, 107–113.

Dunkin, M. J., & Biddle, B. J. *The study of teaching*. New York: Holt, Rinehart & Winston, 1974.

Eastman, C. Behavioral formulations of depression. *Psychological Review*, 1976, *83*, 277–291.

Ebbinghaus, H. *Memory*. Translated by H. A. Ruger & C. E. Bassenius. New York: Teachers College, 1913. Paperback edition, New York: Dover, 1964.

Ebel, R. L. *Measuring educational achievement*. Englewood Cliffs, N.J.: Prentice-Hall, 1965.

Ebel, R. L. Behavioral objectives: A close look. *Educational Technology*, 1970, *10*, 171–173.

Ebel, R. L. *Essentials of Educational Measurement* (3rd ed.). Englewood Cliffs, N.J.: Prentice-Hall, 1979.

Eells, K., Davis, A., Havighurst, R. J., Herrick, V. E., & Tyler, R. *Intelligence and cultural differences: a study of cultural learning and problem solving*. Chicago: University of Chicago Press, 1951.

Eimas, P., Siqueland, E. R., Jusczyk, P., & Vigorito, J. Speech perception in infants. *Science*, 1971, *171*, 303–306.

Eisenberg, T. A., & McGinty, R. L. On spatial visualization in college students. *Journal of Psychology*, 1977, *95*, 99–104.

Eisenberg-Berg, N. The development of children's prosocial moral judgment. *Developmental Psychology*, 1979, *15*, 128–137.

Eisenberg-Berg, N. Development of reasoning regarding prosocial and altruistic behavior. In N. Eisenberg-Berg (Ed.), *The development of prosocial behavior*. New York: Academic Press, 1982. (a)

Eisenberg-Berg, N. *The development of prosocial behavior*. New York: Academic Press, 1982. (b)

Eisenberg-Berg, N., & Hand, M. The relationship of preschoolers' reasoning about prosocial moral conflicts to prosocial behavior. *Child Development*, 1979, *50*, 356–363.

Eisenberg-Berg, N., & Neal, C. Children's moral reasoning about their own spontaneous prosocial behavior. *Developmental Psychology*, 1979, *15*, 228–229.

Eisler, R. M., & Fredericksen, L. W. *Perfecting social skills: A guide to interpersonal behavior development*. New York: Plenum, 1980.

Elashoff, J. D., Snow, R. E., & Jones, C. A. A technically sophisticated reanalysis of the original Pygmalion data. Teachers' expectations have many effects but not, as originally claimed, on IQ. *Pygmalion Reconsidered*. Worthington, Ohio, 1971.

Elkind, D. Quantity conceptions in junior and senior high school subjects. *Child Development*, 1961, *32*, 551–560. (a)

Elkind, D. The development of quantitative thinking: A systematic replication of Piaget's studies. *Journal of Genetic Psychology*, 1961, *98*, 37–46. (b)

Elkind, D. Piagetian and psychometric conceptions of intelligence. In *Environment, heredity, and intelligence*. Compiled from *Harvard Educational Review*, 1969, 321.

Elliot, R., & Vasta, R. The modeling of sharing: Effects associated with vicarious reinforcement, symbolization, age, and generalization. *Journal of Experimental Child Psychology*, 1970, *10*, 8–15.

Erlenmeyer-Kimling, L., & Jarvik, L. F. Genetics

and intelligence: A review. *Science*, 1963, 1477–1479.

Ernest, J. Mathematics and sex. *American Mathematical Monthly*, 1976, *83*, 595–614.

Ervin, S. Imitation and structural change in children's language. Cambridge, Mass.: MIT Press, 1964, 163–189.

Ervin-Tripp, S. Language development. In Hoffman, M., & Hoffman, L. (Eds.), *Review of child development research*, Vol. II. New York: Russell Sage, 1966, 55–105.

Ervin-Tripp, S. Some strategies for the first two years. In T. E. Moore (Ed.), *Cognitive development and the acquisition of language.* New York: Academic Press, 1973.

Ervin-Tripp, S. Speech acts and social learning. In H. Basso & H. Selby (Eds.), *Meaning in anthropology.* Albuquerque: University of New Mexico Press, 1976.

Esposito, D. Homogeneous and heterogeneous ability grouping: Principal findings and implications for evaluating and designing more effective educational environments. *Review of Educational Research*, 1973, *43*, 163–179.

Fairweather, H. Sex differences in cognition. *Cognition*, 1976, *4*, 231–280.

Farnham-Diggory, S. (Ed.). *Information processing in children: The seventh of an annual series of symposia in the area of cognition under the sponsorship of Carnegie-Mellon University.* New York: Academic Press, 1972.

Feffer, M. A developmental analysis of interpersonal behavior. *Psychological Review*, 1970, *77*(3), 197–214.

Feffer, M. H., & Gourevitch, V. Cognitive aspects of role-taking in children. *Journal of Personality*, 1960, *28*, 383–396.

Fennema, E. Influences of selected cognitive, affective, and educational variables on sex-related differences in mathematics learning and studying. In *Women and mathematics: Research perspectives for change.* NIE Papers in Education and Work, Number 8, November 1977.

Fennema, E., & Sherman, J. A. Sex-related differences in mathematics achievement, spatial visualization and affective factors. *American Educational Research Journal*, 1976, *47*(1).

Finke, R. A., & Kosslyn, S. M. Mental imagery acuity in the peripheral visual field. *Journal of Experimental Psychology: Human perception and performance*, 1980, *6*(1), 126–139.

Fischer, W. F. Sharing in preschool children as a function of amount and type of reinforcement.

Genetic Psychology Monographs, 1963, *68*, 215–245.

Flaugher, R. L. The many definitions of test bias. *American Psychologist*, 1978, *33*, 671–679.

Flavell, J. H. *The developmental psychology of Jean Piaget.* New York: Van Nostrand, 1963.

Flavell, J. H. Concept development. In P. H. Mussen (Ed.), *Carmichael's Manual of Child Psychology*, (Vol. I). New York: Wiley, 1970, 983–1059. (a)

Flavell, J. H. Developmental studies in mediated memory. In H. W. Reese & L. P. Lipsett (Eds.), *Advances in child development and behavior* (Vol. 5). New York: Academic Press, 1970. (b)

Flavell, J. H. First discussant's comments: What is memory development the development of? *Human Development*, 1971, *14*, 272–278.

Flavell, J. H. The development of knowledge about visual perception. *Nebraska Symposium on Motivation*, 1976. (a)

Flavell, J. H. Metacognitive aspects of problem-solving. In L. B. Resnick (Ed.), *The nature of intelligence.* Hillsdale, N.J.: Erlbaum, 1976. (b)

Flavell, J. H., Botkin, P. T., Fry, C. L., Wright, J. W., & Jarvis, P. E. *The development of role-taking and communication skills in children.* New York: Wiley, 1968.

Flavell, J. H., Friedrichs, P., & Hoyt, J. Developmental changes in memorization processes. *Cognitive Psychology*, 1970, *1*, 324–340.

Flavell, J. H., & Wellman, H. W. Metamemory. In R. V. Kail & J. W. Kagen (Eds.), *Perspectives on the development of memory and cognition.* Hillsdale, N.J.: Erlbaum, 1977.

Ford, M. The construct validity of egocentrism. *Psychological Bulletin*, 1979, *86*, 1169–1188.

Fox, L. H. The effects of sex role socialization on mathematics participation and achievement. In *Women and mathematics: Research perspectives for change.* NIE Papers in Education and Work, Number 8, November 1977.

Fox, L. H., Fennema, E., & Sherman, J. *Women and mathematics: Research perspectives for change.* NIE Papers in Education and Work, Number 8, November 1977.

Frase, L. T. Questions as aids to reading: Some research and a theory. *American Educational Research Journal*, 1970, *7*, 307–319.

Frase, L. T., & Schwartz, B. J. Effects of question production and answering on prose recall. *Journal of Educational Psychology*, 1975, *67*, 628–635.

Frederiksen, C. H. Effects of task-induced cognitive operations on comprehension and memory processes. In R. O. Freedle & J. B. Carroll (Eds.),

Language comprehension and the acquisition of knowledge. Washington, D.C.: Winston, 1972.

Friedrich, K. L., & Stein, A. H. Prosocial television and young children: The effects of verbal labeling and role playing on learning and behavior. *Child Development,* 1975, *46,* 27–39.

Frieze, I. H. Causal attributions and information seeking to explain success and failure. *Journal of Research in Personality,* 1976, *10*(3), 292–305.

Furth, H. *Thinking without language.* New York: Free Press, 1966.

Furth, H. *Piaget for teachers.* Englewood Cliffs, N.J.: Prentice-Hall, 1970.

Gage, N. L., & Berliner, D. C. *Educational Psychology.* Chicago: Rand McNally, 1979.

Gagne, E. D., & Rothkopf, E. Z. Text organization and learning goals. *Journal of Educational Psychology,* 1975, *67,* 455–460.

Gagne, R. M. *The conditions of learning.* New York: Holt, Rinehart & Winston, 1965.

Gagne, R. M. (Ed.). *Teaching machines and programmed learning. II: Data and directions.* Washington, D.C.: National Education Association, 1965.

Gagne, R. M. The learning basis of teaching methods. In N. L. Gage (Ed.), *The seventy-fifth yearbook of the National Society for the Study of Education.* Chicago: University of Chicago Press, 1976.

Gagne, R. M. *The conditions of learning.* New York: Holt, Rinehart & Winston, 1977.

Gagne, R. M., & Wiegand, V. K. Effects of superordinate context on learning and retention of facts. *Journal of Educational Psychology,* 1970, *61,* 406–409.

Gall, M. D. The use of questions in teaching. *Review of Educational Research,* 1970, *40,* 707–721.

Gall, M. D., Ward, B. A., Berliner, D. C., Cohen, L. S., Winne, P. H., Elashoff, J. D., & Stanton, G. S. Effects of questioning techniques in recitation on student learning. *American Educational Research Journal,* 1978, *15,* 175–199.

Garcia, J. IQ: The conspiracy. *Psychology Today,* 1972, *40.*

Gardner, B. T., & Gardner, R. A. Two-way communication with an infant chimpanzee. In A. Schrier & F. Stollnitz (Eds.), *Behavior of nonhuman primates,* (Vol. IV). New York: Academic Press, 1971, 117–184.

Gardner, H. *The quest for mind; Piaget, Levi-Strauss, and the structuralist movement* (1st ed.). New York: Knopf, 1973.

Gelman, R. The nature and development of early number concepts. In H. Reese (Ed.), *Advances in child development* (Vol. 7). New York: Academic Press, 1972.

Gelman, R., & Gallistel, G. R. *A child's understanding of number.* Cambridge, Mass.: Harvard University Press, 1978.

Ginsburg, H., & Opper, S. *Piaget's theory of intellectual development.* Englewood Cliffs, N.J.: Prentice-Hall, 1969.

Glaser, R. The future of testing: A research agenda for cognitive psychology and psychometrics. *American Psychologist,* 1981, *36*(9), 923–937.

Glass, G. Integrating findings: The meta-analysis of research. *Review of Research in Education,* 1978, *5,* 351–379.

Goldschmid, M., & Bentler, P. M. *Manual: Concept assessment kit, conservation.* San Diego, Calif.: Educational and Industrial Testing Service, 1968.

Good, T. L. Teacher expectations and student perception. *Educational Leadership,* February 1981, *38,* 415–422.

Good, T. L., & Brophy, J. E. Changing teacher and student behavior: An empirical investigation. *Journal of Educational Psychology,* 1974, *66,* 390–405.

Green, D. R., Ford, M. P., & Flamer, G. B. (Eds.). *Measurement and Piaget.* New York: McGraw-Hill, 1971.

Greeno, J. G. Processes of learning and comprehension. In L. W. Gregg (Ed.), *Knowledge and cognition.* Potomac, Md.: Erlbaum, 1974.

Greeno, J. G. Indefinite goals in well-structured problem. *Psychological Review,* 1976, *83,* 491–499.

Greeno, J. G. Notes on problem-solving ability. In W. K. Estes (Ed.), *Handbook of learning and cognitive processes.* Hillsdale, N.J.: Erlbaum, 1978.

Griffiths, J. A., Shantz, C. A., & Siegel, I. E. A methodological problem in conservation studies: The use of relational terms. *Child Development,* 1967, *41,* 205–213.

Groen, G. J. The theoretical ideas of Piaget and educational practice. In P. Suppes (Ed.), *Impact of research on education: Some case studies.* Washington, D. C.: National Academy of Education, 1978.

Grossman, H. (Ed.). *Manual on terminology and classification in mental retardation.* Washington, D.C.: American Association on Mental Deficiency, 1973.

Gruber, H. E., & Voneche, J. J. *The essential Piaget.* New York: Basic Books, 1977.

Grusec, J. E., Saas-Kortsaak, P., & Simutis, Z. M. The role of example and moral exhortation in the training of altruism. *Child Development*, 1978, *49*, 920–923.

Guadalupe v. Tempe School District (F. August 1971, U.S. District Court of Arizona).

Guadia, G. The Piagetian dilemma: What does Piaget really have to say to teachers? In J. F. Magary et al. (Eds.), *Piagetian theory and the helping professions*. Los Angeles: University of Southern California Bookstore, 1977.

Guay, R. B., & McDaniel, E. D. The relationship between mathematics achievement and spatial abilities among elementary school children. *Journal for Research in Mathematics Education*, 1977, *8*(3), 211–215.

Guilford, J. P. *The nature of human intelligence*. New York: McGraw-Hill, 1967.

Guthrie, E. R. *The psychology of learning* (Rev. ed.). New York: Harper & Row, 1952.

Guttman, J. The effects of pictures and partial pictures on children's oral prose learning. *Dissertation Abstracts International*, April 1976, *36* (10-A), 6552.

Haber, R. N., & Erdelyi, M. H. Emergence and recovery of initially unavailable perceptual material. *Journal of Verbal Learning and Verbal Behavior*, 1972, *11*, 278–286.

Hales, L. W., Bain, P. T., & Rand, L. P. An investigation of some aspects of the pass-fail grading system. Paper presented at the meetings of the American Educational Research Association, New York, 1971.

Halliday, M. A. T. *Learning how to mean: Explorations in the development of language*. London: Edward Arnold, 1975.

Harasym, C. R., Boersma, F. J., & Maguire, T. O. Semantic differential analysis of relational terms used in conservation. *Child Development*, 1971, *42*, 767–779.

Harre, R. *An introduction to the logic of the sciences*. New York: Macmillan, 1965.

Harris, J. Sex and language. In E. Donelson & G. Gullahorn (Eds.), *Women: Psychological perspective*. New York: Wiley, 1977.

Harris, M. B., Hassemer, W. G. Some factors affecting the complexity of children's sentences: The effects of modeling, age, sex, and bilingualism. *Journal of Experimental Child Psychology*, 1972, *13*, 447–455.

Hartlage, L. C. Sex-linked inheritance of spatial ability. *Perceptual and Motor Skills*, 1970, *31*, 610.

Hartmann, D. P., Gelfand, D. M., Smith, C. L., Paul, S. C., Cromer, C. C., Page, B. C., & La-

Venta, D. V. Factors affecting the acquisition and elimination of children's donating behavior. *Journal of Experimental Child Psychology*, 1976, *21*, 328–338.

Hartup, W. W., & Coates, B. Imitation of a peer as a function of reinforcement from the peer group and rewardingness of the model. *Child Development*, 1967, *38*, 1003–1016.

Havighurst, R. J., Bowman, P. H., Liddle, G. P., Matthews, G. V., & Pierce, J. V. *Growing up in River City*. New York: Wiley, 1962.

Heider, F. *The psychology of interpersonal relations*. New York: Wiley, 1958.

Heise, D. R. *Causal Analysis*. New York: Wiley, 1975.

Henderson, R. W. Defining goals in open education. In B. Spodek & H. Walberg (Eds.), *Studies in open education*. New York: Agathon Press, 1975.

Henderson, R. W., & Garcia, A. B. The effects of a parent training program on the question-asking behavior of Mexican-American children. *American Educational Research Journal*, 1973, *10*(3), 193–201.

Henderson, R. W., & Merritt, C. B. Environmental backgrounds of Mexican-American children with different potentials for school success. *Journal of Social Psychology*, 1968, *75*, 101–106.

Henderson, R. W., & Swanson, R. A. The application of social learning principles in a field setting: An applied experiment. *Exceptional Children*, September 1974, 53–55.

Henderson, R. W., & Swanson, R. A. The effects of televised skill instruction, instructional system support, and parental intervention on the development of cognitive skills. Final report on Grant No. OCD-CB-479, from the Office of Child Development, Department of Health, Education, and Welfare. Tucson: Arizona Center for Educational Research and Development, The University of Arizona, July 1977.

Henderson, R. W., & Swanson, R. A. Age and directed participation variables influencing the effectiveness of televised instruction on concrete operational behaviors. *Educational Communication & Technology*, 1978, *26*(4), 302–312.

Henderson, R. W., Swanson, R. A., & Zimmerman, B. J. Inquiry response induction in preschool children through televised modeling. *Developmental Psychology*, 1974, *11*(4), 523–524.

Henderson, R. W., Swanson, R. A., & Zimmerman, B. J. Training seriation responses in young children through televised modeling of hierarchically sequenced rule components. *American Educational Research Journal*, 1975, *12*(4), 489–499.

Henderson, R. W., Zimmerman, B. J., Swanson, R. A., & Bergan, J. R. Televised cognitive skill instruction for Papago native-American children. Technical report on Grant No. OCD-CB-479 from the Office of Child Development, Department of Health, Education, & Welfare. Tucson: Arizona Center for Educational Research and Development, The University of Arizona, July 1974.

Herrnstein, R. J. IQ. *Atlantic Monthly*, 1971, *228*(3), 43–64.

Hess, R. D. & Shipman, V. C. Maternal influences upon early learning: The cognitive environments of urban preschool children. In R. D. Hess & R. M. Bear (Eds.), *Early education: Current theory, research, and action*. Chicago: Aldine, 1968.

Hill, C. C. *Problem solving: Learning and teaching*. New York: Nichols Publishing, 1979.

Hively, W. Introduction to domain-referenced testing. *Educational Technology*, 1974, *14*(6), 5–10.

Hoffman, M. L. Sex differences in empathy and related behavior. *Psychological Bulletin*, 1977, *84*, 712–722.

Holstein, C. B. The relation of children's moral judgment level to that of their parents and to communication patterns in the family. In R. C. Smart & M. S. Smart (Eds.), *Readings in child development and relationships*. New York: Macmillan, 1972.

Horan, P. F., & Rosser, R. A. The function of response mode in the coordination of perspectives. *Contemporary Educational Psychology*, in press.

Hull, C. L. Quantitative aspects of the evolution of concepts. *Psychological Monographs*, 1920, *28*, 23.

Hull, C. L. *A behavior system: An introduction to behavior theory concerning the individual organism*. New Haven, Ct.: Yale University Press, 1952.

Huttenlocher, T., & Presson, C. Mental rotation and the perspective problems. *Cognitive Psychology*, 1973, *4*, 277–299.

Hymes, D. Sociolinguistics and the ethnology of speaking. In E. Ardener (Ed.), *Linguistics and social anthropology* (ASA Monograph). London: Travistock Publishers, 1971.

Ianotti, R. J. Effect of role-taking experiences on role-taking, empathy, altruism, and aggression. *Developmental Psychology*, 1978, *14*, 119–124.

Ickes, W. J., & Kidd, R. F. An attributional analysis of helping behavior. In J. H. Harvey, W. J. Ickes, & R. F. Kidd (Eds.), *New directions in attribution research*. Hillsdale, N.J.: Erlbaum, 1976, 311–334.

Inhelder, B., & Piaget, J. *The early growth of logic in the child*. New York: Harper & Row, 1964.

Isaacson, R. L. Relation between achievement, text anxiety, and curricular choices. *Journal of Abnormal and Social Psychology*, 1964, *68*, 447–452.

James, W. *Principles of psychology*. New York: Holt, Rinehart & Winston, 1890.

James, W. *Talks to teachers on psychology*. New York: Holt, Rinehart & Winston, 1899.

Jensen, A. R. Social class, race, and genetics: Implications for education. *American Educational Research Journal*, 1968, *5*, 1–42.

Jensen, A. R. How much can we boost IQ and scholastic achievement? *Harvard Educational Review*, 1969, *39*, 1–23.

Jensen, A. R. Can we and should we study race differences? In J. Hellmuth (Ed.), *Disadvantaged child, Vol. 3, Compensatory education: A national debate*. New York: Brunner/Mazel, 1970.

Jensen, A. R. Do schools cheat minority children? *Educational Research*, 1971, *14*, 3–28.

Jensen, A. R. *Bias in mental testing*. New York: Free Press, 1980.

Johnson, C., & Jenkins, J. Two more incidental tasks that differentially affect associative clustering in recall. *Journal of Experimental Psychology*, 1973, *98*, 203–205.

Johnson, D. L. The influences of social class and race on language test performance and spontaneous speech of preschool children. *Child Development*, 1974, *45*, 517–521.

Johnson, D. W. Affective perspective taking and cooperative predisposition. *Developmental Psychology*, 1975, *11*, 869–870.

Johnson, M. K., Kelley, C. S., Harris, F. R., & Wolf, M. M. An application of reinforcement principles to the development of motor skills of a young child. *Child Development*, 1966, *37*, 379–387.

Jones, R. R., Reid, J. B., & Patterson, M. R. Naturalistic observations in clinical assessment. In P. McReynolds (Ed.), *Advances in psychological assessment* (Vol. 3). San Francisco: Jossey-Bass, 1974.

Joreskog, K. G., & Sorbon, D. *Advances in factor analysis and structural equation models*. Cambridge, Mass.: Abt, 1979.

Joseph, A., Spicer, R., & Chesky, J. *The desert people: A study of the Papago Indians*. Chicago: University of Chicago Press, 1949.

Kail, R., Carter, P., & Pellegrino, J. The locus of sex differences in spatial ability. *Perception & Psychophysics*, 1979, *26*(3), 182–186.

Kamii, C. An application of Piagetian theory to the conceptualization of preschool curriculum. In R.

K. Parker (Ed.), *The preschool in action.* Boston: Allyn & Bacon, 1972.

Kapadia, R. A critical examination of Piaget-Inhelder's view on topology. *Educational Studies in Mathematics,* 1974, *5,* 419–424.

Kazdin, A. E. Statistical analysis for single-case experimental designs. In M. Hersen & D. H. Barlow (Eds.), *Single case experimental designs: Strategies for studying behavior change.* Oxford: Pergamon Press, 1976.

Kendall, P. C., & Hollon, S. D. (Eds.). *Cognitive behavioral interventions: Theory, research and procedures.* New York: Academic Press, 1979.

Kendall, P. C., & Hollon, S. D. *Assessment strategies for cognitive behavioral interventions.* New York: Academic Press, 1981.

Kintsch, W. *The representation of meaning in memory.* Hillsdale, N.J.: Erlbaum, 1974.

Kirk, S. A. Research in education. In H. A. Stevens & R. Heber (Eds.), *Mental retardation: A review of research.* Chicago: University of Chicago Press, 1964.

Kirk, S. A. & Gallagher, J. J. *Educating exceptional children* (3rd ed.). Boston: Houghton Mifflin, 1979.

Klahr, D. Steps toward the simulation of intellectual development. In L. B. Resnick (Ed.), *The nature of intelligence.* Hillsdale, N.J.: Erlbaum, 1976.

Klahr, D. Goal formation, planning, and learning by preschool problem solvers or: "My socks are in the dryer" in Siegler (Ed.), *Children's thinking: What develops?* Hillsdale, N.J.: Erlbaum, 1978.

Klahr, D., & Siegler, R. S. *Advances in child development: An information processing view.* Hillsdale, N.J.: Erlbaum, 1976.

Klahr, D., & Wallace, J. G. *Cognitive development: An information processing view.* Hillsdale, N.J.: Erlbaum, 1976.

Klausmeier, H. J. Publications of the Wisconsin Research and Development Center for Cognitive Learning, Madison, 1970.

Klausmeier, H. J. Individually guided education: 1966–1980. *Journal of Teacher Education,* Fall 1976, *27,* 199–205.

Klausmeier, H. J. Educational experience and cognitive development. *Educational Psychologist,* 1977, *12*(2), 179–196.

Klausmeier, H. J. Origin and overview of IGE. In H. J. Klausmeier, R. Rossmiller, & M. Saily (Eds.), *Individually guided elementary education: Concepts and practices.* New York: Academic Press, 1978.

Klausmeier, H. J., Ghatala, E. S., & Frayer, D. A. *Conceptual learning and development: A cognitive view.* New York: Academic Press, 1974.

Klausmeier, H. J., Rossmiller, R., & Saily, M. *Individually guided elementary education: Concepts and practices.* New York: Academic Press, 1978.

Klineberg, O. *Race differences.* New York: Harper, 1935.

Klineberg, O. Negro-white differences in intelligence test performances: A new look at an old problem. *American Psychologist,* 1963, *18,* 198–203.

Koffka, K. *Principles of Gestalt psychology.* New York: Harcourt Brace & World, 1935.

Kohlberg, L. The development of modes of moral thinking and choice in the years ten to sixteen. Unpublished doctoral dissertation, University of Chicago, 1958.

Kohlberg, L. Stage and sequence: The cognitive developmental approach to socialization. In D. A. Golin (Ed.), *Handbook of socialization theory and research.* Chicago: Rand McNally, 1969.

Kohlberg, L. Moral stages and moralization: The cognitive-developmental approach. In T. Lickona (Ed.), *Moral development and behavior: Theory, research, and social issues.* New York: Holt, Rinehart & Winston, 1976.

Kosslyn, S. M. Information representation in visual images. *Cognitive Psychology,* 1975, *7,* 341–370.

Kosslyn, S. M. Imagery and internal representation. In E. Rosch & B. B. Lloyd (Eds.), *Cognition and categorization.* Hillsdale, N.J.: Erlbaum, 1978.

Kosslyn, S. M., Ball, T. M., & Reiser, B. J. Visual images preserve metric spatial information: Evidence from studies of image scanning. *Journal of Experimental Psychology: Human Perception and Performance,* 1978, *4*(1), 47–60.

Kosslyn, S. M., & Pomerantz, J. R. Imagery, propositions, and the form of internal representations. *Cognitive Psychology,* 1977, *9,* 52–76.

Kosslyn, S. M., & Shwartz, S. P. A data-driven simulation of visual imagery. *Cognitive Science,* 1977, *1,* 265–296.

Kratochwill, T. R. The movement of psychological extras into ability assessment. *Journal of Special Education,* 1977, *11,* 299–311.

Kratochwill, T. R. *Single subject research: Strategies for evaluating change.* New York: Academic Press, 1978.

Kratochwill, T. R. Behavioral assessment of academic and social problems: Implications for the individual education program. *School Psychology Review,* 1980, *9*(3), 199–206.

Kratochwill, T. R. *Selective mutism: Implications for research and treatment.* Hillsdale, N.J.: Erlbaum, 1981.

Kratochwill, T. R., Alper, S., & Cancelli, A. A. Nondiscriminatory assessment in psychology and education. In L. Mann & D. A. Sabatino (Eds.), *Fourth review of special education.* New York: Grune & Stratton, 1980.

Krebs, D. Empathy and altruism. *Journal of Personality and Social Psychology,* 1975, *32*(6), 1134–1146.

Krebs, D., & Gillmore, J. The relationship among the first stages of cognitive development, role-taking abilities, and moral development. *Child Development,* 1982, *53,* 877–886.

Krueger, W. C. F. The effect of overlearning on retention. *Journal of Experimental Psychology,* 1929, *12,* 71–78.

Kuhlmann, F., & Anderson, R. *Kuhlmann-Anderson Intelligence Test.* Seventh Edition, Personnel Press, Princeton, N.J., 1963.

Kuhn, D. Inducing development experimentally: Comments on a research paradigm. *Developmental Psychology,* 1975, *10,* 590–600.

Kuhn, D. Short-term longitudinal evidence for the sequentiality of Kohlberg's early stages of moral development. *Developmental Psychology,* 1976, *12,* 162–166.

Kuhn, T. S. *The structure of scientific revolutions.* Chicago: University of Chicago Press, 1962.

Kulhavy, R. W., & Swenson, I. Imagery instructions and the comprehension of text. *British Journal of Educational Psychology,* 1975, *45,* 47–51.

Kurtines, W., & Greif, E. B. The development of moral thought: Review and evaluation of Kohlberg's approach. *Psychological Bulletin,* 1974, *81,* 453–470.

Labov, W. The logic of nonstandard English. In F. Williams (Ed.), *Language and poverty.* Chicago: Markham, 1970.

Labov, W. The logic of nonstandard English. In Johanna S. Stefano (Ed.), *Language, society, and education: A profile of black English.* Worthington, Ohio: Charles A. Jones Publishing, 1973.

Lahey, B. B. *Behavior therapy with hyperactive and learning disabled children.* New York: Oxford, 1978.

Lamb, C. E. Application of Piaget's theory to mathematics education. In *Piagetian theory and the helping professions.* Los Angeles: University of Southern California Bookstore, 1977.

Laosa, L. M. Nonbiased assessment of children's abilities: Historical antecedents and current issues. In T. Oakland (Ed.), *Psychological and educational assessment of minority children.* New York: Brunner/Mazel, 1977.

LaPointe, K., & O'Donnell, J. P. Number conservation in children below age six: Its relationship to age, perceptual dimensions, and language comprehension. *Developmental Psychology,* 1974, *10,* 422–428.

Larkin, J. H. Teaching problem solving in physics: The psychological laboratory and the practical classroom. In D. T. Tuma & F. Rief (Eds.), *Problem solving and education: Issues in teaching and education.* Hillsdale, N.J.: Erlbaum, 1980.

Larry P. v. Riles, 343 F. Suppl. 1306 (1972).

Lau v. Nichols, 414 U.S. pp. 563–572 (January 21, 1974).

Laurendeau, M., & Pinard, A. *The development of the concept of space in the child.* New York: International Universities Press, 1970.

Lee, E. S. Negro intelligence and selective migration: A Philadelphia test of the Klineberg hypothesis. *American Sociological Review,* 1951, *16,* 227–233.

Lee, L. C. The concomitant development of cognitive and moral modes of thought: A test of selected deductions from Piaget's theory. *Genetic Psychology Monographs,* 1971, *83,* 93–146.

Left, R. Effects of punishment intensity and consistency on the internalization of behavioral suppression in children. *Developmental Psychology,* 1969, *7,* 345–356.

Lenneberg, E. H. A biological perspective of language. In E. H. Lenneberg (Ed.), *New directions in the study of language.* Cambridge, Mass.: MIT Press, 1964.

Lenneberg, E. H. On explaining language: The development of language in children can best be understood in the context of developmental biology. *Science,* 1969, *164,* 635–643.

Lesgold, A., Levin, J., Shimron, J., & Guttman, J. Pictures and young children's learning from oral prose. *Journal of Educational Psychology.* 1975, *67,* 663–667.

Lesgold, A. M., Pellegrino, J. W., Fokkema, S. D., & Glaser, R. (Eds.). *Cognitive psychology and instruction.* New York: Plenum Press, 1978.

Lesh, R. (Ed.). *Recent research concerning the development of spatial and geometric concepts.* ERIC/SMEAC Center for Science, Mathematics, and Environmental Education, 1978.

Lesser, H. *Television and the preschool child.* New York: Academic Press, 1977.

Levin, J., Bender, B., & Lesgold, A. Pictures, repetition, and young children's oral prose learning. *AV Communication Review*, 1976, *24*, 367–380.

Liben, L. S. Performance on Piagetian spatial tasks as a function of sex, field dependence, and training. *Merrill-Palmer Quarterly*, 1978, *24*, 97–110.

Liebert, R. M., Neale, J. M., & Davidson, E. S. *The early window: Effects of television on children and youth*. New York: Pergamon Press, 1973.

Liebert, R. M., Odom, R. D., Hill, J. H., & Huff, R. L. The effects of age and rule familiarity on the production of modeled language constructions. *Developmental Psychology*, 1969, *1*(2), 108–112.

Lohman, D. F. Spatial ability: A review and reanalysis of the correlational literature. Technical report No. 8 on Office of Naval Research and Advanced Research Projects Agency Contract No. N00014-75-C-0882, Stanford University, October 1979. (a)

Lohman, D. F. Individual differences in speed and level. Technical report No. 9 on Office of Naval Research and Advanced Research Projects Agency Contract No. N00014-75-C-0882, Stanford University, October 1979. (b)

Lord, F. M. *Applications of item response theory to practical testing problems*. Hillsdale, N.J.: Erlbaum, 1980.

Luiten, J., Ames, W., & Ackerson, G. A meta-analysis of the effects of advance organizers on learning and retention. *American Educational Research Journal*, 1980, 211–218.

Maccoby, E. E. (Ed.). *The development of sex differences*. Stanford, Calif.: Stanford University Press, 1966.

Maccoby, E. G., & Jacklin, C. N. *The psychology of sex differences*. Stanford, Calif.: Stanford University Press, 1974.

MacMillan, D. L. Special education for the mildly retarded: Servant or savant? *Focus on Exceptional Children*, 1971, *2*, 1–11.

MacMillan, D., Jones, R., & Aloia, G. The mentally retarded label: A theoretical analysis and review of research. *American Journal of Mental Deficiency*, 1974, *79*, 241–261.

Magary, J. F., Poulsen, M. K., Levinson, P. J., & Taylor, P. A. (Eds.). *Piagetian theory and the helping professions*. Los Angeles: University of Southern California Bookstore, 1977.

Mager, R. F. *Preparing instructional objectives*. Belmont, Calif.: Fearon Publishers, 1975.

Mahone, C. H. Fear of failure and unrealistic vocational aspiration. *Journal of Abnormal and Social Psychology*, 1960, *60*, 253–261.

Maier, N. R. F. Reasoning in humans. 1. On direc-

tion. *Journal of Comparative Psychology*, 1930, *10*, 115–143.

Main, S., & Gallagher, D. *Student and faculty evaluations of the new undergraduate grading system: A preliminary report*. Stanford, Calif.: Stanford University Planning Office, 1972.

Mandler, G., & Sarason, S. B. A study of anxiety and learning. *Journal of Abnormal and Social Psychology*, 1952, *47*, 166–173.

Marcus, R. F., Tellen, S., & Roke, E. J. Relation between cooperation and empathy in young children. *Developmental Psychology*, 1979, *15*(3), 346–347.

Markle, S. M. They teach concepts, don't they? *Educational Researcher*, 1975, *4*, 3–9.

Markle, S. M., & Tiemann, P. W. *Really understanding concepts: Or in frumious pursuit of the jabberwock* (3rd ed.). Champaign, Ill.: Stipes, 1970.

Markman, E. H. Factors affecting the young child's ability to monitor his memory. Unpublished doctoral dissertation, University of Pennsylvania, 1973.

Marmor, G. Development of kinetic images: When does the child first represent movement in mental images? *Cognitive Psychology*, 1975, *7*, 548–599.

Martin, F. Questioning skills among advantaged and disadvantaged children in first grade. *Psychological Reports*, 1970, *27*, 617–618.

Martin, J. L. (Ed.). *Space and geometry*. ERIC/SMEAC Center for Science, Mathematics, and Environmental Education, 1976.

Maslow, A. H. *Motivation and personality*. New York: Harper & Row, 1954.

Maslow, A. H. *The farther reaches of human nature*. New York: Viking, 1971.

Mattson, S. L. Spatial ability in young children: The effects of dimensionality. Unpublished doctoral dissertation, The University of Arizona, 1981.

Mauissakalien, M., & Barlow, D. H. *Phobia: Psychological and pharmacological treatment*. New York: Gardner Press, 1980.

Mayer, R. E. Information processing variables in learning to solve problems. *Review of Educational Research*, 1975, *45*(4), 525–541.

McCall, R. B. Challenges to a science of developmental psychology. *Child Development*, 1977, *48*, 333–334.

McCarthy, D. Language development of the preschool child. Minneapolis: University of Minnesota, Institute of Child Welfare, 1930 (Monograph Series No. 4).

McCleary, R., & Hay, A. H. *Applied time series anal-*

ysis for the social sciences. Beverly Hills, Calif.: Sage, 1980.

McClelland, D. C., Atkinson, J. W., Clark, R. A., & Lowell, E. L. *The achievement motive.* New York: Appleton-Century-Crofts, 1953.

McGee, M. G. Human spatial abilities: Psychometric studies and environmental, genetic, hormonal, and neurological influences. *Psychological Bulletin,* 1979, *6*(5), 889–918.

McGuinness, D. Sex differences in the organization of perception and cognition. In B. Lloyd & A. Archer (Eds.), *Exploring sex differences.* London: Academic Press, 1976.

McNeil, J. D. Concomitants of using behavioral objectives in the assessment of teacher effectiveness. *Journal of Experimental Education,* 1967, *36,* 69–74.

McNeill, D. *The acquisition of language: The study of developmental psycholinguistics.* New York: Harper & Row, 1970.

Mehler, J., & Bever, T. G. Quantification, conservation, and nativism. *Science,* 1968, *162,* 979–981.

Mercer, J. R. Sociocultural factors in labeling mental retardates. *Peabody Journal of Education,* 1971, *48,* 188–203.

Mercer, J. R. Implications of current assessment procedures for Mexican-American children. *Journal of the Association of Mexican American Educators,* 1973, *1,* 25–33.

Mercer, J. R., & Ysseldyke, J. Designing diagnostic-intervention programs. In T. Oakland (Ed.), *Psychological and educational assessment of minority children.* New York: Brunner/Mazel, 1977.

Meyer, B. J. F. *The organization of prose and its effect on recall.* Amsterdam: North-Holland Publishers, 1975.

Meyer, B. J. F., & McConkie, G. W. What is recalled after hearing a passage? *Journal of Educational Psychology,* 1973, *65,* 109–117.

Meyers, C., Sundstrom, P., & Yoshida, R. The school psychologist and assessment in special education: A report of the Ad Hoc Committee of APA Division 16. *Monographs of Division 16 of the American Psychological Association,* 1974, *2*(1), 3–57.

Miller, J. F., Chapman, R. S., Branston, M., & Reichle, J. Language comprehension in sensorimotor stages 5 and 6. *Journal of Speech and Hearing Research,* 1980, *23,* 284–311.

Miller, L. Has artificial intelligence contributed to an understanding of the human mind? A critique of arguments for and against. *Cognitive Science,* 1978, *2,* 129–154.

Mischel, W. *Personality and assessment.* New York: Wiley, 1968.

Mischel, W. Toward a cognitive social learning reconceptualization of personality. *Psychological Review,* 1973, *80,* 252–283.

Mischel, W., & Mischel, H. A. A cognitive social-learning approach to morality and self-regulation. In T. Lickona (Ed.), *Moral development and behavior.* New York: Holt, Rinehart & Winston, 1976.

Mitchell, G. D., Arling, G. L., & Moller, G. W. Long-term effects of maternal punishment on the behavior of monkeys. *Psychonomic Science,* 1967, *8,* 209–210.

Montangero, J., & Smock, C. D. Needed research on space in the context of the Geneva group. In J. L. Martin (Ed.), *Space and geometry.* Columbus, Ohio: ERIC Center for Science, Mathematics and Environmental Education, 1976.

Montgomery, G. T., & Landers, W. F. Transmission of risk-taking through modeling at two age levels. *Psychological Reports,* 1974, *34*(3), 1187–1196.

Moore, T. E. (Ed.). *Cognitive development and the acquisition of language.* New York: Academic Press, 1973.

Moore, T. E., & Harris, A. E. Language and thought in Piagetian theory. In L. S. Siegel & C. J. Brainerd (Eds.), *Alternatives to Piaget.* New York: Academic Press, 1978.

Morris, P. E., & Cook, N. When do first letter mnemonics aid recall? *British Journal of Educational Psychology,* 1978, *48,* 22–28.

Morris, R. J., & Kratochwill, T. R. *Behavioral assessment and treatment of children's fears and phobias.* New York: Pergamon, in press.

Mullis, I. V. S. *Educational achievement and sex discrimination.* Denver: National Assessment of Educational Progress, 1975.

Murray, F. B. Acquisition of conservation through social interaction. *Developmental Psychology,* 1972, *6,* 1–6.

Murray, H. *Explorations in personality.* New York: Oxford University Press, 1938.

Mussen, P. H., & Eisenberg-Berg, N. *Roots of caring, sharing, and helping.* San Francisco: Freeman, 1977.

Naremore, R. C. A functionalist approach to the language assessment of Head Start children: Review and justification. Technical Report on Grant HHS/ACYF #105-81-C-008, The University of Arizona, 1982.

Neisser, U., & Weene, P. Hierarchies in concept attainment. *Journal of Experimental Psychology,* 1962, *64,* 640–645.

Nelson, K. Structure and strategy in learning to talk. *Monographs of the Society for Research in Child Development,* 1973, Serial No. 149.

Nelson, R. O., & Bowles, P. E., Jr. The best of two worlds—observations with norms. *Journal of School Psychology,* 1975, *13*(1), 3–8.

Nelson, R. O., & Hayes, S. C. Some current dimensions of behavioral assessment. *Behavioral Assessment,* 1979, *1,* 1–16.

Newell, A., & Simon, H. *Human problem solving.* Englewood Cliffs, N.J.: Prentice-Hall, 1972.

Nunnally, J. C. *Psychometric theory.* New York: McGraw-Hill, 1967.

Oakland, T., & Laosa, L. M. Professional, legislative and judicial influences on psychoeducational assessment practices on schools. In T. Oakland (Ed.), *Psychological and educational assessment of minority children.* New York: Brunner/Mazel, 1977.

Ochs, E., & Schieffelin, B. *Developmental Pragmatics.* New York: Academic Press, 1979.

O'Conner, P., Atkinson, J. W., & Horner, M. Motivational implications of ability grouping in schools. In J. W. Atkinson & N. T. Feather (Eds.), *The theory of achievement motivation.* New York: Wiley, 1966.

Odom, R. D. A perceptual-salience account of decalage relations and developmental change. In L. S. Siegel & C. J. Brainerd (Eds.), *Alternatives to Piaget.* New York: Academic Press, 1978.

Oetzel, R. Classified summary of research in sex differences. In E. Maccoby (Ed.), *The development of sex differences.* Stanford, Calif.: Stanford University Press, 1966.

Otto, H. J., & Sanders, D. C. *Elementary school organization and administration.* Appleton, 1964, 4th Edition.

Paivio, A. Mental imagery in associated learning and meaning. *Psychological Review,* 1969, *76,* 241–263.

Paivio, A. *Imagery and verbal processes.* New York: Holt, Rinehart & Winston, 1971.

Paivio, A. Perceptual comparisons through the mind's eye. *Memory and Cognition,* 1975, *3,* 635–647.

Palermo, D. S. More about less: A study of language comprehension. *Journal of verbal learning and verbal behavior,* 1973, *12,* 211–221.

Parke, R. D. Effectiveness of punishment as an interaction of intensity, timing, agent nurturance, and cognitive structuring. *Child Development,* 1969, *40,* 213–235.

Peeck, J. Effect of prequestion on delayed retention of prose material. *Journal of Educational Psychology,* 1970, *61,* 241–246.

Peeck, J. Retention of pictorial and verbal content of text with illustrations. *Journal of Educational Psychology,* 1974, *66,* 880–888.

Pellegrino, J. W., & Glaser, R. Cognitive correlates and components in the analysis of individual differences. *Intelligence,* 1979, *3*(3), 187–214.

Perfetti, C. A., & Hogaboam, T. The relationship between single word decoding and reading comprehension skill. *Journal of Educational Psychology,* 1975, *67,* 461–469.

Perfetti, C. A., & Lesgold, A. M. Discourse comprehension and individual differences. In P. Carpenter & M. Just (Eds.), *Cognitive processes in comprehension.* Hillsdale, N.J.: Erlbaum, 1978.

Perl, E., & Lambert, W. E. The relation of bilingualism to intelligence. *Psychological Monographs,* 1962, *76,* 1–23.

Peterson, L., Hartmann, D. P., & Gelfand, D. M. Developmental changes in effects of dependency and reciprocity cues on children's moral judgments and donation rates. *Child Development,* 1977, *48,* 1066–1070.

Piaget, J. *The child's conception of physical causality.* Translated by Marjorie Worden. New York: Harcourt Brace, 1927.

Piaget, J. *The moral judgments of the child.* London: Routledge & Kegan Paul, 1932.

Piaget, J. *The psychology of intelligence.* New York: Harcourt Brace, 1950.

Piaget, J. *Construction of reality in the child.* New York: Ballantine Books, 1954.

Piaget, J. *The language and thought of the child.* New York: World Publishing, 1955.

Piaget, J. *Six psychological studies.* New York: Random House, 1967.

Piaget, J. Piaget's theory. In P. H. Mussen (Ed.), *Carmichael's manual of child psychology.* New York: Wiley, 1970.

Piaget, J. Intellectual evolution from adolescence to adulthood. *Human Development,* 1972, *15,* 1–12.

Piaget, J., & Inhelder, B. *The child's conception of space.* London: Routledge & Kegan Paul, 1956.

Piaget, J., & Inhelder, B. *The early growth of logic in the child: Classification and seriation.* London: Routledge & Kegan Paul, 1964.

Piaget, J., & Inhelder, B. *The psychology of the child.* New York: Basic Books, 1969.

Piaget, J., & Inhelder, B. *Mental imagery in the child.* London: Routledge & Kegan Paul, 1971.

Piliavin, I. M., Rodin, J., & Piliavin, J. A. Good

samaritanism: An underground phenomenon? *Journal of Personality and Social Psychology*, 1969, *13*(4), 289–299.

Pinard, A., & Sharp, E. IQ and point of view. *Psychology Today*, 1972, *6*, 65–68.

Poulsen, M. Clinical assessment of semiotic function for the differential diagnosis of young exceptional children. In J. F. Magary et al. (Eds.), *Piagetian theory and the helping professions*. Los Angeles: University of Southern California Bookstore, 1977.

Premack, D. Toward empirical behavior laws: I. Positive reinforcement. *Psychological Review*, 1959, *66*, 219–233.

Pressley, G. M. Imagery and children's learning: Putting the picture in developmental perspective. *Review of Educational Research*, 1976, *47*, 585–622. (a)

Pressley, G. M. Mental imagery helps eight year olds remember what they read? *Journal of Educational Psychology*, 1976, *68*, 355–359. (b)

Pylyshyn, Z. W. What the mind's eye tells the mind's brain: A critique of mental imagery. *Psychological Bulletin*, 1973, *80*, 1–24.

Reder, L. M. The role of elaborations in memory for prose. *Cognitive Psychology*, 1979, *11*, 221–234.

Redfield, D. L. A comparison of the effects of using various types of worksheets on pupil outcomes. Doctoral dissertation, The University of Arizona, 1980.

Reese, H. W. Imagery and contextual meaning. *Psychological Bulletin*, 1970, *73*, 404–414.

Reese, H. W., & Lipsett, L. P. *Experimental child psychology*. New York: Academic Press, 1970.

Reese, H. W., & Overton, W. F. Models of development and themes of development. In L. P. Goulet & P. B. Baltes (Eds.), *Life-span developmental psychology*. New York: Academic Press, 1970.

Reif, F., Larkin, J. H., & Brackett, G. C. Teaching general learning and problem-solving skills. *American Journal of Physics*, 1976, *44*(3), 212–217.

Remstad, R. G. Optimizing the response to a concept attainment task through sequential classroom experimentations. *Dissertation Abstracts*, 1969, *29*(12a), 4336–4337.

Reschly, D. J. Nonbiased assessment. In G. Phye & D. J. Reschly (Eds.), *School psychology: Perspectives and issues*. New York: Academic Press, 1979.

Resnick, L. B. Introduction: Changing conceptions of intelligence. In L. B. Resnick (Ed.), *The nature of intelligence*. Hillsdale, N.J.: Erlbaum, 1976.

Resnick, L. B. Instructional psychology. *Annual Review of Psychology*, 1981, *32*, 659–704.

Resnick, L. B., & Glaser, R. *Problem solving and intelligence*. Pittsburgh: University of Pittsburgh, 1975 (ERIC Document Reproduction Service No. ED 111 727).

Resnick, L. B., & Glaser, R. Problem solving and intelligence. In L. B. Resnick (Ed.), *The nature of intelligence*. Hillsdale, N.J.: Erlbaum, 1976.

Ridberg, E. H., Parke, R. D., & Hetherington, E. M. Modification of impulsive and reflective cognitive styles through observation of film-mediated models. *Developmental Psychology*, 1971, *5*(3), 369–377.

Ripple, R. E., & Rockcastle, V. (Eds.). *Piaget rediscovered: A report of the conference on cognitive studies and curriculum development*. Ithaca, N.Y.: Cornell University Press, 1964.

Rosenhan, D., & White, G. M. Observation and rehearsal as determinants of prosocial behavior. *Journal of Personality and Social Psychology*, 1967, *5*, 424–431.

Rosenthal, R., & Jacobson, L. *Pygmalion in the classroom*. New York: Holt, Rinehart & Winston, 1968.

Rosenthal, T. L., & Zimmerman, B. J. *Social learning and cognition*. New York: Academic Press, 1978.

Rosenthal, T. L., Zimmerman, B. J., & Durning, K. Observationally induced changes in children's interrogative classes. *Journal of Personality and Social Psychology*, 1970, *16*(4), 681–688.

Ross, A. D. *Child behavior therapy: Principles, procedures and empirical basis*. New York: Wiley, 1981.

Rosser, R. A. Social learning theory and the development of prosocial behavior: A system in research integration. In R. W. Henderson (Ed.) *Parent-Child Interaction*. New York: Academic Press, 1981.

Rosser, R. A. Information use by preschool children in altruistic decision-making: An exploratory investigation of donating behavior. *Journal of Genetic Psychology*, 1982, *141*, 19–27.

Rosser, R. A., & Brody, G. H. Acquisition of a concrete operational rule through observational learning: How abstract is the acquired abstraction? *Merrill-Palmer Quarterly*, 1981, *27*(1), 3–13.

Rosser, R. A., & Horan, P. F. Acquisition of multiple classification and seriation from the observation of models: A social learning approach to horizontal decalage. *Child Development*, in press.

Rosser, R. A., Horan, P. F., Campbell, K., Mattson, S., Mazzeo, J., & Swarner, J. The acquisition of spatial competence in young children. Final report on Grant No. NIE-6-79-0091 from the National Institute of Education, The University of Arizona, 1980.

Rothkopf, E. Z. Some theoretical and experimental approaches to problems in written instruction. In J. D. Krumboltz (Ed.), *Learning and the educational process.* Chicago: Rand McNally, 1965.

Rothkopf, E. Z. The concept of mathemagenic activities. *Review of Educational Research*, 1970, *40*, 325–326.

Rotter, J. B. Generalized expectancies for internal versus external control of reinforcement. *Psychological Monographs*, 1966, *80*, 609.

Rubenstein, R. M. A decade of experience in teaching an interdisciplinary problem solving course. In D. T. Tuma & F. Reif (Eds.), *Problem-solving and education: Issues in teaching and education.* Hillsdale, N.J.: Erlbaum, 1980.

Rubin, K. H., & Schneider, F. W. The relationship between moral judgment, egocentrism, and altruistic behavior. *Child Development*, 1973, *44*, 661–665.

Ruch, M., & Levin, J. Pictorial organization versus verbal repetition of children's prose: Evidence for processing differences. *AV Communication Review*, 1977, *25*, 269–279.

Rumelhart, D. E., & Ortony, A. The representation of knowledge in memory. In R. C. Anderson, R. J. Spiro, & W. E. Montague (Eds.), *Schooling and the acquisition of knowledge.* Hillsdale, N.J.: Erlbaum, 1977.

Rushton, J. P. Generosity in children: Immediate and long-term effects of modeling, preaching, and moral judgment. *Journal of Personality and Social Psychology*, 1975, *31*, 349–366.

Rushton, J. P. Socialization and the altruistic behavior of children. *Psychological Bulletin*, 1976, *83*, 898–913.

Sabers, D. L., & Klausmeier, R. D. Accuracy of short-cut estimates for standard deviation. *Journal of Educational Measurement*, 1971, *8*, 335–339.

Salatas, H., & Flavell, J. H. Perspective-taking: The development of two components of knowledge. *Child Development*, 1976, *47*, 103–109.

Salmon-Cox, L., Teachers and Standardized Achievement Tests: What's Really Happening? *Phi Delta Kappan*, May 1981, *63*(9), 631–634.

Salvia, J., & Ysseldyke, J. E. *Assessment in special and remedial education.* Boston: Houghton Mifflin, 1978.

Samuels, S. Effects of pictures on learning to read,

comprehension, and attitudes. *Review of Educational Research*, 1970, *40*, 397–407.

Sattler, J. M. *Assessment of children's intelligence.* Philadelphia: Saunders, 1974.

Scholnick, E. K., & Adams, M. J. Relationship between language and cognitive skills: Passive-voice comprehension, backward repetition, and matrix permutation. *Child Development*, 1973, *44*(4), 741–746.

Sears, R. R., Maccoby, E. E., & Levin, H. *Patterns of child rearing.* Evanston, Ill.: Row, Peterson, 1957.

Seashore, H. (Ed.). *Test Service Bulletin.* Psychological Corporation, 1955, *48*, 8.

Sells, L. W. The mathematics filter and the education of women and minorities. Paper presented at the annual meeting of the American Association for the Advancement of Science, Boston, 1976.

Selman, R. L. The relation of role-taking to the development of moral judgment in children. *Child Development*, 1971, *42*, 79–91.

Selman, R. L., & Byrne, D. F. A structural-developmental analysis of levels of role-taking in middle childhood. *Child Development*, 1974, *45*, 803–806.

Shantz, C., & Watson, J. Spatial abilities and spatial egocentrism in the young child. *Child Development*, 1971, *42*, 171–181.

Shepard, R. N., & Feng, C. A chronometric study of mental paper folding. *Cognitive Psychology*, 1972, *3*, 228–243.

Shepard, R. N., & Metzler, J. Mental rotation of the three-dimensional objects. *Science*, 1971, *161*, 701–703.

Shepard, R. N., & Podgorny, P. Cognitive processes that resemble perceptual processes. In W. K. Estes (Ed.), *Handbook of learning and cognitive processes: V. Human information processing.* Hillsdale, N.J.: Erlbaum, 1978.

Sherman, J. A. Problem of sex differences in space perception and aspects of intellectual functioning. *Psychological Review*, 1967, *74*, 290–299.

Sherman, J. A. *On the psychology of women: A survey of empirical studies.* Springfield, Ill.: Charles C. Thomas, 1971.

Sherman, J. A. *Sex-related cognitive differences.* Springfield, Ill.: Charles C. Thomas, 1978.

Shields, M. Some communication skills of young children: A study of dialogue in the nursery school. In R. Campbell & P. Smith (Eds.), *Recent advances in the psychology of language.* New York: Plenum Press, 1978.

Shuey, A. *The testing of Negro intelligence.* New York: Social Science Press, 1966.

Siegel, I. E., & Cocking, R. *Cognitive development from childhood to adolescence: A constructivist perspective.* New York: Holt, Rinehart & Winston, 1977.

Siegel, L. S. The relationship of language and thought in the preoperational child: A reconsideration of nonverbal alternatives to Piagetian tasks. In L. S. Siegel & C. J. Brainerd (Eds.), *Alternatives to Piaget.* New York: Academic Press, 1978.

Siegel, L. S., & Brainerd, C. J. *Alternatives to Piaget.* New York: Academic Press, 1978.

Siegel, L. S., & Goldstein, A. G. Conservation of number in young children: Recency versus relational response strategies. *Developmental Psychology,* 1969, *1*(2), 128–130.

Siegler, R. S. Three aspects of cognitive development. *Cognitive Psychology,* 1976, *8*, 481–520.

Siegler, R. S. (Ed.). *Children's thinking: What develops.* Hillsdale, N.J.: Erlbaum, 1978. (a)

Siegler, R. S. Reply to "Comment on 'three aspects of cognitive development.' " *Perceptual & Motor Skills,* 1978, *46*(1), 226. (b)

Simon, H. A. Identifying basic abilities underlying intelligent performance of complex tasks. In L. B. Resnick (Ed.), *The nature of intelligence.* Hillsdale, N.J.: Erlbaum, 1976.

Simon, H. A. Information processing models of cognition. *Annual Review of Psychology,* 1979, *30*, 363–396.

Simon, H. A. Problem solving and education. In D. T. Tuma & F. Reif (Eds.), *Problem solving and education: Issues in teaching and education.* Hillsdale, N.J.: Erlbaum, 1980.

Simpson, E. L. Moral development research: A case study of scientific cultural bias. *Human Development,* 1974, *17*, 81–106.

Sinclair, H. *Acquisition du language et development de la pensee.* Paris: Dunod, 1967.

Singer, D. G., & Revenson, T. A. *How a child thinks.* New York: Plume Books, 1978.

Skeels, H. M. Adult status of children with contrasting early life experiences. *Monographs of the Society for Research in Child Development,* 1966, *31*(3).

Skeels, H. M., & Dye, H. B. A study of the effect of differential stimulation on mentally retarded children. *Proceedings of the American Association for Mental Deficiency,* 1939, *44*, 114–136.

Skinner, B. F. *Science and human behavior.* New York: Macmillan, 1953.

Skinner, B. F. *Verbal behavior.* New York: Appleton-Century-Crofts, 1957.

Skinner, B. F. *The technology of teaching.* Englewood Cliffs, N.J.: Prentice-Hall, 1968.

Skinner, B. F. *Beyond freedom and dignity.* New York: Knopf, 1971.

Skinner, B. F. *About behaviorism.* New York: Knopf, 1974.

Skinner, B. F. *Particulars of my life.* New York: Knopf, 1976.

Skodak, M., & Skeels, H. M. A final follow-up study of one hundred adopted children. *Journal of Genetic Psychology,* 1949, *75*, 85–125.

Smith, D. H. The black revolution and education. In R. L. Green (Ed.), *Racial crisis in American education.* Chicago: Follett, 1969.

Snow, R. E., Frederico, P., & Montague, W. E. *Aptitude, learning, and instruction. Vol. I: Cognitive process analysis of aptitude.* Hillsdale, N.J.: Erlbaum, 1980.

Spearman, C. *The abilities of man: Their nature and measurement.* New York: Macmillan, 1927.

Sperling, G. The information available in brief visual presentations. *Psychological Monographs,* 1960, *74* (Whole No. 11).

Spiro, R. J. Constructing a theory of reconstructive memory: The state of the schema approach. In R. C. Anderson, R. J. Spiro, & W. E. Montague (Eds.), *Schooling and the acquisition of knowledge.* Hillsdale, N.J: Erlbaum, 1977. (a)

Spiro, R. J. Remembering information from text: The "state of schema" approach. In R. C. Anderson, R. J. Spiro, & W. E. Montague (Eds.), *Schooling and the acquisition of knowledge.* Hillsdale, N.J.: Erlbaum, 1977. (b)

Spiro, R. J., Bruce, B. C., & Brewer, W. F. (Eds.), *Theoretical issues in reading comprehension.* Hillsdale, N.J.: Erlbaum, 1980.

Spiro, R. J., & Tirre, W. C. Individual differences in schema utilization during discourse processing. Technical report No. 111, National Institute of Education, Contract No. US-NIE-C-400-76-0116, 1980.

Spitzer, D. R. *Concept formation and learning in early childhood.* Columbus, Ohio: Merrill, 1977.

Sproull, L., & Zubrow, D. Standardized testing from the administrative perspective. *Phi Delta Kappan.* May 1981, *62*(9).

Staats, A. W. *Learning, language, and cognition.* New York: Holt, Rinehart & Winston, 1968.

Stafford, R. E. Hereditary and environmental components of quantitative reasoning. *Review of Educational Research,* 1972, *42*(2), 183–201.

Stanley, J. C. Rationale of the study of mathematical precocious youth (SMPY) during its first five years of promoting educational achievement. In J. C. Stanley, W. C. George, & C. M. Solmo (Eds.), *The gifted and the creative: A fifty year perspective.* Baltimore, Md.: Johns Hopkins University Press, 1977.

Staub, E. The use of role playing and induction in children's learning of helping and sharing behavior. *Child Development*, 1971, *42*, 805–816.

Staub, E. *Positive social behavior and morality.* Vol. 2, New York: Academic Press, 1979.

Stein, A. H., & Smithells, J. Age and sex differences in children's sex role standards about achievement. *Developmental Psychology*, 1969, *1*, 252–259.

Sternberg, R. J. *Intelligence, information processing, and analogical reasoning: The componential analysis of human abilities.* Hillsdale, N.J.: Erlbaum, 1977.

Sternberg, R. J., & Weil, E. M. An aptitude x strategy interaction in linear syllogistic reasoning. *Journal of Educational Psychology*, 1980, *72*(2), 226–239.

Struthers, J., DeAvila, E. A. Development of a group measure to assess the extent of prelogical and precausal thinking in primary school age children. Paper presented at the annual convention of the National Science Teachers Association, Detroit, 1967.

Sulzer-Azaroff, B., & Mayer, G. R. *Applying behavior-analysis procedures with children and youth.* New York: Holt, Rinehart & Winston, 1972.

Swanson, R. A., & Henderson, R. W. Achieving home-school continuity in the socialization of an academic motive. *Journal of Experimental Education*, 1976, *44*, 38–44.

Swanson, R. A., & Henderson, R. W. Effects of televised modeling and active participation on rule-governed question production among native-American children. *Contemporary Educational Psychology*, 1977, *2*, 345–352.

Swanson, R. A., & Henderson, R. W. Induction of a concrete operational concept through televised modeling: Evidence and speculation on mediational process. *Contemporary Educational Psychology*, 1979, *4*, 202–210.

Swanson, R. A., Henderson, R. W., & Williams, E. The relative influence on observation, imitative motor activity, and feedback of the induction of seriation. *Journal of Genetic Psychology*, 1979, *136*, 81–91.

Terman, L. M. *Genetic studies of genius* (Volumes 1–5). Stanford, Calif.: Stanford University Press, 1925–1959.

Terman, L. M., & Merrill, M. A. *Stanford-Binet Intelligence Scale: 1972 Norms Edition.* Boston: Houghton Mifflin, 1973.

Thorndike, E. L. *Educational Psychology: The psychology of learning* (Vol. 2). New York: Teachers College, 1913.

Thorndyke, P. W., & Hayes-Roth, B. The use of schemata in the acquisition and transfer of knowledge. *Cognitive Psychology*, 1979, *11*, 82–106.

Thorndyke, P. W., & Yekovich, F. R. A critique of schema-based theories of human story memory. *Poetics*, 1980, *9*, 23–49, North-Holland Publishing.

Thurstone, L., & Thurstone, T. *Primary Mental Abilities Test* (Rev. ed.). Chicago: Science Research Associates, 1962.

Tolman, E. C., & Honzik, C. H. Instruction and removal of reward and maze performance in rats. *University of California, Publications in Psychology.* 1930, *4*, 257–275.

Torrance, E. P. Freedom to manipulate objects and question asking performance of six year olds. *Young Children*, 1970, *26*, 93–97.

Trabasso, T., & Bower, G. H. *Attention in learning.* New York: Wiley, 1968.

Trabasso, T., Isen, A. M., Dolecki, P., McLanahan, A. G., Riley, C. A., & Tucker, T. How do children solve class-inclusion problems? In R. Siegler (Ed.), *Children's thinking: What develops?* Hillsdale, N.J.: Erlbaum, 1978.

Tuddenham, R. D. A Piagetian test of cognitive development. In W. B. Dockrell (Ed.), *On intelligence: The Toronto symposium on intelligence.* London: Methuen, 1970.

Tuddenham, R. D. Theoretical regularities and individual idiosyncracies. In D. R. Green, M. P. Ford, & G. B. Flamer (Eds.), *Measurement and Piaget.* New York: McGraw-Hill, 1971.

Tulving, E. Theoretical issues in free recall. In T. R. Dixon & D. L. Horton (Eds.), *Verbal behavior and general behavior theory.* Englewood Cliffs, N.J.: Prentice-Hall, 1968.

Turiel, E. Social regulations and domains of social concepts. In W. Damon (Ed.), *New Directions for Child Development. Vol 1. Social Cognition.* San Francisco: Jossey-Bass, 1978.

Urberg, K. A., & Docherty, E. M. Development of role-taking skills in young children. *Developmental Psychology*, 1976, *12*, 198–203.

Varma, V. P., & Williams, P. (Eds.). *Piaget, Psychol-*

ogy and Education. Itasca, Ill.: F. E. Peacock, 1976.

Vinacke, W. E. *The psychology of thinking.* New York: McGraw-Hill, 1974.

Vygotsky, L. *Thought and language.* New York: Wiley, 1962.

Walters, G. C. & Grusec, J. E. *Punishment.* San Francisco: W. H. Freeman, 1977.

Walters, R. H., & Parke, R. D. Influence of response consequence to a social model on resistance to deviation. *Journal of Experimental Child Psychology,* 1964, *1,* 269–280.

Watson, J. B. Psychology as a behaviorist views it. *Psychological Review,* 1913, *20,* 158–177.

Watson, J. B. *Behaviorism.* New York: Norton, 1924.

Watts, G. H., & Anderson, R. C. Effects of three types of inserted questions on learning from prose. *Journal of Educational Psychology,* 1971, *62,* 387–394.

Wechsler, D. *Manual for the Wechsler Adult Intelligence Scale.* New York: Psychological Corporation, 1955.

Wechsler, D. *Manual for the Wechsler Preschool and Primary Scale of Intelligence.* New York: Psychological Corporation, 1967.

Wechsler, D. *Manual for the Wechsler Scale for Children-Revised.* New York: Psychological Corporation, 1974.

Weiner, B. *Theories of motivation from mechanism to cognition.* Chicago: Markham, 1972.

Weiner, B. (Ed.). *Achievement motivation and attribution theory.* Morristown, N.J.: General Learning Press, 1974. (a)

Weiner, B. (Ed.). *Cognitive views of human motivation.* New York: Academic Press, 1974. (b)

Weiner, B. A theory of motivation for some classroom experiences. *Journal of Educational Psychology,* 1979, *71*(1), 3–25.

Weiner, B., & Kukla, A. An attributional analysis of achievement motivation. *Journal of Personality and Social Psychology,* 1970, *15,* 1–20.

Weiner, B., Russell, D., & Lerman, D. Affective consequences of causal ascriptions. In J. H. Harvey, W. J. Ickes, & R. F. Kidd (Eds.) *New directions in attribution research* (Vol. 2). Hillsdale, N.J.: Erlbaum, 1978.

White, R. W. Motivation reconsidered: The concept of competence. *Psychological Review,* 1959, *66,* 297–333.

Whitehurst, G. J. The contributions of social learning to language acquisition. *Contemporary Educational Psychology,* 1978, *3,* 2–10.

Whitehurst, G. J., Ironsmith, E. M., & Goldfein, M. R. Selective imitation of the passive construction through modeling. *Journal of Experimental Child Psychology,* 1974, *17,* 288–302.

Whorf, B. L. *Language, thought, and reality.* Cambridge, Mass.: Technology Press, 1956.

Williams, R. Danger: Testing and dehumanizing black children. *Clinical Child Psychology Newsletter,* 1970, *9*(1), 5–6.

Williams, R. Danger: Testing and dehumanizing black children. *The School Psychologist,* 1971, *25,* 11–13.

Winterbottom, M. R. The relation of need for achievement to learning experiences in independence and mastery. In J. W. Atkinson (Ed.), *Motives in fantasy, action and society.* Princeton, N.J.: Van Nostrand, 1958.

Wispe, L. G. Positive forms of social behavior: An overview. *Journal of Social Issues,* 1972, *28*(3), 1–19.

Witkin, H. A., Dyk, R. B., Faterson, H. F., Goodenough, D. R., & Karp, S. A. *Psychological differentiation.* New York: Wiley, 1962.

Wohlwill, J. *The study of behavioral development.* New York: Academic Press, 1973.

Wolff, P., & Levin, J. The role of overt activity in children's imagery production. *Child Development,* 1972, *43,* 537–547.

Yarrow, M. R., Scott, P. M., & Waxler, C. Z. Learning concern for others. *Developmental Psychology,* 1973, *8,* 240–260.

Yoshida, R., & Meyers, E. Effects of labeling as educable mentally retarded on teachers: Expectancies for change in students' performance. *Journal of Educational Psychology,* 1975, *67,* 521–527.

Youniss, J., Furth, H. G., & Ross, B. M. Logical symbol use in deaf and hearing children and adolescents. *Developmental Psychology,* 1971, *5*(3), 511–517.

Ysseldyke, J., & Foster, G. Bias in teachers' observations of emotionally disturbed and learning disabled children. *Exceptional Children,* 1978, *44,* 613–615.

Yussen, S. R., & Levy, V. M., Jr. Developmental changes in predicting one's own span of short-term memory. *Journal of Experimental Child Psychology,* 1975, *19,* 502–508.

Zahn-Waxler, C., Radke-Yarrow, M., & Brady-Smith, J. Perspective-taking and prosocial behavior. *Developmental Psychology,* 1977, *13,* 87–88.

Zigler, E., Abelson, W. D., & Seitz, V. Motivational factors in the performance of economically disadvantaged children on the Peabody Picture Vocabulary Test. *Child Development*, 1973, *44*, 294–303.

Zimmerman, B. J. Modeling influences on children's motivation to solve problems. Paper presented at the annual meeting of American Educational Research Association, Los Angeles, 1981.

Zimmerman, B. J., Beilin, H., Whitehurst, G. J., & Brody, G. H. Papers and discussion. *Contemporary Educational Psychology*, 1978, *3*, 3–31.

Zimmerman, B. J., & Blotner, R. Effects of model persistence and success on children's problem solving. *Journal of Educational Psychology*, 1979, *71*(4), 508–513.

Zimmerman, B. J., & Jaffee, A. Teaching through demonstration: The effects of structuring imitation and age. *Journal of Educational Psychology*, 1977, *69*, 773–778.

Zimmerman, B. J., & Kinsler, K. Effects of exposure to a punished model and verbal prohibitions on children's toy play. *Journal of Educational Psychology*, 1979, *71*, 388–395.

Zimmerman, B. J., & Pike, E. O. Effects of modeling and reinforcement on the acquisition and generalization of question-asking behavior. *Child Development*, 1972, *43*, 892–907.

Zimmerman, B. J., & Ringle, J. Effects of model persistence and statements of confidence on children's self-efficacy and problem solving. *Journal of Educational Psychology*, 1981, *73*(4), 485–493.

Zimmerman, B. J., & Rosenthal, T. L. Conserving and retaining equalities and inequalities through observation and correction. *Developmental Psychology*, 1974, *10*(2), 260–268. (a)

Zimmerman, B. J., & Rosenthal, T. L. Observational learning of rule-governed behavior by children. *Psychological Bulletin*, 1974, *81*(1), 29–43. (b)

Name Index

Subject Index

Ability
  grouping by, 383–384, 390
  intellectual (general), 357
  mathematical, 358, 360, 363
  racial differences and, 364–
    366
  sex differences and, 353–364
  social class and, 365, 366–
    369
  spatial, 358–363, 487–491,
    496–497
  verbal, 357–358
Ability tests. *See* Test(s)
Acceleration programs, 376–
  378. *See also* Individualized instruction
Accommodation, 219–220, 224,
  232, 243
Achievement
  motivation for, 404–408 (*see
    also* Motivation)
  and need achievement
    (*nAch*) scores, 404, 406
Achievement tests. *See* Test(s)
Action
  and language (Piagetian
    view), 271, 281
  statement of, in performance
    objective, 43, 50
  and thought (enactive
    mode), 268
Active constructors (of language structure), 266
Active organism (Piagetian
  theory), 241, 246
Active rehearsal, 147–148. *See
  also* Rehearsal
Adaptation, 219–220, 221, 232,
  266. *See also* Behavior
  and intelligence, 300

motivation (enthusiasm)
  and, 234
Adolescents, 217–218, 358, 514
Advance organizers, 185–186,
  500–501, 504
Age
  and behavior change, 207
  and conservation tasks, 224–
    225, 226, 228, 242–243
  and logic, 212, 226
  and perspective-taking, 521
  and stages or schemes of
    development, 216–218,
    232
Altruism, 512, 515, 516, 534
  defined, 508–509, 518
  studies of, 518–519
American College Testing Program (ACT), 344. *See also*
  Test(s)
Anecdotal records, 590–591
Antecedent stimuli. *See* Stimu-
  lus(i)
Aptitude test. *See* Test(s)
Aptitude-treatment interaction
  (ATI) research, 368
Assimilation
  in cognitive development,
    219–220, 223, 232, 243
  cultural, 292
Association, in learning lan-
  guage, 281
Attention
  by student, 126, 131, 134,
    135, 145, 148, 187–188,
    196
  by teacher, 98–103, 109, 110,
    111, 114, 420
    negative reaction, 400
    question-asking and, 284

Attribution theory of motivation. *See* Motivation
Ausubel, David P., 154, 164–
  168, 170, 178, 185–186,
  283, 436, 438, 453

B = E x P formula. *See* Behavior
Bandura, Albert, 24, 83, 153,
  303, 538; *et al.*, 415
  self-efficacy theory of, 396,
    398, 412–416, 425
  social learning theory of,
    118, 119–120, 121–122,
    128
Baseline record of behavior.
  See Data and data collection
Behavior. *See also* Conse-
  quence(s); Learning
  acquisition of, 121–127, 128,
    131, 133–135, 145
  adaptive (*see* Behavior,
    changes in)
  analysis of, 41
  B = E × P formula for (en-
    vironment and personal
    characteristics effect on),
    6–7, 118, 119, 154, 155,
    201, 208, 295, 431
  changes in, 4–5, 35–36, 37,
    90, 91, 106, 116, 128, 527–
    528. *See also* Adaptation;
    Variable(s)
    age and, 207
  cognitive, 176, 203–233, 266
  collection of data regarding
    (*see* Data and data collec-
    tion)
  conceptual, 431

Engaged learning activity, 96
Enthusiasm, student, 180, 234
Environment. *See also* Cultural
differences; Social class
and behavior (B = E × P)
(*see* Behavior)
and educational opportunity,
365, 366
heredity vs. (*see* Nature-nurture debate)
learning, Piagetian theory
and, 246
-person relationship (*see* Relationships)
variables in (*see* Variable[s])
Environmental contingencies,
120. *See also* Contin-
gency(ies)
Environmental determinism,
205, 206. *See also* Biological determinism
and nature-nurture debate,
311–313
Equilibrium/disequilibrium,
220–221
drives and, 400–401
and equilibration, 221, 242–
244, 245, 513, 524-525,
528, 538
Error
in empirical data, 354–355
halo effect, 545–546, 557,
589
of measurement, standard
(SEM), 329–331, 341, 347,
566
in measuring intelligence,
314–315
personal bias, 589
Essential Piaget, The (Gruber
and Voneche), 236
Evaluation. *See also* Grading;
Performance objectives;
Test(s); Test scores
ability testing and, 351
child's attitude toward, 368
defined (vs. measurement),
324
influences on, 411
normative, 311
outcome of, 373
periodic, combined, 591–593
of personal and social outcomes, 590–591

of products and procedures,
586–589, 590
of special populations, 374–
375
of student progress, 575–599
of teacher (achievement test
results and), 346–347
of tests and test scores, 563–
566, 580–585
Events
mental (*see* Thought)
sequence of (*see* Temporal
sequence of events)
Event sampling 92–93, 94. *See
also* Data and data collection
Evolution, 205, 398, 400. *See
also* Biological determinism
Existing conditions, and hap-
penings/behavior, 17–18,
26, 38
Expectations
of consequences, 130–131
efficacy, 414–415
and expectancy of success or
failure, 405–406, 408, 409–
410, 411, 421–426, 429
response-outcome, 413–414
of student by others, 343,
373, 422–426, 495
Experiment. *See* Method, scientific
Experimentation. *See also* Active organism (Piagetian
theory)
by child, 248
by infant, 223–224
and language, 281
Explanation(s)
of happenings/behavior, 18–
19, 21, 28, 31, 33
verbal, in learning process,
124
Externalization, 31, 42–43
Extinction
of reinforcement or behavior,
78–80, 81, 86, 98, 99, 105–
106, 110–112, 116, 517
vs. punishment, 114, 115

Facilitative effects. *See* Modeling

Factor analysis, 307–310, 319,
321
Feedback
evaluation of student and,
575, 586, 589
use of test results for, 548,
566–567, 573
Field (ecological) studies. *See*
Method, scientific
Forgetting. *See* Retention and
recall
Formal operational period,
216, 232
accomplishments of, 226–
227, 229, 231
Frequency of behavior. *See* Behavior
Freud, Sigmund, 55–56, 404
Function
defined, 218
Piagetian theory of, 218–220,
221, 232
in reinforcement (*see* Reinforcement)
Functional relationships. *See*
Relationships

Gagne, R. M., 436, 444–445,
447, 450, 453, 466, 501
Galton, Francis, 299–304 *pas-
sim*, 307, 310, 312, 315,
319, 320, 321, 397–398
Generalization, 135, 145, 240,
469
of discrimination, 447
Genetic epistemology, 209, 235
Genetics. *See* Biological determinism
Gestalt psychology. *See* Psychology
Goals, 426–429. *See also* Motivation; Outcomes; Perfor-
mance objectives
teacher vs. student, 426–427
Grade equivalent scores, 336–
337, 346. *See also* Test
scores
Grading, 49. *See also* Evaluation; Performance objec-
tives; Test scores
criteria for, 585
"guess method" of, 583
importance of, 599